Artificial Intelligence: Innovations and Applications

Artificial Intelligence: Innovations and Applications

Edited by
Jeremy Rogerson

www.willfordpress.com

Published by Willford Press,
118-35 Queens Blvd., Suite 400,
Forest Hills, NY 11375, USA

ISBN: 978-1-68285-364-1

Cataloging-in-Publication Data

Artificial intelligence : innovations and applications / edited by Jeremy Rogerson.
    p. cm.
Includes bibliographical references and index.
ISBN 978-1-68285-364-1
1. Artificial intelligence. 2. Technological innovations. 3. Neural computers. 4. Remote sensing.
5. Cybernetics. I. Rogerson, Jeremy.
Q335 .A78 2017
006.3--dc23

For information on all Willford Press publications
visit our website at www.willfordpress.com

Printed in the United States of America.

Contents

Preface

This book on artificial intelligence discusses topics related to the principles of artificial intelligence applications and the theories that are relevant for them. Devices based on artificial intelligence aim to fulfill specific functions that may be of great importance. The ever growing need of advanced technology is the reason that has fueled the research in this area in recent times. With state-of-the-art inputs by acclaimed experts of this field, this book targets students and professionals. As this field is emerging at a fast pace, this text will help the readers to better understand the concepts of artificial intelligence.

The researches compiled throughout the book are authentic and of high quality, combining several disciplines and from very diverse regions from around the world. Drawing on the contributions of many researchers from diverse countries, the book's objective is to provide the readers with the latest achievements in the area of research. This book will surely be a source of knowledge to all interested and researching the field.

In the end, I would like to express my deep sense of gratitude to all the authors for meeting the set deadlines in completing and submitting their research chapters. I would also like to thank the publisher for the support offered to us throughout the course of the book. Finally, I extend my sincere thanks to my family for being a constant source of inspiration and encouragement.

Editor

Static Gesture Recognition Combining Graph and Appearance Features

Marimpis Avraam

Computer Science Department
Aristotle University of Thessaloniki, AUTH
Thessaloniki, Greece

Abstract—In this paper we propose the combination of graph-based characteristics and appearance-based descriptors such as detected edges for modeling static gestures. Initially we convolve the original image with a Gaussian kernel and blur the image. Canny edges are then extracted. The blurring is performed in order to enhance some characteristics in the image that are crucial for the topology of the gesture (especially when the fingers are overlapping). There are a large number of properties that can describe a graph, one of which is the adjacency matrix that describes the topology of the graph itself. We approximate the topology of the hand utilizing Neural Gas with Competitive Hebbian Learning, generating a graph. From the graph we extract the Laplacian matrix and calculate its spectrum. Both canny edges and Laplacian spectrum are used as features. As a classifier we employ Linear Discriminant Analysis with Bayes' Rule. We apply our method on a published American Sign Language dataset (ten classes) and the results are very promising and further study of this approach is imminent from the authors.

Keywords— Gesture Recognition; Neural Gas; Linear Discriminant Analysis; Bayes Rule; Laplacian Matrix

I. INTRODUCTION

The purpose of a gesture recognition process is to interpret gestures performed by humans [24]. The domain of such processes can vary significantly, from remote robot control, virtual reality worlds to smart home systems [25]. Most events that are recognized as gestures originate from the body's motions or state, but with most commonly origin the face or the hands.

A topic highly interwoven with gesture recognition and it is equally significant is the sign language recognition (SLR). A sign language is composed of three types of features. Manual features such as, hand shapes, their orientation and movement. Non-manual features are related to arms, the body and the facial expressions. Finally, finger-spelling that corresponds to letters and words in natural languages [19]. Specifically the non manual features are used to both individually form part of a sign or support other signs and modify their bearing meaning [26].

The ultimate purpose of sign language recognition systems is to build automated systems that are able recognize signs and convert them into text or even speech. This could ideally lead to a translation system to communicate with the deaf people. Finally, another challenge in this field is that there is no international sign language, thus every region defines its own

and there is no imposed constraint that is should be based on the spoken language of the region [27].

In the literature have been proposed methods that utilize features extracted in real time and identify the gestures as they are performed. We, on the other, will focus on a series of static images. Our purpose is to demonstrate a novel combination of features, classic appearance-based characteristics and graph descriptors (e.g. adjacency matrix). Through experimentation, we concluded that these features are sufficient to describe in a discriminative way a gesture.

II. RELATED WORK

Soft computing techniques include a plethora of well-established algorithms such as Self-Organizing Neural Gas (SGONG). In [17], the authors employ SGONG by generating an approximation of the hand topology. Based on a number of presumptions such as the hand should be placed vertical, etc they produce a statistical model to recognize the gestures. Moreover, they are able to identify the fingers individually by the number of neighbors that a neuron has. By combining Self-Organizing Maps (SOM) and Markov chains in [18] the authors propose a novel probabilistic classification model. SOMs are used to model the position of the gesture while via a quantization process they describe the hand direction. These features are cast in discrete symbols and then used to construct a Markov model for each hand.

In relation to image processing methods and edge detection methods specifically, in [23] Canny edges in order to produce thinned skeletons of the gestures. While in [19] the Canny edges are further processed by Hough transformation in order to conclude into the gesture features. Simpler but very effective, in [21] the authors utilize the difference between the detected (strong & weak) edges as features. An extensive work, based solely on edges as presented in [20], by which the edges are processed and clip in order to describe the fingers individually. Edges have also been proposed in conjunction with other low level features such as salient points and lines for sparse feature representation in [22].

Each of these proposals manages achieve very high recognition rates utilizing either graph or appearance-based features but not an explicit combination of the two. To our humble knowledge our proposal is one of the few, if not the only one, gesture recognition system (even testing on a simple dataset) that combines appearance-based features and graph properties simultaneously.

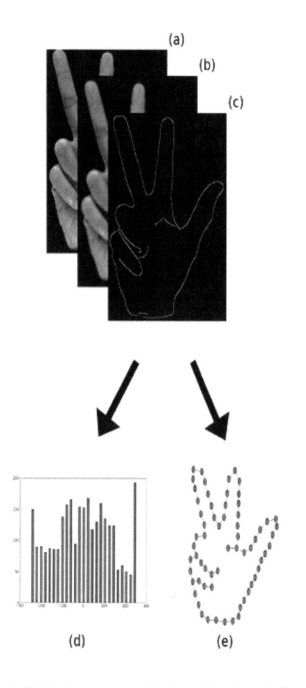

Fig. 1. (a) Orignal gesture image. (b) Grayscaled and passed with a Gaussian Blur filter. (c) Canny edges detected. (e) Histogram of 1 dimensional PCA projection. (f) Graph extracted by Neural Gas with CHL.

III.   PROPOSED METHOD

As stated earlier our method utilizes appearance-based features as well as properties that are induced from graphs. On one hand the Canny edges provide a more general and rich description, without any specificity. On the other, the graph-related features are sufficient to describe the topology of a gesture, but fail to discriminate gestures with similar topographies. We concluded to this combination because these features complement each other.

In the following paragraphs we will provide a detailed description of our system's overview.

A.   Image Preprocessing

Before anything else, we have to segment the hand from the image. Because of the nature of the specific dataset, a simple thresholding is sufficient; the background is just the black color.

The dimensions of the images in the dataset [4] are variable, because a number of transform operations have been applied. Some gestures have bee scaled along the X or Y axis while others have been rotated. The only property that we modify is the dimension of each image. We resize all images to $256x256$ pixels in order to restrict the possible variances of the generated graph topologies.

Finally, in order to restrict the Canny edge detector that we will user later on, we convolve a Gaussian blur kernel with the image as suggested in [16]. This way, we reduce the qualitative resolution of image and the edge detector will highlight only what we have issued to be, the most significant edges on the hand. The edges on the fingers will be greatly enhanced.

B.   Appearance-based features

In Canny edge detector algorithm [3], initially the raw image is convolved with a Gaussian filter in order to reduce its susceptibility to noise. Then, utilizing two filters for each of the directions as in horizontal and vertical it computes the gradient [13]. Finally, it calculates the magnitude and the orientation of the gradient and with the usage a simple threshold technique it suppresses edges with low values.

For our purposes, after the edges are extracted we use PCA [14] and project them into one dimension and calculate the histogram.

C.   Graph-induced features

1) Neural Gas with Competitive Hebbian Learning (NGCHL)

Martinetz and Schulten introduced the Neural Gas manifold learning algorithm in [5] and were inspired by Kohonen's Self Organizing Maps. The most notable difference between these two is that the first does not define explicitly a neighborhood. To overcome this issue an enhanced version of Neural Gas was proposed, integrating Competitive Hebbian Learning (CHL) [1, 2].

This new alternative approach follows closely the description of Neural Gas, that of a feature manifold learning method but through the generation of topology preserving maps. The learning function that is incorporated into the algorithm is described by a gradient descent as in the original algorithm. As in the original Neural Gas, the projection of a feature vector marks the adaptation of all neurons with a step size from the closest to the furthest. The key difference is that the Neural Gas with CHL also creates or destroys the synaptic links between the neurons. Each such connection is described by a synaptic strength. This indicator is used to decide whether or not a connection should be refreshed and kept or removed from the graph.

Below is a short description of the Neural Gas with Competitive Hebbian Learning algorithm. We must declare and set the following parameters: T_{max} (maximum number of iterations), α_T (final edge age), a_0 (initial edge age), e_T (final learning rate), e_0 (initial learning rate), λ_T (initial neighborhood reference), λ_0 (final neighborhood reference).

Create a number of neurons and assign them random positions and with no connections between them (the adjacency matrix is empty).

Step 1: Project $\vec{x}$ (drawn from R^n space) to our network.

Step 2: Sort the nodes based on their distances from $\vec{x}$ (keep the relative index position to k).

Step 3: Adapt the nodes' position vectors ($\vec{w}$) using:

$$N_{\vec{w}} \leftarrow N_{\vec{w}} + [N_{\vec{w}} * e(t) * h(k) * (\vec{x} - N_{\vec{w}})]$$
$$\forall N \in GraphNodes$$

where: $h(t) = \exp \dfrac{-k}{\sigma^2}(t)$, $\sigma^2 = \lambda_0 (\dfrac{\lambda_T}{\lambda_0})^{\frac{t}{T_{max}}}$,

$$e(t) = e_0 (\dfrac{e_T}{e_0})^{\frac{t}{T_{max}}}$$

Step 4: Connect the two closest neurons (according to their distance from $\vec{x}$). If already connected, refresh the age of the connection to 0.

Step 5: Increase the age by 1, of all edges connected with the best matching unit (the neuron closest to $\vec{x}$).

Step 6: Check for old edges in the graph and remove them if their age is exceeding the threshold given by the following formula:

$$\alpha(t) = \alpha_0 (\dfrac{\alpha_T}{\alpha_0})^{\frac{t}{T_{max}}}$$

The above function is a gradient descent. It uses the ranking of nodes in the aggregation of step 3. Increase the iteration counter and repeat from step 2 until the required criteria are met, usually $t = T_{max}$.

2) Graph Spectra

Having obtained an undirected graph from NGCHL we are now able to apply specific linear algebra concepts. One of the most interesting notions in graph theory is the Laplacian matrix [6, 7].

In simple terms, given an adjacency matrix A and a degree matrix D, the Laplacian matrix is given by: $L = D - A$. These matrices have a numerous variations, properties and applications but these topics are out of the scope of this paper.

We would like to use the Laplacian matrix in order to extract its spectrum [8]. The computed Eigenvalues are very important and widely researched (especially the λ_2) [9] in the field of graph analysis and theory and can be employed when comparing graphs [12]. In our case we employ all of the Eigenvalues as a strong discriminative feature.

D. Linear Discriminant Analysis (LDA) and Bayes Optimal Classification

In our proposed method we use LDA to estimate the within class density (based on the assumptions that the distributions are Gaussians and the classes share a common covariance matrix), resulting into a linear classifier model [10, 11].

Based on Bayes' rule, we will assign a gesture to the class with the maximum posterior probability given the feature vector $\vec{X}$. So the conditional probability of class G given X is:

$$\Pr(G = k \mid X = x) = \frac{fk(x)\pi k}{\sum_{l=1}^{k} fl(x)\pi l}$$

Based on the earlier assumption of the normal distributions we can derive the following linear discriminant model:

$$g_i(x) = -\frac{1}{2}(x - \mu_i)^t \Sigma^{-1}(x - \mu_i) + \ln P(\omega_i)$$

This assigns a feature vector x into class i with the maximum g_i. Notice that the above equation contains a term that it is a Mahalanobis distance between the feature vector to and each the c mean vectors, and assign x to the category of the nearest mean [10, 15].

E. American Sign Language Dataset

We applied our proposed in the dataset proposed in [4]. It is a dataset containing 36 American Signs (ASL) each one of which is performed by five different persons. Each gesture is captured using a neutral-colored background (a green background), making the segmentation easier. This enables us to focus our research on the feature extraction and the classification methodology. In order to extend the dataset and provide more realistic (as "in the wild") poses, the original authors of the dataset, rotated each image in different angles and scales resulting into 2425 images.

In this paper, we focus on the ten classes corresponding to the numbering gestures from one to ten. Each class is composed of 65 samples.

IV.   EXPERIMENTAL RESULTS

We applied our proposal in the aforementioned dataset. Ten different gestures (classes), each one a gesture sign counting from zero to nine. The topographical network graph was set in 128 nodes. Finally as far the classification is concerned we followed a 5-fold cross validation scheme. For training we used 50 samples, while the rest 15 composed the testing set. Below we tabulate the results acquired.

TABLE I.   CLASSIFICATION ACCURACY

Bayes Classification	
Gesture Class	*Accuracy Score*
0	93%
1	86%
2	73%
3	65%
4	100%
5	93%
6	86%
7	80%
8	86%
9	69%

a. Mean accuracy of a 5-cross validation procedure.

The results look very promising. Two gestures, namely the "3" and the "9" seem to perform poorly compared to others. The reason for this, is that both gestures are similarly signed (performed) resulting into also similar topographic graphs.

V.   FUTURE WORK

We could possibly improve the performance by considering a method that respects the geodesic distances of the manifold, meaning that the edges would be regulated. This would greatly adjust the generated graphs and ultimately it would refine the quality of the extracted spectrums. We believe that this would result into greater results. In a more extensive work we will integrate a skin detection and segmentation algorithm possible based on a Gaussian Mixture Model that have been widely utilized in the literature. This will help build a more complete system. Another field that enjoys a lot of attention is the usage of wavelets (discrete) in order to extract low approximations of an image. This could result into a new system, in which the edges from the vertical and/or horizontal approximations are used.

VI.   CONCLUSION

In this paper we presented the combination of the some properties and descriptors that can be extracted from a topology graph with Canny edges. A small topology results to a highly connected (or even fully) graph where all nodes are close to each other on the other hand, in a large topology all nodes spread to cover the topology and the connections are sparse, usually limited to their nearest neighbors. Based on the adjacency and degrees matrices we extract the Laplacian spectrum. This fusion yield very satisfactory results based on a five-fold cross validation procedure in a ten-class dataset.

REFERENCES

[1] Martinetz, T., & Schulten, K. (1994). Topology representing networks. Neural Networks, 7(3), 507-522.

[2] Martinetz, T. (1993). Competitive Hebbian learning rule forms perfectly topology preserving maps. In ICANN'93 (pp. 427-434). Springer London.

[3] Canny, J. (1986). A computational approach to edge detection. Pattern Analysis and Machine Intelligence, IEEE Transactions on, (6), 679-698.

[4] Barczak, A. L. C., Reyes, N. H., Abastillas, M., Piccio, A., & Susnjak, T. (2011). A new 2D static hand gesture colour image dataset for asl gestures.

[5] Martinetz, T., & Schulten, K. (1991). A" neural-gas" network learns topologies (pp. 397-402). University of Illinois at Urbana-Champaign.

[6] Newman, M. E. (2006). Modularity and community structure in networks. Proceedings of the National Academy of Sciences, 103(23), 8577-8582.

[7] Newman, M., Barabási, A. L., & Watts, D. J. (Eds.). (2006). The structure and dynamics of networks. Princeton University Press.

[8] Newman, M. (2009). Networks: an introduction. Oxford University Press.

[9] Mohar, B., & Alavi, Y. (1991). The Laplacian spectrum of graphs. Graph theory, combinatorics, and applications, 2, 871-898.

[10] Duda, R. O., Hart, P. E., & Stork, D. G. (2012). Pattern classification. John Wiley & Sons.

[11] Hastie, T., Tibshirani, R., Friedman, J., & Franklin, J. (2005). The elements of statistical learning: data mining, inference and prediction. The Mathematical Intelligencer, 27(2), 83-85.

[12] Koutra, D., Parikh, A., Ramdas, A., & Xiang, J. (2011). Algorithms for Graph Similarity and Subgraph Matching.

[13] Semmlow, J. L. (2004). Biosignal and biomedical image processing: MATLAB-based applications (Vol. 22). CRC press.

[14] Wold, S., Esbensen, K., & Geladi, P. (1987). Principal component analysis. Chemometrics and intelligent laboratory systems, 2(1), 37-52.

[15] Teknomo, Kardi. Discriminant Analysis Tutorial. http://people.revoledu.com/kardi/ tutorial/LDA/

[16] Hai, W. (2002). Gesture recognition using principal component analysis, multi-scale theory, and hidden Markov models (Doctoral dissertation, Dublin City University).

[17] Stergiopoulou, E., & Papamarkos, N. (2009). Hand gesture recognition using a neural network shape fitting technique. Engineering Applications of Artificial Intelligence, 22(8), 1141-1158.

[18] Caridakis, G., Karpouzis, K., Drosopoulos, A., & Kollias, S. (2010). SOMM: Self organizing Markov map for gesture recognition. Pattern Recognition Letters, 31(1), 52-59.

[19] Munib, Q., Habeeb, M., Takruri, B., & Al-Malik, H. A. (2007). American sign language (ASL) recognition based on Hough transform and neural networks. Expert Systems with Applications, 32(1), 24-37.

[20] Ravikiran, J., Mahesh, K., Mahishi, S., Dheeraj, R., Sudheender, S., & Pujari, N. V. (2009, March). Finger detection for sign language recognition. In Proceedings of the International MultiConference of Engineers and Computer Scientists (Vol. 1, pp. 18-20).

[21] MANISHA, L., SHETE, V., & SOMANI, S. (2013). SOFT COMPUTING APPROACHES FOR HAND GESTURE RECOGNITION. International Journal of Computer Science.

[22] Georgiana, S., & Caleanu, C. D. (2013, July). Sparse feature for hand gesture recognition: A comparative study. In Telecommunications and Signal Processing (TSP), 2013 36th International Conference on (pp. 858-861). IEEE.

[23] Barkoky, A., & Charkari, N. M. (2011, July). Static hand gesture recognition of Persian sign numbers using thinning method. In Multimedia Technology (ICMT), 2011 International Conference on (pp. 6548-6551). IEEE.

[24] Chaudhary, A., Raheja, J. L., Das, K., & Raheja, S. (2011). A survey on hand gesture recognition in context of soft computing. In Advanced Computing (pp. 46-55). Springer Berlin Heidelberg.

[25] Chaudhary, A., Raheja, J. L., Das, K., & Raheja, S. (2013). Intelligent approaches to interact with machines using hand gesture recognition in natural way: a survey. arXiv preprint arXiv:1303.2292.

[26] Cooper, H., Holt, B., & Bowden, R. (2011). Sign language recognition. In Visual Analysis of Humans (pp. 539-562). Springer London.

[27] Dreuw, P., Forster, J., Gweth, Y., Stein, D., Ney, H., Martinez, G., ... & Wheatley, M. (2010, May). Signspeak–understanding, recognition, and translation of sign languages. In Proceedings of 4th Workshop on the Representation and Processing of Sign Languages: Corpora and Sign Language Technologies (pp. 22-23).

2

New Hybrid (SVMs-CSOA) Architecture for classifying Electrocardiograms Signals

Assist. Prof. Majida Ali Abed
College of Computers Sciences & Mathematics,
University of Tikrit, Tikrit, Iraq

Assist. Prof. Dr. Hamid Ali Abed Alasad
Computers Sciences Department, Education for Pure
Science College, University of Basra, Basra, Iraq

Abstract—a medical test that provides diagnostic relevant information of the heart activity is obtained by means of an ElectroCardioGram (ECG). Many heart diseases can be found by analyzing ECG because this method with moral performance is very helpful for shaping human heart status. Support Vector Machines (SVM) has been widely applied in classification. In this paper we present the SVM parameter optimization approach using novel metaheuristic for evolutionary optimization algorithms is Cat Swarm Optimization Algorithm (CSOA). The results obtained assess the feasibility of new hybrid (SVMs - CSOA) architecture and demonstrate an improvement in terms of accuracy.

Keywords—Electrocardiograms (ECG); classification; support vector machine; Cat Swarm Optimization

I. INTRODUCTION

In recent years, the automatic classification of Electrocardiogram (ECG) signals has received great attention from the biomedical engineering community. Electrocardiography is an important tool in diagnosing the condition of the heart. The electrocardiogram (ECG) is an electrical signal that is generated during the activities of the heart. ECG provides useful information about the functional status of the heart. ECG analysis is an efficient way of diagnosing the abnormal state of the heart. The methods used to diagnose cardiac conditions require technical knowledge, such as that of a physician. Recently, with the development of computer technology many automatic diagnosis methods have been proposed for ECG analysis, including the standard ECG, Blood and Urine tests, Holter Monitoring, Electro-Physiology Studies (EPS), Event Recorder, an echo-cardiogram, Chest X-Ray, Tilt-table test. Using ECG is a common and the best way for diagnosing arrhythmias [1].

Support Vector Machine (SVM) classifier has been successfully applied to the problem of the automatic classification of ECG signal [2]. For obtaining satisfactory predictive classification accuracy, we can use various SVM kernel parameters. Therefore, it needs to be a convenient and efficient kernel parameter setting method [3]. In this paper, we present the SVM parameter optimization approach based on Cat swarm optimization Algorithm (CSOA). Selection of the parameters is an important factor affecting the performance of the SVM. The CSOA is applied to estimate the optimal parameters of SVM classifier

The next section describes the related work. To describe the Electrocardiograms (ECG) signal, Section III presents the ECG signal as five important component basic activities. Section IV is devoted to the pattern recognition Support Vector Machines (SVMs). In section V, we present a stochastic optimization algorithm which is called Cat swarm optimization (CSOA) to improve classification accuracy. In Section VI we describe our proposed architecture in detail. In Section VII we expose the results obtained from our experiments. Finally Section VIII presents the conclusions.

II. RELATED WORK

Several algorithms have been developed in the literature to improve the detection and classification of Electrocardiogram (ECG) Signals. Better performance depends on features and the methods of classification, early approaches are mostly based on Artificial Neural Networks (ANNs) [4], which have been used in a great number of medical diagnostic decision systems [5, 6]. The most popular neural network is Multi-Layer Perceptron (MLP), fuzzy logic [7], Support Vector Machines SVMs used for Examining feature extraction techniques for ECG classification, Ant colony optimization, k-nearest neighbor [8]. Little research exists that investigates the feasibility of using Evolutionary classifiers for Electrocardiogram (ECG) detection. However, the known methods for Electrocardiograms (ECG) detection mostly focus on differentiating between different Electrocardiogram (ECG) types. Support Vector Machine (SVM) has been used for principal classification but the features' set is evolved through a genetic search. Similarly, some work has done on Electrocardiograms (ECG) signals classification [9].

III. ELECTROCARDIOGRAM (ECG) SIGNAL

Electrocardiogram (ECG) is a non-invasive method of measuring the electrical properties of the heart. It is used to measure the electrical activity and is a common way for detecting heart arrhythmia. These electrical changes that spread through the heart provide information about the functional aspects of the heart and of the cardiovascular system. We must save the ECG signal in order to determine different types of the heart disease. The ECG signal is recorded to identify the change in heartbeat. Every ECG signal consists of five important component basic activities (P, T, Q, S, R waves). All these characteristic points should be detected. QRS wave group complex is ventricular depolarization which has the biggest slop in ECG [10].

- P wave is a trial depolarization

- R is the distance between the peaks of QRS current and previous pulse

- Q is first point before R, which slops less than zero.

- S is first point after R which slops less than zero.

- T wave is ventricular repolarization and equal (R-(Q+S)/2)*0.3+(Q+S)/2

These five important component basic activities (P, T, Q, S, R waves) which are used for the interpretation of the ECG show in Figure (1).

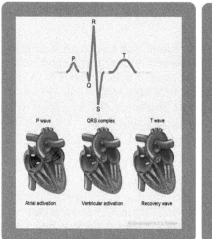 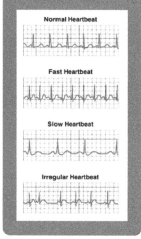

Fig.1. Standard ECG beat, ECG wave form and Process of Heart beat recoding by ECG Signal.

One cycle of ECG signal consists of P-QRS-T wave, six types of beats including Normal Beat, Premature Ventricular Contraction (PVC), Fusion of Ventricular and Normal Beat (F), Atrial Premature Beat (A), Right Bundle Branch Block Beat (R) and Fusion of Paced and Normal Beat (f). Figure(2) shows the ECG signal processing flow. Features such as energy and entropy of the ECG signals, were then extracted from these decomposed signals as feature vectors [11]. The output of Electrocardiography is a graph of two-dimensional plot, the x-axis represents time in seconds and the y-axis represents signal voltage in milli-volts. Conventional ECG machines print their output on grid graph papers, each square grid is 1mm^2.

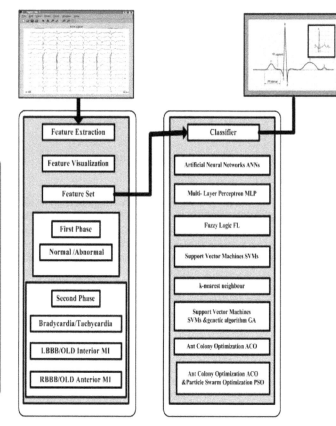

Fig.2. Electrocardiograms ECG Analysis Framework.

IV. SUPPORT VECTOR MACHINES (SVMS)

The Support Vector Machines (SVMs) possess great potential and superior performance as has been shown in many previous researches for efficiently training linear learning machines in kernel-induced feature spaces. SVMs are pattern recognizers that classify data without making any assumptions about the fundamental process by which the explanations were granted. In SVM data can be seen in the form of P-dimensional vector [12]. SVM performs classification tasks by constructing Optimal Separating Hyper-planes (OSH). OSH maximizes the margin between the two nearest data points belonging to two separate classes.

So the following inequality is valid for all input data: The SVMs use hyper- planes to separate the different classes. The SVM approach seeks to find the optimal separating hyper-planes between classes. The hyper- plane is constructed so as to maximize a measure of the 'margin' between classes. Figure (3) The Limitations of SVM are the performance of SVMs which largely depend on the choice of kernels, the choice of kernel functions, which are well suited to the specific problem, is very difficult, speed and size are other problems of SVMs both in training and testing. In terms of running time, SVMs are slower than other neural networks for a similar generalization and performance. For given training data, it is believed that SVS will perform well when the patterns to be classified are not separable and the training data is noisy.

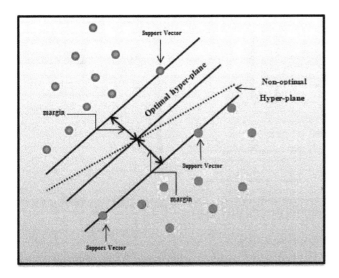

Fig.3.   SVM Model Optimal hyper-plane.

The goal of SVM is to minimize the expectation of the output of sample error. SVM map is a given set of binary labelled of each training sample to a high dimensional feature space and separate the two classes of sample is available with a maximum margin of hyper-plane. SVM algorithm seeks to maximize the margin around a hyper-plane, which separates a positive class from a negative class as shown in equations (1), (2) and (3), [13].

$$f(x) = \big(w.\Phi(x)\big) + b \qquad (1)$$

$$R_{SVM}(c) = c\frac{1}{N}\sum_{i=1}^{N} L_{\varepsilon}(y_i.y_i^\wedge) + \frac{1}{2}w^T.w \qquad (2)$$

$$L_{\varepsilon}(y_i.y_i^\wedge) = |y_i. - y_i^\wedge| - \varepsilon \quad |y_i. - y_i^\wedge| \geq \varepsilon$$

$$= 0 \qquad\qquad otherwise$$

$$^\wedge_{y=f(x)=} \sum_{i=1}^{N}(\propto_i - \propto_i^*)k(x_i, x) + b \qquad (3)$$

$$k(x_i, x) = \exp(\frac{-1}{\delta^2}\left(x_i - x_j\right)^2)$$

Where

$\phi(x)$: is the non-linearity high dimension feature space which mapped from the input space x.

w : is the modifiable model parameter.

b : is the threshold value.

w and b : are estimated by minimizing.

$\propto_i$ and $\propto_i^*$: are the Lagrange multipliers, which are positive real constants. The data points corresponding to   non-zero value for $(\propto_i - \propto_i^*)$ are called support vectors.

$k(x_i, x)$: is the inner product kernel function (Gaussian Kernel).

δ^2 : is the Gaussian kernel factor (the width of the kernel function).

C: positive real constant controls the trade-off between training error and generalization ability and its value is chosen by means of a validation set.

ε: parameter for SVMs.

V.   CAT SWARM OPTIMIZATION ALGORITHM

Many researchers recently found algorithm optimization techniques mimic animal behavior. A new algorithm introduced by Chu, Tsai and Pan in 2006 was named Cat swarm optimization Algorithm (CSOA) [14]. This algorithm is a kind of swarm intelligence that is based on stochastic optimization inspired by social behavior, as well as contributing to computer engineering applications. The problem faced in few researches is how to develop Cat Swarm Optimization algorithm that can be used in data mining, especially for the case of classification, but rarely or never used until now in pattern matching Problems. CSOA has a number of advantages in pattern matching problems of optimization compared to previous techniques such as Genetic algorithm (GA), Ant Colony Optimization Algorithm (ACOA), Particle Swarm Optimization (PSO) and Binary Particle Swarm Optimization (BPSO). With CSO algorithm development, expected produce a faster time and has a better accuracy rate compared to existing algorithms [15].In the CSOA, a set of cat behaviour in two different modes: Searching Mode (TM) and the Tracing Mode (SM) are used to resolve the optimization problem. The first mode of the CSO is to determine how many cats will be used in iteration, then use the cat in the CSOA to resolve the problem. CSOA is an evolutionary optimization algorithm is modelled on two major behavioral traits of cats. These behaviors are termed as seeking mode (Cats move slowly when resting but being alert) and tracing mode (Cats move slowly when resting). In seeking mode, we define four important factors: seeking memory pool (SMP), seeking range of the selected dimension (SRD) (to find a range of selected dimensions), counts of dimension to change (CDC) (to calculate dimensions will change), and self-position considering (SPC) (to consider the position). The tracing mode of CSO algorithm that describes the cat is being followed the lead of the target. Once a cat goes into tracing mode, it moves according to its' own speed for each dimension [16]. The detailed descriptions of these modes are given in the general process of Cat Swarm Optimization Algorithm CSOA in Figure (4). It is explain the two modes of CSO algorithm, the Mixture Ratio (MR) indicates the rate of mixing the seeking mode and the tracing mode. The process of Cat Swarm Optimization Algorithm CSOA is described as follows:

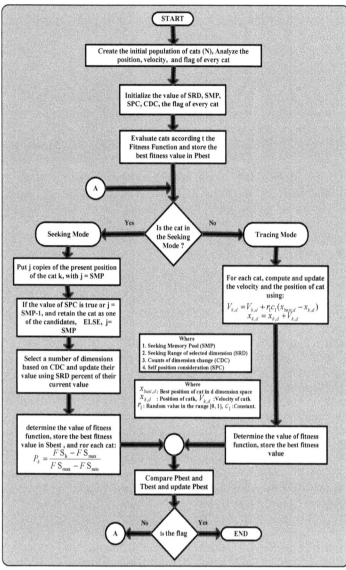

Fig.4.   Figure 4 The general process of Cat Swarm Optimization Algorithm CSOA.

VI.   PROPOSED SYSTEM

The Electrocardiograms ECG electrodes convert heart signals into an electrical signal ranging from 1mV to 5 mV. Every ECG signal has five distinct points (P, Q, R, S and T wave). Figure (5) below explained the Flowchart of CSOA based parameter optimization for SVM classifier of our proposed system which is composed of three stages:

- Pre-processing
- Feature Extraction
- Classification using SVMs

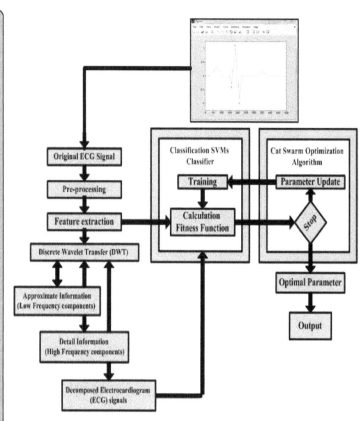

Fig.5.   Flowchart of our proposed system CSOA based parameter optimization for SVM classifier.

A. Pre-processing

The noise of Electrocardiograms ECG signal contains power line interference, baseline wandering effect, and muscle noise. The common noise of raw ECG signals is shown in Figure (6).

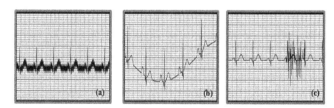

Fig.6.   Examples of different ECG signal noise (a) power line interference, (b) baseline wandering effect(c) muscle noise.

The power-line interference is caused by the electromagnetic field interfering with the ECG equipment cables. Baseline wandering effect causes the entire ECG signal to shift up or down from the normal base at zero y-axis,. A muscle noise is an interference voltage generated whenever a patient contracts a body muscle. These micro-voltages are detected by the electrode and shown in the signal as noise.

To remove all noise from raw ECG signals, we can implement conservative filters. A high-pass filter with 0.5Hz cutoff frequency can be used to remove unwanted low-frequency components of baseline wandering effect. The power-line noise is filtered away by a notch filter, and the muscle noise effect can be removed by a time-varying low-pass filter. in the pretreatment of ECG wave is completed based on a high-pass filter with 0.7Hz and low-pass filter with 100Hz, Figures (7) (a) and (b) [17].

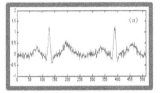 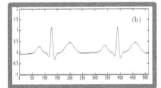

Fig.7.　(a) ECG signal before de-noising, (b) ECG signal after de-noising.

In order to extract and use the feature of the ECG waveform in the classifier design stage of ECG signal analysis, the noise elimination, baseline wanders removal and peak detection (P, Q, R, S and T) [15].

B. Feature extraction

Feature extraction plays an important role in any classification task. The purpose of feature extraction is to select and retain relevant information from the original signals.The feature extraction in this paper uses the Discrete Wavelet Transform (DWT- Daubechies16 (Db16)) [18]. ECG signals were decomposed to the approximate information called low frequency components and detailed information called high frequency components show in Figure (1). Decomposition of the signal is done up to many steps (eight steps). If these steps are high, the low-frequency components of the original signal are better conserved. Low frequency band of the ECG signal is used for the detection of QRS, T, and P waves. For each feature shown in table (1) are calculated. Execution of ECG classifier is done by using SVMs distribution estimation (one-class SVMs).

C. ECG Classification

ECG classification system based on Support Vector Machines SVMs One cycle of ECG signal consists of P-QRS-T wave, six types of beats including Normal sinusrhythm (N), a trial premature beat (A),Ventricular premature beat (V), Right Bundle branch block (RB), Left Bundle branch block (LB), and Paced beat (/).

The ECG signals were first decomposed with the discrete wavelet transform (DWT) after which feature vectors were extracted[19]. These feature vectors were used to classify the signal. In our proposed system we take ten features (QRS Complex ,P-R Segment ,P-R Interval ,S-T segment ,Q-T Interval , R-R Interval, P-P Interval-R and P-P Similarity ,R-R Interval Variance, Heart Beat), they were saved as separate vectors and extracted for each heart beat automatically, then we calculated the difference position between two separate vectors as feature values after detection of the position of Q, R, S, T start, T end, P start and P end. The description of these features has been explained in table (1) below for each heartbeat. The start of the QRS complex was defined as the

beginning of each beat and normal beats which occurred immediately before or after abnormal beats were removed[20].

TABLE I.　　TEN FEATURES DESCRIPTION USED FOR EACH HEART BEAT AUTOMATICALLY.

No.	Feature name	Description of Feature	
1	QRS Complex	Pos(S) - Pos(Q)	Pos position of feature in the ECG signal
2	P-R Segment	Pos(Q) - Pos(Pend)	
3	P-R Interval	Pos(Q) - Pos(Pstart)	
4	S-T segment	Pos(Tstart) - Pos(S)	
5	Q-T Interval	Pos(Tend) - Pos(Q)	
6	R-R Interval	Pos(Rnext) - Pos(R)	
7	P-P Interval	Pos(Pnext) - Pos(P)	
8	R-R and P-P Similarity	ABS((R-R Interval)- (P-P Interval))	
9	R-R Interval Variance	VAR(R-R Interval))	
10	Heart Beat	60/(R-R Interval)	

D. Parameter optimization based on CSOA

To determine the optimized parameter using the CSOA. Randomly generate N solution sets and velocities with D-dimensional space, represented the following parameters of cat swarm optimization algorithm explain in the table (2).

TABLE II.　　PARAMETERS OF CAT SWARM OPTIMIZATION ALGORITHM.

No.	parameter	Description
1	SMP	seeking memory pool
2	SRD	seeking range of the selected dimension
3	CDC	counts of dimension to change
4	MR	mixture ratio
5	NBS	number of best solution sets
6	MR Best	mutation rate for best solution sets
7	NTM	number of trying mutation

We present an CSOA to search the optimal penalty coefficient C_{best} , insensitive loss coefficient ε_{best} and the width of kernel function δ_{best} in the SVM forecast parameters space (C,ε ,δ). Create N cats, regulate N and dusting the adjusted N cats into the 3 dimensional SVM forecast parameter space (C,ε ,δ) evenly by the Even Distribution Process and divide the adjusted N cats into G groups. Randomly generate the Velocities for each dimension V_C, $V\varepsilon$ and V_δ of each cat. This should be in the predefined range. Set the Motion Flag of each cat to make them move into the Parallel Tracing Mode or the Seeking Mode according to the predefined value of MR, where $MR \in [0,1]$ For each cat, take location coordinates (C_i, ,ε_i ,δ_i) into the Fitness Function of SVM, calculate the fitness values respectively, and record the Location coordinates and the fitness values [21-23].

VII. EXPERIMENTS AND RESULTS

This section describes the experimental setup of dataset based on MATLAB. We description the dataset and their training and testing data beats are explained in the two paragraphs below:

- Dataset Description.

- Results and Discussion.

A. Dataset Description

Our experiment conducted on the basis of ECG data from the Public teaching hospital in Tikrit, Heart catheterization suite database, were chosen from the recording of (30) patients, which matched the following files, Table (3) displays the datasets employed in our experiment.

TABLE III.   DISPLAYS THE DATASETS EMPLOYED IN OUR EXPERIMENT.

No. of patient	No. of file	No. of patient	No. of file
1	0100	16	0205
2	0102	17	0206
3	0103	18	0207
4	0104	19	0208
5	0105	20	0209
6	0106	21	0210
7	0107	22	0211
8	0108	23	0212
9	0109	24	0213
10	0110	25	0214
11	0200	26	0215
12	0201	27	0216
13	0202	28	0217
14	0203	29	0218
15	0204	30	0219

B. Results and Discussion

Our proposed system followed the datasets of 30 patients, the number of files for every penitent explained in table (3) which are chosen from Public teaching hospital in Tikrit, to measure the classification accuracy of the proposed hybrid CSOA-SVM method. The measured Electrocardiograms ECG signal refers to succeeding classes of beats:

- Normal sinusrhythm (N)

- Trial premature beat (A)

- Ventricular premature beat (V)

- Right Bundle branch block (RB)

- Left Bundle branch block (LB)

- Paced beat (/).

Our experiment in order to deliver for the classification procedure the two following kinds of features are espoused:

1) ECG morphology features
2) Ten ECG temporal features

The ten features are (QRS Complex, P-R Segment, P-R Interval, S-T segment, Q-T Interval, R-R Interval, P-P Interval-R and P-P Similarity, R-R Interval Variance, Heart Beat). Then, extracting the following ten Temporal features of interest, normalized to the similar length the period of the segmented ECG cycles according to the process reported. To this end, the mean beat length was chosen as the standardized length, which was represented by 300 evenly distributed samples. Accordingly, the total number of morphology and sequential features equals 310 for each beat.

In our experiments, ten different tribunals are performed, each with a new set of randomly selected training beats, while the test set was kept unbothered. The results of these ten tribunals attained on the test set were thus averaged. The thorough amount of training and test beats are described for each class in Figure (8).

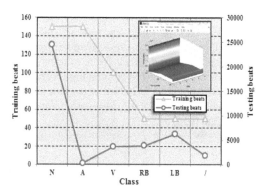

Fig.8.   Numbers of Training and Testing Beats used in our Experiments.

Classification presentation was evaluated in terms of two measures, which are:

1)   Overall Accuracy (OA), which is the percentage of correctly classified Electrocardiograms (ECG) signal among all the beats considered.
2)   Average Accuracy (AA), which is the average over the classification accuracies obtained for the different classes.

Overall Accuracy (OA), Average (AA), and succeeding classes of beats (Normal sinusrhythm (N), Trial premature beat (A), Ventricular premature beat (V), Right Bundle branch block (RB), Left Bundle branch block (LB), Paced beat (/)) Attained on the Test Beats with the Different Investigated Classifiers with a total Number of 550 Training Beats. The accuracy of the intentional system of hybrid CSOA-SVMs may have high accuracy when evaluated with the standard SVMs. The hybrid CSOA-SVMs has high value in all proposed systems. Figure (9) explains the result of our experiment.

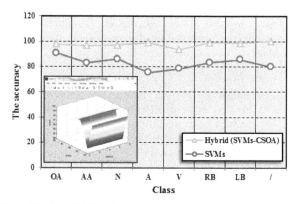

Fig.9.   The hybrid CSOA-SVMs the result of our experiment.

VIII.   CONCLUSION

The natural world secretes many characteristics of different creatures, and all of them have some exceptional behaviors or features to keep them subsist in our paper, CSOA-SVMs approach is proposed for an automatic Electrocardiograms ECG signal classification. This approach presents methods for improving SVMs performance in two aspects: feature selection and parameter optimization.

The new method proposed in this paper is the combination of a support vector machine and cat swarm optimization algorithm (CSOA-SVMs). This hybrid system   is jointly applied to optimize the feature selection and the SVMs parameters (penalty coefficient C_{best} , insensitive loss coefficient ε_{best} and the width of radial basis function kernel function δ_{best} in the SVM prediction parameters space (C, ε ,δ).

REFERENCES

[1] B. Mohammadzadeh Asl, S.K. Setarehdan, and M. Mohebbi, "Support vector machine-based arrhythmia classification using reduced features of heart rate variability signal," Artificial Intelligence in Medicine, vol. 44, no.1, pp. 51-64, 2008.

[2] Osowski, S., Markiewicz, T., & Tran Hoai, L., "Recognition and classification system of arrhythmia using ensemble of neural networks", Measurement, 41, pp. 610-617, 2008.

[3] Polat, K., Akdemir, B., & Günes, S., "Computer aided diagnosis of ECG data on the least square support vector machine", Digital Signal Processing, 18(1), 2008.

[4] Sarkaleh, Maedeh Kiani; Shahbahrami, Asadollah, "A. Classification of ECG Arrhythmias Using Discrete Wavelet Transform and Neural Networks", International Journal of Computer Science, Engineering and Applications, Vol. 2, Issue 1, p1 ,2012.

[5] Javadi M, Ebrahimpoor R, "improving ECG classification accuracy using an ensemble of neural network modules", PLos ONE 6(10).journal.pone.0024386.

[6] Rahat Abbas, Wajid Aziz,   and Muhammad Arif,   "Prediction   of Ventricular Tachyarrhythmia in Electrocardiograph Signals using Neural Network and Modified Nearest Neighbour Method", Proceedings of International Students Conference on Engineering Sciences and Technology (SCONEST), 2004.

[7] Moein, S.T., Advances in Computational Biology: "A MLP Neural Network for ECG Noise Removal Based on Kalman Filter", In: Arabnia, H.R. (ed.). Springer, Heidelberg, 2010.

[8] M. Korürek and A. Nizam, "Clustering MIT-BIH arrhythmias with ant colony optimization using time domain and PCA compressed wavelet coefficients," Digital Signal Processing, vol. 20, no. 4, pp. 1050–1060, 2010.

[9] M. J. del Jesus, F. Hoffmann, L. Junco, L. Sánchez. "Induction of Fuzzy-Rule-Based Classifiers With Evolutionary Boosting Algorithms", IEEE Transactions on Fuzzy Systems 12:3, pp 296-308, 2004.

[10] Bortolan G, Willems JL, "Diagnostic ECG classification based on neural networks", Journal of Electrocardiology, Vol. 26, pp. 75-79, 1994.

[11] Kutlu Y, Kuntalp D., "A multi-stage automatic arrhythmia recognition and   classification   system".   Computers   in   Biology   and Medicine,Vol41(1), pp. 37–45, 2011 .

[12] Wu Q. and Zhou D.-X., "Analysis of Support Vector Machine Classification", International Journal of Computer Analysis and Applications Vol. 8, pp. 99–119, 2006.

[13] Karpagachelvi S, Arthanari M, Sivakumar M., "classification of electrocardiogram signals with support vector machines and extreme learning machine", Neural Computing and Applications, Vol. 21(6), 2012.

[14] S. C. Chu, P. W. Tsai and J. S. Pan, "Cat swarm optimization", proceedings of the 9th   Pacific Rim International Conference on Artificial Intelligence, pp. 854-858, ,2006, Guilin, China.

[15] S. C. Chu and P.W. Tsai, " Computational intelligence based on the behavior of cats", International Journal of Innovative Computing, Information and Control, Vol.3,No.(1), 2007.

[16] J. Paul and T. Yusiong, "Optimizing Artificial Neural Networks using Cat Swarm Optimization Algorithm," I. J. Intelligent Systems and Applications, vol. 1. 2013.

[17] S.Paland M. Mitra, "Detection of ECG characteristic points using multi-resolution wavelet analysis based selective coefficient method", Measurement, Vol.43. 2010.

[18] R. Olszewski, "Generalized feature extraction for structural pattern recognition in time-series data," Ph.D. dissertation, School of Computer Science, Carnegie Mellon University, 2001.

[19] W. Jiang and G. Seong Kong, "Block-Based Neural Networks for Personalized ECG Signal Classification," Neural Networks, IEEE Trans. Vol. 18, No. 6, 2007.

[20] D. Liu, "Research on Quantum Neural Network Model and Its Application to ECG Classification", Master's thesis, Nanjing University of Posts and Telecommunications, 2012.

[21] J. A.Nasiri, M. Sabzekar, H. S. Yazdi, M. Naghibzadeh, and B. Naghibzadeh, "Intelligent Arrhythmia Detection Using Genetic Algorithm and Emphatic SVM(ESVM)," in Third UKSim European Symposium On Computer Modeling and Simulation, pp. 112–117, 2009.

[22] Melgani F, Bazi Y., "Classification of Electrocardiogram Signals with Support Vector Machines and Particle Swarm Optimization", IEEE Trans. On Information Technology in Biomedicine, Vol.2, No. (5), 2008.

[23] Kuan-Cheng Lin, Yi-Hung Huang, Jason C. Hung, and Yung-Tso Lin., "Feature Selection and Parameter Optimization of Support Vector Machines Based on Modified Cat Swarm Optimization", International Journal of Distributed Sensor Networks, 2014.

3

Preliminary Study on Phytoplankton Distribution Changes Monitoring for the Intensive Study Area of the Ariake Sea, Japan Based on Remote Sensing Satellite Data

Kohei Arai
Graduate School of Science and Engineering
Saga University
Saga City, Japan

Toshiya Katano
Institute of Lowland and Marine Research
Saga University
Saga City Japan

Abstract—**Phytoplankton distribution changes in the Ariake Sea areas, Japan based on remote sensing satellite data is studied. Through experiments with Terra and AQUA MODIS data derived chlorophyll-a concentration and suspended solid as well as truth data of chlorophyll-a concentration together with meteorological data and tidal data which are acquired 7 months from October 2012 to April 2013, it is found that strong correlation between the truth data of chlorophyll-a and MODIS derived chlorophyll-a concentrations with R square value ranges from 0.677 to 0.791. Also it is found that the relations between ocean wind speed and chlorophyll-a concentration as well as between tidal effects and chlorophyll-a concentration. Meanwhile, there is a relatively high correlation between sunshine duration a day and chlorophyll-a concentration.**

Keywords-chlorophyl-a concentration; suspended solid; ocean winds.

I. INTRODUCTION

Due to red tide contaminations, water color is changed by an algal bloom. In accordance with increasing of phytoplankton concentration, sea surface color changes from blue to green as well as to red or brown depending on the majority of phytoplankton (Dierssen et al, 2006) so that it is capable to detect red tide using this color changes [1].

MODIS ocean color bands data is used for red tide detection. An iterative approach (Arnone et al., 1998 [2]; Stumpf et al., 2003 [3]) for sediment-rich waters, based on the Gordon and Wang (1994) algorithm [4], is used to correct for the atmospheric interference in the six ocean color bands in turbid coastal waters to obtain water leaving radiance, which are then used in the band-ratio algorithm (O'Reilly et al., 2000 [5]) to estimate Chlorophyll in unit of mg m^{-3}. Also suspended solid is estimated with two bands algorithm (visible minus near infrared bands data). The multi-channels of red tide detection algorithms (in the formula of $C=(R_i-R_j)/(R_k-R_l)$ where R_i, R_j, R_k and R_l are the reflectivity derived from bands i, j, k and l.) are proposed. Also learning approaches based on k-nearest neighbors, random forests and support vector machines have been proposed for red tide detection with Moderate Resolution Imaging Spectro-radiometer: MODIS satellite images (Weijian C.,et al.,2009) [6].

Satellite based red tide detection does work under a fine weather condition but not under cloudy and rainy conditions obviously. Furthermore, revisit period of fine resolution of radiometer onboard satellite orbits are longer than typical red tide propagations so that it is not enough observation frequency if only remote sensing satellite is used for red tide detections. Therefore satellite-and ground-based red tide monitoring system is proposed [7]. In the ground based red tide monitoring system, green colored filtered camera and polarization camera are featured for detection of red tide and discrimination of red tide types [8].

The Ariake Sea is the largest productive area of Nori (*Porphyra yezoensis*) in Japan. In winters of 2012 and 2013, a massive diatom bloom occurred in the Ariake Sea, Japan (Ito et al. 2013). In case of above red tides, bloom causative was *Eucampia zodiacus*. This bloom had been firstly developed at the eastern part of the Ariake Sea. However, as the field observation is time-consuming, information on the developing process of the red tide, and horizontal distribution of the red tide has not yet been clarified in detail. To clarify the horizontal distribution of red tide, and its temporal change, remote sensing using satellite data is quite useful.

In this paper, the chlorophyll-a concentration algorithm developed for MODIS is firstly validated. Then apply the algorithm to MODIS data which are acquired at the Ariake Sea areas, Japan specifically. Also the relations between tidal effects and chlorophyll-a concentration as well as between ocean wind speed and chlorophyll-a concentration together with between sunshine duration a day and chlorophyll-a concentration.

In the next section, the method and procedure of the experimental study is described followed by experimental data and estimated results. Then conclusion is described with some discussions.

II. METHOD AND PROCEDURE

A. The Procedure

The procedure of the experimental study is as follows,

1) Gather the truth data of chlorophyll-a concentration measured at the observation towers in the Ariake Sea areas together with the corresponding areas of MODIS derived chlorophyll-a concentration,

2) Gather the meteorological data which includes sunshine duration a day, ocean wind speed and direction, tidal heights,

3) Correlation analysis between the truth data and MODIS derived chlorophyll-a concentration as well as between geophysical parameters, ocean wind speed, sunshine duration a day, tidal heights and chlorophyll-a concentration is made.

B. MODIS

MODIS stands for The Moderate Resolution Imaging Spectro-radiometer which allows observations of the earth's surface with a variety of wavelength regions ranges from visible to thermal infrared with spatial resolution of 250, 500 and 1000 meters. Major specifications of MODIS are shown in Table 1 and 2.

MODIS is carried on Terra and AQUA satellites with local mean time of 10:30 a.m. and 1:30 p.m. with 2330km of swath width. Therefore, it may cover entire globe within a day. MODIS data is applicable to land surface, ocean surface, and atmosphere observations as is shown in Table 2. In particular for ocean surface observations, bands 8 to 16 data are useful.

TABLE I.   MAJOR SPECIFICATIONS OF MODIS[1]

Orbit:	705 km, 10:30 a.m. descending node (Terra) or 1:30 p.m. ascending node (Aqua), sun-synchronous, near-polar, circular
Scan Rate:	20.3 rpm, cross track
Swath Dimensions:	2330 km (cross track) by 10 km (along track at nadir)
Telescope:	17.78 cm diam. off-axis, afocal (collimated), with intermediate field stop
Size:	1.0 x 1.6 x 1.0 m
Weight:	228.7 kg
Power:	162.5 W (single orbit average)
Data Rate:	10.6 Mbps (peak daytime); 6.1 Mbps (orbital average)
Quantization:	12 bits
Spatial Resolution:	250 m (bands 1-2) 500 m (bands 3-7) 1000 m (bands 8-36)
Design Life:	6 years

TABLE II.   APPLICATION OF MODIS SENSOR DATA[2]

Primary Use	Band	Bandwidth[1]	Spectral Radiance[2]	Required SNR[3]
Land/Cloud/Aerosols Boundaries	1	620 - 670	21.8	128
	2	841 - 876	24.7	201
Land/Cloud/Aerosols	3	459 - 479	35.3	243
Properties	4	545 - 565	29.0	228
	5	1230 - 1250	5.4	74
	6	1628 - 1652	7.3	275
	7	2105 - 2155	1.0	110
Ocean Color/ Phytoplankton/ Biogeochemistry	8	405 - 420	44.9	880
	9	438 - 448	41.9	838
	10	483 - 493	32.1	802
	11	526 - 536	27.9	754
	12	546 - 556	21.0	750
	13	662 - 672	9.5	910
	14	673 - 683	8.7	1087
	15	743 - 753	10.2	586
	16	862 - 877	6.2	516
Atmospheric Water Vapor	17	890 - 920	10.0	167
	18	931 - 941	3.6	57
	19	915 - 965	15.0	250

Primary Use	Band	Bandwidth[1]	Spectral Radiance[2]	Required NE[delta]T(K)[4]
Surface/Cloud Temperature	20	3.660 - 3.840	0.45(300K)	0.05
	21	3.929 - 3.989	2.38(335K)	2.00
	22	3.929 - 3.989	0.67(300K)	0.07
	23	4.020 - 4.080	0.79(300K)	0.07
Atmospheric Temperature	24	4.433 - 4.498	0.17(250K)	0.25
	25	4.482 - 4.549	0.59(275K)	0.25
Cirrus Clouds Water Vapor	26	1.360 - 1.390	6.00	150(SNR)
	27	6.535 - 6.895	1.16(240K)	0.25
	28	7.175 - 7.475	2.18(250K)	0.25
Cloud Properties	29	8.400 - 8.700	9.58(300K)	0.05
Ozone	30	9.580 - 9.880	3.69(250K)	0.25
Surface/Cloud Temperature	31	10.780 - 11.280	9.55(300K)	0.05
	32	11.770 - 12.270	8.94(300K)	0.05
Cloud Top Altitude	33	13.185 - 13.485	4.52(260K)	0.25
	34	13.485 - 13.785	3.76(250K)	0.25
	35	13.785 - 14.085	3.11(240K)	0.25
	36	14.085 - 14.385	2.08(220K)	0.35

[1] Bands 1 to 19 are in nm; Bands 20 to 36 are in μm
[2] Spectral Radiance values are (W/m^2 -μm-sr)
[3] SNR = Signal-to-noise ratio
[4] NE(delta)T = Noise-equivalent temperature difference

Note: Performance goal is 30-40% better than required

There are following many ocean related products[3],

Angstrom Exponent
Aerosol Optical Thickness

[1] http://modis.gsfc.nasa.gov/about/specifications.php
[2] http://modis.gsfc.nasa.gov/about/specifications.php
[3] http://oceancolor.gsfc.nasa.gov/

Chlorophyll a
Downwelling diffuse attenuation coefficient at 490 nm
Level 2 Flags
Photosynthetically Available Radiation
Particulate Inorganic Carbon
Particulate Organic Carbon
Sea Surface Temperature Quality
Sea Surface Temperature Quality - 4um
Remote Sensing Reflectance
Sea Surface Temperature
Sea Surface Temperature 4um

In this study, chlorophyll-a product is used for the experiments.

C. The Intensive Study Areas

Figure 1 shows the intensive study areas in the Ariake Sea area, Kyushu, Japan.

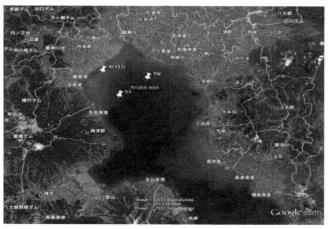

Fig 1.   The Intensive study areas (Yellow pins shows the areas)

There are three observation tower points, TW, S, and A. TW is closely situated to the Saga Ariake Airport and is situated near the river mouth. On the other hand, A is situated most closely to the coastal area while S is situated in the middle point of the Ariake Sea width and is situated most far from the coastal areas and river mouths.

III.   EXPERIMENTS

A. The Data Used

The truth data of chlorophyll-a concentration measured at the observation towers in the intensive study areas in the Ariake Sea areas together with the corresponding areas of MODIS derived chlorophyll-a concentration which area acquired for the observation period of 7 months during from October 2012 to April 2013 are used for the experiments. Also, the meteorological data which includes sunshine duration, ocean wind speed and direction, tidal heights which are acquired for the 7 months are used for the experiments.

Figure 2 shows an example of the chlorophyll-a concentration image which is derived from MODIS data which is acquired on 25 February 2013.

The chlorophyll-a concentration measured at the tower, TW ranges from 52 to 64 ug/l (the highest value in the 7 months). This is red tide (Phytoplankton) blooming period. Such this MODIS derived chlorophyll-a concentration data are available almost every day except cloudy and rainy conditions.

Blooming is used to be occurred when the seawater becomes nutrient rich water, calm ocean winds, long sunshine duration after convection of seawater (vertical seawater current from the bottom to sea surface). Therefore, there must exists relations between the geophysical parameters, ocean wind speed, sunshine duration, tidal heights and chlorophyll-a concentration.

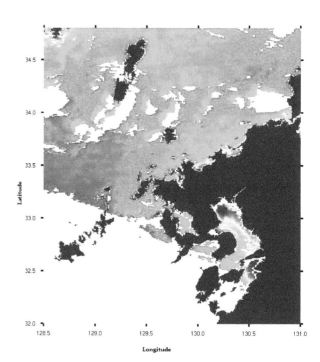

Fig 2.   An example of the chlorophyll-a concentration image which is derived from MODIS data which is acquired on 25 February 2013

B. The Relation Between Truth Data and MODIS Derived Colorophyl-a Concentrations

In order to check validity of the chlorophyll-a concentration estimation algorithm, the relation between truth and MODIS derived chlorophyll-a concentration is investigated. Figure 3 shows the relation between these for intensive study area of S while Figure 4 shows the relation for intensive study area of TW.

In the figures, L and H denote Low and High chlorophyll-a concentration of the day. Also Ch-a denotes chlorophyll-a concentration in unit of μg/l. Linear (L) denotes linear regression line for minimum chlorophyll-a concentration of the day while Linear (H) denotes that for maximum chlorophyll-a concentration of the day.

C. Trend Analysis

MODIS derived chlorophyll-a concentration which are acquired from January 4 2013 to February 28 2013 are shown in Figure 5.

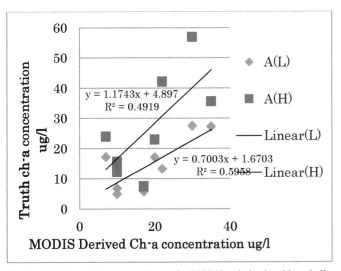

Fig 3. Relation between truth and MODIS derived chlorophyll-a concentrations for the intensive study area of S

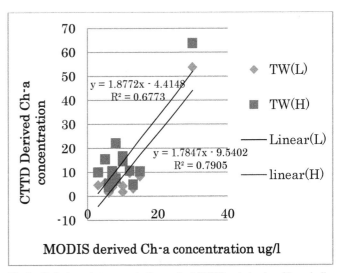

Fig 4. Relation between truth and MODIS derived chlorophyll-a concentrations for the intensive study area of TW

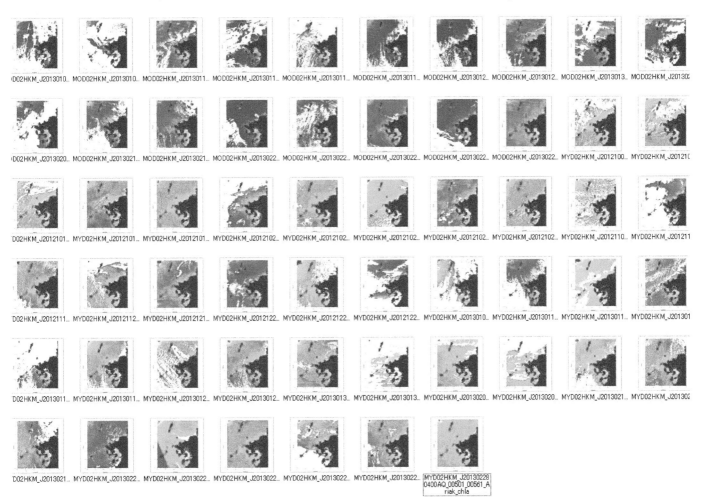

Fig 5. MODIS derived chlorophyll-a concentration in the intensive study areas which are acquired from January 4 2013 to February 28 2013

A massive red tide by large diatom of Eucampia zodiacus occurred from February to April, 2013 in the innermost are of the Ariake Sea. The bloom developing process are clearly detected in Figure 5.

In the first half of the Figure 5, surface chlorophyll-a concentration was low in the sea; however, it obviously increased in the middle of the Figure 5.

Finally, in the later half of the figure, quite high concentrations of chlorophyll-a were detected in the innermost area of the sea, as the Eucampia population developed. To clarify the developing mechanism of this red tide, other environmental variables such as temperature, salinity, nutrient concentrations should be further investigated.

D. Relations between geophysical parameters and chlorophyll-a concentrations

Nutrient rich seawater near the bottom is used to be flown from the sea bottom to the sea surface when the seawater convection is occurred due to ocean wind, and tidal effect. Then chlorophyll-a concentration increases in accordance with sunshine duration with the nutrient rich sea surface water. Therefore, there must exist some relations between the geophysical parameter of ocean wind, tidal effect and sunshine duration.

Figure 6 shows a relatively high relation between accumulated sunshine duration for the past three days and chlorophyll-a concentration. Ocean wind is not so strong, while tidal effect is also not so high. Therefore the relation between accumulated sun appearances time duration is proportional to the truth data of chlorophyll-a concentration.

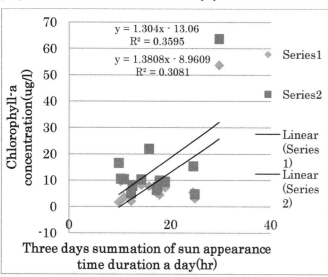

Fig 6.   Relation between accumulated sunshine duration a day for the past three days and chlorophyll-a concentration

It can also be said that there are very weak relation between chlorophyll-a concentration and ocean wind as well as sea level difference a day due to the fact that ocean wind is not so high while tidal effect is not so large. Figure 7 shows the relation between chlorophyll-a concentration and accumulated daily averaged ocean wind speed for the past two days.

Meanwhile, Figure 8 shows the relation between chlorophyll-a concentration and sea surface level difference a day while Figure 9 shows the relation between chlorophyll-a concentration and the accumulated sea surface level difference for the past two days.

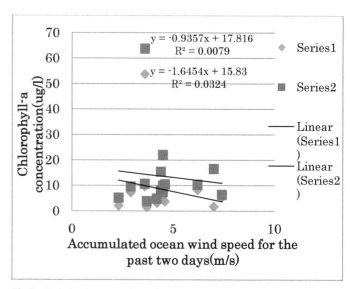

Fig 7.   Relation between chlorophyll-a concentration and accumulated daily averaged ocean wind speed for the past two days.

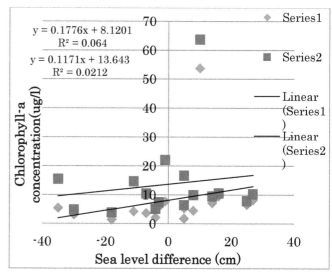

Fig 8.   Relation between chlorophyll-a concentration and sea surface level difference a day

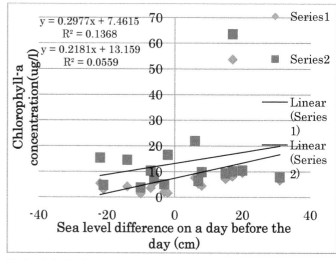

Fig 9.   Relation between chlorophyll-a concentration and the accumulated sea surface level difference for the past two days.

It is confirmed that relation between ocean wind speed and chlorophyll-a concentration is weak. Also, it is confirmed that relation between sea surface level difference a day and chlorophyll-a concentration is weak. It may said that relation between two days accumulated sea surface level difference a day and chlorophyll-a concentration is higher than that between one day sea surface level difference and chlorophyll-a concentration. That is because of the fact that there is time delay of chlorophyll-a increasing after the nutrient rich bottom seawater is flown to the sea surface.

IV. CONCLUSION

Preliminary study on phytoplankton distribution changes monitoring for the intensive study area of the Ariake Sea, Japan based on remote sensing satellite data is conducted. Phytoplankton distribution changes in the Ariake Sea areas, Japan based on remote sensing satellite data is studied.

Through experiments with Terra and AQUA MODIS data derived chlorophyll-a concentration and suspended solid as well as truth data of chlorophyll-a concentration together with meteorological data and tidal data which are acquired 7 months from October 2012 to April 2013, it is found that strong correlation between the truth data of chlorophyll-a and MODIS derived chlorophyll-a concentrations with R square value ranges from 0.677 to 0.791.

Also it is found that the relations between ocean wind speed and chlorophyll-a concentration as well as between tidal effects and chlorophyll-a concentration. Meanwhile, there is a relatively high correlation between sunshine duration a day and chlorophyll-a concentration.

As the results from the experiments, it is found that the followings,

1) the accumulated sun appearances time duration is proportional to the truth data of chlorophyll-a concentration

2) it is confirmed that relation between ocean wind speed and chlorophyll-a concentration is weak,

3) it is confirmed that relation between sea surface level difference a day and chlorophyll-a concentration is weak,

4) it may said that relation between two days accumulated sea surface level difference a day and chlorophyll-a concentration is higher than that between one day sea surface level difference and chlorophyll-a concentration,

5) there is a time delay of chlorophyll-a increasing after the nutrient rich bottom seawater is flown to the sea surface.

ACKNOWLEDGMENT

The authors would like to thank Dr. Yuichi Hayami of Institute of Lowland and Marine Research, Saga University for his great supports through the experiments.

REFERENCES

[1] Dierssen H.M., R.M.Kudela, J.P.Ryan, R.C.Zimmerman, Red and black tides: Quantitative analysis of water-leaving radiance and perceived color for phytoplankton, colored dissolved organic matter, and suspended sediments, Limnol. Oceanogr., 51(6), 2646–2659, E 2006, by the American Society of Limnology and Oceanography, Inc., 2006.

[2] Arnone, R. A., Martinolich, P., Gould, R. W., Jr., Stumpf, R., & Ladner, S., Coastal optical properties using SeaWiFS. Ocean Optics XIV, Kailua Kona, Hawaii, USA, November 10–13, 1998. SPIE Proceedings., 1998.

[3] Stumpf, R. P., Arnone, R. A., Gould Jr., R. W., Martinolich, P. M., & Martinuolich, V., A partially coupled ocean-atmosphere model for retrieval of water-leaving radiance from SeaWiFS in coastal waters. In S. B. Hooker, & E. R. Firestone (Eds.), SeaWiFS Postlaunch Tech. Report Series. NASA Technical Memorandum, 2003-206892, vol. 22 (p. 74), 2003.

[4] Gordon, H. R., & Wang, M., Retrieval of water-leaving radiance and aerosol optical thickness over the oceans with SeaWiFS: A preliminary algorithm. Applied Optics, 33, 443–452, 1994.

[5] O'Reilly, J. E., Maritorena, S., Siegel, D. A., O'Brien, M. C., Toole, D.,Chavez, F. P., et al., Ocean color chlorophyll a algorithms for SeaWiFS, OC2, and OC4: Version 4. In B. Hooker, & R. Firestone (Eds.), SeaWiFS Postlaunch Tech. Report Series. NASA Technical Memorandum 2000-206892, vol. 11 (p. 2000), 2000.

[6] Weijian, C., Hall, L.O., Goldgof, D.B., Soto, I.M., Chuanmin H, Automatic red tide detection from MODIS satellite images, Systems, Man and Cybernetics, 2009. SMC 2009. IEEE International Conference on SMC, 2009.

[7] Kohei Arai and Yasunori Terayama, Polarized radiance from red tide, Proceedings of the SPIE Asia Pacific Remote Sensing, AE10-AE101-14, Invited Paper, 2010

[8] Kohei Arai, *Red tides*: combining satellite- and ground-based detection. 29 January 2011, *SPIE Newsroom*. DOI: 10.1117/2.1201012.003267, http://spie.org/x44134.xml?ArticleID=x44134

[9] Graham LE, Wilcox LW. (2000) Algae. pp. 232-68. Prentice Hall. ISBN 0-13-660333-5

[10] Kroger N, Deutzmann R, Sumper M (1999). "Polycationic peptides from diatom biosilica that direct silica nanosphere formation". *Science* **286** (5442): 1129-32.

[11] Martin-Jezequel V, Hildebrand M, Brzezinski MA (2000). "Silicon metabolism in diatoms: Implications for growth". *J Phycol* **36**: 821-40.

[12] Adl, Sina M.; *et al.* (2005), "The New Higher Level Classification of Eukaryotes with Emphasis on the Taxonomy of Protists", *J. Eukaryot. Microbiol.* **52** (5): 429–493

[13] Adl, Sina M.; *et al.* (2012), "The Revised Classification of Eukaryotes", *J. Eukaryot. Microbiol.* **59** (5): 429–493

4

The Influence of Stubborn Agents in a Multi-Agent Network for Inter-Team Cooperation/Negotiation

Eugene S. Kitamura
Department of Computer Science,
National Defense Academy
Yokosuka, Japan

Akira Namatame
Department of Computer Science,
National Defense Academy
Yokosuka, Japan

Abstract—When teams interact for cooperation or negotiation, there are unique dynamics that occur depending on the conditions. In this paper, a multi-agent system is used under the restrain of a network structure to model two teams of agents interacting for a common consensus, however with the presence of stubborn agents. The networks used were a minimum dumbbell network and two scale-free networks joined together. The network topology, which is a global characteristic, along with the presence of conflicting stubborn agents, can cause various conditions that affect teamwork in cooperation or negotiation. Notable characteristics revealed are boundary role persons (BRPs), lack of unity, need for a third party moderator, coalition formation, and loyalty of the BRP dependent on the distance from the core ideology of the team. Both local and global characteristics of network structures contribute to such phenomenon. The modeling method and corresponding simulation results provide valuable insight for predicting possible social dynamics and outcome when planning cooperation/negotiation tactics.

Keywords—Multi-agent system; consensus problem; stubborn agents; complex network; dumbbell network; Laplacian matrix; boundary role person; coalition formation

I. INTRODUCTION

A. Team dynamics and consensus

The success of an organization depends on how effective its team of agents operate, whether in business or in other social settings. Thus, it is natural for organizational managers to have an interest in understanding group dynamics. A team, as opposed to an individual, is a conglomeration of diverse talents and perspectives, and allows distribution of tasks for efficient operations [1, 2]. Formation of a robust team with diverse agents is especially valued today in business to cope with rapidly changing technological and global markets [3, 4]. However, because of its collective nature of talents and personalities, a team of agents may be exposed to internal conflict and noise in addition to external ones during cooperation or negotiation with another team of agents. Such perturbations can result in unintended consensus dynamics within the team. How does the formation of consensus opinion depend on the locations of stubborn agents in the social network? We would like to be able to predict the outcomes such that we can control or avoid certain situations during the formation of consensus.

To have a holistic view of team dynamics, a manager must consider the *micro* and *macro* properties of a team. *Micro* *properties* considered important are *planning*, which is subdividing tasks among agents, *coordination*, which is the synchronization of agent actions and its continuous monitoring for assessment, and *communication*, which is information exchange among agents [5]. These qualities are micro properties since they are defined for and executed by the agents that form a team. On the other hand, *macro properties* are the network structure that embeds the agent interactions or patterns of relationships within a team [6, 7]. With such network topological aspect, the team dynamics is not only determined by agent characteristics or local interaction rules, but also determined by a global structural restraint. This network formed by the agent team can be considered a macro property since this property ignores the characteristics of each agent and it affects the entire community. For managers and team members to understand and predict team consensus dynamics, they need to observe and evaluate both their micro and macro properties. Failure of such considerations may result in disagreements and formations of coalitions that may impede the team's initial goal.

Consensus dynamics in general have been studied in computer science and control theory for a long time [8]. In a network of agents, consensus is formed when all of the agents agree to a certain parameter state. A consensus algorithm performs a consensus procedure where agents exchange their parameter status among its local neighbors in the agent network so that they may eventually reach an agreement. The analytical foundation of consensus problems for networked systems was presented by Olfati-Saber and colleagues [9]. The consensus problem is also related to synchronization. Synchronization phenomena are seen in diverse settings such as neurons firing, laser cascades, biological cycles, opinion formation, and in chaotic dissipative systems in general. Many such phenomena in nature are realized by synchronization in a constructive manner. However, forming synchronization in a harmful context can cause detrimental effects such as collapse of bridges or causing epileptic seizures [10, 11]. In order to manage such destructive outcomes by synchronization, Louzada [12] studied the use of contrarians to suppress undesired synchronization. Contrarians systematically dephase from the oscillation of their nearest neighbors. Louzada compared the use of contrarians with access to local and global information and concluded that contrarians with local interactions are enough for the most efficient influence. Additionally, when the interacting neighbor number (degree distribution) is relatively even and contrarians are placed at highly connected nodes, the synchronization dephasing performance is significantly improved.

In this paper, instead of contrarians that desynchronize with its neighbors, the presence of stubborn agents that refuse to form consensus with the rest of the agents in the network is considered. Consensus formation of agents under the restriction of a network is observed. In particular, the network used is structured so that it can represent two teams interacting. Two stubborn agents with opposing opinions are used to represent a disagreement in the network. The terms *agent* and *node* are often used interchangeably, where an *agent* may have a stronger social/multi-agent system aspect whereas a *node* may have a complex network connotation.

B. Consensus formation with stubborn agents

Studies of consensus and synchronization under a network structure is important for understanding its dynamics as seen in the previous section. However, there is no guarantee that all of its agents in the network will cooperate. Some agents may lead the team to form a consensus by influencing the rest of the agents or some agents may mislead the consensus formation to an unintended final state. These situations may occur in diverse scenes such as socio-economic situations [13], rendezvous strategies [14], average consensus [15], and sensor deployment [16]. Gupta [17] studied possible scenarios of agent "failure" in the context of distributed algorithms used in the above research presented. The first failure condition is a stopping failure [18] where an agent blacks out and stops communicating with the other agents. The second failure condition is when an agent value becomes stuck at a fixed state. Fagnani [19] showed that if the rest of the agents are non-stubborn, then the agents would converge to this fixed value agent. The third failure condition is when an agent continuously changes its state to erroneous values at every time step, either intentionally or unintentionally [18, 20].

In a social context of stubborn agents, Acemoglu [21] studied the spread of *misinformation* by using "forceful" agents in an agent value averaging model. Forceful agents are not completely stubborn, but under particular conditions they have a strong influence on some of their neighbors such that the terminal consensus value is diverted from the original consensus value without the forceful agents. Spread of misinformation is quantified by measuring the magnitude of this divergence. Instead of forceful agents, Yildiz [22] presented a consensus behavior study with two stubborn agents with opposing opinions with different fixed agent values, using a classical voter model [23, 24]. In this model, the stubborn agent does not affect all of its neighbors, but rather chooses one neighbor randomly, and instead of taking an average value between the two agents, the neighbor agents adopt their neighbor's value. They found that with the presence of opposing stubborn agents, the opinions among the agent society disagree and fluctuate. Finally, Acemoglu [25] uses an inhomogeneous stochastic gossip model of communication. The agents update their belief as a convex combination of their own belief and the belief of their neighbor at the same time step. In addition to finding that consensus process fluctuates and never converges, they demonstrated that in a general network topology the intermediate agents between the stubborn

agents take terminal values which are linear interpolations of the two stubborn agents' beliefs.

In the three above mentioned investigations, they consider dumbbell (barbell) graphs to observe the influence of either single, double, and triple stubborn agents on the rest of the non-stubborn agents. Their dumbbell graphs have two or three cliques of arbitrary agent number. Two small interacting teams can be modeled with a dumbbell graph with complete graphs connected by bridging agents and a link. The smallest complete graphs with three agents are a sufficient condition for a negotiation team [26], since working in small teams allow more flexibility, agility, and adaptability [27, 28]. Modeling of interactions between larger organizations may not be so simple due to its hierarchical structure or the involvements of many sub-divisions in the organization. However, considering that even large organizations would have a small scale working unit or a representative team for negotiations [29], a dumbbell teamwork interaction model is a reasonable and practical consideration. Due to the linking property of a dumbbell graph, special roles are played by bridging agents and link. In graph theoretical terms, these bridging agents have a higher betweenness centrality [30]. In a team cooperation or negotiation context, these bridging agents are called boundary role persons (BRPs) [31] and have a unique role in the team [32]. Later, a modeling of larger teams is also considered by using two scale-free networks connected.

With the presence of one or two stubborn agents, the following questions are investigated: what is the overall dynamics of the society of agents with the presence of stubborn agents? How opinion dynamics are affected with the presence of two stubborn agents holding completely opposite opinions? These are investigated under the constraint of a network structure. First, the time progression of the consensus formation process or stabilization process (if the dynamics is non-convergent) for a minimum dumbbell graph is demonstrated. The time progression shows the various patterns of approach resulting in diverse final outcomes depending on the location of the stubborn agents. Second, the notion of small team dynamics is extended to a team with a larger population and a greater distance of the BRP from the core ideology (stubborn agent) of its team. Two identical scale-free networks with a larger population are used instead of minimum complete graphs. The final states settle as a linear interpolation of agent locations as observed in [25]. However, the time progression shows that the consensus is formed among the local tree modules first, then a global steady state is reached. The presence of two stubborn agents results in the formation of coalitions. The model also supports that the farther away physically and psychologically the BRP is from the core team ideology (stubborn agent), the BRP agent opinion becomes closer to its opponent group [33].

II.   ANALYTICAL FOUNDATION

A. Consensus protocol

The average consensus problem makes use of spectral graph theory and matrix theory [15, 34, 35]. Consider a symmetric (undirected) connected graph $G = (V, E)$ which is the network topology that restricts the agent interactions, where

V is a set of nodes and E is a set of edges. The linear continuous-time consensus protocol used for the network agent dynamics is [15, 35],

$$\dot{x}_i = \sum_{j \in N_i} \alpha_{ij} \left(x_j(t) - x_i(t) \right), \tag{1}$$

where x_i and x_j is the state value of agent i, and its network neighbor j respectively, α_{ij} is the weight of agent i on agent j, N_i is the set of neighbors connected to agent i, and t is time or iterations. Here, $\alpha_{ij} = \alpha_{ji}$ for all i, j, since the graph G is undirected. Consensus is achieved when the agent values converges to a common value based on (1), i.e.,

$$x_1 = x_2 = \cdots = x_n = \alpha, \tag{2}$$

where n is the total number of agents in the network. When there are no stubborn agents or other interferences in the agent network, the value taken by (2) can be expressed by the following equation,

$$\alpha = \frac{1}{n} \sum_{i=1}^{n} x_i(0), \tag{3}$$

where $x_i(0)$ is the initial agent values at $t=0$. In other words, without any bias the consensus converges asymptotically to the average of the initial values. The Laplacian matrix L of the graph network G is explained below. The Laplacian matrix is defined as the following,

$$\mathbf{L} = \mathbf{D} - \mathbf{A}, \tag{4}$$

where $\mathbf{D} = \text{diag}(d_1, d_2, \cdots, d_n)$ is the diagonal matrix with elements $d_i = \sum_j a_{ij}$ and $\mathbf{A}$ is the binary adjacency matrix ($n \times n$ matrix) with elements a_{ij} for all i, j where a_{ij} is 1 if agent i and agent j is connected or 0 if they are disconnected. Then the dynamics of the system in (1) can be expressed as

$$\dot{x} = -\mathbf{L}x(t). \tag{5}$$

B. Stubborn agents

The presence of stubborn agents affects the formation of consensus, and the deviation of this consensus opinion dynamics depends on the network structure and the location of the stubborn agents on that structure. Fagnani [19] shows the analytical framework of consensus dynamics over networks including regular agents and stubborn agents. Consider a symmetric connected graph $G = (V, E)$ introduced earlier. Separate $V = S \cup R$ with the understanding that agents in S are stubborn agents not changing their state while agents in R are regular agents whose state modifies with time according to the consensus dynamics. With the presence of stubborn agents, the whole consensus dynamics can be described by the relation

$$x(t + 1) = P x(t). \tag{6}$$

When the elements in V are ordered in such a way that elements in R come first, the matrix P will exhibit the block structure:

$$P = \begin{bmatrix} Q_1 & Q_2 \\ 0 & I \end{bmatrix}. \tag{7}$$

By splitting the state vector accordingly, $x(t) = (x_R(t), x_S(t))$, the dynamics shown below is obtained.

$$x_R(t + 1) = Q_1 x_R(t) + Q_2 x_S(t)$$

$$x_S(t + 1) = x_S(t) \tag{8}$$

Notice that Q_1 is a sub-stochastic matrix, i.e., all row sums are less than or equal to 1. There is at least one row whose sum is strictly less than one, which is the row corresponding to a regular agent connected to a stubborn one. Using the connectivity of the graph, this easily implies that there exists t such that $(Q_1)^t$ has the property that all its rows have sum strictly less than one. This immediately yields that the matrix is asymptotically stable. Therefore,

$$x_R(t) \to x_R(\infty) \text{ for } t \to +\infty$$

with the limit opinions satisfying the relation which is equivalent to

$$x_R(\infty) = Q_1 x_R(\infty) + Q_2 x_S(0)$$

$$x_R(\infty) = (I - Q_1)^{-1} Q_2 x_S(0). \tag{9}$$

Regular agents settle asymptotically to opinions that are the convex combinations of the opinions of stubborn agents. The above analysis shows, that if all stubborn agents are in the same state x, for instance there is just one stubborn agent, then, consensus is reached by all agents in the opinion of the stubborn agent x. However, typically, consensus is not reached. Few examples modeled by simulation are discussed below. The initial state value of each agent is set as,

$$x_i(0) = i \ (i = 1, 2, \cdots, N). \tag{10}$$

When each agent updates her state value according to (1), the state of each agent converges to a constant value, which is the average of the initial values of all agents. The consensus dynamics in (1) converge to the average of the initial states of all agents without stubborn agents. Additionally, the consensus dynamics profile is different depending on the location of the two stubborn agents.

C. Networks

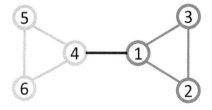

Fig. 1. A diagram of a dumbbell graph. Each clique is composed of 3 agents. The graph contains total of 6 nodes and 7 links. Since each clique consists of a minimum complete graph with 3 nodes, this network is considered a minimum dumbbell network

In the first experiment, we use a dumbbell network. A dumbbell network is a structure with two cliques connected by a single link (Fig. 1). "Simplest" here means the network consists of minimum number of nodes. The definition of a negotiating team is a group of two or more interdependent persons who collaborate to achieve a mutual goal through negotiation and they all attend the bargaining table [36]. The cliques used here consist of three nodes all connected to each other to form a complete graph. One arbitrarily node is chosen from each clique and these nodes are connected by a bridging link. These bridging nodes play a unique role in that they have an absolute influence on their own clique and the greatest influence to the opposite clique when stubborn agents are located at these bridging nodes.

In the second experiment, two scale-free networks were connected. This network was generated to model a greater number of nodes and greater distance between the stubborn agent and the bridge node. Two identical scale-free networks with 50 nodes were generated and the nodes with the least closeness centrality or the most "remote" nodes (Fig. 4, node 50 and 100) were connected. The node chosen for each stubborn agent is the highest alpha-centrality [37] for each scale-free network (nodes 1 and 51). The overall network forms a line network with modular tree structures attached to the nodes on the main line network. A line network is the simplest structure to model the "psychological distance" between the organizational core and the boundary. The entire network is symmetric since two identical networks were connected at identical locations.

III. RESULTS

First, the results from the simplest case of a dumbbell network are presented. On the dumbbell network, where agents are grouped with their clique network, local consensus is promoted in each clique network at first. After that, the global consensus is formed via the bridge link as seen in Fig. 2. Progressively increasing and evenly spaced initial values are assigned to the agents from agent 1through 6 as seen in Fig. 2, except for stubborn agents. Stubborn agents are assigned a node value of either 0 or 100, two extremely opposite values. Without stubborn agents, the agent converges asymptotically, eventually reaching a consensus value of the average of agent values as indicated in (3). Smaller values are assigned to agents in the violet color clique and larger values are assigned to agents in the blue color clique in Fig. 1.

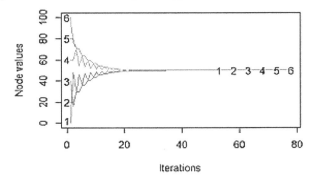

Fig. 2. A consensus progression diagram for the dumbbell graph in Fig. 1. The initial values assigned to agents in each clique are 0 to 50 to one clique and the 51 to100 to the other clique

With the presence of stubborn agents, three types of consensus behavior were noticed for a dumbbell network topology with single and double stubborn agents. The first type is for a single stubborn agent located at node 1 in Fig. 1 (case 1, Fig. 3(a)). This is a trivial solution where all of the agent opinions converge to the stubborn agent, regardless of the location of the stubborn agent. Such dynamics has been analytically modeled by Fagnani [19]. The second type is for two stubborn agents in the same clique. There are two possibilities for this type. The first possibility is when the stubborn agents are located at nodes 2 and 3 so none of the stubborn agents are the bridge agent (case 2, Fig. 3(b)). The rest of the regular agents from both cliques converge to an intermediate value. For the second possibility, the stubborn agents are located at nodes 1 and 2, one of the stubborn agents being a bridge agent (case 3, Fig. 3(c)). The regular agent (agent 3) in the same clique will converge to an intermediate value between the two stubborn agents and all of the agents in the opposite clique without stubborn agents will converge to the bridging stubborn agent node 1. In this case, the regular agents trapped between the stubborn agents converge to an average value between the two stubborn agent values.

The third type is again for two stubborn agents, but one located in each clique. In general, the regular agents in a clique will approach the stubborn agent in their respective cliques, however, under the influence of the stubborn agent of the opposite clique. When one of the stubborn agents is located at node 1 bridge agent (case 4, Fig. 3(d)), this stubborn agent shuts out the rest of the agents in its clique from any influence from the opposite clique. One could say that the stubborn agent at the bridge node "dominates" its clique. Similarly, this bridging stubborn agent will influence the agents in the opposite clique, where its influence will be the strongest with the bridging regular agent node 4, then with indirect and reduced influence with agents beyond the bridge agent of the opposite clique (agent 6), except for the stubborn agent (agent 5). In this case, the regular agents with indirect influence converge to a value between its stubborn agent (agent 5) and the bridging agent (agent 4) as in case 3.

When the two stubborn agents are located at the bridge nodes of their respective cliques, agents 1 and 4 (case 5, Fig. 3(e)), the regular agents will converge to the stubborn agent of their own clique. The regular agents in one clique will never reach a consensus with the regular agents in the opposite clique and vice versa because all influence from the opposite clique is blocked by the stubborn agent at the bridge node of its own clique.

If none of the bridge agents are stubborn (case 6, Fig. 3(f)), the regular agents are not topologically restricted to the influence of a particular stubborn agent. The bridge agents receive the largest influence of the opposite clique and the rest of the regular agents converge to a value between their bridge agent and the stubborn agent in their clique. The regular agents do not converge with the stubborn agent in their clique because of the influence of the stubborn agent in the opposite clique. In general, when the number of agents in the cliques increases while maintaining a complete graph structure, the values of regular agents within the clique tend to attract or "bond" closer together.

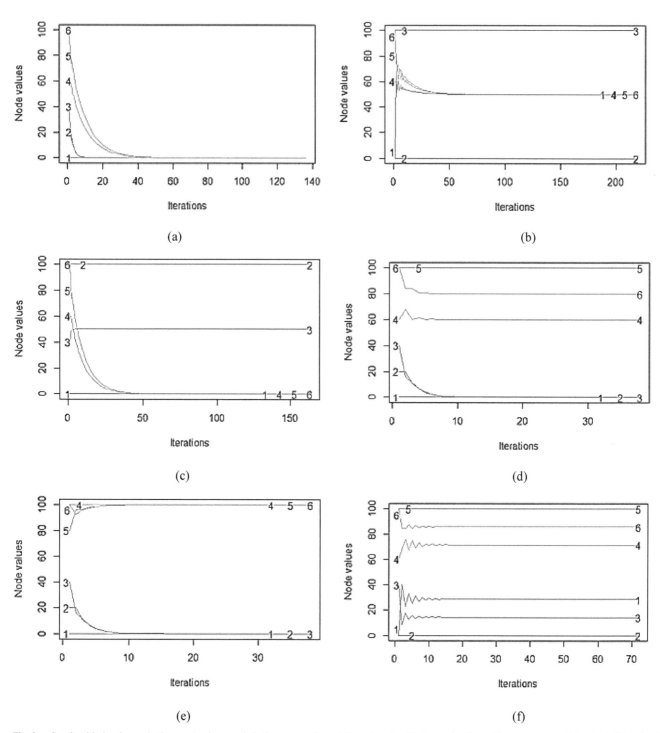

Fig. 3.   Graph with the change in the agent value. x-axis is time step and y-axis is node value. Node number for stubborn agents are (a) node 1, (b) nodes 2 and 3, (c) nodes 1 and 2, (d) nodes 1 and 5, (e) nodes 1 and 4, and (f) nodes 2 and 5. The node numbers are written on the graph lines

Not only that, the value of the regular agents, except for the bridging agents, converge to a single value. The bridging agents of the opposite cliques attract each other so they do not converge completely with the rest of the regular agents in their respective clique. This is also seen in case 4 (Fig. 3(d)). The following is the result from the scale-free network structure (Fig. 4). The number of time steps it took for the agent values to stabilize ($\Delta x_i = 10^{-9}$, which is the difference in the values between two time steps) is close to 6,300 time steps (Fig. 5). The dynamics with two stubborn agents show that consensus is formed locally among the tree module structures branching from the "main" link path connecting the two stubborn agents (a line network). The branching agent is a hub agent for its community. Consensus is formed among such local modules first. When there are no stubborn agents, a global convergence will follow.

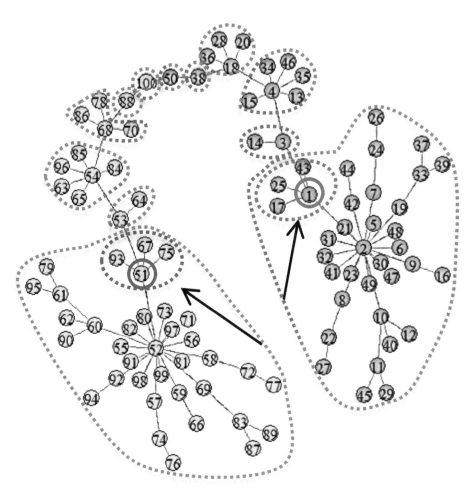

Fig. 4.   Two scale-free networks connected by the most "remote" nodes. The agents forming local consensus are grouped by the gray dotted line. The stubborn agents are marked by the red and blue circles. The red and blue dotted lines are the local consensus initially formed by the tree module community with the stubborn agent as the hub. The black arrow shows that the larger consensus community eventually forms a consensus with the stubborn agent community, a dynamics which can also be observed in Fig. 5

However, when there are two stubborn agents located at the opposite ends of the line network, local consensus never merges together. In fact, the values taken by the local module consensus are essentially the hub agent number evenly dividing the agent value range (Fig. 5), a linear interpolation indicated by [25]. Consequently, the number of consensus settling values equals the number of hub agents along the main link path between the two stubborn agents, in addition to the two stubborn agent values. The order of consensus values associated with the hub communities is consistent with its order along the main link path that connects the two stubborn agents.

One consensus dynamics to notice is the convergence of two tree modules (Fig. 4). Initially, the tree modules of agents 1 and 2 form a consensus among their own modules. Then as time progresses, the consensus of these two modules converges. This occurs because agent 1 is a stubborn agent and all agents in the agent 2 module are regular agents. Therefore all agents in the agent 2 module form a consensus first. Then as time passes, they form a consensus with the stubborn agent 1. The result in the other half of the scale-free network follows a symmetric dynamics with agents 51 and 52.

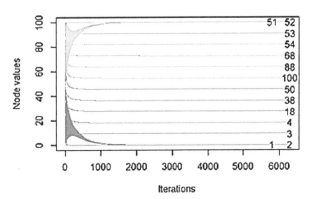

Fig. 5.   Graph with the change in the agent value. x-axis is time step and y-axis is node value. The node numbers written on the agent values are the stubborn agents (1, 51) and the hub agents forming a consensus among their tree module along the main link path between the two stubborn agents

When two stubborn agents are located at the neighboring most "remote" linking agents at nodes 50 and 100, the two scale-free networks form a consensus only within their network community, i.e., the regular agents are attracted to the stubborn agent in their own community.

This is analogous to case 5 in the dumbbell topology dynamics. The value of consensus of each team depends on the value of their respective stubborn agent. Due to the limited node degree of these stubborn agents (agents 50 and 100), the consensus takes almost 10 times longer (about 59,000 time steps) than when the stubborn agents are placed at the nodes with the highest alpha-centrality (agents 1 and 51).

IV. DISCUSSION

This paper investigates the behavior of agents under the influence of opposite opinions or conflicting signals. The agents are caught between dynamics that aggregate and dynamics that are biased. When working in a team, the members must cope with both internal and external noise. Additionally, such local dynamics are met with the global constraint of a network. In the context of team negotiations in business or social settings, an analyst needs to take into account the impact of the social and organizational environments within which agent teamwork dynamics are embedded [38]. The agents' roles, the team characteristics, and agent relationship networks are critical sources of influence within a negotiations setting in particular [39], but this can be applied to other teamwork dynamics as well.

A. Minimum dumbbell team structure

The dumbbell network settings can be used to model a negotiation or a collaborative situation between two teams of agents on a single project. In case 1, a leader with a clear objective, vision, and resource can guide the two teams and the rest will follow (Fig. 3(a)). In case 2, two of the members of the same team may have opposite opinions (two stubborn agents), which is an intra-group conflict situation [40] (Fig. 3(b)). In a real world setting, the teammates are 'not on the same page,' 'confused about goals,' and possess 'conflicting interest within the team' [26]. This may happen when the agents represent different departments and have different goals to achieve. Since the members in the teams must maintain their respective teams (maintain the clique structure), the rest of the agents in both teams take an intermediate opinion and collaborate or find a common ground (form a local consensus) (Fig. 3(b), agents 1, 4, 5, 6). The solution to such intra-team conflict is to have prior preparation for a common agenda [26].

In case 3, the team with stubborn agents will be divided in 3 opinion values, the two stubborn values and the intermediate value of the agent that is connected to the two strong opposite opinions (Fig. 3(c)). If one of the bridge members has a strong vision and leadership (agent 1) and if all the agents in the opposite team are regular agents (agents 4, 5, 6), the opposite team will form an agreement with the bridging member of the team with stubborn agents (agent 1). The bridge agent is known as a boundary role person (BRP). Because such BRPs are often closer to the opposite team, physically and psychologically, they naturally share a relationship with the BRPs of the opposite team. This can potentially weaken the bond of the BRP with their own team [32]. After all, it is often preferable that negotiators have an understanding of and act in a way to accommodate the opponent's needs [31]. The influence of the other team is stronger with individualistic cultures in the occident than in the collectivist cultures in the

orient, because BRP of the individualistic cultures are less bound to their own team [26].

In case 4, one of the bridging members, a BRP, is a stubborn agent or a leader (Fig. 3(d), agent 1). However, there is a strong opposing opinion in the other team which is not a BRP (agent 5). The members of the BRP leader team follow the BRP leader. Although the BRP leader's opinion has an influence on the team members of the other team, where the strongest influence is on the BRP of the other team and less influence on the non-BRP regular agents, the BRP leader cannot completely win over all the agents in the other team due to the opposition member (agent 5) in the other team. This case is a good example to show the extent of influence an agent would have depending on the location in a global network topology. One stubborn agent is a BRP (agent 1) and the other stubborn agent (agent 1) is not. In a team negotiation context, it is known that the quality of the negotiation outcome may be in favor of the BRP that is closer in psychological distance to the core ideologies (stubborn agent) of its own team. Perry [33] has concluded that when one of the negotiators is psychologically distant from their own team, the bargaining outcomes should fall in between the outcomes obtained when the negotiators are either close or far away psychologically. This outcome can be seen in the time progression of Fig. 3(d). Additionally, there is a profound significance to this in a corporate setting. As mentioned earlier, a BRP is located in a privileged position in that it is the only agent to reach the opposite team. Therefore, BRP is an agent that has access to internal as well as external (other corporate) information. Assume that BRP initially does not have any hierarchical authority or a legitimate basis of power. It is just another employee. However, during the time of environmental turbulence for business, due to its unique position in the interaction network of having both internal and external information, the BRP has the potential ability to cope with and absorb uncertainty, and channel or control the flow of information to its own company [41]. Since "power" is defined as an inverse of dependency [42], a BRP could gain power which initially would not have had if it were not a BRP. In fact, the BRP could intentionally generate conflict to maintain the company's dependency on itself and thus keep its power. This is seen again later in this paper.

In case 5, the connecting members of the two teams have opposite opinions (Fig. 3(e), agents 1 and 4). Since the regular agent members (agents 2, 3, 5, 6) of their respective teams are flexible and obedient to their strong leader, the two teams would not reach a consensus and therefore could not collaborate. This is a situation where the intensity of conflict is high. If a consensus of two teams must be achieved, the two teams may need a mediator or an arbitrator [43]. Mediation is where a third party makes a recommendation that is mutually acceptable based on information about the two teams. Arbitration is where the two teams commit to following the third party recommendation. The arbitrator has enforcing means. Both mediators and arbitrators are a third party that intervenes in the negotiation process [44]. In case 6, when there are oppositions by non-bridge members in each team (Fig. 3(f), agents 2 and 5), even though the members are attracted by the other team, they would not form a single consensus. Rather, the opinion of the members would range between the two extreme opinions, where the intermediate BRPs would receive the greatest influence from the other team. Although in case 5 a consensus was formed in their respective cliques, the formation of coalitions is beginning to appear in case 4 and 6. This is more so when we have a tree module line network, which is discussed below.

B. Scale-free network team structure

So far, a model of interaction of small scale teams was considered. The location of stubborn agents and the role of the BRP were examined. When the number of agents increases in a team, there are two things that can change from a smaller group. The first is, as the number of agents increase, there will be more opinions and cultures. The second is, the BRP at the boundary surface may become more distant from the core ideology of their team held by a strong leader (stubborn agent).

First considering the cultural aspect, when the number of cultural diversity increases, the team is exposed to the possibility of forming coalitions within the team. Coalition is a subunit of a team that is consisted of two or more members whose intentions are to fulfill their own goals instead of the goals of the host team [45]. Coalition is said to form among those who have similar social/cultural traits. Here, social/cultural traits are individualism/collectivism, masculinity/femininity, etc. [46]. When the team is culturally homogeneous or completely heterogeneous, the likelihood of coalition formation is less. However, when the diversity of cultures is intermediate, a team is exposed to the possibility of coalition formation [47]. The presence of a coalition in a team can be unproductive because it may cause internal conflict and distancing among members [48]. Coalition makes the team more complex and unstable.

Assuming various cultures exist in a team, such cultures may be modeled as a sub-modular structure in the overall network, as seen in the hub and branch module structure in Fig. 4. When there are two stubborn agents, the agents and their cultural groups positioned between the two stubborn agents may hold varying degrees of sentiments depending on their location. During the consensus procedure, these network modules form a consensus within their cultural module. If there are no stubborn agents or if there is a single stubborn agent, these modules form a global consensus after they have established a local consensus as we have seen in Fig. 2. This two stage convergence is seen also for agents not in between, but "outside" the two stubborn agents, such as agents 2 and 52 community who eventually form a consensus with the agents 1 and 51 community. However, when there are two opposing state values (agent 1 and 51), the local culture modules between the two stubborn agents never converge with the other culture modules due to the influence of the opposing stubborn agents. Thus, multiple coalitions are formed within the team.

Finally, considering the distance of the BRPs from the core ideologies of their team, the farther away they are from the core and closer to the periphery near their opposite team, there is the risk of the negotiation outcome become less attractive for its own team where the BRP belongs and more preferable for the opposite team. There are two reasons why this may happen. First, because of the distance of the BRP from the core, the

negotiator BRP may have an ambiguous understanding of the team's goal because of conflicting information. The second reason is the BRP may set incongruent goals of their team, either unintentionally due to lack of information or intentionally in order to create uncertainty in the situation so that they would be relied upon more by their organization and thus gaining more power. The farther away the BRP is from the core, this trend is stronger [33]. The terminal values taken by the BRP agents in Fig. 5 reflect this situation. The closer the BRP is to their opposite team and farther away they are from their respective "core" stubborn agent values, the BRP values of both teams become closer.

V. CONCLUSION AND SUMMARY

A multi-agent system was used to model the interaction of agents under the restrain of a team structure. The agents have an averaging protocol for consensus formation. However, not all agents are cooperative. The team interaction structures used were a minimum dumbbell network and two scale-free networks connected. All possible outcomes of the minimum dumbbell structure with two stubborn agents were interpreted in a team cooperation/negotiation setting. As indicated by previous literature, the bridging agents or boundary role persons have a unique role to serve. Its position on the network showed that it has a strong influence over the other agents. When stubborn agents are located at both bridging nodes, the agents are strongly united with their team that it is recommended to involve a third party to moderate or arbitrate.

The scale-free line network with tree modules showed the possibility of coalition formation based on the cultural diversity in the team. Such coalition formation dynamics can be seen in the way modular networks form a consensus, that local consensus is formed first and then a global consensus is reached. This shows the influence of both local and global topology that influences the overall characteristics of the network dynamics. The branching agents from the main line nodes can be considered to have the same culture/attitude/mentality. This network can also model the psychological distance between the boundary role person and the core ideology of the team. The farther away they are from the core, and more cultural values there are in between, their ideology becomes closer to the other team. Such a model can be used not only for commercial settings, but also in a political setting in society, between two extreme policies.

REFERENCES

[1] T. H. Cox, Cultural Diversity in Organizations: Theory, Research and Practice. San Francisco, CA: Barrett-Koehler, 1993.

[2] S. Jackson, K. E. May, and K. Whitney, "Understanding the dynamics of diversity in decisions making teams," in Team Effectiveness and Decision Making in Organizations, R. A. Guzzo and E. Salas, Eds. San Francisco, CA: Jossey-Bass, 1995, pp. 204–261.

[3] D. R. Illgen, J. R. Hollenbeck, M. Johnson, and D. Jundt, "Teams in organizations: From I-P-O models to IMOI models," Annual Review, vol. 56, pp. 517–543, 2006.

[4] A. W. Richter, M. A. West, R. van Dick, and J. F. Dawson, "Boundary spanners' identification, intergroup contact, and effective intergroup relations," The Academy of Management Journal, vol. 49, pp. 1252–1269, 2006.

[5] P. L. Curşeu, P. Kenis, J. Raab, and U. Brandes, "Composing effective teams through team-dating," Organ. Stud., vol. 31, pp. 873–894, 2010.

[6]   D. J. Watts and S. H. Strogatz, "Collective dynamics of small-world networks," Nature, vol. 393, pp. 440–442, 1998.

[7]   A. L. Barabási, Linked: The New Science of Networks, Cambridge, MA: Perseus Publishing, 2002.

[8]   A. Pikovsky, M. Rosenblum, and J. Kurths, Synchronization: A Universal Concept in Nonlinear Sciences, Cambridge, UK: Cambridge University presses, 2003.

[9]   R. Olfati-Saber, J. A. Fax, and R. M. Murray, "Consensus and cooperation in networked multi-agent systems", in proc. of IEEE, vol. 95, no. 1, pp.215–233, 2007.

[10] M. Barahona, "Synchronization in small-world systems," Physical Review Letters, vol. 89, 2002.

[11] X. F. Wang and G. Chen, "Synchronization in scale-free dynamical networks: Robustness and fragility", IEEE Transactions on Circuits and Systems I: Fundamental Theory and Applications, pp.54–62, 2001.

[12] V. H. P. Louzada, N. A. Araujo, and H. Herrmann, "How to suppress undesired synchronization," Scientific Reports 2, no. 658, 2012.

[13] D. Acemoglu, G. Como, F. Fagnani, and A. Ozdaglar, "Opinion fluctuations and disagreement in social networks," Mathematics of Operation Research, vol. 38, no. 1, pp. 1–27, 2013.

[14] M. Ji, G. Ferrari-Trecate, M. Egerstedt, and A. Buffa, "Containment control in mobile networks," IEEE Transactions on Automatic Control, vol. 53, no. 8, pp. 1972–1975, 2008.

[15] R. Olfati-Saber and R. M. Murray, "Consensus problems in networks of agents with switching topology and time-delays," IEEE Transactions on Automatic Control, vol. 49, no. 9, pp. 1520–1533, 2004.

[16] J. Cortes, S. Martinez, T. Karatas, and F. Bullo, "Coverage control for mobile sensing networks," IEEE Transactions on Robotics and Automation, vol. 20, no. 2, pp. 243–255, 2004.

[17] V. Gupta, C. Langbort, and R. Murray, "On the robustness of distributed algorithms," in proc. of the 45th IEEE Conference on Decision and Control, 2006.

[18] N. Lynch, Distributed Algorithms. San Mateo, CA: Morgan Kaufmann Publishers, 1996.

[19] F. Fagnani, "Consensus dynamics over networks," 2014.

[20] L. Lamport, R. Shostak and M. Pease, "The Byzantine generals problem,' ACM Transactions on Programming Languages and Systems, vol. 4, no. 3, pp. 382–401, 1982.

[21] D. Acemoglu, A. Ozdaglar, and A. ParandehGheibi, "Spread of (mis)information in social networks," Games and Economic Behavior, vol. 70, no. 2, pp. 194–227, 2010.

[22] E. Yildiz , D. Acemoglu, A. Ozdaglar, A. Saberi, and A. Scaglione, "Discrete opinion dynamics with stubborn agents," 2011.

[23] R. A. Holley and T. M. Liggett, "Ergodic theorems for weakly interacting infinite systems and the voter model," The Annals of Probability vol. 3, no. 4, pp. 643–663, 1975.

[24] P. Clifford and A. Sudbury, "A model for spatial conflict," Biometrika, vol. 60, no. 3, pp. 581–588, 1973.

[25] D. Acemoglu, G. Como, F. Fagnani, and A. E. Ozdaglar, "Opinion fluctuations and disagreement in social networks," Math. Oper. Res. vol. 38, no.1, pp. 1–27, 2013.

[26] K. Behfar, R. Friedman, and J. M. Brett, "The team negotiation challenge: defining and managing the internal challenges of negotiating teams," IACM 21st Annual Conference Paper, November, 2008.

[27] D. S. Alberts and R. E. Hayes, Power to the edge: Command…control…in the information age. Washington: CCRP, 2003.

[28] D. S. Alberts, "Agility, Focus, and Convergence: The Future of Command and Control," The International C2 Journal, vol. 1, pp.1–30, 2007.

[29] S. Brodt and L. Thompson, "Negotiating teams: A levels of analysis approach," Group Dynamics-Theory Research and Practice, vol. 5, no. 3, pp. 208–219, 2001.

[30] M. Barthélemy, "Betweenness centrality in large complex networks," The European Physical Journal B - Condensed Matter and Complex Systems, vol. 38, issue 2, pp. 163–168, 2004.

[31] R. E. Walton and R. B. McKersie, A Behavioral Theory of Labor Negotiations: An Analysis of a Social Interaction System. New York: McGraw-Hill, 1965.

[32] J. S. Adams, "The structure and dynamics of behavior in organization boundary roles," in Handbook of Industrial and Organizational Psychology, M. D. Dunnette, Ed. Chicago: Rand McNally, 1976, pp. 1175–1199.

[33] J. L. Perry and H. L. Angle, "The politics of organizational boundary roles in collective bargaining," The Academy of Management Review, vol. 4, no. 4, pp. 487–495, October 1979.

[34] L. Xiao and S. Boyd, "Fast linear iterations for distributed averaging," Systems & Control Letters, vol. 53, no.1, pp. 65–78, 2004.

[35] W. Ren, R. W. Beard, and E. M. Atkins, "A Survey of Consensus Problems in Multi-agent Coordination," in proc. of the American Control Conference, 2005.

[36] L. Thompson, E. Peterson, and S. Brodt, "Team negotiation: an examination of integrative and distributive bargaining," J. Per. Soc. Psychol., vol. 70, pp. 66–78, 1996.

[37] P. Bonacich and P. Lloyd, "Eigenvector-like measures of centrality for asymmetric relations," Social Networks, vol. 23, pp. 191–201, 2001.

[38] R. M. Kramer and D. M. Messick, Negotiation as a Social Process. Thousand Oaks, CA: Sage, 1995.

[39] M. J. Gelfand and J. M. Brett, The Handbook of Negotiation and Culture. Stanford, CA: Stanford University Press, 2004.

[40] K. Jehn, "A qualitative analysis of conflict types and dimensions in organizational groups," Administrative Science Quarterly, vol. 42, pp. 530–557, 1997.

[41] R. E. Spekman, "Influence and information: An exploratory investigation of the boundary role person's basis of power," Academy of Management Journal, vol. 22, no. 1, 1979.

[42] R. Emerson, "Power dependence relations," American Sociological Review, vol. 22, pp. 31–41, 1962.

[43] M. Goltsman, J. Hörner, G. Pavlov, and F. Squintani, "Mediation, arbitration and negotiation," Journal of Economic Theory, vol. 144, no. 4, pp. 1397–1420, 2009.

[44] R. J. Lewicki, S. E. Weiss, and D. Lewin, "Models of conflict, negotiation and third party intervention: A review and synthesis," Journal of Organizational Behavior, vol. 13, no. 3, pp. 209–252, May 1992.

[45] J. K. Murnighan, "Organizational coalitions: structural contingencies and the formation process," in Research on Negotiation in Organizations, vol. 1, R. J. Lewicki, B. H. Sheppard, and M. Bazerman, Eds. Stanford, CT: JAI Publishing, 1986, pp. 155–173.

[46] G. Hofstede, Culture's Consequences, International Differences in Work-related Values, Beverly Hills, CA: Sage, 1980.

[47] X. Guo and J. Lim, "Negotiation support systems and team negotiations: The coalition formation perspective," Information and Software Technology, vol. 49, pp. 1121–1127, 2007.

[48] S. M. B. Thatcher, K. A. Jehn, and E. Zanutto, "Cracks in diversity research: The effects of diversity faultlines on conflict and performance," Group Decis. Negotiation, vol. 12, pp. 217–241, 2003

5

Cardiac Arrhythmia Classification by Wavelet Transform

Hadji Salah[1]

TIC department
LR SITI ENIT
BP 37 Belvédère 1002 Tunis, Tunisia

Ellouze Noureddine[2]

TIC department
LR SITI ENIT
BP 37 Belvedere 1002 Tunis, Tunisia

Abstract—Cardiovascular diseases are the major public health parameter; they are the leading causes of mortality in the world. In fact many studies have been implemented to reduce the risk, including promoting education, prevention, and monitoring of patients at risk. In this paper we propose to develop classification system heartbeats. This system is based mainly on Wavelet Transform to extract features and Kohonen self-organization map the arrhythmias are considered in this study : N,(Normal),V(PrematureVentricular),A(AtrialPremature),S(Ext rasystolesupraventriculaire),F(FusionN+S),R(RightBundle Branch) .

Keywords—*ECG; QT database; Wavelet Transform; Classification; Kohonen self-organization map*

I. Introduction

The ECG signal is a representation of the electrical heart activity; it is used to analyze the status of the heart. Due to the morphological variability of the different waves of ECG and the presence of noise that interfere with the ECG signal it is so difficult to extract necessary information's from the signal. These difficulties require tools of signal processing and automatic classification of cardiac Arrhythmia. Therefore, many researches were proposed for the automatic classification of the signal heart many methods have been implemented, such as the statistic approach, fuzzy logic and neural networks. In our paper, we have opted for neural classifiers because of their efficiencies were solving problems of classification in the case of large databases dimensions. As classifier, we chose to use the Kohonen topological maps [7,8,9] receives as input 12 parameters characterizing a temporal and morphological ECG beat are mainly: (Length (QRS), amp (Q, R,S) intervals (QT, PR, RR)). In this article, we present in Section II the steps and algorithms used for extracting the characteristic parameters of a heart beat. In Section III, we will describe the methodology adopted for the development of our system classification. In Section IV, we present the main results. A conclusion and outlook for this work are given in Section V.

II. Wavelet Transform

Wavelet Transform is a time-scale representation of signals that has been used in a wide range of applications, including signal analysis and compression. Recently, wavelets have been applied to several problems in Electro cardiology, including data compression, analysis of ventricular late potentials and time localization of ECG characteristics. The Wavelet Transformation (WT) is a linear operation that decomposes a signal into a number of scales related to

frequency components and represents each scale with a fixed time and frequency resolution [12]. WT analysis uses a short time interval for evaluating high frequencies and a long time interval for low frequencies. Wavelet transform of a signal f(t) is defined as the sum of over all time of the signal multiplied by scaled versions of the wavelet function ψ, and is given by :

$$w_{a,b} = \int_{-\infty}^{+\infty} f(t)\psi_{a,b}(t)\delta t \quad (1)$$

$$\psi_{a,b}(t) = \frac{1}{\sqrt{a}} \psi * \left(\frac{t-b}{a}\right) \quad (2)$$

Where * denotes complex conjugation of the mother wavelet $\psi_{a,b}(t)$ and $\psi\left(\frac{t-b}{a}\right)$ is the shifted and scaled version, the constant $\frac{1}{\sqrt{a}}$ is an energy normalization factor. When the scale parameter is the set of integral powers of 2, i.e. $a=2^j$ ($j \in z$, z is an Integer set). The wavelet transform is called dyadic wavelet transform. The wavelet transform at scale 2^j is given by:

$$Wf(2^j, \tau) = \frac{1}{\sqrt{2}} \int_{-\infty}^{+\infty} f(t)\left(\frac{t-\tau}{2^j}\right)\delta\tau \quad (3)$$

A. Stationary wavelet transform

The stationary wavelet transform (SWT: Stationary Wavelet Transform) is an intermediate representation of views between the redundant CWT high redundancy and non-redundant DWT. It retains an almost dyadic sampling continuous and uniform time [12] [59], the coefficients of its decomposition have the appearance of the filtered signals in contrast to the DWT [12]. The SWT is defined by calculating the coefficients: $cd_x(j,k)_{(j,k) \in z^2}$

$$cd_x(j,k) = \int_R x(t)\psi^*_{j,k}(t)dt \quad (4)$$

Where $\psi(t) = 2^{\frac{-j}{2}} \psi_{0,0}(2^{-j}(t-k))$ the relationship between the wavelet bases used in the DWT and SWT is implemented using the following wording:

$$\psi_{j,k}\psi_{j,0}(t - 2^j k), \psi'_{j,k}(t) = \psi_{j,0}(t-k) \quad (5) \text{ with}$$

$$\psi_{j,0}(t) = 2^{\frac{-j}{2}} \psi\left(\frac{t}{2^j}\right)$$

and thus the SWT coincides with the CWT at the uniform grid and the grid dyadic DWT where $cd_x(j,k)$ have the same frequency resolution as dx (j, k), but sharing information on the time axis

$$cd_x(j,k) = cwt_x(a = 2^j, t = k) \qquad (6)$$

$$cd_x(j, 2^j k) = d_x(j,k)$$

The SWT is. Translation invariant in time, what is missing in the DWT and these results from the fact that it has a time sampling of the same signal. This explains the cd$_j$ have the properties of the filtered signal

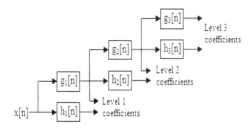

Fig. 1.   3 level decomposition

B. QT database:

The QT is a basic standard database available on the website PhysioNet, which is an international reference in the field of ECG signal processing [11]. The database QT PhysioNet was established by researchers to be used as a reference for validation and comparison of algorithms for segmentation of the ECG. It is known to have a low signal-to-noise ratio with different pathologies leading to accurate detection of waves through this entire base. Therefore, at present, the basic QT is the only database that is annotated appropriately to test our analysis method of long-term recordings. It contains 105 two-channel Holter-recordings primarily (ITNs and V5) of 15 minutes sampled at 250 Hz. These ECG signals were extracted from different databases already existing such as the database arrhythmias MIT-BIH, the database ST-T of the European Society of Cardiology, and several other databases assembled by Boston's Beth medical center

III.   SOM SELF-ORGANIZATION MAP

SOM (Self-organizing Map) is an artificial neural network (ANNA) architecture based on unsupervised, competitive learning [14]. It provides a topology preserving, smooth mapping from a high-dimensional input space to the map units usually arranged as a two-dimensional lattice of neurons (nodes). Thus, the SOM can serve as a tool for cluster analysis of complex, high-dimensional data.   A parametric reference vector m is associated with every node. A data vector x is compared to all reference vectors in any metric and the best matching node is defined, e.g., by the smallest Euclidean distance between the data vector and any of the reference

vectors. During learning, those nodes that are topographically close in the array up to a certain distance will activate each other to learn from the same input:

$$m_i(t+1) = m_i(t) + h_{ci}(t).[x(t) - m_i(y)] \qquad (7)$$

where t is an integer representing time, and h$_{ci}$ is the so-called neighborhood kernel describing the neighborhood that is updated around the best-matching node. Several suitable kernels can be used, e.g. a so-called bubble kernel or a Gaussian kernel, relating to different ways of determining the activating cells. The kernel also includes the learning rate parameter) (t α. With time, the size of the neighborhood and the learning rate are diminished. The described learning process leads to a smoothing effect on the weight vectors in the neighborhood and by continued learning to global ordering of the nodes [14]

The SOM consists of a two-dimensional lattice that contains a number of neurons. These neurons are usually arranged in a rectangular or hexagonal way. The position of the units in the grid, especially the distances between them and the neighborhood relations, are very important for the learning algorithm. A prototype vector (also "model" or "codebook" vector) is associated with each neuron, which is a vector of the same dimension as the input data set. This prototype vector approximates a subset of the sample vectors. The dimension of the sample is called input dimension, and is usually larger than 2, the dimension of the lattice, which is called output dimension. For training and visualization purposes, the sample vectors are assigned to the most similar prototype vector, or best-matching unit (BMU), formally

$$C(x) = \arg\min\{|x - m_i(t)|\} \qquad (7)$$

The learning process itself gradually adapts the model vectors to match the samples and to reflect their internal properties as faithfully as possible, which means that input vectors which are relatively close in input space should be mapped to units that are relatively close on the lattice.

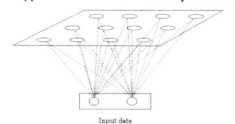

Fig. 2.   Kohonen Network map

A. Parameters extraction

Each ECG beat, consisting of 376 samples centered on the position of the R wave undergoes a SWT on four successive scales using wavelet (db4) as mother wavelet. Subsequently, we calculate the energy of the Stationary wavelet transform each level. Thus it reduces the size of the input vector of 376 elements only 8 for the 4th level gave the best recognition rate. The classification scheme is shown in Figure 3.

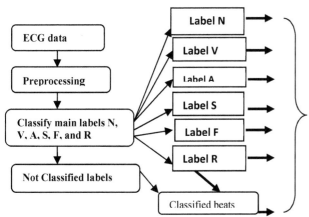

Fig. 3. Classification schème

B. Performance and Measures

The performance of the classification system was measured based on tow standard statistical measures for each class: Sensitivity (Se) and Predectivity (Sp) which are calculated from multi-class classification table [1].

IV. RESULTS

TABLE I. CONFUSION- MATRIX

	N	V	A	S	F	R
N	26792	23	455	458	125	360
V	0	562	0	0	35	6
A	0	0	365	0	4	3
S	1	5	1	235	3	1
F	2	0	0	0	58	0
R	4	3	0	0	0	123

	Se (%)	Sp (%)
N	94,7	99,98
V	93,7	94,7
A	97,4	98,3
S	95,4	98,3
F	96,6	96.6
R	94,4	94,1

Fig. 4. displayed results with SOM

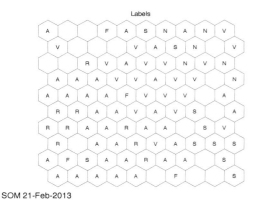

SOM 21-Feb-2013

Fig. 5. cardiac Arrhythmia recognition and displayed by Kohonen map

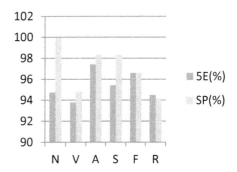

Fig. 6. Histogram variation of recognition rates by wavelet Transform

V. CONCLUSION

In this work we have developed a new method based on wavelet transform decomposition and self organizing map algorithm to classify cardiac arrhythmia labels such as N, A, V, R, F, S, obtained results are very interesting .

The specificity and the Predectivity were higher than 94% in all cases (N, A, S, R, V and F) .This result means that the proposed method is suitable enough for practical clinical use.

REFERENCES

[1] Physiobank Archive Index, QT Database. http://www.physionet.org/physiobank/database

[2] S.Z.Mahmoodabadi,A.Ahmadian and M D. Abolhasan,"ECG Feature Extraction using Daubechies Wavelets", Proceedings of the fifth IASTED International conference on Visualization, Imaging and Image Processing, pp. 343-348, 2005.

[3] Palreddy, S., Hu, Y.H. and Tompkins, W.J. "A patient adaptable ECG beat classifier using a mixture of experts approach", IEEE Trans. on BME, 44(9), 1997, 891–900.

[4] Acr, N. "Classification of ECG beats by using a fast least square support vector machines with a dynamic programming feature selection algorithm", Neural Computing and Applications, 14(4), 2005, 299–309.

[5] P. de Chazal, M. O'Dwyer, and R. Reilly, "Automatic classification of heartbeats using ECG morphology and heartbeat interval features," IEEE Trans. Biomed. Eng., vol. 51, no. 7, pp. 1196–1206, Jul. 2004.

[6] Übeyli, E.D., ECG beats classification using multiclass support vector machines with error correcting output codes Digital Signal Processing, Volume 17, Issue 3, May 2007, 675-68

[7] Osowski, S. and Linh, T.R. "ECG Beat Recognation Using Fuzzy Hybrid Neural Network", IEEE Trans. on BME, 48(11), 2001.

[8] Nadal, J. and Bossan, M. "Classification of cardiac arrhythmia based on principal components analysis and feedforward neural Networks", Comput Cardiol, 1993, 341–344.

[9] Hosseini, H.G., Reynolds, K.J., and Powers, D., "A Multi-stage Neural Network Classifier for ECG Events", Proceedings of the 23rd International Conference of the IEEE Engineering in Medicine and Biology Society, 2001, October 25-28.

[10] Minami, K., Nakajima, H. and Toyoshima, T. "Arrhythmia diagnosis with discrimination of rhythm origin and measurement of heart-rate variation", Comp Cardiol,1997,243–246.

[11] Kohonen, T., (2001). Self-Organizing Maps, 3rd ed., Heidelverg: Springer-Verlag Berlin.

[12] Salah Hadji, "Caractérisation du complexe QRS du signal ECG et Identification des arythmies cardiaques'', Thèse de doctorat de l'université de Tunis Elmanar 3,2012

[13] Kohonen, T.: Self-organizing Maps, Springer-Verlag,1995.

[14] [1Kohonen,T.,Hynninen,J.,Kangas,J.Laaksonen,J.:SOM_PAK - The Self-organizing Map Program Package, 1995.

6

Human Gait Gender Classification using 3D Discrete Wavelet Transform Feature Extraction

Kohei Arai[1]
[1])Graduate School of Science and Engineering
Saga University
Saga City, Japan

Rosa Andrie Asmara[1,2]
[2])Informatics Management Department
State Polytechnics of Malang
Malang, Indonesia

Abstract—Feature extraction for gait recognition has been created widely. The ancestor for this task is divided into two parts, model based and free-model based. Model-based approaches obtain a set of static or dynamic skeleton parameters via modeling or tracking body components such as limbs, legs, arms and thighs. Model-free approaches focus on shapes of silhouettes or the entire movement of physical bodies. Model-free approaches are insensitive to the quality of silhouettes. Its advantage is a low computational costs comparing to model-based approaches. However, they are usually not robust to viewpoints and scale. Imaging technology also developed quickly this decades. Motion capture (mocap) device integrated with motion sensor has an expensive price and can only be owned by big animation studio. Fortunately now already existed Kinect camera equipped with depth sensor image in the market with very low price compare to any mocap device. Of course the accuracy not as good as the expensive one, but using some preprocessing method we can remove the jittery and noisy in the 3D skeleton points.

Our proposed method is to analyze the effectiveness of 3D skeleton feature extraction using 3D Discrete Wavelet Transforms (3D DWT). We use Kinect Camera to get the depth data. We use Ipisoft mocap software to extract 3d skeleton model from Kinect video. From the experimental results shows 83.75% correctly classified instances using SVM.

Keywords—gender gait classification; 3D Skeleton Model; SVM; Biometrics; 3D DWT

I. INTRODUCTION

In recent years, there has been an increased attention on effectively identifying individuals for prevention of terrorist attacks. Many biometric technologies have emerged for identifying and verifying individuals by analyzing face, fingerprint, palm print, iris, gait or a combination of these traits [1]–[3].

Human Gait as the classification and recognition object is the famous biometrics system recently. Many researchers had focused this issue to consider for a new recognition system [4]–[11]. Human Gait classification and recognition giving some advantage compared to other recognition system. Gait classification system does not require observed subject's attention and assistance. It can also capture gait at a far distance without requiring physical information from subjects.

There is a significant difference between human gait and other biometrics classification. In human gait, we should use video data instead of using image data as other biometrics system used widely. In video data, we can utilize spatial data as well as temporal data compare to image data.

There are 2 feature extraction method to be used in gait - classification: model based and free model approach [12]. Model-based approaches obtain a set of static or dynamic skeleton parameters via modeling or tracking body components such as limbs, legs, arms and thighs. Gait signatures derived from these model parameters employed for identification and recognition of an individual. It is obvious that model-based approaches are view-invariant and scale-independent. These advantages are significant for practical applications, because it is unlikely that reference sequences and test sequences taken from the same viewpoint. Model-free approaches focus on shapes of silhouettes or the entire movement of physical bodies. Model-free approaches are insensitive to the quality of silhouettes. Its advantage is a low computational costs comparing to model-based approaches. However, they are usually not robust to viewpoints and scale [13].

Gender classification along with human gait recognition has getting the researchers to find its best methods. Wide implementation make they seem so attractive research. The implementation will not only enhance existing biometrics systems but can also serve as a basis for passive surveillance and control in "smart area" (e.g., restricting access to certain areas based on gender) and collecting valuable demographics (e.g., the number of women entering a retail store, airports, post office, or public smoking area etc. on a given day)

Imaging technology developed quickly this decades. Motion capture (mocap) device integrated with motion sensor has an expensive price and can only be owned by big animation studio. Fortunately now already existed Kinect camera equipped with depth sensor image in the market with very low price compare to any mocap device. Of course the accuracy not as good as the expensive one, but using some preprocessing we can remove the jittery and noisy in the 3D skeleton points. Our proposed method is part of model based feature extraction and we call it 3D Skeleton model. 3D skeleton model for extracting gait itself is a new model style considering all the previous model is using 2D skeleton model. The advantages itself is getting accurate coordinate of 3D point for each skeleton model rather than only 2D point. We use Kinect to get the depth data. We use Ipisoft mocap software to extract 3d skeleton model from Kinect video. Those 3D skeleton model exported to BVH animation standard format file and imported to our programming tool which is Matlab. We use Matlab to extract the feature and use a classifier. We create our own gender gait dataset in 3D environment since there are not exist such a dataset before.

II. PROPOSED METHOD

The classification of gender gait quality in this paper consists of three part, preprocessing, feature extraction, and classification. Figure 1 shows the complete overview of proposed human disable gait quality classification.

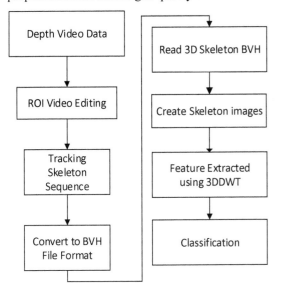

Figure 1: Proposed human gait gender classification

Using Kinect camera have one advantage compare to usual RGB camera. The skeleton created is in 3D space. One can get 2D images from different view angle using only single camera. Figure 2 below shows the 2D skeleton image created from different view angle at the same frame. This is useful to enhance the accuracy of the classification since some paper proposed using multi view image [10], [14]–[16]. However, these papers will only using one view for the analysis.

A. Preprocessing

First, take the Video data using Kinect and IpiRecorder to record the depth data along with RGB video data. To get the video data, there are some recommendation should be considered:

1. Using 9 by 5 feet room space to get best capture.
2. Object should be dressed in casual slim clothing, avoid shiny fabrics.
3. We should ensure that the whole body including arms and legs is visible during the recording states. Beginning from T-Pose and the recording can be started.

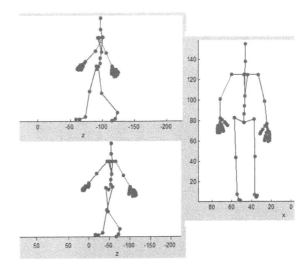

Figure 2. 2D skeleton image created from different view angle at the same frame

Second, processed the depth video data in IPISoft motion capture application. IPISoft will create the 3D skeleton model from video depth recorded using some tracking motion method. The first step is to take only the gait scene, and remove unimportant video scene or we call the Region of Interest (ROI) video. Figure below show the example of video recording.

Third, Create the skeleton 3d model using the tracking motion method, remove the jittery and noises, and export the skeleton model to BVH file format in IPISoft.

Fourth, Read the BVH file, extracted the feature, and classify the feature.

B. Dataset

Unfortunately, there are no Kinect Video Depth gait dataset exists until now. All exist gait dataset is using ordinary RGB camera like USF gait dataset, SOTON gait dataset, and CASIA gait dataset. Figure 3 shows the example of CASIA gait dataset.

Figure 3: Example of CASIA gait dataset

To conduct the experiment, we should prepare the dataset. We will use the Kinect Gait Dataset to analyze and classify gender using gait. The proposed research will search the capability of Kinect and 3D Skeleton model and use their 2D images for gait classification.

Figure 4 below shows the T-pose position before the video recording start. The top right image showing the RGB video sequence. T

he color gradient used to represents the depth in video data. Blue color means the object is close to the camera and red color means the object is far from camera.

Figure 4: T-Pose Position before the recording begin

Figure 5 below show the 3D skeleton tracking motion sequence. First task is specifying subject's physical parameter like gender and height. IpiSoft will detect the ground plane automatically and provide the 3D skeleton in T-Pose position. Our next job is try to put the T-Pose skeleton in the same position with the subject T-Pose position in the first sequence of video.

This time also we should determine the Region of Interest video to be processed. Instead of all the video sequence that we use, we could only take the most important part of the video sequence. Once we put the skeleton to the same position with the subject, we can refitting pose using the application and start tracking. Jittery removal and Trajectory filtering can be done after the tracking finished.

The skeleton sequence result can be import to BVH file standard. Figure 6 and 7 below shows the BVH file result and preview in BVH file viewer and Matlab.

Figure 5: Skeleton motion tracking sequence

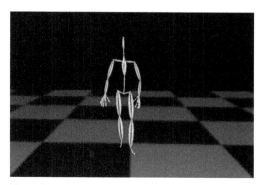

Figure 6: BVH skeleton results

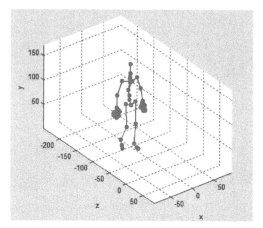

Figure 7: Skeleton model imported in MATLAB

C. 3D Discrete Wavelet Transforms (3D DWT)

3D version of Discrete Wavelet Transform is specially used in volume and video processing. In the 3D case, the 1D analysis filter bank is applied in turn to each of the three dimensions. If the data is of size N1 by N2 by N3, after applying the 1D analysis filter bank to the first dimension one have two sub band data sets, each of size N1/2 by N2 by N3. After applying the 1D analysis filter bank to the second dimension one have four sub band data sets, each of size N1/2 by N2/2 by N3. Applying the 1D analysis filter bank to the third dimension gives eight sub band data sets, each of size N1/2 by N2/2 by N3/2. This is illustrated in the figure 8 below.

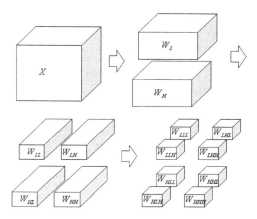

Figure 8. The resolution of a 3-D signal is reduced in each dimension

The block diagram of the 3D analysis filter bank is shown in Figure 9.

D. Feature Extraction

To extract the feature using 3D Discrete Wavelet Transform, we can prepare 2 kind of data. The first data is raw data and the second data is the resized data. The effectiveness and Classification accuracy of each data using statistical feature will be shown in this paper. The resized data have an advantage over the raw data. In Resize data, we can use whole sub bands or decomposition data and process them in the classifier directly.

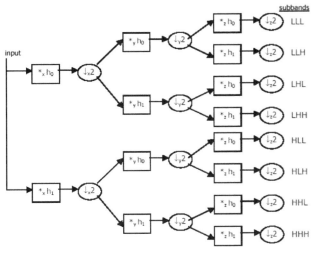

Figure 9. Block diagram of a single level decomposition for the 3D DWT

This can be done because all the dataset have the same dimension. This paper will cover the experimental result of resized data and extracted statistical feature, but this paper will not discuss analyzing of using whole the sub bands feature extraction. To extract the feature in the dataset created, one have to consider about the image size. If all the image is used, it will be costly. One have to extract the skeleton image only and not all the image, thus call it Region of Interest (ROI). One can do automatic ROI using simple image detection since the image is in binary space. After the ROI done, one can extract feature from the data directly or one can resize the data. Thus, there are two kind of data which is raw data and resized data.

Data have to same in image file and frame amount to be used as a resized data. The method used in this paper to create resized data is image resizing and frame cropping. In image resizing, biggest skeleton image ROI will be used as a reference because in this method we don't have to remove some amount of data and those removed data could be valuable information to the system. After finish the image resizing, one can start to crop the frame. This paper will crop the frame based on the smallest amount of video frame, thus all the data have same amount of frame. This paper using middle part of smallest frame amount as a cropped frames. If the smallest frame amount is x, then the video frame crop start at y is round ((total_frame − x)/2) and end in z = y+x.

This paper will used some famous classifier to compare and analyze their best correct classification rate. The decomposition result of Level 1 from 3D DWT of Haar Wavelet will get 8 sub bands which is LLL, LLH, LHL, LHH, HLL, HLH, HHL, and HHH. We will use 3 statistic feature that was used in previous research which is mean, standard deviation, and energy.

The formula for the energy used in Eq.(1) below.

$$E_3 = \sqrt{\sum_{k=1}^{tot_{frame}} \left(\sqrt{\sum_{j=1}^{tot_{col}} \left(\sqrt{\sum_{i=1}^{tot_{row}} (|Wave\ Coef|)^2} \right)^2} \right)^2} \quad (1)$$

From above explanation, we can extract 24 attribute from first and second data type. First 8 attributes is a mean for each sub bands. Second 8 attributes is a standard deviation for each sub bands, and third 8 attributes is an energy for each sub bands. All those 24 attributes namely as mean1_LLL, mean2_LLH, mean3_LHL, mean4_LHH, mean5_HLL, mean6_HLH, mean7_HHL, mean8_HHH, std1_LLL, std2_LLH, std3_LHL, std4_LHH, std5_HLL, std6_HLH, std7_HHL, std8_HHH, e3_LLL, e3_LLH, e3_LHL, e3_LHH, e3_HLL, e3_HLH, e3_HHL, and e3_HHH.

E. Classification

This paper will use two famous classifier which is Naïve Bayes and SVM to analyze and compared the results. SVM (Support Vector Machine) are supervised learning models with associated learning algorithms that analyze data and recognize patterns, used for classification and regression analysis. The basic SVM takes a set of input data and predicts, for each given input, which of two possible classes forms the output, making it a non-probabilistic binary linear classifier.

Given a set of training examples, each marked as belonging to one of two categories, an SVM training algorithm builds a model that assigns new examples into one category or the other. An SVM model is a representation of the examples as points in space, mapped so that the examples of the separate categories are divided by a clear gap that is as wide as possible. New examples are then mapped into that same space and predicted to belong to a category based on which side of the gap they fall on.

III. EXPERIMENTAL RESULT

We start with using Resized data. From 80 dataset with 40 male and 40 female video, we will use SVM and Naïve Bayes as the classifier. First step is we are selecting the best feature in each classifier. There are two method to be use which is Wrapper Method and Ranked Method. We also conduct those two method in two kind of data preprocessing, which is without preprocessing and data after discretization filter preprocessing.

Table 1 is the result of the selected feature using both methods without preprocessing data (raw data type).

TABLE 1. FEATURE SELECTION WITHOUT PREPROCESSING DATA FOR RAW DATA TYPE

	Wrapper Method	Ranked Method
SVM	e3_LLL, e3_LLH	Std1_LLL, e3_HLH, e3_LLL, e3_HLL, e3_HHL, e3_HHH, e3_LHH
Naïve Bayes	mean2_LLH, mean3_LHL, mean6_HLH, mean7_HHL, mean8_HHH, std1_LLL, std3_LHL, std8_HHH, e3_LLL	

Table 2 is the result of the selected feature using both methods with discretization data (raw data type). Table 3 is the result of the selected feature using both methods without preprocessing data (resized data type). Table 4 is the result of the selected feature using both methods with discretization data (resized data type).

TABLE 2. FEATURE SELECTION WITH DISCRETIZATION FILTER DATA FOR RAW DATA TYPE

	Wrapper Method	Ranked Method
SVM	mean5_HLL, mean6_HLH, mean8_HHH, std1_LLL, e3_HLH	e3_HLH, std1_LLL, e3_HHH, e3_LLL, e3_HLL, e3_HHL, std2_LLH
Naïve Bayes	mean2_LLH, mean3_LHL, mean6_HLH, mean8_HHH, std1_LLL, e3_LLL, e3_HLH	

TABLE 3. FEATURE SELECTION WITHOUT PREPROCESSING DATA FOR RESIZED DATA TYPE

	Wrapper Method	Ranked Method
SVM	e3_LLL, e3_LLH, e3_HLL	std6_HLH, std8_HHH
Naïve Bayes	mean6_HLH, std8_HHH, e3_LHL	

TABLE 4. FEATURE SELECTION WITH DISCRETIZATION FILTER DATA FOR RESIZED DATA TYPE

	Wrapper Method	Ranked Method
SVM	mean5_HLL, mean8_HHH, std1_LLL, std7_HHL, std8_HHH, e3_HLL	std6_HLH, std8_HHH, std1_LLL, std4_LHH, e3_HLL, mean5_HLL, e3_LLL, std5_HLL
Naïve Bayes	mean3_LHL, mean4_LHH, mean5_HLL, mean8_HHH, std4_LHH, std8_HHH, e3_LHL, e3_LHH, e3_HHL	

Table 5 shows the result of Correct Classification Rate (CCR) for the selected features (raw data type). Table 6 shows the result of Correct Classification Rate (CCR) for the selected features (resized data type).

TABLE 5. CORRECT CLASSIFICATION RATE FOR EACH SELECTED FEATURE IN EACH CLASSIFIER FOR RAW DATA TYPE

	Wrapper Method		Ranked Method	
	No preprocess	Discretize	No preprocess	Discretize
SVM	68.75%	80%	48.75%	83.75%
Naïve Bayes	77.5%	68.75%	72.5%	76.25%

TABLE 6. CORRECT CLASSIFICATION RATE FOR EACH SELECTED FEATURE IN EACH CLASSIFIER FOR RAW AND RESIZED DATA TYPES

	Wrapper Method		Ranked Method	
	No preprocess	Discretize	No preprocess	Discretize
SVM	45%	76.25%	58.75%	75%
Naïve Bayes	56.25%	61.25%	67.5%	70%

As seen in the tables above, the best CCR is in raw data type using SVM and discretized data and ranked method selected feature. Table 7 is detail accuracy by class using SVM classifier.

TABLE 7. DETAIL ACCURACY BY CLASS USING SVM CLASSIFIER

Class	TP Rate	FP Rate	Precision	Recall	F-Measure	ROC Area
Male	0.775	0.1	0.886	0.775	0.827	0.838
Female	0.9	0.225	0.8	0.9	0.847	0.838
Weighted Average	0.838	0.163	0.843	0.838	0.837	0.838

IV. CONCLUSION

The proposed method uses Kinect depth sensor camera and Ipisoft motion capture software to generate 3D skeleton model. Ipisoft itself is special purpose application to create skeleton so user can use the motion to their computer generated character motion.

The 3D skeleton generated will then extract the 2D image in one view angle and create 2 model data type which is raw and resized video data type. Using Level 1 Haar 3D DWT, we got 8 sub bands and using 3 statistical feature for all 8 sub bands (Mean, Standard deviation, and Energy). By selecting the best feature and classify the results using SVM and Naïve Bayes, the result shows is Table 5 and Table 6. The best result achieved in raw data type using Ranked method feature selection and discretized data which is 83.75% CCR.

ACKNOWLEDGMENT

Portions of the research in this paper is funded by Saga University Japan. Authors would like to thank to Saga University for their providing of the Laboratory and Infrastructures.

REFERENCES

[1] X. Qinhan, "Technology review - Biometrics-Technology, Application, Challenge, and Computational Intelligence Solutions," *IEEE Comput. Intell. Mag.*, vol. 2, pp. 5–25, 2007.

[2] E. Yih, G. Sainarayanan, and A. Chekima, "Palmprint Based Biometric System: A Comparative Study on Discrete Cosine Transform Energy, Wavelet Transform Energy and SobelCode Methods," *Biomed. Soft Comput. Hum. Sci.*, vol. 14, no. 1, pp. 11–19, 2009.

[3] Z. Yang, M. Li, and H. Ai, "An experimental study on automatic face gender classification," *Pattern Recognition, 2006. ICPR 2006. 18th Int. Conf.*, vol. 3, pp. 1099 – 1102, 2006.

[4] N. V. Boulgouris, D. Hatzinakos, and K. N. Plataniotis, "Gait recognition: A Challenging Signal Processing Technology For Biometric Identification," *IEEE Signal Process. Mag.*, vol. 22, no. 6, pp. 78–90, 2005.

[5] M. S. Nixon and J. N. Carter, "Automatic Recognition by Gait," *Proc. IEEE*, vol. 94, pp. 2013–2024, 2006.

[6] D. Cunado, M. S. Nixon, and J. N. Carter, "Automatic Extraction and Description of Human Gait Models for Recognition Purposes," *Comput. Vis. Image Underst.*, vol. 90, no. 1, pp. 1–41, 2003.

[7] X. Li, S. Maybank, and S. Yan, "Gait components and their application to gender recognition," *Syst. Man, Cybern. Part C Appl. Rev. IEEE Trans.*, vol. 38, no. 2, pp. 145–155, 2008.

[8] K. Arai and R. Asmara, "Human Gait Gender Classification using 2D Discrete Wavelet Transforms Energy," *IJCSNS Int. J. Comput. Sci. Netw. Secur.*, pp. 62–68, 2011.

[9] K. Arai and R. Asmara, "Human Gait Gender Classification in Spatial and Temporal Reasoning," *IJARAI Int. J. Adv. Res. Artif. Intell.*, vol. 1, no. 6, pp. 1–6, 2012.

[10] G. Huang and Y. Wang, "Gender classification based on fusion of multi-view gait sequences," *Comput. Vision–ACCV 2007*, vol. 4843, pp. 462–471, 2007.

[11] L. Lee and W. Grimson, "Gait Analysis for Recognition and Classification," in *Proceedings of the Fifth IEEE International Conference on Automatic Face and Gesture Recognition*, 2002, pp. 148–155.

[12] J. Wang, M. She, S. Nahavandi, and A. Kouzani, "A Review of Vision-Based Gait Recognition Methods for Human Identification," *2010 Int. Conf. Digit. Image Comput. Tech. Appl.*, pp. 320–327, Dec. 2010.

[13] K. Arai and R. Asmara, "3D Skeleton model derived from Kinect Depth Sensor Camera and its application to walking style quality evaluations," *Int. J. Adv. Res. Artif. Intell.*, vol. 2, no. 7, pp. 24–28, 2013.

[14] H.-C. Lian and B.-L. Lu, "Multi-view gender classification using multi-resolution local binary patterns and support vector machines.," *Int. J. Neural Syst.*, vol. 17, no. 6, pp. 479–87, Dec. 2007.

[15] W. Kusakunniran, Q. Wu, J. Zhang, and H. Li, "Multi-view Gait Recognition Based on Motion Regression Using Multilayer Perceptron," *2010 20th Int. Conf. Pattern Recognit.*, pp. 2186–2189, Aug. 2010.

[16] Y. Wang, S. Yu, and T. Tan, "Gait recognition based on fusion of multi-view gait sequences," *Adv. Biometrics*, vol. 3832, pp. 605–611, 2005.

7

Diagrammatic Representation as a Tool for Clarifying Logical Arguments

Sabah Al-Fedaghi
Computer Engineering Department
Kuwait University
Kuwait

Abstract—**Knowledge representation of reasoning processes is a central notion in the field of artificial intelligence, especially for knowledge-based agents, because such representation facilitates knowledge of action outcomes necessary for optimum performance by problem-solving agents in complex situations. Logic is the primary vehicle by which knowledge is represented in knowledge-based agents. It involves logical inference that produces answers from what is known based on this inference mechanism. Modus Ponens is the best-known rule of inference that is sound. Recently, a dispute has arisen regarding attempts to show that modus ponens is not a valid form of inference. Part of the cause of the controversy is miscommunication of the involved problem. This paper proposes a diagrammatic representation of modus ponens with the hope that such a representation will serve to clarify the issue. The advantage of this diagrammatic representation is a better understanding of the reasoning process behind this inference rule.**

Keywords—artificial intelligence; diagrammatic representation; conditionals; argument forms; logical argumentation; modus ponens

I. INTRODUCTION

This paper is concerned with the representation of knowledge and the reasoning process, which are central notions in artificial intelligence, especially for knowledge-based agents. The subject is important for artificial agents because they facilitate knowledge of action outcomes necessary for their optimum performance in complex situations and partially observable environments.

Logic is a primary vehicle for representing knowledge. It involves logical inference that produces answers from what is known based on this inference mechanism. In addition to this function of reasoning, an inference mechanism can be utilized for self-learning by artificial agents. Knowledge bases founded on logic consist of statements that accept truth-values with respect to each possible world. They also involve logical *entailment* between statements, where statements follow logically from other statements. Entailment can be used to derive conclusions—that is, to carry out logical inference. An inference rule that derives only entailed sentences is said to be sound or truth preserving.

Modus Ponens (MP) is the best-known rule of inference that is sound or truth preserving and hence can be applied to derive conclusions that lead to the desired goal. History-wise, it has been considered one of the five basic inference rules that are valid without proof (e.g., by the Stoics [1]). Currently, it is

still a central tool; for example, MP is an important forward-chaining inference in a knowledge base of Horn clauses to determine whether a statement is entailed by the knowledge base.

This paper focuses on such MP because recent attempts have been made to show that modus ponens is not a valid form of inference. The paper does not counter or support the logical argument of such an attempt. The underlying thesis is that representation has contributed to such a controversy. This paper aims at proposing a diagrammatic representation of modus ponens with the hope of clarifying the issue in relation to MP.

Current methods of diagrammatic representation of logic formulas incompletely depict the underlying semantics of the formulas, creating a conceptual gap that sometimes causes misinterpretation. The methodology proposed in this paper applies a schematizing of logic formulas in the context of modus ponens. The advantage of this diagrammatic representation is better understanding of the reasoning process at the base of this inference rule.

II. BACKGROUND OF MODUS PONENS

In logic, an indicative conditional statement is a statement that describes implications or hypothetical situations and their consequence, such as *If p then q*, where *p* is called the antecedent, and *q* the consequent; however, in general, such as in natural language, conditional statements are not restricted to this format. In the context of logic, and based on truth conditions, *If p then q,* denoted as p→q, is false when p is true and q is false, otherwise, it is true. "Conditional sentences have attracted concentrated attention of philosophers, although intermittent, since ancient times…" [2].

On the other hand, MP as a principle of inference expresses that: from the conditional if p then q together with its antecedent p, it can be inferred that q. MP is commonly recognized as a basic rule of inference. Along with MP is the Modus Tollens (MT) rule: "we teach them [MP and MT] in introductory logic courses, related to conditional statements. In everyday reasoning, MP and MT can also have important roles, in modes of argumentation" [2]. As mentioned, attempts have been made to show that MP is not a valid form of inference, and these have been based mainly on a number of counterexamples, thus challenging the accepted view in logic that inferences grounded on MP are deductively valid [3-4]. McGee [5] presents the following MP counterexamples:

Opinion polls taken just before the 1980 election showed the Republican Ronald Reagan decisively ahead of the Democrat Jimmy Carter, with the other Republican in the race, John Anderson, a distant third. Those apprised of the poll results believed, with good reason:

a) If a Republican will win the election, then if Reagan will not win, Anderson will win.

b) A Republican will win the election.

c) So, if Reagan will not win, Anderson will win.

But, those apprised of the poll results "did not have reason to believe" conclusion c [5]. This means that c is not obviously true. This application of MP to an ordinary statement leads to a conclusion that is contrary to common-sense expectation. Accordingly, in light of examples such as this, modus ponens is not strictly valid; see discussions in [6-8]. "McGee's [5] attempt to show that modus ponens is not a valid form of inference – and to show this by the help of a counterexample and not by envisaging an evil demon confusing us – is proof of the ingenuity of a philosopher's ability to doubt" [9]. MacFarlane [10] gives two additional examples, as follows:

(a) If that creature is a fish, then if it has lungs, it is a lungfish. (b) That creature is a fish. (c) So, if it has lungs, it is a lungfish.

(a) If Uncle Otto doesn't find gold, then if he strikes it rich, he will strike it rich by finding silver. (b) Uncle Otto won't find gold. (c) So, if Uncle Otto strikes it rich, he will strike it rich by finding silver.

This paper demonstrates diagrammatic construction of MP for the purpose of producing a conceptually complete description of the involved phenomena. The description can provide illustrations and models that might help in facilitating understanding of the MP-based reasoning process. The approach utilizes a diagrammatic apparatus called the Flowthing Model that, for the sake of completeness, will be briefly described in the next section [11-15].

III. USING THE FLOWTHING MODEL

The Flowthing Model (FM) can be related to the notion of fluidity within a web of interrelated *flows* that cross boundaries of intersecting and nested *spheres*. This representation is an apparatus that facilitates flowages (acts of flowing). Ingredients in a flowage include *flowthings* (things that flow), and flow systems (*flowsystems*). So-called objects, concepts, entities, and time are flowthings. A "thing" is defined as a flowthing: "what is created, released, transferred, arrives, is accepted, and processed" while flowing within and among spheres. In spite of use of the term "thing," the fundamental ontology in FM is that "systems are not composed of things, but are rather *defined on* things, and there is a clear distinction between their physical 'thinghood' and logical 'systemhood' properties" [16]. Accordingly, a sphere or subsphere can be any object, any region of logical space that is set apart (mentally) from anything else [16].

A flowthing has a permanent identity but impermanent form. A *flowsystem* constrains the trajectory of flow of flowthings. A particular flowsystem provides the space/time for happenings and existence of flowthings. To flowthings, the

flowsystem is formed of six discontinuities: being created, being released, being transferred, being arrived, being accepted, and being processed.

Flows connect six *stages* that are exclusive for flowthings; i.e., a flowthing can be in one and only one of these six states at a time: Transfer, Process, Creation, Release, Arrival, and Acceptance, as shown in Fig. 1. Where appropriate, we can use Receive as a combined stage of Arrive and Accept. These stages are the elementary basic *actions*. A system manifests itself by engaging in these actions: processing, creating, releasing, receiving, and transferring of flowthings. In Fig. 1, we assume irreversibility of flow, e.g., released flowthings flow only to Transfer.

Note that this conceptualization of stages as elementary *actions* may not coincide with other uses of such terms, e.g., in physics. For example, (model) time and (model) space are simply flowthings in FM that can be created, processed, released, etc.; e.g., a clock is a flowsystem that can create, release, and transfer time.

The lower-level *spheres* where the flows occur are called flowsystems; these include, at most, six stages, as follows:

- *Arrive*: a flowthing reaches a new flowsystem

- *Accepted*: a flowthing is permitted to enter the system.

- *Processed* (changed in form): the flowthing passes through some kind of transformation that changes its form but not its identity (e.g., compressed, colored, compared)

- *Released*: a flowthing is marked as ready to be transferred (e.g., airline passengers waiting to board after completing processing)

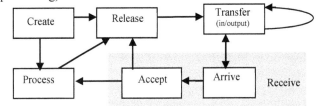

Fig. 1. Flow system

- *Created*: a new flowthing emerges (comes into existence relative to its sphere) in the system (e.g., processing of a neutron generates a proton, electron, and neutrino)

- *Transferred*: the flowthing is en route to somewhere outside the flowsystem (e.g., packets reaching ports in a router, but still not in the arrival buffer).

An additional stage of *Storage* can also be added to any FM model to represent the storage of flowthings; however, storage is a generic stage, not specific, because there can be stored processed flowthings, stored created flowthings, and so on.

A flowsystem may not need to include all the stages because the other stages are irrelevant, have no impact, or are prohibited, e.g., an archiving (storage) system might use only the stages arrive, accept, release, and transfer. Multiple systems captured by FM can interact with each other by triggering interrelated events in their spheres and stages.

IV.   DESCRIBING FORMULAS IN FM

In FM, a formula p can be conceptualized as a sphere formed from two subsystems (Body, Truth), as shown in Fig. 2. Consider the statement *A Republican will win the election* as declared in a logical argument:

1)   ...
2)   ...
3)   p

This indicates that the inference rule, say, MP, processed the premises and reached the conclusion that triggered the creation of p (circles a and b in Fig. 3). As a result of this creation "(3) p" appears in the chain of deduction with its two flowsystems of truth-value and body (c and d).

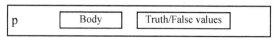

Fig. 2.   p as a sphere with two flowsystems

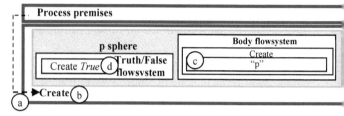

Fig. 3.   p is created as a result of processing premises

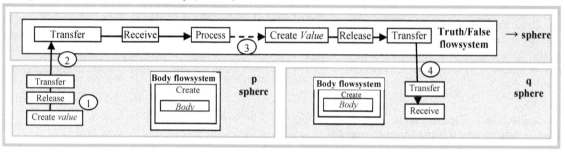

Fig. 4.   FM representation of the implication *p→q*

Fig. 4 shows the FM representation of the implication p→q which is formed from p', q', and →. For simplicity's sake, the truth-value flowsystem (circle 1 in the figure) is not enclosed in a box. The truth-value flows to p', then to the implication (2), where it is processed and, according to the material implication truth table, triggers (3) the creation of a truth-value. This truth-value flows to q' (4). Note that Fig. 4 is an "empty shell" of structure that will be filled when it is triggered. The implication includes p' and q' as shells (place holders) of structure (no assigned truth-values).

Now consider that the modus ponens:

4)   p→q
5)   p

is applied to produce q as shown in Fig. 5. Note that the sphere of the MP involves p, p→q, and q. Such a structure of MP (see Fig. 5) is activated (created) and processed. The antecedent and consequent p' and q' in the figure are "shells" or "place holders" for p and q (loaded with truth-values), in the same way one could give a value to variable *x* in *x* + 200. When p is created then, if its body is similar to the p', the truth-value flows and reaches → to trigger filling of q'; accordingly, the MP "gives birth to" (creates) q.

Fig. 6 shows the complete FM representation of MP, which involves the following:

a) The creation of p→q (shells p' and q', and →), p and q (1, 2, and 3, respectively). Note that true is assigned to the → sphere (2), activating it, analogous to switching an engine ON, as shown in Fig. 7.

b) Assigning a truth-value to p (1)

Accordingly, the *body* of p flows to its corresponding body of the antecedent in the implication (5). If the two bodies are identical (6), then this triggers (7) the flow of truth-value (8 and 9) to the implication to be processed (10) according to the implication truth table.

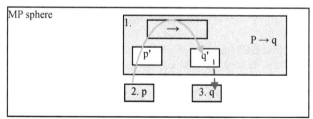

Fig. 5.   The sphere of the MP

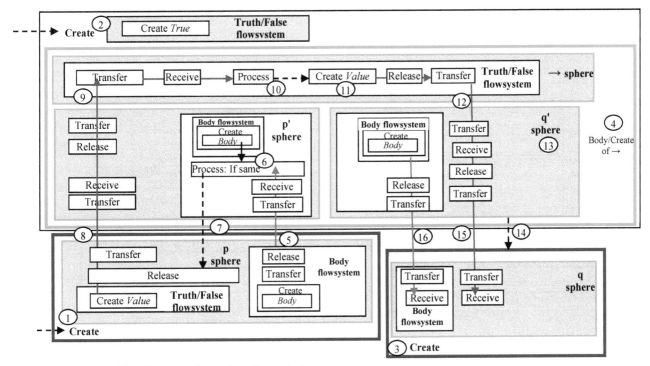

Fig. 6.   FM representation of the MP: p→q, p that produces the conclusion q

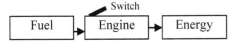

Fig. 7.   Analogy of the activation of MP

The resultant truth-value is created (11) to flow (12) to the sphere of q' (13). This flow to the consequent causes it to trigger (14) the creation of q while "filling" it with a truth-value (15) and body (16).

V.   LEWIS CARROLL

This section shows an example using the FM representation to clarify the mechanism of the modus ponens by drawing it explicitly.

"What the Tortoise Said to Achilles" was written by Lewis Carroll in 1895 as a regress problem that arises from using MP as a deduction rule. It begins by considering the following logical argument:

A: "Things that are equal to the same are equal to each other"

B: "The two sides of this triangle are things that are equal to the same"

Therefore Z: "The two sides of this triangle are equal to each other"

Then, an objection is raised to deducing Z from A and B, based on accepting that A and B are true, but not accepting the principle: *if* A and B are both true, *then* Z must be true. Accordingly, the premises are written as follows.

A: "Things that are equal to the same are equal to each other"

B: "The two sides of this triangle are things that are equal to the same"

C: "If A and B are true, Z must be true"

Therefore Z: "The two sides of this triangle are equal to each other"

However, it is possible to accept premise C while still refusing to accept the expanded argument. In this way, the list of premises continues to grow without end.

(1): "Things that are equal to the same are equal to each other"
(2): "The two sides of this triangle are things that are equal to the same"
(3): (1) and (2) ⇒ (Z)
(4): (1) and (2) and (3) ⇒ (Z)
...
(n): (1) and (2) and (3) and (4) and ... and (n − 1) ⇒ (Z)
Therefore (Z): "The two sides of this triangle are equal to each other."

Fig. 8 shows the FM representation of A, B, and Z. Now consider in the figure:

Refusing to deduce Z from A and B based on accepting that A and B are true, but not accepting the principle: *if* A and B are both true, *then* Z must be true.

The principle that, *if* A and B are both true, *then* Z must be true, is drawn explicitly in the figure as an application of Fig. 6. It seems that refusal is related to the triggering that creates q (*The two sides of this triangle are equal to each other*).

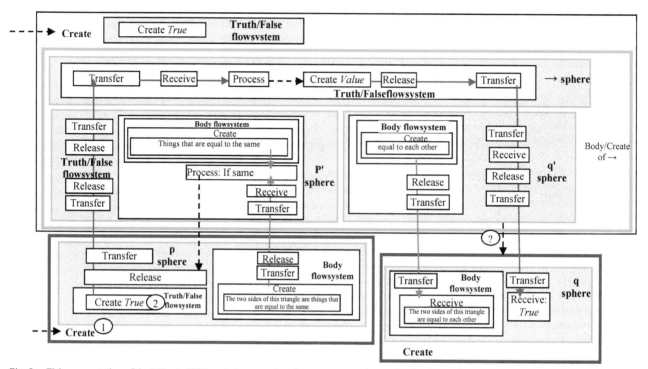

Fig. 8.   FM representation of the MP: A: "Things that are equal to the same are equal to each other," B: "The two sides of this triangle are things that are equal to the same"; therefore Z: "The two sides of this triangle are equal to each other"

As explained when discussing p→q in Fig. 6, p is created (given), and its truth-value (2) flows to the implication → where the truth-value is created according to the truth table (3). Hence, q' is now "pregnant" with full q: *It is true that the two sides of this triangle are equal to each other*. Then, why disbelieve that q' "gives birth" to q? The whole process is a machine-like construction analogous to a machine designed to produce an output.

Another possible objection is disbelieving that the "machine" is designed correctly. What part, then, is the incorrect portion of the machine?

FM representation allows the mechanism of the modus ponens to be explicitly drawn, in contrast to being a "ghost" in such representations as the one shown in Fig. 9.

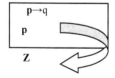

Fig. 9.   Implicit representation of Modus ponens

VI.   McGee's Counterexample

The FM representation can be used to diagram McGee's [5] counterexample mentioned in the introduction.

a) If a Republicans will win the election, then if Reagan will not win, Anderson will win.

b) A Republican will win the election.

c) So, if Reagan will not win, Anderson will win.

Or,

1.   p→(q →t)
2.   p
3.   (q →t)

Fig. 10 shows the corresponding FM representation. The first part, "p→" appears as in the FM description shown in Fig. 6; however, starting with circle 12, the truth-value result, this time, triggers (activates) *another implication* (blue box in the online version): (q →t).

This, in turn, triggers the creation of q (circle 13 in Fig. 10), which is formulated from the body of q' in the implication (14 and 15).

Accordingly, the *true* value of q' (16) flows to the implication in (q' →t') (17), where it is processed (18) to produce a truth-value according to the material implication truth table (19). Since (q' →t') is true and q is true, then the generated truth-value is true. This truth-value flows to (the shell) t' (20) to trigger (21) the creation of t using the body of t' (22).

Now, look at the "internal" MP:

q→t

q

----

t

The situation of (q'→t') (12) being true does not necessarily originate from q is true, as shown in Table1.

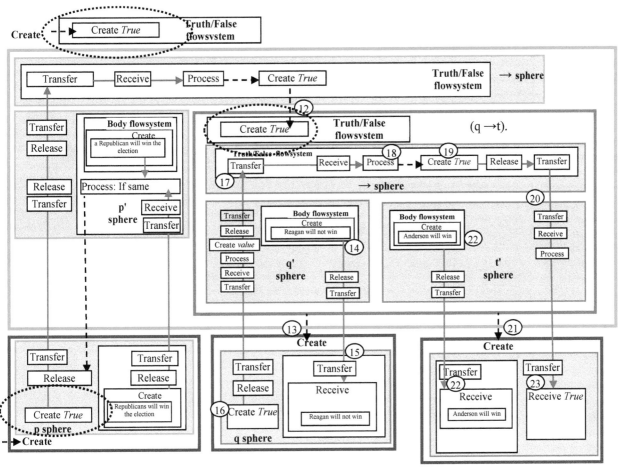

Fig. 10. FM representation of McGee's counterexample

TABLE I.   TRUTH TABLE FOR "q→t" IS TRUE"

	q	t	(q →t)
1	**true**	**true**	**true**
2	false	false	true
3	false	true	true

The true value of (q→t) "means" that q and t could be true or false, as shown in Table 1, relative to the assumed truthfulness of *Reagan will not win*. Accordingly, the implication q→t has three possibilities, all of which satisfy that (q →t) is true:

(Row 1 in Table 1) *A Republican will win the election* → *If Reagan will not win, Anderson will win*

(Row 1 in Table 1) *A Republican will win the election* → *If Reagan will win, Anderson will win*

(Row 1 in Table 1) *A Republican will win the election* → *If Reagan will win, Anderson will not win*

Therefore, the MP should have been written as:

1) If a Republican will win the election, then

(If Reagan will not win, Anderson will win) ∨ (If Reagan will win, Anderson will win) ∨ (If Reagan will win, Anderson will not win)

2) A Republican will win the election

----

3) (If Reagan will not win, Anderson will win) ∨ (If Reagan will win, Anderson will win) ∨ (If Reagan will win, Anderson will not win)

But for all $p_1 \vee p_2 \vee p_3$, $p_1 \vee p_2 \vee p_3$ is true if any of p_1, p_2, or p_3 is true. Accordingly, the consequent (3) is true because (*If Reagan will win, Anderson will not win*). In general, if p_i is true then (p_i ∨ any false statement) is true. The controversy originated with the implication:

p is true → ((q→t) is true)

Subsequently, we can substitute a false statement for q and t and still preserve the truthfulness. If fact, it is a valid deduction that:

1) If a Republican will win the election, then, if The moon is made of green cheese, Anderson will win

2) A Republican will win the election

----

3) (If The moon is made of green cheese, Anderson will win)

This resulted from the definition of material implication [16].

VII. CONCLUSION

This paper proposes a diagrammatic representation of modus ponens with the hope that such a representation can help to clarify issues related to rules of inference, specifically modus ponens. The advantage of this diagram-matic representation as a tool for understanding the reasoning process involved in this inference rule is demonstrated through examples. The results point to the viability of the approach. Further research may confirm such results.

REFERENCES

[1] B. Mates, Stoic Logic. Berkeley: University of California Press, 1953. ISBN 0-520-02368-4

[2] M. M. Dagli, "Modus ponens, modus tollens, and likeness," in Twentieth World Congress of Philosophy, August 10-15, Boston, USA, 1998.

[3] R. Reiter, "On reasoning by default," in Readings in Knowledge Representation, R. J. Brachman and H. J. Levesque, Eds. Los Altos, CA: Morgan Kaufman, 1985, pp. 402-410.

[4] H. Prakken, Logical Tools for Modelling Legal Arguments. Dordrecht: Kluwer, 1997.

[5] V. McGee, "A counterexample to modus ponens." J. Philos., vol. 82, pp. 462-471, 1985.

[6] W. Sinnott-Armstrong, J. Moor, and R. Fogelin, "A defense of modus ponens," J. Philos., vol. 83, pp. 296-300, 1986.

[7] E. J. Lowe, "Not a counterexample to modus ponens," Analysis, vol. 47, pp. 44-47, 1987.

[8] D. E. Over, "Assumptions and the supposed counterexamples to modus ponens," Analysis, vol. 47, pp. 142-146, 1987.

[9] C. Piller, "Vann McGee's counterexample to modus ponens," Philos. Stud., vol. 82, pp. 27-54, 1996.

[10] J. MacFarlane, "McGee on modus ponens," April 21, 2011. http://johnmacfarlane.net/142/mcgee.pdf

[11] S. Al-Fedaghi, "Schematizing proofs based on flow of truth values in logic," in IEEE International Conference on Systems, Man, and Cybernetics (IEEE SMC 2013), October 13-16, Manchester, UK, 2013.

[12] S. Al-Fedaghi, "Visualizing logical representation and reasoning," in 15th International Conference on Artificial Intelligence (ICAI'13), July 22-25, Las Vegas, USA, 2013.

[13] S. Al-Fedaghi, "Schematizing formulas for logic students," Int. J. Intell. Inform. Process., vol. 4, no. 4, pp. 27- 38, 2013.

[14] S. Al-Fedaghi, "On a flow-based paradigm in modeling and programming," Int. J. Advanced Comput. Sci. Appl. (IJACSA), vol. 6, no. 6, pp. 209-217, 2015.

[15] S. Al-Fedaghi, "Conceptualizing effects, and uses of information," in Information Seeking in Context Conference (ISIC 2008), September 17-20, Vilnius. Lithuania, 2008.

[16] G. Sundholm, "'Inference versus consequence' revisited: inference, consequence, conditional, implication," Synthese, vol. 187, pp. 943–956, 2012.

8

Integral Lqr-Based 6dof Autonomous Quadrocopter Balancing System Control

A Joukhadar, BSc, MPhil, PhD
Dept. of Mechatronics Engineering
University of Aleppo, Aleppo-Syria

A Alsabbagh, BSc(Candidate)
Dept. of Mechatronics Engineering
University of Aleppo, Aleppo-Syria

I Hasan, BSc(Candidate)
Dept. of Mechatronics Engineering
University of Aleppo, Aleppo-Syria

M Alkouzbary, BSc(Candidate)
Dept. of Mechatronics Engineering
University of Aleppo, Aleppo-Syria

Abstract—This paper presents an LQR-Based 6DOF control of an unmanned aerial vehicles (UAV), namely a small-scale quadrocopter. Due to its high nonlinearity and a high degree of coupling system, the control of an UAV is very challenging. quadrocopter trajectory tracking in a 3D space is greatly affected by the quadrocopter balancing around its roll-pitch-yaw frame. Lack of precise tracking control about the body frame may result in inaccurate localization with respect to a fixed frame. Thus, the present paper provides a high dynamic control tracking balancing system response. An integral LQR-based controller is proposed to enhance the dynamic system response balancing on roll, pitch and yaw. The control on the hovering angles consists of two-cascaded loops. Namely, an inner loop for the angular speed control of each angular motion around the body frame axes, and an outer loop for the desired position control. In general, the proposed balancing control system on roll, pitch and yaw, has six control loops. The proposed control approach is implemented utilizing an embedded ATMega2560 microcontroller system. Practical results obtained from the proposed control approach exhibits fast and robust control response and high disturbance rejection.

Keywords—Quadrocopter; Balancing Control; Stability of Quadrocopter; LQR; Integral LQR; Modelling of Quadrocopter

I. INTRODUCTION

Control of Unmanned Aerial Vehicles, known as UAVs, has been considered as one of the difficult and complicated challenges, especially controlling those that can perform vertical take-off and landing (VTOL). quadrocopters have become very popular recently due to their simple structure design compared with what they can perform even in a complex environment. Moreover, recent development in high density power storage, integrated miniature actuators and MEMS technology sensors have made the autonomous flying robots possible. However, the quadrocopter is a very nonlinear system; that makes the control of this vehicle not easy to be accomplished.

The movement of the vehicle's body frame with respect to the inertial earth frame is controlled by adjusting the angular speed of the propellers properly. Control laws will lead the vehicle to act in a particular manner as desired. Several control methods have been tested on the quadrocopter to stabilize and track control.

In [1] & [2], authors compared between PID, Sliding mode, LQR and Backstepping, for attitude control only for the quadrocopter. Authors in [1], propose an Integral Backstepping for full position control of the quadrocopter system. LQG controller is applied to control the attitude of quadrocopter [3].

Feedback linearization based technique is proposed to deduce the control law for quadrocopter attitude control, [4]. In [5], a modified Backstepping approach is proposed to control attitude and position of the quadrocopter, where the main contribution was to reduce the number of gains in the control laws.

In [6], a nonlinear control design is combined with an online parameter estimation to develop the control law, in presence of parameter uncertainties and compared with sliding mode control. In [7], Fuzzy Backstepping Sliding Mode Controllers are designed for quadrocopter. However, this control technique is a Backstepping technique where the error signals were determined as the sliding manifold, moreover, a Fuzzy Controler was added instead of sign function in the control law.

The remaining sections are, section II, which briefs the quadrocopter system description. The quadrocopter LQR Controller is discussed in section III. The dynamic model of quadrocopter is given in section IV. Section V explains the design of LQR optimal control design. Practical implementation and results are given in section VI. Section VII discusses the concluded practical results.

TABLE I.   SYMBOLS TABLE

Symbol	Units	Brief description
F_E	None	Earth frame
F_B	None	Body frame
ξ	m	Position vector in the earth frame
X	m	x unit vector in the earth frame
Y	m	y unit vector in the earth frame
Z	m	z unit vector in the earth frame
η	deg	Orientation angle vector in the earth frame
ϕ	deg	Roll Euler angle
θ	deg	Pitch Euler angle
ψ	deg	Yaw Euler angle
$\mathbf{V}_B$	m/s	The prismatic speed vector in the body frame
u	m/s	The prismatic speed on x unit vector in the body frame
v	m/s	The prismatic speed on y unit vector in the body frame
w	m/s	The prismatic speed on z unit vector in the body frame
$\mathbf{v}$	deg/s	The angular speed vector in the body frame
p	deg/s	The angular speed on x unit vector in the body frame
q	deg/s	The angular speed on y unit vector in the body frame
r	deg/s	The angular speed on z unit vector in the body frame
$\mathbf{R}$	None	The transformation matrix from the body frame to the earth frame
$\mathbf{R}^{-1}$	None	The transformation matrix from the earth frame to the body frame
$\mathbf{W}_\eta^{-1}$	None	The transformation matrix of angular speed from the body frame to the earth frame
m	kg	Vehicle flight mass
$\mathbf{T}_B$	m/s	Vector of total force acting on vehicle expressed in the body frame
$\mathbf{G}$	$N.m$	Vector force due to gravity acting on vehicle expressed in the body frame
$\mathbf{I}$	$kg.m^2$	Vehicle flight moment of inertia tensor w.r.t. Center of mass
I_{xx}	$kg.m^2$	x principle moment of inertia
I_{yy}	$kg.m^2$	y principle moment of inertia
I_{zz}	$kg.m^2$	z principle moment of inertia
f_i	N	Vector thrust of rotor i expressed in the body fram
b	$N.s^2$	Thrust factor
d	$N.m.s^2$	Drag factor
Ω_i	deg/s	Scalar rotational speed of rotor i
I_M	$kg.m^2$	Motor moment of inertia
L	m	Horizontal distance: propeller center to cog.
τ	$N.m$	Vector of total torque acting on vehicle expressed in the body frame
Γ	$N.m$	Gyroscopic force vector
J_r	$kg.m^2$	Rotor moment of inertia
Ω_d	deg/s	Overall residual propeller angular speed

II.   QUADROCOPTER SYSTEM DESCRIPTION

The UAV system used for implementation, is shown in Fig. 2. It is aimed to make an autonomous quadrocopter, which can balance itself while flying. To have it done, an Inertial Measurement Unit (IMU) and an altimeter (altitude sensor) are used. The IMU is an MEMS type that measures and reports the quadrocopter's orientation and gravitational forces, using a combination of accelerometer, gyroscope and magnetometer. The altimeter is a fusion sensor that measures the altitude of the quadrocopter. Four BLDC motors, out-runner type, are used. Fig. 2 shows an image of the quadrocopter under investigation in the Lab.

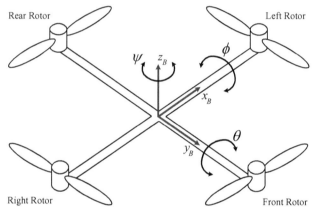

Fig. 1.   Euler angles

Fig. 2.   Quadrocopter system under investigation

The quadrocopter is equipped with an embedded fight controller board, which consists of an ATMega2560 microcontroller and MPU6050 integrated 6-axis motion tracking device, which combines 3-axis gyroscope and 3-axis accelerometer with its dedicated I2C sensor bus. It directly accepts inputs from an external 3-axis compass to provide a complete 9-axis Motion Fusion. Fig. 3 shows the flight controller board. The board also consists of HMC5883L 3-axis digital magnetometer is a surface-mount, multi-chip module designed for low-field magnetic sensing with a digital interface for applications such as low-cost compassing and magnetometry. MS5611-01BA03 is a new generation of high-resolution altimeter sensors from MEAS Switzerland with SPI and I2C bus interface.

Fig. 3. Mircontroller board

III. PROPOSED QUADROCOPTER LQR CONTROL

Fig. 4 shows the proposed entire control system for qaudrocopter balancing and localization. The main goal of the paper is to develop an integral LQR controller to enhance the dynamic control response of the quadrocopter with respect to the quadrocopter body frame. As seen from Fig. 4, the proposed control system consists of two control levels. This includes a low-level control (body frame control), and a high-level control.

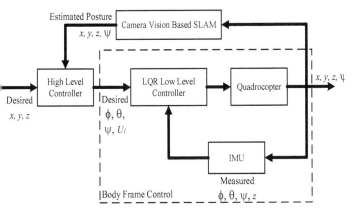

Fig. 4. Proposed Quadrocopter Control System approach

The main task of the low level control, is to improve the dynamic performance of the quadrocopter on the body frame F_B. The low-level control receives the desired command signals, ϕ and θ from the high-level control. While, the control law for the orientation angle ψ considered a high-level control. It is wise mentioning that the goal of the high-level control is to precisely localize the quadrocopter at a desired posture with respect to a fixed earth frame F_E [3].

IV. DYNAMIC MODEL OF A QUADROCOPTER

The non-linear dynamic model of the quadrocopter is provided [8]. It is of 6DOF system, which includes, the position vector ξ with respect to a fixed frame and the orientation vector

η of the body frame F_B relative to a fixed origin of the earth frame F_E. Fig. 5 shows the quadrocopter system with its body frame referenced to a fixed frame [9] & [10].

$$\xi = \begin{bmatrix} x & y & z \end{bmatrix}^T \tag{1}$$

$$\eta = \begin{bmatrix} \phi & \theta & \psi \end{bmatrix}^T \tag{2}$$

$$q = \begin{bmatrix} \xi & \eta \end{bmatrix}^T \tag{3}$$

Equation (3) represents the joint system state space vector of the 6DOF quadrocopter system, which includes the position and the orientation vectors (1) and (2). The linear and the angular velocity vectors are given by (4) and (5), respectively.

$$V_B = \begin{bmatrix} u & v & w \end{bmatrix}^T \tag{4}$$

$$v = \begin{bmatrix} p & q & r \end{bmatrix}^T \tag{5}$$

The rotation matrix R from body frame F_B to earth frame F_E, and the transformation matrix for angular speeds from F_B to F_E, are given by (6) and (7), respectively.

$$R = \begin{bmatrix} C_\psi C_\theta & C_\psi S_\theta S_\phi - S_\psi C_\phi & C_\psi S_\theta C_\phi + S_\psi S_\phi \\ S_\psi C_\theta & S_\psi S_\theta S_\phi + C_\psi C_\phi & S_\psi S_\theta C_\phi - C_\psi S_\phi \\ -S_\theta & C_\theta S_\phi & C_\theta C_\phi \end{bmatrix} \tag{6}$$

$$W_\eta^{-1} = \begin{bmatrix} 1 & S_\phi T_\theta & C_\phi T_\theta \\ 0 & C_\phi & -S_\phi \\ 0 & S_\phi / C_\theta & C_\phi / C_\theta \end{bmatrix} \tag{7}$$

In which, $S_\phi = \sin\phi, C_\phi = \cos\phi, T_\phi = \tan\phi$

And the rotation matrix is orthogonal, i.e., $R^{-1} = R^T$. The physical structure of the quadrocopter is symmetrical about all axes; hence, the inertial matrix is defined as in (8).

$$I = \begin{bmatrix} I_{xx} & 0 & 0 \\ 0 & I_{yy} & 0 \\ 0 & 0 & I_{zz} \end{bmatrix} \tag{8}$$

When rotor i rotates, it generates a lift force f_i, which causes a vertical motion, and an angular torque i around z-axis τ_{Mi} as given in (9) and (10).

$$f_i = b\Omega_i^2 \tag{9}$$

$$\tau_{Mi} = d\Omega_i^2 + I_M\Omega_i \tag{10}$$

As a result, three forces and one torque affect the quadrocopter body and are determined as given by (11), (12), (13) and (14).

$$U_1 = \sum_{i=1}^{4} f_i = b\sum_{i=1}^{4} \Omega_i^2 \tag{11}$$

$$U_2 = b(-\Omega_2^2 + \Omega_4^2) \tag{12}$$

$$U_3 = b(-\Omega_1^2 + \Omega_3^2) \tag{13}$$

$$U_4 = \sum_{i=1}^{4} \tau_{Mi} \tag{14}$$

$$T_B = \begin{bmatrix} 0 & 0 & U_1 \end{bmatrix}^T \tag{15}$$

$$\tau = \begin{bmatrix} lU_2 & lU_3 & U_4 \end{bmatrix}^T \tag{16}$$

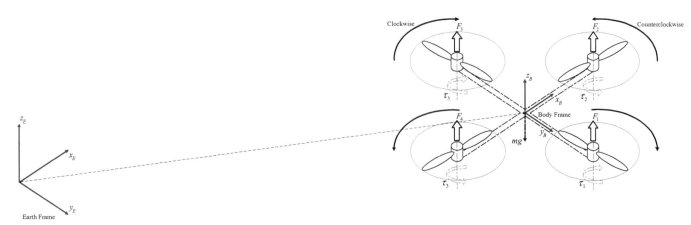

Fig. 5.   Reference frames F_B and F_E, and forces and torques generated by the rotors of the quadrocopter

A. Newton-Euler Equations

It is assumed the quadrocopter to be a rigid body; hence, Newton-Euler equations can be used to describe its dynamics. In the body frame F_B, the force required for the acceleration of mass $m\dot{\mathbf{V}}_B$, and the centrifugal force $\mathbf{v}\times(m\mathbf{V}_B)$ are equal to gravity $\mathbf{R}^T\mathbf{G}$ and the total thrust of the rotors $\mathbf{T}_B$, which is defined in (15), the outcome equation is seen in (18).

$$m\dot{\mathbf{V}}_B + \mathbf{v}\times(m\mathbf{V}_B) = \mathbf{R}^T\mathbf{G} + \mathbf{T}_B \tag{18}$$

In F_E, the centrifugal force is nullified. Therefore, only the gravitational force and the magnitude and direction of the thrust are contributing in the acceleration of the quadrocopter, as in (19) and (20).

$$m\ddot{\xi} = \mathbf{G} + \mathbf{R}\mathbf{T}_B \tag{19}$$

$$\begin{bmatrix} \ddot{x} \\ \ddot{y} \\ \ddot{z} \end{bmatrix} = \begin{bmatrix} 0 \\ 0 \\ -g \end{bmatrix} + \frac{U_1}{m} \begin{bmatrix} C_\psi S_\theta C_\phi + S_\psi S_\phi \\ S_\psi S_\theta C_\phi - C_\psi S_\phi \\ C_\theta C_\phi \end{bmatrix} \tag{20}$$

In F_B, the angular acceleration of the inertia $\mathbf{I}\dot{\mathbf{v}}$, the centripetal forces $\mathbf{v}\times(\mathbf{I}\mathbf{v})$ and the gyroscopic forces $\mathbf{\Gamma}$ are equal to the external torque $\boldsymbol{\tau}$, as in (21), (22) and (23).

$$\boldsymbol{\tau} = \mathbf{I}\dot{\mathbf{v}} + \mathbf{v}\times(\mathbf{I}\mathbf{v}) + \mathbf{\Gamma} \tag{21}$$

$$\mathbf{v}\times(\mathbf{I}\mathbf{v}) = \begin{bmatrix} p \\ q \\ r \end{bmatrix} \times \begin{bmatrix} I_{xx}p \\ I_{yy}q \\ I_{zz}r \end{bmatrix} = \begin{bmatrix} (I_{zz}-I_{yy})qr \\ (I_{xx}-I_{zz})pr \\ (I_{yy}-I_{xx})pq \end{bmatrix} \tag{22}$$

$$\mathbf{\Gamma} = J_r \begin{bmatrix} p \\ q \\ r \end{bmatrix} \times \begin{bmatrix} 0 \\ 0 \\ \Omega_d \end{bmatrix} = J_r \begin{bmatrix} q\Omega_d \\ -p\Omega_d \\ 0 \end{bmatrix} \tag{23}$$

In which,

$$\Omega_d = -\Omega_1 + \Omega_2 - \Omega_3 + \Omega_4 \tag{24}$$

Consequently, the resulted equation can be written as in (25).

$$\begin{bmatrix} \dot{p} \\ \dot{q} \\ \dot{r} \end{bmatrix} = \mathbf{I}^{-1} \left\{ \begin{bmatrix} lU_2 \\ lU_3 \\ U_4 \end{bmatrix} - \begin{bmatrix} (I_{zz}-I_{yy})qr \\ (I_{xx}-I_{zz})pr \\ (I_{yy}-I_{xx})pq \end{bmatrix} - J_r \begin{bmatrix} -q\Omega_d \\ p\Omega_d \\ 0 \end{bmatrix} \right\} \tag{25}$$

$$\begin{bmatrix} \dot{p} \\ \dot{q} \\ \dot{r} \end{bmatrix} = \begin{bmatrix} lU_2/I_{xx} \\ lU_3/I_{yy} \\ U_4/I_{zz} \end{bmatrix} - \begin{bmatrix} (I_{zz}-I_{yy})qr/I_{xx} \\ (I_{xx}-I_{zz})pr/I_{yy} \\ (I_{yy}-I_{xx})pq/I_{zz} \end{bmatrix} - J_r \begin{bmatrix} -q\Omega_d/I_{xx} \\ p\Omega_d/I_{yy} \\ 0 \end{bmatrix} \tag{26}$$

Whereas,

$$\begin{bmatrix} \dot{\phi} \\ \dot{\theta} \\ \dot{\psi} \end{bmatrix} = \begin{bmatrix} 1 & S_\phi T_\theta & C_\phi T_\theta \\ 0 & C_\phi & -S_\phi \\ 0 & S_\phi/C_\theta & C_\phi/C_\theta \end{bmatrix} \begin{bmatrix} p \\ q \\ r \end{bmatrix} \tag{27}$$

B. Nonlinear Dynamic Model Simplification

The transformation between $[\dot{p},\dot{q},\dot{r}]$ and $[\ddot{\phi},\ddot{\theta},\ddot{\psi}]$ for rotational dynamics, is very complex, since it includes many trigonometric functions; therefore, simplification is needed. It is assumed that if perturbations from hover condition are small, body angular rates and rate of change of Euler angles are equal for small values of ϕ and θ, the relation between body angular rates and rate of change of Euler angles becomes as in (28) [10].

$$\begin{bmatrix} \dot{\phi} \\ \dot{\theta} \\ \dot{\psi} \end{bmatrix} = \begin{bmatrix} p \\ q \\ r \end{bmatrix}, \begin{bmatrix} \ddot{\phi} \\ \ddot{\theta} \\ \ddot{\psi} \end{bmatrix} = \begin{bmatrix} \dot{p} \\ \dot{q} \\ \dot{r} \end{bmatrix} \tag{28}$$

According to previous, the complete dynamics of the vehicle is described in (29).

$$\begin{cases} \ddot{\phi} = a_1\dot{\theta}\dot{\psi} + b_1\dot{\theta}\Omega_d + c_1U_2 \\ \ddot{\theta} = a_2\dot{\phi}\dot{\psi} - b_2\dot{\phi}\Omega_d + c_2U_3 \\ \ddot{\psi} = a_3\dot{\theta}\dot{\phi} + c_3U_4 \\ \ddot{x} = (C_\phi S_\theta C_\psi + S_\phi S_\psi)d_1U_1 \\ \ddot{y} = (C_\phi S_\theta S_\psi - S_\phi C_\psi)d_1U_1 \\ \ddot{z} = -g + (C_\phi C_\theta)d_1U_1 \end{cases} \tag{29}$$

Whereas,

$$a_1 = (I_{yy} - I_{zz})/I_{xx}, a_2 = (I_{zz} - I_{xx})/I_{yy}, a_3 = (I_{xx} - I_{yy})/I_{zz}$$

$$b_1 = J_r/I_{xx}, b_2 = J_r/I_{yy}$$

$$c_1 = l/I_{xx}, c_2 = l/I_{yy}, c_3 = l/I_{zz}$$

$$d_1 = 1/m$$

V. LQR OPTIMAL CONTROLLER DESIGN

A. Dynamic Model Linearization

To achieve optimal control algorithm [11] & [12], Linear Quadratic Regular (LQR), the dynamic model, described in (29), must be linearized around a trim condition, which is chosen to be hover condition.

Defining $\mathbf{X} = [\phi, \dot{\phi}, \theta, \dot{\theta}, \psi, \dot{\psi}]^T$ as the state vector of the attitude dynamics whereas, $x_1 = \phi$, $x_2 = \dot{\phi}$, $x_3 = \theta$, $x_4 = \dot{\theta}$, $x_4 = \dot{\theta}$, $x_5 = \psi$, $x_6 = \dot{\psi}$, and $\mathbf{U} = [U_1, U_2, U_3, U_4]^T$ as the input vector. The state space representation of the dynamics can be given by $\dot{\mathbf{X}} = f(\mathbf{X}, \mathbf{U})$ where,

$$f(\mathbf{X}, \mathbf{U}) = \begin{bmatrix} x_2 \\ a_1 x_4 x_6 + b_1 x_4 \Omega_d + c_1 U_2 \\ x_4 \\ a_2 x_2 x_6 - b_2 x_2 \Omega_d + c_2 U_3 \\ x_6 \\ a_3 x_4 x_2 + c_3 U_4 \end{bmatrix} \quad (30)$$

To linearize the system given in (30), and from the Jacobian matrices described in (31) and (32), the linearized system will become as in (33).

$$\mathbf{A}_{n \times n} = \left[\frac{\partial f}{\partial \mathbf{X}} \right]_{(\mathbf{X}_0, \mathbf{U}_0)} = \begin{bmatrix} \frac{\partial f_1}{\partial x_1} & \cdots & \frac{\partial f_1}{\partial x_n} \\ \vdots & \ddots & \vdots \\ \frac{\partial f_n}{\partial x_1} & \cdots & \frac{\partial f_n}{\partial x_n} \end{bmatrix}_{(\mathbf{X}_0, \mathbf{U}_0)} \quad (31)$$

$$\mathbf{B}_{n \times m} = \left[\frac{\partial f}{\partial \mathbf{U}} \right]_{(\mathbf{X}_0, \mathbf{U}_0)} = \begin{bmatrix} \frac{\partial f_1}{\partial u_1} & \cdots & \frac{\partial f_1}{\partial u_m} \\ \vdots & \ddots & \vdots \\ \frac{\partial f_n}{\partial u_1} & \cdots & \frac{\partial f_n}{\partial u_m} \end{bmatrix}_{(\mathbf{X}_0, \mathbf{U}_0)} \quad (32)$$

$$\dot{\mathbf{X}} = \begin{bmatrix} 0 & 1 & 0 & 0 & 0 & 0 \\ 0 & 0 & 0 & 0 & 0 & 0 \\ 0 & 0 & 0 & 1 & 0 & 0 \\ 0 & 0 & 0 & 0 & 0 & 0 \\ 0 & 0 & 0 & 0 & 0 & 1 \\ 0 & 0 & 0 & 0 & 0 & 0 \end{bmatrix} \begin{bmatrix} x_1 \\ x_2 \\ x_3 \\ x_4 \\ x_5 \\ x_6 \end{bmatrix} + \begin{bmatrix} 0 & 0 & 0 \\ c_1 & 0 & 0 \\ 0 & 0 & 0 \\ 0 & c_2 & 0 \\ 0 & 0 & 0 \\ 0 & 0 & c_3 \end{bmatrix} \begin{bmatrix} U_2 \\ U_3 \\ U_4 \end{bmatrix} \quad (33)$$

To stabilize the quadrocopter, the system state, described in (33), will be divided into subsystems as follows:

$$\ddot{\phi} = c_1 U_2 \quad (34)$$

$$\dot{\theta} = c_2 U_3 \quad (35)$$

$$\ddot{\psi} = c_3 U_4 \quad (36)$$

This model could be optimally stabilized using the classical result of LQR.

B. Optimal stabilization of subsystem ϕ

First, the subsystem in (34) is written in a space state form as seen in (37).

$$\begin{bmatrix} \dot{x}_1 \\ \dot{x}_2 \end{bmatrix} = \begin{bmatrix} 0 & 1 \\ 0 & 0 \end{bmatrix} \begin{bmatrix} x_1 \\ x_2 \end{bmatrix} + \begin{bmatrix} 0 \\ c_1 \end{bmatrix} U_2 \quad (37)$$

Fig. 6 shows the suggested LQR controller structure, where a feed forward loop has been added to obtain stabilization at steady state, which supports the control law to maintain the desired angle at its commanded value, and improve the system tracking response. The structure of this control regime was implemented to enhance the quadrocopter balancing system on both roll and pitch angles. It consists of LQR and Integral LQR type controllers. Different control approach structure was proposed for the yaw angle control. Fig. 7 explains the structure of the proposed LQR controller.

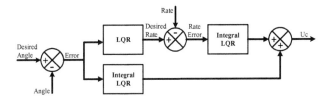

Fig. 6.   Proposed optimal controller for roll and pitch angles control

The system given in (37) should be extended to apply the desired controller, and the extended system is shown in (38).

$$\begin{bmatrix} \dot{x}_1 \\ \dot{x}_2 \\ \dot{\xi}_1 \\ \dot{\xi}_2 \end{bmatrix} = \begin{bmatrix} 0 & 1 & 0 & 0 \\ 0 & 0 & 0 & 0 \\ -1 & 0 & 0 & 0 \\ 0 & -1 & 0 & 0 \end{bmatrix} \begin{bmatrix} x_1 \\ x_2 \\ \xi_1 \\ \xi_2 \end{bmatrix} + \begin{bmatrix} 0 \\ c_1 \\ 0 \\ 0 \end{bmatrix} U_2 \quad (38)$$

$$\mathbf{Q}_\phi = \begin{bmatrix} 170 & 0 & 0 & 0 \\ 0 & 1 & 0 & 0 \\ 0 & 0 & 320 & 0 \\ 0 & 0 & 0 & 0.01 \end{bmatrix}, \mathbf{R}_\phi = \begin{bmatrix} 100 \end{bmatrix} \quad (39)$$

$$\mathbf{K}_\phi = \begin{bmatrix} 1.0333 & 0.447 & -1.791 & -0.7841 \end{bmatrix} \quad (40)$$

C. Optimal stabilization of subsystem θ

$$\begin{bmatrix} \dot{x}_3 \\ \dot{x}_4 \end{bmatrix} = \begin{bmatrix} 0 & 1 \\ 0 & 0 \end{bmatrix} \begin{bmatrix} x_3 \\ x_4 \end{bmatrix} + \begin{bmatrix} 0 \\ c_2 \end{bmatrix} U_3 \quad (41)$$

$$\begin{bmatrix} \dot{x}_3 \\ \dot{x}_4 \\ \dot{\xi}_3 \\ \dot{\xi}_4 \end{bmatrix} = \begin{bmatrix} 0 & 1 & 0 & 0 \\ 0 & 0 & 0 & 0 \\ -1 & 0 & 0 & 0 \\ 0 & -1 & 0 & 0 \end{bmatrix} \begin{bmatrix} x_3 \\ x_4 \\ \xi_3 \\ \xi_4 \end{bmatrix} + \begin{bmatrix} 0 \\ c_2 \\ 0 \\ 0 \end{bmatrix} U_3 \qquad (42)$$

$$\mathbf{Q}_\theta = \begin{bmatrix} 170 & 0 & 0 & 0 \\ 0 & 1 & 0 & 0 \\ 0 & 0 & 320 & 0 \\ 0 & 0 & 0 & 0.001 \end{bmatrix}, \mathbf{R}_\theta = \begin{bmatrix} 100 \end{bmatrix} \qquad (43)$$

$$\mathbf{K}_\theta = \begin{bmatrix} 1.0333 & 0.447 & -1.791 & -0.7841 \end{bmatrix} \qquad (44)$$

D. *Optimal stabilization of subsystem ψ*

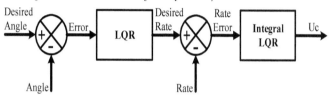

Fig. 7.   The applied optimal controller to control yaw angle

$$\begin{bmatrix} \dot{x}_5 \\ \dot{x}_6 \end{bmatrix} = \begin{bmatrix} 0 & 1 \\ 0 & 0 \end{bmatrix} \begin{bmatrix} x_5 \\ x_6 \end{bmatrix} + \begin{bmatrix} 0 \\ c_3 \end{bmatrix} U_4 \qquad (45)$$

$$\begin{bmatrix} \dot{x}_5 \\ \dot{x}_6 \\ \dot{\xi}_5 \end{bmatrix} = \begin{bmatrix} 0 & 1 & 0 \\ 0 & 0 & 0 \\ 0 & -1 & 0 \end{bmatrix} \begin{bmatrix} x_5 \\ x_6 \\ \xi_5 \end{bmatrix} + \begin{bmatrix} 0 \\ c_3 \\ 0 \end{bmatrix} U_4 \qquad (46)$$

$$\mathbf{Q}_\psi = \begin{bmatrix} 1 & 0 & 0 \\ 0 & 1.1 & 0 \\ 0 & 0 & 0.0001 \end{bmatrix}, \mathbf{R}_\psi = \begin{bmatrix} 2.5 \end{bmatrix} \qquad (47)$$

$$\mathbf{K}_\psi = \begin{bmatrix} 0.8421 & 0.6872 & -0.2067 \end{bmatrix} \qquad (48)$$

VI.   PRACTICAL IMPLEMENTATION AND RESULTS

Practical results obtained from the test bench of the quad-rocopter system, built in Lab, were demonstrated to validate the proposed technique. Intensive practical results were obtained, which demonstrated the applicability of the proposed control approach to work in a robust manner with the ability of disturbance rejection. The practical results were presented in three different categories; angular speed and position control response on roll axis; angular speed and position control response on pitch axis; and angular speed and position control response on yaw axis. To prove the stable high performance balancing control systems on roll, pitch and yaw axes, different desired angular position command on each axis was applied.

A. *Practical Results on Roll-Axis*

This subsection shows the practical results for the balancing control system response on roll axis. It is presumed that there were no motion on the pitch axis i.e., the control balancing system on pitch axis tries to maintain $\theta = \dot{\theta} = 0$ as well as no orientation around yaw axis i.e., $\psi = \dot{\psi} = 0$.

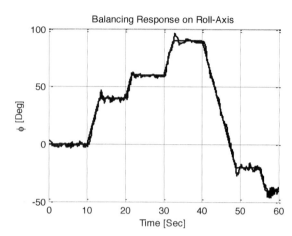

Fig. 8.   Balancing Response on roll-axis

Fig. 8 shows the balancing system response on the roll axis. "Black" is the command signal, and "Blue" is the actual quad-rocopter response. As seen the quadrocopter balancing system exhibited fast tracking response and zero steady state error. As noticed at time t=0➔t=10 sec, the system was balancing at zero roll angle.

B. *Practical Results on Pitch-Axis*

This section explains the dynamic performance of the quad-rocopter balancing for pitch angle control.

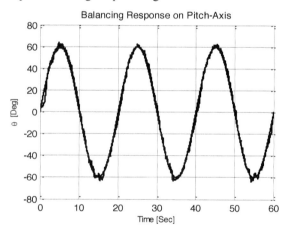

Fig. 9.   Balancing Response on pitch-axis

Fig. 9 shows the response of the quadrocopter control for a sinusoidal changes in the desired command angle. As seen from Fig. 9, "black" is the command and "blue" is the actual system response. There is a very fast command tracking. It is worth mentioning that the peak variation of the quadrocopter around pitch axis is 60°. Hence, the quadrocopter system exhibites a wavey motion with no lack of stability.

Fig. 10 shows the inner angular speed control response. As seen, the integral LQR conroller provides fast angular speed tracking for which the outer position control loop tracks fast the desired position command. Fig. 11 shows the control for the case when controlling the pitch angle, as seen by the angle command profile depicted in Fig. 9. The control law of Fig. 11 is to be sent to the four quadrocopter's rotors, for which stabilization and balancing as desired on pitch axis is achieved.

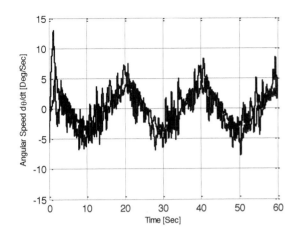

Fig. 10. Angular speed response on pitch-axis

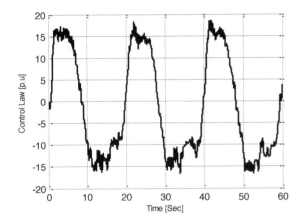

Fig. 11. Control law on pitch-axis

C. Practical Results on Yaw-Axis

The following section provides the experimental results of the quadrocopter balancing system response for yaw angle control.

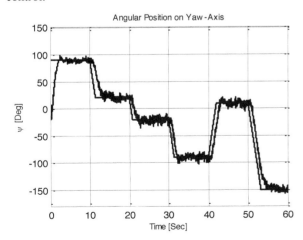

Fig. 12. Angular position response on yaw-axis

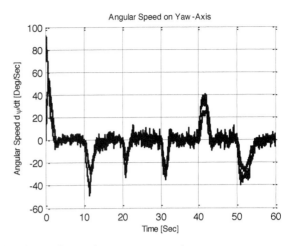

Fig. 13. Angular speed response on yaw-axis

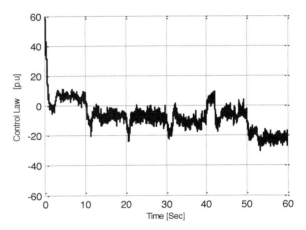

Fig. 14. Control law on yaw-axis

As seen, Fig. 12 and Fig. 13 show the system control response for the outer position control loop and the inner angular speed control loop respectively. "Black" is the command and "blue" is the actual system response. As shown, there is a robust control tracking in both the inner and the outer control loops. Fig. 14 shows the LQR control law generated to maintain stable operation and exact yaw angle tracking as it is desired.

Fig. 15. Real-Time Control of Balancing Quadrocopter System

Fig. 13 shows the test rig of the quadrocopter balancing control system. It has been completely developed by the graduate students in the integration of Mechatronics Systems Lab. As seen, the quadrocopter is linked with a four yellow straps. This is a safety procedure as the quadrocoper is running indoor. This procedure has no effect on the balancing system, as the system is due to work on the body frame angles control and has no motion with respect to the reference fixed earth frame.

VII. CONCLUSION

In this paper, it has been presented a practical implementation of a two-cascaded LQR control loops for position control of the quadrocopter's body frame angles. There are six control loops for the whole quadrocopter balancing control. An LQR and an integral LQR have been proposed for the outer loop (position loop). It has been shown that the proposed control approach, tracks fast the desired commands for roll, pitch and yaw angles in the body frame. It has been also noted that the proposed control approach, exhibits an inherited decoupling control action, for which the control of one axis angle has relieved the dynamic coupling effect on the other two axes. Furthermore, intensive practical results have demonstrated the robustness of the proposed controller. Future work is dedicated for the development of quadrocopter motion control on the Cartesian domain with respect to a fixed frame i.e., high-level control. Referencing to Fig. 4, a vision system assisted-novel SLAM technique is proposed to control and track the localization of the quadrocopter system. Real time implementation of the proposed SLAM technique is done utilizing an Intel® Core^{TM} i5-480M computer machine with a wireless communication system. The communication protocol system is to provide a bi-directional paired communication between the quadrocopter on board control system and the SLAM approach hosted on the computer machine.

ACKNOWLEDGEMENT

The authors would like to thank the Syrian Society for Scientific Research (SSSR) for the financial support provided to cover the IJARAI registration fee

REFERENCES

[1]   S. Bouabdullah "Design and Control of Quadrotors with Application to Autonomous Flying" EPFL, thesis No.3727, 129 pages, 2007.

[2]   A. Eresen – N. İmamoğlu – M. Ö. Efe "Motion Detection and Tracking of classified Objects with Intelligent Systems" 2009 IFAC.

[3]   W. Wang, H. Ma, C. -Y. Sun "Control System Design for Multi-Rotor MAV" Journal of Theoretical and Applied Mechanics, 51, 4, pp. 1027-1038, July 25-27 2013.

[4]   A. A. Saif M. Dhaifullah M. Al-Malki M. El Shafie "Modified Backstepping Control of Quadrotor" 2012 9th International Conference on Systems, Signal and Devices.

[5]   G. -V. Raffo M. -G. Ortega F. -R. Rubio "Backstepping/Nonlinear H∞ Control for Path Tracking of a QuadRotor Unmanned Aerial Vehicle" 2008 American Control Conference, 3356-3361 pp, June 11-13 2008.

[6]   G. Cui – B. M. Chen – T. H. Lee " Unmanned Rotorcraft Systems" Springer, 267 pages, 2011.

[7]   H. Khebbache M. Tadjine "Robust Fuzzy Backstepping Sliding Mode Control for a Quadrotor Unmanned Aerial Vehicle" CEAI, Vol.15, No.2, pp 3-11, 2013.

[8]   T. Luukkonen, "Modelling and control of quadcopter," Independent research project in applied mathematics. pp. 2–4, School of Sience, Espoo, August 22, 2011.

[9]   P. Castillo – R. Lozano – A. E. Dzul "Modeling and Control of Mini Flying Machines" Springer, 251 pages, 2005.

[10] R. Mahony, V. Kuar, P. Corke, "Multirotor Aerial Vehicles: Modeling, Estiation, and Control of Quadcopter," IEEE Robotics & Automation Magazine, vol. 19, no.3, pp. 20-32, Sept. 2012.

[11] A. C. Satici H. Poonawla M. W. Spong "Robust Optimal Control of Quadrotor UAVs" IEEE, Volume 1, pp 79-93, 2013.

[12] O. Santos, H. Romero, S. Salazar and R. Lozano, , "Discrete Optimal Control for a Quadrotor UAV: Experimental Approach," pp. 1139-1141, Orlando, FL, USA, May 27-30, 2014.

[13] K. Nonami - F. Kendoul - S. Suzuki - W. Wang - D. Nakazawa " Autonomous Flying Robots" Springer, 329 pages, 2013.

[14] L. R. G. Carillo - A. E. D. López - R. Lozano - C. Pégard " Quad Rotorcraft Control " Springer, 179 pages, 2013.

[15] H. Khalil " Nonlinear Systems" Prentice Hall, 680 pages, 2002.

[16] M. Krstić I. Kanellakopoulos P. Kokotović "Nonlinear Adaptive Control Design" Springer, 595 pages, 2010.

[17] C. Diao, B. Xian, X. Gu, B. Zhao, J. Guo "Nonlinear Control for an Underactuated Quadrotor Unmanned Aerial Vehicle with Parametric Uncertainties" proceeding of 31st Chinese Conference on Automatic Control, 998-1003 pp, July 25-27 2012.

[18] Z. Yaou Z. Wansheng L. Tiansheng L. Jingsong "The attitude control of the four-rotor unmanned helicopter based on feedback linearization control" WSEAS, Issue 4, Volume 12, April 2013.

[19] L. –X. Wang "Backstepping-Based Inverse Optimal Attitude Control of Quadrotor" Intech, Int J Adv Robotic Sy, 2013, Vol. 10, 223:2013.

[20] M. Önkol and M. Önder Efe. "Experimental Model Based Attitude Control Algorithms for a Quadrotor Unmanned Vehicle", TOBB Economics and Technology University, Turkey, pp 1-6.

[21] A. Ö. Kivrak, "Design of control systems for a quadrotor flight vehicle equipped with inertial sensors", master's thesis in Mechatronics Engineering Atılım University, December 2006, pp 1-37.

[22] M. Rich, "Model development, system identification, and control of a quadrotor helicopter",A thesis submitted to the graduate faculty in partial fulfillment of the requirements for the degree of MASTER OF SCIENCE. Iowa State University Ames, Iowa 2012.

Relation Between Chlorophyll-A Concentration and Red Tide in the Intensive Study Area of the Ariake Sea, Japan in Winter Seasons by using MODIS Data

Kohei Arai [1]
1Graduate School of Science and Engineering
Saga University
Saga City, Japan

Abstract—Relation between chlorophyll-a concentration and red tide in the intensive study area of the back of Ariake Sea, Japan in the recent winter seasons is investigated by using MODIS data. Mechanism of red tide appearance is not so clarified. On the other hand, chlorophyll-a concentration can be estimated with satellite remote sensing data. An attempt is made for estimation of the location and size of red tide appearance. In particular, severe damage due to red tide is suspected in the winter seasons now a day. Therefore, 6 years (winter 2010 to winter 2015) data of MODIS data derived chlorophyll-a concentration and truth data of red tide appearance (the location and the volume) which are provided by Saga Prefectural Fishery Promotion Center: SPFPC (once/10 days of shipment data) have been investigated. As the results of the investigation, it is found that a strong correlation between the chlorophyll-a concentration and red tide appearance together with the possible sources of the red tide.

Keywords—chlorophyl-a concentration; red tide; diatom; MODIS; satellite remote sensing

I. INTRODUCTION

The Ariake Sea is the largest productive area of Nori (Porphyra yezoensis1) in Japan. In winters of 2012, 2013, 2014 and 2015, a massive diatom bloom occurred in the Ariake Sea, Japan [1]. In case of above red tides, bloom causative was Eucampia zodiacus2. This bloom has being occurred several coastal areas in Japan and is well reported by Nishikawa et al. for Harimanada sea areas [2]-[10]. Diatom blooms have recurrently occurred from late autumn to early spring in the coastal waters of western Japan, such as the Ariake Sea [11] and the Seto Inland Sea [12], where large scale "Nori" aquaculture occurs. Diatom blooms have caused the exhaustion of nutrients in the water column during the "Nori" harvest season. The resultant lack of nutrients has suppressed the growth of "Nori" and lowered the quality of "Nori" products due to bleaching with the damage of the order of billions of yen [3].

This bloom had been firstly developed at the eastern part of the Ariake Sea. However, as the field observation is time-consuming, information on the developing process of the red tide, and horizontal distribution of the red tide has not yet been clarified in detail. To clarify the horizontal distribution of red tide, and its temporal change, remote sensing satellite data is quite useful.

In particular in winter, almost every year, relatively large size of diatoms of *Eucampia zodiacus* appears in Ariake Sea areas. That is one of the causes for damage of *Porphyra yezoensis*. There is, therefore, a strong demand to prevent the damage from Nori farmers. Since 2007, *Asteroplanus karianus* appears in the Ariake Sea almost every year. In addition, *Eucampia zodiacus* appears in Ariake Sea since 2012.

The chlorophyll-a concentration algorithm developed for MODIS[3] has been validated [13]. The algorithm is applied to MODIS data for a trend analysis of chlorophyll-a distribution in the Ariake Sea area in winter during from 2010 to 2015 is made [14]. On the other hand, red tide appearance (location, red tide species, the number of cells in unit water volume by using microscopy) are measured from the research vessel of the Saga Prefectural Fishery Promotion Center: SPFPC by once/10 days basis. The location and size of the red tide appearance together with the red tide source would be clarified by using SPFPC data. Match-up data of MODIS derived chlorophyll-a concentrations are used for investigation of relations between MODIS data and truth data of the red tide appearance.

In the next section, the method and procedure of the experimental study is described followed by experimental data and estimated results. Then conclusion is described with some discussions.

II. METHOD AND PROCEDURE

A. The Procedure

The purposes of the research is as follows,

1) At first, MODIS derived chlorophyll-a concentration has to be validated with the truth data (shipment data of the number of cells/ml of red tide species provided by SPFPC),

2) Possible sources of the red tide species has to be estimated,

---

[1] http://en.wikipedia.org/wiki/Porphyra

[2] http://www.eos.ubc.ca/research/phytoplankton/diatoms/centric/eucampia/e_zodiacus.html

[3] http://modis.gsfc.nasa.gov/

3) Spatial relation among several districted sea areas has to be clarified (more precisely, red tide relations between Ariake bay and Isahaya bay as well as Kumamoto offshore have to be clarified),

4) Mechanism of red tide in the intensive study sea areas will be clarified after all.

Therefore, the following procedure of the experimental study is proposed,

1) Gather MODIS data of the Ariake Sea areas together with the chlorophyll-a concentration estimation with the MODIS data,

2) Gather the truth data of red tide appearance (the location and the size of the red tide) together with the red tide species and the number of cells in unit water volume,

3) Investigation on relation between the truth data and the match-up of MODIS data.

B. The Intensive Study Areas

Fig.1 shows the intensive study areas in the Ariake Sea area, Kyushu, Japan.

Fig. 1.   Intensive study areas

III.   EXPERIMENTS

A.   The Data Used (MODIS Data Derived Chlorophyll-a Concentration and Truth Data)

MODIS derived chlorophyll-a concentration which area acquired for the observation period of one month (in January) in 2010 to 2015 is used for the experiments. MODIS data are acquired on these days. MODIS data cannot be acquired on the rest of days due to cloudy condition. White portions in the chlorophyll-a concentration images are cloud covered areas.

These data are acquired on January 4, 6, 7, 8, 9, 9[4], 10, 12, 17, 18, 20, 23, February 1, 3, 6, 9, 13, 14, 20, 27, and March 2 in 2015, respectively. Meanwhile, MODIS data are acquired on January 10, 13, 15, 16, 19, 23, 24, 26, 27, 29, 30 and February 4 in 2014, respectively. In 2013, MODIS data are acquired on January 4, 6, 10, 12, 15, 18, 19, 25, 28, 30, and 31, respectively while, in 2012. MODIS data are acquired on January 2, 6, 7, 12, 17, 20, 21, 23, 26, 29, 30, and 31, respectively. Furthermore, in 2011, MODIS data are acquired on January 1, 2, 7, 8, 14, 17, 22, 26, and 27, respectively while, in 2010, MODIS data are acquired on January 1, 3, 4, 9, 14, 16, 17, 18, 22, 24, 26, 27, and 29, respectively. All the data are shown in the previous paper which deals with "Locality of Chlorophyll-a Distribution in the Intensive Study Area of the Ariake Sea, Japan in Winter Seasons Based on Remote Sensing Satellite Data".

It is found the following red tide at around the Shiota river mouth on January 21 2010,

Asterionella kariana; 3280 cells/ml

Skeletonema costatum: 1330 cells/ml

Fig.2 shows the superimposed image with MODIS data derived chlorophyll-a concentration and truth data which is provided by Saga Prefectural Fishery Promotion Center. The number in the figure denotes the number of red tide cells / ml.

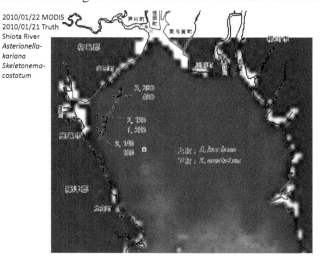

Fig. 2.   Superimposed image with MODIS data derived chlorophyll-a concentration and truth data which is provided by Saga Prefectural Fishery Promotion Center

---

[4] There are two satellites which carry MODIS instruments, Terra and AQUA. Two MODIS data derived chlorophyll-a concentrations can be acquired occasionally.

As shown in the figure, the possible source of red tide would be nutrition rich water flown from the Shiota river mouth. MODIS derived chlorophyll-a concentration is distributed in the whole Ariake bay area while truth data shows red tide is distributed around the Shiota river mouth and Shiroishi offshore.

On January11 2011, it is found the following red tide along with the Shiroishi town offshore to the Shiota river mouth,

Asterionella kariana; 10150 cells/ml

Fig.3 shows the superimposed image with MODIS data derived chlorophyll-a concentration and truth data which is provided by Saga Prefectural Fishery Promotion Center. The number in the figure denotes the number of red tide cells / ml.

Although the truth data say that the red tide is distributed at around Shiota river mouth and Shiroishi offshore, it cannot be seen due to the fact that it is covered with cloud in the MODIS data derived chlorophyll-a concentration.

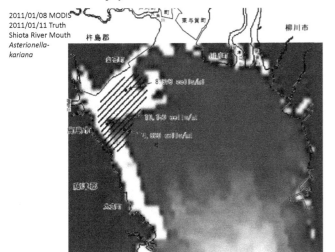

Fig. 3. Superimposed image with MODIS data derived chlorophyll-a concentration and truth data which is provided by Saga Prefectural Fishery Promotion Center

It is found the following red tide at around the Kashima offshore on February 25 2011,

Asterionella kariana; 4950 cells/ml

Fig.4 shows the truth data of red tide distribution which appeared at around Kashima offshore. Unfortunately, MODIS data cannot be acquired on that day.

It is found the following red tide at around the Shiota River Mouth on December 30 2011,

Asterionella kariana; 5150 cells/ml

Fig.5 shows the superimposed image with MODIS data derived chlorophyll-a concentration and truth data which is provided by Saga Prefectural Fishery Promotion Center.

The red tide is distributed Shiota river mouth and Kashima offshore.

On January 23 2012, it is found the following red tide at the Shiroishi offshore,

Skeletonema spp .: 5150 cells/ml

Fig. 4. Truth data of red tide distribution which appeared at around Kashima offshore

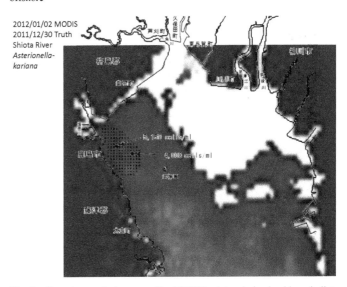

Fig. 5. Superimposed image with MODIS data derived chlorophyll-a concentration and truth data which is provided by Saga Prefectural Fishery Promotion Center

Fig.6 shows the superimposed image with MODIS data derived chlorophyll-a concentration and truth data which is provided by Saga Prefectural Fishery Promotion Center. The red tide is distributed at around Shiota river mouth and Shiroishi offshore.

The following red tide is found widely along with the Kawazoe offshore to the Tara offshore on February 22 2012,

Eucampia zodiacus: 1,090 cells/ml

Fig.7 shows the truth data of red tide distribution which appeared at around Kawazoe offshore. Unfortunately, MODIS data cannot be acquired on that day.

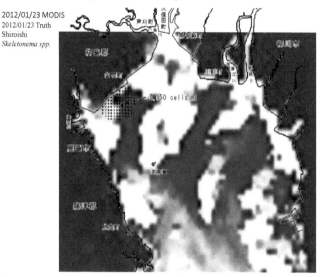

2012/01/23 MODIS
2012/01/23 Truth
Shiroishi
Skeletonema spp.

Fig. 6. Superimposed image with MODIS data derived chlorophyll-a concentration and truth data which is provided by Saga Prefectural Fishery Promotion Center

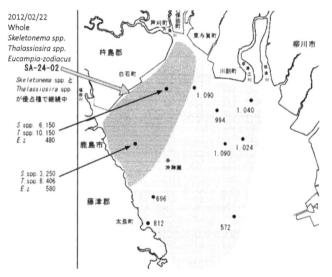

2012/02/22
Whole
Skeletonema spp.
Thalassiosira spp.
Eucampia-zodiacus
SA-24-02

Skeletonema spp. と
Thalassiosira spp.
が優占種で継続中

S.spp. 6.150
T.spp.10.150
E.z   480

S.spp. 3.250
T.spp. 8.406
E.z   580

Fig. 7. Truth data of red tide distribution which appeared at around Kawazoe offshore

Also it is found the following red tide along with the Shiota river mouth to the Kashima offshore on December 31 2012,

Skeletonema spp .: 6110 cells/ml

Fig.8 shows the truth data of red tide distribution which appeared at around Kashima offshore and MODIS data derived chlorophyll-a concentration which is acquired on January 4 2013.

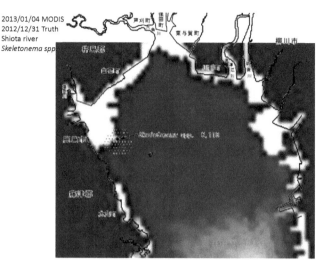

2013/01/04 MODIS
2012/12/31 Truth
Shiota river
Skeletonema spp

Fig. 8. Truth data of red tide distribution which appeared at around Kawazoe offshore and MODIS data derived chlorophyll-a concentration which is acquired on January 4 2013

On January 7 2013, the following red tide are observed along with the Shiota river mouth to the Shiroishi offshore,

Asterionella kariana; 5630 cells/ml

Skeletonema costatum: 3390 cells/ml

Fig.9 shows superimposed image of the truth data and the MODIS data derived chlorophyll-a concentration. The red tide distribution derived from MODIS data is almost coincident to the truth data.

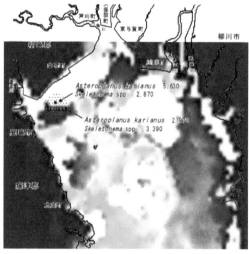

2013/01/10 MODIS
2013/01/07 Truth
Shiota river
Asteroplanus-karianus
Skeletonema spp.

Fig. 9. Superimposed image of the truth data and the MODIS data derived chlorophyll-a concentration

It is found the following red tide at a small area of the Kashima offshore on February 18 2013,

Eutreptia pertyi and Eutreptiella spp.: 116600 cells/ml

Asterionella kariana; 7340 cells/ml

Fig.10 shows the truth data of red tide distribution which appeared at around Kashima offshore. Unfortunately, MODIS data cannot be acquired on that day.

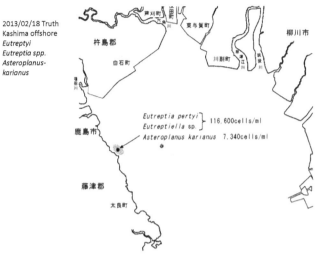

Fig. 10. Truth data of red tide distribution which appeared at around Kashima offshore

On February 26 2013, the following red tide is found almost entire Ariake Bay areas except Rokkaku river mouth,

Eucampia zodiacus: 980 cells/ml

Rhizosolenia setigera: 58 cells/ml

Fig.11 shows the truth data of red tide distribution. Unfortunately, MODIS data cannot be acquired on that day.

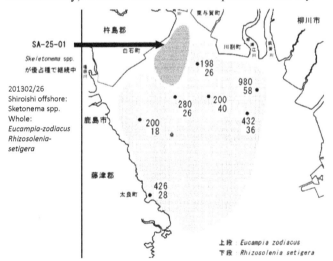

Fig. 11. Truth data of red tide distribution (almost all over the Ariake Bay area)

It is found the following red tide at the Shiraishi offshore on January 6 2014,

Asterionella kariana; 4830 cells/ml

Fig.12 shows the superimposed image of the truth data of red tide and the MODIS data derived chlorophyll-a concentration which is acquired on January 10 2014.

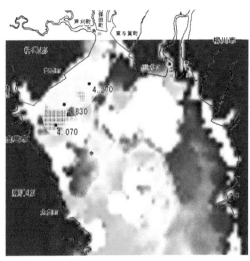

Fig. 12. Superimposed image of the truth data of red tide and the MODIS data derived chlorophyll-a concentration which is acquired on January 10 2014

The following red tide is observed at the Shiroishi offshore on January 16 2014,

Skeletonema spp .: 6110 cells/ml

Thalassiosira spp.: 1510 cells/ml

Fig.13 shows the superimposed image of the truth data of red tide and the MODIS data derived chlorophyll-a concentration which is acquired on January 16 2014. It seems that the red tide which is originated from Rokkaku river mouth and Shiota river mouth propagated to Shiroishi offshore along with the sea water current.

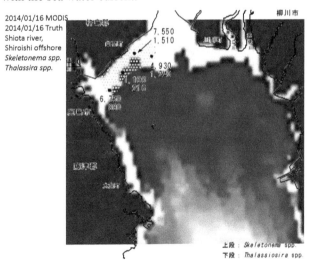

Fig. 13. Superimposed image of the truth data of red tide and the MODIS data derived chlorophyll-a concentration which is acquired on January 16 2014

On February 6 2014, the following red tide is observed almost whole Ariake bay area except the Shiraishi offshore,

Eucampia zodiacus: 568 cells/ml

Fig.14 shows the superimposed image of the truth data of red tide and the MODIS data derived chlorophyll-a concentration which is acquired on February 4 2014.

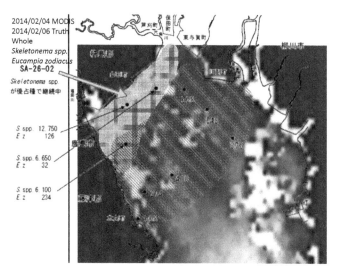

Fig. 14. Superimposed image of the truth data of red tide and the MODIS data derived chlorophyll-a concentration which is acquired on February 4 2014

It is observed the following red tide along with the Shiroishi offshore to the Tara offshore on December 30 2014,

Asterionella kariana; 3890 cells/ml

Skeletonema costatum: 8750 cells/ml

On the other hand, MODIS data is acquired on January 4 2015, clouds are observed almost everywhere in the Ariake bay area though. Fig.15 shows the super imposed image of the truth data of red tide and the MODIS data derived chlorophyll-a concentration which is acquired on January 4 2015. It seems that the red tide which is originated from the Shiota river mouth propagated to the Kashima and Tara offshore and a far beyond along with the sea water current.

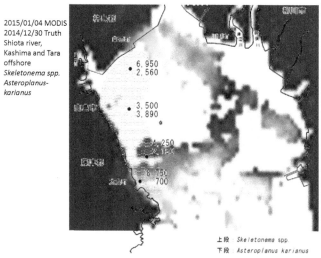

Fig. 15. Superimposed image of the truth data of red tide and the MODIS data derived chlorophyll-a concentration which is acquired on January 4 2015

On March 6 2015, the following red tide is observed along with the Kashima offshore to the Tara offshore,

Eucampia zodiacus: 1310 cells/ml

Fig.16 shows the superimposed image of truth data and the MODIS data derived chlorophyll-a concentration which is acquired on March 5 2015.

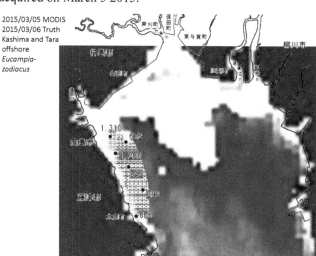

Fig. 16. Superimposed image of truth data and the MODIS data derived chlorophyll-a concentration which is acquired on March 5 2015

B. Trend Analysis in the Case of March 2015

MODIS observed the same sea areas more frequently in this period. Fig.17 shows the superimposed images of the truth data and the MODIS data derived chlorophyll-a concentration which are acquired in the period starting from February 27 to March 5 2015. Chlorophyll-a is distributed densely in the Ariake bay area and Isahaya bay area on February 27. Then the densely distributed chlorophyll-a is flown to the south direction along with the sea water current in the Ariake bay while the densely distributed chlorophyll-a is flown from the Isahaya bay to the Taira-machi and far beyond the Shimabara offshore. Therefore, it may say that the sources of red tide are different between Ariake bay and Isahaya bay.

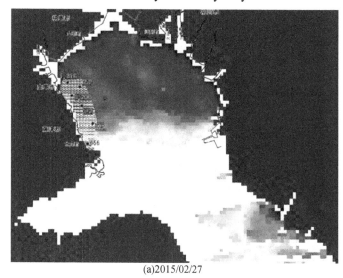

(a)2015/02/27

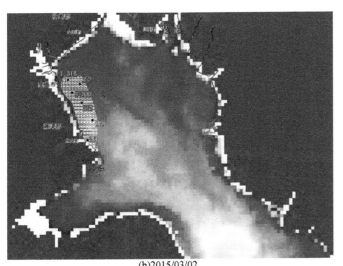

(b)2015/03/02

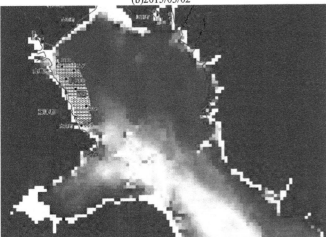

(c)2015/03/04

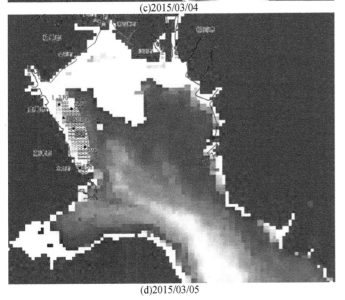

(d)2015/03/05

Fig. 17. Superimposed images of the truth data and the MODIS data derived chlorophyll-a concentration

IV. CONCLUSION

Through experiments with the MODIS data derived chlorophyll-a concentration and the truth data of red tide

(Species and the number of cells/ml) which is provided by the Saga Prefectural Fisher Promotion Center, those are acquired for 6 years (winter 2010 to winter 2015), it is found the followings,

1) Asterionella kariana and Skeletonema costatum are used to be appeared in the Ariake Bay area in the winter seasons followed by Eucampia zodiacus appeared in the early spring every year after 2012 in particular, on February 22 2012, February 26 2013, February 6 2014 and March 6 2015.

2) It seems that the source of Asterionella kariana and Skeletonema costatum are mostly originated from Shiota river mouth and sometime from Rokkaku river mouth.

3) The red tide propagate from the center of Ariake Bay to Kashima, Tara offshore along with the sea water current in the counter clock wise direction.

4) Through the trend analysis with the superimposed images of the truth data and the MODIS data derived chlorophyll-a concentration which are acquired in the period starting from February 27 to March 5 2015, it is found that chlorophyll-a is distributed densely in the Ariake bay area and Isahaya bay area on February 27. Then the densely distributed chlorophyll-a is flown to the south direction along with the sea water current in the Ariake bay while the densely distributed chlorophyll-a is flown from the Isahaya bay to the Taira-machi and far beyond the Shimabara offshore. Therefore, it may say that the sources of red tide are different between Ariake bay and Isahaya bay.

Further investigations are required to clarify the mechanism of red tide appearance with the consideration three dimensional of cross section analysis the red tide source movement.

ACKNOWLEDGMENT

The authors would like to thank Dr. Toshiya Katano of Tokyo University of Marine Science and Technology, Dr. Yuichi Hayami, Dr. Kei Kimura, Dr. Kenji Yoshino, Dr. Naoki Fujii and Dr. Takaharu Hamada of Institute of Lowland and Marine Research, Saga University for their great supports through the experiments.

REFERENCES

[1] Yuji Ito, Toshiya Katano, Naoki Fujii, Masumi Koriyama, Kenji Yoshino, and Yuichi Hayami, Decreases in turbidity during neap tides initiate late winter large diatom blooms in a macrotidal embayment, Journal of Oceanography,69: 467-479. 2013.

[2] Nishikawa T (2002) Effects of temperature, salinity and irradiance on the growth of the diatom *Eucampia zodiacus* caused bleaching seaweed *Porphyra* isolated from Harima-Nada, Seto Inland Sea, Japan. Nippon Suisan Gakk 68: 356–361. (in Japanese with English abstract)

[3] Nishikawa T (2007) Occurrence of diatom blooms and damage tocultured *Porphyra* thalli by bleaching. Aquabiology 172: 405–410. (in Japanese with English abstract)

[4] Nishikawa T, Hori Y (2004) Effects of nitrogen, phosphorus and silicon on the growth of the diatom *Eucampia zodiacus* caused bleaching of seaweed *Porphyra* isolated from Harima-Nada, Seto Inland Sea, Japan. Nippon Suisan Gakk 70: 31–38. (in Japanese with English abstract)

[5] Nishikawa T, Hori Y, Nagai S, Miyahara K, Nakamura Y, Harada K, Tanda M, Manabe T, Tada K (2010) Nutrient and phytoplankton dynamics in Harima-Nada, eastern Seto Inland Sea, Japan during a 35-year period from 1973 to 2007. Estuaries Coasts 33: 417–427.

[6] Nishikawa T, Hori Y, Tanida K, Imai I (2007) Population dynamics of the harmful diatom *Eucampia zodiacus* Ehrenberg causing bleachings of *Porphyra* thalli in aquaculture in Harima- Nada, the Seto Inland Sea, Japan. Harmful algae 6: 763–773.

[7] Nishikawa T, Miyahara K, Nagai S (2000) Effects of temperature and salinity on the growth of the giant diatom *Coscinodiscus wailesii* isolated from Harima-Nada, Seto Inland Sea, Japan. Nippon Suisan Gakk 66: 993–998. (in Japanese with English abstract)

[8] Nishikawa T, Tarutani K, Yamamoto T (2009) Nitrate and phosphate uptake kinetics of the harmful diatom *Eucampia zodiacus* Ehrenberg, a causative organism in the bleaching of aquacultured *Porphyra* thalii. Harmful algae 8: 513–517.

[9] Nishikawa T, Yamaguchi M (2006) Effect of temperature on lightlimited growth of the harmful diatom *Eucampia zodiacus* Ehrenberg, a causative organism in the discoloration of *Porphyra* thalli. Harmful Algae 5: 141–147.

[10] Nishikawa T, Yamaguchi M (2008) Effect of temperature on lightlimited growth of the harmful diatom *Coscinodiscus wailesii*, a causative organism in the bleaching of aquacultured *Porphyra* thalli. Harmful Algae 7: 561–566.

[11] Syutou T, Matsubara T, Kuno K (2009) Nutrient state and nori aquaculture in Ariake Bay. Aquabiology 181: 168–170. (in Japanese with English abstract)

[12] Harada K, Hori Y, Nishikawa T, Fujiwara T (2009) Relationship between cultured *Porphyra* and nutrients in Harima-Nada, eastern part of the Seto Inland Sea. Aquabiology 181: 146–149. (in Japanese with English abstract)

[13] Arai K., T. Katano, Trend analysis of relatively large diatoms which appear in the intensive study area of the ARIAKE Sea, Japan, in winter (2011-2015) based on remote sensing satellite data, Internationa Journal of Advanced Research in Artificial Intelligence (IJARAI), 4, 7, 15-20, 2015.

[14] Arai, K., Locality of Chlorophyll-a Concentration in the Intensive Study Area of the Ariake Sea, Japan in Winter Seasons Based on Remote Sensing Satellite Data, Internationa Journal of Advanced Research in Artificial Intelligence (IJARAI), 4, 8, 18-25, 2015.

10

Using Unlabeled Data to Improve Inductive Models by Incorporating Transductive Models

ShengJun Cheng
School of Computer Science and Technology
Harbin Institute of Technology
Harbin 150001, China
Email: http://hitwer@gmail.com

Jiafeng Liu
Harbin Institute of Technology
Harbin150001, China

XiangLong Tang
Harbin Institute of Technology
Harbin150001, China

Abstract—This paper shows how to use labeled and unlabeled data to improve inductive models with the help of transductive models. We proposed a solution for the self-training scenario. Self-training is an effective semi-supervised wrapper method which can generalize any type of supervised inductive model to the semi-supervised settings. it iteratively refines a inductive model by bootstrap from unlabeled data. Standard self-training uses the classifier model(trained on labeled examples) to label and select candidates from the unlabeled training set, which may be problematic since the initial classifier may not be able to provide highly confident predictions as labeled training data is always rare. As a result, it could always suffer from introducing too much wrongly labeled candidates to the labeled training set, which may severely degrades performance. To tackle this problem, we propose a novel self-training style algorithm which incorporate a graph-based transductive model in the self-labeling process. Unlike standard self-training, our algorithm utilizes labeled and unlabeled data as a whole to label and select unlabeled examples for training set augmentation. A robust transductive model based on graph markov random walk is proposed, which exploits manifold assumption to output reliable predictions on unlabeled data using noisy labeled examples. The proposed algorithm can greatly minimize the risk of performance degradation due to accumulated noise in the training set. Experiments show that the proposed algorithm can effectively utilize unlabeled data to improve classification performance.

Keywords—Inductive model, Transductive model, Semi-supervised learning, Markov random walk.

I. INTRODUCTION

Traditional inductive models like Naive Bayes, CARTs[1], Support Vector Machines are always in supervised settings, which means these model can only be trained on labeled data. Training a good inductive model needs enough labeled examples. Unfortunately, preparing labeled data for such task is often expensive and time consuming, while unlabeled data are readily available. This was the major motivation that led to the arise of semi-supervised paradigm which utilizes few labeled examples and vast amounts of cheap unlabeled examples to learns a model. Semi-supervised learning has achieved considerable success in a wide variety of domains, existing semi-supervised learning methods can be roughly categorized into several paradigms[2], including generative models, semi-supervised support vector machines (S3VMs), graph based methods and bootstrapping wrapper method.

Self-training[3] is a simple and effective semi-supervised algorithm which has been successfully applied to various real-world tasks. It is an wrapper method, which means it can generalize any type of supervised inductive model to the semi-supervised settings[4]. Self-training initially trains a classifier on labeled data and then iteratively augments its labeled training set by adding several newly pseudo-labeled unlabeled examples with most confident predictions of its own. Standard self-training uses the classifier model(trained on labeled examples) to label and select candidates from the unlabeled training set, which may be problematic since the initial classifier may not be able to provide highly confident predictions as labeled training data is always rare. In addition, since self-training utilizes unlabeled data in an incremental manner, early noise introduced to training sets would be reinforced round by round, resulting in severe performance degradation. Although some techniques, e.g. data editing[5], have been employed to alleviate this noise-related problem[6], results are yet undesirable. As a result, it could always suffer from introducing too much wrongly labeled candidates to the labeled training set, which may severely degrades performance. Another drawback of self-training is that the newly added examples are not informative to the current classifier, since they can be classified confidently[7]. As a result, they may only help increase the classification margin, without actually providing any novel information to the current classifier.

In this paper, we show how to use unlabeled data to improve inductive models with the help of transductive models. We proposed a solution for the self-training scenario, a novel self-training style algorithm is proposed. Generally, unlike traditional self-training only using labeled data to label and select unlabeled example for training set augmentation, our algorithm utilizes both labeled and unlabeled data to facilitate the self-labeling process. In detail, all the labeled and unlabeled examples are presented as a graph, where a novel markov random walk with constrains is proposed to label all examples on graph in a transductive setting[8]. This graph-based method satisfy *manifold assumption*that examples with high similarities in the input space should share similar labels. Typically, Most graph based methods output label information to unlabeled data in a transductive setting such as Label propagation, markov random walks, Low density separation[9]. Those methods are designed to utilize unlabeled by representing both the data as a graph, with examples as vertices and similarities of examples as edges. Existing transductive graph-based methods assume all labels on labeled data correct, can not work under training sets subject to noise. While our transductive model can naturally deals with noisy labeled data, which utilize "label smooth" to automatically adjust the potential wrong labels. By incorporating this transductive model to the self-training process, we expect any applied supervised inductive model can be greatly improved.

The main contribution of this paper can be summarized as follows:

- We show that incorporating transductive models to inductive models in semi-supervised settings can improve classification performance.

- We propose a novel self-training algorithm which utilizes a graph-based transductive model for using both labeled and unlabeled data to label and select unlabeled example for training set augmentation.

- We propose a novel transductive model based on graph random walk with constrains. This transductive model can deal with labeled training set with noise and provide more reliable predictions for all unlabeled examples, has strong tolerance to noise in the training set.

- We conduct extensive experiments on several UCI benchmark data sets to evaluate its performance with 3 different inductive model and empirically demonstrate that our algorithm can effectively exploit unlabeled data to achieve better generalization performance.

The rest of this paper is organized as follows. Section 2 describes the problem and gives the algorithm in detail. Section 3 presents the experimental results on UCI data sets when various inductive models are utilized. A short conclusion and future work are presented in Section 4.

mds

January 11, 2007

II. THE PROPOSED ALGORITHM

A. Problem Description and Notation

Let L denote the labeled training set with size $|L|$ and U denote the unlabeled training set with size $|U|$. The goal of our algorithm is to learn a classifier from $L \cup U$ to classify unseen examples. Generally, initial labeled examples are quite few, i.e. $|L| \ll |U|$.

The proposed algorithm learns a inductive model f from labeled and unlabeled data as follows: 1)initialize the model f using labeled set L; 2)use f to predict labels on unlabeled set U; 3)select a subset S from U for which f has the most confident predictions; 4)construct a neighborhood graph G with $L \cup U$ under certain similarity measure; 5)incorporate a transductive model into the self-labeling process: knowing the prior information about labels on $L \cup U$, start a constrained random walk on Graph G to label all the unlabeled examples in U; 6)choose k most confident examples from U for labeled training set augmentation according to the output of random walk; 7)refine f with augmented labeled data. The procedure goes on until there are no unlabeled examples left.

The key distinction between the proposed algorithm and standard self-training is the incorporated transductive model

that utilizes both labeled and unlabeled examples to give prediction on unlabeled data. Most graph based semi-supervised methods are transductive, which are nonparametric and can deal with multi-classification problems. We proposed a novel constrained markov random walk for the transduction purpose. The most desirable property of the proposed transdutive model is that it can work well even if training set contains label-noise. Therefore, it is perfectly suitable for the self-training process, as the pseudo-labeled set S may contain some wrongly labeled examples. At this step, it is expected to yield more reliable predictions on unlabeled data than the classifier does with training set subject to label-noise. Next, we will present the details of the proposed transductive graph-based model.

B. Markov Random Walk with Constrains

Markov random walk is regarded as a transductive graph based approach which exploits manifold assumption to label all the unlabeled examples. Typically, it is given an undirected graph $G = (V, E, W)$, where a node $v \in V$ corresponds to an example in $L \cup U$, an edge $e = (a, b) \in V \times V$ indicates that the label of the two vertices a,b should be similar and the weight W_{ab} reflects the strength of this similarity. In this paper, graph is constructed by using the k nearest neighbor criterion. For each example $v \in L \cup U$, Let $\mathcal{C} = \{1, , m\}$ be the set of possible labels. Two row-vectors $\mathbf{Y}_v, \hat{\mathbf{Y}}_v$ are presented. The first vector $\mathbf{Y}_v$ is the input. The lth element of the vector $\mathbf{Y}_v$ encodes the prior knowledge about label l for example v. For instance, a labeled example v with label c has $\mathbf{Y}_{vc}$ set to 1, and the remaining $m - 1$ elements of $\mathbf{Y}_v$ set to 0. Unlabeled examples have all their elements set to 0, that is $\mathbf{Y}_{vl} = 0$ for $l = 1 \ldots m$. The second vector $\hat{\mathbf{Y}}_v$ is the output of the algorithm, using similar semantics as $\mathbf{Y}_v$. For instance, a high value of $\hat{\mathbf{Y}}_{vl}$ indicates that algorithms believe that the vertex(example) v should have label l.

The constrains of random walks is formalized via three possible actions: inject, continue and abandon(denoted by $inj, cont, abnd$ with pre-defined probabilities $p_v^{inj}, p_v^{cont}, p_v^{abnd}$. Clearly, their sum is unit: $p_v^{inj} + p_v^{cont} + p_v^{abnd} = 1$. To label any example v(either labeled or unlabeled), we initiate a random-walk starting at v facing three options: with probability p_v^{inj} the random-walk stops and return(i.e. $inject$) the pre-defined vector information $\mathbf{Y}_v$. We constrain p_v^{inj} for unlabeled examples. Second, with probability p_v^{abnd} the random-walk abandons the labeling process and returns the all-zeros vector $\mathbf{0}_m$. Third, with probability p_v^{cont} the random-walk continues to one of vs neighbors v' with probability proportional to $W_{v'v}$. Note that by definition $W_{v'v} = 0$ if $(v', v) \notin E$. We summarize the above process with the following set of equations. The transition probabilities are,

$$\Pr[v'|v] = \begin{cases} \dfrac{W_{v'v}}{\sum\limits_{u:(u,v)\in E} W_{uv}}, (v', v) \in E \\ 0, \text{otherwise} \end{cases} \quad (1)$$

The expected score $\hat{\mathbf{Y}}_v$ for node $v \in V$ is given by,

$$\hat{\mathbf{Y}}_v = p_v^{inj} \times \mathbf{Y}_v + p_v^{cont} \times \sum_{v':(v',v)\in E} \Pr[v'|v] \hat{\mathbf{Y}}_{v'} + p_v^{abnd} \times \mathbf{0}_m \quad (2)$$

In this paper, the three probabilities $p_v^{inj}, p_v^{cont}, p_v^{abnd}$ are set using the same heuristics adapted from [10], which are defined by,

$$p_v^{cont} = \frac{c_v}{z_v} \quad ; \quad p_v^{inj} = \frac{d_v}{z_v} \quad ; \quad p_v^{abnd} = 1 - p_v^{cont} - p_v^{inj}$$

(3)

c_v is monotonically decreasing with the number of neighbors for node v in graph G. Intuitively, the higher the value of c_v, the lower the number of neighbors of vertex v and higher the information they contain about the labeling of v. The other quantity d_v is monotonically increasing with the entropy (for labeled vertices). It is noteworthy that abandonment occurs only when the continuation and injection probabilities are low enough. This is most likely to happen at unlabeled nodes with high degree. In effect, high p_v^{abnd} prevents the algorithm from propagating information through high degree nodes.

The final labeling information for all $v \in L \cup U$ can be computed through random walk based on Eq.(2). The algorithm converges when label distribution on each node ceases to change. Note that initial labeled data set L assumes to be noise-free, while the pseudo-labeled dataset S may contain classification noise, hence, certain modification about the transition probabilities needs to be made:

- Since labels on L, which are considered noise-free, should not change during the random walk. For example $v \in L$, the transition probabilities should be fixed as follows: $p_v^{inj} = 1$, $p_v^{cont} = 0$, $p_v^{abnd} = 0$;

- Since examples in S may be wrongly labeled by the classifier, labels on S are allowed to change. For $\forall v \in S$, the transition probabilities should be computed according to Eq.(3);

- For unlabeled example $u \in U - S$, we only constrain $p_u^{inj} = 0$.

Note that the predicted label y_u and labeling confidence $\text{CF}(u, y_u)$ of each example $u \in U - S$ can be easily obtained from $\mathbf{Y}_u$:

$$y_u = \arg\max_l \hat{\mathbf{Y}}_{ul} \; , \; l = 1, ...m$$

(4)

$$\text{CF}(u, y_u) = \hat{\mathbf{Y}}_{uc} , c = y_u$$

(5)

In this paper, our strategy is to incorporates such transductive model into the standard self-training's labeling process, concrete procedures of the proposed algorithm is outlined in **Algorithm 1.** It is noteworthy that size of S only has mediate and minor impact on the final performance. For convenience, $|S|$ is empirically set equal to the number of initial labeled examples,i.e. $|L|$, and we also set k equal to $|L|$, The maximum iteration number M is set to 50.

III. EXPERIMENTS AND DISCUSSION

In this section, we design experiments to verify the efficacy of our algorithm. We mainly focus on the self-training framework, trying to find out how transductive model can improve the semi-supervised inductive model. 12 UCI data sets are used in the experiments[11]. Information on these data sets is shown in Table 1. For each data set, about 25% data are kept as test examples. 10% of the remaining data set is used as the labeled

---

Algorithm 1 Proposed Algorithm

Input:
- $L \cup U$: training sets
- $Learner$: learning algorithm for inducing a classifier
- M: number of iteration

Output:
- f: the returned classifier
  Construct neighborhood graph $G = (V, E, W)$;
2: initialize $p_v^{inj}, p_v^{cont}, p_v^{abnd}$;
  $L' \leftarrow NULL$;
4: **while** $Iter \leq M$ **do**
  Use f to make predictions on U;
6: Select S from U $\{ |S|$ most confident predictions of $f\}$;
  Recompute $p_v^{inj}, p_v^{cont}, p_v^{abnd}$ for $v \in S$ using Eq.(3);
8: Reset prior labeling knowledge $\mathbf{Y}_v$;
  Output $\hat{\mathbf{Y}}_u$ for all $u \in U - S$ by constrained random walk on Graph G;
10: Compute y_u, $\text{CF}(u, y_u)$ for all $u \in U$ using Eq.(4)and Eq.(5)
  Choose the k most confident examples from U based on $\text{CF}(u, y_u)$;
12: Add the chosen pseudo-labeled examples to L';
  $f \leftarrow Learn(L \cup L')$
14: **end while**

TABLE I: Data set summary

Data set	Attribute	Size	Class	Class distribution(%)
australian	14	690	2	55.5/44.5
bupa	6	345	2	42.0/58.0
colic	22	368	2	63.0/37.0
diabetes	8	768	2	65.1/34.9
german	20	1000	2	70.0/30.0
hypothyroid	25	3163	2	4.8/95.2
ionosphere	34	351	2	35.9/64.1
kr-vs-kp	36	3196	2	52.2/47.8
sick	29	3772	2	6.1/93.9
tic-tac-toe	9	958	2	65.3/34.7
vehicle	18	846	4	25.1/25.7/25.7/23.5
wdbc	13	178	3	33.1/39.9/27.0

training set L; the rest examples are treated as the unlabeled set U.

The proposed algorithm is compared with standard self-training and SETRED[6]. SETRED is an improved self-training algorithm by incorporating data editing techniques to help identify and remove wrong labels from the training sets during the self-training process. For fair comparison, the termination criteria used by self-training and SETRED are similar to that used by our algorithm.

we used three supervised inductive model as base learners to perform classifier induction, aiming to investigate how each comparing algorithm behaves along with base learners bearing diverse characteristics. Specifically, Naive Bayes,

TABLE II: Classification error rates of 3 compared algorithms on 12 datasets using naive bayes

| Dataset | Classification error rates: Naive Bayes | | | | | | |
| | initial | proposed algorithm | | SETRED | | Self-training | |
		final	improve/%	final	improve/%	final	improve/%
australian	0.243	0.224	**7.9**	0.234	3.7	0.236	2.9
bupa	0.481	0.442	8.1	0.459	4.6	0.438	**8.9**
colic	0.217	0.207	**4.6**	0.212	2.3	0.221	-1.8
diabetes	0.267	0.257	3.7	0.245	**8.2**	0.264	1.1
german	0.285	0.281	1.4	0.276	**3.2**	0.298	-4.6
hypothyroid	0.024	0.021	**12.5**	0.023	4.2	0.021	**12.5**
ionosphere	0.155	0.129	**16.8**	0.151	2.6	0.166	-7.1
kr-vs-kp	0.142	0.137	3.5	0.143	-0.7	0.128	**9.9**
sick	0.089	0.084	5.6	0.084	5.6	0.079	**11.2**
tic-tac-toe	0.343	0.324	**5.5**	0.328	4.4	0.346	-0.9
vehicle	0.398	0.322	**19.1**	0.367	7.8	0.429	-7.8
wine	0.103	0.096	6.8	0.089	**13.6**	0.116	-12.6
average	–	–	**8.0**	–	4.9	–	1.0

TABLE III: Classification error rates of 3 compared algorithms on 12 datasets using CART

| Dataset | Classification error rates: CART | | | | | | |
| | initial | proposed algorithm | | SETRED | | Self-training | |
		final	improve/%	final	improve/%	final	improve/%
australian	0.222	0.193	**13.0**	0.199	10.4	0.205	7.7
bupa	0.399	0.368	**7.8**	0.391	2.0	0.388	2.8
colic	0.181	0.163	**10.0**	0.174	3.9	0.168	7.2
diabetes	0.316	0.288	8.8	0.272	**13.9**	0.289	8.5
german	0.351	0.324	**7.6**	0.336	4.3	0.336	4.3
hypothyroid	0.012	0.011	**8.3**	0.016	-33.3	0.021	-75
ionosphere	0.155	0.121	**22.0**	0.144	7.1	0.149	3.9
kr-vs-kp	0.035	0.025	28.6	0.018	**48.6**	0.022	37.1
sick	0.024	0.021	**12.5**	0.026	-8.3	0.023	4.2
tic-tac-toe	0.292	0.258	**11.6**	0.268	8.2	0.277	5.1
vehicle	0.254	0.208	**18.1**	0.223	12.2	0.234	7.9
wine	0.085	0.061	**28.2**	0.072	15.3	0.064	24.7
average	–	–	**14.7**	–	7.0	–	3.2

CART, SVM models are used in the experiments. We use LibSVM[12] implementation for SVM. Note that only Naive Bayes is generative model that can yield probabilistic outputs, CART uses the proportion of dominating class in leaf node as probabilistic output and LibSVM is configured to give probabilistic estimates by using the training option "-b 1". For our algorithm and SETRED, we choose a medium number of nearest neighbors, i.e 8 for graph construction, we utilize EUCLIDEAN distance as the similarity measure mainly based on its simplicity and empirical evidences.

Experiments are carried out on each data set for 100 runs under randomly partitioned labeled/unlabeled/test splits. TableII to TableIV present classification errors of these compared algorithms under different inductive models. The "initial" column denotes the average error rates of classification with labeled data only. Columns denoted by "final" and "improve" represent the average error rates and performance improvements of each algorithm respectively.

TableII to TableIV show that proposed algorithm can effectively improve the performance with all the underlying in-

TABLE IV: Classification error rates of 3 compared algorithms on 12 datasets using LibSVM

| Dataset | initial | Classification error rates: LibSVM | | | | | |
| | | proposed algorithm | | SETRED | | Self-training | |
		final	improve/%	final	improve/%	final	improve/%
australian	0.268	0.229	**14.6**	0.234	12.7	0.241	10.1
bupa	0.382	0.353	**7.6**	0.385	-0.8	0.390	-2.1
colic	0.267	0.176	**34.1**	0.198	25.6	0.235	12.1
diabetes	0.421	0.345	**18.0**	0.428	-1.6	0.448	-6.4
german	0.214	0.188	12.1	0.202	5.6	0.179	**16.4**
hypothyroid	0.029	0.024	17.2	0.021	**27.6**	0.026	10.3
ionosphere	0.183	0.164	10.4	0.142	**22.4**	0.181	1.1
kr-vs-kp	0.034	0.027	20.6	0.031	8.8	0.023	**32.4**
sick	0.036	0.034	4.0	0.031	**13.9**	0.033	8.3
tic-tac-toe	0.071	0.036	49.0	0.056	21.1	0.030	**57.7**
vehicle	0.398	0.316	**20.6**	0.367	7.8	0.429	-7.8
wine	0.103	0.048	**53.4**	0.066	36	0.116	-12.6
average	–	–	**21.8**	–	14.9	–	10.0

ductive model. he two-tailed paired t-test under the significant level of 95% shows that all the improvements of performance are significant. The biggest improvements achieved by these three self-training style algorithms have been boldfaced. In fact, if the improvements are averaged across all the data sets, base learners, it can be found that the average improvement of our algorithm is about 14.8%. It is impressive that with all the employed inductive models our algorithm has achieved the biggest improvement among the other 2compared algorithms. Moreover, if the algorithms are compared through counting the number of winning data sets, i.e. the number of data sets on which an algorithm has achieved the biggest improvement among the compared algorithms, our algorithm is almost always the winner. In detail, when Naive Bayes are used, it has 6 winning data sets while self-training has 4 and SETRED has 3; when CARTs are used, our algorithm and SETRED has 10 and 3 winning data sets respectively, while self-training do not have winning data sets; when SVMs are used, our algorithm, SETRED and self-training has 6, 3 and 3 winning data sets respectively.

In particular, comparing to SETRED which utilizes a specific data editing technique to actively identify wrongly-labeled examples in the enlarged training set, the proposed algorithm has achieved better results with no effort for cleaning the training set. This evidence supports our arguments that the incorporated transductive model is robust to noises introduced by the self-labeled process, thus it can achieve stable performance. Moreover, empirical results of on the 2 multi-class datasets(*vehicle,wine*) suggest that our algorithm is superior to self-training and SETRED when dealing with multi-class classification problems. This is mainly due to the fact that it can naturally handle multi-class classification by exploiting manifold assumption to yield confident predictions for training set augmentation.

IV. CONCLUSIONS

This paper shows the benefits of incorporating transdcutive models into semi-supervised bootstrap inductive models, such as self-training. This strategy utilizes both labeled and unlabeled data to yield more reliable predictions for unlabeled examples. We propose a robust self-training style algorithm which exploits manifold assumption to facilitate the self-training process. We adopt a transductive model based on graph random walks to prevent performance degradation due to classification noise accumulation. Empirical results on 12 UCI datasets show that proposed algorithm can effectively exploit unlabeled data to enhance performance.

Graph construction is vital to our algorithm. In this paper, we only use the common EUCLIDEAN distance as the distance measure, there is no guarantee that this is the optimal choice. Generally, the problem of choosing the best distance measure for a specific learning task is very difficult, and some efforts have been made towards tackling this problem under the name of distance metric learning. How to identify or learn the optimal distance measure and how does it affect the performance are worth further investigation.

ACKNOWLEDGMENT

The research is partially supported by National Natural Science Foundation of China under grant number 61173087,61073128. The authors also gratefully acknowledge the helpful comments and suggestions of the reviewers, which have improved the presentation.

REFERENCES

[1] D. Steinberg and P. Colla, "Cart: classification and regression trees," *The Top Ten Algorithms in Data Mining*, pp. 179–201, 2009.

[2] X. Zhu, "Semi-supervised learning literature survey," *Computer Sciences TR 1530, Univ. of Wisconsin*, 2008.

[3] D. Yarowsky, "Unsupervised word sense disambiguation rivaling supervised methods," in *Proceedings of the 33rd annual meeting on Association for Computational Linguistics.* Association for Computational Linguistics, 1995, pp. 189–196.

[4] S. Abney, "Understanding the yarowsky algorithm," *Computational Linguistics*, vol. 30, no. 3, pp. 365–395, 2004.

[5] Y. Wang, X. Xu, H. Zhao, and Z. Hua, "Semi-supervised learning based on nearest neighbor rule and cut edges," *Knowledge-Based Systems*, vol. 23, no. 6, pp. 547–554, 2010.

[6] M. Li and Z.-H. Zhou, "Setred: Self-training with editing," in *Advances in Knowledge Discovery and Data Mining.* Springer, 2005, pp. 611–621.

[7] M.-F. Balcan, S. Hanneke, and J. W. Vaughan, "The true sample complexity of active learning," *Machine learning*, vol. 80, no. 2-3, pp. 111–139, 2010.

[8] T. Joachims *et al.*, "Transductive learning via spectral graph partitioning," in *ICML*, vol. 3, 2003, pp. 290–297.

[9] A. Subramanya and J. Bilmes, "Semi-supervised learning with measure propagation," *The Journal of Machine Learning Research*, vol. 12, pp. 3311–3370, 2011.

[10] S. Baluja, R. Seth, D. Sivakumar, Y. Jing, J. Yagnik, S. Kumar, D. Ravichandran, and M. Aly, "Video suggestion and discovery for youtube: taking random walks through the view graph," in *Proceedings of the 17th international conference on World Wide Web.* ACM, 2008, pp. 895–904.

[11] A. Frank and A. Asuncion, "Uci machine learning repository," 2010.

[12] C.-C. Chang and C.-J. Lin, "Libsvm: a library for support vector machines," *ACM Transactions on Intelligent Systems and Technology (TIST)*, vol. 2, no. 3, p. 27, 2011.

Comparative Study of Feature Extraction Components from Several Wavelet Transformations for Ornamental Plants

Kohei Arai, Indra Nugraha Abdullah, Hiroshi Okumura
Graduate School of Science and Engineering
Saga University
Saga City, Japan

Abstract— Human has a duty to preserve the nature, preserving the plant is one of the examples. This research emphasis on ornamental plant that has functionality not only as ornament plant but also as a medicinal plant. Purpose of this research is to find the best of the particular feature extraction components from several wavelet transformations. It consists of Daubechies, Dyadic, and Dual-tree complex wavelet transformation. Dyadic and Dual-tree complex wavelet transformations have shift invariant property. While Daubechies is a standard wavelet transform that widely used for many applications. This comparison is utilizing leaf image datasets from ornamental plants. From the experiments, obtained that best classification performance attained by Dual-tree complex wavelet transformation with 96.66% of overall performance result.

Keywords—wavelet transformation; shift invariant; rotation invariant; feature extraction; leaf identification.

I. INTRODUCTION

Oxygen is an essential part for all living things in the world. Plant plays an important role to produce oxygen and supply it for their sustainable life. The cycle between human and the plant is the interesting one. Carbon dioxide as the output of human respiratory is needed by plant for photosynthesis activity. Then, this activity is resulting oxygen which vital for human.

According to this cycle, human supposed to preserve the plant to maintain availability of oxygen. Based on International Union for Conservation of Nature and Natural Resources, the number of identified plant species which consist of Mosses, Ferns and Allies, Gymnosperms, Flowering Plants, Green Algae, Red Algae is about 307.674 species. [1].

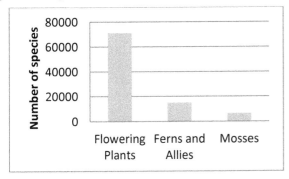

Fig. 1. Column charts number of unidentified plant species

On the other side, the approximate number of unidentified species is 80.500 species. It consists of Flowering Plants with 71.000 species, Ferns and Ales with 15.000 species, Mosses with 6.500 species [2]. Considering the highest number possessed by Flowering Plants, identification of the plants, which include also ornamental plant, has become a challenge for us.

As a recognition step for unidentified species, this research emphasis on ornamental plant, which has medicinal function. However, only few people know about its function as a treatment of the disease. As in Indonesia, this ornamental plant is mostly cultivated in front of the house. If this easiness and its medicinal function are taken into consideration, this plant should be an initial treatment or option towards full chemical-based medicines. In 2005, Gu et al. proposed leaf recognition based on the combination of Haar discrete wavelet transformation and Gaussian interpolation [3]. They used the wavelet to make a leaf skeleton and the extract the feature using run-length feature. Followed by Casanova et al. in 2009, conducted a research with title plant leaf identification using Gabour wavelets [4]. They were used 20 Brazilian plant species, then identified using Gabour wavelets and compared it with Fourier descriptor and co-occurrences matrices.

This research is a sub-research of the main research. The main research is identification ornamental plant based on its color, shape, and texture information. In this study, we want to investigate the best of the particular feature extraction components, which had previously been conducted [5]. For this measurement process, we utilize several wavelet transformations. Start from Daubechies wavelet transformation, and Dyadic wavelet transformation which are the previous researches [6], and then Dual-tree wavelet transformation which is current main focus. Because of there are small numbers of papers dealing with utilization of wavelet transformation for leaf identification. We propose to do comparative study utilizing aforementioned wavelet transformations.

This paper is organized as follows. Section 2 will describe ornamental plant that used in this research. Follow by the next section that explains about the proposed method. Experiments results in section 3. In the end of this paper, there are conclusion and future work.

II. Ornamental Plants

Ornamental plant in this research is not general the ornamental plant, because besides has function as an ornamental plant, also can be used as herbal medicine to cure many diseases. The main focus of this research is to recognize this kind of plant from its leaf.

Image data set of ornamental leaf in this research was obtained from direct acquisition using digital camera. This data set is taken based on tropical ornamental plant that usually cultivated in front of the house in Indonesia. This data set contains 8 classes with 15 images for each class. The classes are Bay (*syzygium polyanthum*), Cananga (*canagium odoratum, lamk*), Mangkokan (*nothopanax scutellarium merr.*), Jasmine (*jasminum sambac [soland]*), Cocor bebek (*kalanchoe pinnuta*), Vinca (*catharanthus roseus*), Kestuba (*euphorbia pulcherrima, willd*), Gardenia (*gardenia augusta, merr*). In order to avoid expensiveness of computation, size of the image is 256 x 256 pixels. The sample images of each class are presented as follow:

Fig. 2. Sample Images from every class inside data set

The Table 1 shows specific medicinal functions of the corresponding ornamental leaf. In Indonesia, there are two mostly used serving ways of these ornamental leaves. Firstly, boils the leaf together with water and apply as drinks. Secondly, put the leaf to the skin surface [7].

TABLE I.   MEDICINAL FUNCTION OF ORNAMENTAL LEAF

Name	Medicinal Function
Bay	Diarrhea, scabies and itching
Cananga	Asthma
Mangkokan	Mastitis, skin injury, hair loss
Jasmine	Fever, head ache, sore eyes
Cocor Bebek	Ulcer, diarrhea, gastritis
Vinca	Diabetes, fever, burn
Kestuba	Bruise, irregular menstrual
Gardenia	Sprue, fever, constipation

III. Proposed Method

A. Wavelet Transformations

1) Daubechies Wavelet Transformation

For $N \in \mathbb{N}$, Daubechies wavelet of class D-*2N* is function $\psi = {}_N\psi \in L^2(R)$ denoted by

$$\psi(x) := \sqrt{2} \sum_{k=0}^{2N-1} (-1)^k h_{2N-1-k} \varphi(2x - k), \quad (1)$$

where $h_0, \dots, h_{2N-1} \in R$ are the constant filter coefficients that fulfilling the conditions

$$\sum_{k=0}^{N-1} h_{2k} = \frac{1}{\sqrt{2}} = \sum_{k=0}^{N-1} h_{2k+1}, \quad (2)$$

similarly, for $l = 0, 1, \dots, N - 1$,

$$\sum_{k=2l}^{2N-1+2l} h_k h_{k-2l} = \begin{cases} 1 & if \ l = 0, \\ 0 & if \ l \neq 0, \end{cases} \quad (3)$$

and where $\varphi = {}_N\varphi : R \rightarrow R$ is the scaling function, given by the recursive equation

$$\varphi(x) = \sqrt{2} \sum_{k=0}^{2N-1} h_k \varphi(2x - k) \quad (4)$$

Daubechies orthogonal wavelets of classes D2 - D20 (only even index numbers) are the wavelets that generally used [8]. The index number belongs to the number *2N* of coefficient. Single wavelet has a number of vanishing moments equal to half the number of coefficients. In this study we propose to use Daubechies D4 wavelets (DB D4), it has two vanishing moments. With these vanishing moments D4 can encodes polynomial of two coefficients, for example constant and linear signal components.

2) Dyadic Wavelet Transformation

The downsampling wavelet, which samples the scale and translation parameters, is often fails when deal with some assignments such as edge detection, features extraction, and image denoising [9,10]. Different with the downsampling wavelet, the dyadic wavelet samples only the scale parameter of a continuous wavelet transform, and does not samples the translation factor. In one side, it creates highly redundant signal representation, but the other side, since it has shift-invariance ability, this method is a convincing candidate as a feature descriptor method.

Let $L^2(R)$ be the space of square integrable functions on real line R, and define the Fourier transform of the function $\psi \in L^2(R)$ by

$$\hat{\psi}(\omega) = \int_{-\infty}^{\infty} \psi(t)e^{-i\omega t} dt \quad (5)$$

If there is exist $A > 0$ and B such that

$$A \leq \sum_{-\infty}^{\infty} \left| \hat{\psi}(2^j \omega) \right|^2 \leq B, \qquad (6)$$

then $\psi(t)$ is called dyadic wavelet function. Dyadic wavelet transform of $f(t)$ is defined using this $\psi(t)$ by

$$Wf(u, 2^j) = \int_{-\infty}^{\infty} f(t) \frac{1}{\sqrt{2^j}} \psi\left(\frac{t-u}{2^j}\right), \qquad (7)$$

from (6), $\hat{\psi}(0) = 0$ must be satisfied, i.e., $\int_{-\infty}^{\infty} \psi(t)dt = 0$. In order to design the dyadic wavelet function, we need a scaling function $\phi(t)$ satisfying a two-scale relation

$$\phi(t) = \sum_k h[k]\sqrt{2}\phi(2t - k). \qquad (8)$$

The scaling function $\phi(t)$ is usually normalized as $\int_{-\infty}^{\infty} \phi(t)dt = 1$.

By (8), the Fourier transform of the scaling function resulting

$$\hat{\phi}(\omega) = \frac{1}{\sqrt{2}} \hat{h}\left(\frac{\omega}{2}\right) \hat{\phi}\left(\frac{\omega}{2}\right), \qquad (9)$$

where $\hat{h}$ denotes a discrete Fourier transform

$$\hat{h}(\omega) = \sum_k h[k]e^{-i\omega t} \qquad (10)$$

Since $\hat{\phi}(0) = 1$, we can apply (9) and (10) to obtain $\hat{h}(0) = \sqrt{2}$. Using the scaling function and the wavelet filter $g[k]$, we define a dyadic function by $\psi(t) = \sum_k g[k]\sqrt{2}\,\phi(2t - k)$.
The Fourier transform of $\psi(t)$,

$$\hat{\psi}(\omega) = \frac{1}{\sqrt{2}} \hat{g}\left(\frac{\omega}{2}\right) \hat{\phi}\left(\frac{\omega}{2}\right), \qquad (11)$$

will be needed later.

Let us denote the discrete Fourier transform of the filters $h[k]$, $h[k]$, $\tilde{h}[k]$, and $\tilde{g}[k]$, by $h(\omega)$, $h(\omega)$, $\hat{\tilde{h}}(\omega)$ and $\hat{\tilde{g}}(\omega)$ respectively.

We suppose that these Fourier transforms satisfy the below condition

$$\hat{\tilde{h}}(\omega)\hat{h}^*(\omega) + \hat{\tilde{g}}(\omega)\hat{g}(\omega) = 2, \quad \omega \in [-\pi, \pi], \qquad (12)$$

where * denotes complex conjugation. This condition called a reconstruction condition.

Under condition (12), we have

$$a_{j+1}[n] = \sum_k h[k]a_j[n + 2^j k]; \, j = 0,1, ..., \qquad (13)$$

$$d_{j+1}[n] = \sum_k g[k]a_j[n + 2^j k]; \, j = 0,1, ..., \qquad (14)$$

here $a_0[n]$ is given by $a_0[n] = \int_{-\infty}^{\infty} f(t)\phi(t - n)dt$.

The (13) and (14) are dyadic decomposition formula for one-dimensional signals.

3) Dual-tree Complex Wavelet Transformation

Problems such as lack of shift invariances and poor directional selectivity that usually appears in DWT can be solved effectively using Dual-tree Complex Wavelet Transformation (DTCWT). Besides that ability, DTCWT also has limited redundancy and efficient order-N computation [12,13].

By doubling the sampling rate at each level of the tree, we can obtain approximate shift invariance with real DWT. This doubling process is done by eliminating the downsampling by 2 after level 1, and this is equal with two parallel fully-decimated trees. The filters in one tree must supply half a sample different of delays from the other tree. Odd-length in one tree and even-length in the other are required for linear phase. The image below is the dual-tree filters for the CWT.

From Fig. 3, tree A is real DWT that gives real part of wavelet transform, and tree B is real DWT that gives imaginary part. These real DWTs use different sets of filters. *h0*, *h1* and *g0*, *g1* denote low-pass/high-pass filter pair for upper filter bank and low-pass/high-pass filter bank for lower filter bank, respectively.

Different with the real DWT which only have three sub images in total. DTCWT decomposes three sub images for each spectral quadrant 1 and 2 and will have six bandpass sub images of complex coefficient at each level. Because of the complex wavelet filters have the ability to separate positive from negative frequency vertically and horizontally, the orientation for these six sub images will cover $\pm 75^0$, $\pm 45^0$, $\pm 15^0$.

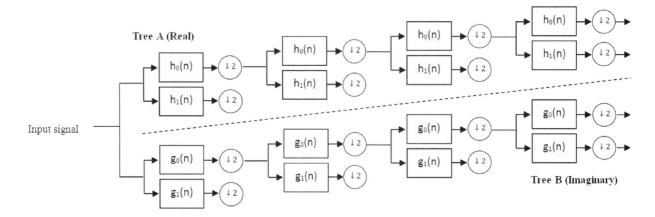

Fig. 3. Dual-tree filters for complex wavelet transformation

The following equation describes the detail:

$$\psi_i(a,b) = \frac{1}{\sqrt{2}}\big(\psi_{1,i}(a,b) - \psi_{2,i}(a,b)\big), \qquad (15)$$

$$\psi_{i+3}(a,b) = \frac{1}{\sqrt{2}}\psi_{1,i}(a,b) + \psi_{2,i}(a,b)) \qquad (16)$$

for $i = 1,2,3$, a denotes row, b denotes column, definition of two separable 2-D wavelet bases are below:

$$\begin{aligned}
\psi_{1,1}(a,b) &= \phi_h(a)\psi_h(b), \\
\psi_{1,2}(a,b) &= \psi_h(a)\phi_h(b), \\
\psi_{1,3}(a,b) &= \psi_h(a)\psi_h(b), \\
\psi_{2,1}(a,b) &= \phi_g(a)\psi_g(b), \\
\psi_{2,2}(a,b) &= \psi_g(a)\phi_g(b), \\
\psi_{2,3}(a,b) &= \psi_g(a)\psi_g(b)
\end{aligned} \qquad (17)$$

The purpose of utilization $1/\sqrt{2}$ is to constitute an orthonormal operation from the sum/difference operation. Through the number of advantages from this DTCWT, we are expecting tight competition of performance with the Dyadic wavelet transformation.

B. SVM Classifier

SVM is a powerful tool for data classification. The indicators are the easiness to apply and impose Structural Risk Minimization (SRM). SRM armed the SVM to have strong ability in generalization of data. Its function is to minimize an upper bound on the expected risk. In principle, SVM learns to obtain optimal boundary with maximum margin that able to separate set of objects with different class of membership.

In order to achieve the maximum margin classifier, we have two options. Hard margin and soft margin are the options that totally depend on linearity of the data. Hard margin SVM is applicable to a linearly separable data set. However, often the data is not linearly separable. Soft margin SVM emerged as its solution [14,15]. The optimization problem for the soft margin SVM presented as below:

$$\min_{w,b} \frac{1}{2}\parallel w \parallel^2 + C\sum_{i=1}^{n}\xi_i$$

$$subject\ to:\ y_i(w^T x_i + b) \geq 1 - \xi_i, \quad \xi_i \geq 0. \qquad (18)$$

where w, C, ξ, b are the weight vectors, the penalty of misclassification or margin errors, the margin error, the bias, respectively.

In (18) can lead us to an efficient kernel methods approach. A kernel method is an algorithm that depends on the data only through kernel function, which computes a dot product in some possibly high dimensional data. Using the function ϕ training vector, the input space x is mapped into higher dimensional space. $K(x_i, x_j) = \phi(x_i)^T\phi(x_j)$ is called kernel function. The degree of the polynomial kernel can control the flexibility of resulting classifier [15]. It will be appropriate with this research when we classify 8 classes of leaf. Polynomial kernel is shown in equation (19).

$$K(x_i, x_j) = (\gamma x_i^T x_j + r)^d, \gamma > 0. \qquad (19)$$

Where γ, r, d are kernel parameters, and i, j denote i^{th}, j^{th} vector in data set.

In this research, we propose to use Sequential Minimal Optimization (SMO). SMO act as efficient solver of the optimization problem in the training of support vector machines. SMO also solves the problems analytically by way of breaks the problems into a series of smallest possible problems.

C. Feature Extraction Components

In this research, we propose to use particular feature extraction components that extracted from the above wavelet transformations. The components are energy, mean, standard deviation and coefficient of variation. These components' values are extracted from four sub images, which are approximation, vertical, horizontal and diagonal sub images for DB D4 and Dyadic wavelet transformations. For DTCWT, those values are obtained from six sub images in real parts tree and six sub images in imaginary parts tree, in total is 12 sub images.

Because wavelet works in the frequency domain, energy is very useful as a feature extraction component. Energy values from several directions and different decomposition levels possibly well-capture the leaf main information which is leaf venation. The other component is mean value, and it can be interpreted as central of tendency of the ornamental leaf data. When standard deviation or predictable dispersion increases in proportion to concentration, we have the other value as a solution called coefficient of variation. Through these comprehensive and fully-related values, we believe that we can gain satisfying results.

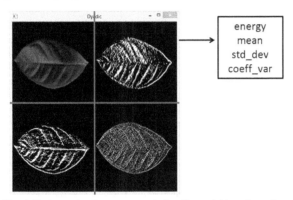

Fig. 4. Feature extraction components for all wavelet transformation

IV. EXPERIMENTS

A. Test Aspects

Test aspects of this research consist of original (no change at all), rotation, scaling, translation, and perspective change. It means we have 5 different datasets with its corresponding test aspect. Inside the rotated dataset, there are images with dissimilar degrees of rotation start from 45^0, 90^0, 135^0, 180^0, 225^0, 270^0, and 315^0. For scaled dataset, we have 30% and 60% downscaled images. Inside the translated dataset, we translated the images to many directions within the original image size. The last is perspective changed dataset with two different perspective changed, are applied to the images.

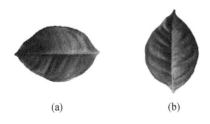

(a)   (b)

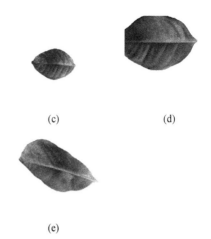

(c)   (d)

(e)

Fig. 5. Test aspects of ornamental leaf images. (a) original, (b) rotation, (c) scaling, (d) translation, (e) perspective change.

B. Comparison Through Classification

TABLE II. BEST DECOMPOSITION LEVEL FOR DB D4

Decomposition level	Level 1	Level 2	Level 3
Original Dataset	**95.83**	94.17	87.5

TABLE III. BEST DECOMPOSITION LEVEL FOR DYADIC

Decomposition level	Level 1	Level 2	Level 3
Original Dataset	**98.33**	97.5	96.67

TABLE IV. BEST DECOMPOSITION LEVEL FOR DUAL-TREE CWT

Decomposition level	Level 1	Level 2	Level 3
Original Dataset	95.83	96.67	**99.17**

According to the result presented in Table 2 and Table 3, it was obtained that decomposition level 1 is the preferable result comparing to the other levels. Then, the best decomposition level for DTCWT was level 3. The reason for those preferable results are from that level was these wavelet transformation could extract very well the leaf main information called leaf venation, in comparison with the other level.

TABLE V.   COMPARISON USING VARIOUS DATASETS

Datasets	Original	Translation	Rotation	Scaling	Perspective	Average
DB D4	95.83	87.5	87.5	90.83	91.67	90.66
Dyadic	98.33	**97.5**	94.17	**96.67**	95	96.33
Dual-tree CWT	**99.17**	95.83	**96.67**	95.83	**95.83**	**96.66**

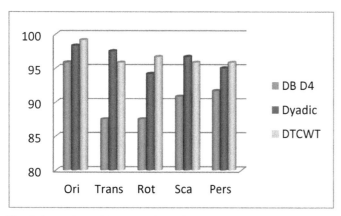

Fig. 6. Comparison of above mentioned feature extraction components using various wavelet transformations.

In Table 5 and Fig. 6 are presented the performance results of previously mentioned test aspects from wavelet transformations. For overall results, DB D4 gave us poor performance in all aspects. As expected, the tight competition came from the Dyadic wavelet transformation and DTCWT. For translation and scaling aspect, the dyadic wavelet transformation is superior to the others. Since sampling only scale parameter of continuous wavelet transformation, made the Dyadic has finer shift invariant property. Because of that reason also, the decomposition image in Dyadic will be exactly same with the input image, and feature extraction components in downscaled image that represent the leaf venation information still could capture.

However, for original, rotation and perspective, the DTCWT is superior. DTCWT has advantages in shift invariant and rotation invariant. Shift invariant property in the DTWCT is not perfect shift invariant but only nearly shift invariant. That reason made the Dyadic results more preferable in the translation dataset.

In the rotation aspect, DTCWT showed its advantages, through the directional selectivity support for six directions in real parts tree and six directions in imaginary parts tree, this DTCWT could give proper results. In original and perspective aspects, the only reason we gained superior results is the effectiveness of utilization 12 feature extraction components. Dissimilar with the DB D4 and Dyadic we only could utilize components from three directions of wavelet decomposition sub images plus one approximation image.

V.   CONCLUSIONS

In this research, we have already measured the performance of Daubechies D4, Dyadic, and Dual-tree wavelet transformations. Daubechies D4 included in real DWT, which has several minus points, from the shift variance until lack of directional selectivity. Different with Daubechies, Dyadic and DTCWT has solutions to solve that shift variance problem. Because of the Dyadic sampling only scale parameter of continuous wavelet transformation, resulting highly redundant signals, but this is the important point when we try to extract information from the leaf for the translation and scaling aspects. Besides possess the nearly shift invariant property, DTCWT also support directional selectivity through six directions for real and imaginary parts, make them is superior for original, rotation and perspective aspect, as well as the overall result.

VI.   FUTURE WORKS

Hence the results from DTCWT outperform in comparison with the others. We still have a deficiency in translation and scaling aspects. Therefore, to find the best in all aspects we plan to conduct the comparative study involving the Double Density wavelet transformation and Double Density Dual-tree Complex wavelet transformation. Double Density wavelet transform has property nearly equal with the DTWCT, and the Double Density Dual-tree is the combination between both.

REFERENCES

[1]   IUCN 2012. Numbers of threatened species by major groups of organisms   (1996–2012). <http://www.iucnredlist.org/documents/summarystatistics/2012_2_RL_Stats_Table_1.pdf >. Downloaded on 21 June 2013.

[2]   Chapman A. D., "Numbers of living species in Australia and the World". Australian Government, Department of the Environment, Water, Heritage, and the Arts. Canberra, Australia, 2009.

[3]   Casanova, D., de Mesquita Sá Junior, J. J. and Bruno, O. M., "Plant leaf identification using Gabor wavelets," Int. J. Imaging Syst. Technol., vol. 19, pp. 236–243, 2009.

[4]   D.S. Huang, X.-P. Zhang, G.-B. Huang, "Leaf recognition based on the combination of wavelet Transform and gaussian Interpolation", ICIC 2005, Part I, LNCS 3644, pp. 253-262, 2005.

[5]   Arai K., Abdullah I. N., Okumura H. and Kawakami R., "Improvement of automated detection method for clustered microcalcification based on wavelet transformation and support vector machine," International Journal of Advanced Research in Artificial Intelligence(IJARAI), 2(4), 2013.

[6]   Arai K., Abdullah I. N., Okumura H., "Image identification based on shape and color descriptors and its application to ornamental leaf", IJIGSP, vol.5, no.10, pp.1-8, 2013.

[7] Hartati Sri, "Tanaman hias berkhasiat obat. IPB Press," 2011. (In Indonesian)

[8] De Vries Andreas, "Wavelets", FH Sudwestfalen University of Applied Sciences, Hagen, Germany, 2006.

[9] Abdukirim T., Nijima K., Takano S. "Lifting dyadic wavelets for denoising," Proceedings of the Third International Workshop on Spectral Methods and Multirate Signal Processing (SMMSP), pp. 147-154. 2003.

[10] Minamoto T., Tsuruta K., Fujii S. "Edge-preserving image denoising method based on dyadic lifting schemes," IPSJ Transactions on Computer Vision and Applications, vol. 2, 48-58, 2010.

[11] Mallat S., "A wavelet tour of signal processing," Academic Press. 1998.

[12] Kingsbury, N. G., "The dual tree complex wavelet transform: a new efficient tool for image Restoration and enhancement," In Proc. EUSIPCO98, Rhodes, Greece, 319-322, 1998.

[13] Selesnick I.W., Baraniuk R.G., and Kingsbury N.G., "The dual-tree complex wavelet transformation", IEEE Signal Processing Magazine, pp. 123-151, November 2015.

[14] Ben-Hur Asa, Weston Jason, "A user's guide to support vector machine. Data Mining Techniques for the Life Science", 223-239, Humana Press, 2010.

[15] Hsu Chih-Wei, Chang Chih-Chuang, Lin Chih-Jen, "A practical guide to support vector classification," Department of Computer Science National Taiwan University, Taiwan, 2010.

[16] Starck Jean-Luc, Murtagh Fionn, Fadili Jalal M. Sparse image and signal processing. Cambridge University Press. 2010.

12

Estimation of Rice Crop Quality and Harvest Amount from Helicopter Mounted NIR Camera Data and Remote Sensing Satellite Data

Kohei Arai [1]
Graduate School of Science and Engineering
Saga University
Saga City, Japan

Osamu Shigetomi [2]
Saga Prefectural Agricultural Research Institute
Saga Prefectural Government,
Japan

Masanoori Sakashita [1]
Information Science, Saga University
Saga, Japan

Yuko Miura [2]
Saga Prefectural Agricultural Research Institute
Saga Prefectural Government, Japan

Abstract—Estimation of rice crop quality and harvest amount in paddy fields with the different rice stump density derived from helicopter mounted NIR camera and remote sensing satellite data is made. Using the intensive study site of rice paddy fields with managing, estimation of protein content in rice crop and nitrogen content in rice leaves through regression analysis with Normalized Difference Vegetation Index: NDVI derived from camera mounted on a radio-control helicopter is made together with harvest amount of rice crops. Through experiments at rice paddy fields which is situated at Saga Prefectural Agriculture Research Institute SPRIA in Saga city, Japan, it is found that protein content in rice crops is highly correlated with NDVI which is acquired with visible and Near Infrared: NIR camera mounted on radio-control helicopter. It also is found that nitrogen content in rice leaves is correlated to NDVI as well. Protein content in rice crop is negatively proportional to rice taste. Therefore rice crop quality can be evaluated through NDVI observation of rice paddy field.

Keywords—Rice Crop; Rice Leaf; Nitrogen content; Protein content; NDVI

I. INTRODUCTION

Vitality monitoring of vegetation is attempted with photographic cameras [1]. Grow rate monitoring is also attempted with spectral reflectance measurements [2]. Bi-Directional Reflectance Distribution Function: BRDF is related to the grow rate for tealeaves [3]. Using such relation, sensor network system with visible and near infrared cameras is proposed [4]. It is applicable to estimate nitrogen content and fiber content in the tealeaves in concern [5]. Therefore, damage grade can be estimated with the proposed system for rice paddy fields [6]. This method is validated with Monte Carlo simulation [7]. Also Fractal model is applied to representation of shapes of tealeaves [8]. Thus the tealeaves can be asse3ssed with parameters of the fractal model. Vitality of tea trees are assessed with visible and near infrared camera data [9]. Rice paddy field monitoring with radio-control helicopter mounting visible and Near Infrared: NIR camera is proposed [10] while the method for rice quality evaluation through nitrogen content in rice leaves is also proposed [11].

The method proposed here is to evaluate rice quality through protein content in rice crop with observation of Normalized Difference Vegetation Index: NDVI which is acquired with visible and NIR camera mounted on radio-control helicopter as well as remote sensing satellite data1. Spatial resolution of Advanced Spaceborne Thermal Emission and Reflection Radiometer: ASTER/Visible to Near Infrared radiometer: VNIR is 15 m and is good enough for evaluation of rice sump density effect on quality and harvest amount.

The fact that protein content in rice crops is highly correlated with NDVI which is acquired with visible and Near Infrared: NIR camera mounted on radio-control helicopter is well reported [10]. It also is reported that nitrogen content in rice leaves is correlated to NDVI as well. Protein content in rice crop is negatively proportional to rice taste. Therefore rice crop quality can be evaluated through NDVI observation of rice paddy field. Relation among nitrogen content in rice leaves, amount of fertilizer, NDVI and protein content in rice crops has to be clarified [11]. There are some indexes which show quality of rice crops, protein content, nitrogen content, etc. in the rice leaves. Meanwhile, there are some indexes for harvest amount, the number of ear in the stump, ear length, crop weight, etc. It should be depending on circumstances of geometric condition, soil condition, meteorological condition, water supply condition, fertilizer amount and rice stump density. Intensive study paddy fields have a variety of conditions. Helicopter mounted NIR camera has a good enough spatial resolution. Therefore, rice crop quality and harvest amount is evaluated as a function of water supply condition and fertilizer amount and rice stump density. Spatial resolution of remote sensing satellite mounted visible to near infrared radiometers, however, are not so fine enough for the rice paddy fields in the sites. Therefore, only stump density influence on rice crop quality and harvest amount is evaluated with remote sensing satellite data.

---

[1] ASTER(Advanced Space based radiometer for Thermal Emission and Reflection)/VNIR(Visible to Near Infrared Radiometer) which is onboard Terra satellite has three spectral channels (Green, Red, and Near Infrared) with 15 m of spatial resolution.

Hiyokumochi rice is our major concern. In the intensive study paddy field, Hiyokumochi rice is planted for the research. Hiyokumochi of rice species is a new species. Therefore, appropriate grow process is unknown. One of the other purposes of this research works is to clarify an appropriate grow process, in particular, the number of ear and the number of rice in a unit area is major concern.

The method used for rice crop quality and harvest amount evaluations is described in the next section followed by experiments. The experimental results are validated in the following section followed by conclusion with some discussions.

II. PROPOSED SYSTEM

A. Radio Controlled Helicopter Based Near Infrared Cameras Utilizing Agricultural Field Monitoring System

The helicopter used for the proposed system is "GrassHOPPER"[2] manufactured by Information & Science Techno-Systems Co. Ltd. The major specification of the radio controlled helicopter used is shown in Table 1. Canon Powershot S100[3] (focal length=24mm) is mounted on the GrassHOPPER. The filter of blue band is replaced to the NIR filter. Therefore, Green, Red and NIR bands of images can be obtained with this camera. It allows acquire images with the following Instantaneous Field of View: IFOV at the certain altitudes, 1.1cm (Altitude=30m) 3.3cm (Altitude=100m) and 5.5cm (Altitude=150m) .

TABLE I.   MAJOR SPECIFICATION OF GRASSHOPPER

Weight	2kg (Helicopter only)
Size	80cm × 80cm × 30m
Payload	600g

Radio wave controlled helicopter mounted near infrared camera imagery data is acquired at A and B paddy fields in SPRIA on 8 October 2014 with the different viewing angle from the different altitudes. Figure 5 shows an example of the acquired near infrared image. There is spectralon[4] of standard plaque as a reference of the measured reflectance in between A and B. Just before the data acquisition, some of rice crops and leaves are removed from the subsection of paddy fields for inspection of nitrogen content. Using the removed rice leaves, nitrogen content in the rice leaves is measured based on the Kjeldahl method[5] and Dumas method[6] (a kind of chemical method) with Sumigraph NC-220F[7] of instrument. The measured total nitrogen content in rice leaves and protein content in rice crops are compared to the NDVI.

B. Rice Crop Field at Saga Prefectural Agriculture Research Institute: SPARI

Specie of the rice crop is Hiyokumochi[8] which is one of the late growing types of rice species. Hiyokumochi is one of low amylase (and amylopectin rich) of rice species (Rice No.216).

Figure 1 shows the Location (a) and (b) Layout of the test site of rice crop field at SPRIA which is situated at 33°13'11.5" North, 130°18'39.6"East, and the elevation of 52 feet on the Google map. B and A in the Figure 1 (b) shows intensive study rice paddy fields. Figure 2 shows the superimposed image of SPARI paddy field layout on Google map. There are the test sites A and B investigation of nitrogen of chemical fertilizer dependency on rice crop quality as shown in Figure 3. There are two types of paddy subsections, densely and sparsely planted paddy fields. Hiyokumochi rice leaves are planted 15 to 20 stumps per m^2 on June 22 2014. Rice crop fields are divided into 10 different small fields depending on the amount of nutrition including nitrogen ranges from zero to 19 kg/10 a/nitrogen.

(a)Google Map

---

[2] http://www.ists.co.jp/?p=789

[3] http://cweb.canon.jp/camera/dcam/lineup/powershot/s100/

[4] https://en.wikipedia.org/wiki/Spectralon

[5] https://en.wikipedia.org/wiki/Kjeldahl_method

[6] https://en.wikipedia.org/wiki/Dumas_method

[7] http://www.hok-chem.co.jp/products/food/NC-220F.html

[8] https://ja.wikipedia.org/wiki/%E3%82%82%E3%81%A1%E7%B1%B3

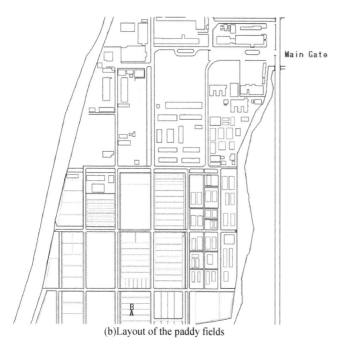

(b)Layout of the paddy fields

Fig. 1. Location of Saga Prefectural Agriculture Research Institute: SPARI on Google map

Nitrogen of chemical fertilizer is used to put into paddy fields for five times during from June to August. Although rice crops in the 10 different small fields are same species, the way for giving chemical fertilizer are different. Namely, the small field No.1 is defined as there is no chemical fertilizer at all for the field while 9, 11, and 13 kg / 10 a/ nitrogen of after chemical fertilizer are given for No.2 to 4, respectively, no initial chemical fertilizer though. Meanwhile, 9, 11, 13 kg /10 a/nitrogen are given as after chemical fertilizer for the small field No.5, 6, and 7, respectively in addition to the 3 kg /10 a/nitrogen of initial chemical fertilizer. On the other hand, 12, 14, and 16 kg /10 a /nitrogen are given for the small fields No.5, 6, 7, respectively as after chemical fertilizer in addition to the initial chemical fertilizer of 3 kg / 10 a/ nitrogen for the small field No. 15, 17, 19, respectively. Therefore, rice crop grow rate differs each other paddy fields depending on the amount of nitrogen of chemical fertilizer.

III. EXPERIMENTS

A. Relations between Measured Indexes and NDVI Measured with Helicopter Mounted NIR Camera

The experiment is conducted on October 3 2014 just before harvest. Figure 4 shows the NIR camera acquired image of the intensive study paddy fields A and B. There are two types of indexes, (1) rice crop quality and (2) harvest amount related indexes are measured. Those are (1) Protein Content in rice crops and SPAD (Greenness of the rice leaves) and (2) Ear Length, the Number of Ear per square meter and Crop Weight per 10a. Namely, protein rich rice crops taste bad while high SPAD means well grown rice leaves (such rice crop with high SPAD tastes good). Regression analysis is made between the measured indexes and the Normalized Difference Vegetation Index: NDVI measured with helicopter mounted NIR camera data.

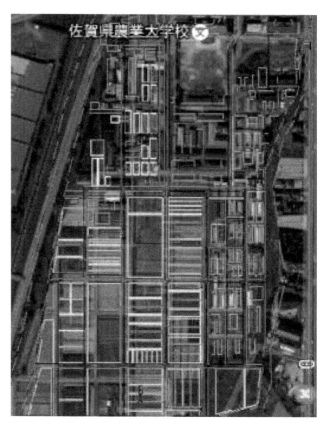

Fig. 2. Superimposed image of SPARI on Google map

A(stump density is 50/3.3m²) B(stump density is 70/3.3 m²)

Fig. 3. Paddy filed layout for investigation of nitrogen of chemical fertilizer dependency on rice crop quality

All the indexes are measured on October 10 2014. Figure 5 shows relations between the measured NDVI and the indexes measured for the intensive study paddy field A.

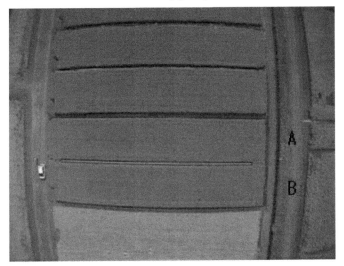

Fig. 4.   NIR camera acquired image of the intensive study paddy fields A and B

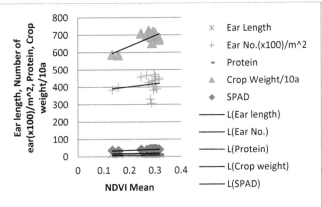

(a)Crop weight/10a and Ear number per m^2

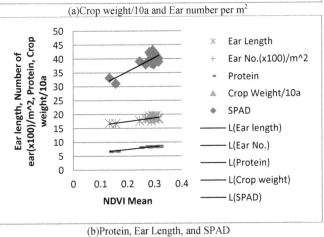

(b)Protein, Ear Length, and SPAD

Fig. 5.   Rice crop quality and harvest amount related indexes

The regressive equation and R^2 for intensive study paddy field A (Stump density is 50/3.3m^2) are shown in equation (1) to (5), respectively. Namely, the equations (1) to (5) are for the Crop Weight / 10a, the Number of Ear(x100) / m^2, SPAD,

the Protein Content in the rice crops and the Ear Length.

$$y = 610.6x + 512.56$$
$$R^2 = 0.6159 \tag{1}$$
$$y = 166.44x + 368.21$$
$$R^2 = 0.0338 \tag{2}$$
$$y = 12.99x + 14.849$$
$$R^2 = 0.643 \tag{3}$$
$$y = 10.252x + 5.3054$$
$$R^2 = 0.919 \tag{4}$$
$$y = 50.017x + 25.383$$
$$R^2 = 0.6904 \tag{5}$$

Also, Figure 6 shows relations between the measured NDVI and the indexes measured for the intensive study paddy field B. Regressive analysis is made for the intensive study paddy field B, The regressive equations and R squares shown in equation (6) to (10), respectively. In comparison of the protein content between intensive study paddy fields A and B, the protein content of A is little bit higher than that of B. Protein rich rice crops are grown in the paddy field with sparse stump density rather than dense stump density. On the other hand, crop weight / 10a of the dense stump density of paddy field is higher than the of the sparse stump density of paddy field.

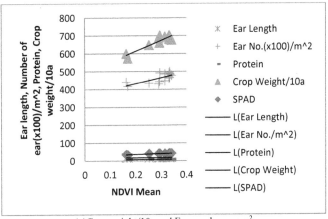

(a)Crop weight/10a and Ear number per m^2

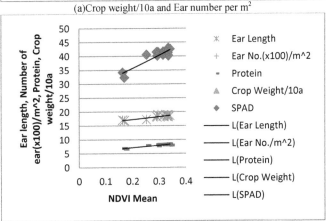

(b)Protein, Ear Length, and SPAD

Fig. 6.   Rice crop quality and harvest amount related indexes

$$y = 616.87x + 490.02$$
$$R^2 = 0.8514 \tag{6}$$
$$y = 332.48x + 365.5$$

$R^2 = 0.5276$ (7)

$y = 10.395x + 15.133$

$R^2 = 0.7926$ (8)

$y = 8.8038x + 5.3074$

$R^2 = 0.8134$ (9)

$y = 47.279x + 26.231$

$R^2 = 0.8168$ (10)

That is the same thing for the Number of Ear(x100) / m². Namely, the number of ear(x100) / m² of the dense stump density of paddy field is greater than the of the sparse stump density of paddy field while SPAD [9] of the dense stump density of paddy field is higher than the of the sparse stump density of paddy field. Meanwhile, the Ear Length of the dense stump density of paddy field is longer than the of the sparse stump density of paddy field.

B. Relations between Protein Content and Harvest Amount and NDVI Measured with Helicopter Mounted NIR Camera

In more detail, there are 8 subdivisions in the same intensive study paddy fields A and B, A1 to A8 and B1 to B8, respectively. Also, the subdivisions are separated into two sets of subdivisions. The protein content and the harvest amount of these 16 different subdivisions are plotted in Figure 7.

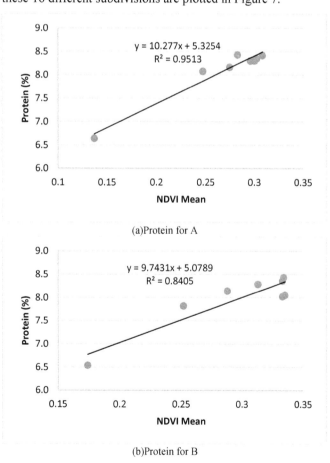

(a)Protein for A

(b)Protein for B

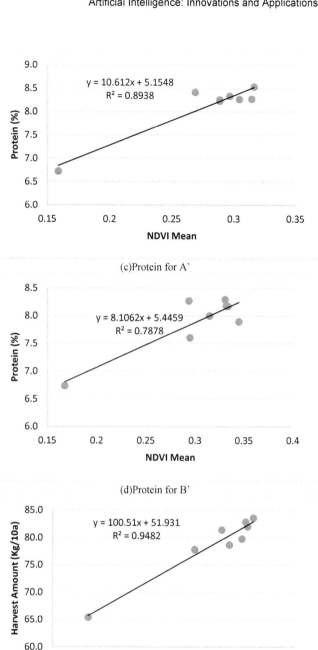

(c)Protein for A'

(d)Protein for B'

(e)Harvest amount for A

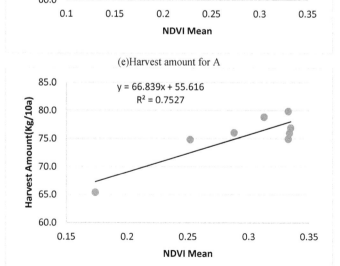

(f)Harvest amount for B

[9] Soil & Plant Analyzer Development： SPAD, chlorophyll meter

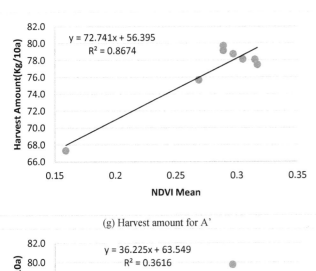

(g) Harvest amount for A'

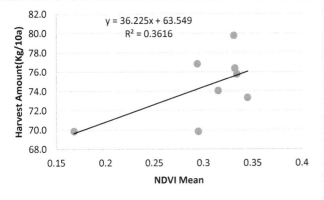

(h)Harvest amount for B'

Fig. 7. Relations between NDVI and protein content as well as harvest amount

The relation between NDVI and protein content is better than that between NVDI and harvest amount. Also, the relations between NDVI and protein content as well as harvest amount for intensive study paddy field A (sparse stump density) are better than those for paddy field B (dense stump density).

C. Relations between Measured Indexes and NDVI Measured with ASTER/VNIR Data

ASTER/VNIR data is acquired on October 8 2014. The small portion of ASTER/VNIR image is shown in Figure 8 (a). In the middle of the image, SPARI is situated. Figure 8 (b) and (c) shows the superimposed image of ASTER/VNIR image on Google map, the superimposed image of ASTER/VNIR image on layout map, and NDVI pixels which correspond to the intensive study paddy fields A and B, respectively. Table 2 shows NDVI of the pixels corresponding to the paddy fields A and B. NDVI of the paddy field A is 15% greater than that of the paddy field B. The result is identical to the result form regressive analysis of protein content with NDVI. These are the same for harvest amount.

TABLE II.　NDVI OF THE PIXELS CORRESPONDING TO THE PADDY FIELDS A AND B

#1	#2	#3	#4	#5	Average
0.3083	0.125	0.125	0.2286	0.2459	0.20656
0.232	0.1818	0.0952	0.0952	0.2462	0.17008

(a)Portion of image of ASTER/VNIR

(b)Superimposed image between Google map and ASTER/VNIR

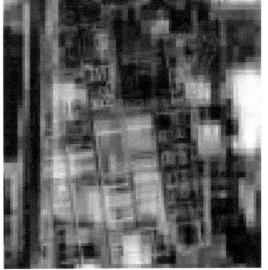

(c)Superimposed image between layout map and ASTER/VNIR

Fig. 8. Images of ASTER/VNIR and Google map and layout image as well as pixels corresponding to the paddy fields A and B

Therefore, the relation between NDVI and rice crop quality which is represented with protein content in rice crops is confirmed with ASTER/VNIR remote sensing satellite data.

D. Most Appropriate Number of Ear and Number of Rice /m²

Relation between NDVI and one of the other concerns of the number of rice / m² is investigated. Figure 9 shows the relation. Although R^2 is not high enough, it is confirmed that the number of rice / m² is proportional to NDVI. Therefore, it is found that around 322 and 348 of the number of rice / m² would be appropriate for stump density 50 and 70 / 3.3 m², respectively. Also, as shown in Figure 7, it is found that 414 and 464 of the number of ear(x100) / m² are appropriate for stump density of 50 and 70 / 3.3 m², respectively. These are estimated with the measured NDVI.

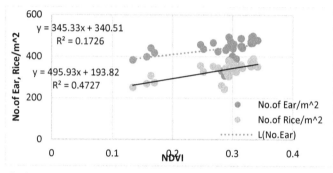

Fig. 9.   Relation between NDVI and one of the other concerns of the number of ear and rice / m²

IV.   CONCLUSION

Estimation of protein content in rice crop and nitrogen content in rice leaves through regression analysis with Normalized Difference Vegetation Index: NDVI derived from camera mounted radio-control helicopter and remote sensing satellite mounted visible to near infrared radiometers made. Through experiments at rice paddy fields which is situated at Saga Prefectural Agriculture Research Institute: SPARI in Saga city, Japan, it is found that protein content and harvest amount of rice crops is highly correlated with NDVI which is acquired with visible and Near Infrared: NIR camera mounted on radio-control helicopter and visible to near infrared radiometer onboard remote sensing satellite.

Protein content in rice crop is negatively proportional to rice taste. Therefore, rice crop quality can be evaluated through NDVI observation of rice paddy field. It is found that harvest amount is linearly proportional to NDVI. Therefore, it is possible to estimate rice crop quality and harvest amount with NDVI. It is also found that rice crop quality of low density of rice stump is better than that of highly dense rice paddy field. It is found that around 322 and 348 of the number of rice /m² would be appropriate for stump density 50 and 70 / 3.3 m², respectively. Also, it is found that 414 and 464 of the number of ear(x100) / m² are appropriate for stump density of 50 and 70 / 3.3 m², respectively. These can be estimated with the measured NDVI.

ACKNOWLEDGEMENT

Authors would like to thank Dr. Satoshi Tsuchida and the other related members of National Institute of Advanced Industrial Science and Technology: AIST, Japan for their providing ASTER/VNIR.

REFERENCES

[1]   Wiegand, C., Shibayama, M, Yamagata, Y, Akiyama, T., 1989. Spectral Observations for Estimating the Growth and Yield of Rice, Journal of Crop Science, 58, 4, 673-683, 1989.

[2]   Kohei Arai, Method for estimation of grow index of tealeaves based on Bi-Directional reflectance function:BRDF measurements with ground based netwrok cameras, International Journal of Applied Science, 2, 2, 52-62, 2011.

[3]   Kohei Arai, Wireless sensor network for tea estate monitoring in complementally usage with Earth observation satellite imagery data based on Geographic Information System(GIS), International Journal of Ubiquitous Computing, 1, 2, 12-21, 2011.

[4]   Kohei Arai, Method for estimation of total nitrogen and fiber contents in tealeaves with grond based network cameras, International Journal of Applied Science, 2, 2, 21-30, 2011.

[5]   Kohei Arai, Method for estimation of damage grade and damaged paddy field areas sue to salt containing sea breeze with typhoon using remote sensing imagery data, International Journal of Applied Science,2,3,84-92, 2011.

[6]   Kohei Arai, Monte Carlo ray tracing simulation for bi-directional reflectance distribution function and grow index of tealeaves estimation, International Journal of Research and Reviews on Computer Science, 2, 6, 1313-1318, 2011.

[7]   Kohei.Arai, Fractal model based tea tree and tealeaves model for estimation of well opened tealeaf ratio which is useful to determine tealeaf harvesting timing, International Journal of Research and Review on Computer Science, 3, 3, 1628-1632, 2012.

[8]   Kohei.Arai, H.Miyazaki, M.Akaishi, Determination of harvesting timing of tealeaves with visible and near infrared cameradata and its application to tea tree vitality assessment, Journal of Japanese Society of Photogrammetry and Remote Sensing, 51, 1, 38-45, 2012

[9]   Kohei Arai, Osamu Shigetomi, Yuko Miura, Hideaki Munemoto, Rice crop field monitoring system with radio controlled helicopter based near infrared cameras through nitrogen content estimation and its distribution monitoring, International Journal of Advanced Research in Artificial Intelligence, 2, 3, 26-37, 2013.

[10]   Kohei Arai, Masanori Sakashita, Osamu Shigetomi, Yuko Miura, Estimation of Protein Content in Rice Crop and Nitrogen Content in Rice Leaves Through Regression Analysis with NDVI Derived from Camera Mounted Radio-Control Helicopter, International Journal of Advanced Research in Artificial Intelligence, 3, 3, 13-19, 2013

[11]   Kohei Arai, Masanori Sakashita, Osamu Shigetomi, Yuko Miura, Estimation of Protein Content in Rice Crop and Nitrogen Content in Rice Leaves Through Regression Analysis with NDVI Derived from Camera Mounted Radio-Control Helicopter, International Journal of Advanced Research in Artificial Intelligence, 3, 3, 13-19, 2013

13

Migration Dynamics in Artificial Agent Societies

Harjot Kaur
Dept of Comp. Sci. and Engg.
GNDU Regional Campus, Gurdaspur
Punjab, INDIA
Email: harjotkaursohal@rediffmail.com

Karanjeet Singh Kahlon
Dept of Comp. Sci. and Engg.
Guru Nanak Dev University, Amritsar
Punjab, INDIA
Email: karanvkahlon@yahoo.com

Rajinder Singh Virk
Dept of Comp. Sci. and Engg.
Guru Nanak Dev University, Amritsar
Punjab, INDIA
Email: tovirk@yahoo.com

Abstract—An Artificial Agent Society can be defined as a collection of agents interacting with each other for some purpose and/or inhabiting a specific locality, possibly in accordance to some common norms/rules. These societies are analogous to human and ecological societies, and are an expanding and emerging field in research about social systems. Social networks, electronic markets and disaster management organizations can be viewed as such artificial (open) agent societies and can be best understood as computational societies. Members of such artificial agent societies are heterogeneous intelligent software agents which are operating locally and cooperating and coordinating with each other in order to achieve goals of an agent society. These artificial agent societies have some kind of dynamics existing in them in terms of dynamics of Agent Migration, Role-Assignment, Norm-Emergence, Security and Agent-Interaction. In this paper, we have described the dynamics of agent migration process, starting from the various types of agent migration, causes or reasons for agent migration, consequences of agent migration, and an agent migration framework to model the its behavior for migration of agents between societies.

I. INTRODUCTION

An *Artificial Agent Society* [8] can be defined as a collection of agents interacting with each other for some purpose and/or inhabiting a specific locality, possibly in accordance to some common norms/rules.These societies are analogous to human and ecological societies, and are an expanding and emerging field in research about social systems. Social networks, electronic markets and disaster management organizations can be viewed as such artificial (open) agent societies and can be best understood as computational societies. The members of such artificial agent societies are heterogeneous intelligent software agents, which are operating locally and cooperating and coordinating with each other in order to achieve goals of an agent society. Artificial Agent Societies can also be viewed as *normative systems*, as in them, the member agents residing have to obey certain rules/norms which are created and abolished from time-to-time in a society and this process is dynamic in nature. Also, the agents residing in the society, while obeying the norms of the society and in order to achieve their individual as well as societal goals move in/between them, and this movement can be termed as *agent migration*.

A. What is Migration?

A **migration system** can be defined as a set of places linked by flows and counter-flows of people, goods, services and information [12], which tends to facilitate further exchange, including migration between the places. And, according to demographers, every act of migration involves an origin, destination, and an intervening set of obstacles [15]. The dictionary meaning of word **Migration** according to Oxford on-line dictionary is

> Movement of people to a new area or country in order to find work or better living conditions.

Considering its *broader demographic perspective*, the term *migration* [19] can also be defined as temporary or permanent move of individuals or groups of people from one geographic location to another for various reasons ranging from better employment possibilities to persecution. Talking in terms of agents (intelligent/software) in artificial agent societies as mentioned above, *agent migration* can be defined as movement of agents in and between societies to new locations for various reasons ranging from societal, economic, social or personal. Although, this movement is selective, but it forms an integral part of the broader process known as *development* of societies, which itself is a linear, universal process consisting of successive stages [12]. The study of migration is not only confined to social sciences, but it has got with a vast and significant importance in the areas of political sciences, economics, anthropology, biology, psychology and artificial intelligence (computer sciences).

In general, migration is considered as a complex dynamic process and a spatial phenomenon with multi-faceted nature and has its own sophisticated theory and dynamics associated with it. The concept of agent migration has been derived from human or animal migration, because like human or animal migration, it has also got associated with it reasons, circumstances, patterns as well as consequences [19] of/for migration. Therefore, various similarities [3] exist between agent, human and animal migration, which are described below.

1) Similarities between agent, human and animal migration: Firstly, both the agent and human/animal migration involve movement in order to migrate, be it in the form of migration in or between societies, and this movement involved in both the cases is linear in nature. Secondly, in the all these type of migrations, a special preparation is initially required for migration, which demands a special allocation of energy from the society. Thirdly, migrating species, whether they are agents, humans or animals, have to maintain a strong commitment to their migration mission or challenge, which is going to keep them undisturbed from all the side temptations. Fourthly, the journey of migration, whether its agent, human or animal migration, has to be continued at all costs.

In the case of human migration, migration can be categorized either as *internal (intra-continental or intraregional)* or *external (inter-continental)* migration [14] [15], talking in same terms, **Agent Migration** can be categorized [17] either as *internal Migration*, (i.e., Migration of agents between two sites in the same society) or as *external Migration*, (i.e., Migration of agents between two different societies). The human migration is normally referred as *immigration*, which is common term used in *demography*, whereas agent migration should be referred by term, *migration* only. In agent migration, the agent who migrates into a new society will be hence termed as *immigrant agent*, and while it is leaving its society of origin to migrate into another, will be termed as *em-migrant agent*.

In addition, to various similarities between agent, human and animal migration, there exist a number of dissimilarities also, which are described below.

2) Dissimilarities between agent, human and animal migration: As explained above, agent and human migration are different with respect to few points also, for instance, agent migration is organized and collective in nature whereas human immigration is disorganized and sporadic. In addition to this, human immigration is downright enigmatic, and this aspect is missing in agent migration in artificial agent societies.

B. Dynamics in Artificial Agent Societies

Artificial agent societies like any other working system have some kind of *dynamics* existing in them, which are in terms of dynamics of *Agent Migration*, *Role-Assignment*, *Norm-Emergence*, *Security* and *Agent-Interaction* [23]. These dynamics are basically changes that occur in the behavioral and emergent properties of the societies due to sensing of a stimulus from an environment as well as due to an external agent, who wants to migrate into the society. Also, these all types of dynamics are in one way or another related to each other as all of them are either directly or indirectly affected by one another.

1) Migration Dynamics in Artificial Agent Societies: The member agents residing in these societies keep on moving between these societies from time-to-time in the same manner as human-beings move between human-societies [20]. And, this movement of agents between artificial agent societies is called Agent Migration. And, all the *internal (related to agent)* and *external (societal)* issues related to agent migration are called agent migration dynamics. In this paper, we have described agent dynamics from their each and every aspect as they play a very pivotal role in the shaping of societies throughout their life time.

2) Why Migration Dynamics: An agent migration is considered as an integral part of development process [12] involved with the growth of artificial agent societies. Therefore, agent migration is one of very essential part of society dynamics, which has to be studied and worked in thoroughly and very less work has been done in this direction. Also, all the other types of society dynamics, (i.e., dynamics of role-assignment, agent interaction, norm emergence, trust and security) [23] are very closely related to it, as all of them are either directly or indirectly affected by migration of agents in/between societies.

Hence, we have focused our research on agent migration dynamics [27] in artificial agent societies in this paper. Our paper focuses on migration dynamics in artificial agent societies because of agent migration process, specifically external migration process, and we have tried to discuss almost everything which can be related to external migration dynamics, i.e., its types, reasons, framework, consequences or problems arising because of external agent migration in this article.

This paper is organized has follows. In section 2, we have discussed background work already performed in the area of agent migration. In section 3, we have covered various aspects of migration dynamics in agent societies. In section 4, we focus on the types of agent migration between agent societies. In section 5, reasons for agent migration between societies are stated. In section 6, consequences arising out of this agent migration are presented and in section 7, we have described an agent migration framework to facilitate migration of agents between agent societies. Then, conclusions and future work are covered in sections 8 and 9 respectively.

II. BACKGROUND AND RELATED WORK

In this section, we have tried to summarize various works, which have been performed and are related to agent migration in artificial agent societies. Also, we have illustrated various possible extensions, which can be performed related to them.

The categorization of agent migration has also been performed by Costa et al [17], as *Internal Migration* and *External Migration* where external migration occurs if agent moves between societies and internal migration occurs if agent moves within a society from one site(group) to another. Also, various consequences related to agent migration are discussed by Glaser and Morignot in [9] and Dignum et al in [6], and they are in terms of *reorganization* of societies that takes place, i.e., society in which agent enters, has to modify (means modification of structure of its organization) itself in order to accommodate the agent in society's already existing roles, which are distributed amongst its member agents. Also, the agent which has joined the society needs to adapt itself so as to internalize in the organization of the society, it now lives in. The type of reorganization demonstrated by Glaser and Morginot is *static reorganization* and by Dignum et al is *dynamic reorganization* as in the case of latter, modifications in structure and behavior of an artificial agent society after addition, removal or substitution of an agent are done to the society while it is executing (i.e., without bringing down the system). This particular type of reorganization is in the form of *dynamic adaptation*.

The works presented by above three authors are one of the basic and initial works done in the area of agent migration dynamics, but all these can be expanded also, by adding more aspects and factors to the agent migration dynamics. For instance, the only types of migration presented by Costa et al [17] are internal and external migration, which are categorized taking into consideration only the factor of geographical distance spanned by an agent while moving from one place to another. But, there are many other factors, which can be considered (i.e., circumstances and adaptability) while agent is to move. Similarly, the only consequence of migration is listed by Dignum et al [6] and Glaser and Morginot [9], as reorganization (static and dynamic) of society, which is one of the societal consequences, where as there are many other societal and individual consequences, which can be explored upon, while working with the process of agent migration.

The basic motivation behind the reorganization of society is either increase in the *agent's utility* or the *society's utility*. Utility [9] of society means what society has gained out of reorganization after the new agent has joined the society and in order to evaluate the utility of convention of society, cost of reorganization and utility of existing structure once without the newly migrated agent and then with newly migrated agent is evaluated in the form of a utility function, where convention means distribution of roles between agents of the society. And, if the utility of the society increases with the above agent migration, reorganization and hence agent migration is considered beneficial for the society.

The utility of an agent depends on the roles it desires, the roles it has committed to and the confidence with which it is playing its roles. Normally, an agent chooses to integrate into that society, which increases its utility and in that case agent is beneficiary. And on the other hand, a society chooses to integrate with an agent, that increases the its utility. Initially, an agent joining an agent society will be consulting the institutional layer [5] of the society to commit itself to certain role, which it has to play in a society and in order to see, whether it satisfies the norms and rules enforced in the society by this layer.

The reorganization, which is an after effect of agent migration, (i.e., integration of a new agent with a society), demonstrated by Dignum et al [6] is dynamic in nature. They have classified it into types, i.e., *Behavioral* and *Structural*. *Behavioral Change* occurs when organizational structure remains the same but the agents enacting roles [4] [24], decide to use different protocols for the same abstract interaction described in the structure, in case an agent leaves the society and a new agent joins it. Therefore, it is only the interaction pattern, that has to be modified, but on the other hand in the case of *Structural Change*, a decision is made concerning the modifications of one of the structural elements, i.e., societies adapt to environmental changes due to addition, deletion or modification of its structural elements (i.e. agents, roles, norms, dependencies, ontologies and communication primitives). Therefore, behavioral changes temporary changes in an organization whereas structural changes can lead to permanent modification in the structure of an organization [18].

Two different *issues* related to agent integration to an existing agent society are described by Eijk et al in [7] and they are based upon open-ended nature of agent societies that allows for the dynamic integration of new agents into an existing open system. These issues are distinguished as **Agent Introduction** and **Agent Creation**. *Agent Introduction* is addition of a new agent which is existing outside the society into a society and *Agent Creation* is similar to object creation, i.e., a newly integrated agent constitutes a previously non-existent entity and is created in a society for agents with limited resources who may face an overloading of tasks to be performed by them. Although, this paper significantly contributes to the process of agent migration, by dynamically integrating new agents into an already existing society, by using an abstract framework in concurrent object oriented language called POOL and its various communication constructs, but still the abstract framework present in this paper for agent introduction and agent creation in a society can be expanded by considering various push-pull factors and the behaviors of the agents which are migrating in/between them, and that also, while the society

TABLE I.   SUMMARY OF RELATED WORK

Author	Work Direction	Key Points	Possible Extensions
Costa et al.	Migration Classification	Internal and External Migration	Various other categories of migration.
Glaser & Morginot	Migration Consequences	Reorganization (Static)	Various other societal and individual consequences.
Dignum et al	Migration Consequences	Reorganization (Dynamic)	Various other societal and individual consequences.
Eijk et al	Migration Issues	Agent Introduction and Creation	A complete migration framework for agent introduction.
Hafizoglu and Sen	Migration Patterns	Conservative, Moderate and Eager Migration	Various other patterns of migration.

is still in running state, i.e., without bringing it down.

When agents migrate between societies, some patterns emerge for migration and they are illustrated by Hafizoglu and Sen in [13] as *Conservative*, *Moderate* and *Eager* migration. These patterns emerge from opinions or choices of agents to migrate. For experimenting between choices and patterns they have used two-dimensional toroidal grid in which simulation proceeds in discrete time steps with agents having two types of opinions, i.e., binary or continuous. In addition to this, many other types of patterns emerging for agent migration process can be studied, like chain, return or step migration of agents amongst societies/groups.

All the above mentioned related works are summarized in table I, which explains various directions followed by various authors in the area of agent migration dynamics, various findings of these research directions as well as how their work can be extended in order to incorporate new aspects in migration dynamics.

Although, migration of agents between societies is discussed in all the above papers, which we have surveyed in this section from different perspectives, but none of them elaborates on the complete migration framework or protocols, which are required and can be used for migration of agents amongst agent societies, i.e., for organizational migration. Our paper focuses on the elaboration of a complete migration framework, which can be used by agents to migrate from one society to another. In addition to that, various dynamics (as mentioned in table I) and their extended forms, in the process of migration will be discussed one by one, in the coming sections.

III.   MIGRATION DYNAMICS IN ARTIFICIAL AGENT SOCIETIES

Agent Migration occurs when an agent moves from one site to another site between a society or an agent moves from one society to another one, that also, physically as well as logically. Agent Migration or the process of entrance of new agent into the society has many issues related with respect to dynamics and structure of an open-agent society (as only in the case of open-agent societies, agents can leave or enter any time). In order to understand properly, all the aspects and behavior of agent migration subsystem [23], which can be viewed as an interdependent dynamic subsystem with its own dynamics, but is interlinked with other subsystems existing in various societies, feedback and adjustments coming from the migration process itself, a proper detailed study of agent migration dynamics is required and that is the main objective of this paper.

The agent migration can be physical as well organizational, because there is a possibility of agents migrating between platforms and that also may be on different computers or same as well, geographically. Our concern in this paper is, only organizational migration, as in the former case, everything is adjusted by network infrastructure for transportation of mobile agents (which are pieces of software), from one site to another. As, the agents in the case of physical migration (agents are mobile in nature), they find standard environments at every site they visit in addition to standard script interpreters for the execution of code and standard communication constructs. Therefore, they face no such problems during and after the physical migration, which are present in the case of organizational migration. Therefore, our main concentration in this paper is only on *organizational* migration and its dynamics.

Basically, dynamics [25] existing in every system can be classified as either *macro dynamics* (i.e., between various societies or inter-societal dynamics) or *micro dynamics* (i.e., inside a single society or intra-societal dynamics). The aspect of internal migration will be considered under micro dynamics and external migration under macro dynamics in agent societies. External Migration is only possible in open agent societies, i.e., society needs to be open internally as well as externally where as in the case of internal Migration society, it need not be a externally open society. This agent mobility actually facilitates efficient collaboration of an agent with other agents at intra-societal (micro dynamics) or inter-societal (macro-dynamics) level. As, we are concerned only with external migration, therefore, the dynamics studied by us will also be of the type of macro-dynamics only. Related to macro or external agent migration dynamics is the *reasons*, *types*, *consequences* and *patterns* adopted for migration. Our paper is dedicated to the illustration of these all dynamics related to agent migration in artificial agent societies, and all of them are covered one by one in the coming sections.

Both internal and external migrations are formally treated as the same kind of processes, since the type of procedures involved are the same. In the case of internal migration, migrating agents will be specialized, non-autonomous agents and in external migration, migrating agents will be fully autonomous agents with full capabilities of their own. The set of external migration dynamics [27] need a multi-dimensional theory and a formulation of proper migration framework. Hence, our main concentration in this paper will be on framework for external migration and study of migration dynamics, because this study have more relevance, when they are considered with respect to external migration. Therefore, all the dynamics related to agent migration, starting from the types, reasons and consequences have been discussed by us in the sections to come. Our next subsection is related to various types of migration, (i.e., migration categorization) in artificial agent societies.

IV. TYPES OF AGENT MIGRATION

Agent migration, as explained above, is similar to human or animal migration because reasons, circumstances, patterns and finally consequences, associated with agent migration are almost same as human/animal migration. Also, Agent migration as inspired from human migration [21] [14] can be classified accordingly into various categories depending upon *three* factors, i.e., *geographical distance spanned, circumstances and adaptability*. These three factors can be stated as follows Firstly, from geographical distance spanned, we mean that the actual distance which is covered by agent while migrating from one place to another. Secondly, from circumstances, we mean all the political, economic and environmental conditions which force the agent to move from one place to another in a same society or another society. Lastly, adaptability means ability of agent to cope up with new surroundings and new place, when agent moves there [22]. The society/site of origin from which agent starts its migration can be termed as **migration source** or **sending society** and the destination society/site to which agent migrates is called **migration sink** or **receiving society**.

The first set of migration categories, which are classified according to *geographical distance* factor are *internal* and *external* migration[1]. Where,

- **Internal Migration** can be defined as migration of agents between two sites in the same society, and

- **External Migration** can be defined as migration of agents between two different societies.

The internal migration in agent societies is similar to intraregional migration in human societies and external migrations in agent societies are analogous to intra-continental and intercontinental (i.e., interregional) migrations in human societies. Therefore, consequences and conflicts arising in agent societies are almost same as consequences and conflicts arising in human societies because of similarities between external and internal migrations in agent societies with inter and intra-regional migrations in human societies.

The second set of migration categories, which are classified according to *circumstances* which lead to migration, they are *forced or involuntary*, *voluntary* or *imposed* migrations. Where,

- **Forced or Involuntary Migration** can be defined as migration in which agent is forced to migrate from source of migration to another society or site due to certain unfavourable circumstances at the migration source.

- **Voluntary Migration** can be defined as migration in which agent voluntarily migrates to another society or migration sink, due to some favourable circumstances there.

- **Imposed Migration** can be defined as migration in which agent is not forced to migrate to another society but due to persistent unfavourable circumstances at the migration source, agent leaves source.

In the case of forced or involuntary migration, agents are left with no choice, they have to migrate, i.e., leave the society. But, in the case of voluntary migration, which can also be termed as *choice migration*, agents by their own will and wish choose to migrate from one place to another. In the third case, i.e., in imposed migration, which can also be termed as *reluctant or impelled* migration, agents are not forced to migrate but it is due to persistent unfavourable circumstances, they decide to migrate from migration source. The concept of agent migration is also related to various reasons which are the root cause behind it and hence they become an essential part of agent migration dynamics, therefore, we have dedicated next section of our paper to various reasons leading to agent migration.

V. REASONS FOR AGENT MIGRATION

Agents are also assumed to be residing in communities like human beings that are connected in some known topological structure [13]. There are always certain *reasons* which are responsible for agent migration, for instance, there are always some social functions and resources needed by an agent which are present in some another society [16], different than its source society for performing that particular job. Agents can migrate because of various reasons, i.e., *social/societal, economical or personal/individual*. These reasons are further based on *push and pull factors* leading to migration of agents amongst agent societies [20] [15]. *Push factors are basically positive attributes perceived by agents, existing at the new location*, i.e., new society or new site to which agent is planning to migrate. Whereas, *pull factors are negative home, i.e., local site or society conditions that impel the agent's decision to migrate to a new society or site.* These push and pull factors are analogous to push and pull factors that result in human migration and can be categorized according to reasons for agents migration as *societal* push-pull factors, *economic* push-pull factors and *individual* push-pull factors.

The *societal* push-pull factors are combination of negative conditions arising in the atmosphere of source society and positive conditions arising in the destination society, as a consequence of which agents migrate between these source and destination agent societies. They are unequal/unfair role-assignment in the source society and comparatively fair/equal role-assignment in the destination society, ineffective security policies in the source society and effective security policies in the destination society. The unequal role-assignment, in a particular society is one of root causes of net overall migration.

Also, when in a particular society some particular role is required to played by an agent and the member agents of that society are incompetent to play that role. And, if that society comes to know, that, there is some particular agent in some other society, and it is fully competent to play the required role. In this case, the destination society, which requires an agent, can also request or pull an agent from its source society to play that particular role in the destination society. This pull factor can be considered as societal pull factor from the side of destination society.

The *economic* push-pull factors are combination of economic benefits received in the form of rewards for playing some specific role, which is existing in some destination society to which agent wants to migrate, and they pull an agent from its residential source society to migrate. Also, rewards obtained by agent for playing the same role in its source society will be lesser in amount as compared to rewards for the same role, which it can obtain in destination society. Therefore, this reward differential will be serving as push factor, which will be pushing an agent to migrate to some other society, where its economic conditions can be better.

The *individual* push-pull factors are combination of individual or personal benefits, which an agent can receive in the destination society to which it migrates. They can be in terms of increased individual agent's utility, autonomy, or role-playing opportunities in destination society as compared to the source society in which it currently resides. This factor is basically related to the favorable conditions, which an agent requires in order to function well in society and in search of these conditions, an agent migrates to that destination society, where these conditions are met.

These push and pull factors, i.e., societal, economic and individual, can also be categorized as *material* and *non-material* incentives related to agent migration, because some of the sub-factors from societal, economic and individual factors [12], result in material benefits/incentives, i.e., can be in terms of economic benefits, whereas others can result in non-material benefits/incentives, which is basically in terms of the chances of self-actualization, for the em-migrant/immigrant agents. After the migration is actualized by an agent or set of agents, *(we are considering here agent or set of agents only because migration is a selective process)*, and only those agents who are interested in undertaking this process, participate. The extent of migration amongst agent societies depends upon all these migration push-pull factors listed above.

VI. CONSEQUENCES OF AGENT MIGRATION

There are several *issues*, *problems* and *consequences* associated with the outcome of agent migration and broadly they can be categorized as issues related to the societies and to the migrating agents. Hence, consequences related to agent migration can be classified as *societal consequences* or *personal consequences*. Here, *Societal consequences* occurring because of agent migration, are *maintenance of functional integrity of a society*, i.e., placing the new immigrant agent in society's already existing social structure [11] whereas personal consequences occurring at the side of *immigrant agent*, are problems of *language and interaction protocols* while conversing with the member agents of the destination society, i.e., the society it has entered into, so that it is considered as a well-behaved agent and problems of *knowledge and performance*, which actually define the ways the agent will behave in order to properly perform the functions (to play the roles) that destination society wants it to perform.

Another set of problems related to an immigrant agent while acting as an em-migrant agent is of helping the society it is leaving, i.e., its source society, to preserve its functional integrity in its absence. An immigrant agent will only be integrating (entering) with a new destination society only if it is sure that it is capable of dealing with the problems that it will face when doing that, i.e., it is prepared to solve problems produced by its entrance or departure. This set of problems can be also considered to fall under personal or individual consequences of agent migration. This section of our paper will be describing all the societal as well individual consequences, related to agent migration.

A. Societal Consequences

Various societal consequences related to agent migration process are:

1) Reorganization: The societies of origin as well as destination always have to *reorganize* structurally as well as behaviorally, when the process of agent migration takes between them. These consequences can also be termed as social consequences arising out of agent migration. These consequences result in terms of constructs of *dynamic role-allocation* to immigrant agent in the destination society and dynamic *role- deallocation* and then *reallocation* in the source society in the place of em-migrant agent. This reorganization can be performed using dynamic role-allocation constructs available in the *role- assignment* module or subsystem for source and destination artificial agent societies.

2) Conflicts: As a result of agent migration process, conflicts will arise in the destination society, to which immigrant agent has entered, because of its integration. The conflicts arising will be *role-conflicts* and *norm-conflicts*. Role-conflicts arise, if an immigrant agent was allocated some role as as em-migrant agent in its society of origin. And, after migration to the destination society, as an immigrant agent, it still wants to play the same role in destination society and in the later, it is not possible. Norm-Conflicts arise, when em-migrant agent moves to some destination society, and there as an immigrant agent, does not wants to obey the norms of the destination society, and still wants to remain associated with the norms of its society of origin. These conflicts are only tolerated for immigrant agent, when its integration with the destination society increases the society's overall utility.

3) Norm Emergence: As a result of migration of agents between societies, the societies also come closer to each other because, when agents following an altogether different set of norms move between them, then *norm emergence* modules of both these societies will execute their respective *norm recognizer* sub-modules to recognize a new set of candidate norms, which later will be functioning as proper or actual norms in the source and destination societies.

B. Individual Consequences

Various individual consequences related to agent migration process are:

1) Interaction Language and Protocol Conflicts : These conflicts arise, when an immigrant agent enters the destination society, and the agent communication language and protocols used in the destination society for agent communication are different from what it was using in its society of origin, and agent is unable to participate in conversations with the member agents of the destination society. In order to resolve such conflicts, language and protocol adaptation at the level of immigrant agent is required in order to adapt already existing communication infrastructure in the destination society. Related to this, very significant amount of work has been performed by Bordini in his doctoral thesis [1] [2], which is dedicated to cultural adaptation being performed at the level of immigrant agents in destination society.

2) Knowledge and Performance Problems: These problems arise when immigrant agent in the destination society is unable to perform the role allocated to it in destination society in a proper manner, because of improper knowledge present with it to perform that role. And, if the problem of performance persists for the immigrant agent, the destination society may can force an immigrant agent to move back to its society of origin.

The outcome of agent's integration with a society is usually an establishment of a new convention between the members of a society and the newly entered agent, i.e., redistribution of roles, performed by role-assignment module which is assigning or distributing roles amongst various member agents in the society. The end result of migration process is a set of relatively stable exchanges, yielding an identifiable geographical structure [13] that persists across space and time. The details of the behavior of migration process are presented by us in the next section.

VII.   AN AGENT MIGRATION FRAMEWORK

Agent Migration is very vital for the development of artificial agent societies, because it is basically agent migration, which will be making the set of existing societies dynamic and in-turn facilitating the movement of agents in/between societies. *An agent migration framework* is vital with respect to facilitation of process of migration of agents amongst agent societies. And, it can be considered to be comprised of a set of societies linked by flows and counter-flows of agents between societies, which tends to facilitate further exchange, including migration between the societies. An agent migration framework in order to facilitate migration in artificial agent societies, requires a migration model [26] which can be used to model the behavior of agents, when they migrate in/between agent societies.

The presentation of migration dynamics [25], is actually involved with modeling migration processes over time, which we have assumed to be comprising of discrete time intervals. An agent migration framework comprises of modeling an agent *migration model*, which in turn uses a *migration function* to facilitate migration of agents from source society or society of origin of agents to destination society. A *migration model* attempts to ascertain the relative importance of various determinants (push-pull factors) leading to migration and also addresses various personal/individual as well as societal consequences resulting after migration. Related to migration model is the term *migration interval*, which is the period of time over which a migratory move is taken by potential em-migrant agents from the source or sending society. This migration interval is also measured in discrete time steps.

The migration model, which we are going to present is an empirical migration model based on combination of gravity model [10] given by Greenwood and social- psychological model of immigration given by Andrew and Zara in [3], and we have given it a name **W5- SGMIM** for *W5 social-gravity migration model* for inter-societal or external migration between agent societies. The characters **W5** which are mentioned in the name of the SGMIM model, are basically **5 W's** *(Who, Whey, Where, What and When)* related to the process of migration and they stand for the following information related to migration model for modeling the behavior of migration process amongst agent societies.

1) *W for Who?* - *Who* amongst the set of member agents residing in the society wants to migrate? This *W* is related to the selection of em-migrant agents in the source society, who are to move to destination society.

2) *W for Why?* - *Why* a particular agent or set of agents want to migrate? This *W* is related to various factors or determinants in source and destination societies, that are leading to agent migration from the source society to destination society.

3) *W for Where?* - *Where* do agent(s) want or plan to migrate? This *W* is related to selection of the destination society to which em-migrant agents in source society, want or plan to migrate and act as immigrant agents there.

4) *W for What?* - *What* will be the consequences of this migration? This *W* is related to various societal and personal consequences, which will be resulting out of this migration in both source and destination societies.

5) *W for When?* - *When* do agent(s) want to migrate? This *W* is related to the description of beginning of *migration interval* of em-migrant agents from the source society to move to destination society.

This model is called a social-gravity model because the migration function used in the migration process is based on gravity model [10] of human migration, which is based on modified version of *Newton's Law of Gravitation*, i.e., the attractive force between two bodies is directly related to their size and inversely related to the distance between them. And, the keyword *social* is added, because, it is based on input of a set of social-psychological factors (push-pull factors), which are the basic determinants of the migration process.

A. A Migration Function

Definition VII.1. (The Agents World)

The Agents World is a set of societies existing in the world of agents, and is defined as $\mathscr{S} = \{\mathscr{S}_1, \mathscr{S}_2, \ldots, \mathscr{S}_n\}$ with a finite number of **n** societies.

Definition VII.2. (Population)

A Population is a set of member agents of any society $\mathscr{S}_i$, and is defined $\mathscr{P}_i = \{\mathscr{A}_{i1}, \mathscr{A}_{i2}, \ldots, \mathscr{P}_{im}\}$, with **m** being finite number of residing member agents in a society $\mathscr{S}_i$.

Definition VII.3. (Roles)

Roles are place-holders assigned to various member agents of the society according to their capability and role-assignment/allocation protocols of the society. They are defined using a finite set $\mathscr{R} = \{\mathbf{r}_1, \mathbf{r}_2, \ldots, \mathbf{r}_k\}$, where **k**, is the number of roles in the role set $\mathscr{R}$.

Definition VII.4. (Agent)

An Agent $\mathbf{a} \in \mathscr{P}_i$ is a tuple $\mathbf{a} = \langle \mathbf{r_{ia}}, \mathbf{u_a}, \mathscr{B}_\mathbf{a} \rangle$, where $\mathbf{r_{ia}}$ is the role allocated to an agent **a**, $\mathbf{u_a}$ is utility function of an agent **a**, and $\mathscr{B}_\mathbf{a}$ is behavior of an agent **a**.

The behavior $\mathscr{B}_\mathbf{a}$ of an agent $\mathbf{a} \in \mathscr{P}_i$, where $\mathscr{P}_i$ is the population of society $\mathscr{S}_i$, describes the behavior of an agent from external point of view. This behavior function is a combination of many external (push-pull) factors, which are existing in the source and destination societies. This behavior

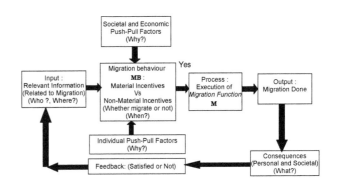

Fig. 1.   The Social- Gravity Migration Model

function, acts as very important decision making factor in the migration process in the form of migration behavior function, in our migration model.

The *migration function* leading to the process of migration can be described as:

Definition VII.5. (A Migration Function)

A Migration function $\mathscr{M}_{i,j}$ for agent $\mathbf{a} \in \mathscr{P}_i$ in source society $\mathscr{S}_i$ for migrating to destination society $\mathscr{S}_j$ at any time $\mathbf{t} \in \mathscr{T}$, where $\mathscr{P}_i$ and $\mathscr{P}_j$ are populations of source and destination society respectively, and $\mathscr{D}_{i,j}$, is distance between them, leading to the process of agent migration amongst them can be defined as

$$\mathscr{M}_{i,j} : (\mathbf{a} \times \mathscr{T}) \to \mathscr{S}_j. \tag{1}$$

Here, $\mathscr{T}$ is a time set comprised of discrete time steps, $\{\mathbf{t}, \mathbf{t} + 1, \ldots, \mathbf{t} + \mathbf{n}\}$.

Also, The Migration Function $\mathscr{M}_{i,j}$ can de written as:

$$\mathscr{M}_{i,j} = \frac{G \mathscr{P}_i \mathscr{P}_j}{\mathscr{D}_{i,j}^2} \tag{2}$$

Where G is constant. and $\mathscr{D}_{i,j}$ is distance between the two societies $\mathscr{S}_i$ and $\mathscr{S}_j$ and it is measured in terms of number of hops agent has to take to move from one society $\mathscr{S}_i$ to $\mathscr{S}_j$.

The above relationship states that *migration function* is directly related to the populations of source and destination societies' population sizes and inversely related to square of distance between them.

B. A Migration Model

The *social- gravity model*, which has been framed by us for the modeling the behavior of migration process occurring between societies, is a multi-dimensional model based on the concepts of system modules of "input, process and output" as described in Figure 1.

1) Input : comprises of relevant information related to the agent or set of agents who want to migrate from their society of origin to some other society of destination. This information also contains the name

and location of the destination society or societies to which agents wish to migrate. Therefore, all the information related to the **"Who?"** and **"Where?"** part of migration process is provided in this module of migration model. This input information launches the individual agent's decision making process, which is known as *migration behavior*, which is going to help agent decide, whether to migrate or not, hence serving a stimulus to migration process.

2) Migration Behavior : comprises of the decision - making part and behavior of agent(s), who want to migrate from their society of origin into some other destination society, and this behavior is affected by societal and personal push- pull factors existing in the source or origin society. In this module, all the *material as well as not-material benefits* related to migration process, are compared with costs which will be incurred for migration, and it is decided by agent, that **"When?"**, it is going to initiate the process of migration. If everything goes well, and benefits over-weigh the costs incurred for migration, then agents initiate the migration process, other wise no migration will be performed and the process of migration will stop altogether.

3) Process : is the module in which migration process is actually realized, and the agent from its society of origin is relocated to the destination society, it has wished for. The theory for the migration function has already been described in the previous subsection by using equations 1 and 2.

4) Societal-Economic Factors : comprise of all the societal and economic push-pull factors existing in source and destination societies, which become very genuine causes and reasons for agents to migrate between them and become very vital **"Why?"** part of migration process. They have already been explained in the section dedicated to them. They help agents to evaluate the *material benefits*, which can be realized from agent migration process.

5) Individual Factors : comprise of personal push-pull factors existing in source and destination societies, which lead to agent migration. These factors also comprise **"Why?"** part of agent migration process and help agents evaluate all the *non-material benefits*, which can be realized from agent migration process.

6) Output : is the outcome of the process of migration, in which agent from its society of origin gets relocated to the destination society, it has chosen as migration sink.

7) Consequences : are various after effects related to the process of migration, which can be categorized at both societal and personal levels of source and destination societies and the agent(s), who have migrated between them. They form **"What?"** part of the agent migration process. All the consequences related to agent migration process have been already illustrated in the previous section, which was dedicated to their description.

8) Feedback : consists of the individual agent's level of satisfaction or dissonance, after it has migrated to the destination society and have become aware of the consequences resulted from the migration process.

This is fed to the member agents of source society, in order to formulate their decision to migrate from the same to any destination society.

The *migration behavior* **MB** can be stated as

$$\mathbf{MB} = f\left(\mathbf{RI} + \mathbf{SE} \text{ factors} + \mathbf{Individual} \text{ factors}\right) \quad (3)$$

where **MB** = migration behavior,

f = is a function of (i.e., result of certain variables and factors),

RI = Relevant Information or input variables,

SE = Societal and Economic Factors,

and **I** = Individual Factors respectively.

The migration model, which has been described by us, is based on migration behavior, which is derived from behavior of an agent, and the migration function, which is facilitating the migration process. There are three parties involved in migration process, i.e., an agent, the society of origin, and the destination society. All three of them help stimulate the process of migration and perpetuate it.

VIII. CONCLUSIONS

In this paper, we have presented, almost all the dynamics related to agent migration process (specifically organizational and external migration process), in artificial agent societies, which have not yet been covered under the dynamics of artificial agent societies. As, mentioned in the related work section, many authors have presented their work on agent migration, but none of them is providing deep insight into the dynamics of agent migration process. All the dynamic aspects which are discussed by us for agent migration are inspired by the dynamic aspects of human migration, as both of them have quite a number of similarities. We have elaborated on various types of agent migration, various causes which lead to agent migration between artificial agent societies and various after effects or consequences of agent migration also. Also, we have formulated in this paper, an empirical agent migration model, i.e., W5 Social-Gravity Model, to model the complex behavior of multi-dimensional, dynamic migration process, which is responsible for moving agents from their society of origin to any other destination society. This migration model uses a two functions, i.e., migration function and migration behavior function for modeling the spatial phenomenon of agent migration process. Also, all the five (5) W's (Who?, Where?, Why?, What?, When?), related to the migration process have described in this model by using its various modules which are based on system's concept of operation.

IX. FUTURE WORK

In this paper, we have covered various types, causes and consequences related to agent migration process and have formulated a 5W Social-Gravity model for agent migration process also, which is used to model the behavior of complex agent migration process for the migration of agents between societies. Although, we tried to cover many aspects of dynamics of agent migration process in our presented literature, but still many aspects such as discussion of migration metrics (which will illustrate the number of agent migrating into and out of the source and sink (destination) agent societies and hence, measuring the net and gross migration of the society can be taken up as future research directions. And, migration protocols, which will be governing the migration process in agent societies can be framed. The discussion of various types of patterns of migration, the concept of re-migration process and emergence of migration norms, can also be considered as few of the future research challenges in agent migration process.

X. Acknowledgements

The authors are really grateful to the reviewers for their valuable suggestions and comments which they have given for this manuscript. They also would like to express thanks to the editor of IJARAI for providing very timely help for publishing this manuscript.

References

[1] R. H. Bordini, *Contributions to an Anthropological Approach to the Cultural Adaptation of Migrant Agents*, Department of Computer Science, University College London, London, U.K., 1999.

[2] R. H. Bordini, *Linguistic Support for Agent Migration*, Universidade Federal do Rio Grands do Sul (UFRGS), Instituto de Informatica, Porto Alegre, RS -BRAZIL, 1995.

[3] D. Z. S. Andrew and M. Zara, *Immigration Bahviour : Towards Social Pscychologial Model for Research*, In Proceedings of ASBBS Annual Conference, ASBBS Annual Conference: Las Vegas, Vol. 20(1), February 2013. ou

[4] M. Dastani and V. Dignum and F. Dignum, *Role-Assignment in Open Agent Societies*, In Proceedings of AAMAS'03: Second International Joint Conference on Autonomous Agents and MultiAgent Systems, Melbourne, Australia, ACM, 2003.

[5] V. Dignum and F. Dignum, *Modeling Agent Societies: Coordination Frameworks and Institutions*, In Proceedings of 10th Portuguese Conference on Progress in AI, Knowledge Extraction, MAS Logic Programming and Constraint Solving, 2001.

[6] V. Dignum and F. Dignum and L. Sonen Berg, *Towards Dynamic Reorganization of Agent Societies*, In Proceedings of CEAS: Workshop on Coordination in Emergent Agent Societies at ECAI2004, Valencia, Spain, September 22-27, 2004.

[7] R. M. Eijk and F. S. de van Boer and W. van der Hoek and Ch. J. J. Meyer, *Open Multi-Agent Systems: Agent Communication and Integration*, In Proceedings of Intelligent Agents VI ATAL 1999, pp. 218-222, 1999.

[8] N. Gilbert and R. Conte, *Artificial Societies: The Computer Simulation of Social Life*, UCL Press, London, 1995.

[9] N. Glasser and P. Morignot, *The Reorganization of Societies of Autonomous Agents*, In Proceedings of 8th European Workshop on Modeling Autonomous Agents in MultiAgent World, Ronneby, Sweden, LNCS 1237, Springer, May 13-16, 1997.

[10] M. J. Greenwood, *Modeling Migration*, Encyclopedia of Social Measurement, Elsevier, Vol. 2, 2005.

[11] H. S. B. Filho and F. B. de Lima Neto and W. Fusco, *Migration and social networks — An explanatory multi-evolutionary agent-based model*, 2011 IEEE Symposium on Intelligent Agent (IA), IEEE, Paris, 11-15 April, 2011.

[12] H. de Haas, *Migration and Development : A theoretical perspective*, International Migration Review, Vol. 44(1), pp. 1-38, 2010.

[13] F. M. Hafizoglu and S. Sen, *Patterns of Migration and Adoption of Choices By Agents in Communities*, Eds. Conitzer, Winikiff, Padgham and van der hock, In Proceedings of the 11th International Conference on Autonomous Agents and Multiagent Systems (AAMAS 2012), International Foundation for Autonomous Agents and MultiAgent Systems, Valencia, Spain, 5-8 June, 2012.

[14] R. King, *Theories and Typologies of Migration*, International Migration and Ethnic Relations, Willy Brandt Series of Working Papers, 3/12, Malmo Institute for Studies of Migration, Diversity and Welfare (MIM), Malmo University, Sweden, 2012.

[15] E. S. Lee, *A Theory of Migration*, Demography, Vol. 3(1), pp. 47-57, 1966.

[16] G. Lekeas and K. Stathis, *Agents acquiring Resources through Social Positions: An Activity Based Approach*, In Proceedings of 1st International Workshop on Socio-Cognitive Grids: the Net as A Universal Human Resource, Santorini, Greece, 1-4 June, 2003.

[17] A.C. da. R. Costa and T.F. Hubener and R. H. Bordini, *On Entering an Open Society*, XI Brazilian Symposium on AI, Fortaleza, Brazalian Computing Society, pp. 535-546, October 1994.

[18] V. Dignum and F. Dignum and V. Furlado A. Melo, *Towards a Simulation Tool for Evaluating Dynamic Reorganization of Agent Societies*, Proceedings of WS. on Socially Inspired Computing, AISB Convention, 2005.

[19] J. R. Weeks, *The Migration Transition*, in *Population : An introduction to concepts and issues*, Ninth Edition, Wadsworth Learning, pp. 273-315, 2005.

[20] J. H. Zanker, *Why do people migrate ? A review of the theoretical literature*, Working Paper MGSoG/2008/WP002MPRA, Munich Personal RePEc Archive, Maastricht University, Maastricht Graduate School of Governance, Netherlands, January 2008.

[21] *Human Migration Guide, Xepeditions, National Geographic Society*, A tutorial.

[22] *Human Migration* , Wikipedia, The Free Encyclopedia

[23] H. Kaur and K.S. Kahlon and R. S. Virk, *A formal Dynamic model of Artificial Agent Societies*, International Journal on Information and Communication Technologies, Vol. 6(1-2), pp. 67-70, Januray-June 2013.

[24] M. Dastani and B. M. van Riemsdijk and J. Hulstijn and F. Dignum and Ch. J. J. Meyer, *Enacting and Deacting Roles in Agent Programming*, Eds. Odell J.J., Giorgini P., Muller J.P, AOSE, LNCS, Vol. 3382, pp. 189-204, Springer Heidelberg, 2004.

[25] R. Brown, *Group Processes: Dynamics Within and Between Groups*, John Wiley and Sons, 1991.

[26] H. S. Filho and F. B. de Lima Neto and W. Fusco, *Migration, Communication and Social Networks - An Agent-Based Social Simulation*, Complex Networks, Studies in Computational Intelligence, Springer Berlin Heidelberg, Vol. 424, pp. 67-74, 2013.

[27] H. de Haas, *The internal dynamics of migration processes: A theoretical inquiry.*, Journal of Ethnic and Migration Studies, Vol. 36(10), pp. 1587-1617, 2010.

Method for Traffic Flow Estimation using On-dashboard Camera Image

Kohei Arai
Graduate School of Science and Engineering
Saga University
Saga, Japan

Steven Ray Sentinuwo
Department of Electrical Engineering
Sam Ratulangi University
Manado, Indonesia

Abstract—This paper presents the method to estimate the traffic flow on the urban roadway by using car's on-dashboard camera image. The system described, shows something new which utilizes only road traffic photo images to get the information about urban roadway traffic flow automatically.

Keywords—traffic flow estimation; on-dashboard camera; computer vision.

I. INTRODUCTION

Due to the increasing of the traffic densities nowadays, there exists a growing demand for advanced systems that can provide the essential traffic and travel information for the drivers to improve the traffic quality and travel optimization. The comprehensive and accurate of traffic information is the important aspect in order to manage the roadway network and to provide the navigation service for the road users. The density value measurement is one of the important aspect of transportation management. Intelligent Transportation System is a breakthrough technology that combines components of information management systems to create better transportation system. Currently, demands on the system are growing rapidly with an estimated travel demand increase of 30% over the next ten years[1]. The efficient of transportation system can be an alternative to increase the roadway capacity in order to prevent the traffic congestion at current levels from getting worse.

Vehicle detection and surveillance technologies are an integral part of ITS, since they gather all or part of the data that is used in ITS. There is an estimation that an investment in ITS will allow for fewer miles of road to be built, thus reducing the cost of mitigating recurring congestion by approximately 35 percent nationwide. New vehicle detection and surveillance technologies are constantly being developed and existing technologies improved, to provide speed monitoring, traffic counting, presence detection, headway measurement, vehicle classification, and weigh-in-motion data.

There are many methods and technologies for traffic measurement. However, the conventional measurement methods, such as "in-situ" technologies which are measure traffic data by locating detectors or sensors along the roadway, have some drawbacks. The use of these conventional methods for collecting data is necessary but not sufficient because of their limited coverage area and expensive costs of implementation and maintenance. Then as the alternative to the conventional methods there are alternative methods, such as based on the vehicle location or Floating Car Data method (FCD), and collecting data from "in-vehicle" devices.

This paper proposes a method for traffic measurement using the approach of collecting data from "in-vehicle" device which is by utilizing camera device that located on the car's dashboard. The image that captured by digital camera photo then was analyzed to get the estimation value of roadway traffic flow condition. A traffic measurement using digital camera device can be a practical and low cost solution compare to the conventional traffic measurement methods.

This paper is organized as follow. The brief description about traffic flow measurement methods and procedures is quick review in Section 2. Section 3 described some previous research that taking into account traffic monitoring models. In Section 4, the proposed method of traffic flow measurement using on-dashboard camera image is explained. Section 5 and Section 6 show the results of simulation study and experiment in the real traffic condition, respectively. Finally, in Section 7, we present the conclusion and the future works.

II. TRAFFIC FLOW MEASUREMENT

Researchers in the area of Intelligent Transportation System have been greatly interested in the various of traffic management and monitoring applications. For several years, under growing pressure for improving traffic management, a wide variety of applications have been developed. Some researchers focus on the theoretical aspect that involves driver behavior into the transportation model [2][3][4][5]. While the other focus on the development of application and tools of intelligent transportation system.

There are some items of interest in traffic theory, have been the following[6]:

- Rates of flow, which evaluates the number of vehicles per unit of time;
- Speeds, which evaluates the distance per unit time;
- Travel time over a known length of road, or sometimes refer to the invers of speed;
- Occupancy, that is percent of time a point on the road is occupied by vehicles;
- Density, which is refer to the number of vehicles per unit distance.
- Time headway between vehicles (time per vehicle);

- Spacing, or space headway between vehicles (distance per vehicles);
- Concentration, that is measured by density of occupancy.

The capability of traffic measurement to gather transportation data have changed over the nearly sixty year span of interest in traffic flow measurement. And to be more growing which there have been a large number of freeway and number of population. Indeed, traffic measurement methods are still changing, there are five common procedures in this area:

- Measurement at a point;
- Measurement over a short section, by which meant less than about 10 meters (m);
- Measurement over a length of road, usually at least 0.5 kilometers (km);
- Using moving observer along the traffic stream;
- Wide-area samples obtained simultaneously from a number of vehicles, as part as the Intelligent Transportation System (ITS).

In moving observer method, there are two common approaches[6]. The first one is the simple floating car data procedure (FCD). This approach intends to record speeds and travel times as the function of time and location along the road. The intention of this approach is the floating car as the observer car behaves as an average vehicle within the traffic stream. However, this approach cannot give provide average speed data. This one just effective for producing a qualitative information about roadway conditions and operations. One form of this approach uses a person in the floating car to record speeds and travel times. The second form uses a modified recording speedometer of the type regularly used in long-distance trucks or buses. While the drawback of this approach is that it means there are usually significantly fewer speed observations than volume observations.

The second one introduced by Wardrop et.al.[7] for urban traffic measurements. This approach intends to obtain both speed and volume measurements simultaneously. This method is based on an observation vehicle that travels in both direction on the roadway. The formulae allow one to estimate both speeds and flows for one direction of travel. The formulae are as follow :

$$= \frac{(x+y)}{(t_a+t_w)} \qquad (1)$$

$$\bar{t} = t_w - \frac{y}{q} \qquad (2)$$

where,

- q, is the estimated flow on the road in the direction of interest,
- x, is the number of vehicles traveling in the direction of interest, which are met by the observation car while traveling in the opposite direction,

- y, is the net number of cars that overtake the observation car while traveling in the direction of interest,
- t_a, is the travel time taken for the trip against the stream,
- t_w, is the travel time for the trip with the stream,
- $\bar{t}$, is the estimate of mean travel time in the direction of interest.

In 1973, Wright revised the theory behind this method[8]. His paper finds that the method gives biased results, although the degree of bias is not significant in practice, and can be overcome. His paper proposed that the driver should fix the journey time in advance then stops along the way would not matter. He found also that the turning traffic (exiting or entering) can upset the calculation done using this method. A suggestion also said that a large number of observations are required for reliable estimation of speeds and flow rates in order to get the precision value.

III. ROAD TRAFFIC MONITORING MODELS

Most of the road traffic monitoring system are based on motion detection to make a segmentation to the region of the image. Zhu et.al[9]. presented VISATRAM, a system for automatic traffic monitoring using 2D spatio-temporal images. A TV cam- era is mounted above a highway to monitor the traffic through two slice windows, and a panoramic view image and an epipolar plane image are formed for each lane. If the regions contain the appropriate characteristics, vehicles are considered and can be counted or tracked as desired. Out of the motion detection techniques defined so far, the two most frequently used in road-traffic monitoring are the image difference method and the motion detection technique based on features.

The other system uses image difference technique[10]. This technique based on the fact that the differences between two frames captured at different time instants reveal regions in motion. An image difference I is generated by calculating the absolute difference between two frames (I_1 and I_2) and thresholding the result.

$$I(x,y) = \begin{cases} 0, & \text{if } |I_1(x,y) - I_2(x,y)| \leqslant \theta \\ 1, & \text{otherwise} \end{cases} \qquad (3)$$

where θ is an appropriate threshold. In the case of traffic monitoring, it is usual for I_1 to be the input frame and I_2 to be the reference frame (background). The reference frame is an image from the scene, without cars. The purpose of the threshold is to reduce the effects of noise and changes in the scene's lighting. The latter is a great problem in computer vision and it is usually necessary to use methods of dynamic updating of the reference frame to adapt to the scene's lighting.

Some complete traffic monitoring systems are available to date. The system that called TRIP (Traffic Research using Image Processing)[11] is designed to count vehicles traveling in a two-lane, two- way highway. The camera is placed in the highway, looking vertically onto the scene.

By using a reference image, the input images are differentiated and the result is thresholded. This leads to a binary image where vehicles in motion should appear.

The greatest effort in the development of ITS was probably made by the U.S. Department of Transportation when it requested Mitretek Systems, Inc.[1] to carry out several ITS projects. The ones that stand out are those meant for a metropolitan ITS infrastructure, to which the following systems belong: Arterial Roads Control System, Highway Control System, Transit Control System (meant for public transportation in cities), Incident Control System, Emergency Control System, Electronic Collection System for Toll Roads (freeways), Electronic Fares Payment System (in-cities), Intersections between Freeways and Railroad Tracks, Regional Information for travelers and Integrated Systems. The subject continues to arouse a lot of interest, as can be seen in the article on vehicle detection and classification[12], where a six-stage system is proposed: (1) segmentation, (2) region tracking, (3) recovery of vehicle parameters, (4) vehicle identification, (5) vehicle tracking and (6) vehicle classification.

IV. TRAFFIC FLOW ESTIMATION USING ON-DASHBOARD CAMERA IMAGE

As stated before, the purpose of this paper is to present a visual system which estimate the traffic flow by utilize digital camera which located on the car's dashboard to capture the road scenery image. Figure 1 shows the schematic diagram of the concept.

Figure. 1. Schematic diagram of the concept

This system uses a camera mounted on the car's dashboard which capture real traffic image.

V. REAL TRAFFIC EXPERIMENT

Empirical data is used in this experiment. Figure 2 shows the location of this experiment. The on-dashboard camera then capture the front scenery information. In this example, which is showed by Figure 3, we captured the real traffic situation and investigated for the opposite lane direction of the observer car.

This system uses four sub-step to identified the car. In the initial step, this system crop the raw image to get only the opposite direction lane image. This preprocessed image is showed by Figure 3. In the second step, the preprocessed image is gray-scaled. After that the threshold is applied to the image. Then the car is detected by using blob detection and some morphology step.

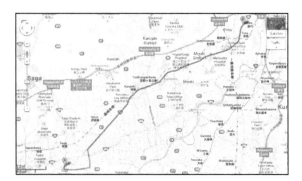

Figure. 2. The Location of Observation

Figure. 3. Road traffic monitoring image

Figure. 4. Preprocessed Image

In the Figure 6, the difference matrix is applied to a threshold. The gray levels greater and lower than the threshold is updated as 1 and 0, respectively. Which leads the car objects to be represented as black pixels.

Figure. 5. Real Image in gray scales

Figure. 6. Segmented Image

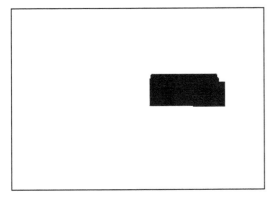

Figure. 7. Processed Image

(a)Original

(b)Canny filter summation

Figure 8. Example of images of which it is hard to count the number of cars in front of the car in concern

As shown in Figure 8 (a) and (b), it is hard to count the number of cars in front of the car in concern because some cars are overlapped just a behind of the car just in front of the car in concern. It, however, the hidden cars (occluded cars) are appeared when they are observed in curved roads or in sloped roads as shown in Figure 9 (a) and (b). Where the image (a) shows the original image while the image (b) shows Canny filter with summation is applied for segmentations.

(a)Original

(b)Canny filter summation

Figure 9. Example of images of which it is possible to count the number of cars in front of the car in concern

VI. CONCLUSION AND FUTURE WORKS

Automatic traffic flow estimation through on-dashboard camera is the new approach for the intelligent transportation system domain. This paper proposes a method for traffic measurement using the approach of collecting data from "in-vehicle" device which is by utilizing camera device that located on the car's dashboard. The image that captured by digital camera photo then was analyzed to get the estimation value of roadway traffic flow condition. A traffic measurement using digital camera device can be a practical and low cost solution compare to the conventional traffic measurement methods.

The future step needs the effective solution on how to remove the noise background and shadow that occur on the real traffic image.

REFERENCES

[1]   T. Proper, A, "Intelligent transportation system benefits," *US Dep. Transp. Washingt. DC.*

[2]   A. Schadschneider, "The Nagel-Schreckenberg model revised," *Eur. Phys. J. B*, vol. 10, no. 3, pp. 573–582, 1999.

[3]   K. Arai and S. R. Sentinuwo, "Effect of Driver Scope Awareness in the Lane Changing Maneuvers Using Cellular Automaton Model," *Int. J. Adv. Res. Artif. Intell.*, vol. 2, no. 7, pp. 6–12, 2013.

[4]   K. Arai and S. R. Sentinuwo, "Validity of Spontaneous Braking and Lane Changing with Scope of Awareness by Using Measured Traffic Flow," *Int. J. Adv. Res. Artif. Intell.*, vol. 2, no. 7, pp. 13–17, 2013.

[5]   K. Arai and S. R. Sentinuwo, "Validity of Spontaneous Braking and Lane Changing with Scope of Awareness by Using Measured Traffic Flow," *Int. J. Adv. Res. Artif. Intell.*, vol. 2, no. 7, pp. 13–17, 2013.

[6]   F. Hall, "Traffic stream characteristics," Washington, DC, 1975.

[7]   J. . Wardrop and G. Charlesworth, "A Method of Estimating Speed and Flow of Traffic from a Moving Vehicle," in *Proceedings of the Institution of Civil Engineers, Part II, Vol. 3*, 1954, pp. 158–171.

[8]   C. Wright, "A Theretical Analysis of the Moving Observer Method," *Transp. Res. 7*, pp. 293–311, 1973.

[9]   Z. Zhu, G. Xu, B. Yang, D. Shi, and X. Lin, "VISATRAM: A real-time vision system for automatic traffic monitoring," *Image Vis. Comput.*, 2000.

[10] M. Sonka, V. Hlavac, and R. Boyle, *Image processing, analysis, and machine vision*. Chapman & Hall, 1999.

[11] K. Dickinson and C. Wan, "Road traffic monitoring using the TRIP II system," *Road Traffic Monit. 1989*

[12] S. Gupte and O. Masoud, "Detection and classification of vehicles," *Intell. Transp. Syst.*, vol. 3, no. 1, pp. 37–47, 2002.

15

Predicting Quality of Answer in Collaborative Question Answer Learning

Kohei ARAI
Graduate School of Science and Engineering,
Saga University
Saga Japan[1]

ANIK Nur Handayani
Electrical and Information Technology,
State University of Malang
Malang, Indonesia

Abstract— Studies over the years shown that students had actively and more interactively involved in a classroom discussion to gain their knowledge. By posting questions for other participants to answer, students could obtain several answers to their question. The problem is sometimes the answer chosen by student as the best answer is not necessarily the best quality answer. Therefore, an automatic recommender system based on student activity, may improve these situations as it will choose the best answer objectively. On the other side, in the implementation of collaborative learning, in addition to sharing information, sometimes students also need a reference or domain knowledge which relevant with the topic. In this paper, we proposed answer quality predictor in collaborative question answer (CQA) learning, to predict the quality of answer either from recommender system based on users activity or domain knowledge as reference information.

Keywords— *collaborative question answer learning; domain knowledge; answer quality predictor; recommender.*

I. INTRODUCTION

The concept of Collaborative Learning is two or more people learn or attempt to learn something together than independent. Different with individual learning, in collaborative learning student can exploit and share their resources and skills by asking, evaluating, monitoring one another's information and idea, etc [1]. Collaborative Learning is a model that knowledge can be created by sharing experiences within a population where members actively interact [2] [3]. Including both directly with face-to-face conversations [5] or using computer discussions (online forums, chat rooms, etc.) [6].

In [3] authors indicate that when they found some problem, students learn better when they learn together more frequently than working individually as members in a group. Indeed, the effectiveness of collaborative learning on the internet has been identified by various studies. Interaction among students is fostered as communication over the internet is unpretentious and convenient when addressing to a single user or multiple users. By posting questions for other participants to answer, students could obtain several answers to their question. The problem is sometimes the answer chosen by student as the best answer is not necessarily the best quality answer. The decision of an asker is influenced by subjective reasoning such as the relations between students, the asker's own point of view, his lack on the subject and others [7]. Therefore, an automatic recommender system may improve these situations as it will choose the best answer objectively. On the other side, in the implementation of collaborative learning, in addition to sharing information, sometimes students also need a reference or domain knowledge which relevant with the topic. The function of domain knowledge is used as knowledge about the environment in which the target information operates as a reference. In [11], we had developed collaborative question answer (CQA) using domain knowledge and answer quality predictor. Besides providing answer quality predictor as a recommender, the system also provides an answer that is taken from the domain knowledge as a reference.

In this paper, we proposed answer quality predictor in collaborative question answer (CQA) learning, to predict the quality of answer either from recommender system based on users activity or domain knowledge as reference information. With the proposed system right after collaborative answer, then answer quality predictor will give recommendation from the entire student's answer. And in the same time QA tools will extract answer from domain knowledge. The information from domain knowledge and answer quality predictor will be reprocess in the recommender system to predict as a bad, medium, or good answer. The paper is organized as follows. First is introduction for the question and answering system. Section 2 presents the proposed method. Section 3 explains implementation and result. Finally section 4 is summary and conclusion of this paper.

II. PROPOSED METHOD

Our proposed method in this paper consists of four parts. There are data collection, annotator, feature extraction, and coefficient correlation with answers. We explored Decision Trees classifier to get high precision on the target class (Weka framework used in this study [15]). Figure 1 shows the architecture of the system.

A. Data Collection

There are two kind of data, first is data that derived from Indonesian Yahoo! Answers (http://id.answers.yahoo.com/) and choosing the internet and computer category. This data had been processed through the answer quality predictor [9] [10]. For the domain knowledge we used id.wikipedia [8], there were over 100.000 articles in the Indonesian Wikipedia project. We collected 556 data from answer yahoo that could be processed in the QA tools to extract answer from domain knowledge [11].

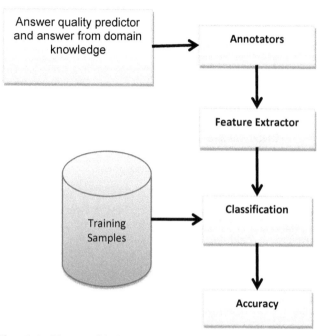

Figure1. Architecture of the System

TABLE 1. DATA COLLECTION

Category	Internet and Computer
Domain Knowledge	id.wikipedia
QA pairs	id.answeryahoo
Question	350
Answer	350
Data Training	250
Data Testing	100

The quality of a Q&A depends on the question part and answer part. For the question part we use most popular resolved question. Users could not get any useful information from bad questions. The reality bad questions always lead to bad quality answers. Therefore we decide to estimate the good answer by using annotators, and for all we got 350 Q&A pair. Table 1 shows the data collection of the research proposed.

B. Annotator

The quality of a question answer depends on both the question part and the answer part. It is often impossible to gather evaluative data about answers from the askers themselves, and that was the case here. The information of collaborative question answer is typically complex and subjective. We use annotators for manual judgment of answer quality and relevance. General, good answers tend to be relevant, information, objective, sincere and readable. We may separately measure these individual factors and combine scores to calculate overall the quality of the answer. Our annotators read answers, consider all of the above factors and specify the quality of answers in three levels: Bad, Medium and Good. Consider factors are as follows,

1. This answer provides enough information for the question. (informative)
2. This answer is polite (not offending). (polite)
3. This answer completely answers the whole question. (complete)
4. This is an easy to read answer. (readable)

5. This answer is relevant to the question. (relevant)
6. The answer contains enough detail. (detailed)
7. This answer is useful or helpful to address the question. (helpful)

C. Feature Extraction

A number of features have been identified in the literature for predicting the quality of answer. In this research, we used text feature and readability feature to predict the quality of answer. The selection of these two kinds of features based on the first Q&A pairs is already processed in the answer quality predictor; second there is internal reviewer from in term of domain knowledge system.

1) Text features are those extracted from the textual content of the articles used by [12] [13] [14]. The general intuition behind them is that a mature and good quality text is probably neither to short, which could indicate incomplete topic coverage, nor excessively long, which could indicate verbose content. We use the following features :

a) Character length: Number of characters for the answer.

b) World length: Number of words for the answer.

c) Sentences length: Number of sentences for the answer.

2) Readability Feature

These features, first used in [15], are intended to estimate the age or US grade level necessary to comprehend a text. They comprise several metrics combining counts of words and sentences. The intuition behind these features is that good information should be well written, understandable, and free of unnecessary complexity. The features are;

a) Automatic readability index (t_{rari}) : This metric was proposed in [16] and consists of using the average of word per sentence and the average of characters per words to estimate the readability.

$$t_{rari} = 4.71 \frac{characters}{words} + 0.5 \frac{words}{sentences} - 21.43 \dots (1)$$

b) Coleman Liau (t_{rcl}): This metric was proposed in [84] and consists of the average of characters per word and the number of sentences in a fragment of 100 words (w_f).

$$t_{rari} = 5.89 \frac{characters}{words} + 0.5 \, wf - 15.48 \dots (2)$$

c) The compound is a compound word or a combination of all of the basic morpheme that existed as a word that has a specifically pattern of phonological, grammatical, and semantic according to the rules of the language. The specific pattern distinguishes as a phrase or combination of words. For example, in Indonesian, kamar mandi is a compound word, while the baju hijau is the phrase while in English; the blackbird is a compound word, while the black bird is the phrase. [17]

d) Loan word is a word that derived from foreign languages that has been integrated into an Indonesian and generally accepted to be used. Indonesian has absorbing many words from other languages, especially those that have direct contact with the community, either through tarding (Sanskrit, Chinese, Arabic), or colonialism (Portuguese, Dutch, Japanese), as well as the development of science (English). [17]

e) Abstract noun is a type of noun (to explain the names of objects) which the existence could not be captured using human eyes and can only be imagined. The examples of abstract nouns are science, dreams, ideas, inspiration, happiness and others. [17]

f) Conjunction:In grammar, conjunction (abbreviated conj or cnj) is a part of speech that connects two words, sentences, phrases or clauses.

A discourse connective is a conjunction joining sentences. This definition may overlap with that of other parts of speech, so what constitutes a "conjunction" must be defined for each language. In general, a conjunction is an invariable grammatical particle, and it may or may not stand between the items it conjoins.[17]

D. Correlation Coefficient

The function of the correlation coefficient is to know how closely one variable is related to another variable [18], in this case the correlation between individual features and the annotators scores (good answers have higher scores: Bad = 0, Medium = 1, Good = 2). Table 2 shows coefficient correlation with the quality of answer. Surprisingly, all of feature has the strongest correlation with the quality of the answer, except for Auto read index and Coleman liau index.

From the calculation of Corr, we can see that text feature and readability feature affects the quality of the answers. In this study (Computer and Internet) using a lot of loan word (eg. Computer → komputer, Processor → prosesor, etc) , abstract noun word (eg. Principle →prinsip, definition → definisi, etc), and compound word (database, how it work →carakerja, etc). Auto read index and Coleman liau index is a feature used to calculate English language readability parameter. Several intelligent of United States of America used this parameter to measure readability of electronic letter. This convinced us that the character of one language is different one another.

TABLE 2. COEFFICIENT CORRELATION

Features	Correlation
Number of loan word	0.948
Number of Abstract noun word	0.999
Number of conjunction	0.828
Number of compound word	0.861
Number of char	0.971
Number of word	0.961
Number of sentence	0.928
Auto read index	0.0088
Coleman liau index	0.0002

The formula for Pearson's Correlation Coefficient:

$$r_{xy} = \frac{\sum XY - \frac{(\sum X)(\sum Y)}{n}}{\sqrt{\left[\sum X^2 - \frac{(\sum X)^2}{n_x}\right]\left[\sum Y^2 - \frac{(\sum Y)^2}{n_y}\right]}} \quad (3)$$

III. IMPLEMENT AND RESULT

We will implement the proposed methods to the Q&A pair of data. There are four kind data for the classification, first is data that acquired from the entire feature, data with high correlation (> 0.1 and > -0.1), text feature data, and readability feature data. We build the predictor using 250 training data and 100 testing data.

TABLE 3. ACCURACY OF ALL FEATURE AND CORR FEATURE

Feature	Training Set	Data Test	CV		
			5	10	15
All Feature	93.6	72.8	88.4	88.4	88.4
Corr Feature	93.2	71.2	88	88.4	88.4
Text Feature	90.4	70.4	84.4	84	83.2
Readability Feature	93.2	73.6	87.6	86.4	87.6

Table 3 shows prediction accuracy for the different implementation of answer quality, in particular comparing the choice in classifier algorithm, feature sets (using all feature, Correlation feature, text feature, and readability feature) and test option. By using C4.5 results, the best performance of the entire variant feature is all features with 93.6 of accuracy slightly adrift of 0.4 with Corr feature. We can conclude that text feature is a part of readability feature because some text feature parameter are count character, word, and sentence. For the count word parameter, in the computer and internet subject mostly users used Loan word. Another interesting result from the table 3 we could see that the differences between all features, Correlation feature and readability feature, is not too significant for accuracy it is about 0,4. This indicates that feature which does not have high correlation is not too pretty significant impact for classification results. Figure.2 shows the result classification on training data using Weka framework.

Figure 2. Result of Classification on Training Data

IV. CONCLUSION

In this paper we presented our knowledge to quantify and predict quality of answer in collaborative question answer (CQA) learning, especially for Indonesian. Beyond developing models to select best answer and evaluate the quality of answers, there are several important lessons to learn here for measuring content quality in CQA. We find that domain knowledge information sometime isn't providing good answer. On the other side students answer better than domain knowledge answer.

With appropriate features, we could build models that could have significantly higher probability of identifying the best answer class than classifying a non-best answer. From the entire system from 9 features, we conclude as following:

1) From the four existing feature, the highest accuracy exist on all feature set (comparing with correlation coefficient set, text feature set and readability feature set).

2) The best performance for all feature set by using C4.5 classifier, with averaged accuracy 93.6 for training set, 72.8 data test and 88.4 for cross validation.

In the future our models and predictions could be useful for predictor quality information as a recommender system to complete collaborative question answer learning.

ACKNOWLEDGMENT

The authors wish to thank to the students of Electrical and Information Technology State University of Malang Indonesia, who contributed and supported to the experiments.

REFERENCES

[1] Dillenbourg, P. (1999). Collaborative Learning: Cognitive and Computational Approaches. Advances in Learning and Instruction Series. New York, NY: Elsevier Science, Inc.

[2] Chiu, M. M. (2000). Group problem solving processes: Social interactions and individual actions. Journal for the Theory of Social Behavior, 30, 1, 27-50.600-631.

[3] Chiu, M. M. (2008).Flowing toward correct contributions during groups' mathematics problem solving: A statistical discourse analysis. Journal of the Learning Sciences, 17 (3), 415 – 463

[4] Mitnik, R., Recabarren, M., Nussbaum, M., & Soto, A. (2009). Collaborative Robotic Instruction: A Graph Teaching Experience. Computers & Education, 53(2), 330-342.

[5] Chiu, M. M. (2008). Effects of argumentation on group micro-creativity. Contemporary Educational Psychology, 33, 383 – 402.

[6] Chen, G., & Chiu, M. M. (2008). Online discussion processes. Computers   and Education, 50, 678 – 692

[7] Wang, C.C., Hung J.C., Yang C.Y., Shih T.K. (2006). An Apllication of Question Answering System for Collaborative Learning.   IEEE Conference on ICDCSW'06

[8] Kohei Arai, Anik Nur Handayani, Question Answering System for an Effective Collaborative Learning. (IJACSA) Vol 3. No.1, 2012. Page 60-64.

[9] Kohei Arai, Anik Nur Handayani, Predicting Quality of Answer in Collaborative Q/A Community. (IJARAI), Vol 2. No.3, 2013. Page 21-25.

[10] Kohei Arai, Anik Nur Handayani, Question Answering for Collaborative Learning with Answer Quality Predictor. (IJMECS), Vol 5. No.5, 2013. Page 12-17.

[11] Kohei Arai, Anik Nur Handayani, Collaborative Question Answering System Using Domain Knowledge and Answer Quality Predictor (IJMECS), Vol. 5 Number 11, 2013. Page 21-27

[12] Watzlawick, P. (1967) Pragmatics of Human Communications: A Study of Interactional Patterns. Pathologies and Paradoxes. W.W. Norton, New York.

[13] Smith, B. L., & MacGregor, J. T. (1992). "What Is Collaborative Learning?". National Center on Postsecondary Teaching, Learning, and Assessment at Pennsylvania State University

[14] Chiu, M. M. (2004). Adapting teacher interventions to student needs during cooperative learning. American Educational Research Journal, 41, 365-399.

[15] L. Rassbach, T. Pincock, and B. Mingus. Exploring the feasibility of automatically   rating   online   article   quality. http://upload.wikimedia.org/wikipedia/wikimania2007/d/d3/RassbachPincockMingus07.pdf.

[16] E. A. Smith and R. J. Senter. Automated readability index. 1967.

[17] http://id.wiktionary.org/wiki/Kategori:Kata_bahasa_Indonesia

[18] Chiu, M. M. (2000). Group problem solving processes: Social interactions and individual actions. for the Theory of Social Behavior, 30, 1, 27-50.600-631.

A Novel Control-Navigation System-Based Adaptive Optimal Controller & EKF Localization of DDMR

Dalia Kass Hanna, Bsc, Msc(Candidate)
Mechatronics Department
University of Aleppo
Aleppo-Syria

Abdulkader Joukhadar, Bsc, MPhil, PhD
Mechatronics Department
University of Aleppo
Aleppo-Syria

Abstract—This paper presents a newly developed approach for Differential Drive Mobile Robot (DDMR). The main goal is to provide a high dynamic system response in the joint space level, the low level control, as well as to enhance the DDMR localization. The proposed approach depends on a Linear Quadratic Regulator (LQR) for the low level control and an Adaptive LQR for the high level control. The investigated DDMR is considered highly nonlinear system due to uncertainty exhibited by the mobile robot incorporated with actuators nonlinearity. DDMR's uncertainty leads to erroneous localization. An Extended Kalman Filter (EKF) -based approach with fusion sensors is used to enhance the robot degree of belief for its posture. Intensive simulation results obtained from the developed uncertain model and the proposed approach have shown very good dynamic performance on the low level control and very good convergence to the desired posture of the mobile robot path with the presence of robot uncertainty.

Keywords—DDMR modelling; Localization; LQR; Adaptive LQR; EKF; System Uncertainty

I. INTRODUCTION

The question of "where am I?" exhibited by mobile robots, in general, remains challenging and incompletely covered in academics. The topic of mobile robot localization has been paid wide attention by academics and industry to enhance the robot performance in different aspects for which the robot can perform its motion towards any desired posture with as minimum error as possible. Different techniques proposed to enhance trajectory tracking of wheeled mobile robots. [1, 2, 3, 4] utilize EKF algorithm with fusion sensors and gyroscope to localize the robot system as close as possible to the desired posture. The disadvantages of the work presented in [1, 2] do not pay attention to the dynamic performance of the system due to robot uncertainty but they considered only the noise affecting the proprioceptive and the exteroceptive sensors.

However, in [2, 3] researchers use fusion sensors and vision sensor to help the system to be located correctly in a specific location. People in [3] implement EKF-based algorithm assisted with a gyroscope sensor to enhance the robot localization. Researchers in [3, 4] consider the proprioceptive sensors provide exact information about the robot motion in which the robot's posture is considered correct but noisy. Thus [3, 4] use EKF to purify the information about the robot's

localization. [6, 8] have proposed trajectory tracking algorithm but considered the information comes from the proprioceptive sensors is correct enough to determine the robot's posture with no lack of accuracy. The uncertainty of the mobile robot due to inaccuracy in the mechanical robot design and due to joint space inaccuracy exhibited by the mobile robot actuators lead to accumulated drift and divergence from the desired robot's posture.

This paper focuses on a novel control approach utilizing Linear Quadratic Regulator for joint space control of robot actuators as well as proposing EKF-assisted optimal controller to overcome the problem of robot uncertainty, which may lead to robot posture divergence. The proposed approach is supported by fusion sensors consisted of a gyroscope sensor (rate & accelerometer) which is fixed to the robot's center of gravity and robot's on board sensors (odometry sensors). The onboard sensors (proprioceptive sensors) assumed noisy, in addition to the robot's mechanical parameters also considered highly uncertain.

It is presumed, as well, that the mobile robot is due to some random disturbance represented by τ_d which is very common in the system control areas [3]. The remaining sections of the paper are as follows: Section II provides details about the dynamic model of the mobile robot incorporating the actuators dynamics; section III explains the design of the proposed controller for the joint space control system i.e., low level control; section IV discusses mobile robot navigation and localization; section V exhibits intensive simulation results with different system uncertainty and section VI provides a conclusion for the presented work.

II. DIFFERENTIAL DRIVE MOBILE ROBOT MODEL

A. Mobile Robot Motion Description:

The HBE-RoboCar wheeled mobile Robot (WMR) has four driving wheels, which determine the moving direction of the robot through the rotating direction and speed of wheels. This WMR uses 4-DC geared motors for operation, and each wheel has one motor mounted. The wheels in the same side (left or right) are operated together as shown in Fig.1 to follow a certain robot trajectory. Such wheeled robots called Differential Drive Mobile robot (DDMR). In this section a mathematical description of DDMR moving on a planar surface is presented.

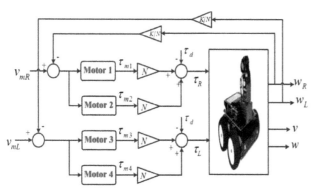

Fig.1.   Block diagram of DDMR with actuators.

Usually, the DDMR's posture is determined in its environment based on two coordinate frames: the Global frame {G} and Local Frame {L}. The global frame is fixed in the environment in which the robot moves in. The local frame attached to the DDMR at the middle point A between two back wheels. The movement of point A represents the movement of the robot [9].

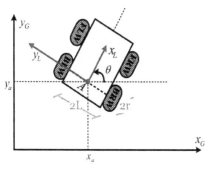

Fig.2.   DDMR Coordinates Systems

As shown in Fig.2, x_a and y_a coordinate denote the position of DDMR in the global frame. The angle θ between the moving direction of the DDMR and the positive direction of the x-axis of the global coordinate frame denotes the orientation. Symbols used in this section are listed in Table1:

TABLE I.   KINEMATIC & DYNAMIC MODEL VARIABLES:

Parameter:	Description:
$2L$	Distance between two wheels (m)
C	The center of mass
A	the middle point between two back wheels
d	Distance between A and C (m)
r	Wheel radius (m)
ω_R, ω_L	The angular velocity of the wheels ($rad.s^{-1}$)
v	The linear velocity of DDMR ($m.s^{-1}$)
ω	The angular velocity of DDMR ($rad.s^{-1}$)
N	Gear ratio
K	back emf constant ($vs.rad^{-1}$)
M	Robot mass (kg)
J	Robot moment of inertia ($kg.m^2$)
F_{uR}, F_{uL}	Tangential forces exerted on DDMR by the wheels.
F_{wR}, F_{wL}	Radial forces exerted on DDMR by the wheels.

The study of DDMR motion is divided into three parts including kinematics, dynamics and drivers [8, 9].

B. Kinematic Model of the DDMR:

Kinematics is the most basic study of how mechanical systems behave in order to model, analyze and simulate any control system design. The motion of this type of wheeled robot is classified as non-holonomic, which means, the motion constraint equations are needed to introduce into the DDMR's motion equations based on two main assumptions [9]:

- The robot can't move sideward. These non-holonomic constraints are taken into account by defining the velocity of the center point A in the local frame and forcing it to be zero. This constraint introduces in the global frame related to the velocity of point A by the following equation (1):

$$-\dot{x}_a^G \sin(\theta) + \dot{y}_a^G \cos(\theta) = 0 \qquad (1)$$

Where $q^G = \begin{bmatrix} x_a^G & y_a^G & \theta \end{bmatrix}^T$ is the coordinate of point A in the global frame.

- To simplify the model, it is assumed that each wheel has one contact point with the ground and there is no slippage in its longitudinal axis and lateral axis. The velocities of the contact points in the local frame are related to the wheel velocities by (2):

$$\begin{aligned} V_R &= r\omega_R \\ V_L &= r\omega_L \end{aligned} \qquad (2)$$

The linear and angular velocities of the DDMR related to the wheels velocities and the geometric parameters of the robot are given as follows (3):

$$\begin{aligned} v &= (V_R + V_L)/2 \\ \omega &= (V_R - V_L)/2L \end{aligned} \qquad (3)$$

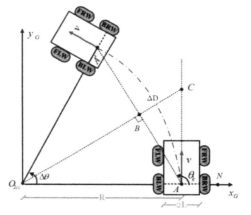

Fig.3.   The DDMR new position and orientation

To determine the new DDMR's position and orientation it is considered that the robot moves from the point A with a position (x_{-1}, y_{-1}), and orientation ($\theta_{-1} = \angle NAC$) to A' through a circular arc with an Instantaneous Center of Curvature (ICC) [2].

The increment of distance denoted by (ΔD) and orientation denoted by ($\Delta\theta$). As shown in Fig.3, based on triangular relationship the angle ($\angle CAB = \Delta\theta/2$) and the new orientation of DDMR given by (4):

$$\theta = \theta_{-1} + \Delta\theta/2 \qquad (4)$$

Considering that the increment of distance and orientation is small then $AA' = \Delta D$ and the DDMR kinematic equation is given by (5):

$$q = \begin{bmatrix} x \\ y \\ \theta \end{bmatrix} = \begin{bmatrix} x_{-1} + \Delta x \\ y_{-1} + \Delta y \\ \theta_{-1} + \Delta\theta \end{bmatrix}$$
$$= \begin{bmatrix} x_{-1} + \Delta D\cos(\theta_{-1} + \Delta\theta/2) \\ y_{-1} + \Delta D\sin(\theta_{-1} + \Delta\theta/2) \\ \theta_{-1} + \Delta\theta/2 \end{bmatrix} \qquad (5)$$

Equation (5) is called Navigation Equation also. The navigation system analysis and design are based on equation (5). Another form for the kinematic model describes the robot behavior relative to the linear and angular velocities of the DDMR which can be written as follows (6):

$$\begin{bmatrix} \dot{x}_A^G \\ \dot{y}_A^G \\ \dot{\theta} \end{bmatrix} = \begin{bmatrix} \cos\theta & 0 \\ \sin\theta & 0 \\ 0 & 1 \end{bmatrix} \begin{bmatrix} v \\ \omega \end{bmatrix} \qquad (6)$$

The velocities of the center of mass C represented in the global inertial frame are given by (7):

$$\begin{bmatrix} \dot{x}_C^G \\ \dot{y}_C^G \\ \dot{\theta} \end{bmatrix} = \begin{bmatrix} \cos\theta & -d\sin\theta \\ \sin\theta & d\cos\theta \\ 0 & 1 \end{bmatrix} \begin{bmatrix} v \\ \omega \end{bmatrix} \qquad (7)$$

Equation (7) is the relation between the velocities in local and global frames named as Guidance matrix G.

C. Dynamic Model of the DDMR:

In this subsection, the dynamic behavior of DDMR mechanisms based on Newton-Euler approach is presented [9].

By considering the free body diagram of DDMR; Fig.4 shows the forces acting on the DDMR [9].

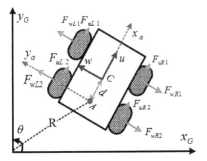

Fig.4.   Active Forces of the DDMR.

From Fig.4 the DDMR position, velocity and acceleration represented in the global frame using polar coordinate system and the equations (8) are divided using Newton's laws of motion in the robot frame:

$$M\dot{v} - Md\omega^2 = 2(\tau_R + \tau_L)/r$$
$$(Md^2 + J)\dot{\omega} + Md v\omega = 2L(\tau_R - \tau_L)/r \qquad (8)$$

where F_{uR}, F_{uL} is linearly dependent on the wheel control input as follows:

$$F_{uR} = \tau_R/r, F_{uL} = \tau_L/r$$

Equations (8) represent the dynamic model of DDMR taking into account the non-holonomic constraints [9].

III.   CONTROLLER SYSTEM DESIGN:

In this section, a controller design based on solving quadratic optimal control problem has been presented to improve the dynamic performance of the DDMR for accurate trajectory tracking.

Classical control methods are first designed and then their stability is examined. In optimal control, based on Liapunov approach the conditions for stability are formulated first and then the system is designed within these limitations. Thus, the designed system has a configuration with inherent stability characteristics [12].

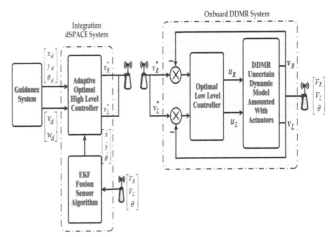

Fig.5.   Optimal High and Low Level Control Structure Based DDMR.

The proposed control scheme shown in Fig.5 has two main controllers; high level control based on kinematic model of DDMR, that; correct the robot position and orientation to follow the commanded trajectory; and low level control based on dynamic model of DDMR which follows the velocities commands given by the high level controller. Both controllers employ quadratic optimal control approach.

A. Low Level Controller:

It is presumed in subsection (II, B) that, the linear and angular velocity of the DDMR related to the wheels velocities are given by (3) then the accelerations terms of the robot velocity and orientation angular speed are given by (9):

$$\dot{v} = (\dot{V}_R + \dot{V}_L)/2$$
$$\dot{w} = (\dot{V}_R - \dot{V}_L)/2L \qquad (9)$$

By substituting (9) equations in the dynamic equation of DDMR (8):

$$\dot{V}_R = 2A\tau_R + 2B\tau_L - \eta_1 + \eta_2$$
$$\dot{V}_L = 2B\tau_R + 2A\tau_L + \eta_1 + \eta_2 \qquad (10)$$

Where η_1, η_2 are the coupling terms between the left and the right wheels. An integral optimal control is proposed to control right and left wheels velocities by inserting an integrator in the feed forward path between the error comparator and the plant.

Fig.6 shows the block diagram of the DDMR with optimal low level control.

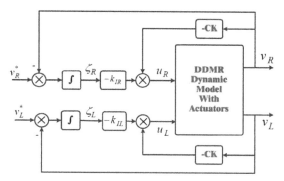

Fig.6.   DDMR with optimal low level control.

The vector control u_{op} which minimizes a selected cost function J given in (11) is determined as follow to solve the quadratic optimal control problem for the system given in (9):

$$J = \int_0^\infty (x^T Q x + u^T R u)dt \qquad (11)$$

Where:

$x_{4\times 1}$: System state vector.

$u_{2\times 1}$: Vector control.

$Q_{4\times 4}$: Positive semi-definite symmetric matrix determines the relative importance of the error.

$R_{2\times 2}$: Positive definite symmetric matrix determines the relative importance of the expenditure of the energy of the control signals.

The optimal control law is given as follows (12):

$$u_{op} = -R^{-1}B_1^{\ T}Px \qquad (12)$$

$P_{4\times 4}$ is the state covariance matrix which can be obtained from Reccati equation which is given as follows (13):

$$A^T P + PA - PB_1 R^{-1}B_1^{\ T}P + Q = 0 \qquad (13)$$

By designing the low level control system to have exponentially stable dynamic response with high dynamic performance response, the high level controller can be designed, considering linear dynamic response in the low level.

B. High Level Controller:

A proposed Adaptive Discrete Quadratic Optimal Controller formula based on DDMR kinematic system is described in this subsection. To derive the high level controller, the mathematical model of DDMR kinematic will be used. As

seen the velocities of the center of mass C represented in the global frame are given by (7).

It should be noted that the kinematic model of this type of wheeled robot is classified as nonlinear and involves non-holonomic constraints. To apply the optimal controller, a linear model of DDMR kinematic needs to be obtained. But if the linearization was about a stationary operating point the system become not controllable (In case that $\theta = 0$ and the DDMR move straightforward the information about y axes is lost. A novel technique is developed and applied on DDMR) by Adapting the discrete quadratic optimal algorithm to include this type of nonlinear systems using linear error model system along a desired trajectory [7].

First, equation (7) is discretized using the backward Euler method with sampling time T_s. The discretized form of DDMR kinematic model is obtained as shown in (14):

$$x_k = (v_k \cos\theta_{k-1} - dw_k \sin\theta_{k-1})T_s + x_{k-1}$$
$$y_k = (v_k \sin\theta_{k-1} + dw_k \cos\theta_{k-1})T_s + y_{k-1} \qquad (14)$$
$$\theta_k = w_k T_s + \theta_{k-1}$$

or :

$$x_k = f(x_{k-1}, u_k)$$

where $x_k = \begin{bmatrix} x_k & y_k & \theta_k \end{bmatrix}^T$ is the system state vector and $u_k = \begin{bmatrix} v_k & w_k \end{bmatrix}^T$ is the input vector.

Second, defining the same equations for a desired trajectory generated by Guidance System as follows (15):

$$x_{dk} = f(x_{dk-1}, u_{dk-1}) \qquad (15)$$

The posture error vector e_{xk} is given by (16):

$$\begin{bmatrix} e_{xk} & e_{yk} & e_{\theta k} \end{bmatrix}^T = \begin{bmatrix} x_{dk} & y_{dk} & \theta_{dk} \end{bmatrix}^T - \begin{bmatrix} x_k & y_k & \theta_k \end{bmatrix}^T \qquad (16)$$

The velocities error vector e_{uk} is given by (17):

$$\begin{bmatrix} e_{vk} & e_{wk} \end{bmatrix}^T = \begin{bmatrix} v_{dk} & w_{dk} \end{bmatrix}^T - \begin{bmatrix} v_k & w_k \end{bmatrix}^T \qquad (17)$$

The linear error model is given by (18):

$$e_{xk} = F_x e_{xk-1} + F_u e_{uk} \qquad (18)$$

Where:

$$F_x = \begin{bmatrix} 1 & 0 & (-v_{dk}\sin(\theta_{dk}) - dw_{dk}\cos(\theta_{dk}))T_s \\ 0 & 1 & (v_{dk}\cos(\theta_{dk}) - dw_{dk}\sin(\theta_{dk}))T_s \\ 0 & 0 & 1 \end{bmatrix}$$

$$\qquad (19)$$

$$F_u = \begin{bmatrix} T_s\cos(\theta_{dk}) & -dT_s\sin(\theta_{dk}) \\ T_s\sin(\theta_{dk}) & dT_s\cos(\theta_{dk}) \\ 0 & T_s \end{bmatrix}$$

F_x, F_u are the Jacobian matrices of the system with respect to e_{xk-1}, e_{uk} respectively which was derived around a desired trajectory. Now, considering the following discrete cost function:

$$J = \sum_0^\infty e_k^T Q e_k + u_k^T R u_k \qquad (20)$$

The closed loop system state space will be (21):

$$e_{xk} = (F_x - F_u K)e_{xk-1} \quad (21)$$

Where K is the optimal control gain vector. These errors in position and orientation of DDMR are represented in the global frame, then the errors in the local frame have been found as follows (22):

$$e_{uk} = G^{-1}e_{xk} \quad (22)$$

The velocities commands which tracked by the low level control given by (23):

$$v_R^* = (v_{dk} + e_{vk}) + L(w_{dk} + e_{wk})$$
$$v_L^* = (v_{dk} + e_{vk}) - L(w_{dk} + e_{wk}) \quad (23)$$

IV. NAVIGATION SYSTEM AND LOCALIZATION:

The robot navigation is the task of an autonomous robot to move safely from one location to another [13]. To make a truly autonomous robot an accurate localization is a key problem for successful navigation systems [4, 11].

The objective is to accurately determine DDMR's posture involving sensor noise uncertainties and potential failures in an optimal way with respect to a global or local frame of reference by integrating (fusing) kinetic information received from proprioceptive sensors (odometry and gyroscope) which give the robot feedback about its driving actions and obtaining knowledge about DDMR's environment [13].

In mobile robot navigation systems, onboard navigation sensors based on dead-reckoning are widely used. Dead reckoning is the process of calculating DDMR's current position by using a previously determined position and estimated speeds over the elapsed time [2, 5].

In the present section, EKF sensor fusion method is used for the estimation of DDMR's accurate posture and eliminates the effect of uncertainty associated with the system.

The Extended Kalman filter (EKF) is a recursive optimum stochastic state estimator which can be used for parameter estimation of a non-linear dynamic system in real time by using noisy monitored signals that are disturbed by random noise [14, 15, 16].

The EKF has been widely used for mobile robot navigation and system integration to address the nonlinearity in the system kinematic.

The goal of the EKF is to estimate the unmeasurable state (e.g. DDMR's posture) by using measured states, and also statistics of the noise and measurement (i.e. covariance matrices Q, R, P of the system noise vector, measurement noise vector, and system noise vector respectively) [15, 16, 17]. So the problem of mobile robot localization can usually not be sensed directly. The robot has to integrate data over time to determine its pose as accurate as possible using EKF fusion sensors method [4].

In order to apply the EKF algorithm [15], first, a discrete time Navigation Model for the DDMR based on equation (6) using the backward Euler method with sampling time T_s has been obtained (24):

$$\begin{bmatrix} x_k \\ y_k \\ \theta_k \end{bmatrix} = (1/2)\begin{bmatrix} T_s\cos(\theta) & T_s\cos(\theta) \\ T_s\sin(\theta) & T_s\sin(\theta) \\ T_s/L & -T_s/L \end{bmatrix}\begin{bmatrix} V_{Rk} \\ V_{Lk} \end{bmatrix} + \begin{bmatrix} x_{k-1} \\ y_{k-1} \\ \theta_{k-1} \end{bmatrix} \quad (24)$$

Second, note that equation (24) is nonlinear. So, in order to apply EKF algorithm, a linear approximation of Navigation Equation using Taylor series have to be obtained as follows (25):

$$x_k = J_x x_{k-1} + J_u u_k \quad (25)$$

where:

$$x_k = \begin{bmatrix} x_k & y_k & \theta_k \end{bmatrix}$$
$$u_k = \begin{bmatrix} V_{Rk} & V_{Lk} \end{bmatrix}$$

The terms J_x, J_u are the Jacobian which are obtained by differentiating equation (24) with respect to the state vector and input vector respectively (26):

$$J_x = \begin{bmatrix} 1 & 0 & -v_k T_s\sin(\theta) \\ 0 & 1 & v_k T_s\cos(\theta) \\ 0 & 0 & 1 \end{bmatrix}$$

$$J_u = (1/2)\begin{bmatrix} T_s(\cos(\theta) - \frac{v_k}{2L}\sin(\theta)) & T_s(\cos(\theta) + \frac{v_k}{2L}\sin(\theta)) \\ T_s(\sin(\theta) + \frac{v_k}{2L}\cos(\theta)) & T_s((\sin(\theta) - \frac{v_k}{2L}\cos(\theta)) \\ T_s/L & -T_s/L \end{bmatrix} \quad (26)$$

The EKF algorithm contains basically two main stages [10], Fig.7:

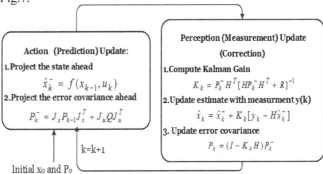

Fig.7. EKF Fusion Sensors Recursive Algorithm.

1) Action (or prediction) update:

Having a priori knowledge implies that x_{k-1}, P_{k-1} are initializing, the robot moves and estimates its position through its ideal proprioceptive sensors u_k.

$$\hat{x}_k^- = f(x_{k-1}, u_k) \quad (27)$$

The covariance matrix after moving is given by (28):

$$P_k^- = J_x P_{k-1} J_x^T + J_u Q J_u^T \quad (28)$$

During this step, the robot uncertainty grows.

2) Perception (or measurements) update:

The robot makes an observation using its uncertain model and corrects its position by opportunely combining its belief before the observation with the probability of making exactly that observation. The Kalman gain is chosen to minimize the estimation error variance of the states to be estimated.

$$K_k = P_k^- H^T [HP_k^- H^T + R]^{-1} \qquad (29)$$

The predicted state estimate $\hat{x}_k$ (and also its covariance matrix P_k) is corrected recursively through a feedback correction scheme which is the product of the Kalman gain K and the deviation of the estimated measurement output vector and the actual output vector ($y - \hat{y}$) that makes use of the actual measured quantities.

$$\hat{x}_k = \hat{x}_k^- + K_k [y_k - H\hat{x}_k^-]$$
$$P_k = (I - K_k H)P_k^- \qquad (30)$$

During this step, the DDMR uncertainty shrinks. If one looks at the problem of probabilistically, one can say that the robot has a degree of belief (*bel*) about where it is [5].

The goal of localization is to make this belief get as close as possible to the real distribution of the robot location. The robot incorporates these measurements into its belief to form a new belief about where it is [5].

The determinant of P_k provides a good measure of uncertainty as it is proportional to the volume of the deviation error ellipsoid. [5]

The degree of belief is given by (31):

$$bel = 1 - \sqrt{\det(P_k)} \quad where \quad 0 < bel \le 1 \qquad (31)$$

The higher $det(P_k)$ is the less degree of belief there is in the measurements.

V.   SIMULATION RESULTS:

This section, several test results are demonstrated for the proposed control-navigation system based DDMR using MATLAB/ SIMULINK and C code.

The kinematics and dynamics model of the DDMR described in section II are used. The simulation is carried out by tracking different 3 DOFs desired paths with the high and low level control system of the DDMR. The proposed control-navigation system is implemented based on the structures shown in Fig. 5.

The DDMR with optimal low level control has been tested. Fig. 8.a shows the time response of the right and left motor wheels linear velocities and their corresponding control law i.e., actuator voltage control respectively to a step input command simulated using MATLAB/ Simulink.

As seen from Fig. 8(a, b) the dynamic system response for the right and left wheels is high, and they converge to the desired set value exponentially with no overshot in the system response i.e., the equivalent damping ratio of the system is $\zeta=1$. It is noted that the low level dynamic system is exponentially stable and shows high dynamic performance response with the limitation of $\pm 12 volt$

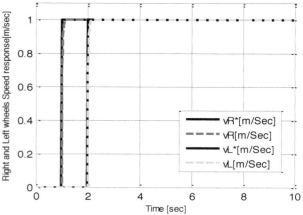

a.   Time Response for step commend

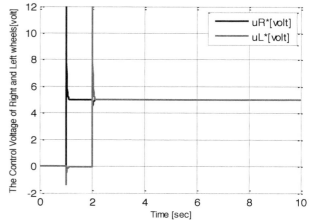

b.   Motors voltages for left and right wheels

Fig.8.   Time responses of the right and left wheels velocity

Two experiments were performed and compared for DDMR with adaptive optimal high level control, with several trajectories to examine the robot dynamic performance, one was implemented utilizing only the onboard sensors data, and the other used EKF assisted fusion sensors method as navigation system considering different system uncertainty.

A. Square Trajectory Tracking:

This section demonstrates the mobile robot control performance to a square path with a side length of 1 meter. Fig. 9 shows the system dynamic response for the high-level control. As seen in Fig 9 that the system exhibited advancement trajectory tracking with a high degree of localization belief has explained by Fig. 10.

As observed in Fig. 10 that the mobile robot system control in the high-level is very certain in its location i.e., where I am, since the degree of belief is high which is also very convincing indicator since the trajectory tracking error is negligible.

Fig. 11 shows the mobile robot speed response, as seen in Fig. 11 the robot moved with maximum speed value 0.14 m.sec^{-1}

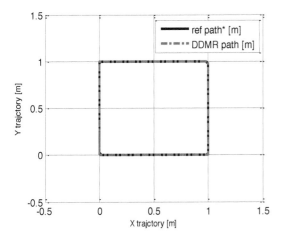

Fig.9. Square Trajectory EKF sensor fusion performance

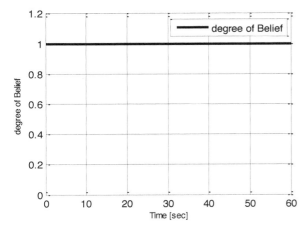

Fig.10. The Degree of Belief for System Navigation

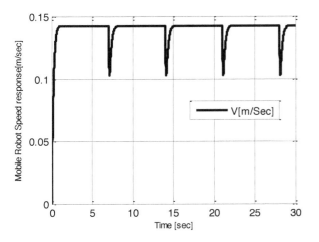

Fig.11. Speed Response of Mobile Robot

B. Eight Shape Trajectory Tracking:

This section provides two case simulation results for 8-shape. These are simulation without system uncertainty and with system uncertainty. As seen in Fig. 12, the robot system tracks correctly the system the desired path (blue) and (red) real trajectory.

The result, in this case, of Fig. 12, was obtained assuming the system is certain and there is no need to use any correction technique to correct the trajectory tracking.

It is seen that the system exhibited a very good convergence to the desired posture of DDMR. The same system is now tested presuming such uncertainty the robot model. It is to kindly remind the reader that the system is to work with no correction technique.

As seen in Fig. 13 the robot dynamics showed a remarkable divergence in the system trajectory tracking (see 'black' reference trajectory and 'blue' real trajectory).

Fig. 14 shows the robot's dynamic performance for an 8-shape with presence of uncertainty in the mobile robot, but the control system was supported with a correction technique for posture correction ('blue' is the reference trajectory, and 'cyan' the real trajectory).

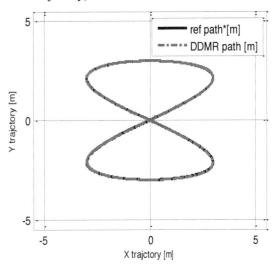

Fig.12. DDMR Trajectory Tracking with Adaptive Optimal Control.

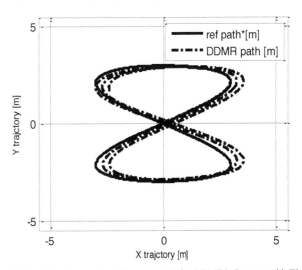

Fig.13. The Accumulated Divergence in the DDMR's Posture with Time

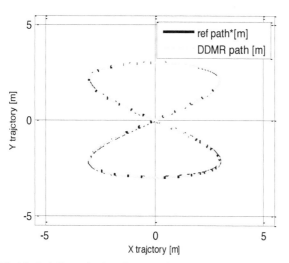

Fig.14. Path Correction based EKF Fusion Sensors Algorithm.

Fig. 15 shows that the proposed Control-Navigation system enhances the robot's belief at different points in time. The solid line displays the actions, and the ellipsoids represent the uncertainty effects on the robot's dynamic performance for the trajectory.

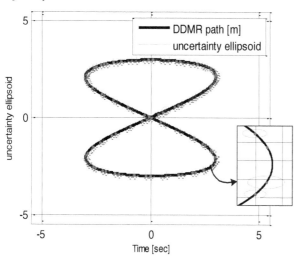

Fig.15. The Posture Believe's DDMR for 8 Shape.

C. Flower Shape Trajectory Tracking:

More complex trajectory is used to examine the robot dynamic performance without the presence of uncertainty and with uncertainty. The system dynamic performance is shown in Figures 16, 17, 18 and 19. As noticed in Fig. 19 that the system showed high dynamic performance control for which is the system is capable to correctly track the desired path and even ensure high degree of belief for the robot posture.

It can be observed that better performance control in real time has been obtained by integrating the control system (Low and high levels) with EKF fusion sensors approach to make the control system sensitive to the effects of the environment and able to eliminate the uncertainty effect.

VI. CONCLUSION

This paper has proposed a newly developed approach to enhance the dynamic response of a differential drive mobile robot with the presence of huge system uncertainty. The developed approach has considered a low-level system control developed on the joint space level (the actuators control level) and on the Cartesian space level control i.e., high-level control. For low-level control optimal type controllers (optimal and integral optimal) have been proposed for the actuator velocity control. It has been shown that the dynamic control response of the actuators is high and robust to system uncertainty.

In the high-level control, the system has been incorporated with Extended Kalman Filter (EKF) to estimate, as accurate as possible, the mobile robot posture. Simulation results obtained from the developed control system have shown that a large divergence was due to occur because of system uncertainty, which may lead to erroneous system localization as well as exhibited low degree of belief in the robot location. The proposed control approach in high-level domain overcomes the problem of robot's posture mismatch and tries to correct and compensate the trajectory tracking which may happen due to uncertainty.

The interactive navigation process with the degree of belief, which reflects how the present robot's posture is close to the desired one. The validation of the proposed approach for low-level and high-level control has been confirmed through intensive simulation results obtained for different cases in which the robot has been imposed with uncertainty. As explained the proposed technique has given very encouraging results and has provided very good target tracking with high degree of belief for the robot localization. This work presented in this paper is basis for future. It is to be used for real time implementation for Mobile robot localization system control on the high and low levels identification e.g. UKF in real time utilizing **dSPACE** system board.

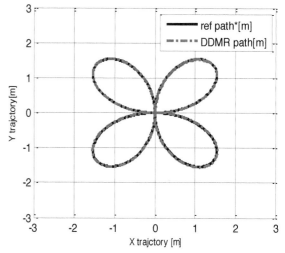

Fig.16. DDMR Trajectory Tracking with Adaptive Optimal Control

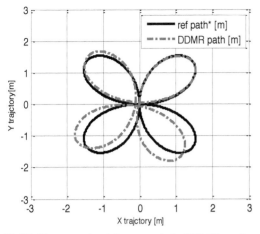

Fig.17. The accumulated divergence in the DDMR's posture with time.

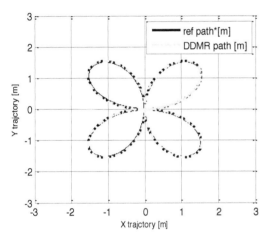

Fig.18. Path Correction based EKF Fusion Sensors Algorithm.

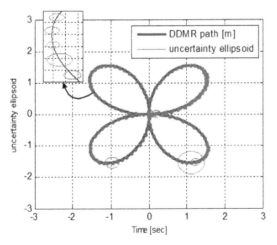

Fig.19. The Posture Believe's DDMR for flower shape.

ACKNOWLEDGEMENT

The authors would like to thank the Syrian Society for Scientific Research (SSSR) for the financial support provided to cover SAI conference registration fee.

REFERENCES

[1] Q. Meng, Y. Sun and Z. Cao "Adaptive Extended Kalman Filter (AEKF)-Based Mobile Robot Localization Using Sonar," Robotica (2000), United Kingdom, Cambridge University Press, vol. 18, pp. 459-473, (December 1999).

[2] Y. Liu, Navigation and Control of Mobile Robot Using Sensor Fusion, Robot Vision, Ales Ude (Ed.), InTech, Available from: http://www.intechopen.com/books/robot-vision/navigationand-control-of-mobile-robot-using-sensor-fusion, (2010).

[3] S. Panich and N. Afzulpurkar "Mobile Robot Integrated with Gyroscope by using IKF," International Journal of Advanced Robotic Systems, vol. 8, No. 2, pp. 122-136, (2011).

[4] R. Negenborn, "Robot Localization and Kalman Filters On Finding Your Position in a Noisy World", UTRECHT UNIVERSITY (september 2003).

[5] S. Thrun, D. Fox and W. Burgard, "PROBABILISTIC ROBOTICS" Massachusttes Institute of Technology (2006).

[6] P. Jensfelt, "Approaches to Mobile Robot Localization in Indoor Environments", Royal Institute of Technology (KTH), (2001).

[7] F. Kühne,W.F.Lages and Gomes da Silva Jr, "Model Predictive Control of a Mobile Robot using Linearization,", IEEE Latin-American Robotics Symposium, pp. 525-530, (2005).

[8] K. Kozlowski and D. Pazderski, "Modeling and Control of a 4-wheel Skid- Steering Mobile Robot,", Int. J. Appl. Math. Comput. Sci., vol. 14, pp. 477-496, (2004).

[9] R. Dhaouadi and A. Abu Hatab "Dynamic Modelling of Differential-Drive Mobile Robots using Lgrange and Newton-Euler Methodologies: AUnified Framework," Advance in Robotics & Automation, vol. 2, (Autom 2013).

[10] S. Haykin, "Kalman Filtering and Neural Networks", A Wiley-Interscience Publication, (2001).

[11] R. Siegwart and I. R. Nourbakhsh, "Introduction to Autonomous Mobile Robots", The MIT Press,Cambridge, Massachusetts London, England, (2004).

[12] K. Ogata, "Designing Linear Control Systems With MATLAB", Prentice Hall,(1994).

[13] P. Corke, " Robotics, Vision and Control Fundamental Algorithms in MATLAB", Springer Tracts in Advanced Robtics, vol 73, (2011).

[14] J.P. Norton, "An Introduction to Identification", Harcourt Brace Jovanovich, Publishers,(1986)

[15] P.S.Maybeck,"Stochastic models, estimation, and control", Harcourt Brace Jovanovich, Publishers,(,vol 1, (1982)

[16] P.S.Maybeck,"Stochastic models, estimation, and control", Harcourt Brace Jovanovich, Publishers,(,vol 2, (1982)

[17] P.S.Maybeck,"Stochastic models, estimation, and control", Harcourt Brace Jovanovich, Publishers,(,vol 3, (1982)

A Design of a Multi-Agent Smart E-Examiner

Khaled Nasser ElSayed

Computer Science Department, Umm AlQura University

Abstract—this paper proposes a design of an application of multi agent technology on a semantic net knowledge base, to build a smart e-examiner system. This e-examiner could be used in building and grading a personalized special on-line e-assessment. The produced e-assessment should cover the majority of examined topics and material. It should cover various levels of difficulties and learners profile(s). The e-examiner will use a semantic net question bank, to emphasize on the structuring categories of all course domains. This task is done through four different intelligent agents: control agent, personal agent, examiner agent, and grading agent. The system might select questions from a bank of questions for several courses. It could be used in different education levels and natures. Also, it will produce a key for the produced exam, to be used latter in grading, and giving final marks of e-assessments.

Keywords—m-Learning; e-Assessments; Multi-agent; Semantic net; Examiner

I. INTRODUCTION

The e-learning and m-learning are considered the important ways to respond to the needs of the d-learning. Many traditional learning styles should be applied together with the learner-centered approach to represent the needs of the e-learning system [1].

Software educational systems have become highly complex in both concept and design in the education of most sciences. In these systems, there is a wide difference between the role of the computer from solely a transmitter of knowledge and using it as a tool that aids in the construction of knowledge, as in [2].

There are an increasing number of AI algorithms and applications that are applied in tutoring and education systems. One of the AI techniques is the intelligent agent, which could be widely used in education. An intelligent agent is an autonomous calculated entity.

An intelligent agent could collect personal interests of the learner (s) and user (s) to give instance response according to the pre-specified demands of them. A personal one can discover their personal interests easily without disturbing them. So, it is suitable for personalized e-learning by recommending selected suitable learning materials [3].

An agent could detect by its sensors and perform actions on its environment by actuators to achieve target goals. The intelligent agent could learn new knowledge and uses it in achieving target goals. It might be simple procedure or program to perform simple goal or task. Also, it could be a complicated system working as a group of persons co-operated together towards a target goal [4].

A multi-agent system is constructed from a several intelligent agents, cooperated and interacted together to achieve target goal(s) within an environment. It could solve problems that are difficult be solved with an individual agent [5].

Adaptive learning is a learner-centric and individualized learning. The target of this learning may be certain learner or group of learner have a public feature(s). According to that, each learner could select chapters, exercises, and remedial actions even the curriculum relative to his individual's mental state. Then the learning system can maintain a dynamic knowledge for learners. It monitors the learner's behavior and stores his mental model which could be used in identifying the causes of the student performance [6].

Nowadays, there are many tools help in producing assessments. Advanced eLearning Builder [7] is an Authoring tool designed for creating e-learning materials such as e-tests, tutorials and quizzes in visual mode and compiling them in EXE form. Also, MicroGrade and Micro Test [8] are desktop applications with built-in access to hosted Internet sites for secure test delivery and grade posting for Windows and Macintosh compatible. While, OnlineTesting offers in [9] software and programming services to offer online quizzes and tests through the Internet or within an Intranet.

There are many other software tools for producing assessments like; ProPrfos [10], Adit Sofware [11], Quizworks [12] and ExamJet [13]. Majority of those software tools enable the human examiner to select questions or the question are selected randomly.

This paper presented a design of a multi-agent based smart e-examiner system. This design is for building a personalized e-assessment according to the study, level and profile of the learner(s). It builds its semantic net as object oriented knowledge base (question KB) to be filled with questions that cover the materials of topics of courses. Then it is running its four agents (control agent, personal agent, examiner agent and grading agent) on that question KB to select questions and building e-assessments according to learner(s) education level and profile data. The e-examiner agent gets its intelligence from watching and learning from the human examiner to enhance the selection of questions. It is designed for education in academic institutions, training centers, human resources departments. Also, it can help human examiners in producing their own assessments.

II. CATEGORIES OF GENERATED QUESTIONS

Questions are the infrastructure of the system, which could be generated for building an e-assessment. These questions and their answers from several e-courses construct the semantic net question KB. There are four categories of exercises; each includes a number of questions of that category.

- **The Multiple Choice Category**; where a question could be a text (sentence), while the answer is one correct choice from available four multiple choices (might be less). The answer of this category will be checked and graded by the e-examiner system, as shown in Figure 1-a.

a.

1	Which of the following languages have case-sensitive names?
T	❑ C++
	❑ COBOL
	❑ Fortran
	❑ Pascal

b. Verifies whether or not the string can be generated by grammar.
    Answer: ☐ **True** ☐ **False**

c. A.......... determines the order in which operators of equal Precedence are evaluated when they occur in the same expression
(Associativity, Availability, Precedence, Mandatory)

d. Consider the following XX **grammar:**
    LP → LP FUNC (PAR ; PAR) | LP (PAR) | exec
    FUNC → ID
    PAR → LP | NUM

    Note: (**NUM** is the token for numbers and **ID** is the token for identifiers).
    Answer the following questions:
- Give the equivalent grammar after removing the left

    recursion from the above grammar

- Derive the following string from LP.

            exec svg (exec max (2 ; 5) ; 4)

Fig. 1.   Examples of Question Types stored in Question KB

- **The True/False Category**; where a question could be a text (sentence), while the answer should be one of two options (true or false), it is a logical choice. The answer of this category will be checked and graded by the e-examiner system. An example of this category is shown in Figure 1-b.

- **The Fill in the Blanks Category**; where a question could be a text (sentence), while the answer is one-word/simple-sentence to be selected from a pool-from 2 to 10- of words/small sentences. So, the process of filling in the spaces looks like matching certain question with a suitable answer. The answer of this category will be checked and graded by the e-examiner system. An example of this category is shown in Figure 1-c.

- **The General Category**; where a question could be in a form differs than each of the above 3 forms. It could be a long or short text, including graphs, equations, or numbers. Also, it could be imported from an external file. While the answer could be a free text including graphs, equation, or whatever the examined person want to write. Answer of this category of question should be checked and graded manually, by the examiner/ instructor. An example of this category is shown in Figure 1-d.

III. Main Components of the E-Examiner

The proposed e-examiner system consists mainly, as shown in Figure 2, of four components; each component cooperates with each other to prove the system generality.

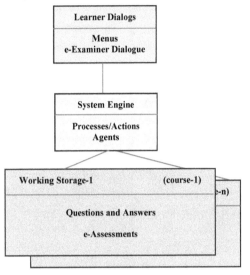

Fig. 2.   Structure of the e-examiner system

- **Learner Dialog**; which is a menu-driven dialog for easing learner interaction with the e-examiner system directly. After finishing certain topics or certain course or part of course, he will navigate this dialog, thin the e-examiner will start creation of a personalized e-assessment special to that learner. After passing answers of a learner to the e-examiner, it will check and grade his answers, and update the profile of that learner.

- **System Engine**; which involves four intelligent agents, as shown in Figure 3. The first agent is the control agent, which controls the process and agents. The second intelligent agent creates, fills and updates personal profiles of the examined learners. While the third agent will serve in selecting questions and create a personalized e-assessment and learns from the instructor examiner by watching him and gets from his experience, at editing questions or at creating exams. The fourth agent is the grading agent, which is responsible of checking and grading learner answers.

- **Question Bank Knowledge Base**; which is a semantic network KB, as shown in Figure 4. It consists of nodes like: exams, exercise, questions, answers and links (relations between nodes). Its structure is based on object oriented analysis of application domains. It holds an indexing structure used by the inference engine to locate questions. Each node or link is represented by an object of a suitable class.

- **Working Storages**; where each working storage is assigned to certain topic, chapter or course. The e-examiner system can be switched from one working storage to another.

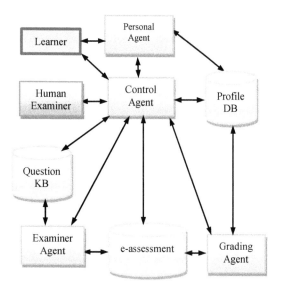

Fig. 3.   Intelligent Agents in e-examiner system Agent

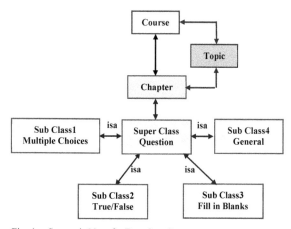

Fig. 4.   Semantic Net of e-Examiner System

IV.   BUILDING THE QUESTION KB

A topic (course) material as application domain is analyzed using object oriented techniques to be used to create e-assessment. This e-assessment should cover that material completely or even a part(s) of it the learner profile and studying. Each domain is defined as objects like courses, topics, chapters, assessment exercises, questions, attributes, answers and relationships between these objects.

This question KB is designed, as shown in Figure 4, to be instantiated for several course, one course at a time. In the first use of the e-examiner, name of college or institute, department, and courses could be identified. Then, questions and their answered could be edited.

A. Organization of the Question KB

Questions to select from, should be distributed over the question KB, which designed and organized in certain manner that enables the e-examiner to select questions randomly according the learner(s) profile and e-assessment factors, which are supervised by the intelligent agents.

At editing questions to be acquired, the editor will provide the KB with certain information to be used later as a basis for the e-examiner to select a set of questions for certain e-assessment. It should takes in consideration, that the e-assessment should cover majority or even specified parts of course material and should include various levels of difficulties.

The KB is designed to deal with the categories of question listed in the previous section. Its entity classes are fulfilled with attributes that lead it to be suitable to acquire the knowledge learned from the examiner at building e-assessments. It has one Super Class and 4 Sub Classes, which has to be suitable to hold all categories of question listed in the previous section.

*1) **The Super Class question** is the base for all categories of questions. It has some important attributes that are inherited by the other four sub classes. These attributes include a string attribute for the question text, pointer to the chapter or topic related to, and pointers to two lists of links (relations). It also, includes an attribute for learner answer of that question.*

The first type of links are to the reminded questions – questions that are suggested to be with that a certain question in the same e-assessment. While, the second type of links are to the rejected questions –questions that are not allowed to be with that a certain question in the same e-assessment. The other four sub classes should have the inherited attributes of the super class, in addition to special attributes as listed below.

*2) **The Sub Class for Multiple Choice Questions**; which have many special attributes: four string attributes for predicted choices, and character attribute to denote the correct choice.*

*3) **The Sub Class for True/False Questions**; which have only one special attribute, which is a binary attribute. This attribute will hold the answer, which is 1 (for True question text) or 0 (for False Question text).*

*4) **The Sub Class for Filling in Blanks Questions**; which have only one special attribute, which is a string attribute to hold the correct text to be filled in the spaces.*

*5) **The Sub-Class for General Questions**; which have only one special attribute, to hold the complete answer of the generic question. Contents of this attributes could be imported from an external file. This answer could be edited or imported from a file.*

B. Filling the Question KB

Question KB should be initiated for each course individually by certain information, like course code and name, department and/or institute offering that course; number of predicted chapter (could be modified latter by increasing or decreasing certain chapter). For each chapter, questions and their answers according to the four previous question types, listed before in section II, could be supplied to the system.

The human examiner starts supplying questions to the e-examiner. First, he selects the course, topic, chapter, and one question type of those listed in section II. Then, he supplies the question text, accompanied with all needed information as described in section III. Then, e-examiner will fill the KB tables with questions and their related knowledge.

Knowledge within the two lists of links could be acquired at entering a new question or be learnt from the human examiner when he add/rejects certain question.

V. Intelligent Agents and an E-Assessment

The process of building an e-assessment should emphasize that each course include a number of chapters/topics. Some or all of these chapters could be covered by the e-assessment. This will help the e-examiner in selecting questions from the specified chapters or topics. Also, dividing a course into chapters helps to divide assessment into logical parts and "accumulate" assessment question KB (for example, you have 500 questions, but single e-assessment consists of 20 questions that are randomly selected from the KB).

A. Role of Agents in the e-Examiner System

As seen in Figure 3, the e-examiner system has four agents; each of them has its important role in the main process of building and grading of an e-assessment, as described below:

- **Control Agent (CA)** is responsible of managing the process of building and grading of e-assessments. It controls and initiates other agents.

- **Personal Agent (PA)** is responsible of gathering information about learner and saving it in profile file. It also retrieves and updates his profile file.

- **Examiner Agent (EA)** is responsible of **selection** of question from question KB. It uses random and mathematical functions in additions to the knowledge resides in the relations between different questions to pick the best choices from many enumerated possibilities. It manipulates questions and other objects and the in-between relations in a standard way with all presented topic(s) or chapter(s). It watches the examiner when he requests to remove/add certain questions from/to the e-assessment produced by the system (in the training phase). It has its actions on the knowledge in the relation between questions for next e-assessment building.

- **Grading Agent (GA)** is responsible of checking and grading e-assessments passed by certain learner(s). It compares answers of learner with answers stored with questions in question KB. Then, it updates profiles of examined learner(s), according to grading results.

B. Criteria of an e-Assessment

The presented e-examiner is a comprehensive solution for building e-assessments on the Internet and Intranet and grading those e-assessments. It can easily select all exercises types and format the text, add graphics, formulas in offline and online e-assessments.

In the offline e-assessments, the tool can produces an e-assessment to be printed and copied to be distributed over students in a class. Also, it will produce a key for each e-assessment, to help the examiner to check answers of the examined people, and grading their e-assessment.

E-examiner does the process of building an e-assessment, as shown in Fig. 5, it emphasized the following criteria:

- The heading interface of the e-assessment is fully customizable.

- E-examiner supports multi-language.

- Questions and answers could be shuffled randomly (for every particular question), to avoid any fraud by people who pass your tests.

- Unlimited number of questions in a single test and up to 4 answers in multiple choices.

- E-examiner system is trained in the beginning under supervision of the human examiner.

- Then the whole process is fully automated.

C. Initiating the e-examiner System

Before using the e-examiner system on-line with learners to generate e-assessment(s), it has to be initialized and trained to be ready for its work. Also, it will be adjusted to produce off line assessments.

For producing assessments using e-examiner system, the human examiner should initiate the assessment by supplying some information like the name, top introduction, bottom conclusion, and logo of the examining institute. Then, he should provide course name and chapters to be covered in the assessment to be selected from those available in the question KB.

Some optional data -could be applied to the system like: Academic year, Semester, Student sections, e-assessment duration, maximum score, e-assessment type (midterm, quiz, final), sort of e-assessment (A, B), total mark. While for online/offline assessment, the human examiner should specify the types of exercises in the assessment, number of question in each, and the mark specified for each exercise.

VI. Building and Grading an E-Assessment

The e-examiner system can start production of offline/online assessments under the supervision the human examiner. Then it can generate e-assessment alone with no need to guidance from human examiner.

A. Training of the e-Examiner by Human Examiner

In first use of the e-examiner system, it should passes through a training session to build e-assessments under the supervision of a human examiner, as seen in the algorithm shown in Figure 5.

The EA agent will get its experience by watching the human examiners, in two different situations.

First, at editing a question; when the human examiner specifies that some question(s) are preferred to be in the same e-assessment or should prevented from being in the same e-assessment with that question.

Secondly, at building an e-assessment, when the human examiner asks to remove certain question(s) or adds certain ones.

1. **PA agent GETS e-Assessment Data:** Course, Chapters covered, From Learner(s) profile
2. **CA agent GETS Exercise Data:** number of exercises, type, number of questions in each exercise from Human examiner
3. **CA agent CALCULATES** Number of questions in each exercise from each Chapter.
4. **For each exercise in the e-assessment Do**
5.   **Do Until end of questions in the exercise**
        EA agent SELECTS a question using Random function & Links
        EA agent CHECKS Reminding & Rejection links in the relationships of the question KB net.
6.   **CA agent DISPLAY** Complete exercise to the human examiner.
7.   **IF NOT APPROVED** (by human examiner)
8.   **EA agent GETS** rejections and reasons, suggestions and reasons (reminding), **UPDATE** links of the question KB, and **UPDATES** exercise.
9.   **ELSE CONTINUE** (go to 4)
10. **CA agent CONSULTS complete e-Assessment to human examiner**

Fig. 5.   Algorithm for Training the e-Examiner System

At beginning a session to build an e-assessment from the question KB, e-examiner system performs its task through several steps, which incorporates knowledge acquisition and learning with knowledge retrieval from its question KB, based on intelligent agents.

The e-examiner asks the examiner about type of each exercise and its number of questions. It calculates number of questions per each chapter by mathematical functions.

Then, EA agent starts a process of selection questions, one by one, until finishing selecting. This selection is based on random function and according to the reminding and rejecting knowledge resides in the links between each question and other questions in the question KB.

The e-examiner consults selection results in a complete exercise to the human examiner for approval. Sometimes, she/he removes certain question or adds another question. In this case, the EA agent asks her/him for explanation.

 This explanation is acquired to a rejecting knowledge in case of refusing certain question, and to a reminding knowledge in case of adding certain questions. This knowledge will reside in the links between any requested question and other questions in the question KB.

After performing the requested modification, the tool, finally, produces a file including the final form of the e-assessment or the quiz. This e-assessment version should be reviewed by the human examiner. Also, the e-examiner system produces a key for questions.

B. The e-Examiner Builds an e-Assessment

After the e-examiner passed about 50 training sessions in building e-assessments, under the supervision of a human examiner, it is ready to build its own e-assessment, depending on his knowledge. It builds its e-assessments, as shown in Figure 6, depending on the learner profile data and the regulations acquired from before the human examiner.

C. e-Examiner Grades an e-Assessment

The grading process of an e-assessment is done so easily by the e-examiner system. At selecting certain question to add to an e-assessment, the EA agent retrieves its answer from the question KB, attached with it. Then the GA agent compares the answer of learner with the answer retrieved from the question KB. If they are the same, it accumulates a one degree to the total degrees collected by the learner in that e-assessment. Finally, it gives the total degree to the PA agent to update the learner profile data.

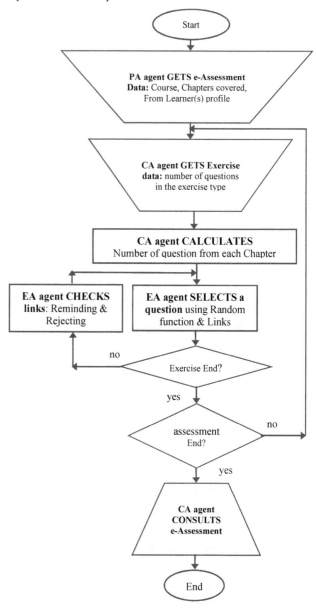

Fig. 6.   Building an e-assessment by the e-examiner system

VII. Conclusions

The presented paper presented a design of a smart e-examiner system, which is running four intelligent agents on a semantic net of question KB. Its agents; control agent, personal agent, examiner agent, and grading agent co-operated together to perform its task of producing and grading personalized e-assessment, depending on learner studying and level.

The system should start its work under the supervision of human examiner. The examiner agent (EA) got experience by watching the human examiner, in two different situations: at editing a question; when the he specifies that some question(s) are preferred to/not-to be prevented from being in the same e-assessment with that question, and at building e-assessment; when the examiner asks to remove certain question(s) or add certain ones.

The e-examiner system could be used on various education level and nature to generate e-assessments for employees and students in training courses. Also, it produced a key for the produced e-assessment, to be used in grading, and giving final marks of e-assessments. Future work will include enhancing system architecture and improving its security and reading IP address of learner.

REFERENCES

[1] Zhi Liu & Bo Chen, "Model and Implement an Agent Oriented E-Learning System", the International Conference on Computational Intelligence for Modeling, Control and Automation, and International Conference Intelligent Agents, Web Technologies and Internet Commerce, Vienna (CIMCA-IAWTIC'05) 0-7695-2504-0/05, 28-30 Nov.2005, pp. 859–864. http://doi.ieeecomputersociety.org/10.1109/CIMCA.2005.1631576

[2] J. Anderson, F. Boyle, A. Corbett, and M. Lewis, "Cognitive Modeling and Intelligent Tutoring", Elsevier Science Publishers, Journal Artificial Intelligence, Special issue on artificial intelligence and learning environments archive, vol. 42, no. 1, pp. 7-49, Feb. 1990. http://act-r.psy.cmu.edu/wordpress/wp-content/uploads/2012/12/119CogMod_IntTut.pdf

[3] Jin-Ling Lin and Ming-Hung Chen, "An Intelligent Agent for Personalized E-Learning", 8th Inter. Conference on Intelligent Systems Design and Applications - Volume 01, Kaohsiung, 26-28 Nov. 2008, pp. 27-31. http://ieeexplore.ieee.org/xpl/articleDetails.jsp?arnumber=4696172

[4] S. J. Russell, and P. Norvig, (2009, Dec. 11), *Artificial Intelligence – A Modern Approach*, 3rd Ed., Prentice Hall. http://stpk.cs.rtu.lv/sites/all/files/stpk/materiali/MI/Artificial%20Intellig ence%20A%20Modern%20Approach.pdf

[5] M. Niazi and A. Hussain, "Agent-based Computing from Multi-agent Systems to Agent-Based Models: A Visual Survey". Springer Scientometrics, vol. 89, no. 2, pp. 479–499, 2011. doi: 10.1007/s11192-011-0468-9.

[6] S. A. Agarwal and M. Sinha," Multi Agent Adaptive E-Learning System", International Journal of Advanced Research in Computer Science and Software Engineering, vol. 3, no. 7, pp. 242-246, IJARCSSE, July 2013.

[7] Advanced eLearning Builder, "Authoring tool designed for creating e-learning materials", 2015. http://www.eduiq.com/elearning.htm

[8] MicroGrade and MicroTest,"desktop applications", 2015. http://www.chariot.com/

[9] OnlineTesting,"software and programming services", 2015. http://www.onlinetesting.net/

[10] ProfProf, "Create Online Tests & Quizzes Easily", 2015. http://www.proprofs.com/quiz-school/

[11] AditSofware," Exams, Tests and Quizzes Made Easy", 2015. http://www.aditsoftware.com/

[12] Quizworks, " Build online exams with our fun & easy to use tool", 2015. "https://www.onlineexambuilder.com/

[13] ExamJet Quiz Maker," Quiz maker software made with love", 2015. https://www.igneon.com/

18

Creation of a Remote Sensing Portal for Practical Use Dedicated to Local Goverments in Kyushu, Japan

Kohei Arai [1]

[1] Graduate School of Science and Engineering
Saga University
Saga City, Japan

Masaya Nakashima [1]

[1] Department of Information Science
Saga University
Saga City, Japan

Abstract—Remote sensing portal site for practical uses which is dedicated to local governments is created. Key components of the site are (1) links to data providers, (2) links to the data analysis software tools, (3) examples of actual uses of the satellite remote sensing data in particular for local governments. Users' demands for remote sensing satellite data are investigated for the local governments situated in Kyushu, Japan. According to the users' demands, the remote sensing portal site is created with the aforementioned key components. For the examples of remote sensing data applications, creation of land use maps, disaster mitigations, forest maps, vegetation index map for evaluation of vitality of agricultural fields and forests, etc. are taken into account. In particular for forest map creation, it is created with free open source software: FOSS of classifiers together with open data API derived training samples applied to Landsat-8 OLI data. On the other hand, volcanic eruption is featured for disaster relief with 3D representation by using open data derived DEM data. In accordance with the users' evaluation reports, it is found that the proposed portal site is useful.

Keywords—Remote Sensing; Satellite data; Land use map creation; Disaster prevention; Normalized Difference Vegetation Index: NDVI; Forest map; Volacanic eruption; 3D representation with Digital Elevation Model: DEM; Open data API

I. INTRODUCTION

There are many remote sensing portals in the world. Most of them are dedicated to scientific research based data driven portal sites. The most famous and useful site among them is Geoss portal which allows access to the data servers through the portal. On the other hand, most of space agencies create their own remote sensing satellite data servers. Meanwhile, Free Open Source Software: FOSS of data analysis software tools is also available through the different software providers. It seems that there is no portal site which allows remote sensing satellite data access, FOSS of software access, examples of data analysis and instructions of data analysis procedure with government providing open data in particular for practical use of the remote sensing satellite data dedicated to local governments. For instance, federal and state governments provide open data together with open data API. By using such government providing open data, practical use of remote sensing satellite data can be done easily.

There are many previously proposed methods for information and image retrievals in particular for remote sensing satellite data [1]-[20]. This paper is intended to provide the aforementioned purpose of remote sensing portal site for practical uses which is dedicated to local governments is

created. Key components of the site are (1) links to data providers, (2) links to the data analysis software tools, (3) examples of actual uses of the satellite remote sensing data in particular for local governments. Users' demands for remote sensing satellite data are investigated for the local governments situated in Kyushu, Japan. According to the users' demands, the remote sensing portal site is created with the aforementioned key components. For the examples of remote sensing data applications, creation of land use maps, disaster mitigations, forest maps, vegetation index map for evaluation of vitality of agricultural fields and forests, etc. are taken into account. In particular for forest map creation, it is created with FOSS of classifiers together with open data API derived training samples applied to Landsat-8 OLI data. On the other hand, volcanic eruption is featured for disaster relief with 3D representation by using open data derived DEM data. In accordance with the users' evaluation reports, it is found that the proposed portal site is useful.

This paper is organized as (1) investigation of users' demands on practical uses of remote sensing satellite data in particular for the local governments which are situated in Kyushu, Japan, (2) design of the proposed remote sensing portal site, (3) examples of practical uses of remote sensing satellite data utilizing open data which are provided by the government, and (4) concluding remarks together with some discussions.

II. PROPOSED PORTAL SITE FOR PRACTICAL USES OF REMOTE SENSING SATELLITE DATA

A. Hearing of the Users' Demands on Practical Uses of Remote Sensing Satellite Data from the Local Governments in Kyushu, Japan

Investigation is conducted for clarifying users' demands on practical uses of remote sensing satellite data from the local governments in Kyushu, Japan. The followings are users' demands,

(1)Agricultural and forestry applications
Rice crop quality map
High quality of tealeaves map
Total nitrogen content in agricultural fields
Agricultural productivity map
Forest inventory map
Forest type and age estimations
Bamboo forest map
(2)Water resources and quality monitoring

Run-off water resource map
Water resource management
(3)Disaster
Disaster mitigation
Hazard map
Volcanic monitoring
Tsunami prediction
Illegal disposal findings
(4)Atmospheric environment
Air pollution map
Solar irradiance estimation
(5)Ocean monitoring
Ocean monitoring
Renewable resources monitoring
Nutrient rich water map
Red tide
River and coastal area monitoring and planning

The largest users' demands are agricultural and forest monitoring followed by disaster monitoring. The reason for this is the fact that the largest industry in Kyushu is agriculture and forest resources. Ocean monitoring and water resources as well as atmospheric environment are followed by. The Kyushu is surrounded by the ocean. Therefore, fishery is a major industry in Kyushu. In Kyushu, there are so many active volcanoes. It is so frequently that typhoon hit Kyushu. This is because the disaster related users' demands are dominated. Other than these, there is strong demand on solar energy monitoring for solar power plantation of electricity provides. Also, air pollution comes from the Asian continent. Therefore, air pollutions including PM2.5 is major concern for Kyushu.

B. Design Concept

There are four major key components for the proposed portal site. Those are as follows,

1) Links to the major remote sensing satellite data providers

2) Links to the major sites for data analysis software providers

3) Links to the major sites for open data which are applicable to remote sensing data analysis

4) Examples of practical uses of remote sensing satellite data.

Namely, the proposed portal site is intended to provide the aforementioned four major links and information, data providers, software providers, open data providers, and examples of practical uses of the remote sensing satellite data for local governments.

C. The Links to the Remote Sensing Satellite Data Providers

There are many remote sensing satellite data providers. Local governments need solar reflectance wavelength region of the surface reflectance channels of data with a high spatial resolution (higher than 30 m) with free of charge (downloadable from their sites freely). Therefore, Landsat ETM+, TM, OLI, ASTER/VNIR, ASTER/SWIR are candidates. Such these users' requirements are matched to the following sites,

1) Unite State Geological Survey: USGS[1]
2) National Institute of Advanced Industrial Science and Technology: AIST[2]
3) Libra[3]
4) Reverb | ECHO[4]
5) JAXA G-Portal[5]

Screen shot images of the data providers are shown in Fig.1. Fig.1 (a) shows USGS site followed by AIST of Landsat viewer in Fig.1 (b). In particular for AIST site, there is a comprehensive map utilizing retrieval site as shown in Fig.1 (c). Fig.1 (d) shows Libra site provided by Libra development seed organization. NASA/EOSDIS provides the Reverb | ECHO as shown in Fig.1 (e). Meanwhile, Fig.1 (f) shows JAXA G-Portal which allows remote sensing satellite data by application fields and by mission instruments.

(a)USGS

(b)AIST

[1] http://landsatlook.usgs.gov/
[2] http://landbrowser.geogrid.org/landbrowser/index.html
[3] http://libra.developmentseed.org/
[4]
http://reverb.echo.nasa.gov/reverb/#utf8=%E2%9C%93&spatial_map=satellite&spatial_type=rectangle
[5] https://www.gportal.jaxa.jp/gp/date-and-area.html?F1108489815937N0QOGR=_

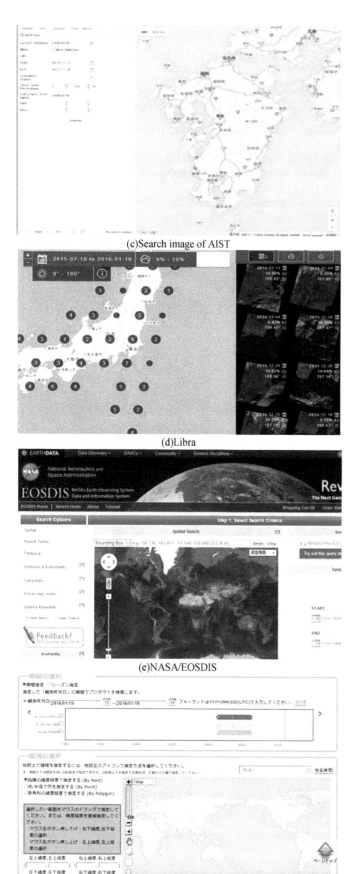

(c)Search image of AIST

(d)Libra

(e)NASA/EOSDIS

(f)JAXA G-Portal

Fig. 1.   Examples of the remote sensing satellite data retrieval sites

D. The Links to the Open Data Providers

Open data[6] is available and is useful for remote sensing satellite data analysis. For instance, training samples for land uses of the open data is useful for land use map creations. Open data initiative of Japan[7] is launched in 2012. The home page of the open data site in Japan is as shown in Fig.2 (a). Through the home page, the open data provided by ministries and local governments are accessible as shown in Fig.2 (b).

(a)Home page

(b)List of the available open data

Fig. 2.   Open data initiative in Japan (Home page and the list of available data of the open data)

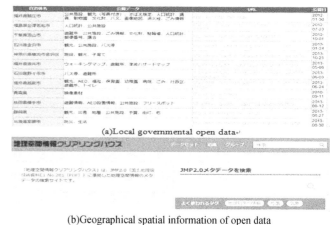

(a)Local governmental open data

(b)Geographical spatial information of open data

Fig. 3.   Screen shots of local governmental open data and geographical statial information

6 https://en.wikipedia.org/wiki/Open_data
7 http://www.data.go.jp/?lang=english

A portion of available open data provided by the local governments in Japan is shown in Fig.3 (a) while the home page of the clearing house of geographical spatial information is shown in Fig.3 (b). Links to the local government open data sites of URLs are available from the site of Fig.3 (a) while JMP2.0 based metadata search is available for the clearing house.

E. The Links to the Software Providers

Most of local governments prefer Free Open Source Software: FOSS of analysis software tools rather than commercially available software. MultiSpec[8] is one of those of FOSS. Meanwhile, RSP [9] is sophisticated image analysis software dedicated to the remote sensing satellite data analysis which is provided by the Aoyama construction company limited. On the other hand, QGIS[10] is sophisticated software which is developed by QGIS development team. One of the specific features of QGIS is available programming languages, C++, Python[11], Qt[12]. Therefore, it is relatively easy to utilize the software with the uses' developed software. Furthermore, QGIS is cross platform FOSS which allows refers, edit, and analyze the imagery data on GIS (Geographical Information System).

Common functionalities of these software tools are as follows,

1) File manipulations including format conversion, image portion extraction, pan-sharpening, color composite, etc.

2) Geometric corrections including Affine transformation, pseudo Affine transformation, etc.

3) Filtering processing which includes mask processing, median filter, edge extraction, etc.

4) Image operation processing including add, subtract, multiply, division, NDVI calculation, etc.

5) Analysis including correlation analysis, principal component analysis, etc.

6) Color information manipulations which include enhancing, binarization, histogram manipulations, pseudo color representation, multi-level slicing, etc.

7) Image display which includes enlargement, shrinking, etc.

8) Image classification including maximum likelihood classification, clustering, etc.

9) Geographical analysis including Digital Elevation Model: DEM representation, DEM editing, slope elevation and azimuth angle calculation, etc.

F. Examples of Practical Uses of Remote Sensing Satellite Data

Major concerns of local governments have to be referred through the proposed portal site. In the site, (1) NDVI calculation for forest vitality monitoring, (2) forest inventory map creation which includes forest type classification, (3) sediment disaster due to volcanic eruptions, etc. are referred.

1) NDVI calculation for forest vitality monitoring

NDVI is expressed as follows,

$$NDVI = (NIR-Red)/(NIR+Red) \qquad (1)$$

where NIR, Red denote leaf surface reflectance at Near Infrared wavelength region (more than 700nm) and that at red color wavelength (around 600nm), respectively. NDVI represents vitality of the tree and or the forest. In Kyushu, most of prefectural local governments concern forest vitality. NDVI has positive correlation to total nitrogen content in the leaves and has negative correlation to fiber content in the leaves. Total nitrogen content is highly correlated to tree or forest vitality while fiber content is highly correlated to age of the leaves. Therefore, total vitality of tree or forest can be estimated with NDVI. By using the correlations, quality of agricultural products, in particular, tea trees vitality and quality of tealeaves can be estimated.

Fig.4 shows an example of the NDVI estimated with Terra/ASTER/VNIR data which are acquired in the winter seasons. In the winter season, tea trees are patients for the next coming sprinter season maintaining their vitality. In such season (approximately five months), a fine condition of remote sensing satellite data can be acquired.Fig.5 (a) to (e) shows NDVI images in 2011 to 2015 which are estimated with the VNIR image of Ureshino district, Saga, Kyushu, Japan in where many tea farm areas are situated. Thus quality of new fresh tealeaves can be estimated. These NDVI images can be created with image operations and manipulations using RSP, QGIS and the other remote sensing imagery data processing software.

Fig. 4.   Example of NDVI image of Southern Kyushu, Japan

[8] http://itcweb.cc.affrc.go.jp/affrit/sidab-info/satellite/multispec

[9] http://rs.aoyaman.com/soft/item.html

[10] http://www.qgis.org/ja/site/forusers/download.html

[11] https://www.python.org/

[12] https://ja.wikipedia.org/wiki/Qt

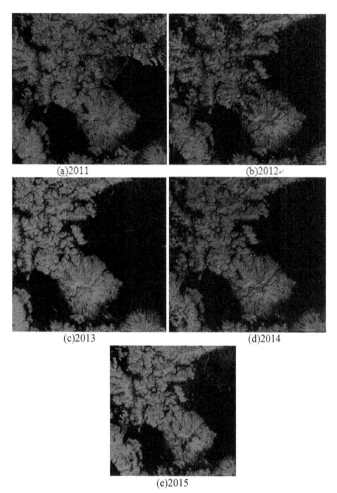

(a)2011   (b)2012

(c)2013   (d)2014

(e)2015

Fig. 5.   NDVI images of Ureshino city Saga Japan in the winter seasons of 2011 to 2015

2) Forest inventory map creation which includes forest type classification

Landsat-8/OLI imagery data which is acquired on May 2 2015 can be retrieved and download through AIST site. One of the examples of false color representation of image is shown in Fig.6 (a). Meanwhile, classified image is easily created with RSP software (class#1: Ocean, class#2: River water, class#3: vegetated areas, class#4: Bare soil, class#5: Urbanized areas) as shown in Fig.6 (b). It is possible to extract training samples for classification through referring Open Data of previously classified image with Open Data API.

Forest type classification is also available with previously created open data of forest map (Fig.7 (a)) for forest inventory provided by prefectural local government which is downloaded through Open Data portal with Open Data API. Example of the classified result is shown in Fig.7 (b) with the legends as shown in Fig.7 (c). By using DEM data provided by geological survey of Japan through Open Data portal, bird view image of classification result can be created easily as shown in Fig.7 (d). Therefore, classified results can be represented from different aspects with QGIS software.

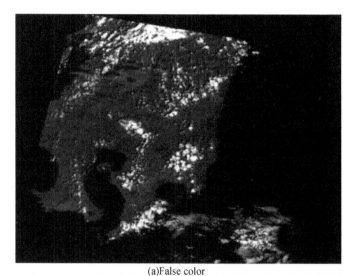

(a)False color

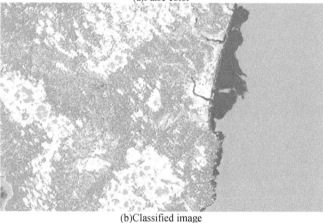

(b)Classified image

Fig. 6.   Example of downloaded image of Landsat-8/OLI and classified image

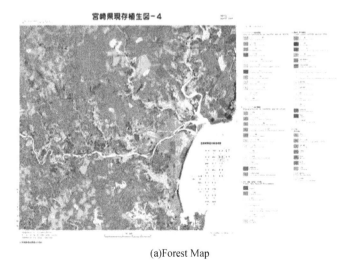

(a)Forest Map

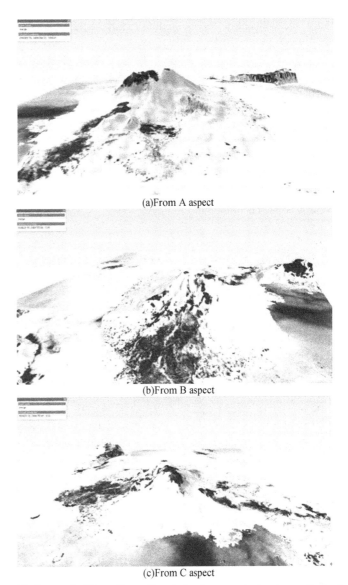

(a)From A aspect

(b)From B aspect

(c)From C aspect

Fig. 8. Land slide and/or sediment disaster areas (red color portion) of Sakurajima Mountain in August 2015

(b)Classified image

(c)Legend of the classification

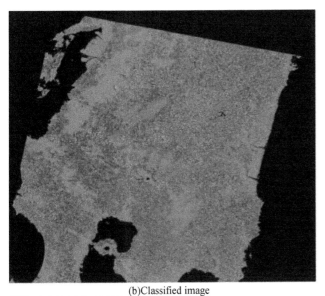

(d)3D representation of classified image

Fig. 7. Forest inventory application of remote sensing satellite data

3) Sediment disaster due to volcanic eruptions

Land slide (sediment disaster) due to volcanic eruption can be detected by extracting land cover changes from vegetated areas to non-vegetated areas (bare soil) form the two different remote sensing satellite imagery data which are acquired before and after the eruption. Active volcano of Sakurajima Mountain, Kagoshima, Kyushu, Japan is erupted during August 9 and September 10 2015. On August 15, caution level is raised from 3 to 4 and then that is dropped from 4 to 3 on September 1. By comparing two Landsat-8/OLI images which are acquired on August 9 and September 10, land slide areas are detected. Using QGIS, land slide areas which are colored in red can be detected and represented as shown in Fig.8 (a) to (c) from the different aspects. Through comparison between analyzed land slide areas and local government provided land slide data (truth data), it is found that they show a good coincident.

III. CONCLUSION

Remote sensing portal site for practical uses which is dedicated to local governments is created. Key components of the site are (1) links to data providers, (2) links to the data analysis software tools, (3) examples of actual uses of the satellite remote sensing data in particular for local governments. Users' demands for remote sensing satellite data are investigated for the local governments situated in Kyushu, Japan. According to the users' demands, the remote sensing portal site is created with the aforementioned key components. For the examples of remote sensing data applications, creation of land use maps, disaster mitigations, forest maps, vegetation index map for evaluation of vitality of agricultural fields and forests, etc. are taken into account. In particular for forest map creation, it is created with free open source software: FOSS of classifiers together with open data API derived training samples applied to Landsat-8 OLI data. On the other hand, volcanic eruption is featured for disaster relief with 3D representation by using open data derived DEM data. In accordance with the users' evaluation reports, it is found that the proposed portal site is useful.

Further investigation is required for increasing application examples in particular for matching to the prefectural local government need.

ACKNOWLEDGMENT

The author would like to thank all the participants to this project (Kyushu Aeronautical and Space Development Promotion Committee Members) and Mr.Masanori Sakashita of Graduate School of Science and Engineering of Saga University in Japan for his effort to conduct users' demand investigations and simulation studies.

REFERENCES

[1] Shin-ichi Sobue, Kohei Arai, Osamu Ochiai, Inter-Operable Protocol for Earth Observation Satellite Data Retrievals, Journal of Information Processing Society of Japan, Vol.39, No.3, 222-228, Mar.1998.

[2] Kohei Arai, Manabu Arakawa, Hirofumi Etoh, Fuzzy Search of Earth Observation Data Retrievals Using Physical and Spatial features Based on Fuzzy Theory, Journal of Japan Society of Photogrammetry and Remote Sensing,, Vol.38, No.4, pp.17-25, Aug.1999.

[3] Hirofumi Etoh, Takahiro Yamamoto, Kohei Arai, Indexing Method for Image Database Retrievals by Means of Spatial Features, Journal of Japan Society of Photogrammetry and Remote Sensing,, Vol.39, No.3, pp.14-20,(2000).

[4] Kohei Arai, Bu Kenkyo, Image portion retrievals in large scale imagery data by using online clustering taking into account pusuite algorithm based Reinforcement learning and competitive learning, Journal of Image Electronics Society of Japan, 39, 3, 301-309, 2010

[5] Kohei Arai, Visualization of 3D object shape complexity with wavelet descriptor and its application to image retrievals, Journal of Visualization, DOI:10.1007/s, 12650-011-0118-6, 2011.

[6] K.Arai, C.Rahmad, Wavelet based image retrieval method, International Journal of Advanced Computer Science and Applications, 3, 4, 6-11, 2012.

[7] K.Arai, DP matching based image retrieval method with wavelet Multi Resolution Analysis: MRA which is robust against magnification of image size, International Journal of Research and Review on Computer Science, 3, 4, 1738-1743, 2012.

[8] K.Arai, Free Open Source Software: FOSS based GIS for spatial retrievals of appropriate locations for ocean energy utilizing electric power generation plants, International Journal of Advanced Computer Science and Applications, 3, 9, 95-99, 2012.

[9] K.Arai, Visualization of link structure and URL retrievals utilization of interval structure of URLs based on brunch and bound algorithms, International Journal of Advanced Research in Artificial Intelligence, 1, 8, 12-16, 2012.

[10] Kohei Arai, Method for image portion retrieval and display for comparatively large scale of imagery data onto relatively small size of screen which is suitable to block coding of image data compression, International Journal of Advanced Computer Science and Applications, 4, 2, 218-222, 2013.

[11] Kohei Arai, Cahya Rahmad, Content based image retrieval by using multi-layer centroid contour distance, International Journal of Advanced Research in Artificial Intelligence, 2, 3, 16-20, 2013.

[12] Kohei Arai, Remote sensing satellite image database system allowing image portion retrievals utilizing principal component which consists spectral and spatial features extracted from imagery data, International Journal of Advanced Research in Artificial Intelligence, 2, 5, 32038, 2013.

[13] Kohei Arai, Image retrieval and classification method based on Euclidian distance between normalized features including wavelet descriptor, International Journal of Advanced Research in Artificial Intelligence, 2, 10, 19-25, 2013.

[14] Kohei Arai, Numerical representation of web sites of remote sensing satellite data providers and its application to knowledge based information retrievals with natural language, International Journal of Advanced Research in Artificial Intelligence, 2, 10, 26-31, 2013.

[15] K.Arai, Indra Nugraha Abudullar, Hiiroshi Okumura, Image retrieval based on color, shape and texture for ornamental leaf with medicinal functionality, International journal of Image, Graphics and Signal Processing, Vol.6, No.7, June 2014

[16] Cahya Rahmad, K.Arai, Comparison contour extraction based on layered structure and Fourier descriptor on image retrieval, International Journal of Advanced Research on Artificial Intelligence, 4, 12, 71-74, 2015.

[17] S.Sobue and K.Arai, Metadata Definition and Retrieval of Earth Observation Satellite Data, Proceedings of the IEEE Meatadata Conference, (1997)

[18] Kohei Arai, Open GIS with spatial and temporal retrievals as well as assimilation functionality, Proceedings of the Asia Pacific Advanced Network Natural Resource Workshop, Utilization of Earthy Observation Satellite-Digital Asia Special Session 1,p8, 2003.

[19] Kohei Arai, Yuji Yamada, Image retrieval method based on hue information and wavelet description based shape information as well as texture information of the objects extracted with dyadic wavelet transformation, Proceedings of the 11th Asian Symposium on Visualization, ASV-11-08-10, 1-8, 2011.

[20] K.Arai, C.Rahmad, Wavelet based image retrievals, Proceedings of the 260th conference in Saga of Image and Electronics Engineering Society of Japan, 243-247, 2012.

19

An Implementation of Outpatient Online Registration Information System of Mutiara Bunda Hospital

Masniah

College of Informatics and Computer Management

STMIK Banjarbaru

Banjarbaru, Indonesia

Abstract—Outpatient care is one of the medical services in Mutiara Bunda hospital. The management of outpatient registration of Mutiara Bunda Hospital used conventional way. Within 1 hour serving, 5 patients were enrolled with an average time of 13 minutes per patient. This caused the registration queue to get outpatient services. The study was conducted with the aim to produce outpatient online registration information system design of Mutiara Bunda Hospital in order to increase outpatient registration service and to manage data in getting medical care.

The patients register on Outpatient Online Registration Information System without having to come first to the hospital and get a queue number, so they can estimate the waiting time in the hospital to get medical care at Mutiara Bunda Hospital; while the patients who come to the hospital are served directly by the registrar.

From the results of the research, it can be concluded that the application of Outpatient Online Registration Information System help in managing and processing data of patient registration to be able to get medical care immediately at Mutiara Bunda Hospital.

Keywords—*Online Registration; Outpatient; Information System*

I. INTRODUCTION

Mutiara Bunda Hospital is a private hospital which provides medical services to the community including a Home Care Unit, Emergency Room (ER), Inpatient, Outpatient, Clinical Laboratory, Pharmacy, and Medical Check Up. In 2015, the outpatient service consists of four polyclinics: General polyclinic has 8 doctors, Obstetrics and Gynecology polyclinic has 3 doctors, Medical and Aesthetic Acupuncture polyclinic has one doctor and Psychology polyclinic has 2 doctors.

In managing outpatient registration, Mutiara Bunda Hospital used conventional way in which patients came directly and patient data is recorded on a sheet of paper. This caused the registration queue in getting outpatient medical care.

The study was conducted with the aim to produce outpatient online registration information system design in Mutiara Bunda Hospital in order to increase outpatient registration service and to manage data in getting medical care.

II. THEORITICAL BASIS

A system is a network of interconnected procedures, cohere to perform an activity or to accomplish a particular goal (Jogiyanto HM, 2009).

An information system is a man-made system which provides an integrated set of manual components and computerized components in order to collect data, process data, and generate information for users (Sidarta, 1995).

A patient is a person who consults health problems to obtain the necessary health services either directly or indirectly to the doctor or dentist. Hospital Management Information System or HMIS is a communication information technology system which processes and integrates the entire workflow process of Hospital services in the form of coordination network, reporting and administrative procedures for obtaining information appropriately and accurately; and is part of the Health Information System (Permenkes No: 269, 2008).

Outpatient is a patient care for observation, diagnosis, treatment, medical rehabilitation and other health services without staying in the hospital (Menkes No: 560, 2003).

A good service quality must be provided by a service business. With the rise of new competitors will lead to intense competition in obtaining consumers as well as retaining customers. The observant consumers will naturally choose the good quality goods and services (Nova, 2010).

Hospital as a public service institution requires the existence of an information system which is accurate and reliable, and sufficient to improve services to patients as well as other relevant environment. With such a broad scope of services, of course, there are many complex problems which occur in the process of hospital services. The numbers of variables in the hospital determine the speed of the information flow needed by the users and the hospital environment (Handoyo etc, 2008).

According to Lidia Andriani (2009) in her research entitled Outpatient Registration Information System in Hospital by Using a Computer Program, by using Outpatient Registration Information System, the registration process of outpatients can be done easily and quickly; avoids double medical record numbers because this system can detect if there is any identical medical record numbers; facilitates registrar in printing medical cards, patients' identity and patient visit; provides information of daily and monthly reports quickly and the type of report may vary according to the needs; and saves time and energy of the patient registrars.

Dwi Parawanto (2012), in his research entitled Patient Administration and Registration Information Systems in SADEWA Mother and Child Hospital, generated Patient Administration and Registration Information Systems which processes data of patients, doctors, employees, examinations and administrations. The data then was considered as references for decision making by the doctors or the hospital, thus the services to patients would be improved.

According to Gunawan Susanto and Sukadi (2012), in their journal entitled Medical Record Information Systems On Regional Public Hospital (RPH) of Pacitan Web-Base Based, by developing a web-based medical record information system in RPH of Pacitan double medical records can be reduced and searching of medical record status can be done quickly, this overcame the medical record keeping system which has been used previously. The previous system stored the patients' medical records locally where the patients were examined and treated, this did not allow the direct data exchanging. This medical record information system helps medical personnel to carry out health services to patients.

Bambang Eka Purnama and Sri Hartati (2012), in their journal entitled Conveniences and Benefits of Patient Medical Database and Elasticity for Therapy Accessibility in Different Locations, explained that the Medical Record Information System which has been developed based on the standard among hospitals and clinics provides the benefits of conveniences and records of patient's medical history so that the number misdiagnosis and malpractices can be pressed.

Ahmad Anshari and Bambang E P (2013), in their journal entitled Distributed Data Patient In Medical Record Information System, with the Information system will be able to overcome the problem of data search quickly at a hospital. Patients who visit any hospital will feel comfortable and Mall practice would be suppressed because can easily find previous patient history data, so as to determine the subsequent diagnosis becomes easier.

III.   SYSTEM ANALYSIS AND DESIGN

A. Problem Analysis

In the system of patient registration processing at Mutiara Bunda Hospital, there were several constraints in the processing and reporting of patient registration data. Based on interviews with registrar, revealed that the records of outpatients data used conventional way in which the data was written on sheets of paper in a large book. The number of patients in a doctor's practice schedule has been determined. Searching in the book caused the patients who came directly did not get queued at their desire. The long queues of patients caused the requirement of an online information system so the registration process will be faster and more efficient

B. System Design

a) Context Diagram

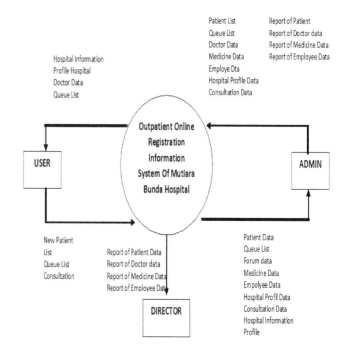

Fig. 1.   Context Diagram

b) Use Case Diagram

Use Case diagram illustrates the common features of the Outpatient Online Registration Information System of Mutiara Bunda Hospital. To get into the system, the user must log in first.

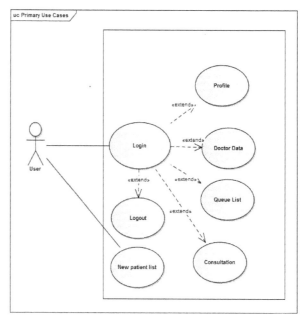

Fig. 2.   Use Case of User

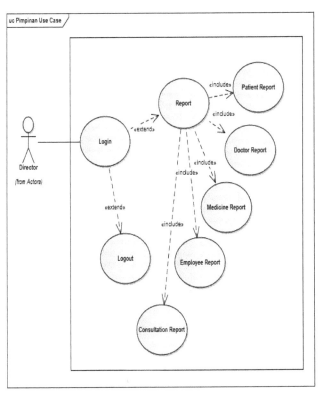

Fig. 3.   Use Case of Director

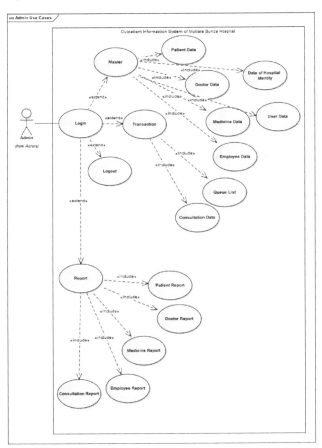

Fig. 4.   Use Case of Admin

c) Activity Diagram

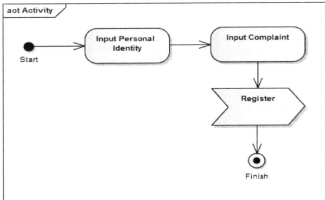

Fig. 5.   Diagram Activity of Queue List

Fig 5. Activity diagram of queue list describes the process when the user enrolls for registration queue to get treatment or consultation with a doctor in Mutiara Bunda hospital.

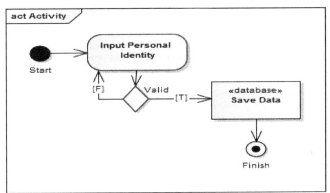

Fig. 6.   Diagram Activity New of Patient List

Fig 6. Activity diagram of patient list illustrates the process of registering as new patients on Web page of Outpatient Online Registration Information System of Mutiara Bunda Hospital.

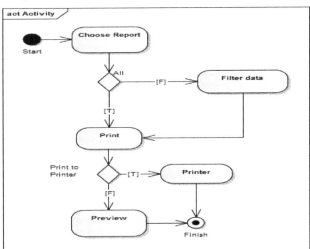

Fig. 7.   Diagram Activity of Report

Fig 7. Activity diagram of report describes the activity processes of making a report to printing the report.

d) Sequence Diagram

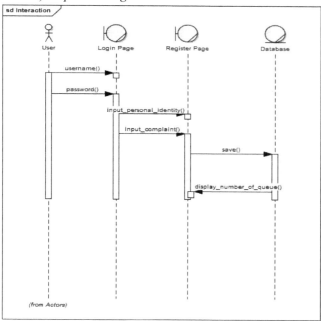

Fig. 8.   Sequence Diagram of Queue List

Fig 8. Sequence Diagram of Queue list describe the process when the user enrolls for registration queue to get treatment or consultation with a doctor in Mutiara Bunda hospital.

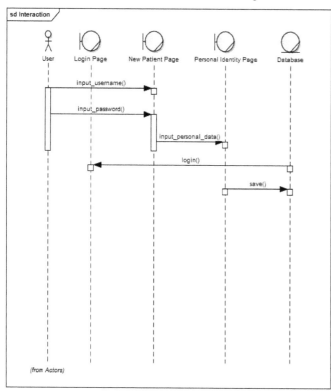

Fig. 9.   Sequence Diagram of Patient List

Fig 9.Sequence diagram of Patient List illustrate the process of registering as a new patient on Outpatient Online Registration Information System Web page of Mutiara Bunda Hospital.

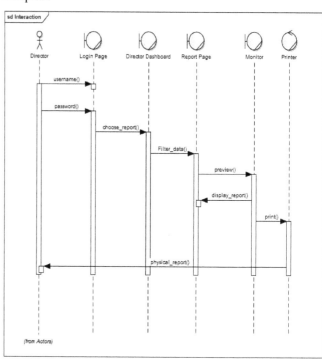

Fig. 10. Sequence Diagram of Report

Fig 10. Sequence Diagram of Report describes the activity processes of making to printing a report.

e) Database Model

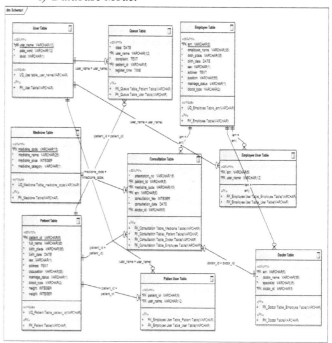

Fig. 11. Database Model

f) Database Design

TABLE I.   TABLE USER

Field Name	Type	Information
user_name	varchar(12)	PRIMARY
pass_word	varchar(12)	-
Level	varchar(1)	Director, user & admin

TABLE II.   TABLE QUEUE

Field Name	Type	Information
Date	Date	-
user_name	varchar(12)	FOREIGN
Complaint	Text	-
patient_id	varchar(5)	-
register_time	Time	-

TABLE III.   TABLE EMPLOYEE

Field Name	Type	Information
ERN	varchar(5)	PRIMARY
employee_name	varchar(35)	-
birth_place	varchar(35)	-
birth_date	Date	-
sex	varchar(1)	-
address	Text	-
position	varchar(55)	-
marriage_status	varchar(1)	-
blood_type	varchar(2)	-

TABLE IV.   TABLE MEDICINE

Field Name	Type	Information
medicine_code	varchar(15)	PRIMARY
medicine_name	varchar(25)	-
medicine_price	int(11)	-
medicine_category	varchar(1)	-

TABLE V.   TABLE DOCTOR

Field Name	Type	Information
ERN	varchar(5)	FOREIGN
doctor_name	varchar(35)	Name
Specialist	varchar(35)	-
doctor_id	varchar(5)	PRIMARY

TABLE VI.   CONSULTATION

Field Name	Type	Information
prescription_no	varchar(15)	-
patient_id	varchar(5)	FOREIGN
medicine_code	varchar(15)	FOREIGN
ERN	varchar(5)	FOREIGN
consultation_fee	int(11)	-
consultation_date	Date	-
doctor_id	varchar(5)	FOREIGN

TABLE VII.   PATIENT USER

Field Name	Type	Information
patient_id	varchar(5)	FOREIGN
user_name	varchar(12)	FOREIGN

TABLE VIII.   PATIENT

Field Name	Type	Information
patient_id	varchar(5)	PRIMARY
full_name	varchar(35)	-
birth_place	varchar(35)	-
birth_date	Date	-
Sex	varchar(1)	-
Address	Text	-
occupation	varchar(55)	-
marriage_status	varchar(1)	-
blood_type	varchar(2)	-
Height	int(11)	-
Weight	int(11)	-

TABLE IX.   TABLE EMPLOYEE USER

Field Name	Type	Information
ERN	varchar(5)	FOREIGN
user_name	varchar(12)	FOREIGN

TABLE X.   IDENTITY HOSPITAL

Field Name	Type	Information
hospital_name	varchar(35)	Hospital Name
phone_no.	varchar(15)	Phone Number
E-mail	varchar(35)	-
Address	Text	-
Owner	varchar(35)	-
license_no.	varchar(35)	Number of Licensing
Website	varchar(35)	Hospital Website

g) Interface Design

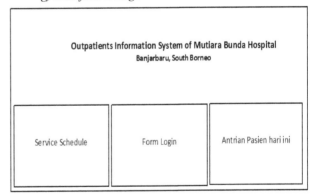

Fig. 12. Home Page

Fig. 13. Login Form

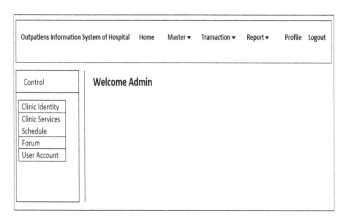

Fig. 14. Admin Dashboard

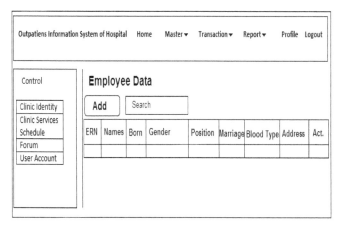

Fig. 15. Employee Dashboard

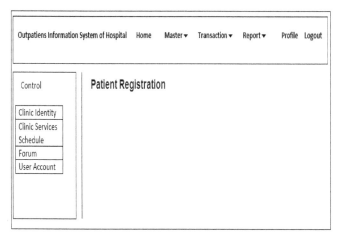

Fig. 16. Patient Registration Dashboard

IV.   IMPLEMENTATION OF THE SYSTEMS

A.   The Users of Outpatients Online Registration Information System

The users of outpatient online registration information system are administrator who is the holder of the highest privileges in the system, doctors, staff and patients.

B.   Display Interface

Fig. 17. Display of Homepage

Fig 17. Display of Homepage Outpatients Online Registration Information System has a main page which contains the login form used to authenticate the user in order to access the system, a link to the registration form (register now) used for user registration, and display of the service schedule and the number of queues.

Fig. 18. Display of Form Login

Fig 18. Display the Login Form, user must enter a user name and password in order to access the Outpatients Online Registration Information System. If the user is a patient, then the user who has not been registered can register an account by clicking "Register now".

Fig. 19. Display of the Employee Data Page

Fig 19. Display the Employee Data Page, the user can control the data by adding, changing, or deleting the data of employees.

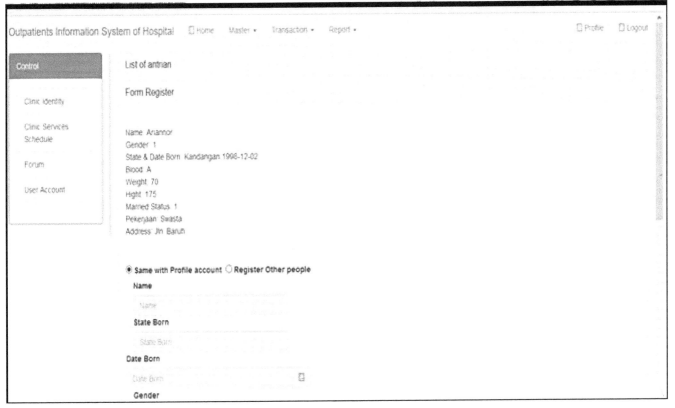

Fig. 20. Display of Outpatients Online Registration

Fig 20. Display of outpatients online registration, the patients who have filled the form on Outpatients Online Registration Information System will get queue numbers which can be be printed.

V. CONCLUSION

From the results of research, it can be concluded that:

1) The average time of outpatient registration in Mutiara Bunda Hospital conventionally per patient was 13 minutes which includes acceptance of patients, recording the patient's identity, storing data, and taking medical records of patients. Within 1 hour, only about 5 patients registration can be served.

2) On the Outpatients Online Registration System, the patients can register online without having to come to the hospital first, and they get queue numbers so they can estimate waiting time in the hospital to get medical care from Mutiara Bunda Hospital. While the patients who come directly to the hospital will received by the registrar.

3) After applying the Outpatient Online Registration Information System, number of patients served in 1 hour is approximately 12 patients. This means the application of Outpatient Online Registration Information System help to manage and process of patient registration data to be able to get medical care at Mutiara Bunda Hospital immediately.

REFERENCES

[1] Jogiyanto, HM., Perancangan Sistem Informasi Pengenalan Komputer. Yogyakarta: Pustaka Pelajar, 2009.

[2] Sidharta, Pengantar Sistem Informasi Bisnis, P.T. ELEX Media Komputindo, Jakarta, 1995.

[3] Kementerian Kesehatan Republik Indonesia. 2007. Peraturan Menteri Kesehatan Republik Indonesia Nomor 269/Menkes/Per/III/2008 Tentang Rekam Medis.

[4] Keputusan Menteri Kesehatan Republik Indonesia Nomor 560/MENKES/SK/IV/2003. 2003 Tentang Tarif Perjan Rumah Sakit.

[5] Nova, R. F. Pengaruh Kualitas Pelayanan Terhadap Kepuasan Pasien Rawat Inap Pada Rumah Sakit Pku Muhammadiyah Surakarta. Skripsi, 21, 2010.

[6] Handoyo, E., Budi Prasetijo, A., & Noor Syamhariyanto, F. Aplikasi sistem informasi rumah sakit berbasis web pada sub-sistem farmasi menggunakan framework prado. Vol. 7 No. 1 Januari - Juni 2008, 1,2010.

[7] Andriani, Lidya et al. Sistem Informasi Pendaftaran Pasien Rawat Jalan Di Rumah Sakit Dengan Menggunakan Program Komputer. USU Repository © 2009.

[8] Parawanto, Dwi. Sistem Informasi Administrasi dan Pendaftaran Pasien pada Rumah Sakit Ibu dan Anak SADEWA, 2012.

[9] Susanto,Gunawan & Sukadi. Sistem Informasi Rekam Medis Pada Rumah Sakit Umum Daerah (RSUD) Pacitan Berbasis Web Base." Speed – Sentra Penelitian Engineering dan Edukasi 9(3): 40–46, 2012.

[10] Purnama., Eka, Bambang., & Hartati, Sri.Convenience and Medical Patient Database Benefits and Elasticity for Accessibility Therapy in Different Locations." International Journal of Advanced Computer Science and Applications 3(9): 54–60, 2012.

[11] Ana Nur Cahyanti, Bambang Eka Purnama, Pembangunan Sistem Informasi Manajemen Puskesmas Pakis Baru Nawangan, Jurnal Speed Volume 9 No 2 – Agustus 2012 , ISSN 1979 – 9330

[12] Bambang Eka Purnama, Ahmad Ashari (2013), Distributed Data Patient In Medical Record Information System, IJSTR - International Journal Of Scientific & Technology Research Volume 2, Issue 8, August 2013 ISSN 2277-8616

[13] Ernawati, Bambang Eka Purnama, Implementasi Sistem Informasi Puskesmas Pembantu Desa Nglaran, Jurnal IJNS Volume 3 No 3 Juli 2014, ISSN: 2302-5700 (Print) 2354-6654 (Online), ijns.apmmi.org

[14] Hendik Mulyanarko Bambang Eka Purnama Sukadi, Pembangunan Sistem Informasi Billing Pada Rumah Sakit Umum Daerah (Rsud) Kabupaten Pacitan Berbasis Web, Jurnal TIK Provisi Vol 4, No 2 Agustus 2013

[15] Bambang Eka Purnama, Ahmad Ashari, Distributed Data Patient In Medical Record Information System, International Journal Of Scientific & Technology Research Volume 2, ISSUE 8, AUGUST 2013 ISSN 2277-8616

20

Naive Bayes Classifier Algorithm Approach for Mapping Poor Families Potential

Sri Redjeki, M. Guntara, Pius Anggoro
Informatics Engineering Department
STMIK AKAKOM
Yogyakarta, Indonesia

Abstract—The poverty rate that was recorded high in Indonesia becomes main priority the government to find a solution to poverty rate was below 10%. Initial identification the potential poverty becomes a very important thing to anticipate the amount of the poverty rate. Naive Bayes Classifier (NBC) algorithm was one of data mining algorithms that can be used to perform classifications the family poor with 11 indicators with three classifications. This study using sample data of poor families a total of 219 data. A system that built use Java programming compared to the result of Weka software with accuracy the results of classification of 93%. The results of classification data of poor families mapped by adding latitude-longitude data and a photograph of the house of the condition of poor families. Based on the results of mapping classifications using NBC can help the government in Kabupaten Bantul in examining the potential of poor people.

Keywords—*Data Mining; Naive Bayes; Poverty Potential; Mapping*

I. INTRODUCTION

Poverty in Indonesia has a number that is still quite high, above 10% [12]. It is becoming a top priority for the government to find solutions to reduce the poverty rate is below 10% [2]. Central Statistics Bureau (BPS) defines poverty as the inability to meet the minimum standards of basic needs that include food and non-food needs. BPS showed that the poverty rate in Indonesia, in September 2014, was still high at about 27.7 million people, or approximately 10.96% [11]. The poverty data graph shown in Figure 1.

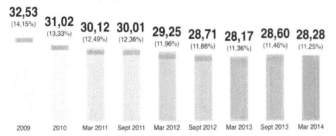

▸ Tren 2009 - 2014 (dalam juta jiwa)

Fig. 1. Poverty Data Graph in Indonesia (bps.go.id)

The number of poor people in Indonesia are mostly locate in Java island with a total of 57.8% of the total number of poor people in Indonesia, and it is located in Yogyakarta province. Poverty measurement in each country or even in every region that does not have the same size [8][9]. The poverty measurement that called as the poverty indicator becomes the most important part in determining poverty status [8][9]. In Bantul, which is one district in Yogyakarta has a fairly high poverty rate, above 14%.

The determination in classifying the poverty status of someone is the tough section that needs hard effort because it must represent the accurate results. Naive Bayes Classifier is one of the data mining algorithms that uses probabilistic approach [1][4][5]. This research will discuss how Naive Bayes Classifier algorithm can classify the status of poor families to identify potential poverty based on existing indicators. There were 11 indicators of poor families used in this study, and each of them has certain value [10]. The indicators were food, clothing, shelter, income, health, education, wealth (rupiah), property (land), water, electricity and the number of family members. While the classification used is very poor, poor and vulnerable poor [10][12].

II. LITERATURE REVIEW

A. Poverty

Poverty is a matter of deprivation or problematic deficiencies. Poverty is a condition where a person or a family is in a state of deprivation [2][9]. From these definitions, poverty can be divided into two parts: absolute and relative,

a) Absolute poverty is defined as the inability to achieve a minimum standard of life. Understanding the needs of different minimum standards in each country.

b) Relative poverty, on the other hand, is defined as the inability to achieve the standards of contemporary needs , which is linked to the welfare-rata average or average income community planning at the time.

Based on the data, the factors are distinguished into the data that affect poverty in the countryside and in urban areas, too. The comparison is important because poverty does not only happen in rural area but also in urban area. Based on this geographical approach, then poverty can be differentiated into poverty in rural and urban areas.

a) Rural poverty is a poverty which has the characteristics such as: i) limited access to the ground facilities and irrigation, ii) the slow adaptation to modern technology, iii) too large burden borne, iv) limited human capital, v) only concentrated in rural areas and vi) only concentrated on certain ethnic minorities [9].

b) Urban poverty is a poverty which has the characteristics such as: i) have limited access to resources and services, ii) limited human resources quality, iii) too large burden borne, iv) the low wages earned, v) big amount of the disorganized small enterprises and vi) a big amount of groups that do not have the capability [9].

B. Data Mining

Data Mining as a process to obtain useful information from a data warehouse [6] [7]. The term data mining is often called knowledge discovery. One technique that is made in data mining is to explore existing data to build a model and then use that model in order to identify the pattern of other data that is not stored in the database [6].

C. Naive Bayes Classifer (NBC)

Naive Bayes Classifier estimates the conditional class opportunities which assume that the attributes are conditionally independent and given the class label Y [3][5] Conditional independent assumptions can be expressed in the following form :

$$P(X|Y=y)=\prod_{i=1}^{d}P(X_i|Y=y) \quad\cdots\cdots\cdots\cdots\cdots\cdots (1)$$

each set of attributes consisting of d attributes. There is a special treatment before the features with numeric data types are put into Naive Bayes. The first way is to use discretization and the assumption of a Gaussian distribution. Gaussian distribution was chosen to represent the conditional probability that a continuous feature in a class independency $P(Xi|Y)$. This Gaussian distribution approach was used by the researcher to obtain a probability value of each poverty indicator.

Generics Naive Bayes Classifier Algorithms:

1) Read attributes and class of the data set.

2) Calculate the posterior probability of each attribute to an existing class.

3) Calculate the probability pior of existing classes.

4) Calculate the multiplication value of the posterior probability of each class and the value prior to all existing classes.

5) Find the greatest probability value in step four as the final classification.

III.   METHODOLOGY

The data has used in this study taken from the poor families in the Kabupaten Bantul. The overall system can be seen in the block diagram that existed at Figure 2.

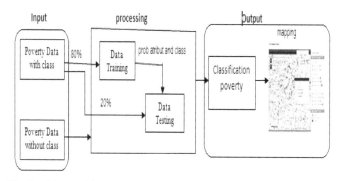

Fig. 2.   Diagram Block System

The block diagram system represented in Figure 2 was divided into three parts. The first part was the data input which was consisted of three classes of poverty (poverty status) and the poverty data which would be used for identification. Poverty classes consist of very poor, poor and vulnerable poor. The number of parameters for classification was composed from 11 indicators as presented on Table 1.

TABLE I.   POVERTY INDICATOR

No	Indicator	Indicator Score
1	Food	(0,12)
2	Clothing	(0,9)
3	Shelter	(0,9)
4	Income	(0,35)
5	Health	(0,6)
6	Education	(0,6)
7	Wealth (Rupiah)	(0,5)
8	Property (Land)	(0,6)
9	Water	(0,4)
10	Electricity	(0,3)
11	Number of Familly members	(0,5)

There were 219 data which were divided into two parts: 80% (175 data) were used for training data and 20% (approximately 44 data) were used for data testing. The second part was the main process of Naive Bayes Classifier that calculated a probability value to be used for classification. The calculated data was the training data set. The training phase results were in the form of probability values which would be used for testing.

Phase testing was done to see the accuracy of the obtained classification. The third section resulted the classification of the poverty class which would be mapped to see the poverty potential in an area by using Google Maps.

The training process (training) on the algorithm of Naive Bayes Classifier (NBC) can be seen in Figure 3.

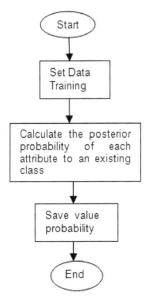

Fig. 3.   Training Fase Naive Bayes

Figure 3, showed the step-by-step process of Naïve Bayes Classifier algorithm which included reading the data sets. The display of training data is shown in Figure 4.

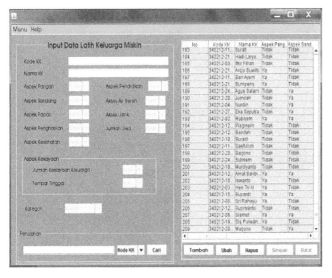

Fig. 4.   Data Training Display

The training input from the indicators was Yes and No category which can be seen in Figure 4. Input yes represent value a score largest while value not represent value a score smallest (see. indicator score in table 1). Whereas for the testing process can be shown in Figure 5. The data used for testing were as much as 20% which was approximately 44 data from 219 data.

The results of the testing phase was used to calculate the probability of each classification by using a probability value obtained in the training phase to determine the poverty classification results by taking the smallest probability. In the testing phase, it can be seen that the high accuracy of the identification of the poor people status in Kabupaten Bantul. Figure 6 represented the display of testing menu interface.

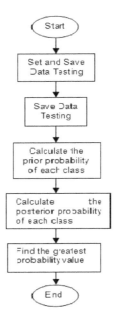

Fig. 5.   Testing Fase Naive Bayes

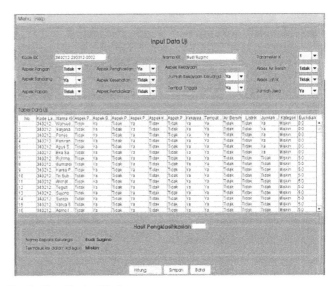

Fig. 6.   Data Testing Display

IV.   RESULT AND DISCUSSION

The implementation of Naïve Bayes algorithm to determine the classification of poverty was built using Java. These results were used as the input for mapping poor families.These results would be mapped using Google Maps by adding the data ordinates (latitude and longitude) location of a poor family. The results of testing the classification of the data shown in Figure 7 were presented in the form of recapitulation.

From the results of the data testing, the accuracy of the data was 92.5% which came from the data of 44 poor people from the total amount of 219 poor residents. Results of existing data were also compared with the results from the Weka software. Before the data were being processed, preprocessing the data was done previously. This stage was done to look at the description of the data which needs to be processed using NBC. The description of statistical data showed that the data to be processed had an average value 1.804 and a standards deviation value of 2.869. From this value, it was indicated that the deviation of the data is very high. After preprocessing being done, then classification analysis was done using Naive Bayes Classifier (NBC) algorithm. From Weka data testing results in Figure 8, it was shown that the classification results had the accuracy of 93.18%.

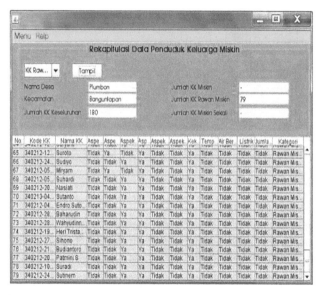

Fig. 7. Result Testing Rekapitulation

From 44 data tested using Weka, there were 41 data that could be recognized correctly, while there were 3 data that could not be identified. The results of the classification in Figure 7 were used as the input for mapping the poor families by adding the data latitude and longitude as well as home photo of the poor families.

inst#,	actual,	predicted,	error,	probability distribution	
1	2:M	1:RM	+	*0.817 0.183	0
2	2:M	2:M		0.003 *0.997	0
3	2:M	2:M		0.027 *0.973	0
4	2:M	2:M		0.011 *0.989	0
5	2:M	2:M		0 *1	0
6	1:RM	1:RM		*0.824 0.176	0
7	1:RM	1:RM		*0.84 0.16	0
8	2:M	2:M		0.191 *0.809	0
9	2:M	2:M		0.21 *0.79	0
10	1:RM	1:RM		*0.824 0.176	0
11	1:RM	1:RM		*0.84 0.16	0
12	1:RM	1:RM		*0.824 0.176	0
13	2:M	2:M		0.006 *0.994	0
14	1:RM	1:RM		*0.824 0.176	0
15	2:M	1:RM	+	*0.974 0.026	0
16	2:M	2:M		0.191 *0.809	0
17	2:M	2:M		0.001 *0.999	0
18	2:M	2:M		0.011 *0.989	0
19	2:M	2:M		0.21 *0.79	0
20	2:M	2:M		0.018 *0.982	0
21	2:M	2:M		0.186 *0.814	0
22	2:M	2:M		0.003 *0.997	0
23	2:M	2:M		0.001 *0.999	0
24	1:RM	1:RM		*0.84 0.16	0
25	2:M	2:M		0.001 *0.999	0
26	1:RM	1:RM		*0.84 0.16	0
27	2:M	2:M		0.21 *0.79	0
28	1:RM	1:RM		*0.84 0.16	0
29	2:M	2:M		0.191 *0.809	0
30	2:M	2:M		0.001 *0.999	0
31	1:RM	1:RM		*0.824 0.176	0
32	1:RM	1:RM		*0.84 0.16	0
33	2:M	2:M		0.003 *0.997	0
34	1:RM	1:RM		*0.824 0.176	0
35	2:M	2:M		0.135 *0.865	0
36	2:M	2:M		0.001 *0.999	0
37	1:RM	1:RM		*0.84 0.16	0
38	2:M	2:M		0.002 *0.998	0
39	1:RM	1:RM		*0.84 0.16	0
40	2:M	1:RM	+	*0.817 0.183	0
41	2:M	2:M		0.001 *0.999	0
42	1:RM	1:RM		*0.824 0.176	0
43	2:M	2:M		0.005 *0.995	0
44	1:RM	1:RM		*0.994 0.006	0

```
=== Evaluation on test split ===
=== Summary ===

Correctly Classified Instances      41           93.1818 %
Incorrectly Classified Instances     3            6.8182 %
Kappa statistic                     0.8594
Mean absolute error                 0.1021
```

Fig. 8. Weka Output

The mapping displays of the poor families were shown in Figure 9 and Figure 10. Figure 9 shows the location mapping of the poor families for all categories of poverty in a certain area. This mapping information will describe the potential of the existing poverty in a certain region. Figure 10 provides detailed information about a poor family that includes Family Identification Number, Name of the head of the family, the home location and home photos of poor families.

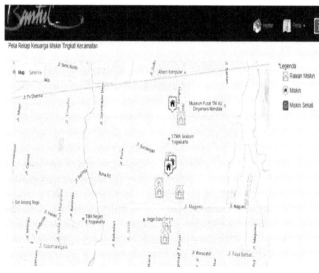

Fig. 9. Poverty Mapping

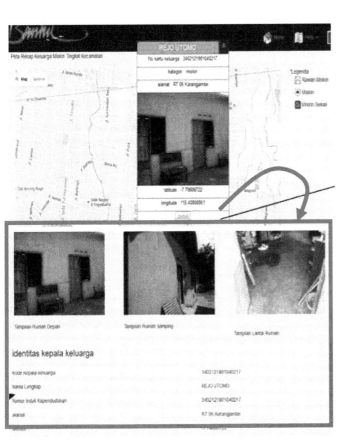

Fig. 10. Detail Information Poor Family

This detailed data will provide benefits for decision makers in providing aid or poverty reduction solutions.

V. CONCLUSION

From the explanation that is in chapter before it can be taken conclusion on the results of the study among other:

a) Method Naive Bayes Classifier can do classifications the determination of their position in the family poor with the accuracy 93%.

b) Classifications produced on data testing only two classifications that are 25 poor and 19 prone to poor, where 41 data recognizable by right and 3 data could not identified.

c) Mapping and detailed information from the classifications into Google Maps can inform us about the potential of poverty in areas.

d) The implementation of Naive Bayes Classifier algorithm built use Java used by the decision makers who is in Kabupaten Bantul.

ACKNOWLEDGMENT

We want to thank to SKPD BKKPPKB in Kabupaten Bantul which has given the opportunity to do research in the field of poverty.

REFERENCES

[1] Addin, O., Sapuan, S. M., Mahdi, E., & Othman, M. "A Naive-Bayes classifier for damage detection in engineering materials", Materials and Design, 2007, pp. 2379-2386.

[2] BKKBN,2006, Kependudukan dan Pembangunan, http://www.bkkbn.go.id/news-detail.php?nid790, diakses tanggal 14 Februari 2013.

[3] Chang-Hwan Lee, Fernando G, Dejing D, 2011, Calculating Feature Weights in Naive Bayes with Kulback-Leibler Measure, 11th IEEE International Conference on Data Mining,1550-4786/11.

[4] Congle Zhang,Gui-Rong Xue,Yong Yu and Hongyuan Zha, 2009, web-Scale Classification with Naive Bayes, Poster Season, April 22, 2009, Madrid, Spain. ACM 978-160558-487-4/09/04

[5] Daniela Xhemali, Christopher J. Hinde and Roger G. Stone, Naive Bayes vs Decision Trees vs Neural Network in the Classification of Training Web Pages, IJCSI International Journal of Computer Science Issues, Vol. 4, No. 1, 2009, ISSN (Online): 1694-0784, ISSN (Print): 1694-0814

[6] Eko Prasetyo, 2012, Data Mining : Konsep dan Aplikasi menggunakan Matlab, Penerbit Andi Yogyakarta.

[7] Jiawei Han, Micheline Kamber, Data Mining : Concepts and Techniques, Morgan Kaufmann Publisher, Microsoft research,2007.

[8] Manurung, Martin, 2005, Measuring Poverty: The Prominent and Alternative Indicators, Mimeo, University of East Anglia.

[9] Pernia, Ernesto M dan M.G. Quibra, 1999, Poverty in Developing Countries, Handbook of Regional and Urban Economics Vol 3. Amsterdam: Elseiver

[10] Peraturan Bupati Bantul Nomor 21A Tahun 2007.

[11] Yeffriansyah Salim, 2012, Penerapan Algoritma Naive Bayes untuk Penentuan Status Turn-Over Pegawai. Media Sains, Volume 4, Nomor 2.

[12] Badan Pusat Statistik, 2013, Jumlah Penduduk Miskin, Persentase Penduduk Miskin dan Garis Kemiskinan, http://bps.go.id/linkTabelStatis/view/id/1494

[13] BPS Kabupaten Bantul, Penduduk Miskin, http://bantulkab.bps.go.id/Subjek/view/id/23#subjekViewTab1

21

Analytical Study of Some Selected Classification Algorithms in WEKA Using Real Crime Data

Obuandike Georgina N.
Department of Mathematical Sciences and IT
Federal University Dutsinma
Katsina state, Nigeria

Audu Isah
Department of Mathematics and Statistics
Federal University of Technology
Minna, Niger State

John Alhasan
Department of Computer Science
Federal University of Technology,
Niger State, Nigeria

Abstract—Data mining in the field of computer science is an answered prayer to the demand of this digital age. It is used to unravel hidden information from large volumes of data usually kept in data repositories to help improve management decision making. Classification is an essential task in data mining which is used to predict unknown class labels. It has been applied in the classification of different types of data. There are different techniques that can be applied in building a classification model. In this study the performance of these techniques such as J48 which is a type of decision tree classifier, Naïve Bayesian is a classifier that applies probability functions and ZeroR is a rule induction classifier are used. These classifiers are tested using real crime data collected from Nigeria Prisons Service. The metrics used to measure the performance of each classifier include accuracy, time, True Positive Rate (TP) Rate, False Positive (FP) Rate, Kappa Statistic, Precision and Recall. The study showed that the J48 classifier has the highest accuracy compared to other two classifiers in consideration. Choosing the right classifier for data mining task will help increase the mining accuracy.

Keywords—Data Mining; Classification; Decision Tree; Naïve Bayesian; Tp Rate; component; formatting

I. INTRODUCTION

In this era of digital age and with the improvement in computer technology, many organizations usually gather large volumes of data from operational activities and after which are left to waste in data repositories. That is why [1] in his book said that we are drowning in data but lack relevant information for proactive management decision. Any tool that will help in the analysis of these large volumes of data that is being generated daily by many organizations is an answered prayer. It was this demand of our present digital age that gave birth to the field of data mining in computer science [2].

Data Mining is all about the analysis of large amount of data usually found in data repositories in many organizations. Its application is growing in leaps and bounds and has touched every aspect of human life ranging from science, engineering to business applications [3]. Data mining can handle different kinds of data ranging from ordinary text and numeric data to image and voice data. It is a multidisciplinary field that has applied techniques from other fields especially statistics, database management, machine learning and artificial intelligence [3].

With the aid of improved technology in recent years, large volumes of data are usually accumulated by many organizations and such data are usually left to waste in various data repositories. With the help of data mining such data can now be mined using different mining methods such as clustering, classification, association and outlier detection method in order to unravel hidden information that can help in improved decision making process [4].

Crime is a social sin that affects our society badly in recent times. Thus, to control this social sin, it is needful to put in place effective crime preventive strategies and policies by analyzing crime data for better understanding of crime pattern and individuals involved in crime using data mining techniques. Understanding the capability of various methods with regards to the analysis of crime data for better result is crucial. Classification is the data mining technique of focus in this paper. The performance of some selected classifiers such as J48, zeroR and Naïve Bayes are studied based on metrics such as accuracy, True Positive (TP) Rate, False Positive (FP) Rate, Kappa statistics, precision, recall and time taken to build the classification models.

The rest of the sections are discussions on the classifiers and their performance analysis with real crime data collected from the Nigeria Prisons Service in 2014.

II. CLASSIFICATION

Classification is the act of looking for a model that describes a class label in such a way that such a model can be used to predict an unknown class label [3]. Thus, classification is usually used to predict an unknown class labels. For instance, a classification model can be used to classify bank loans as either safe or unsafe. Classification applies some methods like decision tree, Bayesian method and rule induction in building its models. Classification process involves two steps. The first step is the learning stage which involves building the models while the second stage involves using the model to predict the class labels.

A record E with $n -$ attributes can be represented as $E = (e_1, e_2, \dots e_n)$ each of the records E belongs to a class of attributes $(A_1, A_2, \dots A_n)$. An attribute with discrete value is termed categorical or nominal attribute and this is normally referred to as class labels. The set of records that are used to build classification models are usually referred to as training records. The model can be represented as a function Y = F(e) which denotes the attribute Y of a particular record E. This function can be represented as rules, decision trees or mathematical formulae.

III. DECISION TREE

It is a well known classification method that takes the form of tree structure and it is usually made up of:

1) Testing node which holds the data for testing the condition

2) Start node is the parent and usually top most node.

3) Terminal node (leaf node): is the predicted class label

4) Branches: represents results of a test made on an attribute.

Figure 1: is a sample decision tree that predicts the purchasing interest of a customer in computer. Rectangular shapes are used for testing nodes while oval shapes are used for result nodes. It is mostly binary while others are non binary.

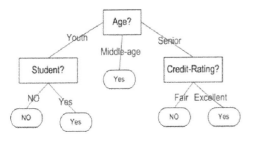

Fig. 1. A simple Decision Tree

Source: (Jiawei et al, 2011)

B. Building Decision Tree

Decision tree can be built using different methods, the first method developed was ID3 (Interactive, Dichotomiser) which later metamorphosed into C4.5 classifier. J48 classifier is an improved version of C4.5 decision tree classifier and has become a popular decision tree classifier. Classification and Regression Trees (CART) was later developed to handle binary trees. Thus, ID3, J48 and CART are basic methods of decision tree classification [5].

C. Decision Tree Algorithm

Algorithm
Parameters
Dataset *T* and its fields
Set of Attributes *A*
Selection Technique for the Attribute
Result
Tree Classifier
Procedure
1) A node is Created (call it *E*)
2) Check if all records *R* is in one group *G* and write node

Algorithm
E as
the last node in the that Group *G*
3) If *A* = 0 (no attribute)
4) then write E as the last node
5) Use Selection technique for attributes on (R, A) to get the
Best splitting condition
6) Write the condition on node E
7) Check if attribute is discrete and allows multiway split then
It is not strictly binary tree
8) For all output O from splitting condition, divide the records and build the tree
9) Assign R_0 = *Set of all records in output O*
10) If R_o = 0 then
11) Node E is attached with a leaf labelled with majority class R
12) Otherwise node E is attached with node obtained from Generate Decision Tree (R_o, A)
13) Next
14) Write E

Fig. 2. Decision Tree Algorithm

Source: (jiawei, et al, 2011)

IV. NAÏVE BAYESIAN

This is a classification method that is based on Bayes' theorem which is used to predict class labels. This classifier is based on probability theorem and is named after Thomas Bayes who is the founder of the theorem [6].

Suppose R is a record set, it is considered as evidence in Bayesian theorem and R depends on n-features. Assume rule T implies that R ∈ K class, the condition that T is true if R ∈ K is given by P(T ∩ R).

For example, suppose a dataset R is described by age and educational qualification and R is a person within the age of 20 - 34 and has no educational qualification and T is a rule that someone within that particular age limit and educational qualification is likely to commit an offense then P(T ∩ R) implies that someone is likely to commit an offense if its age and educational qualification is within the limit.

P(T) is a general probability which implies that anyone is likely to commit offense not minding the age and educational qualification and other things that might be considered thus P(T) is not dependent on R. In order words, P(T ∩ R) is the probability of R when satisfied rule T. That is to say that a person is likely to commit an offense if the age and educational qualification is within the rule. P(R) is the probability that someone from the given dataset is within the age limit and a given educational qualification level. Bayes' theorem is given as in equation 1.

$$P(T \cap R) = \frac{P(R \cap T)P(T)}{P(R)}, \text{ provided } P(R) > 0 \qquad (1)$$

V. ZEROR CLASSIFIER

It is a rule based method for data classification in WEKA. The rule usually considers the majority of training dataset as real Zero R prediction. Thus, it focuses on targeted class labels and ignores others. Zero R is not easily predictable; it only serves as a baseline for other classifiers [7].

VI. ABOUT WEKA

It is machine learning software developed at university of Waikato in New Zealand. It is an open source software and can be freely downloaded from this web site address http://www.cs.waikato.ac.nz. It accepts its data in ARFF (Attribute Related File Format). It has different algorithms for data mining and can work in any platform. The Graphical User Interface (GUI) is as shown in figure 3 [8].

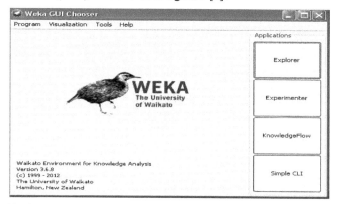

Fig. 3.   WEKA GUI Chooser

VII. EXPERIMENTS

A. Evaluation Metrics

The parameters considered while evaluating the selected classifiers are:

1) Accuracy: This shows the percentage of correctly classified instances in each classification model

2) Kappa: Measures the relationship between classified instances and true classes. It usually lies between [0, 1]. The value of 1 means perfect relationship while 0 means random guessing.

3) TP Rate: Is the statistics that shows correctly classified instances.

4) FP Rate: Is the report of instances incorrectly labelled as correct instances.

5) Recall: Measures the percentage of all relevant data that was returned by the classifier. A high recall means the model returns most of the relevant data.

6) Precision: Measures the exactness of the relevant data retrieved. High precision means the model returns more relevant data than irrelevant data.

7) Time: Time taken to perform the classification [9;10].

B. Datasets

A real crime data collected from selected prisons in Nigeria were used to perform this experiment. The dataset were converted to Attribute Related File Format (ARFF) form for easy processing by WEKA. The dataset was divided into two: training set and test set. The former was used to train the model while the other was used to test the built model. A cross validation process was applied in dividing the dataset into

training and test set. The process divides the data into equal parts usually k = 10 and the model was trained using k − 1 fold and kth fold was used as test set. The process was repeated K times to allow for both training and testing of each set.

C. Testing of J48 Classifier on crime data

J48 classifier is an enhanced version of C4.5 decision tree classifier and has become a popular decision tree classifier. It builds its model using a tree structure which usually made up of the following:

1) Testing node which holds the data for testing the condition

2) Start node is the parent and usually top most of the node.

3) Terminal node (leaf node): is the predicted class label

4) Branches: represents results of a test made on an attribute.

```
=== Run information ===

Scheme:weka.classifiers.trees.J48 -C 0.25 -M 2
Relation:    Combined_Prisons
Instances:   1733
Attributes:  4
             Offence
             Age
             Edu-Qualification
             Occupation

Time taken to build model: 0.76 seconds

=== Stratified cross-validation ===
=== Summary ===

Correctly Classified Instances      1025        59.146 %
Incorrectly Classified Instances    708         40.854 %
Kappa statistic                     0.1516
Mean absolute error                 0.2760
Root mean squared error             0.3783
Relative absolute error             93.9487 %
Root relative squared error         98.5845 %
Total Number of Instances           1733

=== Detailed Accuracy By Class ===

TP Rate  FP Rate  Precision  Recall  F-Measure  ROC Area  Class
0.266    0.09     0.515      0.266   0.351      0.627     Secondary
0        0.003    0          0       0          0.663     Tertiary
0.022    0.013    0.2        0.022   0.04       0.586     Primary
0.913    0.758    0.613      0.913   0.733      0.61      NONE
0.591    0.456    0.51       0.591   0.514      0.613     weighted Avg

=== Confusion Matrix ===

   a   b   c   d   <-- classified as
 122   2  10 324 |  a = Secondary
  10   0   2  51 |  b = Tertiary
  30   0   5 193 |  c = Primary
  75   3   8 898 |  d = NONE
```

Fig. 4.   Run information for J48 classifier

D. Naïve Bayes Classifier evaluation on Crime data

```
=== Run information ===

Scheme:weka.classifiers.bayes.NaiveBayes
Relation:     Combined_Prisons
Instances:    1733
Attributes:   4
              Offence
              Age
              Edu-Qualification
              Occupation
Test mode:10-fold cross-validation

=== Classifier model (full training set) ===


Naive Bayes Classifier


Time taken to build model: 0.09 seconds

=== Stratified cross-validation ===
=== Summary ===

Correctly Classified Instances       984         56.7802 %
Incorrectly Classified Instances     749         43.2198 %
Kappa statistic                        0.0813
Mean absolute error                    0.279
Root mean squared error                0.3771
Relative absolute error               94.6346 %
Root relative squared error           98.2498 %
Total Number of Instances           1733

=== Detailed Accuracy By Class ===

TP Rate  FP Rate  Precision  Recall  F-Measure  ROC Area  Class
0.157    0.077    0.424      0.157   0.229      0.643     Secondary
0        0.002    0          0       0          0.709     Tertiary
0.031    0.015    0.233      0.031   0.054      0.612     Primary
0.92     0.834    0.592      0.92    0.72       0.634     NONE
0.568    0.496    0.478      0.568   0.477      0.636     Weighted Avg

=== Confusion Matrix ===

  a   b   c   d   <-- classified as
 72   0  10 376 |  a = Secondary
  7   0   2  54 |  b = Tertiary
 24   2   7 195 |  c = Primary
 67   1  11 905 |  d = NONE
```

Fig. 5.   Run Information for Naïve Bayes Classifier

E. ZeroR Classifier Evaluation

It is a simple classification method that works with mode for the prediction of nominal data and mean for the prediction of numeric data. It is usually referred to as majority class method.

```
=== Run information ===

Scheme:weka.classifiers.rules.ZeroR
Relation:     Combined_Prisons
Instances:    1733
Attributes:   4
              Offence
              Age
              Edu-Qualification
              Occupation
Test mode:10-fold cross-validation

=== Classifier model (full training set) ===

ZeroR predicts class value: NONE

Time taken to build model: 0.09 seconds

=== Stratified cross-validation ===
=== Summary ===

Correctly Classified Instances       984         56.7802 %
Incorrectly Classified Instances     749         43.2198 %
Kappa statistic                        0
Mean absolute error                    0.2948
Root mean squared error                0.3838
Relative absolute error              100      %
Root relative squared error          100      %
Total Number of Instances           1733

=== Detailed Accuracy By Class ===

TP Rate  FP Rate  Precision  Recall  F-Measure  ROC Area  Class
0        0        0          0       0          0.497     Secondary
0        0        0          0       0          0.483     Tertiary
0        0        0          0       0          0.495     Primary
1        1        0.568      1       0.724      0.498     NONE
0.568    0.568    0.322      0.568   0.411      0.497     Weighted Avg

=== Confusion Matrix ===

  a   b   c   d   <-- classified as
  0   0   0 458 |  a = Secondary
  0   0   0  63 |  b = Tertiary
  0   0   0 228 |  c = Primary
  0   0   0 984 |  d = NONE
```

Fig. 6.   Run Information for ZeroR

VIII. RESULT DISCUSSION

Table 1 shows the tabulation of various results obtained from the three classifier used in this work while figure 7 is the graphical representation of the results.

TABLE I.   TABULATED RESULT

Evaluation Metrics	J48	Naïve Bayes	ZeroR
Time	0.76 Secs	0.09 Secs	0.09 Secs
Accuracy	59.15%	56.78%	56.78%
`TP Rate	0.591	0.568	0.568
FP Rate	0.456	0.496	0.568
Kappa	0.15	0.0813	0
Precision	0.51	0.478	0.322
Recall	0.591	0.568	0.568

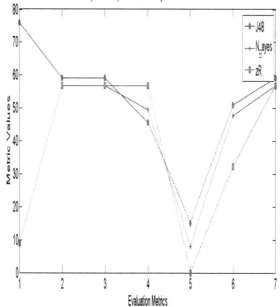

Fig. 7.   Graph of the three Classifiers

The study shows that the J48 classifier has higher accuracy of 59.15 while both Naïve Bayesian and ZeroR classifier has accuracy of 56.78 each. The J48 though took more time of 0.76 seconds to build the model compare to 0.09 seconds each for both Naïve Bayesian and ZeorR classifier, where time is not the main metric for evaluation of the performance, the j48 classifier can be said to have performed better than Naïve Bayesian and ZeroR classifiers.

IX.   CONCLUSION

The advancement in data mining has been accompanied with development of various mining techniques and algorithms. Choosing the right technique for a particular type of data mining task is now becoming difficult. The best way is to perform a particular task using different techniques in order to choose the one that gives the best result. This work performed a comparative analysis of three classification techniques J48, Naïve Bayesian and zeroR to see which one that will give the best result using real crime data collected from some selected Nigerian prisons. There by proposing a frame work for choosing a better algorithm for data mining tasks. The J48 seems to have performed better than Naïve Bayesian and ZeroR classifiers using crime dataset and thus can be recommended for the classification of crime data. However, further work can be carried out using a different dataset and other classification techniques in WEKA mining tool or any other mining tool.

REFERENCES

[1]   J. Naisbitt " *Megatrends* ", 6th ed., Warner Books, New York. 1986.

[2]   T. ZhaoHui and M. Jamie "Data Mining with SQL Server 2005",Wiley Publishing Inc, Indianapolis, Indiana, 2005.

[3]   H. Jiawei, K. Micheline, and P. Jian "Data mining: Concept and Techniques" 3rd edition, Elsevier, 2011.

[4]   M. Goebel and L.Gruenwald "A survey of data mining and knowledge discovery software tools", ACM SIGKDD Explorations Newsletter, v.1 n.1, p.20-33, 1999.

[5]   Aman Kumar Sharma, Suruchi Sahni, "A Comparative Study of Classification Algorithms for Spam Email Data Analysis", IJCSE, Vol. 3, No. 5, 2011, pp. 1890-1895

[6]   Anshul Goyal, Rajni Mehta, "Performance Comparison of Naive Bayes and J48 Classification Algorithms", IJAER, Vol. 7, No. 11, 2012, pp.

[7]   S. K. Shabia and A. P. Mushtag " Evaluation of Knowledge Extraction Using Variou Classification Data Mining Techniqes", IJARCSSE, Vol. 3, Issue 6, pp. 251 – 256 , 2013.

[8]   I. Witten and E. Frank " Data mining: Practical Machine Learning Tools and Techniques with Java Implementations", San Francisco: Morgan Kaufmann publishers, 2000.

[9]   Hong Hu, Jiuyong Li, Ashley Plank, "A Comparative Study of Classification Methods for Microarray Data Analysis", published in CRPIT, Vol. 61, 2006.

[10]   Milan Kumari, Sunila Godara, "Comparative Study of Data Mining Classification Methods in cardiovascular Disease Prediction", IJCST, Vol. 2, Issue 2, pp. 304-308, 2011.

22

Recognition of Similar Wooden Surfaces with a Hierarchical Neural Network Structure

Irina Topalova

Faculty of German Engineering Education and Industrial Management
Technical University of Sofia, Bulgaria
Sofia, Bulgaria

Abstract—The surface quality assurance check is an important task in industrial production of wooden parts. There are many automated systems applying different methods for preprocessing and recognition/classification of surface textures, but in the most cases these methods cannot produce very high recognition accuracy. This paper aims to propose a method for effective recognition of similar wooden surfaces applying simple preprocessing, recognition and classification stage. The method is based on simultaneously training two different neural networks with surface image histograms and their second derivatives. The combined outputs of these networks give an input training set for a third neural network to make the final decision. The proposed method is tested with image samples of seven similar wooden texture images and shows high recognition accuracy. The results are analyzed, discussed and further research tasks are proposed.

Keywords—recognition; preprocessing; neural network; wooden surface

I. INTRODUCTION

Many modern automated inspection systems in wooden industry are developed for inspection of the wooden surface quality. All of them have costly hardware solutions and are compatible with the specific company production equipment. The existing software products for texture recognition are not intended for implementation in common purpose programmable logic controllers widely used in technological processes control. A specific task in wooden industry is the sorting of similar tiles having identical textures but with different shades or including some defects. It is difficult to obtain high classification accuracy in this case because of the high correlated texture parametrical descriptions.

In some cases the surface textures have to be recognized in movement, because of the production process specifics. Thus the motion blur noise is added to the similarities of the textures and some other kind of noise with Gaussian or uniform distribution. Thus de-correlation of the texture descriptions in the preprocessing stage is needed, as these descriptions usually feed the recognition structure itself. That is the reason to develop effective methods and algorithms aiming high recognition accuracy for different kinds of similar textures when evaluating them in production environment. As well optimal (considering the proportion between classification accuracy, calculation simplicity and cost) methods, software and hardware system solutions have to be sought, suitable for implementation in real time systems.

Taking into consideration the above discussion, a method for recognition of similar wooden surfaces applying simple preprocessing, recognition and classification stage is presented. The method is based on preliminary analyzing the correlation between different wood texture descriptions, followed by a simultaneously training two different neural networks with surface image histograms and their second derivatives. The combined outputs of these networks give an input training set for a third neural network to take the final decision. The proposed method is tested with image samples of seven similar wooden classes and many exemplars of their noisy images. The obtained results are presented and discussed.

II. RELATED WORKS

The most research in the wood product industry has been applied in the development of automatic visual inspection systems, based on the quality of the wood and the presence of defects. Usually these technologies use devices and technologies that are rather complex and expensive. A wood classification system based on several Multi-layered perceptron (MLP) neural network models has been developed and discussed in [1]. The MLP structure has been trained by the authors, using 20 input features such as angular second moment, contrast, correlation, inverse difference moment, entropy, etc., for five different image rotations [1]), extracted from the texture. In this case, the authors have obtained 1sec overall computation time and 95% accuracy. Other methods for defect detection in textured wood surfaces rely on the analysis and fusion of image series with variable illumination [2, 3]. These methods can be considered as filter-based, where the filters or feature detectors are learned from a set of training surfaces. It spends 0.5 to 1.6 seconds to process an image of 256x256 pixels and is tested in Mat Lab. The method represented in [4] is based on applying a length histogram that embodies the width and height of the grey level texture histogram and gives a maximum of 86.6% recognition accuracy. Considering the existing texture classification methods [1, 2, 3, 4] and technologies, we came to the conclusion that they are not effective for textures having identical structures, they need significant computational time, and in the most cases cannot obtain high recognition accuracy. The existing neural network software for texture recognition is applicable for simulating and testing the methods but is not intended for implementation in real time systems for control of different automated technological processes in industry.

III. HIERARHICAL NEURAL NETWORK RECOGNITION STRUCTURE

When investigating recognition and classification of a preliminary known texture classes, more suitable is to apply an adaptive recognition method and a supervised learning scheme, since this method gives the more accurate results. In this instance the best variant is to choose neural networks (NN) because of the good NN capabilities to adapt to changes in the input vector, to set precisely the boundaries between the classes therefore offering high recognition accuracy and fast computations in the recognition phase [5].

After choosing a NN for combination between a supervised learning scheme and utilization of the histogram parameters, the more important thing is the right choice of the input NN data. This choice is influential for the right and fast convergence of the NN, for the number of parameters in the input vector and the whole NN topology. The initial choice of variables is guided by intuition. Next the number of NN input parameters has to be optimized, developing a suitable method for their reduction aiming to preserve only the informative parameters without loose of any information useful for accurate class determination. The preprocessing stage in the recognition systems with visual image acquisition is intended for image quality enhancement, for feature extraction and constituting a feature parametrical vector. This vector is provided for feeding the chosen recognition structure with input data. Some important requirements to the input vector are: precisely description of the class using distinguishing features, high input vector correlation between different samples of the same class and high de-correlated input vectors representing different classes.   Before taking the decision what kind of appropriate texture recognition method to apply, it is necessary to evaluate the similarity i.e. the correlation between the estimated description vectors [6]. As the histograms give an integral characteristic of the texture image, they are very appropriate to be used as initial parametrical description vectors of the image.

A. The proposed method

The proposed method aims high recognition accuracy of similar wooden surfaces applying simple preprocessing to obtain different input parametrical vectors for feeding two neural networks (NN) on the first recognition stage. The first stage NN outputs constitute the input vector for feeding the second stage NN, designed for making the final decision. Considering the real-time working of the system, the influence of the production technology specifics is reflected in the chosen input training set, i.e. motion blur and Gaussian noise are added to the images. Many recent developed methods use texture histograms, DCT or Wavelet transform over the texture histogram as NN input training sets [6, 7].

The proposed method here combines two different input training vectors aiming to reflect simultaneously the translations or stretches along the argument axis together with changing the function values. The translation of the histogram because of brightening or darkening of the image and the histogram stretches because of adding motion blur are the most possible reasons for histogram changes along the argument (grey levels) axis. As the image histograms are an

integral presentation of the image texture and reflect the above mentioned image changes, they could be used as input training vectors for a recognition structure. The first and second derivatives of the image histogram represent the changes in the function values, i.e. in the height of the grey level texture histogram for each grey level point. The present research shows that the second derivative over the image texture histogram meets better the requirements for low inter class correlation, in comparison to other previous tested by the author NN input training sets [6, 7, 8]. The NNs are capable of setting precisely the boundaries between overlapping classes in the parametrical feature space. But feeding the NN with de-correlated input vectors already in the preprocessing stage, would give assistance to the training process and respectively to the recognition accuracy.

The proposed recognition structure is shown in Fig. 1. NN1 is trained with a set of histogram values H(g) representing different samples of the examined texture classes for each grey level g. NN2 is trained with a set of second derivative over the histogram values $d^2H(g)/dg^2$ representing different samples of the same texture classes. The outputs of NN1 and NN2 constitute the input training vector for the third NN3 which is intended to make the final decision, increasing the recognition accuracy. The proposed method and the hierarchical recognition structure was trained and tested with many samples of seven similar texture images with their species numbers, shown in Fig.2.

B. Preprocessing stage

In the preprocessing stage the correlation of different texture image parametrical descriptions between each two species was calculated. The inter class correlation coefficient of classes (species) i and j is r_{ij} and was calculated according to (1), where $H_i(g)$ is the histogram value for grey level g and $\bar{H}_i$ is the mean of all histogram values for class i. Next the coefficient r_{ij} was calculated when the parametrical descriptions of all species are DCTs over their histograms $DCT[H(g)]$ as it is given in (2).

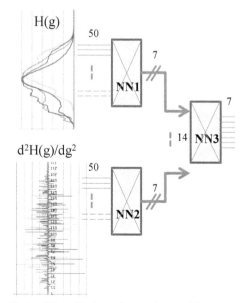

Fig. 1.   Hierarchical neural network recognition structure

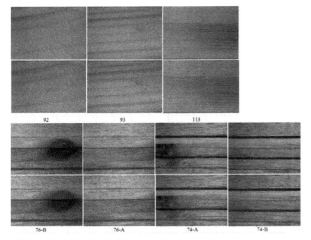

Fig. 2. Seven tested similar texture images

$$r_{ij} = \frac{\sum_{g=1}^{256}(H_i(g)-\bar{H}_i)(H_j(g)-\bar{H}_j)}{\sqrt{\sum_{g=1}^{256}(H_i(g)-\bar{H}_i)^2 \sum_{g=1}^{256}(H_j(g)-\bar{H}_j)^2}} = \frac{\sigma_{ij}^2}{\sigma_{ii}\sigma_{jj}} \quad (1)$$

$$DCT[H(g)] = DCT(w) = c_w \sum_{k=0}^{N} H(g) \cos\left(\frac{(2k+1)}{2N}\right) \quad (2)$$

$$for\ w = \{0, \ldots, N-1\},$$

$$c_w = \begin{cases} \dfrac{1}{\sqrt{N}}, for\ w = 0 \\ \sqrt{\dfrac{2}{N}}, for\ w > 0 \end{cases}$$

The correlation coefficient r_{ij} between each two texture species was also calculated for the first $dH(g)/dg$ and second derivative $d^2H(g)/dg^2$ over the texture histogram values. Fig. 3 represents the four r_{ij} between each two wooden species over their $H(g)$,

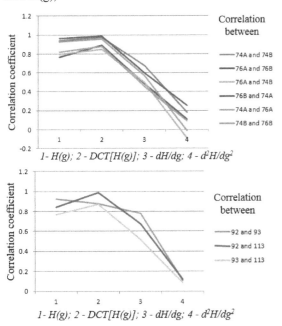

Fig. 3. Correlation coefficients between each two texture species

$DCT[H(g)]$, $dH(g)/dg$ and $d^2H(g)/dg^2$. Obviously r_{ij} decreases considerably for the first and second histogram

derivative. So it seems reasonable to use $d^2H(g)/dg^2$ as input training set because of its low inter class correlation and its capability to reflect the vertical histogram changes for each grey level g. Thus the both parametrical descriptions H(g) as an integral grey level distribution and $d^2H(g)/dg^2$ are used as input vectors for NN1 and NN2.

IV. EXPERIMENTS AND RESULTS

The texture image histograms of the seven investigated species are normed through division of each histogram value by

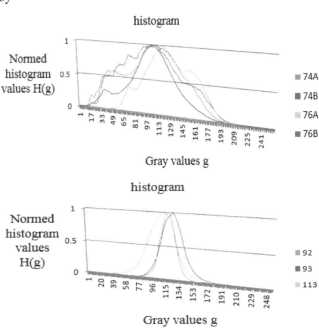

Fig. 4. Normed histogram values for the tested similar texture images

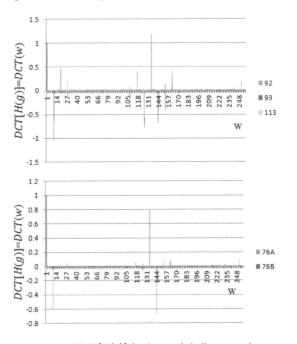

Fig. 5. Normed $DCT[H(g)]$ for the tested similar texture images

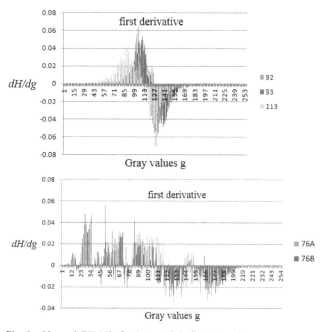

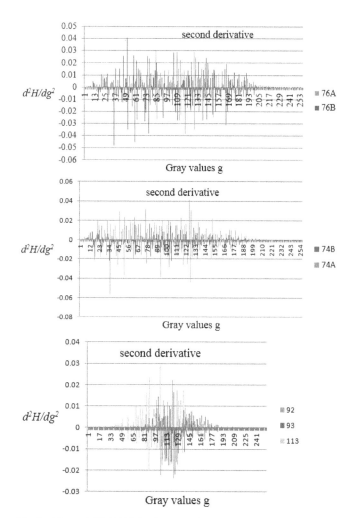

Fig. 6.   Normed dH(g)/dg for the tested similar texture images

the maximum $H_{max}(g)$ value. Thus the NN1 input training set is in the argument range of the NN activation function. They are represented in Fig.4. All of the rest descriptions - $DCT[H(g)]$, dH(g)/dg and $d^2H(g)/dg^2$ are also normed in this way on account of better correlation analysis and NNs argument fitting. Fig.5 shows the normed histogram $DCT[H(g)]$ for the tested similar texture images, respectively Fig.6 shows the normed first dH(g)/dg derivatives for the same images.

A. Training the NN structure

The images were captured with a CCD camera Nikon D7100 with CMOS 23.5x15.6 sensor and resolution of 4494x3000 pixels. The suggested hierarchical NN recognition structure is trained, tested and validated with 40 samples representing each one of the seven species given in Fig.2. Some normed d2H(g)/dg2 for the tested similar texture images are represented in Fig.7. The samples were generated adding respectively different amount - between 5 and 25 Pix - motion blur to simulate the effect of image acquisition in movement. Also 3% or 5% Gaussian noise was added to some of the images. According to the requirements of the sampling theorem [9] the number of values in H(g) and $d^2H(g)/dg^2$ were reduced to 50 points to facilitate the real-time work of the NN structure. The most frequently used proportion between training, cross validating and testing set of 60%-15%-25% of the general sample number is used in the research [10]. The 60% of the samples for each specie were randomly given to the corresponding NN1 – H(g) and to NN2 - $d^2H(g)/dg^2$. The NN1 was trained to mean square error of $\varepsilon=0.001$, NN2 to $\varepsilon=0.01$ and NN3 to $\varepsilon=0.03$. Each NN has only one hidden layer with 20 neurons. The three NNs were trained applying Backpropagation (BPG) learning algorithm since it seems to give the most promising results. *Neuro Solution software* package [10] was used, because it offers DLL export of the trained NN structure and an opportunity for implementation in different

Fig. 7.   Normed $d^2H(g)/dg^2$ for the tested similar texture images

Programmable Logic Controllers (PLC) for real-time work. Three different BPG algorithms [10] were probed aiming best accuracy in the recognition phase: *static* where the output of a network is strictly a function of its present input, *trajectory* where each exemplar has a temporal dimension defined by its forward period and *fixed point where* each exemplar represents a static pattern that is to be embedded as a fixed point of a recurrent network [10]. The best recognition accuracy in the recognition phase was obtained applying the static BPG learning algorithm.

B. Results and discussion

The achieved recognition accuracy when testing the trained NN structure with 10 samples (i.e. 25% of the general sample number) of each class/specie is represented in Table 1. It is visible that NN1 gives recognition accuracy between 50 and 70%, NN2 – between 70 and 90% (because the input vectors are better de-correlated), but NN3 on the last stage gives between 90% and 100%. Thus each NN contributes to the training and to the recognition accuracy in the test phase. NN3 on the second stage sets precisely the boundaries between similar texture images and classifies accurately the tested samples. Fig.8 represents NNs output values in dependence of variations of two characteristic points – $max[d^2H(g)/dg^2]$ and $VH_{(g)\,max\text{-}diff}$.

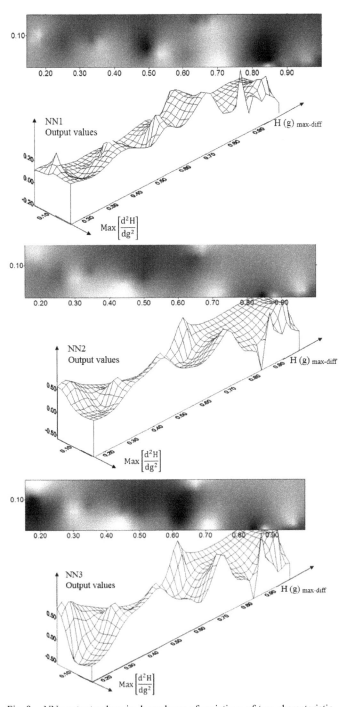

TABLE I.   RECOGNITION ACCURACY OF EACH NN IN THE STRUCTURE

Recognition accuracy [%]	Recognized Classes						
	74-A	74-B	76-A	76-B	92	93	113
NN1	63	66	70	66	73	66	76
NN2	83	86	86	83	90	86	90
NN3	90	93	96	100	96	96	100

V. CONCLUSION

The main benefits of the proposed method and NN recognition structure is the achieving of high recognition accuracy by very simple preprocessing calculations. Only H(g) and $d^2H(g)/dg^2$ are calculated. Feeding different NNs with different parametrical input vectors and combining the results of the first recognition stage into input feeding vector for the second stage contributes to the precisely separating the similarities in the classes.

The obtained accuracy is between 90 and 100% even for very similar texture images. The utilized software package offers good opportunity for real-time implementation in different kinds of PLCs. To generalize the method, further research is planned with the intention of testing with much more different samples of much more texture images.

REFERENCES

[1] K. Marzuki, et al., "Design of an Intelligent Wood Species Recognition System", IJSSST, Vol. 9, No. 3, pp. 9-19, September, 2008.

[2] A.P. Grassi, et al., "Illumination and model-based detection of finishing defects", Reports on Distributed Measurement Systems, Shaker Verlag, pp. 31-35, 2008.

[3] F. Puente and K. Dostert, "Reports on Industrial Information Technology", Karlsruhe Institute of Technology, Vol 12, pp. 35-54, 2010.

[4] Hang-jun Wang, Guang-qun Zhang and Heng-nian Qi, "Wood Recognition Using Image Texture Features", PLoS One, Open Access Research,http://dx.doi.org/10.1371/journal.pone.0076101,October, 2013.

[5] M. Sartori and P. Antsaklis, A simple method to derive bounds on the size and to train multi-layer neural networks, IEEE Trans. Neural Networks, vol. 2, no. 4, pp. 467-471, 1991.

[6] I. Topalova and A. Tzokev, "Automated Texture Classification of Marble Shades with Real-Time PLC Neural Network Implementation", WCCI 2010 IEEE World Congress on Computational Intelligence, July, pp.1031-1038, ISBN 978-1-4244-8126-2/10, Barcelona, Spain, 2010.

[7] I. Topalova, "Automated Marble Plate Classification System Based on Different Neural Network Input Training Sets and PLC Implementation", IJARAI – International Journal of Advanced Research in Artificial Intelligence, May, pp. 50-56, Volume1, Issue2, ISSN: 2165-4069, 2012.

[8] I. Topalova, A. Mihailov and A. Tzokev, "Automated classification of heat resistant steel structures based on neural networks", IEEE 25-th Convention of Electrical and Electronics Engineers'08, December, pp. 437- 440, ISBN: 978-1-4244-2482-5, Eilat, ISRAEL, 2008.

[9] E. W. Weisstein, "Sampling Theorem." From MathWorld--A Wolfram Web Resource. http://mathworld.wolfram.com/SamplingTheorem.html

[10] NeuroSolutions, User Manual, pp. 84-85, Copyright © 2014 by NeuroDimension, 2015.

Fig. 8.   NNs output values in dependence of variations of two characteristic points – $\text{Max}\left[\frac{d^2H}{dg^2}\right]$ and H (g) max-diff

These points correspond to the maximum value of the second derivative and to the histogram point where the difference between the histogram values of the tested samples is maximal. It is visible according to Figure 8, that NN3 separates and isolates better the classes in comparison to NN1 and NN2 applying closer final fitting, steeper slopes, deeper hollows and sharper boundaries.

23

Implement Fuzzy Logic to Optimize Electronic Business Success

Fahim Akhter

Department of Management Information Systems
College of Business Administration
King Saud University, Saudi Arabia

Abstract—Customers are realizing the importance and benefits of shopping online such as convenience, comparison, product research, larger selection, and lower prices. The dynamic nature of e-commerce evokes online businesses to make alterations in their business processes and decisions making to satisfy customers' needs. Online businesses are adopting Business Intelligence (BI) tools and systems with the collaboration of fuzzy logic system to forecast the future of the e-commerce. With the aid of BI, businesses have more possibilities to choose types and structures of required information to serve customers. The fuzzy logic system and BI capabilities would allow both customers and vendors to make right decisions about online shopping. Many experts believe that trust and security are critical risk factors for the embracement of e-commerce. Online trust may be influenced by factors such as usability, familiarity and conducting business with unknown parties. This paper discusses fuzzy logic and BI approach to gauge the level of trust and security in online transactions. The paper further addresses the issues and concerns related to the equilibrium of trust, security, and usability in online shopping.

Keywords—Business Intelligence; Fuzzy Logic; Electronic Business; Trust; Security; Usability

I. INTRODUCTION

E-commerce is a widely accepted way of doing business, and within a relatively short time, its services have risen to become a core element of the Internet. The Census Bureau of the Department of Commerce declared that the estimate of U.S. retail e-commerce sales for the fourth quarter of 2015 was $89.1 billion, an increase of 2.1 percent (±0. 9%) since the third quarter of 2015 [1]. E-commerce sales in the USA are projected to reach $482 billion by 2018 [2], accounting for approximately 9% retail sales within the country. The number of digital buyers reached 171 million in 2015 and continues to increase, with the total number of digital buyers projected to surpass 190 million by 2018. Credit and debit cards (73%) are the payment method of choice for USA online shoppers with digital payments (16%) increasing in popularity [2]. The growth of e-commerce is not alone in the US, but the sign points towards continued growth globally. To this end, we aimed at identifying major elements that back the acceptance of e-commerce among the users. This study established the elements that contribute to the growth of users' trust, leading them to complete online retail sales in the United States transactions.

Consumers perceive security threats from different perspectives, for example, whether the web server is owned and operated by a legitimate company, how one can verify that the web pages do not contain malicious code, or how one can ensure that the Web server will not distribute the information to a third party. Similarly, it is important to be able to confirm that the information sent back and forth between the server and the user's browser has not been altered. These concerns illustrate the types of a security issue that can arise in e-commerce transactions. The importance of security implementation is reflected in the policies and actions of the company. Consumers analyze the security policies of vendors mainly through the company's statements on their homepage. These statements normally describe the terms and conditions of the vendor's security policies. For example, through the introduction of security features such as the presence of a secure socket layer, encryption, password and third party security seals. Some companies explain these security policies to alleviate consumers concern while some make these issues hard to find and difficult to understand.

The effectiveness of communicating a commitment to consumers by the use of the latest technology such as third party verification programs, encryption methods, and data protection is important for online companies to appreciate. Previous studies [3] have found no negative correlation between the presence of security statements and the perceived risk of a site. Research also revealed that security statements of Web based companies do show a positive correlation with an increased likelihood that consumers' will purchase from those companies. However, it is not clear during the decision making process, under what conditions the consumer considers security features more important than 'pleasure' features such as convenience, ease of use, and ease of navigation.

An expert has argued that the growth of online e-commerce is attributed not only to ease of use, but also to the fact that they provide reputation and feedback systems that help marketplace platforms create trust [4]. Security features are complex to understand by consumers, but, provided they are properly handled, consumers will confidently conduct their purchase online. Thus, the second hypothesis suggests that the security indicators are the leading factors in the customer's decision to purchase online when compared to design features.

II. LITERATURE REVIEW

An expert has argued that the operational Business Intelligence supports an analysis and control of business processes by an integration of information systems from a technical and business perspective [5]. BI enables the web-based business to make informed business decisions and thus can be the source of competitive advantages. This advantage is necessary to improve the timeliness and quality of information to serve consumers 'needs. The access to current and accurate information could eliminate the vagueness within a business process. Due to the vagueness and ambiguous information, consumers' find the decision-making process hard and painful. BI would enhance coordination among business process and enable the business to respond timely to consumers' concern and expectations.

Fuzzy logic provides a means for coping with the ambiguity and vagueness that are often present in B2C commerce [4]. Indeed, it was reported that qualitative and fuzzy type information is commonly used in the trust evaluation process [6]. MATLAB was used because of the built-in support that assisted in understanding the intrinsic relationships between the driving parameters and their effects on the degree of B2C transactions in e-commerce. In conclusion, this study has provided a deeper insight into the factors affecting consumer perception of B2C commerce. Nowadays, consumers have many online alternatives to explore and make a sensible and safe purchase decision. They could find the same items offered by different online retailers with different price options in a matter of a couple of clicks. Consumers buying decision could be influenced by different factors such as trustworthiness, brand, reputation, familiarity, third party seal, security and privacy, fulfillment, presentation and many more. Consumers have to analyze and compare these factors to make a final decision of pursuing online transactions. The purpose of research is to uncover hidden relationships between the critical factors and their effect on the human decision process.

The study [7] provides a review of the literature on the trust issue mainly considering organizational level relationships. The review highlights trust evaluation being a multi-layer, multi-criteria and often a context-dependent process which commonly uses various sources of evidence to judge the trustworthiness of trustees. It has been mentioned [8] that trust has been the most important factor for consumers to do business with each other Contrarily, the trustworthiness of a system provides assurance for consumers to choose a particular e-commerce platform in the first place. They have proposed a fuzzy hybrid multi-criteria analysis approach to measure the trustworthiness of e-commerce systems.

It's extremely critical to acknowledge and understand the trust issues that are associated with the websites which hold the customer back from shopping online [9]. They believe that the consumers' concerns have to be acknowledged in respect of security, usability and trust parameters that leads to the development of the fuzzy system. The researchers has [10] presented and discussed a fuzzy logic based reputation system that assessed the consumers and vendors through the exploitation of a fuzzy trust model which takes into account a set of metrics and a fuzzy based reputation aggregation taking into account credibility concept to discriminate false trust values.

III. METHODOLOGY

This study adopts a fuzzy logic approach and utilizes a mathematical research toolset known as Matlab fuzzy logic toolbox® to achieve its objectives. The rationale for choosing the fuzzy logic approach is based on the underlying reasoning process behind B2C transactions, which is based on human decision-making. Though many factors influence the decision process of B2C transactions, the perception of an influencing feature is more important than the actual level of the feature itself. For example, if the perceived security level is higher than its actual implementation, then it will contribute positively to the level of B2C outcome. There may be cases where the inverse is true as well, but for such cases, a high level of persuasion will be needed to alter the perception level.

The concept of a linguistic variable is paramount to fuzzy logic, where values of a linguistic variable are expressed as words rather than numerical values. For example, the statement 'e-commerce successfully implies that the linguistic variable *e-commerce* takes the linguistic value *successful*. The term *rule* in Fuzzy logic, which is the most commonly used types of knowledge representation, can be defined as an IF-THEN structure that relates has given information or facts in the IF part to some action in the THEN part [11]. A rule provides some description of how to solve a problem. The rules are relatively easy to create and understand. Any rule consists of two parts: the IF part, called the *antecedent* (premise or condition) and the THEN part called the consequent (conclusion or action). Furthermore, a rule can have multiple antecedents joined by the keywords AND (conjunction), OR (disjunction) or a combination of both.

Fuzzy reasoning includes two distinct parts: (1) evaluating the rule *antecedent* and (2) implication or applying the result to the *consequent*. In the classical expert system, if the rule antecedent is true, then the consequent is also true. In fuzzy systems, where the antecedent is a fuzzy statement, all rules fire to some extent, or in other words, they fire partially. This can also be understood as that if the premise is true to some degree, then the conclusion will also be true to the same degree. It is required to examine the various hedges of this set, which will automatically create some additional subset of the trust indicators. In order to get a complete picture of the fuzzy expert system, an inference diagram can give a detailed explanation of the processes involved.

It should be noted that the initial input(s) are a crisp set of numbers. These values are converted from a numerical level to a linguistic level. Following that, the fuzzy rules are applied and fuzzy inference engine is executed. This will result in a given B2C level as varying degree of membership of fuzzy subsets of the B2C superset. The last step is the defuzzification process, which provides a numeric value for the likelihood of the B2C transaction, such as how is this system useful to the consumer and what benefits can the B2C vendor expect from utilizing such a tool? For the consumer who is unaware or unable to reach a sound buying decision this tool will assist him/her in understanding the parameters that could influence or ascertain the strength and weaknesses of the B2C site. Similarly, the B2C vendor can use this tool to discover the critical factors on which consumer bases a B2C transaction irrespective of the product/services offered. Consequently, a more realistic picture can be drawn of the factors influencing a consumer's B2C decision.

IV. DISCUSSION & ANALYSIS

The raw data from the survey has been entered into the worksheet and no interpretation is provided. In the security worksheet, a linguistic input has been assigned a numeric value such as 2, 1 or 0 to calculate the accumulated security level. Accumulated security level is the total sum of the four numeric values and maximum is the percentage of the sum (x/8 multiply by 100). This security level is then calculated as a percentage of a maximum value (usually 8) and from that, a linguistic security level is drawn. It was decided to express the security level as one of three linguistic values, namely low, moderate, and high. The percentage of maximum is evenly distributed to establish a linguistic security level such as low (0-33), moderate (34-66), and high (67-100). The Familiarity worksheet followed the same pattern as used in the security worksheet. The Usability worksheet also followed the same pattern except the linguistic design level was labeled as poor (0-33), moderate (34-66), and good (67-100). In the linguistic data worksheet, trust data have been entered and aligned with security, familiarity, and usability levels by expressing them in terms of linguistic parameters as explained earlier. A Visual Basic language was used to extract and organized data. Trust and other categories are labeled as very low, low, moderate, high, very high and fair, moderate and highly respectively. In the trust rules worksheet, a maximum of twenty-seven unique rules could be identified from respondents input by sorting the security, familiarity and usability columns in alphabetic order. The rules describing the basis for a given trust level were based on degrees of security, familiarity, and usability. These degrees were formulated in terms of their linguistic variables such as low, moderate and high. The degree for usability level was expressed in terms of poor, moderate and good. Similarly, the degree for a trust level was ranging from very low to very high, in five distinct fuzzy sets.

These rules were derived from the survey data after a thorough organization and analysis represent the users' views of the Trust level of a given website based on the given factors. A rule can be extracted such as if (security = high) and (familiarity = low) and (usability = moderate) then (trust = moderate trust). In order to fully understand the contributions from various factors contributing to the Trust level, it is required that we examine the contribution of each factor separately. Figure 1 shows the contribution to Trust of a given website originating from the Security. Therefore, the contribution from Familiarity and Usability has been kept constant at three levels, namely: low, moderate and high corresponding to numeric values for Familiarity and Usability of (1 - 4 and 7). The figure 8 shows that Trust level is monotonically increasing for increasing the perceived security of a website for any given level of Familiarity and Usability (F&U). However, when both F&U is "High" (numeric value of 7) the Trust level is at its maximum for maximum Security. The three curves have one common feature that they exhibit a

"staircase shaped" curvature. It is interesting to note that for "low" and "moderate" levels of F&U the developed Trust is almost identical up to a Security level of about 5. Then there is a sharp change on the Trust level between "low" and "moderate", and the perceived Trust for "moderate" F&U is approaching that of "high". A general observation is that the Trust is positively related to Security for any given value of Familiarity and Usability. This observation is also plausible to the human mind. One feature that is disclosed from this figure is that for "high" levels of Security the Trust difference is less significant for "moderate" and "high" levels of F&U. This result could not be anticipated from the outset.

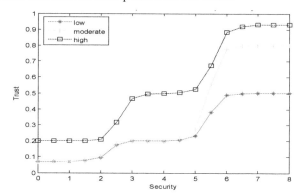

Fig. 1.   Trust versus Security for constant familiarity and design

The study has attempted to visualize the Trust level as a continuous function of its input parameters. It should be noted that since the contribution of Familiarity and Usability is identical, it suffices to view Trust as a function of Security and one other factor say Familiarity. The figure 3 attempts to portray variation of Trust as encapsulated in the rules for the Trust.

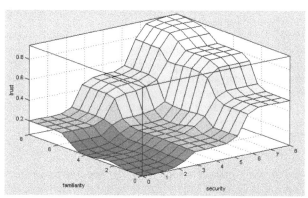

Fig. 2.   The trust level is positively related to Levels of Security and Familiarity

The figure 2 shows that Trust level is positively related to Levels of Security and Familiarity. That is when Familiarity and Security are low, then Trust is also low. Furthermore, the Trust is at its maximum when the both Security and Familiarity are maximized. Since the low Familiarity Trust is increasing in "steps" with increasing Security, attaining its maximum at a level of about 0.5. Looking at figure 3 from its topmost point the gradient perpendicular to Security is less than that which is perpendicular to Familiarity axis. This suggests that lowering the Security level has a greater detrimental effect on Trust than that attained when decreasing Familiarity levels of similar magnitude. The highest gradient for the Trust is when Familiarity is "moderate" and Security is "moderate" to "high". This suggests that when people are somewhat familiar with a website then a small increase in security levels from between moderate to high security will boost their trust in a significant way. Looking at figure 5 diagonally for (low, low) to (high, high) levels of Security and Familiarity one observes three plateaus where the last one is around 0.925 and remains at that level even when the input factors are increased further. This result is somehow unexpected and may be due to the fuzzy nature of the expert system where a "Trust" or "Truth" level of 100 % is unrealistic. The contributions of Familiarity and Usability levels on Trust are similar and, in fact, identical. This can also be deduced from the figure 3, showing complete mirror symmetry of the Trust mapping. One interesting point to note however is that for maximum Familiarity and Usability the Trust level is never higher than 0.5. This plateau is also reached fairly rapidly with high gradients from both sides of the input variables.

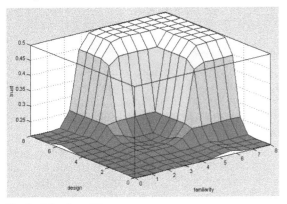

Fig. 3.   Mapping of Trust

Consumers generally perceive online shopping as a risky option due to presents of numerous risks. Lack of trust is one of the major risk factors for consumers for not purchasing from online. Security and privacy issues have become an another leading risk factors major for consumers as well business due the growth of the Internet and the complex nature of e-commerce. Strong encryption and authentication are useful in terms of helping to build the trustworthiness of transactions over the Internet but are not yet sufficient for customers to use e-commerce with confidence. Many consumers do not trust an available security option for online transactions and neither trust e-commerce systems, nor believe they will be able to evaluate or control their information when providing them. The issue of trust is very important, especially when the success of e-commerce relies on the profitable exchange of business and consumer relationship.

Fuzzy logic based decision support system, containing BI tools, supports business and organizational decision-making relationship. A properly designed system is an interactive software-based system intended to help consumers' to gauge

the level of risk factors in a given website. The proposed system in this study could compile useful information from raw data, documents, personal knowledge, and from business models to create rules to identify the potential risk factors in respect of conducting online transactions. Online business required a current and precision information about the consumers' background, needs and perception of the business process. In this respect, the fuzzy logic approach is capable of collaborating with BI to collect and process the consumers' information. This partnership will assist in creating the rules for making right decisions.

The proposed system is also beneficial to web-based businesses. It allows the businesses to reach out the consumers' possibly by BI. The recommendations and suggestions of the proposed systems would assist the management to address the needs of the customers, ability to act on market drivers, optimization of business and customer retention.

REFERENCES

[1]   U.S. Census Bureau News. Quarterly Retail E-Commerce Sales 4th Quarter 2015. Available at: https://www.census.gov/retail/mrts/www/data/pdf/ec_current.pdf (Accessed: 2 March 2016).

[2]   PFS web. eCommerce Summary. Available at: http://www.pfsweb.com/pdf/global-ecommerce-book/2016-Global-eCommerce-Book-USA.pdf (Accessed: 5 March 2016).

[3]   Fahim Akhter and Wafi Albalawi, "Online Trust and Young Entrepreneurs: A case Study of Saudi Arabia", International Journal of Theoretical and Applied Information technology, E-ISSN 1817-3195 / ISSN 1992-8645, 2016.

[4]   S. Tadelis, "The Economics of Reputation and Feedback Systems in E-Commerce Marketplaces," in IEEE Internet Computing, vol. 20, no. 1, pp. 12-19, Jan.-Feb. 2016

[5]   T. Hänel and C. Felden, "An Empirical Investigation of Operational Business Intelligence Perspectives to Support an Analysis and Control of Business Processes," System Sciences, 2015 48th Hawaii International Conference on, Kauai, HI, 2015, pp. 4722-4731.

[6]   Z. M. Husseini, M. H. Fazel Zarandi and S. M. Moattar Husseini, "Trust evaluation for buyer-supplier relationship concerning fuzzy approach," Fuzzy Information Processing Society held jointly with 2015 5th World Conference on Soft Computing, 2015 Annual Conference of the North American, Redmond, WA, 2015, pp. 1-6.

[7]   Husseini, Z.M.; Fazel Zarandi, M.H.; Moattar Husseini, S.M., "Trust evaluation for buyer-supplier relationship concerning fuzzy approach," in Fuzzy Information Processing Society, 2015 Annual Conference of the North American, vol., no., pp.1-6, 17-19 Aug. 2015

[8]   Zhengping Wu; Lifeng Wang, "Trustworthiness Measurement of E-commerce Systems Using Fuzzy Hybrid Multi-criteria Analysis," in Trustcom/BigDataSE/ISPA, 2015 IEEE, vol.1, no., pp.668-675, 20-22 Aug. 2015

[9]   Kaur, B.; Madan, S., "A fuzzy expert system to evaluate customer's trust in B2C E-Commerce websites," in Computing for Sustainable Global Development (INDIACom), 2014 International Conference on, vol., no., pp.394-399, 5-7 March 2014

[10] Fahim Akhter and Zakaria Maamar. "Evaluation of Fuzzy Models to Support Online-Trust Assessment." Comparison-Shopping Services and Agent Designs. IGI Global, 90-100, 2009

[11] Zadeh, L. Outline of a new approach to the analysis of the complex system and decision processes. IEEE Transactions on System, Man, and Cybernetics, SMC-3 (1), 1974. 28-44.

24

Language Identification by Using SIFT Features

Nikos Tatarakis , Ergina Kavallieratou
Dept. of Information and Communication System Engineering,
University of the Aegean,
Samos, Greece

***Abstract*—Two novel techniques for language identification of both, machine printed and handwritten document images, are presented. Language identification is the procedure where the language of a given document image is recognized and the appropriate language label is returned. In the proposed approaches, the main body size of the characters for each document image is determined, and accordingly, a sliding window is used, in order to extract the SIFT local features. Once a large number of features have been extracted from the training set, a visual vocabulary is created, by clustering the feature space. Data clustering is performed using K-means or Gaussian Mixture Models and the Expectation - Maximization algorithm. For each document image, a Bag of Visual Words or Fisher Vector representation is constructed, using the visual vocabulary and the extracted features of the document image. Finally, a multi class Support Vector Machine classification scheme is used, to score the system. Experiments are performed on well-known databases and comparative results with another established technique, are also given.**

Keywords—Document image processing; language identification; SIFT features; bag of Visual Words; Fisher Vector

I. Introduction

There is no doubt that nowadays all services tend to become even more digitalized. There is a growing trend for many multinational companies or organizations to digitalize their old documents or books and store them in digital databases. These documents could be either handwritten or machine printed and usually in various languages. Google Books [1] is an example. Language identification is a very important task, as it could help to index and/or sort a big digital document corpus in a convenient way.

In the area of optical character recognition (OCR), most of the works assume that the language of the document is known beforehand. In this case, document language identification could be used as a valuable pre-processing task, in order to determine the correct language and eventually utilize the appropriate OCR engine for text extraction, translation and/or indexing.

The difficulty of language identification is highly dependent on the languages themselves. For example, a machine printed Chinese document is easily separated from a machine printed English document, since the local language structure, words and the shape of the letters, differ vastly in these two languages. Many papers have been published to address this issue.

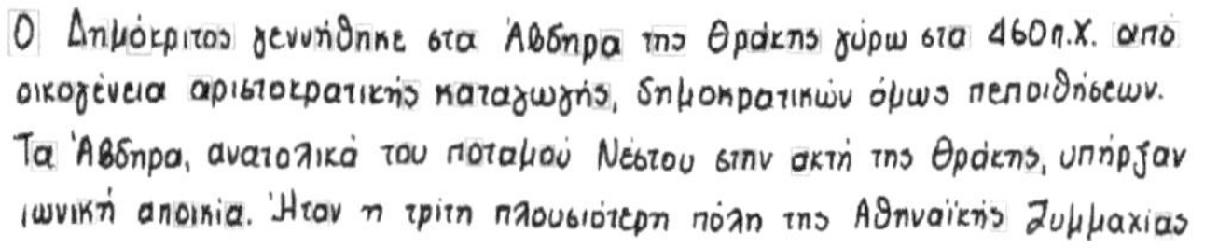
Ο Δημόκριτος γεννήθηκε στα Άβδηρα της Θράκης γύρω στα 460π.Χ. από
οικογένεια αριστοκρατικής καταγωγής, δημοκρατικών όμως πεποιθήσεων.
Τα Άβδηρα, ανατολικά του ποταμού Νέστου στην ακτή της Θράκης, υπήρξαν
ιωνική αποικία. Ήταν η τρίτη πλουσιότερη πόλη της Αθηναϊκής Συμμαχίας

Fig. 1. Handwritten Greek text

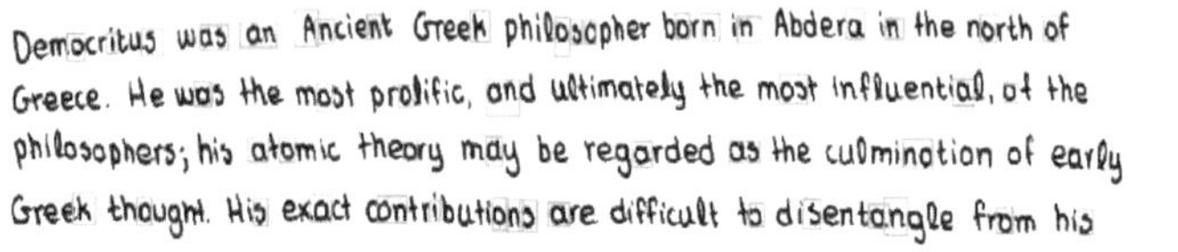
Democritus was an Ancient Greek philosopher born in Abdera in the north of
Greece. He was the most prolific, and ultimately the most influential, of the
philosophers; his atomic theory may be regarded as the culmination of early
Greek thought. His exact contributions are difficult to disentangle from his

Fig. 2. Handwritten English text

In this paper, we focus on languages that are not very distant from each other and even share many common letters, like e.g. English and Greek. In Fig 1 and 2, common letters are noted, to show the very small intra-class variation.

To the best of our knowledge, most of the published work puts great emphasis on machine printed text that is also very linguistically diverse. The proposed works could be classified considering the methodology they are based on: a) Template Matching [2,3] b) Texture Analysis [4,5] and c) Shape Codebooks [6].

Hochberg et al. [2-3] presented a system for language identification matching cluster-based templates. In this work, they aim to discover repeating linguistic features like characters and word shapes in each script. To do so, they create fixed-size templates (textual symbols) from the training set, by clustering similar symbols together and representing each cluster by its centroid. They score the system by matching a subset of symbols to the templates. The reported results show high accuracy on a machine printed text corpus.

Texture analysis has also been proposed for the task of language identification. In [4], G. S. Peake et al. propose a segmentation-free approach. They used grey level co-occurrence matrices and Gabor filters in order to extract features. For classification, a K-NN classifier is used and they reported fair results on machine printed content. In [5], A. Busch et al. extracted wavelet co-occurrence features from small blocks of machine printed text and used a Gaussian Mixture Model (GMM) classifier to score the system. They reported good results, but on small machine printed textual regions and not on the whole document pages. More similar work on texture analysis can be found in [7, 8].

In [6], Zhu et al. propose a segmentation-free language identification system for both handwritten and machine printed documents for 8 languages. They extract local features that called Triple Adjacent Contours (TAS) from document images and form a shape codebook by clustering that feature space. They use that codebook to create an image descriptor for each document image. This descriptor is basically a statistical representation of the frequency that each TAS feature occurs on the image. They use a Support Vector Machine (SVM) for the classification process. They don't show how it performs on languages with low intra class-variation like Greek and English, but they report exceptional results on a wide language variety.

Apart from the aforementioned work, there are also a considerable number of other papers trying to address this problem, based mostly on line analysis of textual features. Projection profiles are being explored in [9] and upward concativities in [10]. These approaches usually require some preprocessing, like skew correction.

In this paper, two systems for the task of Language identification are presented. The first one is based on the Bag of Visual Features (BoVF) [11]. The second approach is based on representing the images using Fisher Vectors (FV) [12-13] created by a GMM visual vocabulary. For these two approaches, a Support Vector Machine classification scheme is used to score the system. Both methods share many similarities, however they perform differently.

The two systems are presented in the sections II and III, respectively, while the experimental results are analyzed in section IV. Finally our conclusions are drawn in section V.

II. LANGUAGE IDENTIFICATION USING BAG OF VISUAL FEATURES

The Bag of Visual Features (BoVF) is one of the suggested methods for generic Image categorization based on image content. This particular method is widely applied in scene and object categorization as well as image retrieval [14-15]. The Bag of Visual Features has been inspired from the Bag of Words of the area of Natural Language Processing that is used for text classification. Generally speaking, the mentioned systems are trying to extract relevant features from the images in order to create a histogram representation of every image (Fig.3) that will be used as input to a classifier.

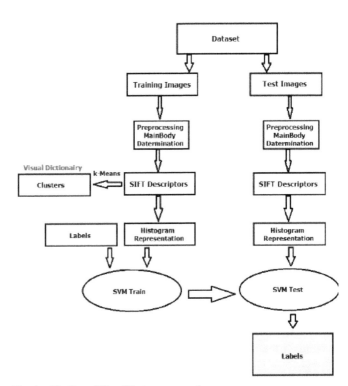

Fig. 4. The Bag of Visual Features approach

The BoVF system that we implement consists of the following steps:

1) A Preprocessing step for every document image that determines the Main Body size of the characters.

2) Feature Extraction for every document image.

3) Creation of a visual vocabulary using k-means.

4) Histogram creation for every document image, which represents the frequency of the visual features in the image.

5) Training of an SVM classification scheme that will be fed with the histograms. The BoVF is a method that only the feature appearance frequency is used from the image without taking into consideration the natural position of every feature on the image. However, in our application, the position of the objects is not important. In Fig.4, the proposed Bag-of-Visual-Feature approach is shown.

The first step consists of the application of the Main Body detection algorithm, described in [16], to the document image. This will return a number n which indicates how tall is the main body of the majority of the characters in the image. During the feature extraction procedure, this information is used in order to create a nxn sliding window to dense sample the image for SIFT features using the algorithm in [17].

1) The SIFT Descriptor is a spatial histogram with 4x4 bins. By setting the size of sliding window to nxn, which is given by the main body detection algorithm, actually the SIFT descriptor is computed in a 4nx4n pixel area (Fig.5).

Democritus was an Ancient I x7

Greece. He was the most pr

philosophers; his atomic the → e x7

Greek thought. His exact cor → a x5

mentor Leucippus, as they

Fig. 3. To represent an image as a Bag of Visual Features, each feature is mapped to the nearest image feature/word cluster. All the information of each document image is finally included in e.g. 300 features, out of the e.g. 500-1000 clusters of Visual Features

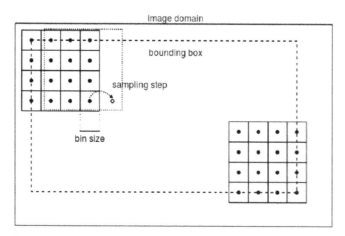

Fig. 5.   Dense SIFT descriptor geometry [18]

This step proved to be particularly important as the document images within a class (same language) have quite similar main body estimations. This scheme creates a more personalized and more sophisticated local descriptor within a class, which creates more unique patterns inside the data and maximizes the inter-class variation, while at the same time the intra-class variation is minimized.

The SIFT descriptor is used, since it is sufficiently robust against noise, as well as scale and rotation invariant, which is very important, especially when we have to deal with badly scanned document images. Finally, the SIFT descriptor is 128-dimensional, which maintains as much information as possible and a more distinctive image representation is achieved.

The visual vocabulary can be thought as a big dictionary that contains visual words (features) from the training set. After a feature is extracted from an image, the visual vocabulary is used in order to map this image feature to the closest cluster. An extreme approach would be to compare every image feature to every feature from the training space. However, this is quite unlikely to happen as the feature space from the training set is extremely large and such a task would be computationally expensive. In order to shrink the feature space and create a comprehensive codebook, k-means is used. As usually, it is hard to define how many clusters are enough for the task. Tests with several k values have to be performed to decide, which the correct value for our data is (section 4).

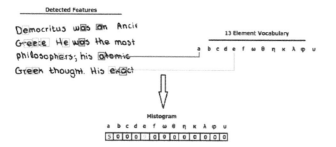

Fig. 6.   Histogram creation

Once the visual vocabulary is created, the image representation follows. For every image, the features are extracted. For every feature, the closest entry in the visual vocabulary is detected. The Euclidean distance is used to

define how close the visual feature to each cluster is. The size of the resulting histogram for each image equals to the size of the dictionary (Fig.6). However, the histogram is usually very sparse, since most of the words of the visual vocabulary are too distant to match with an image feature, especially if they belong to a different language. As a result, some bins of the histogram are overpopulated, while all the others have small or null values. This high variance could cause trouble to the classifier so the histogram is normalized to *1*.

The Classification is the last task of the proposed system. An one- against -all SVM classification is used. The idea behind one-against-all approach is, to train Support Vector Machine models each one separating one class from the rest. Every time, the classifier with the largest decision value is chosen. During training, the classifier is fed with the training histograms and their labels (1/-1). During the testing process, the test histograms are provided and the predicted label is received.

III.   LANGUAGE IDENTIFICATION USING FISHER VECTOR

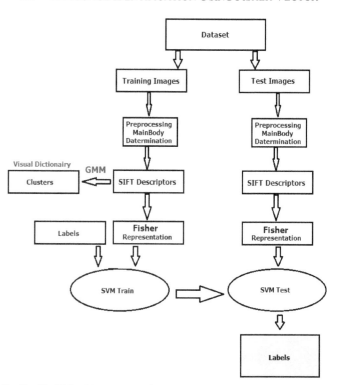

Fig. 7.   The Fisher Vector approach

The Fisher Vector (FV) system is basically an extension to the Bag of Visual Features approach. However, it differs a lot, when it comes to create the visual vocabulary and to represent the images. Here, the visual vocabulary is created by training clusters using the Gaussian Mixture Models (GMM). Following the clustering, the images are represented by Fisher Vectors. In this section, the procedure that builds a Fisher vector, using the clustering given by a GMM, is presented. The other tasks have been analyzed in the previous section.

Thus, Fisher Vector pipeline consists of the following steps:

- A Preprocessing step for every document image that help us to determine the Main Body size of the characters.

- Feature Extraction for every document image.

- Creation of a visual vocabulary using Gaussian Mixture Models.

- Fisher Vector representation is created for every document image.

- Training of an SVM classification scheme that will be fed with the Fisher vectors.

In Fig.7 the proposed approach is shown.

In [13], a new algorithm for image representation using the FV is introduced, given local image descriptors and a GMM probabilistic vocabulary. This algorithm as it is used in our approach is described in Fig.8. The dimensionality of this image descriptor is K(2D+1), where K is the number of GMM clusters and D the dimensions of the local image descriptor. Thus, the D is 128, due to the SIFT descriptor, but the K also needs to be determined through experiments (section 4).

Input:

- Local image descriptors $X = \{ x_t \in R^D, t = 1, \ldots T \}$,
- Gaussian Mixture model parameters $\lambda = \{w_k, \mu_k, \sigma_k, k = 1, \ldots, K\}$

Output:

- Normalized Fisher Vector representation $G_\lambda^X \in R^{K(2D+1)}$

1. **Compute Statistics**
   - For $k = 1, \ldots, K$ initialize accumulators
     - i. $S_k^0 = 0, S_k^1 = 0, S_k^2 = 0$
   - For $t = 1, \ldots T$
     - i. Compute $\gamma_t(k)$ using (3.4.1.1.1 formula, 6)
     - ii. For $k = 1, \ldots T$
       - $S_k^0 = S_k^0 + \gamma_t(k)$,
       - $S_k^1 = S_k^1 + \gamma_t(k)x_t$,
       - $S_k^2 = S_k^2 + \gamma_t(k)x_t^2$

2. **Compute Fisher Vector Signature**
   - For $k = 1, \ldots, K$:

     $G_{\alpha_k}^X = (S_k^0 - Tw_k)/\sqrt{w_k}$

     $G_{\mu_k}^X = (S_k^1 - \mu_k S_k^0)/\sqrt{w_k}\sigma_k$

     $G_{\sigma_k}^X = (S_k^2 - 2\mu_k S_k^1 + (\mu_k^2 - \sigma_k^2)/\sqrt{2w_k\sigma_k^2}$
   - Concatenate all Fisher vector components into one vector

     $G_\lambda^X = (G_{\alpha_1}^X, \ldots, G_{\alpha_K}^X, G_{\mu_1}^X, \ldots, G_{\mu_K}^X, G_{\sigma_1}^{X'}, \ldots, G_{\sigma_K}^X)$

3. **Apply normalizations**
   - For $i = 1, \ldots, K(2D + 1)$ apply power normalization

     $$[G_\lambda^X]_i \leftarrow sign([G_\lambda^X]_i \sqrt{[G_\lambda^X]_i})$$
   - Apply $l_2 - normalization$

     $$G_\lambda^X = G_\lambda^X / \sqrt{G_\lambda^{X'} G_\lambda^X}$$

Fig. 8.   The algorithm for the Fisher Vector system

IV. EXPERIMENTAL RESULTS

In order to evaluate these systems, three different datasets are used. The first is a labmade dataset that consists of machine printed text in Greek, English and Arabic document images that have been taken randomly from papers and e-books all over the web. It contains 120 test images, 40 from each language, and 180 training images, 60 from each language. This is a high resolution dataset. The second is the dataset of ICDAR2013 Handwriting Segmentation Contest [19]. This one also consists of high resolution images of handwritten text in English, Greek and Indian. It contains 150 test images, 50 from each language, and 200 training images, 75 from each language. The third dataset was intended to be as close as possible to the one described in [6], in order to give comparative results. In order To evaluate the performance of our multiclass SVM classifier and to score the system, confusion matrixes and the accuracy rate were used.

A. The Bag of Visual Feature System

First, it examined how the results are affected by the window size. The goal is to determine the window size in relation to the main body size, as a natural normalization of the writing style. Once the optimal size is determined, then, additional experiments will be performed in order to evaluate the size of the vocabulary.

Roughly, around 600-700 SIFT features are extracted from each image. This step of the algorithm is particularly time consuming, since the images have been taken in high resolution. However, trying to keep preprocessing as low as possible, image resizing techniques that would probably cause valuable information loss were not applied.

In this experiment, the size of the codebook was kept relatively small at the fixed value of k=50, while performing experimenting with the following rectangular window sizes: main body x 1, main body x 2 and round(main body x 0.5). In tables 1-3, the results are shown on Labmade dataset, while in Fig.9 the accuracy graph for those values is presented.

TABLE I.   DATA SET = LABMADE, K=50, WINDOW=MAIN BODY X 1, SVM C PARAMETER = 0.0001

Labmade Data Set		Predicted Class		
		Greek	English	Arabic
Actual Class	Greek	0.525	0.35	0.125
	English	0.3	0.55	0.15
	Arabic	0.175	0.125	0.70
Mean Diagonal Accuracy : 59.16%				

TABLE II.   DATA SET= LABMADE, K=50, WINDOW = MAIN BODY X 2 , SVM C PARAMETER = 0.0001

Labmade Data Set		Predicted Class		
		Greek	English	Arabic
Actual Class	Greek	**0.475**	0.325	0.20
	English	0.35	**0.525**	0.125
	Arabic	0.2	0.125	**0.675**
Mean Diagonal Accuracy : 55.83%				

TABLE III.   DATA SET= LABMADE, K=50, WINDOW =ROUND(MAIN BODYX0.5), SVM C PARAMETER = 0.0001

Labmade Data Set		Predicted Class		
		Greek	English	Arabic
Actual Class	Greek	**0.45**	0.35	0.20
	English	0.375	**0.475**	0.15
	Arabic	0.175	0.15	**0.675**
Mean Diagonal Accuracy : 53.33%				

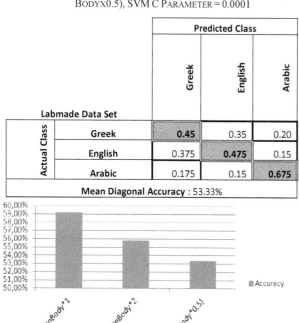

Fig. 9.   Collective Accuracy Graph

It is clear that the highest accuracy was obtained by using the rectangular window with size main bodyx1. The results look quite low, since the visual vocabulary contained 50 visual words, only. In the following experiments the sliding window will constantly set at this size, while the vocabulary size will be increased from 100 to 2000 features. The results of this experiment are presented in tables 4-8, while the accuracy graph is shown in Fig.10.

TABLE IV.   DATA SET= LABMADE, *K*=100, *WINDOW = MAIN BODY X 1,* SVM *C* PARAMETER = 0.0001

Labmade Data Set		Predicted Class		
		Greek	English	Arabic
Actual Class	Greek	**0.65**	0.225	0.125
	English	0.175	**0.675**	0.15
	Arabic	0.2	0.075	**0.725**
Mean Diagonal Accuracy : 68.33%				

TABLE V.   DATA SET= LABMADE, K=200, WINDOW = MAIN BODY X 1, SVM C PARAMETER = 0.0001

Homemade Data Set		Predicted Class		
		Greek	English	Arabic
Actual Class	Greek	**0.70**	0.20	0.10
	English	0.175	**0.75**	0.075
	Arabic	0.10	0.075	**0.825**
Mean Diagonal Accuracy : 75.83%				

TABLE VI.   DATA SET= LABMADE, K=500, WINDOW = MAIN BODY X 1, SVM C PARAMETER = 0.0001

Homemade Data Set		Predicted Class		
		Greek	English	Arabic
Actual Class	Greek	**0.8**	0.15	0.05
	English	0.125	**0.825**	0.05
	Arabic	0.075	0.025	**0.9**
Mean Diagonal Accuracy : 84.16%				

TABLE VII.   DATA SET= LABMADE, K=1000, $WINDOW$ =$MAIN BODY X 1$, SVM C PARAMETER = 0.0001

	Predicted Class		
Labmade Data Set	Greek	English	Arabic
Actual Class Greek	**0.85**	0.125	0.025
English	0.1	**0.875**	0.025
Arabic	0.025	0.025	**0.95**
Mean Diagonal Accuracy : 89.16%			

TABLE VIII.   DATA SET= LABMADE, K=2000, $WINDOW$ = $MAIN BODY X 1$, SVM C PARAMETER = 0.0001

	Predicted Class		
Labmade Data Set	Greek	English	Arabic
Actual Class Greek	**0.875**	0.075	0.05
English	0.075	**0.90**	0.025
Arabic	0.025	0.025	**0.95**
Mean Diagonal Accuracy : 90.83%			

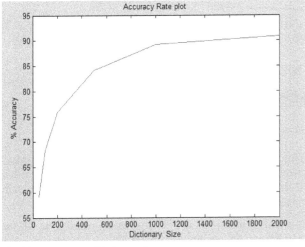

Fig. 10. Accuracy vs. Dictionary size

Apparently, the dictionary size is a very important parameter because it highly affects the overall performance. For the Labmade dataset, the highest score was achieved by using a relatively large dictionary of 2000 centers. It is worth noting that after 1000 centers the accuracy is getting marginally better. Therefore, anything over 2000 is expected to increase performance cost rather than the accuracy.

TABLE IX.   DATA SET= ICDAR 2013, K=2000, $WINDOW$ = $MAIN BODY$, SVM C PARAMETER = 0.0001

	Predicted Class		
ICDAR 2013	Greek	English	Indian
Actual Class Greek	**0.86**	0.12	0.02
English	0.14	**0.84**	0.02
Indian	0.04	0.02	**0.94**
Mean Diagonal Accuracy : 88%			

Similarly, on the ICDAR 2013 dataset the best results obtained for window size = *main body x 1* and *k=2000* (table 9).

Regarding ICDAR2013 dataset, the best performance for the Bag Of Visual Features model is a bit lower than the best result of the labmade dataset, since this dataset is much harder as it contains only handwritten documents images.

B. The Fisher Vector System

For this approach, the optimal dictionary size among our experiments on the ICDAR dataset proved to be 256 elements (tables 10-12, Fig.11), since for more elements the whole system gets very slow and eventually it runs out of memory. Similarly, in [20] they also suggest a codebook of 256 clusters. Again, the window of size=*main body x 1* was used. Finally, in table 13, the results for the Labmade dataset are given.

TABLE X.   DATA SET= ICDAR2013, K=64, $WINDOW$ = $MAIN BODY X 1$, SVM C PARAMETER = 0.0001

	Predicted Class		
ICDAR 2013	Greek	English	Indian
Actual Class Greek	**86**	10	4
English	12	**86**	2
Indian	2	0	**98**
Mean Diagonal Accuracy : 90%			

TABLE XI.   DATA SET= ICDAR2013, K=128, WINDOW = MAIN BODY X 1, SVM C PARAMETER = 0.0001

	Predicted Class		
ICDAR 2013	Greek	English	Indian
Actual Class Greek	**88**	12	0
English	8	**92**	0
Indian	2	0	**98**
Mean Diagonal Accuracy : 92.66%			

TABLE XII.   DATA SET= ICDAR2013, K=256, WINDOW = MAIN BODY X 1, SVM C PARAMETER = 0.0001

		Predicted Class		
		Greek	English	Indian
ICDAR 2013				
Actual Class	Greek	**0.92**	0.08	0
	English	0.06	**0.94**	0
	Indian	0	0	**1**
Mean Diagonal Accuracy : 95,33%				

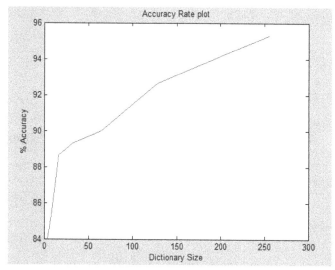

Fig. 11. Accuracy vs. Dictionary size

TABLE XIII.   DATA SET= LABMADE, K=256, WINDOW = MAIN BODY X 1, SVM C PARAMETER = 0.0001

		Predicted Class		
		Greek	English	Arabic
Labmade				
Actual Class	Greek	**0.925**	0.05	0.025
	English	0.025	**0.95**	0.025
	Arabic	0.025	0	**0.975**
Mean Diagonal Accuracy : 95%				

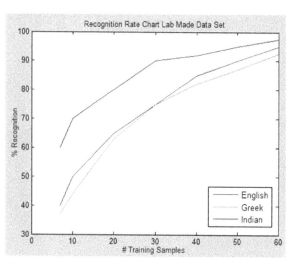

Fig. 12. Recognition Rate for the Labmade dataset

These results are quite surprising since they give higher scores in ICDAR 2013 dataset, which is objectively a harder handwritten dataset compared to the Labmade. However, by a closer look on the data in the labmade results, the scores regarding the Greek and English documents are slightly higher than their handwritten equivalent ones (Fig.12-13).

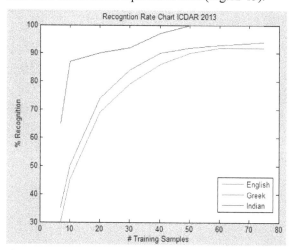

Fig. 13. Recognition Rate for the ICDAR 2013

This proves that languages with very distinctive features like Arabic and Indian are much easier to separate. Even with a small amount of training samples it is enough to obtain acceptable recognition rates.

It was mentioned that the dimensionality of a Fisher Vector representation is given by the formula $K(2D+1)$, where K is the number of GMM clusters and D the local image descriptor dimensions. Suppose that we have formed a GMM dictionary of $K=256$ centers like above. As the SIFT descriptor is 128-

dimensional, every image is represented by a vector of $256 \cdot (2 \cdot 128 + 1)$, or 65792 elements. A good idea to shrink the Fisher vector is the application of PCA to the 128-D SIFT descriptors [20]. This would lead to a more computationally efficient classification scheme as the SVM would have to deal with smaller Fisher Vectors. In [21], they propose to apply PCA on SIFT descriptors to reduce their dimension from 128 to 64. This would cut down the final Fisher Vector to 33024 elements instead of 65792, which makes the system much more efficient and less memory starving. In [20] they report some increase in their overall classification performance after applying PCA, about 4%. In of our system, regarding the effect of PCA, apart of the faster computation and less memory demands, the overall performance was slightly dropped (Fig.14).

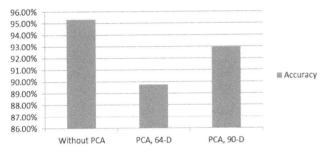

Fig. 14. Considering PCA for the proposed system

In any case, the reported results were already pretty high, so it was quite expected that PCA wouldn't help drastically. In fact, it didn't help at all. This also could mean that the extracted features are of high quality and very discriminative and contain very small amounts of redundant data, if any at all.

C. Comparative results

In this section, comparative results to the system presented in [6] are given.

Maryland + IAM 3.0	Predicted Class (Percentages)							
	Thai	Cyrillic	Chinese	Hindi	Korean	Japanese	Arabic	English
Thai	100	0	0	0	0	0	0	0
Cyrillic	0	97.5	0	0	0	0	2.5	0
Chinese	0	0	97.5	0	2.5	0	0	0
Hindi	0	0	2.5	97.5	0	0	0	0
Korean	0	0	0	0	100	0	0	0
Japanese	0	0	6.65	0	0	66.7	26.65	0
Arabic	0	0	0	0	8.70	0	91.30	0
English	0	1	0	0	0	0	0.5	98.5
Mean Diagonal Accuracy : 93.62%								

Fig. 15. Confusion matrix for the BoFV system

Maryland + IAM 3.0	Predicted Class (Percentages)							
	Thai	Cyrillic	Chinese	Hindi	Korean	Japanese	Arabic	English
Thai	100	0	0	0	0	0	0	0
Cyrillic	0	100	0	0	0	0	0	0
Chinese	0	0	97.5	0	2.5	0	0	0
Hindi	0	0	0	100	0	0	0	0
Korean	0	0	0	0	100	0	0	0
Japanese	0	0	0	0	0	80	20	0
Arabic	0	0	0	0	0	0	100	0
English	0	0	0	0	0	0	0	100
Mean Diagonal Accuracy : 97.18%								

Fig. 16. Confusion matrix for the FV system

Maryland + IAM 3.0	Predicted Class (Percentages)							
	Thai	Cyrillic	Chinese	Hindi	Korean	Japanese	Arabic	English
Thai	96.3	0	0.3	0.9	0.3	0.6	0	1.6
Cyrillic	0.4	97.1	0	0	0	0	0.5	2
Chinese	0.2	0.7	85	1	1	6.7	1.4	4
Hindi	0	0	0.2	98.8	0	0.8	0.2	0
Korean	0.1	0.5	0.8	1.9	96	0.5	0	0.1
Japanese	0	0	1.3	0.2	1.3	96.2	0	1
Arabic	0	0	0.3	0	0	0	99.7	0
English	0.6	0.6	0	0.2	1.1	0	1.6	95.9
Mean Diagonal Accuracy : 95.6%								

Fig. 17. Confusion matrix for the system in [6]

To evaluate objectively the proposed systems, they are compared to the current state of the art system presented by G. Zhu et al. in [6] by using the same databases; The IAM handwriting DB3.0 database [22] as well as the University of Maryland multilingual database [23]. The dataset contains over 1000 document images from both databases in 8 languages (Thai, Cyrillic, Chinese, Hindi, Korean, Japanese, Arabic and English). The comparative results are given (Fig.15-17) in the form of confusion tables.

V. CONCLUSIONS

In this paper, two systems for the task of Language Identification based on document Images have been proposed. To evaluate the performance of the proposed systems, three datasets were used. From the experimental results, it is concluded that both of these systems have high potential, although the Fisher Vector approach proved to be much better and more accurate than the Bag of Visual Features. It is also safe to claim that the Fisher Vector method is able to outperform the current state of the art approach for the task of Language Identification as it is shown in section 4.3.

The main advantages of the Fisher Vector (FV) image representation over Bag of Visual Features (BoVF) representation, is, that the former, using a much smaller dictionary, that contains only 256 clusters, it significantly outperforms the BoVF system which needs at least a 1000-words dictionary to perform well, as it was proved in our experiments. Therefore, the FV system has a lower computational cost as it requires a much smaller dictionary to obtain acceptable recognition accuracy. The only issue with Fisher vectors is that they are quite dense compared to the sparse BoVF histograms, which makes them unappealing, in case we have to deal with a lot of data, as the storage and I/O requirements will increase dramatically.

Another very important fact is that even with a small number of training samples, it can perform exceptionally well, especially if the document language includes very distinctive features.

Finally, the choice to include a preprocessing task like the main body estimation is of high importance. This task helped to extract very distinctive, personalized and relevant features from every image and increased the overall accuracy of our system.

In the future, we are going to experiment with more techniques inspired from Natural Language Processing for the document Image Processing tasks.

REFERENCES

[1]   L. Vincent, "Google book search: Document understanding on a massive scale", In Proc. Int. Conf. Document Analysis and Recognition, pages 819–823, 2007.

[2]   J. Hochberg, L. Kerns, P. Kelly, T. Thomas, "Automatic script identification from images using cluster-based templates", Proceedings of Third International Conference on Document Analysis and Recognition, Vol.1, pp. 378, 1995.

[3]   J. Hochberg, P. Kelly, T. Thomas, L. Kerns, "Automatic Script Identification From Document Images Using Cluster-Based Templates", IEEE Transactions on Pattern Analysis and Machine Intelligence, pp. 176-181, 1997.

[4]   G. S. Peake, T.N. Tan, "Script and Language Identification from Document Images", Proceedings of the Workshop on Document Image Analysis, pp.10-17, 1997.

[5]   A. Busch, W. W. Boles, and S. Sridharan, "Texture for script identification" IEEE Transactions on Pattern Analysis and Machine Intelligence, 27(11):1720–1732, 2005.

[6]   G. Zhu, X. Yu, Y. Li, and D. Doermann, "Unconstrained Language Identification Using A Shape Codebook", ICFHR2008, p.13–18, 2008.

[7]   T. Tan, "Rotation Invariant Texture Features And Their Use In Automatic Script Identification", IEEE Transactions on Pattern Analysis and Machine Intelligence, 20(7):751–756, 1998.

[8]   V. Singhal, N. Navin, and D. Ghosh, "Script-based classification ofhand-written text document in a multilingual environment," in Proc. ofInt. Workshop on Research Issues in Data Eng., 2003, pp. 47–54. -

[9]   S. L. Wood, Xiaozhong Yao, K. Krishnamurthi, L. Dang, Language identification forprinted text independent of segmentation, Proceedings of the International Conference onImage Processing, vol.3, pp.3428-3431, 1995. -

[10] A. L. Spitz, "Determination of the Script and Language Content of Document Images", IEEE Trans. Pattern Analysis and Machine Intelligence, pp. 235-245, 1997.

[11] G.Csurka, C. Dance, L. Fan, J. Willamowski, C. Bray, "Visual categorization with bags of keypoints", ECCV'04 workshop on Statistical Learning in Computer Vision, pp. 59-74, 2004.

[12] F. Perronnin and C. Dance. Fisher kernels on visual vocabulariesfor image categorization. In CVPR, 2007. -

[13] J. Sanchez, F. Perronnin, T. Mensink, and J. Verbeek, "Image classification with the Fisher vector: Theory and practice", IJCV, 105(3):222–245, June 2013.

[14] J. Winn, A. Criminisi, and T. Minka. Object categorizationby learned universal visual dictionary.In International Conference on Computer Vision,2005.=

[15] J. Liu. Image retrieval based on bag-of-words model. InarXiv preprint arXiv:1304.5168, 2013. -

[16] P. Diamantatos, V. Verras, E. Kavallieratou. Detecting Main Body Size in Document Images. ICDAR, 2013.

[17] D.G.Lowe, "Distinctive image features from scale-invariant keypoints", International Journal of Computer Vision, 60:91–110, 2004.

[18] A. Vedaldi and B. Fulkerson. VLFeat library. http://www.vlfeat.org/, 2008.

[19] N.Stamatopoulos, B.Gatos, G.Louloudis, U.Pal, A.Alaei, "ICDAR 2013 handwriting segmentation contest", 12th International Conference on Document Analysis and Recognition (ICDAR), pp. 1402-1406, 2013.

[20] K. Chatfield, V. Lempitsky, A. Vedaldi, and A. Zisserman. The devil is in the details: an evaluation of recent feature encoding methods. In BMVC, 2011.

[21] Y. Ke and R. Sukthankar. PCA-SIFT: A more distinctive representation for local image descriptors. In Proc. CVPR, 2004. L. Vincent, "Google book search: Document understanding on a massive scale", In Proc. Int. Conf. Document Analysis and Recognition, pages 819–823, 2007.

[22] J. Hochberg, L. Kerns, P. Kelly, T. Thomas, "Automatic script identification from images using cluster-based templates", Proceedings of Third International Conference on Document Analysis and Recognition, Vol.1, pp. 378, 1995.

[23] J. Hochberg, P. Kelly, T. Thomas, L. Kerns, "Automatic Script Identification From Document Images Using Cluster-Based Templates", IEEE Transactions on Pattern Analysis and Machine Intelligence, pp. 176-181, 1997.

[24] G. S. Peake, T.N. Tan, "Script and Language Identification from Document Images", Proceedings of the Workshop on Document Image Analysis, pp.10-17, 1997.

[25] A. Busch, W. W. Boles, and S. Sridharan, "Texture for script identification" IEEE Transactions on Pattern Analysis and Machine Intelligence, 27(11):1720–1732, 2005.

[26] G. Zhu, X. Yu, Y. Li, and D. Doermann, "Unconstrained Language Identification Using A Shape Codebook", ICFHR2008, p.13–18, 2008.

[27] T. Tan, "Rotation Invariant Texture Features And Their Use In Automatic Script Identification", IEEE Transactions on Pattern Analysis and Machine Intelligence, 20(7):751–756, 1998.

[28] V. Singhal, N. Navin, and D. Ghosh, "Script-based classification ofhand-written text document in a multilingual environment," in Proc. ofInt. Workshop on Research Issues in Data Eng., 2003, pp. 47–54. -

[29] S. L. Wood, Xiaozhong Yao, K. Krishnamurthi, L. Dang, Language identification forprinted text independent of segmentation, Proceedings of the International Conference onImage Processing, vol.3, pp.3428-3431, 1995. -

[30] A. L. Spitz, "Determination of the Script and Language Content of Document Images", IEEE Trans. Pattern Analysis and Machine Intelligence, pp. 235-245, 1997.

[31] G.Csurka, C. Dance, L. Fan, J. Willamowski, C. Bray, "Visual categorization with bags of keypoints", ECCV'04 workshop on Statistical Learning in Computer Vision, pp. 59-74, 2004.

[32] F. Perronnin and C. Dance. Fisher kernels on visual vocabulariesfor image categorization. In CVPR, 2007. -

[33] J. Sanchez, F. Perronnin, T. Mensink, and J. Verbeek, "Image classification with the Fisher vector: Theory and practice", IJCV, 105(3):222–245, June 2013.

[34] J. Winn, A. Criminisi, and T. Minka. Object categorizationby learned universal visual dictionary.In International Conference on Computer Vision,2005.=

[35] J. Liu. Image retrieval based on bag-of-words model. InarXiv preprint arXiv:1304.5168, 2013. -

[36] P. Diamantatos, V. Verras, E. Kavallieratou. Detecting Main Body Size in Document Images. ICDAR, 2013.

[37] D.G.Lowe, "Distinctive image features from scale-invariant keypoints", International Journal of Computer Vision, 60:91–110, 2004.

[38] A. Vedaldi and B. Fulkerson. VLFeat library. http://www.vlfeat.org/, 2008.

[39] N.Stamatopoulos, B.Gatos, G.Louloudis, U.Pal, A.Alaei, "ICDAR 2013 handwriting segmentation contest", 12th International Conference on Document Analysis and Recognition (ICDAR), pp. 1402-1406, 2013.

[40] K. Chatfield, V. Lempitsky, A. Vedaldi, and A. Zisserman. The devil is in the details: an evaluation of recent feature encoding methods. In BMVC, 2011.

[41] Y. Ke and R. Sukthankar. PCA-SIFT: A more distinctive representation for local image descriptors. In Proc. CVPR, 2004.

25

Applying Swarm Optimization Techniques to Calculate Execution Time for Software Modules

Nagy Ramadan Darwish
Department of Computer and
Information Sciences, Institute of
Statistical Studies and Research,
Cairo University, Cairo, Egypt

Ahmed A. Mohamed
Department of Information System,
Higher Technological Institute,
10th of Ramadan City,
Egypt

Bassem S. M. Zohdy
Department of Business Technology,
Canadian International College,
Cairo, Egypt

Abstract—This research aims to calculate the execution time for software modules, using Particle Swarm Optimization (PSO) and Parallel Particle Swarm Optimization (PPSO), in order to calculate the proper time. A comparison is made between MATLAB Code without Algorithm (MCWA), PSO and PPSO to figure out the time produced when executing any software module. The proposed algorithms which include the PPSO increase the speed of executing the algorithm itself, in order to achieve quick results. This research introduces the proposed architecture to calculate execution time and uses MATLAB to implement MCWA, PSO and PPSO. The results show that PPSO algorithm is more efficient in speed and time compared to MCWA and PSO algorithm for calculating the execution time.

Keywords—Particle Swarm Optimization; Parallel Particle Swarm Optimization; MATLAB Code without Algorithm

I. INTRODUCTION

Testing is a crucial phase that is performed during software development. It is a primary technique which is used to gain consumer confidence in the software. It is conducted by executing the program developed with test inputs and comparing the observed output with the expected one [1, 2]. Testing is the writing and applying all software tests to ensure the confidence in the operation of the program. Testing is the phase of development that is carried out after the main coding efforts [3].

Execution time is the time during which software is running. Calculating execution time is very important in many fields, such as; medical system, army system, and airlines system … etc., Where any time delay in these software misfortunes may occur.

This research selects primary studies that published between 2005 and 2015, while searching many electronic databases in order to determine if similar work had already been performed, and locates potentially relevant studies.

C. Mao [4] proposed a search-based test data generation solution for software structural testing using particle swarm optimization (PSO) technique. A. Windisch, S. Wappler and j. Wegener [5] applied a particle swarm algorithm for evolutionary structural testing. R. Ding and H. Dong [6] proposed a hybrid particle swarm genetic algorithm to apply in software testing using case automate generations. A. S. Andreou, K. A. Economides and A. A. Sofokleous [7] proposed an enhanced testing framework that combines data flow graphs with genetic algorithms (GA) to generate optimum test cases. P. Palangpour, G.K. Venayagamoorthy, and S.C. Smith [8] presented a pipelined architecture for hardware particle swarm optimization (PSO) implementation to achieve much faster execution times than possible in software. A. Mansoor [9] developed AI technique based on genetic algorithm for the optimization of software test data. M. Syafrullah and N. Salim [10] proposed a new approach based on particle swarm optimization techniques in order to improve the accuracy of term extraction results. J. H. Andrews, T. Menzies, and F.Li [11] described a system that is based on a genetic algorithm (GA) to find parameters for randomized unit testing that optimize test coverage. J. CHANG and J. Pan [12] presented a Parallel Particle Swarm Optimization (PPSO) algorithm and a three communication strategies. D. Arora, A. S. Baghel [1] presented a method that uses genetic algorithm and particle swarm optimization for optimizing software testing by finding the most error prone paths in the program.

The method used here in this research is to calculate execution time for software modules, this could be achieved by using the Particle Swarm Optimization (PSO) techniques, as the each population in each iteration search for best execution time through particles in this population, and finally compare the best solution to produce the best execution time, also the use of parallel particle swarm optimization helps to run the populations and particles in distributed processing systems to help find the best solution in parallel, then selecting the best execution time. It is very crucial phase for any software to determine its quality and ability to meet requirements, which could be achieved through test this software, testing as a phase of software engineering process, literally takes about 40~50% of the development efforts in software houses [13].

It is noteworthy that life critical software could use more efforts and resources, if it is not tested perfectly, the software may cause dangerous consequences as timetable delays, cost overrun. Also software community aims to deliver high quality software to customers, to ensure that the software will run perfect with no delays in execution time, as this is the aim of this research is to calculate the execution time [14, 15, 16]. Also the proposed algorithm in this research is done automatically through a testing tool that produces the results of execution time, also trials have been done and the results of sample code is depicted below in implementation part.

The paper is organized as follows: in part II an introduction and brief description of PSO algorithm, in part III brief description of the two types of PPSO techniques, in part IV description of the proposed PSO and PPSO algorithms, followed by the implementation in part V, and then analysis and results in part VI, the conclusion and future work in part VII.

II. PARTICLE SWARM OPTIMIZATION

Modelling of swarms was initially proposed by Kennedy to simulate the social behaviour of fish and birds, the optimization algorithm was presented as an optimization technique in 1995 by Kennedy and Eberhart, PSO has particles which represent candidate solutions of the problem, each particle searches for optimal solution in the search space, each particle or candidate solution has a position and velocity. A particle updates its velocity and position based on its inertia, own experience and gained knowledge from other particles in the swarm, aiming to find the optimal solution of the problem [17].

The particles update its position and velocity according to the following Equation:

$$v_i^{k+1} = wv_i^k + c_1 \text{rand}_2 \times (\text{pbest}_i - s_i^k) + (\text{gbest}_i - s_i^k) \qquad (1)$$

Where:

v_i^{k+1} = Velocity of agent i at iteration k,
w = Weighting function,
cj = Weighting factor,
rand = Random number between 0 and 1,
S_i^k = Current position of agent iteration k,
pbesti = Pbest of agent i,
gbesti = gbest of the group.

The weighting function used in Equation 1:

$$w = w_{max} - \frac{w_{max} - w_{min}}{\text{iter}_{max}} \times \text{iter} \qquad (2)$$

Where:

Wmax= Initial weight,
Wmin= Final weight,
itermax= Maximum iteration number,
Iter = Current iteration number.

According to more than ninety modifications are applied to original PSO [17, 18].

III. PARALLEL PARTICLE SWARM OPTIMIZATION

PSO is optimized to be implemented on distributed systems, the iterations and particles within each iterations of the PPSO are independent of each other, so results could be parallel analysed. PPSO could be divided into two types [19, 20, 21]:

1) Synchronous Parallel Particle Swarm Optimization

PSO parallel implementation is to simply evaluate the particles (solutions), or in other words the execution time produced within each iteration in parallel, without changing the overall logic of the algorithm itself. In this implementation, all particles within design iteration are sent to the parallel computing environment, and the algorithm waits for all the analyses to complete before moving to the next iteration. This implementation is referred to as a synchronous implementation. This method is used in this research [22, 23].

2) Asynchronous Parallel Particle Swarm Optimization Algorithm

Considering an asynchronous algorithm means that particles (solutions) or as mentioned before execution time produced in the next iteration are analysed before the current design iteration is completed. The goal is to have no idle processors as one move from one iteration to the next. [22]

The key to implementing an asynchronous parallel PSO algorithm is to separate the update actions associated with each point and those associated with the swarm as a whole. These update actions include updating the inertia value and the swarm and point histories. For the synchronous algorithm, all the update actions are performed at the end of each design iteration. For the asynchronous algorithm, researchers want to perform point update actions after each point is analysed and the swarm updates actions at the end of each design iteration. The parts of the algorithm that need to be considered when looking at the update actions are the velocity vector, and the dynamic reduction of the inertia value. [22]

The velocity vector is the centre point of any PSO algorithm. For each design point, the velocity vector is updated using the following dynamic properties for that point: the previous velocity vector; the current position vector; and the best position found so far. In addition, the updated inertia value and the best position for the swarm as a whole are also required. To do the velocity update in an asynchronous fashion, researchers need to update the position vector and the best position found so far for each design point directly after evaluating that point. For the best position in the swarm, researchers have two choices:

Use the best position in the current iteration, or use the best position found so far. To keep the best position for the swarm current when moving to the next design iteration, before the current iteration is completed, it is necessary to use the best position found so far rather than the best position in the current iteration. This setup allows the algorithm to update all required dynamic properties of the velocity vector directly after evaluating each design point, except for the inertia value. The inertia value is the only iteration level update required to compute the velocity vector and is updated at the end of each design iteration. The craziness operator is the only other iteration level update and is also performed at the end of each design iteration. [23]

The asynchronous algorithm is thus very similar to the synchronous algorithm, except that researchers update as much information as possible after each design point is analysed. The inertia is only applied when design iteration is completed. Of course, this could result in some points of the next design iteration being analysed before the inertia operator is applied for that design iteration. However, the influence on the overall performance of the algorithm seems to be negligible [24].

IV.   PROPOSED PSO & PPSO ALGORITHMS

The proposed architecture is based on PSO and PPSO algorithms to calculate execution time depicted below in figure 1. Additionally, in order to evaluate the execution time for software module, a proposed PPSO (Parallel PSO) algorithm to calculate execution time also introduced and the recommended execution time strategy is determined for implementing this PPSO algorithm.

- The PSO Algorithm to Calculate Execution Time can be listed in following steps:

A. *Initialize the population with N Particles. And Set iterations counter I = 0.*

B. *Apply Fitness function: Calculating the fitness value by calculating the percentage of this particle will share in minimizing the total processing time to find the optimal solution.*

C. *Compare the calculated fitness value of each particle with its (lbest). If current value is better than (gbest), then reset (gbest) to the current index in particle array. Select the best particle as (gbest).*

D. *Calculated fitness value among the neighboured particles in the network achieved so far in the iteration.*

E. *Update each Particle Velocity and position according to Eq. (1).*

$$v_1^{k+1} = wv_1^k + c_1 \text{rand}_2 \times (\text{pbest}_i - s_i^k) + (\text{gbest}_i - s_i^k) \quad (1)$$

Where I= 0, 1, 2… M-1

To prevent the velocity from becoming too large, researchers set a maximum value to limit the range velocity as

$$-\text{VMAX} \leq \text{V} \leq \text{VMAX}$$

F. *Cost function assigns the highest fitness value in the iteration and which has a current position (xi).*

t = t +1.

G. *End While.*

H. *Stop.*

So these recursive steps continue until reaching the termination condition, and the termination condition achieved when the cost function finishes the execution, and finds the optimal time and solution.

In PPSO, computation time of PSO can be reduced with the parallel structure. Parallel processing aims at producing the same results achievable using multiple processors with the goal of reducing the run time. The same steps described in PSO will be applied, but in step (a) PPSO will define how many group of processors needed for the cost function to be executed, because it can be designed to be 2n sets.

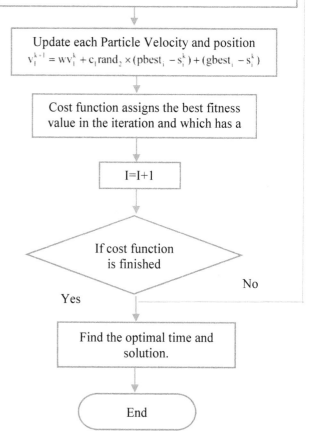

Fig. 1.   Proposed PSO Based Algorithm to Calculate Execution Time

The performance of the Parallel PSO can be evaluated using Amdahl's Law Eq. [25].

Speedup $(S_p) = 1/f_s + f_p/p$

Where:

f_s= serial fraction of code

f_p= parallel fraction of code

P= number of processors

Suppose serial fraction of code (0.5), parallel fraction of code (0.5) and number of processors (2, 4, 8, 16, 32, 64, 128, 256, 512, and 1024).

If P=2: Sp= 1 / (0.5+0.25) = 1.33

TABLE I. Ppso Algorithm

P	SP	Elapsed Time
2	1.33	0.02
4	1.60	0.017
8	1.79	0.012
16	1.89	0.008
32	1.96	0.005
64	2.00	0.003
128	2.00	0.002
256	2.00	0.001
512	2.00	0.001
1024	2.00	0.0003

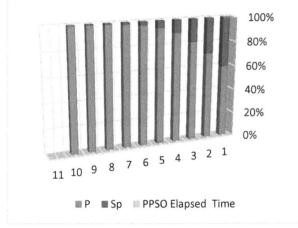

Fig. 2. PPSO Algorithm

This figure shows that the increase of number of processors, increase in speed results and decrease in elapsed time.

V. IMPLEMENTATION OF THE PROPOSED ALGORITHM

This section introduces implementation of MCWA, PSO and PPSO where cost function (CF) is:

```
CF: function z=Sphere(x)
    z=sum (x. ^2);
    end
```

This paper implementation proposed cost function uses MCWA, PSO and PPSO. The first implementation uses MCWA where results are shown below in table 2:

TABLE II. RESULTS OF MCWA

Iteration	CF	Elapsed Time(ET)
1	1	16.16
2	4	97.15
3	9	109.26
4	16	118.05
5	25	126.38
6	36	133.59
7	49	140.11
8	64	147.25
9	81	157.59
10	100	169.34

In table 2 each test case (iteration) to optimize the cost function but elapsed time increased and shown below in figure3:

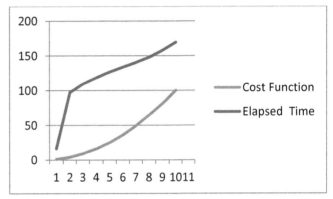

Fig. 3. Releationship between CF and ET in MCWA

In figure 3 shown relationships between CF and ET where found positive relationship between them.

The second implementation uses PSO where results are shown below in table 3:

TABLE III. RESULTS OF PSO

Iteration	CF	ET
1	58.73	0.04
2	24.48	0.07
3	15.00	0.10
4	5.85	0.13
5	5.85	0.16
6	5.85	0.19
7	5.34	0.21
8	2.73	0.24
9	2.73	0.27
10	2.73	0.30

In table 3 each test case (iteration) to optimize the cost function but elapsed time decreased compared with MCWA and shown in figure 4.

In figure 4 shown relationships between CF and ET where found inverse relationship between them.

The third implementation uses PPSO where results are shown in table 4.

In table 4 each test case (iteration) to optimize the cost function but elapsed time decreased compared with MCWA, PSO and shown in figure 5.

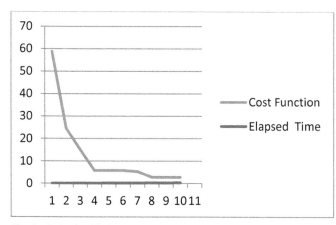

Fig. 4.   Releationship between CF and ET in PSO

TABLE IV.   RESULTS OF PPSO

x	P	Sp	CF	ET
1	2	1.33	58.73	0.02
2	4	1.60	24.48	0.017
3	8	1.79	15.00	0.012
4	16	1.89	5.85	0.008
5	32	1.96	5.85	0.005
6	64	2.00	5.85	0.003
7	128	2.00	5.34	0.002
8	256	2.00	2.73	0.001
9	512	2.00	2.73	0.001
10	1024	2.00	2.73	0.0003

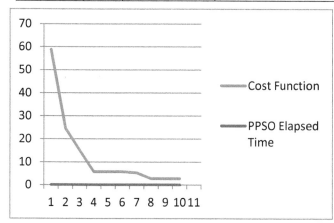

Fig. 5.   Releationship between CF and ET in PPSO

In figure 5 shown relationships between CF and ET where found inverse relationship between them.

This paper introduces compared between PSO and PPSO where shown in figure 6.

In figure 7 shown inverse relationships between SP, PSO and PPSO Whenever an increase in speed occur where decreased in PSO and also more decreased in PPSO.

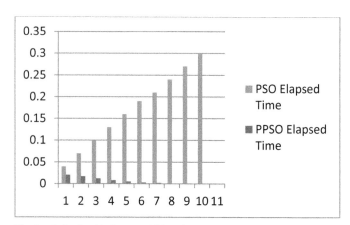

Fig. 6.   Releationship between PSO and PPSO

In figure 6 shown relationships between PSO and PPSO where elapsed time in PPSO decreased compared with PSO. In figure 7 shown relationships between SP, PSO and PPSO.

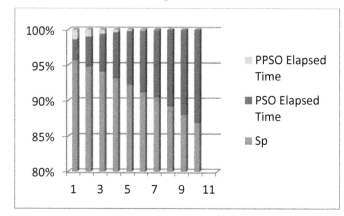

Fig. 7.   Releationship between SP, PSO and PPSO

VI.   ANALYSIS AND RESULTS

This paper presented the results of PSO and PPSO. In PSO, the results show inverse relationship between CF & ET, although the optimizing, the cost function elapsed time decreased compared with MCWA. In PPSO found that there is an inverse relationship between CF & ET although optimizing the cost function, but elapsed time decreased compared with MCWA and PSO. This paper shows the relationship between PSO and PPSO where elapsed time in PPSO decreased compared with PSO and shows inverse relationship between SP, PSO and PPSO Whenever an increase in speed occur it decreased in PSO and also time decreased more in PPSO.

VII.   CONCLUSION AND FUTURE WORK

PSO is relatively recent heuristic approach; it is similar to PPSO in a way that they both are population based evolutionary algorithms.

The research presents the application of PSO and PPSO. The proposed research described the basic concepts of PSO and PPSO, calculating execution time for software modules for using PSO and PPSO and how they are useful in finding the optimal solution to the problem. Comparative study is done between both the algorithm where PPSO can be useful, and showing how PPSO overcome the drawback of PSO. This paper shows that PPSO algorithm is more efficient in speed and time compared with MCWA and PSO algorithm to calculate the execution time.

In future, the researchers aim to apply the proposed approach using ante colony optimization (ACO) and cat optimization (CO) and compare the results with other results produced from other evaluation techniques of swarm optimization algorithms. In addition, the researchers aim to enhance the proposed approach by examining more hybrid techniques to calculate execution time for software modules.

REFERENCES

[1] D.Arora, A.Baghel "Application of Genetic Algorithm and Particle Swarm Optimization in Software Testing "Journal of Computer Engineering , Volume 17, PP 75-78 ,2015.

[2] James H. Andrews, Tim Menzies, Felix C.H. Li, "Genetic Algorithms for Randomized Unit Testing", IEEE Transactions on Software Engineering, vol.37, no. 1, pp. 80-94, January/February 2011.

[3] Nagy Ramadan Darwish "Towards An Approach For Evaluating The Implementation Of Extreme Programming Practices" International Journal of Intelligent Computing and Information Science, Volume 13, PP 55-67,2013.

[4] C. Mao, "Generating Test Data for Software Structural Testing Based on Particle Swarm Optimization," Arabian Journal for Science and Engineering, vol. 39, pp. 4593-4607, 2014.

[5] A. Windisch, S. Wappler and j. Wegener, "Applying Particle Swarm Optimization to Software Testing," in Proc. 9th Conf. Genetic and evolutionary computation, 2007, pp. 1121-1128.

[6] R. Ding and H. Dong "Automatic Generation of Software Test Data Based on Hybrid Particle Swarm Genetic Algorithm," in Electrical & Electronics Engineering (EEESYM), 2012, pp. 670 - 673.

[7] A. S. Andreou, K. A. Economides and A. A. Sofokleous "An Automatic Software Test-Data Generation Scheme Based on Data Flow Criteria and Genetic Algorithms," in 7th Int. Conf. Computer and Information Technology, 2007.

[8] P. Palangpour, G.K. Venayagamoorthy, and S.C. Smith, "Particle Swarm Optimization: A Hardware Implementation," in Proc. Int. Conf. Computer Design, 2009.

[9] A. Mansoor, "Automated Software Test Data Optimization Using Artificial Intelligence," International Journal of Information and Communication Trends, vol. 1, pp. 1-60, 2014.

[10] M. Syafrullah and N. Salim, "Improving Term Extraction Using Particle Swarm Optimization Techniques," Journal of Computing, vol. 2, 2010.

[11] J. H. Andrews, T. Menzies, and F.Li, "Genetic Algorithms for Randomized Unit Testing," IEEE Transactions on Software Engineering, vol. 37, no. 1, 2011.

[12] J. CHANG and j. Pan, "A Parallel Particle Swarm Optimization Algorithm with Communication Strategies," Journal of Information Science and Engineering, vol. 21, pp. 809-818, 2005.

[13] Jovanovic and Irena,"Software TestingMethods and Techniques," May 26, 2008.

[14] Saswat Anand, Edmund Burke, Tsong Y. Chen, et al., "An Orchestrated Survey on Automated Software Test Case Generation" Journal of Systems and, Software, 2013.

[15] "Addressing Software Testing Costs, Complexity and Challenges: Sogeti UK's Annual TestExpo Survey", Survey Report, Sogeti Inc., 2013.

[16] Myers, Glenford J., IBM Systems Research Institute, Lecturer in Computer Science, Polytechnic Institute of New York, "The Art of Software Testing", Copyright 1979. by John Wiley & Sons, Inc.

[17] Aly, Walid; Yousif, Basheer; Zohdy, Bassem "A Deoxyribonucleic Acid Compression Algorithm Using Auto-Regression and Swarm Intelligence". Journal of Computer Science, 690-698, 9(6), 2013.

[18] Syafrullah M., Salim N., 2010, "Improving Term Extraction Using Particle Swarm Optimization Techniques", Journal of Computing, Vol. 2, Issue2, pages 116-120, 2010.

[19] Chang, J.F., Chu, S.C., Roddick, J.F., Pan, J.S., "A parallel particle swarm optimization algorithm with communication strategies", Journal of information science and engineering. 21, 809–818, 2005.

[20] Shu-Chuan, Chu et al. "Parallel Particle Swarm Optimization Algorithms With Adaptive Simulated Annealing", Springer, 31, 2006.

[21] Venter G, Sobieszczanki-Sobieksi J. A parallel particle swarm optimization algorithm accelerated by asynchronous evaluations. Journal of Aerospace Computing, Information, and Communication. 6th World Congresses of Structural and Multidisciplinary Optimization, 2005

[22] Şaban Gülcü, and Halife Kodaz, "A novel parallel multi-swarm algorithm based on comprehensive learning particle swarm optimization," Engineering Applications of Artificial Intelligence, vol. 45, pp. 33–45, 2015.

[23] R. V. Kulkarni and G. K. Venayagamoorthy, "Particle swarm optimization in wireless-sensor networks: a brief survey," IEEE Transactions on Systems, Man and Cybernetics Part C, vol. 41, no. 2, pp. 262–267, 2011.

[24] C. A. Voglis , K. E. Parsopoulos , I. E. Lagaris, "Particle swarm optimization with deliberate loss of information", Soft Computing - A Fusion of Foundations, Methodologies and Applications, v.16 n.8, p.1373-1392, August 2012.

[25] Herb Sutter, "The Free Lunch is Over: A Fundamental Turn Toward Concurrency in Software", Dr. Dobb's Journal, 30(3), March 2005.

26

An Expert System-Based Evaluation of Civics Education as a Means of Character Education Based on Local Culture in the Universities in Buleleng

Dewa Bagus Sanjaya[1]
Lecturer of Civics Education
Ganesha University of Education
Singaraja, Bali, Indonesia

Dewa Gede Hendra Divayana[2]
Lecturer of Information Technology Education
Ganesha University of Education
Singaraja, Bali, Indonesia

Abstract—Civics education as a means of character education based on local culture has the mission to develop values and attitudes. In the educational process, various strategies and methods of value education can be used. In Civics Education characters are developed as the impact of education and also as its nurturing effect. Meanwhile, other subjects, which formally have the major mission other than character development have to develop activities that have the nurturing effect of character development in the students. However, in the educational process this has not run well. Hence, there is a need to evaluate educational programs at public as well as private universities in Buleleng regency. One of the evaluation techniques that can be used is the CIPP model combined with certainty factor method in expert system. The CIPP Model can evaluated the Civics education processes at all the public and private universities in Buleleng regency objectively, especially in probing local culture in character educational development. Meanwhile, the certainty factor method is used to determine the extent or degree of certainty of a component being evaluated in Civics educational processes.

Keywords—Evaluation of Civics Education; Character; Local culture; Expert System; Certainty Factor

I. INTRODUCTION

Civics Education (PKn) has a very vital status and very strategic in fostering patriotism, nationalism and in nation and carácter building. However, in its implementation, it is very susceptible to practical political bias of the authority that tends to be an instrument used by the authority rather a means of the nation character building. The same thing occurs in developing countries as stated by Cogan (1998). He states: It (citizenship education) has also often reflected the interests of those in power in a particular society and thus has been a matter of indoctrination and the establishment of ideological hegemony rather than of education [1].

Various efforts have been done such discussion, conference, *sarasehan*, and other activities of that are like them that are vercommon all over the regions of Indonesia, a strong indicator that all of the components of the nation have a strong national commitment. However, there is a need for a comprehensive national policy, that is coherent, and sustainable that encourages the government to take an initiative to prioritize the nation character development. This implies that every effort of development has to always be directed to give a positive effect to the nation character development. In this modern world, as stated by Lickona (1991) we tend to forget the virtuous life, including in it self-oriented virtues or virtues to oneself, such as self control and moderation; and other-oriented virtues such a generosity and compassion or willingness to share and feel virtues[2].

As the consequence, the nation character building has a very wide scope and a multidimensional urgency level. Winataputra (2006) stresses that the nation character development has to be focused on three broad levels.,i.e., (1) to foster and strengthen the nation identity, (2) to keep the Unification of Republic of Indonesia (NKRI), and (3) to develop Indonesian man and womans and Indonesian community that have good ethics and a nation with dignity[3].

Civics Education as a means of character education based on local culture has the mission to develop values and attitudes. In the educational process it can use various strategies and value education methods. Civics Education develop character as the effect of the education and also as the dampak pengiring. Meanwhile, other subjects which formally have the major missions other than the character development, have to develop activities that have dampak pengiring of the development of character in the students. However, the education process has not run well.

For that reason, there is a need for evaluating the educational processes at the public and private universities in Buleleng regency. One of the techniques of evaluation that can be used is CIPP model combined with certainty factor in the expert system. The CIPP Model can evaluate the Civics Education process in all the public and private universities in Buleleng regency objectively, especially in probing the local culture in developing character education.

Meanwhile certainty factor method is used to determine the extent of certainty of one component which is being evaluated in the Civics Education process.

II. LITERATURE REVIEW

A. Evaluation

In [4], evaluation is a systematic collection of fact to determine whether in fact there is a change in students and establish the extent of change in the individual student.

In [5], Evaluation is an activity in collecting, analysing, and presenting information about an object of research and the results can be used to take a decision. In [6], Evaluation can be defined as the determination of conformity between the results achieved and the objectives to be achieved. In [7], Evaluation is an activity to gather information about the workings of something, which then the information is used to determine the appropriate alternative in making decisions.

From the opinions of the above can be concluded in general that the evaluation is an activity for data collecting, data analysing and data presenting into information about a particular object under study so that the results can be used to take a decision.

B. CIPP Model

In [8], the CIPP evaluation there are four components that must be passed is the evaluation of the component context, the evaluation of input component, the evaluation of process components, and the evaluation of product components.

In [9], CIPP model is a model in its activities through four stages of evaluation are: evaluation of the component context, input, process and product.

From the above opinions can be concluded in general that the CIPP model is a model that essentially has four stages of evaluation are: evaluation of the component context, component input, component process and component product.

C. Expert System

In [10], an expert system is considered as a computer simulation of human expertise. In [11], Expert System is a program that behaves like some experts, and have limited domains of application in certain problems.

In [12], an expert system is a computer program that stimulates an evaluation and behaviors of human or organization that has knowledge and experiences of experts in a certain field.

In [13], Expert system is an artificial intelligence system that combines the basics of knowledge and inferential motor in such a way that it can adopt the ability of an expert into the computer, so that the computer can solve problems such as those often done by experts.

In [14], Expert system is made only in certain knowledge domain to approximate human ability only in one field.

In [15], Expert system is a kind of contemporary software that makes computer more useful than before.

From the various opinion above it can be concluded that artificial intelligence that combines the basics of knowledge and inferential machine in order it can adopt the ability experts into an instrument to solve problems like what experts do.

D. Certainty Factor (CF)

Certainty Factor (CF) is one of the methods used to show the extent of certainty of facts or rules. 16]. The notation of certainty factor caused by one fact is as follows:

$$CF[H,E] = MB[H,E] - MD[H,E].............................1$$

In which:

$CF[H,E]$ = certainty/ confidence factor about hypothesis H towards fact E (between -1 and 1)

$MB[H,E]$ = the extent of confidence towars hypothesis H with fact E (between 0 and 1)

$MB[H,E]$ = the extent of nonconfidence towards hypothesis H with fact E (between 0 and 1)

Meanwhile factor notation of certainty facts that are caused by more than one fact is as follows:

$$CF[H,E1^\wedge E2] = MB[H,E1^\wedge E2] - MD[H,E1^\wedge E2].........2$$

In which:

$MB[H,E1^\wedge E2] = MB[H,E1]+MB[H,E2]*(1-MB[H,E1])$

$MD[H,E1^\wedge E2] = MD[H,E1]+MD[H,E2]*(1-MD[H,E1])$

In which:

$CF[H,E1^\wedge E2]$ = certainty/confidence factor about hypothesis H towards fact E1 and E2 (between -1 and 1)

$MB[H,E1^\wedge E2]$ = the extent of confidence towards hypothesis H with facts E1 and E2 (between 0 and 1)

$MB[H,E1^\wedge E2]$ = the extent of nonconfidence towards hypothesis H with facts E1 and E2 (between 0 and 1)

III. METHODOLOGY

A. Object dan Research Site

1) Research Object is Civics Education program as the means for character education.

2) Research Site at universities in Buleleng regencies.

B. Data Type

In this research, the authors use primary and secondary data, quantitative and qualitative data.

C. Data Collection Techniques

In this research, the authors use data collection techniques such as observation, interviews, and documentation.

D. Evaluation Model

Evaluation model used in this research is CIPP model and combined with the certainty factor method.

E. Aspect of Evaluation

The aspects that were evaluated in Civics Education can be seen in the table of evaluation criteria as follows.

TABLE I. EVALUATION CRITERIA

No	Component	Aspects
1.	Context	The status of Civics Education in university curriculums
		Visions and Missions of Civics Education
2.	Input	Description of Civics Education
		Human resources
		Infrastructures and facilities
3.	Process	Planning for Civics Education
		Implementation of Civics Education
		Assessment of Civics Education
4.	Product	Effect of the implementation of Civics Education
		Results expected from the implementation of Civics Education

IV. RESULT AND DISCUSSION

A. Result

1) Result of analysis from CIPP Model

The result of analysis using CIPP model can be explained as follows:

a) In the Context components: Civics Education at universities in Buleleng regency has followed the curriculum written in each respective institution.

b) In the Input components: Civics Education at universities in Buleleng regency has followed the descriptions offered by the Ministry of Research, Technology and Higher Education. The educational background of the lecturers of Civics Education at the universities in Buleleng regency is minimally Master degree in the Department of Pancasila and Civics Education Department.

c) In the Process components: The universities in Buleleng regency have appreciated, accommodated, and internalized local culture based character education through Civics Education that is stipulated in the curriculum. In the effort to internalize and transform character education in the educational process, the lecturers of Civics Education have used multi-approaches multi-strategies, and multi-methods. One of the dominant approaches practiced in education is contextual approach.

d) In the Product components: The realization of contextual approach is the probing of local wisdoms of Baliese community that can be used as the model in developing character education, which among other things include:

i. *Tri hita karana* ideology terminologically, the concept of *tri hita karana* comes from the word *tri* that means three;; *hita* prosperity, happiness; and *karana* that means source of cause. Thus *tri hita karana* means three sources of cause of the prosperity and happiness in life and the life of all creatures of God [17]. The prosperity of life can be realized if there is a harmony between human beings and the creator (God), human beings and their fellow human beings, and human beings and the natural environment. *Tri hita karana* then developed into the teaching of harmony, and balance and at the same time also the interdependence in a life system. This is based on the awareness that the universe is a complexity of elements which form a system of universe. The major principle of balance and harmony in the relationship between human beings and God, human beings and their fellow human beings, and human beings and the natural environment becomes the philosophy of life of the Balinese community, both in developing the system of knowledge, the patterns of behavior, attitudes, values, tradition, art, etc. This is very useful for Balinese community in the effort to meet the needs and solving problems of life that are faced both in interpersonal and intergroup relations. Since these major principles become the basis for the development of attitudes, values, behaviors, values, and social relationship in Balinese community, and these principles have been internalized and

institutionalized in the social life of the Balinese social structure. At the individual level, Balinese as the microcosmic environment (*buana alit*), for example, it is believed that human life is a dynamic manifestation of relational motion of *atman* (spirit), *prana* (power, strength), and *sarira* (physical body element). The broader social institutions of the Balinese is the environment of the macrocosmic environment of the individual, from the family organization as the smallest social institution, group of kinship (clan), *desa pakraman*, *subak* organization, *seke teruna-teruni, seke manyi, seke gong*, up to the Balinese community as a whole, apply the same pattern in creating the harmony among the three elements above in developing a daily cultural activity by reinforcing the concepts of *parhyangan, pawongan, dan palemahan*[18]. Through the concept of *parahyangan*, Balinese man and woman and Balinese community believe that everything in this world including human beings come from and because of this will come to God. This awareness encourages Balinese man and woman and Balinese community to improve their *crada dan bhakti* (belief and devotion) to God *(Ida Sang Hyang Widhi Waca)* in accordance with the teachings of the religion, beliefs and traditions that they practice in life. It is not surprising since at each level of the Balinese social institution are erected holy places of worshipping God the places that function as a means for human beings to relate themselves with God. It is also believed that all cultural products and human civilization and also Balinese community are created as offerings to God and spirits that are often called *yadnya*. We can see, for example, from the religiously symbolic meanings hidden and contained in the implementation of *yadnya*, the traditional or customary activities, and Balinese art and cultural works. Through the concept of *pawongan*, then, Balinese man and woman and Balinese community believe that naturally, human beings are equal as the creature and servants of God who are cultured and as a consequence, need to develop the attitude of *asah, asih, dan asuh* and work together to achieve the goal of human life, humans as social creature. The third element from the *tri hita karana* teaching is *palemahan*. Through this concept, Balinese man and Balinese community believe that there is a need for a harmonic relationship between human being and the other elements and powers of nature. Such relationship is symbolized with the expression "*kadi manik ring cecepu*" (like a baby in its mother's womb) [19]. Balinese man and woman are aware that human beings cannot be separated from the nature, since it is the nature that gives humans prosperity. Even they believe that the elements and power of this nature are the siblings of human beings as symbolized that every baby born it is always together with its four siblings (placenta, amniotic fluid, lamas/ placenta wrapping pembunga kus arib-ari and blood). The manifestation of love of Balinese man and woman towards these elements and powers of the universe is expressed in a sacrifice ceremony to *bhuta (butha yadnya)*, in addition to actively maintaining and preserving the natural environment.

ii. The *tat twam asi* teaching which literally means "he or she is you too". With the teaching of *tat twam asi* is meant that actually all human beings are one and the same creature of God. Thus, it is believed that to help other people means to help oneself, and to hurt others means to hurt oneself too [20]. Balinese man and woman believe and appreciate the differences in the characteristics of the life of human beings as the result of *rwabhineda* ties themselves.

iii. The concept of *Nyama braya*. *Nyama braya* is a concept that comes from the community cultural system. The cultural value system is the highest level and the most abstract of the customs. This is caused by the fact that the cultural values are concepts about what is life in the thinking of most of the people of a particular community about what they consider valuable, important and correct that have to be done in the life in this world, these high values are expected to function as a guide that gives a direction and orientation to the people of Bali, both those who live in complex towns or cities and those who live in villages and mountains with a simple life, there are some cultural values that are related with each other to form a system, and this system serves as a guideline from the ideal concepts in the culture as a strong motif for the direction in life of the community members. *Nyama braya* is the application of the concept of *rukun*. The word *rukun* contains the meanings close, peaceful, and do not fight with each other, thus it is likened to the life of a couple in a family that is *rukun*, it means harmonious and peaceful. The most essential meaning of *kerukunan hidup* is to protect harmony in the community that is multicultural by fostering the attitude of mutual respect and mutual complementing since to be aware that human beings are the best of all the creatures that God created. There is no absolutely perfect human being *(tan hana wong swasta nulus)*. Human beings need the help from each other *(paras paros sarpanaya, salunglung sabhayantaka, saling asah, asih dan asuh)*.

Differences/varieties are a must *(rwabhineda)*. The awareness in practicing the teaching of religion is tested when one is aware of life plurality *(tattwamasi)*. To show an attitude towards differences as human right of each individual *(sarva santhu niramayah)* as long as it does not violate the other's right.

2) Result of Analysis of Certainty Factor Method

TABLE II.　　SCORE OF DETERMINING THE DEGREE OF CERTAINTY OF A COMPONENT EVALUATED IN CIVICS EDUCATION PROCESS

No	Respon-Dent	Component of Evaluation								CF Value	
		C (%)		I (%)		P (%)		P (%)		Dec	%
		B	U	B	U	B	U	B	U		
1	R1	90	10	98	2	95	5	98	2	0,82	82
2	R2	97	3	99	1	99	1	99	1	0,94	94
3	R3	95	5	95	5	95	5	99	1	0,80	80
4	R4	95	5	95	5	95	5	99	1	0,80	80
5	R5	97	3	99	1	99	1	99	1	0,94	94
6	R6	97	3	99	1	99	1	99	1	0,94	94
7	R7	95	5	95	5	95	5	99	1	0,80	80
8	R8	90	10	98	2	95	5	98	2	0,82	82
9	R9	97	3	99	1	99	1	99	1	0,94	94
10	R10	95	5	95	5	95	5	99	1	0,80	80
11	R11	97	3	99	1	99	1	99	1	0,94	94
12	R12	90	10	98	2	95	5	98	2	0,82	82
13	R13	97	3	99	1	99	1	99	1	0,94	94
14	R14	95	5	95	5	95	5	99	1	0,80	80
15	R15	95	5	95	5	95	5	99	1	0,80	80

Explanation:
B　: The extent of belief/faith in component
U　: The extent of disbelief/Unfaith in component
C　: Context component
I　: Input component
P　: Process component
P　: Product component

B. Discussion

1) Working Principle of Certainty Factor (CF)

The working principle of *certainty factor* (CF) is by doing a substraction between the extent of disbelief in hypothesis H with Fact E (MB[H,E]) and the extent of belief in hypothesis H with fact E (MD[H,E]). In addition, there is also the principle of *certainty factor* (CF) that is used to determine a hypothesis based on some evidence, i.e., by substracting the extent of disbelief in hypothesis H with facts E1 and E2 (MB [H, E1^E2]) terhadap the extent of belief in hypothesis H with facts E1 and E2 (MD [H,E1^E2]).

2) Certainty Factor (CF)Working Procedures

Referring to the result in table II above, for respondent RI then its Certainty Factor (CF) following the following procedures:

a) Determining Certainty Factor (CF) of the success of the context component caused by the aspect of Civics Education status in the curriculum of Higher Learning, and Vision and Missions of Civics Education Course

CF [H,E] = MB[H,E] – MD[H,E]
CF [H,E] = 0.9-0. 1 = 0. 8

b) Determining Certainty Factor (CF) of the success of the input component caused by the aspect of description of Civics Education, human resources, infrastructure and facilities

CF [H,E1^E2] = MB[H,E1^E2] - MD[H,E1^E2]
MB[H,E1^E2] = MB[H,E1]+MB[H,E2]*(1-MB[H,E1])
MB[H,E1^E2] = 0. 9+0. 98*(1-0. 9) = 0. 998
MD[H,E1^E2] = MD[H,E1] + MD[H,E2]*(1-MD[H,E1])
MD[H,E1^E2] = 0. 1+0.02*(1-0. 1) = 0. 118
CF [H,E1^E2] = 0. 998 – 0.118 = 0. 880

c) Determining Certainty Factor (CF) of the success of the process component caused by the aspect of planning of Civics Education, implementation of Civics Education and assessment of Civics Education

CF [H,E1^E2^E3] =MB[H,E1^E2^E3] – MD[H,E1^E2^E3]
MB[H,E1^E2^E3] =MB[H,E1^E2] + MB[H,E3]*(1-MB[H,E1^E2])
MB[H,E1^E2^E3] = 0.998+0.95*(1-0.998) = 0.999
MD[H,E1^E2^E3] = MD[H,E1^E2] + MD[H,E3]*(1-MD[H,E1^E2])
MD[H,E1^E2^E3] = 0.118+0.05*(1-0.118) = 0.162
CF [H,E1^E2^E3] = 0.999 – 0.162 = 0.837

d) Determining Certainty Factor (CF) of the success of the product component caused by the aspect of effect of implementation of Civics Education as the means of character education based on local culture, and the result expected from the implementation of Civics Education.

CF [H,E1^E2^E3^E4] = MB[H,E1^E2^E3^E4] –
                MD[H,E1^E2^E3^E4]
MB[H,E1^E2^E3^E4] = MB[H,E1^E2^E3] + MB[H,E4] * (1-
                MB[H,E1^E2^E3])
MB[H,E1^E2^E3^E4] = 0.999+0.98*(1-0.999) = 0.999
MD[H,E1^E2^E3^E4] = MD[H,E1^E2^E3] + MD[H,E4] * (1-
                MD[H,E1^E2^E3])
MD[H,E1^E2^E3^E4] = 0.162+0.02*(1-0.162) = 0.179
CF [H,E1^E2^E3^E4] = 0.999 – 0.179 = 0.82

From the calculation the value of CF for respondent RI to determine the degree of certainty of components evaluated in Civics Education process using CIPP is 0.82 or 82%.

Following the same steps of calculation above for data from other respondents produced results as shown in table above.

V. CONCLUSIONS

Based on the analysis that has been made and the results of the discussion in the previous section, then some conclusions can be drawn as follows:

a) Imperatively, institutes of higher learning are one of the places for character education that is developing the nation character. The character development in the institutes of higher learning also constitutes a pillar in the institute of higher learning tridharma, i.e., education that covers curricular instructional, co-curicular and extra-curricular activities, research, and community service. In the educational activity in the classroom, the development of character is done using integrated approaches in all lectures. Especially for Civics Education, in keeping with its co-curricular mission that it develops values and attitudes, then the character development has to become the main focus that can use various strategies/methods of character education. Civics Education in the institute of higher learning, epistemologically even strengthens the basis of its ontological basis. The first content

confirms the academic and ideological substantive dimensions. While the second confirms the psycho-pedagogical and socio-cultural dimensions of the discipline of civics education.

b) Using the CIPP model in evaluating Civics Education processes in all public and private universities in Buleleng regency makes the evaluation more objective, especially in proving local culture in developing character education.

c) Using certainty factor method in determining the extent or degree of certainty of a component that is being evaluated in Civics Education process will produce a more objective and optimal evaluation.

REFERENCES

[1] J.J. Cogan, and B.J. Derricott, Multidemensional Civic Education, Tokyo, 1998.

[2] T. Lickona, Educating for Character. New York: Bantams Books, 1991.

[3] U.S. Winataputra, Concepts and Strategies of Citizenship Education in Schools: Review of Psycho-Pedagogical. Jakarta: Directorate General of Primary and Secondary Education of the Republic of Indonesia, 2006.

[4] Bloom, *Evaluation to Improve Learning.* San Fransisco: McGraw Hill Book Company, 1981.

[5] I.M. Sundayana, "Implementation of Computer Assisted CIPP Model for Evaluation Program of HIV/AIDS Countermeasures in Bali," in International Journal of Advanced Research in Artificial Intelligence, Vol. 4, No. 11, 2015, pp. 27-29.

[6] D. Mardapi, Measurement, Assessment, and Evaluation of Education (1st Edition). Yogyakarta: Nuha Medika, 2012.

[7] S. Arikunto, Basics of Education Evaluation. Jakarta: Bumi Aksara, 2010.

[8] Wirawan, Evaluation Theory, Model, Standards, Applications, and Profession (1st Edition). Jakarta: Rajawali Pers,2011.

[9] I.M. Sundayana, "Implementation of Computer Assisted CIPP Model for Evaluation Program of HIV/AIDS Countermeasures in Bali," in International Journal of Advanced Research in Artificial Intelligence, Vol. 4, No. 11, 2015, pp. 27-29.

[10] P. Isaki, and S.P. Rajagopalan, "The Expert System Design To Improve Customer Satisfaction," in Advanced Computing: An International Journal (ACIJ), Vol. 2, No. 6, 2011, pp. 69-84.

[11] S.T. Deepa, and S.G. Packiavathy, "Expert System for Car Troubleshooting," in International Journal For Research in Science & Advanced Technologies, Vol. 1, No. 1, 2012, pp. 46-49.

[12] M.S. Josephine, and V. Jeyabalaraja, "Expert System and Knowledge Management for Software Developer in Software Companies," in International Journal of Information and Communication Technology Research, Vol. 2, No. 3, 2012, pp. 243-247.

[13] D.G.H. Divayana, "Development of Duck Diseases Expert System with Applying Alliance Method at Bali Provincial Livestock Office, " in International Journal of Advanced Computer Science and Applications, Vol. 5, No. 8, 2014, pp. 48-54.

[14] S. Hartati, and S. Iswanti, Expert System and It's Development.Yogyakarta: Graha Ilmu, 2008.

[15] N.Y. Asabere, "mMES: A Mobile Medical Expert System for Health Institutions in Ghana," in International Journal of Science and Technology, Vol. 2, No. 6, 2012, pp. 333-344.

[16] S. Kusumadewi, Artificial Intelligence (Techniques and It's Application). Yogyakarta: Graha Ilmu, 2003.

[17] I.G.K. Kaler, Why Corpse Burned? Denpasar: Yayasan Dharma Narada, 1993.

[18] I.G.N. Gorda, Hindu Ethics and Organizational Behavior. Denpasar: Widya Kriya Gematama, 1996.

[19] Griya, Orientation Balinese Cultural Values in Development. Denpasar: Research Center of Udayana University, 1998.

[20] M. Titib, Bali Cultural values; Implementation in The Institute of Higher Learning Tridharma. Denpasar: Udayana University, 1995.

27

Improved Text Reading System for Digital Open Universities

Mahamadou ISSOUFOU TIADO
Department of Mathematics and
Computer Science,
University of Abdou Moumouni,
UAM
Niamey, Niger

Abdou IDRISSA
University Institute of Technology
University of Tahoua
Tahoua, Niger

Karimou DJIBO
Department of Mathematics and
Computer Science,
University of Abdou Moumouni,
UAM
Niamey, Niger

Abstract—The New Generation of Digital Open Universities (DOUNG) is a recently proposed model using m-learning and cloud computing option and based on an integrated architecture built with open networks as GSM and Internet. The goal of achieving the ubiquitous ability of the m-learning is having the large number of languages as a serious issue. It needs to use many teachers in order to repeat the same course in various languages. In this paper, an extended system is proposed under the consideration of the low capacities of the cell-phone device in terms of computing and visualization. The model uses the possibility to build a voice warehouse which can be used to generate the audio format of every course provide in a text format and in a particular language. The Advanced Text Reading System (ATRS) is proposed to use that voice warehouse and to produce the audio format of a course, giving facility to teachers to easily overcome the constraints of language barrier. The new proposed model is described and its contributions are discussed.

Keywords—m-learning; distance learning; digital open universities; cloud-computing; audio warehouse

I. INTRODUCTION

The advent of the New Generation of Digital Open Universities was previously proposed to achieve the goal of realizing the conversion of the traditional distance learning to digital solutions with multiple options. Some of the DOUNG options allow to record the sessions given by a teacher in a multimedia format or to convey the multimedia stream instantly through the network towards the learners. In this operating model, the saved multimedia files contain a particular course in a specific language. An incoming limitation is related to the need to deliver the same course in another language. The nowadays solution uses another session given by a teacher chosen according to the targeted language, with also another work of recording to do. That operating model becomes heavier and generates more issues when addressing large public of learners around the world according to the ubiquitous nature of the m-learning. Thus, the learner's language becomes a barrier for the teacher and another parameter for recording new sessions. The goal of providing courses to a wide public of learners around the world in as many languages as possible brings to the proposition of the audio warehouse and its exploitation script. They are used to facilitate the conversion of the courses in audio format within a selected language. In addition, this new operating model that

generates audio format of courses meets the constraints of the extension of the DOUNG services over GSM network.

After presenting the basic concepts of the distance education in point II, the hybrid model of the DOUNG is presented in point III. The point IV presents the voice warehouse with its building process. The point V highlights the ATRS algorithm used on the cloud computing architecture to improve the DOUNG offered services. The point VI presents the cloud computing architecture of the DOUNG improved by the audio warehouse and the ATRS.

II. BASIC CONCEPTS OF THE DISTANCE EDUCATION

The distance education is implemented with various techniques such as the use of the e-learning by the means of computers network. Following the evolution process, the e-learning techniques and the mobile learning [1] bring to the advent of the m-learning technology. The new concept integrates the expansion of the education including mobile learners that use a wireless network without architecture (ad hoc technology) interconnected to the initial Internet backbone. The m-learning uses a wide range of mobile devices including wireless technologies, different protocols and applications. The designed architecture operates under the service-oriented technology philosophy. The increasing number of mobile devices becomes a favorable factor for the implementation and the extension of the m-learning, particularly because of the interconnection between wired and wireless networks, and between telecommunications and computer networks.

In a second side, the technological evolution process brings to the advent of the cloud computing technique that allows to optimize the use of the computers in a network. The cloud computing provides the possibility to put in common the overall storage capacity and processing power of the computers in the network. With this technique, the network becomes a channel that carries program and data from one point to another to ensure remote collaboration between nodes seamlessly to the user. The cloud computing allows to design a configurable architecture of computing resources in the network such as storage servers, applications, and services. Following the success of the cloud computing, the technology evolution process brings to the advent of the cloud learning. The cloud learning is a service offering distance learning based on cloud computing. It uses the availability of network servers offering data that contains sources and training documents in different formats such as text, multimedia, images. The environment used to design the system is called Cloud Learning Environment (CLE). It is free of an organization and put together learners and trainers.

At the third side, the Virtual Private Network [2][3][4][5] (VPN) has emerged and becomes another technology of distance education used by many centers. The VPN technique uses several remote computers, in the image of a real private Local Area Network (LAN), but communicating by using a public infrastructure. The computers operate by creating a tunnel and imposing the constraints of (1) user authentication, (2) encryption of the data, (3) access keys management and (4) multi-protocol availability. The following protocols are used to ensure the VPN operation. The Point to Point Tunneling Protocol (PPTP) creates a virtual private network by using the Point to Point Protocol (PPP) and the Internet Protocol (IP). The Internet Protocol Security (IPsec) [6] or the Multi-Protocol Label Switching (MPLS) [7] are used at the level 3. The Secure Sockets Layer (SSL) [8] is used at level 4 and ensures the security and the confidentiality of the communication through the network. The SSL protocol uses a socket connection to associate clients to server stations. It can be used by any application for securing the traffic such as Hyper Text Transport Protocol (HTTP). Other applications are used to offer multiple choices to the learners such as File Transfer Protocol (FTP), Telnet [9], Internet Relay Chat (IRC) ...

III.   THE HYBRID MODEL OF THE DOUNG

A. The DOUNG architecture

As defined in [10], it is designed to achieve the ubiquitous faculty of the m-learning associated to the capacities offered by the cloud computing. The architecture is based on the hybrid model with set of solutions based on computers and telecommunication networks. The model interconnects teachers and learners within a course produce in a support made available for learner's access. The package 10 in 1 that summarizes the set of solutions gives different format of the link between the teacher and the learner. It includes also the format of the content of the course, the course medium and the methods of the course production. The DOUNG is designed with various method destined to make the course available (broadcast and/or storage). It is designed with the definition of many kinds of learner access (synchronous and/or asynchronous transfer files). The definition of the nature of the channel that can be used completes the description of the DOUNG services. The transmission channel consists of a backbone network connected to the Internet, accessible via Internet and GSM. The course can be subjected to immediate transmission in multimedia stream, or stored as multimedia files, treated text files, untreated text files or pdf files. The operation of the DOUNG is based on the cloud computing with the goal to achieve the balancing of the servers load in the network combines to the need to incorporate the limited capacity of mobile devices.

At the learner side, the required materials consist of a computer with Internet access or a cellular phone. Among many choices offered by the DOUNG, the learner can use multimedia applications (real time and deferred time), or file

transfer mode with file displaying applications according to their format [1].

B. The DOUNG applications

The implementation tools of the DOUNG are previously defined in [10] with hardware, protocols and applications. The wide range of applications is given by the m-learning and is extended by the use of the cloud computing, making helpful their grouping into categories. The applications used to produce the courses are grouped in category (1). The second (2) category contains applications used to make those courses available. The applications allowing the learner to access the DOUNG services are grouped in the third (3) category. The fourth (4) category regroups applications used for the visualization of the courses by the learner and the fifth (5) category concerns the applications of exchange between teacher and learner.

The list of applications used by the DOUNG is extended because of the need to integrate the new proposed voice warehouse. As previously stated, the first list of applications of the category (1) regroups multimedia stream capture and recording applications, text processing applications, spreadsheets and pdf file generator. The category (2) still remains in multimedia recording with instant transmission server and an ftp server. Immediate multimedia viewer and ftp clients are used for the category (3). Deferred visualization multimedia client, word processing application, spreadsheets and pdf viewers are used for the category (4).

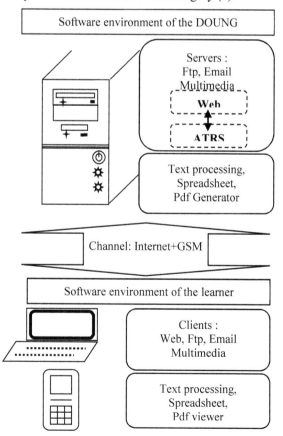

Fig. 1.   The improved DOUNG software environment

The category (5) concerning applications used for the exchange between learner and teacher includes multimedia clients, multimedia servers with instantaneous transmission, Internet telephony applications, email clients and servers applications. A web server is still being suitable to be used for its multifunctional operating mode that incorporates web pages containing courses, multimedia content, ftp site, search of archives, … The following figure 1 shows the improvement of the DOUNG software environment when integrating the ATRS.

IV. THE VOICE WAREHOUSE

A language can be singularly defined as a set of reserved words and a set of rules that explain how to put the language words together. The set of words define a dictionary which is usually available in a text format. Every word used to build sentences that composed a text in a particular language is provided by the dictionary. The voice warehouse is here a kind of dictionary containing the audio format of each word in a given language. A difference that can be stated is that words that have the same pronunciation generate the same audio file, even if their orthography is different.

The idea given as part of the main contribution of this paper is to improve the options offered by the DOUNG to a learner. In the improved scheme, the DOUNG provides in addition to the previous courses format, the same courses in audio format and in different language through the Advanced Text Reading System. The ATRS is implemented as a script that uses the audio warehouse containing the pronunciation of every word given by the dictionary of a selected language. The script is written to follow the words juxtaposition in a text and for each word, it will select the corresponding audio file from the warehouse. After the selection step, the audio file is played by using the loudness parameters defined later to help to take the punctuation into account. The audio flow produced is conveyed through the network (Internet + GSM) to the cell-phone of the learner as in the case of the VPN multimedia traffic between Internet and GSM. The audio flow can be also converted in a multimedia file so that a learner having a cell-phone with appropriate option (multimedia client) can download the file and play it locally. This means that another course in multimedia format can be produced by the ATRS without imposing to the teacher the constraints to record again the same course given in the text format.

Such kind of association between a word and its associated audio file can simply be made by given to the audio file, the same character composition of the word regardless to the upper or lower cases of the characters. This brings to make the script more intelligent so that it can resolve the cases of words having different orthography with the same pronunciation. A faire organization can be made in the storage of the sound in the warehouse. The audio dictionary of a language will be put into a separate directory different to the other language one. This may help to facilitate the language word selection while the language itself becomes an input parameter of the ATRS script. It can be assumed that if the text is well written in a particular language, by following the language grammar and its orthography constraints, the ATRS will also produce the correct reading of that text.

The precedent list of applications of category (1) is extended to integrate the ATRS script. The performance of the production of the sound by the ATRS is subjected to the capacity of the computer to run fast that conversion program. Another solution can be implemented used by multimedia applications. It concerns the use of the anticipation window that allows to early provide new sounds by accessing to the warehouse when the precedent audio words are being played. Thus by using the cloud computing mechanism, the task will remain on the server of the GSM provider. And then, the flow of sound provided by the ATRS will be conveyed to the cell-phone through GSM channel as in the case of the transmission of the normal audio emission. The cell-phone will receive the text, but also the sound, and the learner can choose freely to replay the sound unlimitedly, with more connection benefit in the case of a downloaded multimedia file.

Three processes are used to build the entire system. The first process is related to the building of the voice warehouse, the second process allows to implement the ATRS algorithm, and then the third process includes the running of the ATRS script by the learner.

The process of building the voice warehouse as the first step is conduct by recording an audio file for each word in a selected language. The file represents a word and is put in the warehouse. The warehouse is subdivided into folders with a separate folder for each language. A folder contains all the necessary voice files of a language that are previously recorded. Thus the whole audio warehouse becomes an audio dictionary.

V. THE ADVANCED TEXT READING SYSTEM

The encoding of the ATRS script is realized by following some steps in order to facilitate its evolution through new versions. The first step allows the script to take a language as an input parameter. It sets the language folder in the warehouse as default and current folder to avoid the searching of the file path during every warehouse access. The second step of the encoding of the ATRS system brings to write the script that reads the text by following the words sequence inside the course provides in text format. For the next step, the script realizes the conversion of the extracted word into its audio format by accessing to the appropriate part of the warehouse and selecting the audio file corresponding to the word. The encoding of the ATRS script is realized within the text reading algorithm with taking care of punctuation and performing another algorithm for reading numbers. The running of the ATRS script by a learner is managed by the use of the web server.

A. The text reading algorithm

Let assume that the course is produced in the web page format and the ATRS system has to skim the text with the word recognition philosophy by using separators. It is useful to integrate the difference between the word of the course and the reserved words of the Hyper Text Markup Language (HTML) so that, the HTML reserved words must not be pronounced by the ATRS script. The algorithm will use the beacon format in the HTML language to distinguish the reserved words of the language and the course words. The text will be read character by character. Between HTML beacon characters starting with "<" and ending with ">", the words are ignored. Outside the range of the HTML beacon containing eventually attributes and delimited by the precedent characters, each character not includes in the list of separator is put in a string. The string is built by considering the characters between two separators. The extracted string triggered the loading and the running of the corresponding audio file from the voice warehouse. This is referenced here by the term "resolving the word sound". The text reading algorithm can be written in a low level language as the C language used in the development of the Linux version and the other open sources.

B. Integrating the punctuation in the ATRS

When reading the text, taken care of the punctuation offers the guarantee to make the reading understandable. We will consider two kinds of influence of the punctuation. The first influence is related to the break time before continuing the reading; the second one is related to the sound volume at the end of sentences. When reading the text, the ATRS will use the Normal Inter Words (NIW) interval time that allows the listener to distinguish the "space" separator between words. The speed level of reading can be set according to a value evolving inside an interval given by [LS, HS], where LS is the allowed Low Speed value and HS the allowed High Speed value. These parameters are paramount important for the regulation of the speed of the words resolution in the warehouse. They must be chosen according to the minimum time that can take the system to resolve the word in the warehouse, even if an anticipation window can be used at the convenience of the implementation. When encountering a coma (","), the ATRS will use the Short Inter Words (SIW) interval time. When encountering a full stop character ("."), the algorithm will use the Long Inter Words (LIW) interval time. When playing the pronunciation of the words extracted from a text, the algorithm will use a Normal Loudness Level (NLL). But the pronunciation of the word that comes before the full stop will use a Decrease Loudness Level (DLL) from the NLL level to the Limit of Hearing Level (LHL). The association of the NLL and the LIW at the end of a sentence can give the pronunciation of the question mark "?". Thus, LS, HS, NIW, SIW, LIW, NLL, DLL, LHL are classified in the range of the algorithm parameters that can be adjusted to bring an improved listening quality.

C. The left-to-right reading numbers algorithm

A particular algorithm must be used to read numbers differently to the reading of strings. A string is delimited by separators and its audio format is in a single file. A number is also a string delimited by separators but need to be read digit by digit and by mixing the ten powers showing the position of the digit inside the number. When reading a number, also sub numbers that are in the language base must be detected. Every language has its own base containing digits (single numbers) and sub numbers composed with digits and having their own name. The ten powers are particular sub numbers that are in the base and are usually used to determine the position of the precedent number in the sequence forming one string number. For example, 2345 can be read as follow: two thousand three hundred forty five. Thousand and hundred are the ten powers and two, three and five are digits, then forty is a sub number.

For recognizing a sub number when reading a string number, the script must take into account the current digit and the number of the remaining digits that follows it. If the system crosses a digit that begins a basic sub number, and if the number of symbols (digits) that follows the current digit allows to recognize the sub number, the system will get the other next digits before resolving the word sound. The number of symbols that follows the current digit is also used to determine the time at which the correspondent ten power must be used. For example, for "23", the system recognizes first the digit "2" and then detects that the number of the remaining digits allows to recognize a sub number. The script waits to the get the next digit before resolving the word sound. The algorithm will resolve "20" before "3". It will pronounce after getting the digit "3": twenty three. But in the case of the number "230", after recognizing the digit "2", the number of the remaining digits can't allow to recognize a sub number. Then the system will resolve "2" with using the ten power "100" and adding "30". It will pronounce: two hundred thirty.

A string that consists of characters and numbers is assumed to be a string and can be read in two ways: (1) by spelling the characters that compose the string or (2) by pronouncing the substring formed by the characters and spelling the integrated number digit by digit. For example, the string "MAN123" can be read "M-A-N-one-two-three" or "MAN-one-two-three".

The need to integrate the reading of numbers brings to the completion of the warehouse by including digit sound files, ten powers sound files, and by extension, all the sub numbers that are in the numeric base and that have their own name. For example for the English language, the base consists of the digits from zero to nine, the sub number from eleven to twenty, and thirty, forty, fifty, sixty, seventy, eighty, ninety, hundred, thousand, million, billion.

D. Reading extra language words

In a text, all the words are not necessary given by the language dictionary because of names of objects or technical names that can be used. Two kinds of solution can be implemented when during the resolution of the word in the audio warehouse the ATRS doesn't find the correspondent audio file. The first solution useful for the words in capital letter is to spell the word character by character. This means that the resolution is done for every character in the audio warehouse; not for the entire word. For example, "HTML" will be pronounced "H-T-M-L". The second solution is to put the text under test after producing the course so that the script can early detect the additional words to be put in the language dictionary and thus, in the audio warehouse. This will let the dictionary becoming richer. Anyway, it is assumed that after producing a course, the author must perform the ATRS script and listen to the reading of the text to detect anomalies. It is also possible for the author to adjust the text reading parameters to make his message understandable at his convenience. The access of the text reading parameters given as input to the ATRS script can also be let at the convenience of the learner.

E. Integrating new other language subtleties

Dependent to the robustness of the ATRS, the DOUNG can offer many courses in many languages, regardless to the evolution of the content of the course. This is made possible because of the separation between a course and its content provided in text format in one side, and in the other side the audio warehouse containing audio files of the basic words of a language. The ATRS is used to read any course provide in the language. This contribution is different to the case by which a particular course is recorded in audio format as in the case of the course provide with the multimedia captors and recorded in an audio file. In that case, when the content of the course changes another audio file must be recorded. The audio warehouse offers flexibility to teachers without the constraints to record any course or to record again when the content of the course changes. The ATRS must be designed as an evolving algorithm because every language has its own subtleties. Thus, it is paramount important to let the possibility to make the ATRS system becoming more robust among versions so that it can integrate other particular languages pronunciation of words. The following figure 2 shows the operating mechanism of the ATRS script.

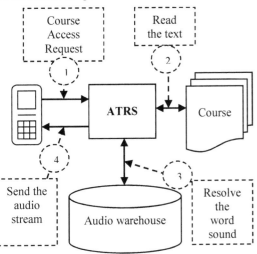

Fig. 2.   Interactions between the learner, the ATRS and the courses

VI.   IMPROVING THE CLOUD COMPUTING ARCHITECTURE OF THE DOUNG

The DOUNG services are designed to operate on a cloud computing architecture in a completely transparent manner to the learner. The cloud computing is integrated to achieve a minimum level of quality of service when the learner is monitoring the courses. The Sotfware as a Service (SaaS) part of the cloud computing in the DOUNG architecture allows to subdivide the applications in elementary modules freely assembled. A web service is suggested to be used for assembling a course in image format, video format, and fixed text format or by extracting information from a database. For an advanced use of that component of the cloud computing, the ATRS script will accompany a web page by providing the audio format of the transferred text on the learner's device. The same initial advantage is maintained, that is to fit the case of GSM supports more suitable for the audio transmission. This additional ATRS script provides help for the cell devices by offering a solution to the problem inherent to their limited capacity of installing and running applications.

The Data as a Service (DaaS) of the cloud computing used by the DOUNG consists initially of available courses in a warehouse. The warehouse is implemented on different servers to resolve the limited capacity problem of data storage of the cellular devices. The contribution of the ATRS system brings to the improvement of the new version of the DaaS part of the services offered by the DOUNG. The courses warehouse in HTML format (text, image, video) is having as neighbor, the audio warehouse that is used to generate the voice format of courses in different languages. The same transparent location is maintained within a collaborative exchange between the DOUNG servers and all GSM partners.

The Platform as a Service (PaaS) part of the DOUNG services provides a support for processing. In the case of the ATRS, the PaaS is improved by the offered option to the learner to run the script of the translation of a course from its text format to its equivalent in audio format. That audio format can be easily conveyed through the GSM network. By considering the limitation of the text traffic in the GSM network, the audio format is assumed to provide an appropriate framework for the learner to follow his courses. The improved PaaS service by the integration of the remote ATRS system will help to overcome the problem of the limited processing capabilities inherent to mobile devices.

The Infrastructure as a Service (IaaS) is provided in [10] with the interfacing between the web service and other scripts. The example of CGI scripts is given which are written in low level programming languages and which execution extends to files access. The case of ATRS script is illustrative of the implementation of that part of the DOUNG service for the need of reading the text file, the need of recognizing words and selecting the appropriate audio file in the voice warehouse. The illustration is extended to the running of the audio file and its transmission through GSM channel.

VII.   CONCLUSION

The e-learning, the m-learning, the VPN, and the cloud computing are techniques used in an integrated architecture using Internet and GSM for the advent of the DOUNG with the goal to cover large world areas. The initial model on which the DOUNG is operating let appears some complementary work of re-recording lessons according to the language of learners or according to some changes that occurs in recorded sessions. To overcome these limitations, the new model integrates the use of an audio warehouse with its ATRS exploitation script. An audio warehouse is an audio dictionary of a chosen language, recorded in a particular folder with a fair organization associating each language to a specific folder. The ATRS script is designed to read a course produced in the HTML format by extracting words, and accessing to the language audio warehouse. It then gives the correct pronunciation of the text. The system conveys the voice stream through the network. That format is more suitable for the GSM, while the cloud-computing gives facility to cell-devices used by to follow a course according to his own budget and time table. An incoming work to be conduct is to integrate many languages constraints in the ATRS. The second work is related to the adding of the language translation module. Then, the performances of the whole system must be evaluated under simulations with specific criterions.

REFERENCES

[1] LeCavé, A.D. Salamin, "Mobile Learning : Les avantages du papier virtuel," FI 1, 3 Février 2004, pp.7-9.

[2] H. Jeng, J. Uttaro, L. Jalil, B. Decraene, Y. Rekhter, R. Aggarwal, "Virtual Hub-and-Spoke in BGP/MPLS VPNs", October 2013, RFC 7024

[3] Y. Cai, E. Rosen, IJ. Wijnands, "IPv6 Multicast VPN (MVPN) Support Using PIM Control Plane and Selective Provider Multicast Service Interface (S-PMSI)", RFC 6516, February 2012

[4] B. Davie, F. Le Faucheur, A. Narayanan, " Support for the Resource Reservation Protocol (RSVP) in Layer 3 VPNs ", RFC 6016, October 2010

[5] E. Rosen, Y. Cai, I. Wijnands, "Cisco Systems' Solution for Multicast in BGP/MPLS IP VPNs", RFC 6037, October 2010

[6] S. Frankel, S. Krishnan, "IP Security (IPsec) and Internet Key Exchange (IKE) Document Roadmap", RFC 6071, February 2011

[7] K. Lam, S. Mansfield, E. Gray, "Network Management Requirements for MPLS-based Transport Networks", RFC5951, September 2010

[8] A. Freier, P. Karlton, P. Kocher, "The Secure Sockets Layer (SSL) Protocol version 3.0", RFC 6101, August 2011

[9] T. Murphy, P. Rieth, J. Stevens, "IBM's iSeries Telnet Enhancements", RFC 4777, November 2006

[10] Issoufou Tiado, H. Saliah-Hassane, "Cloud-Computing based architecture for the advent of a New Generation of Digital Open Universities in m-learning", ICEER 2013 conference Proceedings, pp572-579, Marrakesh – Morocco, July 2013

28

Improving Performance of Free Space Optics Link Using Array of Receivers in Terrible Weather Conditions of Plain and Hilly Areas

Amit Gupta
Professor, Department of ECE
Chandigarh University,
Gharuan, India

Shaina
Research Scholar, Department of ECE
Chandigarh University,
Gharuan, India

Surbhi Bakshi
Associate Professor, Department of ECE
Chandigarh University,
Gharuan, India

Mandeep Chaudhary
School of Engineering & Digital arts
University of Kent
Canterbury,UK

Abstract—Free-space optical (FSO) communication is a cost effective and high data rate access technique, which has been proving itself a best alternative to radio frequency technology. FSO link provides high bandwidth solution to the last mile access bottleneck. However, for terrestrial communication systems, the performance of these links is severely degraded from atmospheric loss mainly due to fog, rain and snow. So, a continuous availability of the link is always a concern. This paper investigates the dreadful weather effects such as rain, fog, snow, and other losses on the transmission performance of FSO systems. The technique of using an array of receivers for improving the performance of FSO links is explored in this paper. It involves the deployment of multiple photo detectors at the receiver end to mitigate effects of various weather conditions. The performance of the proposed system is evaluated in terms of bit error rate, received signal power, Q- factor and height of eye diagram. The influence of various weather conditions of plain and hilly areas are taken into consideration and results are compared with conventional FSO links.

Keywords—Free space optics (FSO) communication; Array of photo detectors; Bit Error Rate (BER); Eye diagram; Quality factor (Q factor); Bad weather effects

I. INTRODUCTION

The optical wireless communication (OWC) systems have attracted a lot of interest of the users because they can solve the last mile problem in urban environments. OWC, also recognized as free space optical (FSO) communication, has emerged as a commercially feasible alternative to radio frequency (RF) and millimetre waves wireless communication for reliable and rapid deployment of data and voice networks. FSO communication using high bandwidth transmission links has enormous potential to serve for requirements of high data rate transmissions. License free bandwidth, high carrier frequency (range 20 THz- 375Thz), easy deployment, appreciable security of data, avoiding electromagnetic pollution, low power consumption enables FSO links to provide high data rates communications[1]. Its various advantages over existing Radio Frequency (RF) technologies like wider bandwidth that can support a large number of users without any delay or interference in communication, have increased its demand in the market.

Despite of being on the list of most desirable technologies of the next generation, its deployment is highly dependent on atmospheric variations thus related to its reliability and availability issues. Fog, snow and clouds scatter or absorb the optical signal, which causes transmission errors. Maintaining a clear line of sight (LOS) between transmitter and receiver is also one of the major challenges in establishing optical wireless links in the free space [6]. The LOS is disturbed due to atmospheric influences like fog, rain, snow, dust, sleet, clouds or temporary physical obstructions like birds and airplanes. Various researchers have come up with the results that optical attenuation can reach up to 128dB/km in heavy fog and snow conditions in different areas [7]. The scattering, absorption and refraction of light signals reduce the link capacity and availability in different weather conditions.

To lessen these effects, techniques like using multiple transmit lasers and multiple receive apertures can be applied [8-9]. The performance of FSO links in the presence of atmospheric turbulence had been analyzed using spatial diversity [10-11]. To calculate the error rate performance, outage probability and diversity gain for multi-input multi-output FSO links, the combined effect of atmospheric turbulence and misalignment was also considered [12-13]. Then the effect of weather conditions was taken into account using array of receivers [14-16].

But the effect of weather conditions of hilly areas like heavy fog, wet snow, dry snow etc was not discussed by researchers in previous literature. The consideration of these parameters cannot be ignored while installation of FSO link especially in hilly areas. In this paper a comprehensive analysis of FSO link in all weather conditions has been performed using one of the most important approaches of array of photo detectors to reduce the effects of attenuation on received signal. At an ideal case, the only cause of signal attenuation is distance of transmission. So, the additional losses we have taken into account are due to weather conditions only and other losses are considered to be 0 dB/km. The study of bit error rate, height of eye diagram, Q factor and maximum received power is taken into account for studying the performance of FSO link.

The paper is organized as: After the introduction of FSO systems, system analysis of proposed FSO model is provided and various parameters that affect the quality of the signal in the link are discussed in section II. In Section III, the results obtained after simulations are evaluated for both hilly and plain areas using array of receivers. Finally, conclusions are drawn in Section IV.

II. SYSTEM ANALYSIS

A synoptic diagram of the considered system model is depicted in Figure 1 below. The block diagram shows the three key function elements of FSO system that are the transmitter, the atmospheric channel and the receiver. The transmitter which is used for converting electrical signal into optical signal consists of a modulator, a laser driver, a laser and a power meter.

The modulator used in the link converts the information into the desired signal and controls the amplitude of an optical signal. Laser driver provides the power to the laser for its proper functioning and helps to prevent aging and other environmental effects of laser. The range of the link for evaluating the performance is chosen as 500m and the transmission wavelength chosen for the working of laser is 1550 nm which is the 3rd optical window of wireless transmission. It is chosen to work on this wavelength as the functioning of FSO link is more robust and safe for human eye at this value [2-3].

The information signal is transmitted over FSO channel where it undergoes attenuation and power loss as a result of absorption, scattering and turbulence. At the receiver end, the signal is amplified and detected by an array of receivers which improve the overall efficiency and accuracy of the system. The filter and regenerator are used to preserve the wave shape of the signal. Power meter and BER analyser are used to measure the parameters of received signal. The data rates up to 100 Gb/s can be achieved using FSO technology [4-5].

Attenuation present in the atmosphere of the system can affect its performance. Atmospheric attenuation and geometric losses constitute all attenuation. It is the effect of particles present in the air for e.g. haze, rain, fog, snow etc. These particles can stay a longer time in the atmosphere. So, attenuation values depend upon the visibility level at that time. To reduce these effects, a system is proposed that can work properly under these conditions. The value of parameters on which the system is operating is mentioned in table 1.

The total attenuation of wireless medium communication system can be estimated [17] as:

$$\alpha = \alpha fog_\gamma + \alpha snow_\gamma + \alpha rain_\gamma + \alpha scattering_\gamma, dB/km \tag{1}$$

where, α=attenuation and

γ=is transmission wavelength in μm

The main attenuation factor for optical wireless links is fog, but the attenuation caused by an effect of rain cannot be ignored, especially in environments where rain is more frequent than fog.

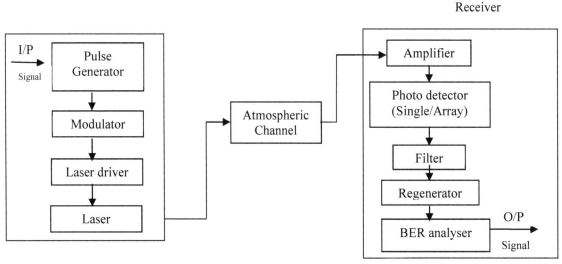

Fig. 1.   Block diagram of FSO link

TABLE I.   PROPOSED OPERATING PARAMETERS FOR FREE SPACE OPTICAL COMMUNICATION SYSTEMS

Operating parameters	Value
Signal transmitted power (plain areas)	1mW
Signal transmitted power (hilly areas)	20 W
Attenuation (plain areas)	0-43 dB
Attenuation (hilly areas)	110-128 dB
No. of photo detectors used	8
Range of Link	500 m
Operating signal wavelength,	1550 nm
Transmitter lens diameter	100 cm
Receiver aperture diameter	50 cm

Let $\overline{R}$ be the rain rate in mm/h, the specific attenuation of optical wireless link is given by [18]:

$$\alpha_{rain} = 1.076 \ R^{0.67} \quad dB/km \qquad (2)$$

If S is the snow rate in mm/h then specific attenuation in dB/km is given by [19] as:

$$\alpha_{dry\ snow} = aS^b \quad dB/km \qquad (3)$$

If λ is the wavelength, the parameters a and b for dry snow is given as the following:

$a = 5.42 \times 10 - 4\lambda + 5.495876$, b = 1.38

The specific attenuation in the case of wet snow can be expressed as the following formula [20]:

$$\alpha_{wet\ snow} = h \ S^g \quad dB/km \qquad (4)$$

The parameters h and g for wet snow are as, h $= 1.023 \times 10 - 4\lambda + 3.7855466$, g = 0.72

The amount of received power is proportional to the amount of power transmitted and the area of the collection aperture but inversely proportional to the square of the beam divergence and the square of the link range. It is also inversely proportional to the exponential of the product of atmospheric attenuation coefficient times the link range [21-22].

$$P_{received} = P_{received} * \frac{d_2^2}{[d1 + (D*R)]^2} * 10^{(-a*r/10)} \qquad (5)$$

Where, P = power,

d1 = transmit aperture diameter (m),

d2 = receive aperture diameter (m),

D = beam divergence (mrad), R = range (km),

a = atmospheric attenuation factor (dB/km).

Also, the bit error rate can also be expressed in terms of signal to noise ratio (SNR) as:

$$BER = \frac{2}{\pi.SNR} . \exp\left(-\frac{SNR}{8}\right) \qquad (6)$$

III.   RESULTS AND PERFORMANCE EVALUATION

The model has been investigated to show the weather effects on the transmission and overall performance on free space communication in hilly and plain areas by using single photo detector and an array of photodetectors. FSO system with link range 500m operating at a wavelength of 1550 nm is considered such that it can show useful results over a wide range of weather conditions. The values of attenuation effecting information signal considered in table 2 are taken from [6].

TABLE II.   COMPARISON OF OUTPUTS OF BER ANALYSER IN PLAIN AREAS

Attenuation	Weather conditions	Output using single receiver	Output using array of receivers
0.43 dB	Clear air		

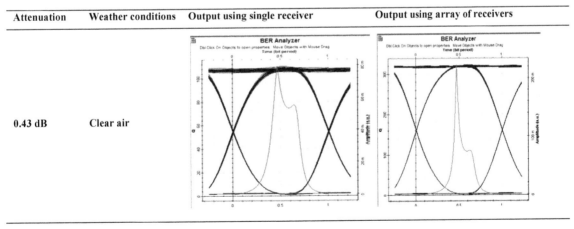

4.2 dB	Haze		
5.8 dB	Moderate rain		
9.2 dB	Heavy rain		
20 dB	Light fog		
42.2 dB	Moderate fog		

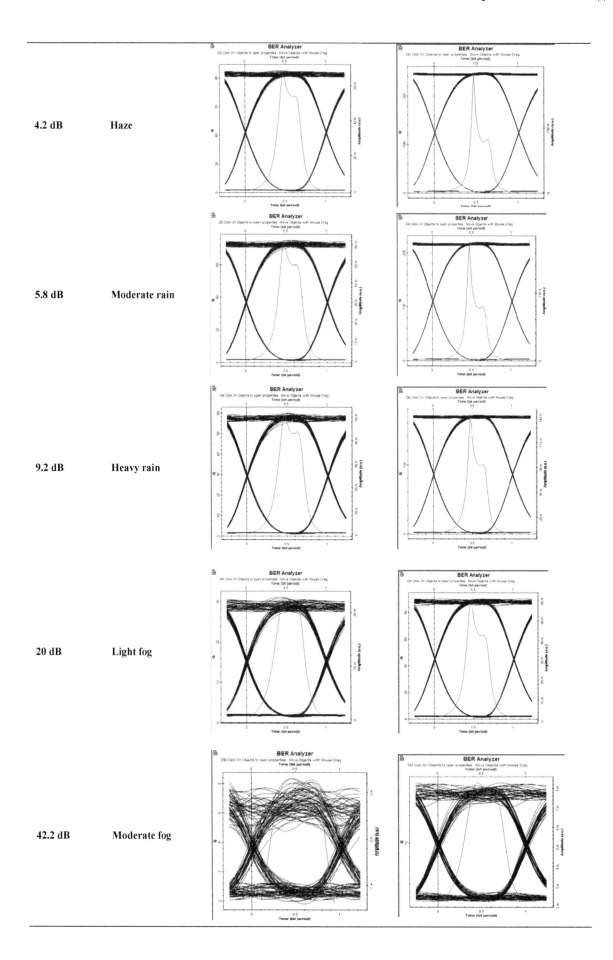

Table 2 shows the output of BER analyser for FSO link located in plain areas. The comparison is showing the improvement in the output when more than one receivers are inserted in the link. It can be seen than width and height of eye have increased and curve of Q factor has become sharp after using array of receivers at different values of attenuation. Figures in the table have proved that received signal power decreases with increasing atmospheric attenuation for in the presence of bad weather effects. But using an array of photo detectors has presented the highest received signal power compared to a single receiver. From the above discussion it is clear that array of receivers is giving better results in these weather conditions also. So, this technique can be further implied on the weather conditions of hilly areas too.

TABLE III.   COMPARISON OF OUTPUTS OF BER ANALYSER IN HILLY AREAS

Attenuation	Weather conditions	Output using single receiver	Output using array of receivers
110 dB	Wet snow		
125 dB	Heavy fog		
128 dB	Dry snow		

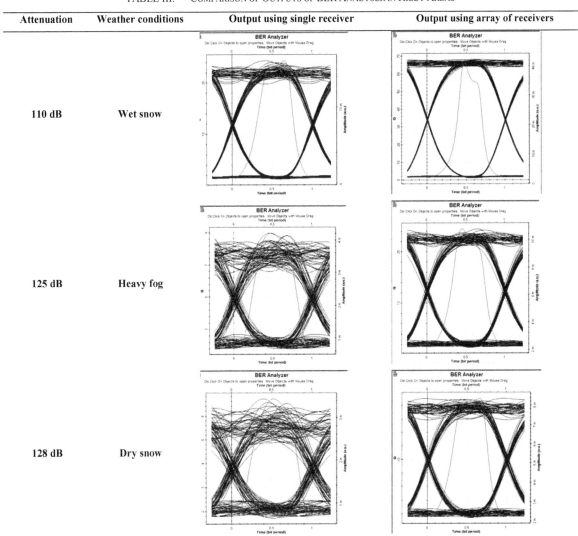

Similarly, Table 3 is the comparison of the output of BER analyzer in hilly areas. The values of attenuation of the signal effecting communication considered in table 3 in taken from [7]. The value of attenuation in hilly areas is very large as compared to plain areas.

So using an array of receivers in hilly areas gives very effective results by improving values of simulation parameters far better than optimum values.

The figures show that even in high attenuation conditions FSO systems can be deployed reliably by slightly modifying the conventional FSO systems.

The system operation characteristics have been plotted under varying weather conditions using different simulation parameters. A brief comparison is made to show the improvement in all simulation parameters using more than one receiver for receiving the information signal.

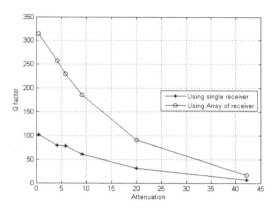

Fig. 2.   Comparison of Q factor in weather conditions of plain areas using single and array of Photo detectors

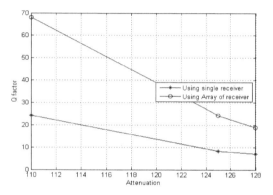

Fig. 3.   Comparison of Q factor in weather conditions of hilly areas using single and array of Photo detectors

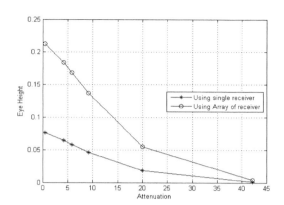

Fig. 4.   Comparison of Eye height in weather conditions of plain areas using single and array of Photo detectors

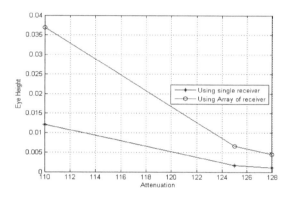

Fig. 5.   Comparison of eye height in weather conditions of hilly areas using single and array of Photo detectors

The graphs in figure 2 and 3 show the comparison of various values of Q factor of system model, as a result of using single receiver and array of receivers at different weather conditions of plain areas and hilly areas. The curve in figure 2 shows that, at transmitter power of 1mW there is a large difference in output signals of both the cases. Below 20 dB attenuation the technique employed is improving the quality of the received signal in huge ratio. After 20 dB the results start decreasing linearly with increasing attenuation and for the values above 40 dB there are not many variations in the results.

In figure 3 also, the results have assured that the Q factor of the system increases with increasing number of photo detectors in the link. It is observed that the quality of a signal received using an array of receivers is much better than the quality of the signal using single detector under different attenuation conditions. There is a significant difference in the value of Q factor at 128 dB, thus improving the reliability of the communication in bad weather conditions.

Figures 4 and 5 have demonstrated that the width of eye increases after the use of array of receivers in the link in both plain as well as hilly areas because the resultant signal is chosen such that it have maximum signal to noise ratio thus the opening of eye is more as compared to signal detected with single photo detector.

In figure 4, there is a significant difference in the values before 20 dB attenuation but after 20 dB it is almost same. But figure 5 illustrates that in hilly areas using this technique is quite helpful in removing the noise and jitter from the signal.

At 128 dB, the value of eye height in the conventional system is 0.0012 which is improved to 0.0036 using array of receivers.

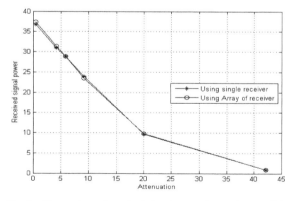

Fig. 6.   Comparison of received signal power in weather conditions of plain areas using single and array of Photo detectors

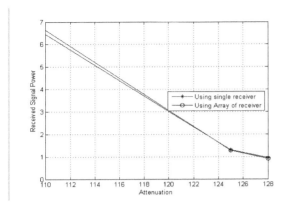

Fig. 7. Comparison of received signal power in weather conditions of hilly areas using single and array of Photo detectors

Figures 6 and 7 are indicating that with an increase in a number of photo detectors at the receiver end, there is a slight increase in received signal power because the multiple numbers of detectors are detecting the same signal independently. The final signal obtained is the maximum value of all detected signals.

Finally, a comprehensive comparison has been presented in an organized manner among the performances of links having single photo detector and multiple photo detectors in tabular form. Table 4 is illustrating the values of simulation parameters analyzed in plain areas with transmission power one mW. It can be clearly visualized that in the case of an array of photo detectors, there is a significance decrease in bit error rate. Also the values of Q factor, the height of eye and received signal power increases with the introduction of more than one photo detectors in the link.

TABLE IV.   EVALUATION OF FSO LINK IN PLAIN AREAS WITH POWER 1 MW

		Max. Q factor	Min. BER	Eye height	Received signal power(mW)
Single photo detector	Clear air (0.43	102.192	0	0.076034	36.7936
	Haze (4.2dB)	79.0142	0	0.0647861	30.911234
	Moderate rain (5.8dB)	78.2872	0	0.0583843	28.845105
	Heavy rain (9.2dB)	60.5079	0	0.0461851	23.91591
	Light fog (20 dB)	30.7312	7.34165e-208	0.0184382	9.69035
	Moderate fog (42.2 dB)	6.93705	1.83037e-12	0.00107621	0.90622
Array of photo detectors	Clear air (0.43	314.806	0	0.21236	37.388885
	Haze (4.2dB)	257.198	0	0.183567	31.362605
	Moderate rain (5.8dB)	229.584	0	0.168624	28.845105
	Heavy rain (9.2dB)	186.242	0	0.136811	23.480854
	Light fog (20 dB)	90.6124	0	0.055339	9.8212256
	Moderate fog (42.2 dB)	17.0842	8.87462e-66	0.00437094	0.920583

TABLE V.   EVALUATION OF FSO LINK IN HILLY AREAS WITH POWER 20W

		Max. Q factor	Min. BER	Eye height	Received signal power(mW)
Single photo detector	Wet snow (110 dB)	24.2834	1.12641e-130	0.0121424	6.4458854
	Heavy fog (125 dB)	8.19081	1.13342e-16	0.0017453	1.3038745
	Dry snow (128 dB)	7.04754	8.40774e-13	0.0011057	0.9438791
Array of photo detectors	Wet snow (110 dB)	68.0498	0	0.0369363	6.6352527
	Heavy fog (125 dB)	24.1941	2.00845e-104	0.0065796	1.2833537
	Dry snow (128 dB)	19.0077	8.40774e-13	0.0044685	0.9144441

The performance of link in hilly areas for different cases is summarized in Table 5. It shows the values of various parameters in hilly areas, where attenuation is very high as compared to plain areas. So, the power used for transmission of signal in hilly areas is 20W. The quality of received signal is improving as the values of simulation parameters are attaining optimum values.

It can be clearly visualized from the above results that as the number of photo detectors are increased at the receiver end; it is possible to obtain performance that may not be possible by using other techniques like increasing the transmitter power or aperture averaging.

IV. CONCLUSION

In this paper, the performance of the free space optical communication systems under the effects of bad weather conditions especially for heavy rain, fog, dry and wet snow has been analyzed. The performance of link is investigated for these conditions and is further improved by the technique of using an array of receivers. The results reveal that use of array of receivers is advantageous over that of a single receiver in FSO link for detecting the signal more accurately as the quality factor of received signal is improved by approximately 28% in all the cases under consideration. With further research and development, communication in FSO system can also be enhanced at higher data rate over a longer link range under all weather conditions and atmospheric turbulences to enhance the usage of free space optics technology.

REFERENCES

[1] F. Nadeem, V. Kvicera, M. S. Awan, E. Leitgeb, S. S. Muhammad, G. Kandus, "Weather Effects on Hybrid FSO/RF Communication Link," IEEE J. On selected areas in Comm., Vol.27, No. 9, pp. 1687-1696, Dec. 2009

[2] H.H. Refai, J.J. Sluss Jr., H.H. Refai, "Comparitive study of performance of analog fiber optic links versus free- space optical links" J. of Optical Engineering, Vol. 45, No.2, Feb. 2006

[3] S. Saini, A. Gupta," Investigation to find optimal modulation format for low power inter-satellite optical wireless communication (LP-IsOWC)", Eleventh International conference on Wireless and Optical Communication Networks, pp. 1-4, 2014

[4] V. Sarup, A. Gupta" Performance analysis of an ultra high capacity 1 Tbps DWDM-RoF system for very narrow channel spacing", Eleventh International conference on Wireless and Optical Communication Networks, pp. 1-5, 2014

[5] N. Cvijetic, Q. Dayou, Y. Jianjun, H. Yue-Kai, W. Ting, "100 Gb/s per channel free space optical transmission with coherent detection and MIMO processing,"in Proc. ECOC, pp.1-2, 2009

[6] B. He, R. Schober," Bit-Interleaved Coded Modulation for Hybrid RF/FSO Systems", IEEE Trans. on Comm., Vol. 57, No. 12,pp. 3753-3763, Dec. 2009

[7] A.N.Z. Rashed, M.M.E. El-Halawany, "Transmission characteristics evaluation under bad weather conditions in optical wireless links with different optical transmission windows", Wireless Personal Communications, Springer, Vol. 71, No. 2, pp. 1577-1595, July 2013

[8] A. K. Majumdar and J. C. Riclkin, "Free-space laser communications," in Principles and Advances. New York, NY, USA: Springer-Verlag, 2007.

[9] M. M. Ibrahim and A. M. Ibrahim, "Performance analysis of optical receivers with space diversity reception," IEE Proc. Commun., vol. 143, no. 6, pp. 369–372, Dec. 1996.

[10] S. Saini, A. Gupta," Modeling and Performance Analysis of DWDM Based 100 Gbps Low Power Inter-satellite Optical Wireless Communication (LP-IsOWC) System", SOP transactions on signal processing, Vol. 2, No. 1, 2015

[11] M. Khalighi, N. Schwartz, N. Aitamer, and S. Bourennane, "Fading reduction by aperture averaging and spatial diversity in optical wireless systems," J. Opt. Commun. Netw., vol. 1, no. 6, pp. 580–593, Nov. 2009.

[12] H. G. Sandalidis, T. A. Tsiftsis, G. K. Karagiannidis, and M. Uysal, "BER performance of FSO links over strong atmospheric turbulence channels with pointing errors," IEEE Commun. Lett., vol. 12, no. 1, pp. 44–46, Jan. 2008.

[13] A. A. Farid and S. Hranilovic, "Diversity gain and outage probability for MIMO free-space optical links with misalignment," IEEE Trans. Commun., vol. 60, no. 2, pp. 479–487, Feb. 2012.

[14] P. Kaur, V. K. Jain, and S. Kar," Performance Analysis of FSO Array Receivers in Presence of Atmospheric Turbulence", IEEE Photonics Technology Letter, Vol. 26, No. 12, pp. 1165-1168, June, 2014

[15] A. Gupta , R S Kaler, H Singh, "Investigation of OBS assembly technique based on various scheduling techniques for maximizing throughput", Optik-International Journal for Light and Electron Optics, 124(9), pp. 840–844, 2013

[16] A Gupta, RS Kaler, H Singh," An inimitable scheduling technique for optical burst switched networks", Optik-International Journal for Light and Electron Optics, vol. 124, no. 8, pp.689-692, 2013

[17] A. K.Majumdar& J. C. Ricklin, "Free space laser communications, principles and advantages", Berlin: Springer, 2008

[18] S. Muhammad, B. Flecker, E. Leitgeb, & M. Gebhart, "Characterization of fog attenuation in terrestrial free space optical links" Journal of Optical Engineering, vol. 46, no. 4, pp.1–9, 2007

[19] Akiba, M., Ogawa, K., Wakamori, K., Kodate, K., & Ito, S, "Measurement and simulation of the effect of snowfall on free space optical propagation", Journal of Applied Optics, Vol. 47, No. 31, pp. 5736– 5743, 2008

[20] Betti, S., Carrozzo, V., & Duca, E. "Over stratospheric altitude optical free space links: System performance evaluation transparent optical networks". In ICTON, International Conference on Transparent Optical Networks, July 2007

[21] S. Bloom, E. Korevaar, J. Schuster and H. Willebrand, "Understanding the performance of free-space optics", Journal of Optical Networking, Vol. 2, No. 6, June 2003.

[22] M. Jeong, J. Lee, S. Kim, S. Namgung, J. Lee, M. Cho, S. Huh, Y. Ahn, J. Cho, and J. Lee, "Weather-Insensitive Optical Free-Space Communication Using Gain-Saturated Optical Fiber Amplifiers", IEEE Journal of Lightwave Technology, Vol. 23, No. 12, 2005.

[23] A. E. N. A Mohamed, H. A. Sharshar, A. N. Z. Rashed & A. El-Nabawy, " Integrated service quality enhancement of wireless optical communication systems for long haul transmission distances" Canadian Journal on Electrical and Electronics Engineering, vol. 2, no. 12, pp.-557–570, 2011

[24] A Gupta, H Singh, J Kumar," A novel approach to reduce packet loss in OBS networks" International Journal of Computer Applications, vol. 58, no. 3, 2012

[25] N. Vinayak, A gupta," Comparative analysis of WDM system using Cascaded amplifiers in Optical wireless channel over a distance of 10000 km", SOP Transactions on Signal Processing, Vol. 1, No. 1, pp.25-32, 2014

29

Blurring and Deblurring Digital Images Using the Dihedral Group

Husein Hadi Abbas Jassim
Faculty of Computer Science and Mathematics
University of Kufa
Najaf, Iraq

Hind R.M Shaaban
Faculty of Computer Science and Mathematics
University of Kufa
Najaf, Iraq

Zahir M. Hussain
Faculty of Computer Science and Mathematics
University of Kufa
Najaf, Iraq
Adj. Prof., School of Engineering, ECU, Australia

Kawther B.R. Al-dbag
Faculty of Computer Science and Mathematics
University of Kufa
Najaf, Iraq

Abstract—**A new method of blurring and deblurring digital images is presented. The approach is based on using new filters generating from average filter and H-filters using the action of the dihedral group. These filters are called HB-filters; used to cause a motion blur and then deblurring affected images. Also, enhancing images using HB-filters is presented as compared to other methods like Average, Gaussian, and Motion. Results and analysis show that the HB-filters are better in peak signal to noise ratio (PSNR) and RMSE.**

Keywords—Dihedral group; Kronecker Product; motion blur and deblur; digital image

I.   INTRODUCTION

This template, There are three main categories of image processing, image enhancement, image compression and restoration and measurement extraction [3,6]. A digital image is divided into pixels. Each pixel has a magnitude that represents intensity. The camera uses the recorded image as a faithful representation of the scene that the user saw, but every image is more or less burry. Blurring may arise in the recording of image, because it is unavoidable the scene information "spills over" to neighboring pixels. When there is motion between the camera and image objects during photographing, the motion blur the image. In order to recover motion-blurred images, mathematical model of blurring process are used [1]. Many authors studied motion blur. Often, it is not easy or convenient to eliminate the blur technically. Mathematically, motion blur is modeled as a convolution of point spread function (filters) denoted by (PSF) with the image represented by its intensities. The original image must be recovered by using mathematical model of the blurring process which is called image deblurring [7]. Many researchers introduced algorithms to remove blur such as Average filter AF (or Mean filter), Gaussian filter (GF). The Gaussian filter is equivalent to filtering with a mask of radius R, whose weights are given by Gaussian function: $(x, y) = \frac{1}{2\pi\sigma^2} e^{\frac{-(x^2+y^2)}{2\sigma^2}}$, $x \in R$; where σ is stander deviation of the Gaussian: large σ for more intensive smoothing) [2]. Motion Blur effect filter is a filter that makes the image appear to be moving by adding a blur in a specific direction [10]. The largest subgroup H of dihedral group D_n is found in [4].

In this work, Markov basis *HB* is used to introduce a new filters from Average filter for adding and removing motion blur of image, denoted by *HB*-filters.

II.   PRELIMINARY CONCEPTS

This section reviews the preliminaries about H-filters, Dihedral group, Convolution and Deconvolution processes.

A.   H-Filters

H-filters are 18 elements as per the following set [5].

$$\mathbf{z}_1 = \begin{bmatrix} 1 & -1 & 0 \\ -1 & 1 & 0 \\ 0 & 0 & 0 \end{bmatrix}; \mathbf{z}_2 = \begin{bmatrix} 0 & 0 & 0 \\ 1 & -1 & 0 \\ -1 & 1 & 0 \end{bmatrix};$$

$$\mathbf{z}_3 = \begin{bmatrix} 1 & 0 & -1 \\ -1 & 0 & 1 \\ 0 & 0 & 0 \end{bmatrix}; \mathbf{z}_4 = \begin{bmatrix} 0 & 0 & 0 \\ 1 & 0 & -1 \\ -1 & 0 & 1 \end{bmatrix};$$

$$\mathbf{z}_5 = \begin{bmatrix} 0 & 1 & -1 \\ 0 & -1 & 1 \\ 0 & 0 & 0 \end{bmatrix}; \mathbf{z}_6 = \begin{bmatrix} 0 & 1 & -1 \\ 0 & 0 & 0 \\ 0 & -1 & 1 \end{bmatrix};$$

$$\mathbf{z}_7 = \begin{bmatrix} 0 & 0 & 0 \\ 0 & 1 & -1 \\ 0 & -1 & 1 \end{bmatrix}; \mathbf{z}_8 = \begin{bmatrix} 1 & -1 & 0 \\ 0 & 0 & 0 \\ -1 & 1 & 0 \end{bmatrix};$$

$$\mathbf{z}_9 = \begin{bmatrix} 1 & 0 & -1 \\ 0 & 0 & 0 \\ -1 & 0 & 1 \end{bmatrix}; \mathbf{z}_{10} = \begin{bmatrix} -1 & 1 & 0 \\ 1 & -1 & 0 \\ 0 & 0 & 0 \end{bmatrix};$$

$$\mathbf{z}_{11} = \begin{bmatrix} 0 & 0 & 0 \\ -1 & 1 & 0 \\ 1 & -1 & 0 \end{bmatrix}; \mathbf{z}_{12} = \begin{bmatrix} -1 & 0 & 1 \\ 1 & 0 & -1 \\ 0 & 0 & 0 \end{bmatrix};$$

$$\mathbf{z}_{13} = \begin{bmatrix} 0 & 0 & 0 \\ -1 & 0 & 1 \\ 1 & 0 & -1 \end{bmatrix}; \mathbf{z}_{14} = \begin{bmatrix} 0 & -1 & 1 \\ 0 & 1 & -1 \\ 0 & 0 & 0 \end{bmatrix};$$

$$\mathbf{z}_{15} = \begin{bmatrix} 0 & -1 & 1 \\ 0 & 0 & 0 \\ 0 & 1 & -1 \end{bmatrix}; \mathbf{z}_{16} = \begin{bmatrix} 0 & 0 & 0 \\ 0 & -1 & 1 \\ 0 & 1 & -1 \end{bmatrix};$$

$$\mathbf{z}_{17} = \begin{bmatrix} -1 & 1 & 0 \\ 0 & 0 & 0 \\ 1 & -1 & 0 \end{bmatrix}; \mathbf{z}_{18} = \begin{bmatrix} -1 & 0 & 1 \\ 0 & 0 & 0 \\ 1 & 0 & -1 \end{bmatrix};$$

B. Definition 1: Dihedral Group

Let n be a positive integer greater than or equal to 3. The group of all symmetries of the regular polygon with n sides, including both rotations and reflections, is called **dihedral group** and denoted by D_n[13]. The 2n elements in D_n can be written as: $\{e, r, r^2, \ldots, r^{n-1}, s, sr, sr^2, sr^{n-1}\}$, where e is the identity element in D_n. In general, we can write D_n as: $D_n = \{s^j r^k : 0 \le k \le n - 1, 0 \le j \le 1\}$ which has the following properties:

$$r^n = 1, \quad sr^k s = r^{-k}, \quad (sr^k)^2 = e, \text{ for all } 0 \le k \le n - 1.$$ The composition of two elements of the D_n is given by $r^i r^j = r^{i+j}$, $r^i s r^j = sr^{j-i}$, $sr^i r^j = sr^{i+j}$, $sr^i s r^j = r^{j-i}$.

C. 2D Convolution

Assume two discrete 2-dimensional images $f(x, y)$ and $h(x, y)$. Their *convolved* (or *folded*) *sum* is the image $g(x, y)$, the convolution of these two functions is defined as [12]:

$g(x,y) = f(x,y) \otimes h(x,y)$, so
$$f(x,y) \otimes h(x,y) = \sum_{m=0}^{M-1} \sum_{n=0}^{N-1} f(m,n) h(x-m, y-n) \tag{1}$$

For $0 \le x, m \le M - 1$; $0 \le y, n \le N - 1$,

where $M \times N$ is a size of $h(x,y)$.

III. 2D DISCRETE FOURIER TRANSFORM

The two-dimensional *discrete Fourier transform* (DFT) of the image function $f(x, y)$ is defined as,

$$F(u,v) = \sum_{x=0}^{M-1} \sum_{y=0}^{N-1} f(x,y) e^{-j2\pi(\frac{ux}{M} + \frac{vy}{N})} \tag{2}$$

where $f(x, y)$ is a digital image of size $M \times N$, and the discrete variable u and v in the ranges: $u = 0, 1, 2, \ldots, M\text{-}1$ and $v = 0, 1, 2, \ldots, N\text{-}1$[11].

Given the transform $F(u, v)$, we can obtain $f(x, y)$ by using the *inverse discrete Fourier transform* (IDFT):

$$f(x,y) = \frac{1}{MN} \sum_{u=0}^{M-1} \sum_{v=0}^{N-1} F(u,v) e^{j2\pi(\frac{ux}{M} + \frac{vy}{N})} \tag{3}$$

It can be shown by direct substitution into Eq. 2 and Eq. 3 that the *Fourier transform* pair satisfies the following translation properties:

$$f(x-m, y-n) \Longleftrightarrow F(u,v) e^{-i2\pi(\frac{um}{M} + \frac{vn}{N})} \tag{4}$$

Now, interested in finding the Fourier transform of Eq. 1:

$\mathcal{F}(f(x,y) \otimes h(x,y)) =$
$\sum_{x=0}^{M-1} \sum_{y=0}^{N-1} [\sum_{m=0}^{M-1} \sum_{n=0}^{N-1} f(m,n) h(x-m, y-n)] e^{-j2\pi(\frac{ux}{M} + \frac{vy}{N})}$, so by Eq. 4 we have,
$\mathcal{F}(f(x,y) \otimes h(x,y)) =$
$\sum_{m=0}^{M-1} \sum_{n=0}^{N-1} f(m,n) H(u,v) e^{-j2\pi(\frac{ux}{M} + \frac{vy}{N})} = F(u,v) H(u,v)$.

This result of the *convolution theorem* is written as:

$$f(x,y) \otimes h(x,y) \Longleftrightarrow F(u,v) H(u,v) \tag{5}$$

The transform of the original image simply by dividing the transform of the degraded image $G(u, v)$, by the degradation function $H(u, v)$ is

$$\hat{F}(u,v) = \frac{G(u,v)}{H(u,v)} \tag{6}$$

that's called inverse filter [9].

A. Fourier Spectrum

Because the 2-D *DFT* is complex in general [8], it can be expressed in polar form: $F(u,v) = |F(u,v)| e^{-i\emptyset(u,v)}$

where the magnitude,

$$|F(u,v)| = [R^2(u,v) + I^2(u,v)]^{\frac{1}{2}} \tag{7}$$

is called the Fourier (or frequency) spectrum. The power spectrum is defined as,

$$P(u.v) = |F(u,v)|^2 = R^2(u,v) + I^2(u,v).$$

As before, R and J are the real and imaginary parts of $F(u, v)$ and all computations are carried out for the discrete variables $u = 0, 1, 2, \ldots, M\text{-}1$ and $v = 0, 1, 2, \ldots, N\text{-}1$. Therefore,

$|F(u,v)|$, $\emptyset(u,v)$, and $P(u,v)$ are arrays of size $M \times N$.

B. Image Restoration based on Wiener Deconvolution

The method considers images and noise as random variables, and the objective is to find an estimate $\hat{f}$ of the uncorrupted image f such that the mean square error *(MSE)* between them is minimized. This error measure is given by:

$$e^2 = E\left\{(f - \hat{f})^2\right\} \tag{8}$$

Based on these conditions, the minimum of the error function in Eq. 8 is given in the frequency domain by the expression:

$$\hat{F}(u,v) = \left[\frac{H^*(u,v)S_f(u,v)}{S_f(u,v)|H(u,v)|^2 + S_\eta(u,v)}\right] G(u,v)$$
$$= \left[\frac{1}{H(u,v)} \frac{|H(u,v)|^2}{|H(u,v)|^2 + S_\eta(u,v)/S_f(u,v)}\right] G(u,v) \tag{9}$$

The terms in Eq. 9 are as follows:

$H(u,v)$ = degradation function & $H^*(u,v)$ = complex conjugate of H(u, v) & $|H(u,v)|^2 = H^*(u,v)H(u,v)$ & $S_\eta(u,v) = |N(u,v)|^2$ = power spectrum of the noise & $S_f(u,v) = |F(u,v)|^2$ = power spectrum of the original image & $G(u, v)$ = the transform of the degraded image. Note that if the noise is zero, then the noise power spectrum vanishes and the Wiener filter reduces to the inverse filter.

IV. THE PROPOSED APPROACH

H-filters are used to generate **HB-filters** by adding each element in **H-filters** to the average filter, so we got some **HB-filters** with dimensions *3-by-3* and each of which has type of blur different from the other.

Then the **HB-filters** can be extended using tenser product (by operation $\circledast$) to larger sizes, in order to get a higher degrees of blur in digital images. Take any one of **HB-filters** $h(x,y)$ of dimension *3-by-3* and extend it by identity matrix I_n, *n-by-n* where n is an odd number greater than or equals 3, by Tensor Product T:

$$T(x,y) = h(x,y) \circledast I_n(x,y)$$
$$= \begin{bmatrix} h_{11} \times I_n & h_{12} \times I_n & h_{13} \times I_n \\ h_{21} \times I_n & h_{22} \times I_n & h_{23} \times I_n \\ h_{31} \times I_n & h_{32} \times I_n & h_{33} \times I_n \end{bmatrix}_{3n \times 3n}$$

This filter will be called *extended HB-filter* generated from **HB-filter** $h(x,y)$ and I_n.

Example 1.

Choose any one of **H-filters**: $z_2 = \begin{bmatrix} 0 & 0 & 0 \\ 1 & -1 & 0 \\ -1 & 1 & 0 \end{bmatrix}$

Divide z_2 by 9, and add it to the average filter (A_f) as follows:

$$h_1 = z_2 + A_f = \begin{bmatrix} 0 & 0 & 0 \\ 1 & -1 & 0 \\ -1 & 1 & 0 \end{bmatrix}/9 + \begin{bmatrix} 1 & 1 & 1 \\ 1 & 1 & 1 \\ 1 & 1 & 1 \end{bmatrix}/9 =$$

$\begin{bmatrix} 1 & 1 & 1 \\ 2 & 0 & 1 \\ 0 & 2 & 1 \end{bmatrix}/9$. So, $h_1 = \begin{bmatrix} 1 & 1 & 1 \\ 2 & 0 & 1 \\ 0 & 2 & 1 \end{bmatrix}/9$ it's one of **HB-filters**.

Now use the action largest subgroup $\mathcal{H} = \{e, r^{\frac{n}{3}}, r^{\frac{2n}{3}}, sr, sr^{1+\frac{n}{3}}, sr^{1+\frac{2n}{3}}\}$ of dihedral group [4], to generate other **HB-filters**. So, h_1 can be represented as 9-dimensional column vector,

$$h_1 = \begin{bmatrix} 1 \\ 1 \\ 1 \\ 1 \\ 2 \\ 0 \\ 1 \\ 0 \\ 2 \end{bmatrix}/9 \in \mathbb{Z}^9 ,$$

and calculate element of $\mathcal{H}$ in D_9 as

$$r^{\frac{n}{3}} = r^3$$

$$= \left(1 \ \frac{n}{3}+1 \ \frac{2n}{3}+1\right)\left(2 \ \frac{n}{3}+2 \ \frac{2n}{3}+2\right)...\left(\frac{n}{3} \ \frac{2n}{3} \ n\right)$$

$$= (1\ 4\ 7)(2\ 5\ 8)(3\ 6\ 9).$$

To find $T_{r^3}h_1$, one has:

$$T_{r^3} = \begin{bmatrix} 0 & 0 & 0 & 0 & 0 & 0 & 1 & 0 & 0 \\ 0 & 0 & 0 & 0 & 0 & 0 & 0 & 1 & 0 \\ 0 & 0 & 0 & 0 & 0 & 0 & 0 & 0 & 1 \\ 1 & 0 & 0 & 0 & 0 & 0 & 0 & 0 & 0 \\ 0 & 1 & 0 & 0 & 0 & 0 & 0 & 0 & 0 \\ 0 & 0 & 1 & 0 & 0 & 0 & 0 & 0 & 0 \\ 0 & 0 & 0 & 1 & 0 & 0 & 0 & 0 & 0 \\ 0 & 0 & 0 & 0 & 1 & 0 & 0 & 0 & 0 \\ 0 & 0 & 0 & 0 & 0 & 1 & 0 & 0 & 0 \end{bmatrix},$$

then

$$T_{r^3}h_1 = \begin{bmatrix} 0 & 0 & 0 & 0 & 0 & 0 & 1 & 0 & 0 \\ 0 & 0 & 0 & 0 & 0 & 0 & 0 & 1 & 0 \\ 0 & 0 & 0 & 0 & 0 & 0 & 0 & 0 & 1 \\ 1 & 0 & 0 & 0 & 0 & 0 & 0 & 0 & 0 \\ 0 & 1 & 0 & 0 & 0 & 0 & 0 & 0 & 0 \\ 0 & 0 & 1 & 0 & 0 & 0 & 0 & 0 & 0 \\ 0 & 0 & 0 & 1 & 0 & 0 & 0 & 0 & 0 \\ 0 & 0 & 0 & 0 & 1 & 0 & 0 & 0 & 0 \\ 0 & 0 & 0 & 0 & 0 & 1 & 0 & 0 & 0 \end{bmatrix} \cdot \begin{bmatrix} 1 \\ 1 \\ 1 \\ 1 \\ 2 \\ 0 \\ 1 \\ 0 \\ 2 \end{bmatrix}/9$$

$$= \begin{bmatrix} 1 \\ 0 \\ 2 \\ 1 \\ 1 \\ 1 \\ 1 \\ 2 \\ 0 \end{bmatrix}/9 = h_2 ,$$

So, $h_2 = \begin{bmatrix} 1 & 0 & 2 \\ 1 & 1 & 1 \\ 1 & 2 & 0 \end{bmatrix}/9 \in HB$

Similarly, one obtains

$$r^{\frac{2n}{3}} = sr^6$$

$$= \left(1 \ \frac{2n}{3}+1 \ \frac{n}{3}+1\right)\left(2 \ \frac{2n}{3}+2 \ \frac{n}{3}+2\right)...\left(\frac{n}{3} \ n \ \frac{2n}{3}\right)$$

$$= (1\ 7\ 4)(2\ 8\ 5)(3\ 9\ 6) \cdot h_1 = \begin{bmatrix} 1 & 2 & 0 \\ 1 & 0 & 2 \\ 1 & 1 & 1 \end{bmatrix}/9 = h_3 .$$

$$sr = (1\ n)(2\ n-1)...\left(\frac{n}{3} \ \frac{2n}{3}+1\right)\left(\frac{n}{3}+1 \ \frac{2n}{3}\right)...\left(\frac{n-1}{2} \ \frac{n+3}{2}\right)$$

$$= (1\ 9)(2\ 8)(3\ 7)(4\ 6)(4\ 6) \cdot h_1 = \begin{bmatrix} 2 & 0 & 1 \\ 0 & 2 & 1 \\ 1 & 1 & 1 \end{bmatrix}/9 = h_4 .$$

$$sr^{\frac{n}{3}+1} = sr^4$$

$$= \left(1 \ \frac{2n}{3}\right)\left(2 \ \frac{2n}{3}-1\right)...\left(\frac{n}{3} \ \frac{n}{3}+1\right)\left(\frac{2n}{3}+1 \ n\right)...$$

$$...\left(\frac{5n-3}{6} \ \frac{5n+9}{6}\right)$$

$$= (1\ 6)\ (2\ 5)(3\ 4)\ (7\ 9)(7\ 9) \cdot h_1 = \begin{bmatrix} 0 & 2 & 1 \\ 1 & 1 & 1 \\ 2 & 0 & 1 \end{bmatrix}/9 = h_5 .$$

$$sr^{\frac{2n}{3}+1} = \left(1 \ \frac{n}{3}\right)\left(2 \ \frac{n}{3}-1\right)...\left(\frac{n-3}{6} \ \frac{n+9}{6}\right)\left(\frac{n}{3}+1 \ n\right) \times$$

$$\times \left(\frac{n}{3}+2 \ n-1\right)...\left(\frac{2n}{3} \ \frac{2n}{3}+1\right)$$

$$= (1\ 3)\ (2\ 2)\ (1\ 3)\ (4\ 9)\ (5\ 8)\ (6\ 7) \cdot h_1$$

$$= \begin{bmatrix} 1 & 1 & 1 \\ 2 & 0 & 1 \\ 0 & 2 & 1 \end{bmatrix}/9 = h_6$$

All of these filters belong to **HB-filters**.

Most **HB-filters** can be obtained using other **H-filters**. For example the *extended HB-filters* generated from **HB-filter**

$$h(x,y) = \begin{bmatrix} 2 & 0 & 1 \\ 0 & 2 & 1 \\ 1 & 1 & 1 \end{bmatrix}$$ with I_3 is given by

$$T(x,y) = h(x,y) \circledast I_3(x,y) = \begin{bmatrix} 2 & 0 & 1 \\ 0 & 2 & 1 \\ 1 & 1 & 1 \end{bmatrix} \circledast \begin{bmatrix} 1 & 0 & 0 \\ 0 & 1 & 0 \\ 0 & 0 & 1 \end{bmatrix}$$

$$= \begin{bmatrix} 2 & 0 & 0 & 0 & 0 & 0 & 1 & 0 & 0 \\ 0 & 2 & 0 & 0 & 0 & 0 & 0 & 1 & 0 \\ 0 & 0 & 2 & 0 & 0 & 0 & 0 & 0 & 1 \\ 0 & 0 & 0 & 2 & 0 & 0 & 1 & 0 & 0 \\ 0 & 0 & 0 & 0 & 2 & 0 & 0 & 1 & 0 \\ 0 & 0 & 0 & 0 & 0 & 2 & 0 & 0 & 1 \\ 1 & 0 & 0 & 1 & 0 & 0 & 1 & 0 & 0 \\ 0 & 1 & 0 & 0 & 1 & 0 & 0 & 1 & 0 \\ 0 & 0 & 1 & 0 & 0 & 1 & 0 & 0 & 1 \end{bmatrix}_{9\times 9}$$

A. Blurring

This sub-section describes the standard filters algorithm for addition blur of an image by using the convolution theorem.

Blur algorithm

Consider an image matrix $f(x, y)$ of dimension m-by-n, which can be written as follows:

$$f(x,y) = \begin{bmatrix} f_{11} & \cdots & f_{1n} \\ \vdots & \ddots & \vdots \\ f_{m} & \cdots & f_{mn} \end{bmatrix}_{m\times n}$$. And **HB-filter** $h(x,y)$ p-by-q

dimension defined as, $h(x,y) = \begin{bmatrix} h_{11} & h_{12} & \cdots & h_{1q} \\ h_{21} & h_{22} & \cdots & h_{2q} \\ \vdots & \vdots & \ddots & \vdots \\ h_{p1} & h_{p2} & \cdots & h_{pq} \end{bmatrix}_{p\times q}$.

Step1: In the beginning add $f(x,y)$ by p-1 rows with zeros from up and down, and p-1 columns with zeros from left and right, such that the result is $\{m+2(p-1)\}$-by-$\{n+2(q-1)\}$ dimensions, as follows:

$$f(x,y) = \begin{bmatrix} 0 & 0 & 0 & \cdots & 0 & 0 & 0_{1j} \\ \vdots & \vdots & \vdots & 0 & 0 & 0 \\ 0 & \cdots & f_{11} & f_{1n} & \vdots & \vdots \\ \vdots & & \vdots & \ddots & \vdots & \\ 0 & 0 & f_{m1} & f_{mn} & 0 & 0 \\ 0_{i1} & 0 & 0 & 0 & 0 & 0_{ij} \end{bmatrix}_{i\times j} ,$$

where $i= m+2(p-1)$ and $j= m+2(q-1)$.

Step2: Reverse $h(x,y)$ (that used in blurring) for two directions,

$$h(x,y) = \begin{bmatrix} h_{11} & h_{12} & \cdots & h_{1q} \\ h_{21} & h_{22} & \cdots & h_{2q} \\ \vdots & \vdots & \ddots & \vdots \\ h_{p1} & h_{p2} & \cdots & h_{pq} \end{bmatrix}$$

$$\xrightarrow{rev} h(x,y) = \begin{bmatrix} h_{pq} & \cdots & h_{p2} & h_{p1} \\ h_{2q} & \cdots & h_{22} & h_{21} \\ \vdots & \ddots & \vdots & \vdots \\ h_{1q} & \cdots & h_{12} & h_{11} \end{bmatrix}_{p\times q}$$

Step3: Make the two arrays as follows:

$$h(x,y) = \begin{bmatrix} h_{pq} & \cdots & h_{p2} & h_{p1} \\ h_{2q} & \cdots & h_{22} & h_{21} \\ \vdots & \ddots & \vdots & \vdots \\ h_{1q} & \cdots & h_{12} & h_{11} \end{bmatrix}$$

$$f(x,y) = \begin{bmatrix} 0 & \cdots & 0_{1q} & 0 & 0 & \cdots & 0 \\ 0 & \cdots & & 0 & 0 & 0 & 0 \\ \vdots & \ddots & \vdots & \vdots & \vdots & 0 & 0 \\ 0_{p1} & \cdots & f_{11} & f_{12} & 0 & 0 & 0 \\ \vdots & \cdots & \vdots & \vdots & & 0 & \vdots \\ 0 & & f_{m1} & f_{m2} & \ddots & \vdots & \vdots \\ 0 & \vdots & \vdots & \vdots & \vdots & 0 & 0 \\ 0 & 0 & 0 & 0 & 0 & 0 & 0 \end{bmatrix}_{i\times j} .$$

Step4: Calculate the convolution equation for all pixels of blurred matrix $g(x,y)$:

$$g(x,y) = f(x,y) \otimes h(x,y) = \sum_{i=1}^{p}\sum_{j=1}^{q} f(i,j)h(i,j)$$

So,

$$\begin{aligned} g(1,1) &= \left(0 \times h_{pq}\right) + \left(0 \times h_{p2}\right) + \left(0 \times h_{p1}\right) + \left(0 \times h_{2p}\right) \\ &\quad + \cdots + (0 \times h_{22}) + (0 \times h_{21}) + (0 \times h_{1q}) \\ &\quad + \cdots + (0 \times h_{12}) + (f_{11} \times h_{11}) \\ &= (f_{11} \times h_{11}). \end{aligned}$$

After that shift the filter $h(x,y)$ as much as one column as follows:

$$h(x,y) = \begin{bmatrix} h_{pq} & \cdots & h_{p2} & h_{p1} \\ h_{2q} & \cdots & h_{22} & h_{21} \\ \vdots & \ddots & \vdots & \vdots \\ h_{1q} & \cdots & h_{12} & h_{11} \end{bmatrix}$$

$$f(x,y) = \begin{bmatrix} 0 & 0 & \cdots & 0 & \cdots & 0 & 0 & 0_{1j} \\ \vdots & \vdots & \ddots & \vdots & \cdots & 0 & 0 & 0 \\ 0 & 0 & f_{11} & f_{12} & f_{1n} & \vdots & \vdots \\ \vdots & \vdots & \vdots & \vdots & \ddots & \vdots & \vdots \\ 0 & 0 & f_{m1} & f_{m2} & f_{mn} & 0 & 0 \\ 0 & 0 & 0 & 0 & 0 & 0 & 0 \\ 0_{i1} & 0 & 0 & 0 & 0 & 0 & 0_{ij} \end{bmatrix}_{i\times j}$$

Also,

$$\begin{aligned} g(1,2) &= \left(0 \times h_{pq}\right) + \cdots + \left(0 \times h_{p2}\right) + \left(0 \times h_{p1}\right) \\ &\quad + \left(0 \times h_{2q}\right) + \cdots + \left(0 \times h_{22}\right) + \left(0 \times h_{21}\right) \\ &\quad + \cdots + \left(0 \times h_{1q}\right) + \cdots + \left(f_{11} \times h_{12}\right) \\ &\quad + \left(f_{12} \times h_{11}\right) = \left(f_{11} \times h_{12}\right) + \left(f_{12} \times h_{11}\right) \end{aligned}$$

Now repeat step 4 to obtain digital image convolution $g(x,y)$ at all times that the two arrays overlap. We continue until we find $g(r, c)$, where r & $c=m+ (p-1)$, then the final form of the blurred matrix $g(x,y)$ is:

$$g(x,y) = \begin{bmatrix} g_{11} & \cdots & g_{1c} \\ \vdots & \ddots & \vdots \\ g_{r} & \cdots & g_{rc} \end{bmatrix}_{r\times c} .$$

Step5: Delete from $g(x,y)$ as much as $\frac{p-1}{2}$ rows from up and down, and $\frac{p-1}{2}$ columns from left and right, such that the blurred matrix $g(x,y)$ becomes m-by-n in dimension:

$$g(x,y) = \begin{bmatrix} g_{11} & \cdots & g_{1n} \\ \vdots & \ddots & \vdots \\ g_{m} & \cdots & g_{mn} \end{bmatrix}_{m\times n} .$$

Example 2.

Suppose the image matrix $f(x,y)$ is:

$$f(x,y) = \begin{bmatrix} 209 & 90 & 60 \\ 0 & 77 & 30 \\ 100 & 46 & 20 \end{bmatrix}_{3\times3}$$. We blur this matrix with one

of the **HB-filters**: $h(x,y) = \begin{bmatrix} 2 & 0 & 1 \\ 0 & 2 & 1 \\ 1 & 1 & 1 \end{bmatrix}/9$.

Step1: Add two rows from up and down, and two columns from left and right of zeros for the matrix $f(x, y)$, such that becomes *7-by-7* dimension, as follows:

$$f(x,y) = \begin{bmatrix} 0 & 0 & 0 & 0 & 0 & 0 & 0 \\ 0 & 0 & 0 & 0 & 0 & 0 & 0 \\ 0 & 0 & 209 & 90 & 60 & 0 & 0 \\ 0 & 0 & 0 & 77 & 30 & 0 & 0 \\ 0 & 0 & 100 & 46 & 20 & 0 & 0 \\ 0 & 0 & 0 & 0 & 0 & 0 & 0 \\ 0 & 0 & 0 & 0 & 0 & 0 & 0 \end{bmatrix}_{7\times7}$$.

Step2: Reverse the filter $h(x,y)$ for two directions:

$$h(x,y) = \begin{bmatrix} 2 & 0 & 1 \\ 0 & 2 & 1 \\ 1 & 1 & 1 \end{bmatrix}/9 \overset{rev}{\Longrightarrow} \begin{bmatrix} 1 & 1 & 1 \\ 1 & 2 & 0 \\ 1 & 0 & 2 \end{bmatrix}/9$$

Step3: Make the two arrays, as the following form:

$$h(x,y) = \begin{bmatrix} 1 & 1 & 1 \\ 1 & 2 & 0 \\ 1 & 0 & 2 \end{bmatrix}/9$$

$$f(x,y) = \begin{bmatrix} 0 & 0 & 0 & 0 & 0 & 0 & 0 \\ 0 & 0 & 0 & 0 & 0 & 0 & 0 \\ 0 & 0 & 209 & 90 & 60 & 0 & 0 \\ 0 & 0 & 0 & 77 & 30 & 0 & 0 \\ 0 & 0 & 100 & 46 & 20 & 0 & 0 \\ 0 & 0 & 0 & 0 & 0 & 0 & 0 \\ 0 & 0 & 0 & 0 & 0 & 0 & 0 \end{bmatrix}_{7\times7}$$

Step4: Calculate the convolution equation for all pixels of blurred matrix $g(x,y)$:

$$g(x,y) = f(x,y) \otimes h(x,y) = \sum_{m_1=1}^{3}\sum_{n_1=1}^{3} f(m_1,n_1)h(m_1,n_1)$$

Now, $g(1,1) = (209 \times 0.2222) = 26.4444$

After that, shift the filter $h(x,y)$ as much as one column, then repeat the same step.

So, $g(1,2) = (90 \times 0.2222) = 20$
$g(1,3) = (209 \times 0.1111) + (60 \times 0.2222) = 36.5556$
⋮
$g(5,5) = (20 \times 0.2222) = 2.2222$

The final form of the blurred matrix $g(x,y)$ is:

$$\begin{bmatrix} 46.4444 & 20 & 36.5556 & 10 & 6.6667 \\ 0 & 63.5556 & 94.8889 & 31.8889 & 10 \\ 45.4444 & 43.4444 & 72.5556 & 37 & 12.2222 \\ 0 & 30.7778 & 33.2222 & 21.4444 & 5.5556 \\ 11.1111 & 16.2222 & 18.444 & 7.3333 & 2.2222 \end{bmatrix}_{5\times5}$$

Step5: Delete from $g(x,y)$ as much as *one* row from up and down, and *one* column from left and right, such that the result is the blurred matrix $g_1(x, y)$ *3-by-3* dimension,

$$g_1(x,y) = \begin{bmatrix} 63.5556 & 49.39 & 31.57 \\ 43.4444 & 72.5556 & 37 \\ 30.7778 & 33.2222 & 21.4444 \end{bmatrix}_{3\times3}$$.

B. Deblurring

Here we express the proposed deblurring method.

Deblur Algorithm

Weiner deconvolution for the matrix $g(x,y)$ and $h(x,y)$ is given by:

$$\hat{F}(u,v) = \left[\frac{1}{H(u,v)}\frac{|H(u,v)|^2}{|H(u,v)|^2+S_\eta(u,v)/S_f(u,v)}\right]G(u,v)$$.

Suppose there is no noise (i.e. $\frac{S_\eta(u,v)}{S_f(u,v)} = 0$), then the noise of power spectrum vanishes and the Weiner reduces to the invers filter, so one has: $\hat{F}(u,v) = \frac{G(u,v)}{H(u,v)}$.

Step 1: Find Fourier transform of the blurred matrix $g(x,y)$ *r-by-c* dimensions,

$$G(u,v) = \sum_{x=1}^{m}\sum_{y=1}^{n} g(x,y)\, e^{-j2\pi(\frac{ux}{M}+\frac{vy}{N})}$$.

Step 2: Find Fourier transform of **HB-filter** h(x,y).

$$H(u,v) = \sum_{x=1}^{m}\sum_{y=1}^{n} h(x,y)\, e^{-j2\pi(\frac{ux}{M}+\frac{vy}{N})},$$

If the dimension of $h(x,y)$ is less than dimension of $g(x,y)$, we will add zeros for $h(x,y)$ to create as same as the dimension of the image matrix $g(x,y)$ before doing the transform, such that the result is *m-by-n* in dimension.

Step 3: Calculate the transform of estimated image $\hat{F}(u,v)$.

Step 4: Find estimated image $\hat{f}(x,y)$ by taking inverse Fourier transform of $\hat{F}(u,v)$, by follows:

$$\hat{f}(x,y) = \frac{1}{MN}\sum_{u=1}^{m}\sum_{v=1}^{n} \hat{F}(u,v)\, e^{j2\pi(\frac{ux}{M}+\frac{vy}{N})}$$.

Step 5: Remove zeros from $\hat{f}(x,y)$ as much as $(p-1)/2$ of last rows and columns, where resulted dimensions equal to dimensions original image matrix $f(x,y)$.

Example 2. We will take blurred matrix $g(x,y)$ from ex.2,
$g(x,y) =$

$$\begin{bmatrix} 46.4444 & 20 & 36.5556 & 10 & 6.6667 \\ 0 & 63.5556 & 94.8889 & 31.8889 & 10 \\ 45.4444 & 43.4444 & 72.5556 & 37 & 12.2222 \\ 0 & 30.7778 & 33.2222 & 21.4444 & 5.5556 \\ 11.1111 & 16.2222 & 18.444 & 7.3333 & 2.2222 \end{bmatrix}_{5\times5}$$,

with **HB-filter**, $h(x,y) = \begin{bmatrix} 2 & 0 & 1 \\ 0 & 2 & 1 \\ 1 & 1 & 1 \end{bmatrix}/9$.

Now, from the Weiner equation, suppose that $\frac{S_\eta(u,v)}{S_f(u,v)} = 0$, then the Weiner reduces to the invers filter as following, $\hat{F}(u,v) = \frac{G(u,v)}{H(u,v)}$.

Step 1: Find Fourier transform of the matrix $g(x,y)$,

$$G(u,v) = \sum_{x=1}^{m}\sum_{y=1}^{n} g(x,y)\, e^{-j2\pi(\frac{ux}{M}+\frac{vy}{N})}$$

Now, $G(1,1) = \sum_{x=1}^{5}\sum_{y=1}^{5} g(x,y)\, e^{-j2\pi\left(\frac{x}{5}+\frac{y}{5}\right)}$

$= \left(g(1,1)e^{-j2\pi\left(\frac{1}{5}+\frac{1}{5}\right)}\right) + \left(g(1,2)e^{-j2\pi\left(\frac{1}{5}+\frac{2}{5}\right)}\right)$

$\qquad + \left(g(1,3)e^{-j2\pi\left(\frac{1}{5}+\frac{3}{5}\right)}\right)$

$\qquad + \left(g(1,4)e^{-j2\pi\left(\frac{1}{5}+\frac{4}{5}\right)}\right) + \cdots$

$\qquad + \left(g(5,5)e^{-j2\pi\left(\frac{5}{5}+\frac{5}{5}\right)}\right)$

$= 46.4444e^{-j\left(\frac{4}{5}\right)\pi} + 20e^{-j\left(\frac{6}{5}\right)\pi} + 36.5556e^{-j\left(\frac{8}{5}\right)\pi}$

$\qquad + 10e^{-j2\pi} + \cdots + 2.2222e^{-j4\pi} = 632 + 0j$

$G(1,2) = \sum_{x=1}^{5}\sum_{y=1}^{5} g(x,y)\, e^{-j2\pi\left(\frac{x}{5}+\frac{2y}{5}\right)}$

$\qquad = -89.44 - 191.15j$

$G(1,3) = \sum_{x=1}^{5}\sum_{y=1}^{5} g(x,y)\, e^{-j2\pi\left(\frac{x}{5}+\frac{3y}{5}\right)}$

$\qquad = 30.94 + 17.24j$

$\vdots$

$G(5,5) = \sum_{x=1}^{5}\sum_{y=1}^{5} g(x,y)\, e^{-j2\pi\left(\frac{5x}{5}+\frac{5y}{5}\right)}$

$\qquad = -1.13 - 45.84j$

So, the final form of $G\,(u,v)$ be

$$\begin{bmatrix} 632+0j & -89.44-191.15j & 30.94+17.24j & 30.94-17.24j & -89.44+191.15j \\ -59.29-165.44j & -1.13+45.84j & 7.69+13.15 & 17.02+4.9j & 101.27+20.83j \\ 42.45-55.03j & 31.43+42.17j & 42.35+97.85j & 98.29+36.24j & 42.97+17.47j \\ 42.45-55.03j & 42.97-17.47j & 98.29-36.24j & 42.35-97.85j & 31.43-42.17j \\ -59.29+165.44j & 101.27-20.83j & 17.02-4.9j & 7.69-13.15j & -1.13-45.84j \end{bmatrix}_{5\times5}$$

Step 2: Because of the dimension of $h(x,y)$ is less than dimension of $g(x,y)$, then add zeros for $h(x,y)$ to create as same as the dimensions of the image matrix $g(x,y)$, so we have:

$$h(x,y) = \begin{bmatrix} 2 & 0 & 1 & 0 & 0 \\ 0 & 2 & 1 & 0 & 0 \\ 1 & 1 & 1 & 0 & 0 \\ 0 & 0 & 0 & 0 & 0 \\ 0 & 0 & 0 & 0 & 0 \end{bmatrix}_{5\times5} \Big/ 9,$$

After that, we are doing the Fourier transform of $h(x,y)$:

$H(u,v) = \sum_{x=1}^{m}\sum_{y=1}^{n} h(x,y)\, e^{-j2\pi\left(\frac{ux}{M}+\frac{vy}{N}\right)}$

Now, $H(1,1) = \sum_{x=1}^{5}\sum_{y=1}^{5} h(x,y)\, e^{-j2\pi\left(\frac{x}{5}+\frac{y}{5}\right)}$

$= \left(h(1,1)e^{-j2\pi\left(\frac{1}{5}+\frac{1}{5}\right)}\right) + \left(h(1,2)e^{-j2\pi\left(\frac{1}{5}+\frac{2}{5}\right)}\right)$

$\qquad + \left(h(1,3)e^{-j2\pi\left(\frac{1}{5}+\frac{3}{5}\right)}\right)$

$\qquad + \left(h(1,4)e^{-j2\pi\left(\frac{1}{5}+\frac{4}{5}\right)}\right) + \cdots$

$\qquad + \left(h(5,5)e^{-j2\pi\left(\frac{5}{5}+\frac{5}{5}\right)}\right)$

$= 2e^{-j\left(\frac{4}{5}\right)\pi} + 0e^{-j\left(\frac{6}{5}\right)\pi} + 1e^{-j\left(\frac{8}{5}\right)\pi} + 0e^{-j2\pi} + \cdots + 0e^{-j4\pi}$

$\qquad = 1 + 0j$

$H(1,2) = \sum_{x=1}^{5}\sum_{y=1}^{5} h(x,y)\, e^{-j2\pi\left(\frac{x}{5}+\frac{2y}{5}\right)}$

$\qquad = 0.1667 - 0.5129j$

$H(1,3) = \sum_{x=1}^{5}\sum_{y=1}^{5} h(x,y)\, e^{-j2\pi\left(\frac{x}{5}+\frac{3y}{5}\right)}$

$\qquad = 0.1667 + 0.1211j$

$\vdots$

$H(5,5) = \sum_{x=1}^{5}\sum_{y=1}^{5} h(x,y)\, e^{-j2\pi\left(\frac{5x}{5}+\frac{5y}{5}\right)}$

$\qquad = -0.2828 + 0.0249j$

So, the final form of $H(u,v)$ is:

$H(u,v)$

$= \begin{bmatrix} 1+0j & 0.1667-0.5129j & 0.1667+0.1211j & 0.1667-0.1211j & 0.1667+0.5129j \\ 0.1667-0.5129j & -0.2828-0.0249j & 0.1667+0.171j & 0.1667+0.0404j & 0.4444+0j \\ 0.1667+0.1211j & 0.1667+0.171j & 0.3383+0.2767j & 0.4444+0j & 0.1667-0.0404j \\ 0.1667-0.1211j & 0.1667+0.0404j & 0.4444+0j & 0.3383-0.2767j & 0.1667-0.171j \\ 0.1667+0.5129j & 0.4444-0j & 0.1667-0.0404j & 0.1667-0.171j & -0.2828+0.0249j \end{bmatrix}_{5\times5}$

Step 3: Calculate the Fourier transform of estimated image.

$\hat{F}(u,v)$
$= G(u,v)/H(u,v) =$

$\begin{bmatrix} 632+0j & 285.83-267.23j & 170.67-20.58j & 170.67+20.58j & 285.83+267.23j \\ 257.77-199.34j & -10.23-161.21j & 61.93+15.37j & 103.17+4.41j & 227.85+46.87j \\ 323.73+94.98j & 218.33+29.01j & 216.73+111.98j & 221.15+81.54j & 219.57+158.02j \\ 323.73-94.98j & 219.57-158.02j & 221.15-81.54j & 216.73-111.98j & 218.33-29.01j \\ 257.77+199.34j & 227.85-46.87j & 103.17-4.41j & 61.93-15.37j & -10.23+161.21j \end{bmatrix}_{5\times5}$

Step 4: Find inverse Fourier transform with only real numbers $\hat{f}(x,y)$ of an array $\hat{F}(u,v)$.

$\hat{f}(x,y) = \frac{1}{MN}\sum_{u=1}^{m}\sum_{v=1}^{n} \hat{F}(u,v)\, e^{j2\pi\left(\frac{ux}{M}+\frac{vy}{N}\right)}$,

So,

$\hat{f}(1,1) = \frac{1}{5\times5}\sum_{u=1}^{m}\sum_{v=1}^{n} \hat{F}(u,v)\, e^{j2\pi\left(\frac{u}{5}+\frac{v}{5}\right)}$

$\qquad = \frac{1}{5\times5}\left(\hat{F}(1,1)e^{j2\pi\left(\frac{1}{5}+\frac{1}{5}\right)}\right.$

$\qquad\quad + \hat{F}(1,2)e^{j2\pi\left(\frac{1}{5}+\frac{2}{5}\right)} + \hat{F}(1,3)e^{j2\pi\left(\frac{1}{5}+\frac{3}{5}\right)} + \cdots$

$\qquad\quad \left. + \hat{F}(5,5)e^{j2\pi\left(\frac{5}{5}+\frac{5}{5}\right)}\right)$

$\qquad = \frac{1}{25}\Big((632+0j)e^{j\left(\frac{4}{5}\right)\pi} + (285.83$

$\qquad\quad - 267.23j)e^{j\left(\frac{6}{5}\right)\pi} + (170.67$

$\qquad\quad - 20.58j)e^{j\left(\frac{8}{5}\right)\pi} + \cdots + (-10.23$

$\qquad\quad + 161.12j)e^{j4\pi}\Big) = 209$

$\hat{f}(1,2) = 90$
$\hat{f}(1,3) = 60$
$\vdots$
$\hat{f}(5,5) = 0$

Now, the final of estimated image $\hat{f}(x,y)$ is $\hat{f}(x,y) =$

$$\begin{bmatrix} 209 & 90 & 60 & 0 & 0 \\ 0 & 77 & 30 & 0 & 0 \\ 100 & 46 & 20 & 0 & 0 \\ 0 & 0 & 0 & 0 & 0 \\ 0 & 0 & 0 & 0 & 0 \end{bmatrix}_{5\times5}.$$

Step 5: Remove the last two rows and columns of zeros from $\hat{f}(x,y)$:

$\hat{f}(x,y) = \begin{bmatrix} 209 & 90 & 60 \\ 0 & 77 & 30 \\ 100 & 46 & 20 \end{bmatrix}_{3\times3}$, where the original matrix

$f(x,y)$ is: $g(x,y) = \begin{bmatrix} 209 & 90 & 60 \\ 0 & 77 & 30 \\ 100 & 46 & 20 \end{bmatrix}_{3\times3}$.

Now, we give the (original, blurred, estimated) block image to explain the image enhancement in ex.2 and ex.3 as shown in Fig.1.

Fig. 1. Image blocks in ex.2 & ex.3. Left: original image f(x,y). Middle: blurred g(x,y). Right: estimated image $\hat{f}(x,y)$

TABLE I. THE COMPARISON OF BETWEEN DIFFERENT FILTERS

	Degree of blur	Image blur	Aver. filter	Gauss. filter	Motion filter	Proposed filter
PSNR	9×9	21.44	7.25	21.45	13.78	45.53
	21×21	18.03	7.01	18.04	12.7	49.9
	27×27	17.02	7.03	17.02	11.79	46.23
RMSE	9×9	21.61	110.66	21.58	52.18	1.35
	21×21	31.98	113.72	31.96	59.1	0.81
	27×27	35.95	113.45	35.94	65.65	1.24

C. Comparison with other filters

HB-filters are compared in PNSR (in dB) and RMSE with the (*AF, GF,* and *MF*) filters. The proposed method and the other methods are applied on (256× 256) Pepper RGB image, by using (jpg. format) as in Table I. The application of proposed method and some other methods on the color images (in jpg. format) of different blur is shown in Fig.2.

V. CONLCLUSION

Nlur has been added and removed from digital images using HB-filters. The HB-filters perform well for grayscale, binary and color (jpg, png) images with different blur degrees. Results show that the HB method has higher PSNR and less RMSE than Average, Gaussian and Motion methods.

ACKNOWLEDGMENT

We would like to thank the University of Kufa for financial support.

Fig. 2. Application on Pepper (jpg. format) RGB image with degree of blur 27*27. Top Left: Original. Top Right: Blur image PSNR=17.02, RMSE=35.95. Middle Left: A.F, PSNR=7.03, RMSE=113.45. Middle Right: G.F, PSNR=17.02, RMSE =35.94> Bottom Left: M.F, PSNR=11.79, RMSE =65.65. Bottom Right: Proposed, PSNR=46.23, RMSE=1.24

REFERENCES

[1] B. Jiang, A. Yang, C. wang, and Z. Hou, "Comparison of Motion-blurred Image Restoration Using Wiener Filter and Spatial Difference Technique", International Journal of Signal Processing, vol. 7, pp.11-22, 2014.

[2] D. Majerova, "Image Processing by Means of Lukasiewicz Algebra with Square Root", Institute of Chemical Technology, Pregue, Department of Computing and Control Engineering, 2004.

[3] Gonzalez, R.C., Woods, R.E., "Digital Image Processing", 2nd Ed, Prentice-Hall of India Pvt. Ltd, 2002.

[4] H. H. Abbass, and H. S. Mohammed Hussein "An Invariant Markov basis Under the Action of Largest Subgroup of Dihedral Group D_{3^m} ", European Journal of Scientific Research, Vol. 125, pp. 265-277, 2014.

[5] H. H. Abbass, and H. S. Mohammed Hussein " On Toric Ideals for $3 \times \frac{n}{3}$ -Contingency Tables with Fixed Two Dimensional Marginals n is a multiple of 3", European Journal of Scientific Research, Vol. 123, pp. 83-98, 2014.

[6] Madasu Hanmandlu Member IEEE and Devendra Jha "An Optimal Fuzzy System for color image Enhancement" , IEEE Trans image process , 2006.

[7] M. Dobes, L.Machala, and T. Furst, "Digital Signal Processing", Elsevier Inc, 1677-1686, March, 2010.

[8] R. C. Gonzalez and R. E. Woods , " Digital Image Processing ", Prentice Hall,3rd Edition, 2008.

[9] R. C. Gonzalez "Digital Image Processing", ISBN 0201180758, 9780201180756 ,prentice Hall , 2002.

[10] S. Aoki, A. Takemura, "The Largest Group of Invariance for Markov Bases and Toric ideals", J. Symbolic Computation ,pp. 342–358, 2008.

[11] W. K. Pratt, " Digital Image Processing", A Wiey-Inters-Cience Publication, ISBN: 978-0-471-76777-0, TA 1632.p 7, 4 Edition, 2007.

[12] X. Jiany, D. Cheng, S. Wachenfeld, and K. Rothaus, "Image Processing and Pattern Recognition", Department of Mathematics and Computer Science, University of Muenster, Winter, 2005.

[13] W. J. Gilbert," Modern Algebra With Application ",John Wiley, Inc., New Jersey, U.S.A, 2004.

30

Application of K-Means Algorithm for Efficient Customer Segmentation: A Strategy for Targeted Customer Services

Chinedu Pascal Ezenkwu, Simeon Ozuomba, Constance kalu

Electrical/Electronics & Computer Engineering Department, University of Uyo, Uyo, Akwa Ibom State, Nigeria

Abstract—The emergence of many business competitors has engendered severe rivalries among competing businesses in gaining new customers and retaining old ones. Due to the preceding, the need for exceptional customer services becomes pertinent, notwithstanding the size of the business. Furthermore, the ability of any business to understand each of its customers' needs will earn it greater leverage in providing targeted customer services and developing customised marketing programs for the customers. This understanding can be possible through systematic customer segmentation. Each segment comprises customers who share similar market characteristics. The ideas of Big data and machine learning have fuelled a terrific adoption of an automated approach to customer segmentation in preference to traditional market analyses that are often inefficient especially when the number of customers is too large. In this paper, the k-Means clustering algorithm is applied for this purpose. A MATLAB program of the k-Means algorithm was developed (available in the appendix) and the program is trained using a z-score normalised two-feature dataset of 100 training patterns acquired from a retail business. The features are the average amount of goods purchased by customer per month and the average number of customer visits per month. From the dataset, four customer clusters or segments were identified with 95% accuracy, and they were labeled: High-Buyers-Regular-Visitors (HBRV), High-Buyers-Irregular-Visitors (HBIV), Low-Buyers-Regular-Visitors (LBRV) and Low-Buyers-Irregular-Visitors (LBIV).

Keywords—machine learning; data mining; big data; customer segmentation; MATLAB; k-Means algorithm; customer service; clustering; extrapolation

I. INTRODUCTION

Over the years, the increase in competition amongst businesses and the availability of large historical data repositories have prompted the widespread applications of data mining techniques in uncovering valuable and strategic information buried in organisations' databases. Data mining is the process of extracting meaningful information from a dataset and presenting it in a human understandable format for the purpose of decision support. The data mining techniques intersect areas such as statistics, artificial intelligence, machine learning and database systems. The applications of data mining include but not limited to bioinformatics, weather forecasting, fraud detection, financial analysis and customer segmentation. The thrust of this paper is to identify customer segments in a retail business using a data mining approach. Customer segmentation is the subdivision of a business customer base into groups called customer segments such that each customer segment consists of customers who share similar market characteristics. This segmentation is based on factors that can directly or indirectly influence market or business such as products preferences or expectations, locations, behaviours and so on. The importance of customer segmentation include, inter alia, the ability of a business to customise market programs that will be suitable for each of its customer segments; business decision support in terms of risky situation such as credit relationship with its customers; identification of products associated with each segments and how to manage the forces of demand and supply; unravelling some latent dependencies and associations amongst customers, amongst products, or between customers and products which the business may not be aware of; ability to predict customer defection, and which customers are most likely to defect; and raising further market research questions as well as providing directions to finding the solutions.

Clustering has proven efficient in discovering subtle but tactical patterns or relationships buried within a repository of unlabelled datasets. This form of learning is classified under unsupervised learning. Clustering algorithms include k-Means algorithm, k-Nearest Neighbour algorithm, Self-Organising Map (SOM) and so on. These algorithms, without any knowledge of the dataset beforehand, are capable of identifying clusters therein by repeated comparisons of the input patterns until the stable clusters in the training examples are achieved based on the clustering criterion or criteria. Each cluster contains data points that have very close similarities but differ considerably from data points of other clusters. Clustering has got immense applications in pattern recognition, image analysis, bioinformatics and so on. In this paper, the k-Means clustering algorithm has been applied in customer segmentation. A MATLAB program (Appendix) of the k-Means algorithm was developed, and the training was realised using z-score normalised two-feature dataset of 100 training patterns acquired from a retail business. After several iterations, four stable clusters or customer segments were identified. The two features considered in the clustering are the average amount of goods purchased by customer per month and the average number of customer visits per month. From the dataset, four customer clusters or segments were identified and labelled thus: High-Buyers-Regular-Visitors (HBRV), High-Buyers-Irregular-Visitors (HBIV), Low-Buyers-Regular-Visitors (LBRV) and Low-Buyers-Irregular-Visitors (LBIV). Furthermore, for any input pattern that was not in the training set, its cluster can be correctly extrapolated by normalising it and computing its similarities from the cluster centroids associated with each of the clusters. It will hence be assigned to any of clusters with which it has the closest similarity.

II. LITERATURE REVIEW

A. Customer Segmentation

Over the years, the commercial world is becoming more competitive, as such organizations have to satisfy the needs and wants of their customers, attract new customers, and hence enhance their businesses [1]. The task of identifying and satisfying the needs and wants of each customer in a business is a very complex task. This is because customers may be different in their needs, wants, demography, geography, tastes and preferences, behaviours and so on. As such, it is a wrong practice to treat all the customers equally in business. This challenge has motivated the adoption of the idea of customer segmentation or market segmentation, in which the customers are subdivided into smaller groups or segments wherein members of each segment show similar market behaviours or characteristics. According to [2], customer segmentation is a strategy of dividing the market into homogenous groups. [3] posits that "the purpose of segmentation is the concentration of marketing energy and force on subdivision (or market segment) to gain a competitive advantage within the segment. It's analogous to the military principle of concentration of force to overwhelm energy." Customer or Market segmentation includes geographic segmentation, demographic segmentation, media segmentation, price segmentation, psychographic or lifestyle segmentation, distribution segmentation and time segmentation [3].

B. Big Data

Recently, research in Big data has gained momentum. [4] defines Big data as " the word describing the large volume of both structured and unstructured data, which cannot be analyzed using traditional techniques and algorithm." According to [5], "the amount of data in our world has been exploding. Companies capture trillions of bytes of information about their customers, suppliers, and operations, and millions of networked sensors are being embedded in the physical world in devices such as mobile phones and automobiles, sensing, creating, and communicating data." Big data has demonstrated the capacity to improve predictions, save money, boost efficiency and enhance decision-making in fields as disparate as traffic control, weather forecasting, disaster prevention, finance, fraud control, business transaction, national security, education, and health care [6]. Big data is mainly characterised by three V's namely: volume, variety and velocity. There are other 2V's available - veracity and value, thus making it 5V's [4]. Volume refers to the vast amount of data in Zettabytes or Brontobytes being generated per minute; velocity refers to speed at which new data is created or the speed at which existing data moves around; variety refers to different types of data; veracity describes the degree of messiness or trustworthiness of data; and value refers to the worth of information that can be mined from data. The last V, value is what makes Big data and data mining interesting to businesses and organisations.

C. Clustering and k-Means Algorithm

According to [7], clustering is the unsupervised classification of patterns (observations, data items, or feature vectors) into groups (clusters). [8] opined that clustering algorithms generate clusters having similarity between data objects based on some characteristics. Clustering is extensively used in many areas such as pattern recognition, computer science, medical, machine learning. [6] states that "formally cluster structure is represented as a set of subset $C=C1,\ldots\ldots.Ck$ of S, such that $S=\cup_{i=1}^{k} Ci$ and $C_i \cap Cj=\emptyset$ for $i \neq j$. Consequently, instances in S belong to exactly one and only one subset". Clustering algorithms have been classified into hierarchical and partitional clustering algorithms. Hierarchical clustering algorithms create clusters based on some hierarchies. It is based on the idea of objects being more related to nearby objects farther away [6]. It can be top-down or bottom-up hierarchical clustering. The top-down approach is referred to as divisive while the bottom-up approach is known as agglomerative. The partitional clustering algorithms create various partitions and then evaluate them by some criterion. k-Means algorithm is one of most popular partitional clustering algorithm[4]. It is a centroid-based algorithm in which each data point is placed in exactly one of the K non-overlapping clusters selected before the algorithm is run.

The k-Means algorithm works thus: given a set of d-dimensional training input vectors { x_1, x_2,.., x_n }, the k-Means clustering algorithm partitions the n training examples into k sets of data points or clusters $S = \{S_1, S_2, \ldots, S_k\}$, where k≤n, such that the within cluster sum of squares is minimised.

That is,

$$\underset{S}{argmin} \sum_{i=1}^{k} \sum_{x \in s_i} \|x - \mu_i\|^2 \qquad (1)$$

where, μ_i is the centroid or mean of data points in cluster s_i .

Generic k-means clustering Algorithms:

1) Decide on the number of clusters, k.

2) Initialize the k cluster centroids

3) Assign the n data points to the nearest clusters.

4) Update the centroid of each cluster using the data points therein.

5) Repeat steps 3 and 4 until the changes in positions of centroids are zero.

III. METHODOLOGY

The data used in this paper was collected from a mega retail business outfit that has many branches in Akwa Ibom state, Nigeria. The dataset consists of 2 attributes and 100 tuples, representing 100 selected customers. The two attributes include average amount of goods purchased by customer per month and average number of customer visits per month. In this paper, four steps were adopted in realising an accurate result. They include feature normalisation alongside centroids initialisation step, assignment step and updating step, which are the three major generic steps in the k-Means algorithms.

A. Feature normalisation

This is a data preparation stage. Feature normalisation helps to adjust all the data elements to a common scale in order to improve the performance of the clustering algorithm. Each data point is converted to the range of -2 to +2. Normalisation techniques include Min-max, decimal scaling and z-score. The z-score normalisation technique was used to normalise the features before running the k-Means algorithm on the dataset. Equation (2) gives the formulae for normalisation using the z-score technique.

$$x_{norm} = \frac{x - \mu_f}{\sigma_f} \qquad (2)$$

where, x_{norm} is the normalised value of x in feature vector **f**, μ_f is the meant of the feature vector **f**, and σ_f is the standard deviation of feature vector **f**.

B. Centroids Initialisation

The initial centroids or means were chosen. Figure 1 presents the initialisation of the cluster centres. Four cluster centres shown in different shapes were selected using Forgy method. In Forgy method of initialisation k (in this case k=4) data points are randomly selected as the cluster centroids.

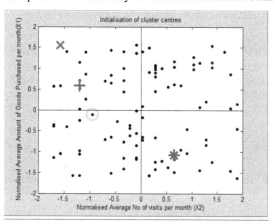

Fig. 1.   The initialization stage of k-Means algorithm

C. Assignment Stage

In the assignment stage, each data point is assigned to the cluster whose centroid yields the least within cluster sum of squares compared with other clusters. That is, the square Euclidean norms of each data point from the current centroids are computed. Thereafter, the data points are assigned membership of the cluster that gives the minimum square Euclidean norm.

This has been mathematically explained in equation (3)

$$s_i^{(t)} = \{x_p : \|x_p - \mu_i^{(t)}\|^2 \leq \|x_p - \mu_j^{(t)}\|^2 \ \forall j, 1 \leq j \leq k\} \ (3)$$

where each data point x_p is assigned to only one cluster or set $s^{(t)}$ at the iteration t.

D. Updating Stage

After each iteration, new centroid is computed for each cluster as the mean of all the data points present in the cluster as shown in equation (4)

$$\mu_t^{(t+1)} = \frac{1}{|s_i^{(t)}|} \sum_{x_j \in s_i^{(t)}} x_i \qquad (4)$$

where, $\mu_t^{(t+1)}$ is the updated centroid.

Fig. 2 presents the positions of the centroids and the updated assignment of their cluster members after the 30th iteration. The each cluster members assume the same shapes as their cluster centroid. Table II shows the changes in the cluster centroids from the initialisation stage (0th iteration) to the 5th iteration.

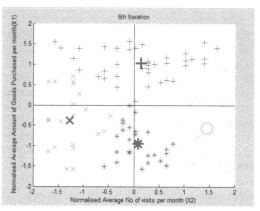

Fig. 2.   Positions of the centroids and their cluster members after the 30th iteration

TABLE I.   INITIALISATION AND UPDATING OF THE CLUSTER VECTORS OR CENTROIDS)

Iteration	INTIALISED CLUSTER CENTROIDS:						
	Cluster Centre +		Cluster Centre *		Cluster Centre O		Cluster Centr
0	-0.0892	1.3654	0.6541	-1.0856	-0.2131	-0.3669	-0.2131	-0.3
	UPDATED CLUSTER CENTROIDS:						
1	0.5656	1.0971	0.8733	-0.9508	-0.6306	-0.6728	-0.6306	-0.6728
2	0.5798	1.0456	0.9976	-0.9639	-0.5466	-0.8295	-0.5466	-0.8295
3	0.5502	1.0346	1.0376	-0.9348	-0.5600	-0.9284	-0.5600	-0.9284
4	0.5502	1.0346	1.0376	-0.9348	-0.5641	-0.9557	-0.5641	-0.9557
5	0.5502	1.0346	1.0376	-0.9348	-0.5901	-0.9894	-0.5901	-0.9894

IV.   RESULTS AND DISCUSSION

The k-Means clustering algorithm converged after 100 iterations. That is, the cluster centroids became stable. Figure 3 shows the graph of the converged data points and centroids. After this, the k-Means algorithm was able to cluster almost the entire data points correctly. The centroids or the cluster vectors after convergence are:

*Cluster Centre +   Cluster Centre *   Cluster Centre* **O**   *Cluster Centre* **X**
[-0.8325 0.9574] [0.7403 -1.0926] [-0.8279 -0.7217] [0.8444 0.8412]

Each of the clusters represents a customer segment. From Figure 3, the data points at the right hand top corner represent HBRV; the data points left hand top corner represent the HBIV; the data points at the right hand lower corner represent LBRV; while those at the left hand lower corner represent the LBIV. This is clearly shown in Table II.

TABLE II.   DESCRIPTION OF EACH CLUSTER IN TERMS OF THE CUSTOMER SEGMENT

HBIV	HBRV
Cluster +	Cluster **X**
LBIV	LBRV
Cluster **O**	Cluster *

V.   PERFORMANCE EVALUATION

Purity measure was used to measure the extent to which a cluster contains of class of data points. The purity of each cluster is computed with equation (5).

$$purity(D_i) = \max_j \left(P_i(C_j) \right) \tag{5}$$

Where, $P_i(C_j)$ is the proportion of class C_j data points in cluster i or D_i.

The total purity of the whole clustering i.e. considering all the clusters is given by equation (6).

$$Purity_{total}(D) = \sum_{i=1}^{k} \frac{|D_i|}{|D|} \, X \, purity(D_i) \tag{6}$$

Where, D is the total number of data points being classified.

The confusion matrix is presented in Table III.

TABLE III.   CONFUSION MATRIX

Cluster	HBIV	HBRV	LBIV	LBRV	Purity
Cluster +	21	1	0	0	0.954
Cluster X	0	28	0	0	1.000
Cluster O	2	0	24	1	0.889
Cluster *	0	0	1	22	0.957
Total	23	29	25	23	0.950

Since, $Purity_{total}(D) = 0.95$(from row 6, column 6 of Table 3), the clustering algorithm was 95% accurate in performing the customers segmentation.

VI.   CONCLUSIONS

This paper has presented a MATLAB implementation of the k-Means clustering algorithm for customer segmentation based on data collected from a mega business retail outfit that has many branches in Akwa Ibom state, Nigeria. The algorithm has a purity measure of 0.95 indicating 95% accurate segmentation of the customers. Insight into the business's customer segmentation will avail it with the following advantages: the ability of the business to customise market programs that will be suitable for each of its customer segments; business decision support in terms of risky situations such as credit relationship with its customers; identification of products associated with each segments and how to manage the forces of demand and supply; unravelling some latent dependencies and associations amongst customers, amongst products, or between customers and products which the business may not be aware of; ability to predict customer defection and which customers are most likely to defect; and raising further market research questions as well as providing directions to finding the solutions.

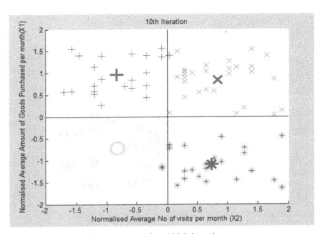

Fig. 3.   The centroids converge after 100th iteration

REFERENCES

[1] Puwanenthiren Premkanth, "Market Segmentation and Its Impact on Customer Satisfaction with Especial Reference to Commercial Bank of Ceylon PLC." Global Journal of Management and Business Research Publisher: Global Journals Inc. (USA). 2012. Print ISSN: 0975-5853. Volume 12 Issue 1.

[2] Sulekha Goyat. "The basis of market segmentation: a critical review of literature". European Journal of Business and Management www.iiste.org. 2011. ISSN 2222-1905 (Paper) ISSN 2222-2839 (Online).Vol 3, No.9, 2011

[3] By Jerry W Thomas. "Market Segmentation". 2007. Retrieved from www.decisionanalyst.com on 12-July, 2015.

[4] T.Nelson Gnanaraj, Dr.K.Ramesh Kumar N.Monica. "Survey on mining clusters using new k-mean algorithm from structured and unstructured data". International Journal of Advances in Computer Science and Technology. 2007. Volume 3, No.2.

[5] McKinsey Global Institute. Big data. The next frontier for innovation, competition, and productivity. 2011. Retrieved from www.mckinsey.com/mgi on 14 July, 2015.

[6] Jean Yan. "Big Data, Bigger Opportunities- Data.gov's roles: Promote, lead, contribute, and collaborate in the era of big data". 2013. Retrieved from http://www.meritalk.com/pdfs/bdx/bdx-whitepaper-090413.pdf on 14 July 2015.

[7] A.K. Jain, M.N. Murty and P.J. Flynn."Data Clustering: A Review". ACM Computing Surveys. 1999. Vol. 31, No. 3.

[8] Vaishali R. Patel1 and Rupa G. Mehta. "Impact of Outlier Removal and Normalization Approach in Modified k-Means Clustering Algorithm". IJCSI International Journal of Computer Science Issues, Vol. 8, Issue 5, No 2, September 2011 ISSN (Online): 1694-0814

[9] Md. Al-Amin Bhuiyan and Hiromitsu Hama, "Identification of Actors Drawn in Ukiyoe Pictures", Pattern Recognition, Vol. 35, No. 1, pp. 93-102, 2002.

[10] S. O. Olatunji, M. Al-Ahmadi, M. Elshafei, and Y. A. Fallatah, "Saudi arabia stock prices forecasting using artificial neural networks," pp.81-86, 2011.

[11] Q. Wen, Z. Yang, Y. Song, and P. Jia, "Automatic stock decision support system based on box theory and svm algorithm," Expert System Application, vol. 37, no.2, pp. 1015–1022, Mar. 2010.[Online]. Available: http://dx.doi.org/10.1016/j.eswa.2009.05.093.

[12] P.-C. Chang, C.-Y. Fan, and J.-L. Lin, "Trend discovery in financial time series data using a case based fuzzy decision tree," ExpertSystem Application, vol. 38, no. 5, pp. 60706080, May 2011. [Online]. Available: http://dx.doi.org/10.1016/j.eswa.2010.11.006

APPENDIX

```
clc;clf;close;clear all;
load CustData % Data file containing 100-by-2 training examples, X
%Normalisation and Selection of initial centroids
```

```
X=[(X(:,1)-mean(X(:,1)))/std(X(:,1))    (X(:,2)-
mean(X(:,2)))/std(X(:,2))];
j = 1;k=1;l=1;
i = randi(length(X));
while j==i
    j=randi(length(X));
end
while k==i|k==j
    k =randi(length(X));
end
while l==i|l==j|l==k;
    l =randi(length(X));
end
centr1 = X(i,:);centr2 = X(j,:); centr3 = X(k,:);centr4 = X(l,:);
%Initial plots of points and position of initial centroids
plot(X(:,1),X(:,2),'.k','MarkerSize',15)
hold on
plot(centr1(1),centr1(2),'+r','MarkerSize',18,'LineWidth',3)
plot(centr2(1),centr2(2),'*b','MarkerSize',18,'LineWidth',3)
plot(centr3(1),centr3(2),'Og','MarkerSize',18,'LineWidth',3)
plot(centr4(1),centr4(2),'Xm','MarkerSize',18,'LineWidth',3)
title('Initialisation of cluster centres')
xlabel('Normalised Average No of visits per month (X2)')
ylabel('Normalised Average Amount of Goods Purchased per
month(X1)')
hold off;
%Iterations to update Centroids and assign clusters members
count = 1;
while count <=10
    d1=(X-[ones(length(X),1)*centr1(1)
        ones(length(X),1)*centr1(2)]).^2;
    d2=(X-[ones(length(X),1)*centr2(1)
        ones(length(X),1)*centr2(2)]).^2;
    d3=(X-[ones(length(X),1)*centr3(1)
        ones(length(X),1)*centr3(2)]).^2;
    d4=(X-[ones(length(X),1)*centr4(1)
        ones(length(X),1)*centr4(2)]).^2;
    d11 = d1(:,1)+d1(:,2);
    d22 = d2(:,1)+d2(:,2);
    d33 = d3(:,1)+d3(:,2);
    d44 = d4(:,1)+d4(:,2);
    row1 = d11<d22 & d11<d33 & d11<d44;
    row2 = d22<d11 & d22<d33 & d22<d44;
    row3 = d33<d22 & d33<d11 & d33<d44;
    row4 = d44<d22 & d44<d11 & d44<33;
    cluster1 = X(row1,:);
    cluster2 = X(row2,:);
    cluster3 = X(row3,:);
    cluster4 = X(row4,:);
    centr1 = [mean(cluster1(:,1)) mean(cluster1(:,2))];
    centr2 = [mean(cluster2(:,1)) mean(cluster2(:,2))];
    centr3 = [mean(cluster3(:,1)) mean(cluster3(:,2))];
    centr4 = [mean(cluster4(:,1)) mean(cluster4(:,2))];
    count = count + 1;
end
% Plot the final centroids positions and cluster data points
figure; hold on;
plot(cluster1(:,1),cluster1(:,2),'+r','MarkerSize',10)
plot(cluster2(:,1),cluster2(:,2),'*b','MarkerSize',10)
plot(cluster3(:,1),cluster3(:,2),'og','MarkerSize',10)
plot(cluster4(:,1),cluster4(:,2),'Xm','MarkerSize',10)
plot(centr1(1),centr1(2),'+r','MarkerSize',18,'LineWidth',3)
plot(centr2(1),centr2(2),'*b','MarkerSize',18,'LineWidth',3)
plot(centr3(1),centr3(2),'Og','MarkerSize',18,'LineWidth',3)
plot(centr4(1),centr4(2),'Xm','MarkerSize',18,'LineWidth',3)
plot([-2 0 2],[0 0 0],'-k')
plot([0 0 0],[-2 0 2],'-k')
title('100th Iteration')
xlabel('Normalised Average No of visits per month (X2)')
ylabel('Normalised Average Amount of Goods Purchased per
month(X1)')
```

31

Differential Evolution Enhanced with Eager Random Search for Solving Real-Parameter Optimization Problems

Miguel Leon
School of Innovation, Design and Egineering
Malardalen University
Vasteras, Sweden

Ning Xiong
School of Innovation, Design and Egineering
Malardalen University
Vasteras, Sweden

Abstract—**Differential evolution (DE) presents a class of evolutionary computing techniques that appear effective to handle real parameter optimization tasks in many practical applications. However, the performance of DE is not always perfect to ensure fast convergence to the global optimum. It can easily get stagnation resulting in low precision of acquired results or even failure. This paper proposes a new memetic DE algorithm by incorporating Eager Random Search (ERS) to enhance the performance of a basic DE algorithm. ERS is a local search method that is eager to replace the current solution by a better candidate in the neighborhood. Three concrete local search strategies for ERS are further introduced and discussed, leading to variants of the proposed memetic DE algorithm. In addition, only a small subset of randomly selected variables is used in each step of the local search for randomly deciding the next trial solution. The results of tests on a set of benchmark problems have demonstrated that the hybridization of DE with Eager Random Search can substantially augment DE algorithms to find better or more precise solutions while not requiring extra computing resources.**

Keywords—Evolutionary Algorithm, Differential Evolution, Eager Random Search, Memetic Algorithm, Optimization

I. INTRODUCTION

Evolutionary algorithms (EAs) are stochastic and biologically inspired techniques that provide powerful and robust means to solve many real-world optimization problems. They are population-based optimization approaches [1] which perform parallel and beam search, thereby exhibiting strong global search ability in complex and high dimensional spaces. Another merit of EAs is that they dont need the derivative information of objective functions. This is very attractive for wide applications of EAs in various situations without requiring the problem space to be continuous and differentiable. Many variants of EAs have been developed to deal with real-parameter continuous optimization problems, including evolution strategies [2], real-coded genetic algorithms [3], [4], differential evolution (DE) [5], [6], and particle swarm optimization [7] and [8].

Differential evolution presents a class of evolutionary techniques to solve real parameter optimization tasks with nonlinear and multimodal objective functions. Despite sharing common concepts of EAs, DE differs from many other EAs in that mutation in DE is based on differences of pair(s) of individuals randomly selected from the population. Thus, the direction and magnitude of the search is decided by the distribution of solutions instead of a pre-specified probability density function. DE has been used as very competitive alternative in many practical applications due to its simple and compact structure, easy use with fewer control parameters, as well as high convergence in large problem spaces. However, the performance of DE is not always excellent to ensure fast convergence to the global optimum. It can easily get stagnation resulting in low precision of acquired results or even failure [9].

Recent researches have shown that hybridization of EAs with other techniques such as metaheuristics or local search techniques can greatly improve the efficiency of the search. EAs that are augmented with local search for self-refinement are called Memetic Algorithms (MAs) [[10], [11]]. In MAs, a local search mechanism is applied to members of the population in order to exploit the most promising regions gathered from global sampling done in the evolutionary process. Memetic computing has been used with DE to refine individuals in their neighborhood. Norman and Iba [12] proposed a crossover-based adaptive method to generate offspring in the vicinity of parents. Many other works apply local search mechanisms to certain individuals of every generation to obtain possibly even better solutions, see examples in ([13], [14], [15], [16]), [17]).

This paper proposes a new memetic DE algorithm by incorporating Eager Random Search (ERS) to enhance the performance of a conventional DE algorithm. ERS is a local search method that is eager to move to a position that is identified as better than the current one without considering other opportunities in the neighborhood. This is different from common local search methods such as gradient descent [18] or hill climbing [19] which seek local optimal actions during the search. Forsaking optimality of moves in ERS is advantageous to increase randomness and diversity of search for avoiding premature convergence. Three concrete local search strategies within ERS are introduced and discussed, leading to variants of the proposed memetic DE algorithm. In addition, only a small subset of randomly selected variables is used in every step of the local search for randomly deciding the next trial point. The results of tests on a set of benchmark problems have demonstrated that the hybridization of DE with

Eager Random Search can bring improvement of performance compared to pure DE algorithms while not incurring extra computing expenses.

The rest of the paper is organized as follows. Section 2 briefly presents the related works. Section 3 introduces the basic DE algorithm. Then, the proposed memetic DE algorithm in combination with Eager Random Search is presented in details in Section 4. Section 5 gives the results of tests for evaluation. Finally, concluding remarks are given in Section 6.

II. RELATED WORK

Since the first proposal of DE in 1997 [20], a lot of works have been done to improve the search ability of this algorithm, resulting in many variants of DE. A brief overview on some of them is given in this section.

Ali, Pant and Nagar [13] proposed two different local search algorithms, namely Trigonometric Local Search and Interpolated Local Search, which were applied to refine the best solution and two random solutions in every generation respectively.

Local search differential evolution was developed in [14] where a new local search operator was used on every individual in the population with a probability. The search strategy attempted to find a random better solution between trial vector and the best solution in the generation.

Dai, Zhou, Zhang and Jiang [15] combined Orthogonal Local Search with DE in the so-called OLSDE (Orthogonal Local Search Differential Evolution) algorithm. Therein two individuals were randomly selected from the population in each generation and they were used to generate a group of trial solutions with the orthogonal method. Then the best solution from the group of trial solutions replaced the worst individual in the population.

Jia, Zheng and Khan [9] proposed a memetic DE algorithm in combination with chaotic local search (CLS). The adaptive shrinking strategy embedded within CLS enabled the DE optimizer to explore large space in the early search phase and to exploit small regions in the later phase. Moreover, the chaotic iteration produced a higher probability to move into a boundary field, which appeared helpful for avoiding premature convergence to some extent. A similar work of utilizing chaotic principle based local search in DE was presented in [21].

Poikolainen and Neri [22] proposed a DE algorithm employing concurrent fitness based local search (DEcfbLS). The local search was applied to multiple promising solutions in the population, and the selection of individuals for local improvement was based on a fitness-based adaptation rule. Further, the local search operator was realized by making trial moves successively on single dimensions. But there was not much variation in the step sizes of the moves for different variables within an iteration of the search.

III. BASIC DE

DE is a stochastic and population based algorithm with Np individuals in the population. Every individual in the population stands for a possible solution to the problem. One of the Np individuals is represented by $X_{i,g}$ with $i = 1, 2, ., N_p$

and g is the index of the generation. DE has three consecutive steps in every iteration: mutation, recombination and selection. The explanation of these steps is given below:

MUTATION. N_p mutated individuals are generated using some individuals of the population. The vector for the mutated solution is called mutant vector and it is represented by $V_{i,g}$. There are some ways to mutate the current population, but only three will be explained in this paper. The notation to name them is $DE/x/y/z$, where x stands for the vector to be mutated, y represents the number of difference vectors used in the mutation and z stands for the crossover used in the algorithm. We will not include z in the notation because only the binomial crossover method is used here. The three mutation strategies (random, current to best and current to rand) will be explained below. The other mutation strategies and their performance are given in [23].

- Random Mutation Strategy:

Random mutation strategy attempts to mutate three individual in the population. When only one difference vector is employed in mutation, the approach is represented by DE/rand/1. A new, mutated vector is created according to Eq. 1

$$V_{i,g} = X_{r_1,g} + F \times (X_{r_2,g} - X_{r_3,g}) \qquad (1)$$

where $V_{i,g}$ represents the mutant vector, i stands for the index of the vector, g stands for the generation, $r_1, r_2, r_3 \in \{1,2,\ldots,N_p\}$ are random integers and F is the scaling factor in the interval [0, 2].

Fig. 1 shows how this mutation strategy works. All the variables in the figure appear in Eq. 1 with the same meaning, and d is the difference vector between $X_{r_2,g}$ and $X_{r_3,g}$.

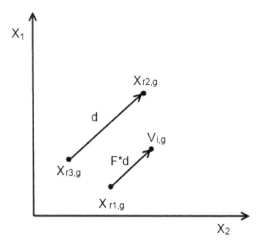

Fig. 1: Random mutation strategy

- Current to Best Mutation Strategy:

The current to best mutation strategy is referred as DE/current-to-best/1. It moves the current individual towards the best individual in the population before being disturbed with a scaled difference of two randomly selected vectors. Hence the mutant vector is created by

$$V_{i,g} = X_{i,g} + F1 \times (X_{best,g} - X_{i,g}) + F2 \times (X_{r_1,g} - X_{r_2,g}) \quad (2)$$

where $V_{i,g}$ stands for the mutant vector, $X_{i,g}$ and $X_{best,g}$ represent the current individual and the best individual in the population respectively, $F1$ and $F2$ are the scaling factors in the interval $[0, 2]$ and $r_1, r_2 \in \{1, 2, \ldots, N_p\}$ are randomly created integers.

Fig. 2 shows how the DE/current-to-best/1 strategy works to produce a mutant vector, where $d1$ denotes the difference vector between the current individual $X_{i,g}$, and $X_{best,g}$, $d2$ is the difference vector between $X_{r_1,g}$ and $X_{r_2,g}$.

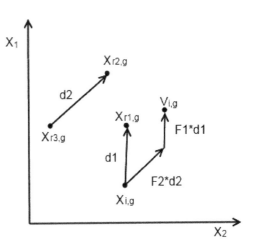

Fig. 3: Current to rand mutation strategy

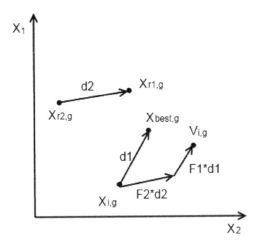

Fig. 2: Current to best mutation strategy

- Current to Rand Mutation Strategy:

The current to rand mutation strategy is referred to as DE/current-to-rand/1. It moves the current individual towards a random vector before being disturbed with a scaled difference of two randomly selected individuals. Thus the mutant vector is created according to Eq. 3 as follows

$$V_{i,g} = X_{i,g} + F1 \times (X_{r_1,g} - X_{i,g}) + F2 \times (X_{r_2,g} - X_{r_3,g}) \quad (3)$$

where $X_{i,g}$ represents the current individual, $V_{i,g}$ stands for the mutant vector, g stands for the generation, i is the index of the vector, $F1$ and $F2$ are the scaling factors in the interval $[0, 2]$ and $r1, r2, r3 \in \{1, 2, \ldots, N_p\}$ are randomly created integers.

Fig. 3 explains how the DE/current-to-rand/1 strategy works to produce a mutant vector, where $d1$ is the difference vector between the current individual, $X_{i,g}$, and $X_{r_1,g}$, and $d2$ is the difference vector between $X_{r_3,g}$ and $X_{r_2,g}$.

CROSSOVER. In step two we recombine the set of mutated solutions created in step 1 (mutation) with the original population members to produce trial solutions. A new trial vector is denoted by $T_{i,g}$ where i is the index and g is the generation.

Every parameter in the trial vector is calculated with equation 3

$$T_{i,g}[j] = \begin{cases} V_{i,g}[j] & \text{if } rand[0,1] < CR \text{ or } j = j_{rand} \\ X_{i,g}[j] & \text{otherwise} \end{cases} \quad (4)$$

where j stands for the index of every parameter in a vector, CR is the probability of the recombination and j_{rand} is a randomly selected integer in $[1, N_p]$ to ensure that at least one parameter from the mutant vector is selected.

SELECTION. In this last step we compare a trial vector with its parent in the population with the same index i to choose the stronger one to enter the next generation Therefore, if the problem to solve is a minimization problem, the next generation is created according to equation 4

$$X_{i,g+1} = \begin{cases} T_{i,g} & \text{if } f(T_{i,g}) < f(X_{i,g}) \\ X_{i,g} & \text{otherwise} \end{cases} \quad (5)$$

where $X_{i,g}$ is an individual in the population, $X_{i,g+1}$ is the individual in the next generation, $T_{i,g}$ is the trial vector, $f(T_{i,g})$ stands for the fitness value of trial solution and $f(X_{i,g})$ is the fitness value of the individual in the population.

The pseudocode for basic DE is given in Alg. 1. First of all we create the initial population with randomly generated individuals. Then we evaluate every individual in the population with a fitness function. Afterward we perform the three main steps: mutation, recombination and selection. First we mutate the population according Eq. 1, Eq. 2 or Eq. 3, then we recombine mutant vectors and their parents to get trial vectors according to Eq. 4, which are also called offspring. Finally we compare the offspring with their parents and the better individuals get into the updated population. From step 3 to step 7 we need to repeat it until the termination condition is satisfied.

Algorithm 1 Differential Evolution

1: Initialize the population with ramdomly created individuals
2: Calculate the fitness values of all individuals in the population
3: **while** The termination condition is not satisfied **do**
4:    Create mutant vectors using a mutation strategy in Eq. 1, Eq. 2 or Eq. 3
5:    Create trial vectors by recombining mutant vectors with parents vector according to Eq. 4
6:    Evaluate trial vectors with their fitness function
7:    Select winning vectors according to Eq. 5 as individuals in the next generation
8: **end while**

IV. DE INTEGRATED WITH ERS

This section is devoted to the proposal of the memetic DE algorithm with integrated ERS for local search. We will first introduce ERS as a general local search method together with its three concrete (search) strategies, and then we shall outline how ERS can be incorporated into DE to enable self-refinement of individuals inside a DE process.

A. Eager Random Local Search (ERS)

The main idea of ERS is to immediately move to a randomly created new position in the neighborhood without considering other opportunities as long as this new position receives a better fitness score than the current position. This is different from some other conventional local search methods such as Hill Climbing in which the next move is always to the best position in the surroundings. Forsaking optimality of moves in ERS is beneficial to achieve more randomness and diversity of search for avoiding local optima. Further, in exploiting the neighborhood, only a small subset of randomly selected variables undergoes changes to randomly create a trial solution. If this trial solution is better, it simply replaces the current one. Otherwise a new trial solution is generated with other randomly selected variables. This procedure is terminated when a given number of trial solutions have been created without finding improved ones. The formal procedure of ERS is given in Algorithm 2, where α denotes the portion of variables that are subject to local changes and M is the maximum number of times a trial solution can be created in order to find a better position than the current one.

The next more detailed issue with ERS is how to change a selected variable in making a trial solution in the neighborhood. This corresponds to the way to assign a possible value for parameter k in line 7 of Algorithm 2. Our idea is to solve this issue using a suitable probability function. We consider three probability distributions (uniform, normal, and Cauchy) as alternatives for usage when generating a new value for a selected parameter/variable. The use of different probability distributions lead to different local search strategies within the ERS family, which will be explained in the sequel.

1) Random Local Search (RLS): In Random Local Search (RLS), we simply use a uniform probability distribution when new trial solutions are created given a current solution. To be more specific, when dimension k is selected for change, the

---

Algorithm 2 Eager Random Local Search

1: Set $i = 1$;
2: **while** $i <= M$ **do**
3:    $candidates = 1, 2, \ldots, \text{dimension}$;
4:    Set $j = 1$;
5:    **while** $j < \alpha * dimension$ **do**
6:       Randomly select k from candidates;
7:       Assign a random possible value to parameter k of the vector;
8:       Remove k from $candidates$;
9:       Set $j = j + 1$;
10:   **end while**
11:   **if** This new solution is better than the parent **then**
12:      Replace the parent solution with the new one;
13:      Set $i = 1$;
14:   **else**
15:      Set $i = i + 1$;
16:   **end if**
17: **end while**

---

trial solution X' will get the following value on this dimension regardless of its initial value in the current solution:

$$X'[k] = rand(a_i, b_i) \tag{6}$$

where $rand(a_i, b_i)$ is a uniform random number between a_i and b_i, and a_i and b_i are the minimum and maximum values respectively on dimension k.

As equal chance is given to the whole range of a variable when changing a solution, RLS is more likely to create new points with large variation, thus increasing the opportunity to jump out from a local optimum. The disadvantage of RLS lies on its fine tuning ability to reach the exact optimum.

2) Normal Local Search (NLS): In Normal Local Search (NLS), we create a new trial solution by disturbing the current solution in terms of a normal probability distribution. This means that, if dimension k is selected for change, the value on this dimension for trial solution X' will be given by

$$X'[k] = X[k] + N(0, \delta) \tag{7}$$

where $N(0, \delta)$ represents a random number generated according to a normal density function with its mean being zero.

Owing to the use of the normal probability distribution, NLS usually creates new trial solutions that are quite close to the current one. This may, on one hand, bring benefit for the fine-tuning ability to reach the exact optimum. But, on the other hand, it will make it more difficult for the local search to escape from a local optimum.

3) Cauchy Local Search (CLS): In this third local search strategy, we apply the Cauchy density function in creating trial solutions in the neighborhood. It is called Cauchy Local search (CLS). A nice property of the Cauchy function is that it is centered around its mean value whereas exhibiting a wider distribution than the normal probability function, as is shown in Fig. 3. Hence CLS will have more chances to make big moves in attempts to find possibly better positions and to leave away from local minima. Regarding the fine-search ability, CLS will be better than RLS though it is not expected as good as NLS.

More concretely, a Cauchy probability density function is defined by

$$f(x) = \frac{1}{\pi} \times \frac{t}{t^2 + x^2}, t > 0 \qquad (8)$$

Its corresponding cumulative probability function is given by

$$F(x) = \frac{1}{2} + \frac{1}{\pi} \times arctan(\frac{x}{t}) \qquad (9)$$

It follows that, on a selected dimension k, the value of trial solution X' will be generated as follows:

$$X'[k] = X[k] + t \times tan(\pi \times (rand(0,1) - 0.5)) \qquad (10)$$

where $rand(0,1)$ is a random uniform number between 0 and 1.

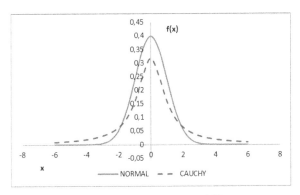

Fig. 4: Distribution probability

B. The Proposed Memetic DE Algorithm

Here with we propose a new memetic DE algorithm by combining basic DE with Eager Random Search (ERS). ERS is applied in each generation after completing the mutation, crossover and selection operators. The best individual in the population is used as the starting point when ERS is executed. If ERS terminates with a better solution, it is inserted into the population and the current best member in the population is discarded. The general procedure of the proposed memetic DE algorithm is outlined in Algorithm 3.

Finally, different strategies within ERS can be used for local search in line 9 of Algorithm 3. We use DERLS, DENLS, and DECLS to refer to the variants of the proposed memetic DE algorithm that adopt RLS, NLS, and CLS respectively as local search strategies.

Algorithm 3 Memetic Differential Evolution

1: Initialize the population with randomly created individuals
2: Calculate the fitness values of all individuals in the population
3: **while** The termination condition is not satisfied **do**
4:   Create mutant vectors using a mutation strategy in Eq. 1, Eq. 2 or Eq. 3
5:   Create trial vectors by recombining mutant vectors with parents vector according to Eq. 4
6:   Evaluate trial vectors with their fitness function
7:   Select winning vectors according to Eq. 5 as individuals in the next generation
8:   Identify the best individual X_{best} in the population
9:   Perform local search from X_{best} using a ERS strategy
10:   **if** the result from local search X_r is better than X_{best} **then**
11:     replace X_{best} by X_r in the population
12:   **end if**
13: **end while**

V. EXPERIMENTS AND RESULTS

To examine the merit our proposed memetic DE algorithm compared to basic DE, we tested the algorithms in thirteen benchmark functions [24] listed in Table 1. Functions 1 to 7 are unimodal and functions 8 to 13 are multimodal functions that contain many local optima. Table 1 gives the definition of every function. The most difficult functions are 8, 9 and 10, which are shown in Figs. 5, 6 and 7 respectively.

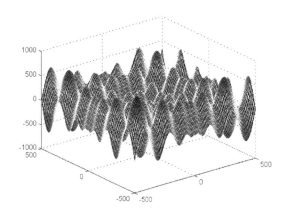

Fig. 5: Function 8 with two dimensions

A. Experimental Settings

DE has three main control parameters: population size (N_p), crossover rate (CR) and the scaling factor (F) for mutation. The following specification of these parameters was used in the experiments: $Np = 60$, $CR = 0.85$ and $F, F1, F2 = 0.9$. All the algorithms were applied to the benchmark problems with the aim to find the best solution for each of them. Every algorithm was executed 30 times on every function to acquire a fair result for the comparison. The condition to finish the execution of DE programs is that the error of the best result found is below 10e-8 with respect to the true minimum or the number of evaluations has exceeded

TABLE I: The thirteen functions used in the experiments

FUNCTION
$f1(x) = \sum_{i=1}^{n} x_i^2$
$f2(x) = \sum_{i=1}^{n} |x_i| + \prod_{i=1}^{n} |x_i|$
$f3(x) = \sum_{i=1}^{n} (\sum_{j=1}^{i} x_j)^2$
$f4(x) = max_i\{|x_i|, 1 \le i \le n\}$
$f5(x) = \sum_{i=1}^{n-1} [100 \times (x_{i+1} - x_i^2)^2 + (x_i - 1)^2]$
$f6(x) = \sum_{i=1}^{n} \lfloor (x_i + 0.5)^2 \rfloor$
$f7(x) = \sum_{i=1}^{n} i \times x_i^4 + random[0, 1)$
$f8(x) = \sum_{i=1}^{n} -x_i \times sin(\sqrt{|x_i|})$
$f9(x) = \sum_{i=1}^{n} [x_i^2 - 10 \times cos(2 \times \pi \times x_i) + 10]$
$f10(x) = -20 \times exp(-0.2 \times \sqrt{\frac{1}{n} \times \sum_{i=1}^{n} x_i^2}) - exp(\frac{1}{n} \times \sum_{i=1}^{n} cos(2\pi x_i)) + 20 + e$
$f11(x) = \frac{1}{4000} \times \sum_{i=1}^{n} x_i^2 - \prod_{i=1}^{n} cos(\frac{x_i}{\sqrt{i}}) + 1$
$f12(x) = \frac{\pi}{n} \times \{10sin^2(\pi y_i) + \sum_{i=1}^{n-1}((y_i - 1)^2[1 + 10sin^2(\pi y_{i+1})]) + (y_n - 1)^2\} +$ $+ \sum_{i=1}^{n} u(x_i, 10, 100, 4)$, where $y_i = 1 + \frac{1}{4}(x_i + 1)$ $u(x_i, a, k, m) = \begin{cases} k(x_i - a)^m, & x_i > a \\ 0, & -a \le x_i \le a \\ k(x_i - a)^m, & x_i < -a \end{cases}$
$f13(x) = 0.1 \times \{sin^2(3\pi x_1) + \sum_{i=1}^{n-1}((x_i - 1)^2[1 + sin^2(3\pi x_{i+1})]) +$ $+(x_n - 1)[1 + sin^2(2\pi x_n)]\} + \sum_{i=1}^{n} u(x_i, 5, 100, 4)$

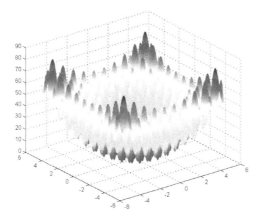

Fig. 6: Function 9 with two dimensions

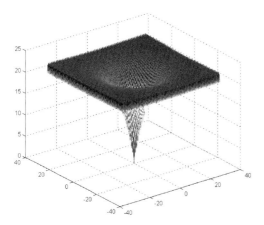

Fig. 7: Function 10 with two dimensions

300,000. The parameters in DECLS are $t = 0.2$, $M = 5$ and $\alpha = 0.1$.

The results of experiments will be presented as follows: First we will compare the performance (the quality of acquired solutions) of the various DE approaches with random mutation strategy, secondly we will compare the performance of the same approaches using the current to rand mutation strategy and third we will compare the performance of the same approaches using the current to best mutation strategy.

B. Performance of the Memetic DE with random mutation strategy

First, random mutation strategy (DE/rand/1) was used in all DE approaches to study the effect of the ERS local search strategies in the memetic DE algorithm. The results can be observed in Table 2 and the values in boldface represent the lowest average error found by the approaches.

In Table 3 there is a ranking among all the approaches for every function. The last row represents the average of the rankings.

We can see in Table 2 and Table 3 that DECLS is the best in all the unimodal functions except on Function 4 that is the second best. In multimodal functions, DERLS is the best on Functions 8, 10 and 11. DECLS found the exact optimum all the times in Functions 12 and 13. The basic, DE performed the worst in multimodal functions. According to the above analysis, we can say that DECLS improve a lot the performance of basic DE with random mutation strategy and also we found out that DERLS is really good in multimodal functions particularly on Function 8, which is the most difficult function. Considering all the functions and the average ranking in Table 3, the best algorithm is DECLS and the weakest one is the basic DE.

TABLE II: Average error of the found solutions on the test problems with random mutation strategy

FUNC.	DE	DERLS	DENLS	DECLS
f1	**0,00E+00**	**0,00E+00**	**0,00E+00**	**0,00E+00**
	(4,56E-14)	(6,80E-13)	(1,21E-13)	(1,33E-14)
f2	1,82E-08	5,30E-08	2,26E-08	**1,42E-08**
	(1,13E-08)	(2,39E-08)	(1,32E-08)	(1,07E-08)
f3	6,55E+01	8,01E+01	1,11E+00	**6,54E-01**
	(3,92E+01)	(4,88E+01)	(1,10E+00)	(1,47E+01)
f4	6,22E+00	2,37E+00	1,80E-02	**5,66E-01**
	(5,07E+00)	(1,87E+00)	(7,28E-01)	(3,68E-01)
f5	2,31E+01	2,27E+01	2,65E+01	**2,03E+01**
	(2,00E+01)	(1,81E+01)	(2,41E+01)	(2,62E+01)
f6	**0,00E+00**	**0,00E+00**	**0,00E+00**	**0,00E+00**
	(0,00E+00)	(0,00E+00)	(0,00E+00)	(0,00E+00)
f7	1,20E-01	1,15E-02	1,23E-02	**1,05E-02**
	(3,79E-03)	(3,16E-03)	(3,29E-03)	(3,61E-03)
f8	2,72E+03	**2,31E+02**	1,86E+03	1,58E+03
	(8,15E+02)	(1,50E+02)	(5,46E+02)	(5,16E+02)
f9	1,30E+01	1,28E+01	**6,17E+00**	7,72E+00
	(3,70E+00)	(3,72E+00)	(2,06E+00)	(2,43E+00)
f10	1,88E+01	**1,87E+00**	4,94E+00	5,50E+00
	(4,28E+00)	(4,76E+00)	(8,11E+00)	(7,53E+00)
f11	**8,22E-04**	**8,22E-04**	1,49E-02	1,44E-02
	(2,49E-03)	(2,49E-03)	(2,44E-02)	(2,70E-02)
f12	3,46E-03	3,46E-03	1,04E-02	**0,00E+00**
	(1,86E-02)	(1,86E-02)	(3,11E-02)	(8,49E-15)
f13	3,66E-04	**0,00E+00**	**0,00E+00**	**0,00E+00**
	(1,97E-03)	(2,14E-13)	(1,31E-14)	(3,37E-15)

TABLE IV: Average error of the found solutions on the test problems with current to rand mutation strategy

FUNC.	DE	DERLS	DENLS	DECLS
f1	**0,00E+00**	**0,00E+00**	**0,00E+00**	**0,00E+00**
	(1,20E-16)	(5,50E-15)	(2,53E-16)	(5,23E-17)
f2	**0,00E+00**	**0,00E+00**	**0,00E+00**	**0,00E+00**
	(6,79E-10)	(2,68E-09)	(1,65E-09)	(8,09E-10)
f3	1,96E+01	1,99E+01	**3,89E-01**	4,46E-01
	(9,93E+00)	(1,16E+01)	(2,94E-01)	(3,29E-01)
f4	3,30E+00	1,39E+00	6,19E-01	**9,44E-02**
	(2,81E+00)	(1,66E+00)	(1,64E+00)	(2,14E-01)
f5	1,57E+01	1,91E+01	2,70E+01	**1,49E+01**
	(1,48E+01)	(1,82E+01)	(2,70E+01)	(1,94E+01)
f6	**0,00E+00**	**0,00E+00**	**0,00E+00**	**0,00E+00**
	(0,00E+00)	(0,00E+00)	(0,00E+00)	(0,00E+00)
f7	9,64E-03	9,36E-03	9,57E-03	**9,04E-03**
	(9,93E-03)	(2,63E-03)	(2,21E-03)	(3,22E-03)
f8	6,71E+03	**1,20E+03**	5,17E+03	4,02E+03
	(2,93E+02)	(2,78E+02)	(6,33E+02)	(6,01E+02)
f9	1,08E+01	1,37E+01	1,04E+01	**1,01E+01**
	(2,39E+00)	(4,45E+00)	(3,72E+00)	(3,41E+00)
f10	1,93E+01	**4,62E-01**	6,92E+00	1,59E+00
	(3,58E+00)	(2,49E+00)	(9,22E+00)	(4,86E+00)
f11	**2,47E-04**	4,93E-04	9,04E-03	3,77E-03
	(1,33E-03)	(1,84E-03)	(2,09E-02)	(7,87E-03)
f12	**0,00E+00**	**0,00E+00**	3,46E-03	**0,00E+00**
	(1,61E-17)	(5,02E-17)	(1,86E-02)	(9,99E-18)
f13	**0,00E+00**	**0,00E+00**	**0,00E+00**	**0,00E+00**
	(1,85E-13)	(1,68E-11)	(2,48E-12)	(6,99E-15)

TABLE III: Ranking of all DE approaches with random mutation strategy

FUNCTION	DE	DERLS	DENLS	DECLS
f1	**2,5**	**2,5**	**2,5**	**2,5**
f2	2	4	3	**1**
f3	3	4	2	**1**
f4	4	3	**1**	2
f5	3	2	4	**1**
f6	**2,5**	**2,5**	**2,5**	**2,5**
f7	3	2	4	**1**
f8	4	**1**	3	2
f9	4	3	**1**	2
f10	4	**1**	2	3
f11	**1,5**	**1,5**	4	3
f12	2,5	2,5	4	**1**
f13	4	2	2	2
average	3,076923	2,384615	2,692308	**1,846154**

TABLE V: Ranking of all approaches with current to rand mutation strategy

FUNCTION	DE	DERLS	DENLS	DECLS
f1	**2,5**	**2,5**	**2,5**	**2,5**
f2	**2,5**	**2,5**	**2,5**	**2,5**
f3	3	4	**1**	2
f4	4	3	2	**1**
f5	2	3	4	**1**
f6	3	4	2	**1**
f7	2	4	3	**1**
f8	3,5	**1**	3,5	2
f9	4	3	2	**1**
f10	4	**1**	3	2
f11	**1**	2	4	3
f12	2	2	4	**2**
f13	**2,5**	**2,5**	**2,5**	**2,5**
average	2,846152	2,461538	2,769231	**1,923077**

C. Performance of the Memetic DE with Current to Rand Mutation Strategy

The next mutation strategy used in our experiments was current to rand mutation strategy (DE/current-to-rand/1) and the results are illustrated in Table 4. The first column of this table shows the functions that we used for testing and the results for every algorithm are given in Columns 2-5.

Table 5 shows the ranking of all the approaches for every test function with current to rand mutation strategy.

We can see in Table 4 and Table 5 that in unimodal functions the best algorithm is DECLS except in Function 3 DENLS is the best. In multimodal functions, basic DE is the worst, because it has the worst results in Functions 8 and 10, two of the most difficult functions and basic DE did not find good result in Function 9. The best algorithms in multimodal functions are DECLS and DERLS. According to this analysis we can say that DECLS is most desirable as it appeared to be competent in all functions, also in the average ranking DECLS gets the best result.

D. Performance of the Memetic DE with Current to Best Mutation Strategy

The last experiments were related with current to best mutation strategy (DE/current-to-best/1). This mutation strategy was used in all DE approaches to study the effect of our proposed ERS strategies in the memetic DE algorithm. The results can be observed in Table 6 and the values in boldface represent the lowest average error found by the approaches.

In Table 7 there is a ranking among all the approaches for every function. The last row represents the average of the rankings.

We can see in Table 6 and Table 7 that DECLS got the best results in most unimodal functions. DERLS is the best on Functions 8 and 10, always finding the true optimum in Function 10. DECLS is the best algorithm in Function 9 and only this algorithm always found the true optimum in Functions 12 and 13. According to the above analysis, we can say that DECLS is the best algorithm, because it is competitive in almost all unimodal and multimodal functions. DECLS also

TABLE VI: Average error of the found solutions on the test problems with current to best mutation strategy

FUNC.	DE	DERLS	DENLS	DECLS
f1	**0,00E+00**	**0,00E+00**	**0,00E+00**	**0,00E+00**
	(1,81E-34)	(8,64E-32)	(1,14E-33)	(1,04E-33)
f2	**0,00E+00**	**0,00E+00**	**0,00E+00**	**0,00E+00**
	(9,16E-20)	(5,69E-19)	(7,19E-19)	(3,02E-19)
f3	**2,73E-03**	7,27E-03	5,97E-02	5,09E-03
	(2,57E-03)	(8,06E-03)	(3,21E-01)	(2,64E-02)
f4	6,42E-04	2,69E-03	2,98E-04	**1,86E-04**
	(5,95E-04)	(4,72E-03)	(2,47E-04)	(1,93E-04)
f5	4,10E-01	4,34E-01	1,97E+00	**1,07E+00**
	(1,19E+00)	(1,23E+00)	(3,64E+00)	(1,75E+00)
f6	2,33E-01	2,67E-01	6,67E-02	**0,00E+00**
	(4,23E-01)	(5,12E-01)	(2,49E-01)	(0,00E+00)
f7	7,94E-03	8,54E-03	8,33E-03	**7,77E-03**
	(2,45E-03)	(2,21E-03)	(3,40E-03)	(2,40E-03)
f8	2,35E+03	**3,10E+02**	2,35E+03	2,10E+03
	(8,66E+02)	(1,86E+02)	(5,85E+02)	(5,75E+02)
f9	2,18E+01	2,02E+01	1,23E+01	**1,08E+01**
	(4,47E+00)	(5,13E+00)	(6,08E+00)	(3,72E+00)
f10	1,06E+01	**0,00E+00**	2,78E+00	1,99E+00
	(9,89E+00)	(1,28E-15)	(6,44E+00)	(5,87E+00)
f11	**4,76E-03**	9,52E-03	1,16E-01	1,01E-01
	(5,28E-03)	(8,59E-03)	(8,04E-02)	(6,79E-02)
f12	2,76E-02	1,04E-02	1,42E-01	**0,00E+00**
	(5,31E-02)	(3,11E-02)	(3,21E-01)	(8,22E-33)
f13	1,83E-03	3,66E-04	4,36E-04	**0,00E+00**
	(4,09E-03)	(1,97E-03)	(1,64E-03)	(2,57E-09)

TABLE VII: Ranking of all DE approaches with random mutation strategy

FUNCTION	DE	DERLS	DENLS	DECLS
f1	**2,5**	**2,5**	**2,5**	**2,5**
f2	**2,5**	**2,5**	**2,5**	**2,5**
f3	**1**	3	4	2
f4	3	4	2	**1**
f5	**1**	2	4	3
f6	3	4	2	**1**
f7	2	4	3	**1**
f8	3,5	**1**	3,5	2
f9	4	3	2	**1**
f10	4	**1**	3	2
f11	**1**	2	4	3
f12	3	2	4	**1**
f13	4	3	3	**1**
average	2,653846	2,538462	3,038462	**1,769231**

gets the best ranking among others. Besides, DERLS is shown to be competitive in multimodal functions.

VI. CONCLUSIONS

In this paper we propose a memetic DE algorithm by incorporating Eager Random Search (ERS) as a local search method to enhance the search ability of a pure DE algorithm. Three concrete local search strategies (RLS, NLS, and CLS) are introduced and explained as instances of the general ERS method. The use of different local search strategies from the ERS family leads to variants of the proposed memetic DE algorithm, which are abbreviated as DERLS, DENLS and DECLS respectively. The results of the experiments have demonstrated that the overall ranking of DECLS is superior to the ranking of basic DE and other memetic DE variants considering all the test functions and various mutation strategies used. In addition, we found out that DERLS is much better than the other counterparts in very difficult multimodal functions.

In future work, we intend to improve our proposed algorithms with adaptive parameters in mutation, crossover and

local search and attempting to hybridize both alternatives to take advantage of the best features from each of them. Moreover, we will also apply and test our new computing algorithms in real industrial scenarios.

ACKNOWLEDGMENT

The work is funded by the Swedish Knowledge Foundation (KKS) grant (project no 16317). The authors are also grateful to ABB FACTS, Prevas and VOITH for their co-financing of the project. The work is also partly supported by ESS-H profile funded by the Swedish Knowledge Foundation.

REFERENCES

[1] N. Xiong, D. Molina, M. Leon, and F. Herrera, "A walk into meta-heuristics for engineering optimization: Principles, methods, and recent trends," *International Journal of Computational Intelligence Systems*, vol. 8, no. 4, pp. 606–636, 2015.

[2] N. Hansen and A. Ostermeier, "Completely derandomized self-adaptation in evolution strategies," *Evolutionary Computation*, vol. 9, no. 2, pp. 159–195, 2001.

[3] F. Herrera and M. Lozano, "Two-loop real-coded genetic algorithms with adaptive control of mutation step size," *Applied Intelligence*, vol. 13, pp. 187–204, 2000.

[4] E. Falkenauer, "Applying genetic algorithms to real-world problems," *Evolutionary Algorithms*, vol. 111, pp. 65–88, 1999.

[5] R. Storn and K. Price, "Differential evolution - a simple and efficient heuristic for global optimization over continuous spaces," *Journal of Global Optimization*, vol. 11, no. 4, pp. 341 – 359, 1997.

[6] J. Brest, S. Greiner, B. Boskovic, M. Mernik, and V. Zumer, "Self-adapting control parameters in differential evolution: A comparative study on numerical benchmark problems," in *IEEE Transaction on Evolutionary Computation*, vol. 10, 2006, pp. 646–657.

[7] J. Kenedy and R. C. Eberhart, "Particle swarm optimization," in *In Proc. IEEE Conference on Neural Networks*, 1995, pp. 1942–1948.

[8] G. Venter and J. Sobieszczanski-Sobieski, "Particle swarm optimization," *AIAA Journal*, vol. 41, pp. 1583–1589, 2003.

[9] D. Jia, G. Zheng, and M. K. Khan, "An effective memetic differential evolution algorithm based on chaotical search," *Information Sciences*, vol. 181, pp. 3175–3187, 2011.

[10] D. Molina, M. Lozano, A. M. Sanchez, and F. Herrera, "Memetic algorithms based on local search chains for large scale continuous optimization problems: Ma-ssw-chains," *Soft Computing*, vol. 15, pp. 2201–2220, 2011.

[11] N. Krasnogor and J. Smith, "A tutorial for competent memetic algorithms: Model, taxonomy, and design issue," *IEEE Transactions on Evolutionary Computation*, vol. 9, no. 5, pp. 474–488, 2005.

[12] N. Norman and H. Ibai, "Accelerating differential evolution using an adaptive local search," in *IEEE Transactions on Evolutionary Computation*, vol. 12, no. 1, 2008, pp. 107 – 125.

[13] M. Ali, M. Pant, and A. Nagar, "Two local search strategies for differential evolution," in *Proc. Bio-Inspired Computing: Theories and Applications (BIC-TA), 2010 IEEE Fifth International Conference, Changsha, China*, 2010, pp. 1429 – 1435.

[14] G. Jirong and G. Guojun, "Differential evolution with a local search operator," in *Proc. 2010 2nd International Asia Conference on Informatics in Control, Automation and Robotics (CAR), Wuhan, China*, vol. 2, 2010, pp. 480 – 483.

[15] Z. Dai and A. Zhou, "A diferential ecolution with an orthogonal local search," in *Proc. 2013 IEEE congress on Evolutionary Computation (CEC), Cancun, Mexico*, 2013, pp. 2329 – 2336.

[16] X. Weixeng, Y. Wei, and Z. Xiufen, "Diversity-maintained differential evolution embedded with gradient-based local search," *soft computing*, vol. 17, pp. 1511–1535, 2013.

[17] K. Bandurski and W. Kwedlo, "A lamarckian hybrid of differential evolution and conjugate gradients for neural networks training," *Neural Process Lett*, vol. 32, pp. 31–44, 2010.

[18] M. Avriel, "Nolinear programming: Analysis and methods," in *Dover Publishing*, 2003.

[19] S. Russel and P. Norvig, "Artificial intelligence: A moder approach," in *New Yersey: Prentice Hall*, 2003, pp. 111–114.

[20] R. Storn and K. Price, "Differential evolution - a simple and efficient adaptive scheme for global optimization over continuous spaces," Comput. Sci. Inst., Berkeley, CA, USA, Tech Rep. TR-95-012, 1995.

[21] W. Pei-chong, Q. Xu, and H. Xiao-hong, "A novel differential evolution algorithm based on chaos local search," in *Proc. International conference on information Engineering and Computer Science, 2009. ICIECS 2009. Wuhan, China*, 2009, pp. 1–4.

[22] I. Poikolainen and F. Neri, "Differential evolution with concurrent fitness based local search," in *Proc. 2013 IEEE Congress on Evolutionary Computation (CEC), Cancun, Mexico*, 2013, pp. 384–391.

[23] M. Leon and N. Xiong, "Investigation of mutation strategies in differential evolution for solving global optimization problems," in *Artificial Intelligence and Soft Computing.* springer, June 2014, pp. 372–383.

[24] X. Yao, Y. Liu, and G. Lin, "Evolutionary programming made faster," in *Proc. IEEE Transactions on Evolutionary Computation*, vol. 3, no. 2, 1999, pp. 82–102.

32

Effect of Sensitivity Improvement of Visible to NIR Digital Cameras on NDVI Measurements in Particular for Agricultural Field Monitoring

Kohei Arai [1]
1Graduate School of Science and Engineering
Saga University
Saga City, Japan

Takuji Maekawa [2]
2 LSI Production Headquarters
Rohm Co., Ltd.
Kyoto City, Japan

Toshihisa Maeda [2]
2 LSI Production Headquarters
Rohm Co., Ltd.
Kyoto City, Japan

Hiroshi Sekiguchi [2]
2 LSI Production Headquarters
Rohm Co., Ltd.
Kyoto City, Japan

Noriyuki Masago [2]
2 LSI Production Headquarters
Rohm Co., Ltd.
Kyoto City, Japan

Abstract—Effect of sensitivity improvement of Near Infrared: NIR digital cameras on Normalized Difference Vegetation Index: NDVI measurements in particular for agricultural field monitoring is clarified. Comparative study is conducted between sensitivity improved visible to near infrared camera of CuInGaSe: CIGS and the conventional camera. Signal to Noise: S/N ratio and sensitivity are evaluated with NIR camera data which are acquired in tea farm areas and rice paddy fields. From the experimental results, it is found that S/N ratio of the conventional digital camera with NIR wavelength coverage is better than CIGS utilized image sensor while the sensitivity of the CIGS image sensor is much superior to that of the conventional camera. Also, it is found that NDVI derived from the CIGS image sensor is much better than that from the conventional camera due to the fact that the sensitivity of the CIGS image sensor in red color wavelength region is much better than that of the conventional camera.

Keywords—CuInGaSe; SiCMOS; NDVI; Rice crop; Tealeaves; S/N ratio; Sensivity

I. INTRODUCTION

Most of the commercially available digital cameras use Silicon utilized SiCMOS or CCD for the detector. The material of these detectors is silicon. Therefore, wavelength regions are limited up to around 900nm due to restriction of silicon image sensor of responsibility. Although these visible to 900nm wavelength region of digital cameras are acceptable for the general purposes, there are strong demands for acquisition of camera images with visible to near infrared region in particular for biometric security system, medical check system, agricultural and forestry application fields. In order to improve the sensitivity of the detector, CuInGaSe: CIGS image sensor is developed by Rohm Co., Ltd. in Japan [1]-[7]. The sensitivity of the image sensor covers from visible to 1200nm with the acceptable quantum efficiency.

One of application fields of the CIGS image sensor is vegetation monitoring. Importantly, vegetation monitoring needs wide wavelength coverage with an acceptable sensitivity. There are so many types of commercially available digital cameras. These, however, are not enough for monitoring of vegetation index which needs an acceptable sensitivity at red color wavelength and NIR wavelength regions. Usually, spectral reflectance of vegetation shows very low at the red color wavelength and quite high in the NIR region. Due to the fact that sensitivity of the commercially available digital cameras is not enough in NIR region while the reflectance of vegetations in red color wavelength is low, it would be better to improve the sensitivity of the digital camera in NIR wavelength region together with red color region. The CIGS image sensor gives one of solutions for solving the above mentioned problem.

Tea farm areas and rice paddy fields are selected for showing an effectiveness of the CIGS image sensor in particular for improving sensitivity in red to near infrared regions. The most important thing for tealeaves monitoring is NDVI estimation [8]-[20]. Amino acid contents containing in tealeaves depends on NDVI. Amino acid rich tealeaves taste good. Also, tealeaf growing stage monitoring needs fiber content estimation. Depending on growing stage, fiber content is getting large. Therefore, it is possible to estimate fiber content in tealeaves.

Meanwhile, protein content in rice crops is highly correlated with nitrogen content in rice leaves [21]-[26]. Protein content rich rice crops taste bad. Therefore, it is possible to estimated rice crop quality once protein content in rice crops is estimated. Nitrogen content in rice leaves depends on rice leaf reflectance. Therefore, it is capable to estimate protein content in rice crops through estimation of nitrogen content in rice leaves which is done with visible to near infrared camera data.

In order to estimate NDVI, leaf reflectance has to be measured in red and near infrared wavelength regions. The sensitivity of the CIGS image sensor in these wavelength regions is much better than those of the conventional digital cameras which utilized SiCMOS or CCD with silicon materials. Therefore, it is expected that NDVI estimation accuracy is improved. More than that, the sensitivity of the CIGS image sensor is better than that of the conventional digital cameras. This paper clarified these improvements quantitatively.

The next section describes the specification of the CIGS image sensor followed by the method and procedure of the experiments Then experimental results are described followed by conclusions with some discussions.

II. CIGS IMAGE SENSOR

A. Specific Features of the CIGS Image Sensor

One of the specific features of the CIGS image sensor is wide spectral coverage ranges from 430 to 1025nm with the sensitivity level (Quantum Efficiency) of 30. The wavelength coverage of the conventional SiCMOS image sensor ranges from 400 to 750nm. Fig.1 shows wavelength coverage of the CIGS image sensor and the conventional SiCMOS image sensor while Fig.2 shows outlook of the CIGS image sensor.

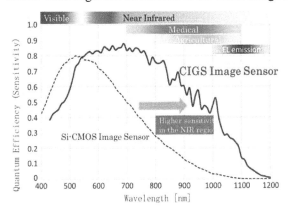

Fig. 1. Wavelength coverage of the CIGS and the conventional SICMOS image sensors

Fig.3 shows structural difference between the CIGS image sensor and the conventional SICMOS sensor. In particular, detector surface reflectance of the CIGS image sensor is much lower than that of the conventional SiCMOS image sensor. Also, aperture ratio of the CIGS image sensor is much higher than that of the conventional SiCMOS image sensor which results in high sensitivity in visible to near infrared wavelength regions.

Fig. 2. Outlook of the CIGS image sensor

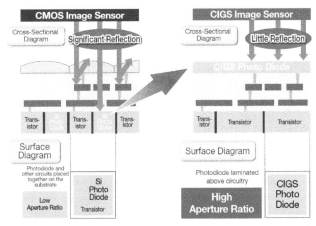

Fig. 3. Structural difference between the CIGS image sensor and the conventional SICMOS sensor

B. Specific Applications of the CIGS Image Sensor

Fig.4 (a) and (b) shows examples of applications of the CIGS image sensor for biometric sensors and for vegetation monitoring, respectively. Vein patterns of human hands can be detected by the CIGS image sensor as a biometric sensor for identification of the registered persons for security reason. On the other hand, vegetation monitoring can be done with the CIGS image sensor as shown in Fig.4 (b) because the reflectance of vegetation is very high in near infrared wavelength region.

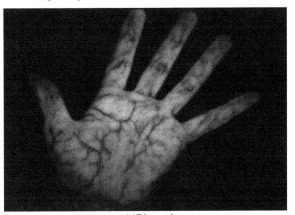

(a)Biometric sensor

(b)Vegetation

Fig. 4. Examples of the CIGS image sensor

Fig.4 (b) left shows the outdoor scenery of vegetation acquired by CIGS image sensor without any filter while Fig.4 (b) right shows that with visible wavelength coverage cut filter. It is quite obvious that vegetated areas are brighter for the CIGS image sensor image than those areas for the CIGS image sensor with visible wavelength coverage cut filter image (NIR image).

III. EXPERIMENTS

A. Method and Procedure

Signal to Noise ratio: S/N ratio is evaluated by assuming the mean of the small portion of the acquired image where is seemed to be homogeneous pixel values must be the signal and by assuming the standard deviation of the same area of image is the noise. On the other hand, sensitivity can be evaluated by taking ratio between mean values of the different homogeneous portions of images.

Comparisons of S/N ratio and sensitivity are carried out between the CIGS image sensor and the conventional SiCMOS image sensor of Canon S100 with the replaced NIR filter to the originally blue filter. Spectral response of the S100 camera used is shown in Fig.5.

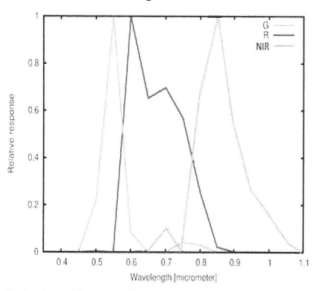

Fig. 5. Spectral Response of S100 Camera of which Blue Filter is Changed to NIR filter

B. Intensive Study Araeas

The experiments are conducted at the tea farm areas of the Saga Prefectural Institute of Tea: SPIT which is situated in Ureshino city, Saga Japan and the Saga Prefectural Institute of Agriculture: SPIA which is situated in Saga city, Saga Japan. Outlooks of SPIT and SPIA are shown in Fig.6 (a) and (b), respectively. The third tea farm field at the North tea farm areas of Yabukita Tea at SPIT is selected as tealeaf example while Hiyokumochi of sticky rice paddy field is also chosen as rice leaves example.

(a)SPIT

(b)SPIA

Fig. 6. Outlooks of the SPIT and SPIA

C. S/N Ratio and Sensitivity Evaluations

Fig.7 (a) shows top view of the acquired image of a small portion of the Yabukita Tea field on October 4 2015. Meanwhile, Fig.7 (b) shows the acquired image with the CIGS image sensor of the tiny portion of a piece of tealeaf together with histogram of the rectangle area of the tiny portion (m1 and s1 denotes the mean and the standard deviation of this portion of image, respectively) while Fig.7 (c) shows that of the different rectangle portion of the tiny portion (m2 and s2 denotes the mean and the standard deviation of this portion of image, respectively). On the other hand, Fig.7 (d) shows the acquired image with the S100 camera of the almost same portion of the tealeaf (m3 and s3 denotes the mean and the standard deviation of this portion of image, respectively) while Fig.7 (e) shows that of the different portion of the tealeaf on October 7 2015 (m4 and s4 denotes the mean and the standard deviation of this portion of image, respectively). All these images are acquired by the CIGS image sensor and the S100 image sensor with NIR filter.

(a)Top view of Yabukita tealeaf

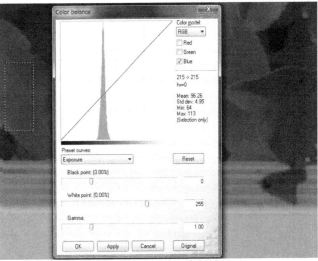

(d)Tiny portion of image with S100 camera

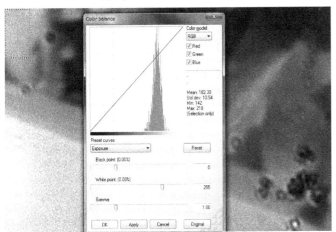

(b)Tiny portion of image with CIGS camera

(e)Different portion of image with S100 camera

Fig. 7.   Acquired images of Yabukita tealeaves with CIGS and S100 cameras

Fig.8 (a) shows slant view of the acquired image of a small portion of the Hiyokumochi rice paddy field. Meanwhile, Fig.8 (b) shows the acquired image with the CIGS image sensor of the tiny portion of a piece of rice leaf together with histogram of the rectangle area of the tiny portion (M1 and S1 denotes the mean and the standard deviation of this portion of image, respectively) while Fig.8 (c) shows that of the different rectangle portion of the tiny portion (M2 and S2 denotes the mean and the standard deviation of this portion of image, respectively). On the other hand, Fig.8 (d) shows the acquired image with the S100 camera of the almost same portion of the rice leaf (M3 and S3 denotes the mean and the standard deviation of this portion of image, respectively) while Fig.8 (e) shows that of the different portion of the rice leaf (M4 and S4 denotes the mean and the standard deviation of this portion of image, respectively).

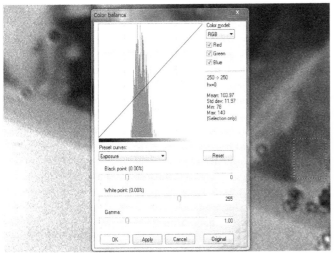

(c)Different portion of image with CIGS camera

(a)Slant view

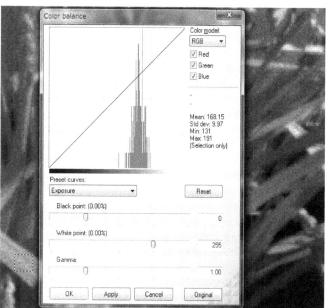

(b)Tiny portion of image with CIGS

(c)Different portion of image with CIGS

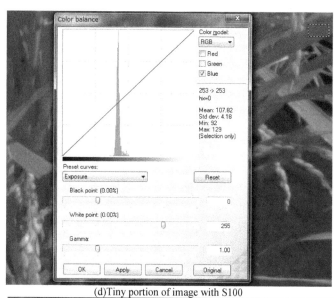

(d)Tiny portion of image with S100

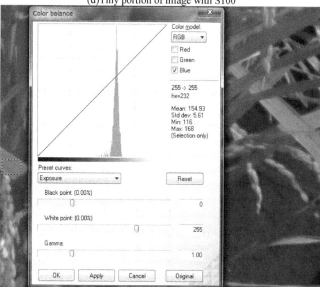

(e)Different portion of image with S100

Fig. 8. Acquired images of Hiyokumochi rice leaves with CIGS and S100 cameras

From these mean values and standard deviations, the normalized sensitivities and the normalized S/N ratios can be calculated as follows,

a) Yabukita tealeaf

CIGS: Normalized Sensitivity:$m1/m2=182.3/103.97=1.753$ Normalized S/N=$m1/s1=182.3/10.54=17.296(24.76dB)$, $m2/s2=103.97/11.97=8.686(18.78dB)$

S100: Normalized Sensitivity:$m3/m4=96.26/75.03=1.283$ Normalized S/N=$m3/s3=96.26/4.55=20.277(26.14dB)$, $m4/s4=75.03/4.19=17.907(25.06dB)$

b) Hiyokumochi rice leaf

CIGS: Normalized Sensitivity:$M1/M2=168.15/109.46=1.536$ Normalized S/N:$M1/S1=168.15/9.97=16.866(24.54dB)$, $M2/S2=109.46/12.34=8.87(18.96dB)$

S100: Normalized Sensitivity:M3/M4=154.93/107.82=1.437
Normalized S/N:M3/S3=154.93/5.61=27.617(28.82dB),
M4/S4=107.82/4.18=25.794(28.23dB)

As the results, it may say that sensitivity of the CIGS image sensor is 10 to 50 % better than that of the S100 image sensor while S/N ratio of the S100 image sensor is 50 to 100 % better than that of the CIGS image sensor.

D. NDVI Estimation Accuracy Evaluations

Measured spectral reflectance of Yabukita tealeaves and Hiyokumochi rice leaves on October 4 and 7 are shown in Fig.9 (a) and (b), respectively.

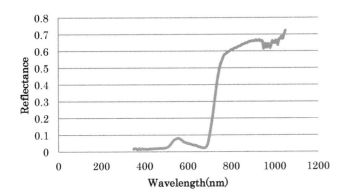

(a)Yabukita Tealeaves

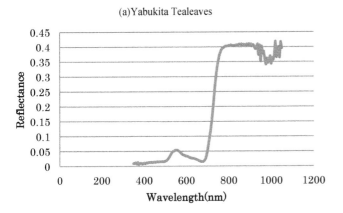

(b)Hiyokumochi Rice Leaves

Fig. 9.　Spectral reflectance of the Yabukita tealeaves and Hiyokumochi rice leaves

From the spectral reflectance and the measured S/N ratios, it is capable to predict NDVI estimation accuracy improvement by the improvement of S/N ratio as shown in Table 1. From the S/N ratio, it becomes available to calculate noise level. By considering the calculated noise, NDVI estimation accuracy can be evaluated as shown in Table 1.

In these cases, plus minus 10% of noise levels for each red and NIR wavelength regions are added in the NDVI equation. Then as shown in Table 1, -9 to 8 % of NDVI is deviated from the NDVI without 10% of noise for tealeaves while -2 to 2 % of NDVI is deviated from the NDVI without 10% of noise for rice leaves (red colored values show improvement of NDVI calculations due to 10% improvement of S/N of the CIGS image sensor in comparison to the S100 image sensor.

TABLE I.　Improvement of NDVI Estimation Accuracy by Improvement of S/N Ratio

Tealeaf	Reflectance	S/N(dB)	Noise	NDVI+	NDVI-
870nm	0.61	24.28	0.0373	0.8485	
600nm	0.05	25.04	0.0028	0.8492	0.8477
Rice leaf				0.07988	-0.0903
870nm	0.4	31.95	0.0101	0.9048	
600nm	0.02	32.58	0.00047	0.9049	0.90456
				0.01713	-0.01802

Quantum efficiency in red wavelength is 0.75 for the S100 image sensor while that for the CIGS image sensor is 0.81. On the other hand, quantum efficiency in NIR (870nm) is 0.19 for the S100 image sensor while that of the CIGS image sensor is 0.63. Therefore, S/N influence of quantum efficiency difference on NDVI calculation is as follows,

$$(CIGS): (N \pm 1/0.19 - R \pm 1/0.75)/ (N \pm 1/0.19 + R \pm 1/0.75)$$
$$(1)$$
$$(S100): (N \pm 1/0.63 - R \pm 0.81)/(N \pm 1/0.63 + R \pm 1/0.81)$$
$$(2)$$

where N and R denotes the signal level in NIR and red wavelength regions, respectively. Fig.10 shows the calculation results. When S/N ratio at red wavelength region is improved by 10%, NDVI is not so changed and improved.

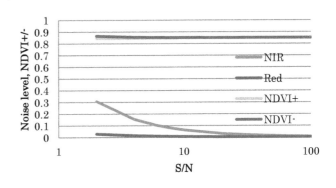

(a)10% improvement

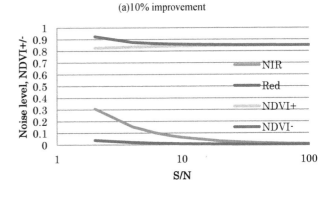

(b)50% improvement

Fig. 10. Noise level and NDVI improvement for the cases that S/N ratio at red wavelength region is improved by 10 and 50 %

Meanwhile, when S/N ratio at red wavelength region is improved by 50%, then NDVI is improved by 10%. More than that, quantum efficiency of the CIGS image sensor is 7 times and twice much higher than those of S100 image sensor in NIR and red wavelength regions, respectively. Therefore, it is expected that estimated NDVI is 10 to 50 % accurate.

IV. CONCLUSION

Effect of sensitivity improvement of Near Infrared: NIR digital cameras on Normalized Difference Vegetation Index: NDVI measurements in particular for agricultural field monitoring is clarified. Comparative study is conducted between sensitivity improved visible to near infrared camera of CuInGaSe: CIGS and the conventional camera.

Signal to Noise: S/N ratio and sensitivity are evaluated with NIR camera data which are acquired in tea farm areas and rice paddy fields. From the experimental results, it is found that S/N ratio of the conventional digital camera with NIR wavelength coverage is better than CIGS utilized image sensor while the sensitivity of the CIGS image sensor is much superior to that of the conventional camera. Also, it is found that NDVI derived from the CIGS image sensor is much better than that from the conventional camera due to the fact that the sensitivity of the CIGS image sensor in red color wavelength region is much better than that of the conventional camera.

ACKNOWLEDGEMENTS

Authors would like to thank Dr. Hideo Miyazaki of Saga Prefectural Institute of Tea and Dr. Osamu Shigetomi of Saga Prefectural Institute of Agriculture and their research staff for their efforts to conduct the experiments and valuable discussions.

REFERENCES

[1] Matsushima, O., Miyazaki, K., Takaoka, M., Maekawa, T., Sekiguchi, H., Fuchikami, T., ... & Niki, S. (2008, December). A high-sensitivity broadband image sensor using CuInGaSe 2 thin films. In Electron Image sensors Meeting, 2008. IEDM 2008. IEEE International (pp. 1-4). IEEE.

[2] K. Miyazaki, O. Matsushima, M. Moriwake, H. Takasu, S. Ishizuka, K. Sakurai, A. Yamada and S. Niki:Thin Solid Films517(2008) 7.

[3] Minoura, S., Maekawa, T., Kodera, K., Nakane, A., Niki, S., & Fujiwara, H. (2015). Optical constants of Cu (In, Ga) Se2 for arbitrary Cu and Ga compositions. Journal of Applied Physics, 117(19), 195703.

[4] Hara, T., Maekawa, T., Minoura, S., Sago, Y., Niki, S., & Fujiwara, H. (2014). Quantitative Assessment of Optical Gain and Loss in Submicron-Textured C u I n 1− x G a x S e 2 Solar Cells Fabricated by Three-Stage Coevaporation. Physical Review Applied, 2(3), 034012.

[5] A.M. Gabor, J. R. Tuttle, D. S. Albin, M. A. ContreasandR. Noufi:Appl. Phys. Lett.65(1944) 198-200.

[6] N. Kohara, T. Negami, M. Nishitani and T. Wada:Jpn. J. Appl. Phys. 34(1995) 1141-1144.

[7] K. Sakurai, R. Hunger, R. Scheer, C. A. Kaufmann, A. Yamada, T. Baba, Y. Kimura, K. Matsubara, P. Fons, H. NakanishiandS. Niki: Prog. Photovolt. Res. Appl.12(2004) 2.

[8] Kohei Arai, Method for estimation of grow index of tealeaves based on Bi-Directional reflectance function: BRDF measurements with ground based network cameras, International Journal of Applied Science, 2, 2, 52-62, 2011.

[9] Kohei Arai, Wireless sensor network for tea estate monitoring in complementally usage with Earth observation satellite imagery data based on Geographic Information System(GIS), International Journal of Ubiquitous Computing, 1, 2, 12-21, 2011.

[10] Kohei Arai, Method for estimation of total nitrogen and fiber contents in tealeaves with ground based network cameras, International Journal of Applied Science, 2, 2, 21-30, 2011.

[11] Kohei Arai, Monte Carlo ray tracing simulation for bi-directional reflectance distribution function and grow index of tealeaves estimation, International Journal of Research and Reviews on Computer Science, 2, 6, 1313-1318, 2011.

[12] K.Arai, Fractal model based tea tree and tealeaves model for estimation of well opened tealeaf ratio which is useful to determine tealeaf harvesting timing, International Journal of Research and Review on Computer Science, 3, 3, 1628-1632, 2012.

[13] Kohei Arai, Hideo Miyazaki, Masayuki Akaishi, Tea tree vitality evaluation method and appropriate harvesting timing determination method based on visible and near infrared camera data, Journal of Japan Society of Photogrammetry and Remote Sensing, 51, 1, 38-45, 2012

[14] Kohei Arai, Method for tealeaves quality estimation through measurements of degree of polarization, leaf area index, photosynthesis available radiance and normalized difference vegetation index for characterization of tealeaves, International Journal of Advanced Research in Artificial Intelligence, 2, 11, 17-24, 2013.

[15] K.Arai, Optimum band and band combination for retrieving total nitrogen, water, and fiber in tealeaves through remote sensing based on regressive analysis, International Journal of Advanced Research in Artificial Intelligence, 3, 3, 20-24, 2014.

[16] Kohei Arai, Kyushu small satellite for remote sensing (QSAT/EOS) and value added tealeaves "Eisei-no-megumi Ureshino-cha", Journal of Society for Instrument Control Engineering of Japan, 53, 11, 988-996, 2014

[17] Kohei Arai, Yoshihiko Sasaki, Shihomi Kasuya, Hideto Matsuura, Appropriate tealeaf harvest timing determination based on NIR images of tealeaves, International Journal of Information Technology and Computer Science, 7, 7, 1-7, 2015

[18] Kohei Arai, Yoshihiko Sasaki, Shihomi Kasuya, Hideo Matsuura, Appropriate harvest timing determination referring fiber content in tealeaves derived from ground based NIR camera images, International Journal of Advanced Research on Artificial Intelligence, 4, 8, 26-33, 2015.

[19] Kohei Arai and Long Lili, BRDF model for new tealeaves on old tealeaves and new tealeaves monitoring through B RDF measurement with web cameras, Abstract of the 50th COSPAR(Committee on Space Research/ICSU) Congress, A3.1-0008-08 ,992, Montreal, Canada, July, 2008

[20] Kohei Arai, Estimation method for total nitrogen and fiber contents in tealeaves as well as grow index of tealeaves and tea estate monitoring with network cameras, Proceedings of the IEEE Computer Society, Information Technology in Next Generation, ITNG, 595-600, 2009

[21] Kohei Arai, Osamu Shigetomi, Yuko Miura, Hideaki Munemoto, Rice crop field monitoring system with radio controlled helicopter based near infrared cameras through nitrogen content estimation and its distribution monitoring, International Journal of Advanced Research in Artificial Intelligence, 2, 3, 26-37, 2013.

[22] Kohei Arai, Rice crop quality evaluation method through regressive analysis between nitrogen content and near infrared reflectance of rice leaves measured from near field radio controlled helicopter, International Journal of Advanced Research in Artificial Intelligence, 2, 5, 1-6, 2013.

[23] K.Arai, Masanori Sakashita, Osamu Shigetomi, Yuko Miura, Estimation of protein content in rice crop and nitrogen content in rice leaves through regressive analysis with NDVI derived from camera mounted radio-control helicopter, International Journal of Advanced Research in Artificial Intelligence, 3, 3, 7-14, 2014.

[24] Kohei Arai, Masanori Sakashita, Osamu Shigetomi, Yuko Miura, Relation between rice crop quality (protein content) and fertilizer amount as well as rice stump density derived from helicopter data, International Journal of Advanced Research on Artificial Intelligence, 4, 7, 29-34, 2015.

[25] Kohei Arai, Masanori Sakashita, Osamu Shigetomi, Yuko Miura, Estimation of Rice Crop Quality and Harvest Amount from Helicopter Mounted NIR Camera Data and Remote Sensing Satellite Data, International Journal of Advanced Research on Artificial Intelligence, 4, 9, , 2015.

[26] Kohei Arai and Yui Nishimura, Degree of polarization model for leaves and discrimination between pea and rice types leaves for estimation of leaf area index, Abstract of the 50th COSPAR(Committee on Space Research/ICSU) Congress, A3.1-0010-08 ,991, Montreal, Canada, July, 2008

33

Packrat Parsing: A Literature Review

Manish M. Goswami
Research Scholar,
Dept. of Computer Science and
Engineering,
G.H.Raisoni College of Engineering,
Nagpur, India

Dr. M.M. Raghuwanshi,
Professor,
Department of Computer
Technology,
YCCE,
Nagpur, India

Dr. Latesh Malik,
Professor,
Dept. of CSE,
G.H.Raisoni College of Engg.,
Nagpur, India

Abstract—**Packrat parsing is recently introduced technique based upon expression grammar. This parsing approach uses memoization and ensures a guarantee of linear parse time by avoiding redundant function calls by using memoization. This paper studies the progress made in packrat parsing till date and discusses the approaches to tackle this parsing process efficiently. In addition to this, other issues such as left recursion, error reporting also seems to be associated with this type of parsing approach and discussed here the efforts attempted by researchers to address this issue. This paper, therefore, presents a state of the art review of packrat parsing so that researchers can use this for further development of technology in an efficient manner.**

Keywords—Parsing Expression Grammar; Packrat Parsing; Memoization; Backtracking

I. INTRODUCTION

Parsing consists of two processes: lexical analysis and parsing. The job of the lexical analysis is to break down the input text (string) into smaller parts, called tokens. The lexical analyzer then sends these tokens to the parser in sequence. During parsing, the parser takes the help of a grammar to decide whether to accept the input string or reject .i.e. whether it is a subset of the accepting language or not. A set of grammar rules or productions is used to define the language of grammar. Each production can then, in turn, compose of several different alternative productions. These productions guide the parser throughout the parsing to determine whether to accept the input string or to reject it. Top-down parsing is a parsing strategy that attempts left-to-right leftmost derivation (LL) for the input string. This can be achieved with prediction, backtracking or a combination of the two. LL(k) top-down parser makes its decisions based on lookahead, where the parser attempts to "look ahead" k number of symbols of the input string. A top-down parser that uses backtracking instead evaluates each production and its choices in turn; if a choice/production fails the parser backtracks on the input string and evaluates the next choice/production, if the choice/production succeeds the parser merely continues. The bottom-up parsing is a parsing method that instead attempts to perform a left-to-right rightmost derivation (LR) in reverse of the input string. Shift-reduce parsing is widely used bottom-up parsing technique. A shift-reduce parser uses two different actions during parsing: shift and reduce. A shift action takes a number of symbols from the input string and places them on a stack. The reduce action reduces the symbols on the stack based on finding a matching grammar production for the

symbols. The decisions regarding whether to shift or reduce are done based on lookahead. Several different parsing techniques have been developed over the years, both for parsing ambiguous and unambiguous grammars. One of the latest is packrat parsing [5]. Packrat parsing is based upon a top-down recursive descent parsing approach with memoization that guarantees linear parse time. Memoization employed in the packrat parsing eliminates disadvantage of conventional top-down backtracking algorithms which suffer from exponential parsing time in the worst case. This exponential runtime is due to performing redundant evaluations caused by backtracking. Packrat parsers avoid this by storing all of the evaluated results to be used for future backtracking eliminating redundant computations. This storing technique is called memoization which ensures guaranteed linear parsing time for packrat parsers. The memory consumption for conventional parse algorithms is linear to the size of the maximum recursion depth occurring during the parse. In the worst case it can be the same as the size of the input string. In packrat parsing, the memory consumption for a packrat parser is linearly proportional to the size of the input string. Packrat parsing is based upon parsing expression grammars (PEGs) which have the property of always producing unambiguous grammars. It has been proven that all LL(k) and LR(k) grammars can be rewritten into a PEG[7]. Thus, packrat parsing is able to parse all context-free grammars. In fact, it can even parse some grammars that are non-context-free [7].

Another characteristic of packrat parsing is that it is scannerless i.e. a separate lexical analyzer is not needed. In packrat parsers, they are both integrated into the same tool, as opposed to the Lex[10]/Yacc[9] approach where Lex is used for the lexical analysis and Yacc for parsing phase of the compiler.The founding work for packrat parsing was carried out in 1970 by A. Birman et. al.[4]. Birman introduced a schema called the TMG recognition schema (TS). Birman's work was later refined by A. Aho and J. Ullman et. al.[2], and renamed into generalized top-down parsing language (GTDPL). This was the first top-down parsing algorithm that was deterministic and used backtracking. Due to deterministic nature of resulting grammar they discovered that the parsing results could be saved in a table to avoid redundant computations. However, this approach was never put into practice, due to the limited amount of main memory in computers at that time [10,14]. Another characteristic of GTDPL is that it can express any LL(k) and LR(k) language, and even some non-context-free languages[2,3]. Rest of the paper consists of introduction to Parsing Expression grammar along with discussion on its properties followed by the work carried out by researchers in this area. Finally the paper focuses upon the open problems in packrat parsing and concluded with future work.

II. PARSING EXPRESSION GRAMMAR

As an extension to GTDPL and TS, Bryan Ford introduced PEGs [7]. CFGs (which were introduced mainly for usage with natural language [7]) may be ambiguous and thereby either (1) produce multiple parse tree's, which is not necessary due to only one is needed, and (2) produce a heuristically chosen one, which might not even be correct[8]. However, one of the characteristics of PEGs is that they are by definition unambiguous and thereby provides a good match for machine-oriented languages (since programming languages supposed to be deterministic). It is also shown that PEGs, similar to GTDPL and TS, can express all LL(k) and LR(k) languages, and that they can be parsed in linear time with the memoization technique [7].

A. Definitions and Operators

PEGs, as defined in [7], are a set of productions of the form A <- e where A is a nonterminal and e is a parsing expression. The parsing expressions denote how a string can be parsed. By matching a parsing expression e with a string s, e indicates success or failure. In case of a success, the matching part of s is consumed. If a failure is returned, s is matched against the next parsing expression. Together, all productions form the accepting language of the grammar. The following operators are available in PEG productions: [7,14]

Ordered choice: $e_1/.../e_n$, expression e1,...,en is evaluated in this order, to the text ahead, until one of them succeeds and possibly consumes some text. If one of the expressions succeeded, indicate success. Otherwise indicate failure and input is not consumed.

Sequence: $e_1,...,e_n$, expressions $e_1,...,e_n$, is evaluated in this order, to consume consecutive portions of the text ahead, as long as they succeed. If all succeeded, success is indicated. Otherwise indicate failure and input is not consumed.

And predicate: &e, if expression e matches the text ahead; indicate success otherwise indicate failure. Text is not consumed.

Not predicate:!e, if expression e matches the text ahead, failure is indicated; otherwise, indicate success. Do not consume any text.

One or more: e+, expression e is repeatedly applied to match the text ahead, as long as it succeeds. Matched Text is consumed if any and success is indicated if there is at least one match. Otherwise failure is indicated.

Zero or more: e*, As long as expression e matches text ahead it is applied repeatedly and consumed the matched text (if any). Always report success.

Zero or one: e?, if expression e matches the text ahead, consume it. Always report success.

Character class: [s], character ahead is consumed if it appears in the sting s and success is indicated. Otherwise

failure is indicated.

Character range: [c1- c2], if the character ahead is one from the range c1 through c2, consume it and indicate success. Otherwise indicate failure.

String:'s', if the text ahead is the string s, consume it and success is indicated. Otherwise failure is indicated.

Any character: (dot), if there is a character ahead, consume it and indicate success. Otherwise (that is, at the end of input) indicate failure.

B. Ambiguity

The unambiguousness of a PEG comes from the ordered choice property. The choices in CFGs are symmetric, i.e., the choices need not be checked in any specific order. However, the choices in a PEGs are asymmetric, i.e., the ordering of the choices determines in which order they are tested. For a PEG the first expression that matches are always chosen. This means that a production such as A<-a/aa is perfectly valid and unambiguous. However, it only accepts the language {a} on the contrary, a CFG production A->a|aa is ambiguous but accepts the language {a,aa}.

A traditional example that is hard to express with the use of CFGs is the dangling else problem. Consider the following if-statement:

if cond then if cond then statement else statement

This statement can be matched in the following two ways:

if cond then (if cond then statement else statement) if cond then (if cond then statement) else statement

If the intended matching is the former of the two (in fact, this is how it is done in the programming language C[8]) then the following PEG production is sufficient:

Stmt<- 'if' Cond 'then' Stmt 'else' Stmt

| | /'if' | Cond | 'then' | Stmt |
| /... | | | | |

Note: Matching the outermost if with the else-clause is believed not to be possible with a PEG. However, no source to either prove or contradict this statement was found.

Discovering if a CFG production is ambiguous is sometimes a non-trivial task. Similarly, choosing the ordering of two expressions in a PEG production without affecting the accepting language is not always straightforward [7].

C. Left Recursion

Left recursion is when a grammar production refers to itself as its left-most element, either directly or indirectly. Similar to the conventional LL(k) parsing methods, left recursion proves to be an issue for PEGs, and therefore a problem also for packrat parsing [10,7]. Consider the following alteration of the production:

A<-Aa / a

For a CFG, this modification is not a problem. However, for a PEG, parsing of nonterminal A requires testing that A matches, which requires testing that A matches etc, producing an infinite recursion. However, it was early discovered that a left-recursive production can always be rewritten into an equivalent right-recursive production [1], and thus making it manageable for a packrat parser. However, if there is indirect left recursion involved, the rewriting process may become fairly complex.

D. Syntatic Predicates

PEGs allow the use of the syntactic predicates! and &. Consider the following grammar production:

$$A <- !B\ C$$

Every time this production is invoked it needs to establish if the input string matches a B and if it does, signal a failure. If there is no match the original input string is compared with the nonterminal C. This ability to "look ahead" an arbitrary amount of characters combined with the selective backtracking gives packrat parsers unlimited lookahead [10, 6, 7, 13].

E. Memoization

The introduction of memoization was treated as a machine learning method in 1968 by D. Michie et. al. [11]. By storing calculated results, the machine "learned" it. The next time it was asked for the same result, the machine merely"remembered" it by looking up the previously stored result. The storage mechanism used was a stack. This makes the look-up process become linear. However, insertions of results are constant; they are merely pushed on top of the stack. In packrat parsing, the results are instead stored in a matrix or similar data structure that provides constant time look-ups (when the location of the result is already known) and insertions [10]. For every encountered production this matrix is consulted; if the production has already occurred once the result is thereby already in the matrix and merely needs to be returned; if not, the production is evaluated and the result is both inserted into the matrix and returned. Conventional recursive descent parsers that use backtracking may experience exponential parsing time in the worst case. This is due to redundant calculations of previously computed results caused by backtracking. However, memoization avoids this problem due to the fact that the result only needs to be evaluated once. This gives packrat parsing a linear parsing time in relation to the length of the input string (given that the access and insertion operations in the matrix are done in constant time). Let us look at the following trivial PEG, taken from [10]:

Additive <- Multitive '+' Additive / Multitive

Multitive <- Primary '*' Multitive / Primary

Primary <- '(' Additive ')' / Decimal

Decimal <- [0-9]

With this grammar and the input string 2*(3+4) the following memoization matrix can be produced:

The columns correspond to each position of the input string; the rows correspond to each of the parsing procedures. To make it clear that the rows are in fact procedures they have been given a prefix 'p'. Each cell contains either a number that represents how much of the input string that have been consumed by a previous call to the procedure, or the cell

pAdditive	7	-1	5	3	-1	1	-1	-1
pMultitive	7	-1	5	1	-1	1	-1	-1
pPrimary	1	-1	5	1	-1	1	-1	-1
pDecimal	1	-1	-1	1	-1	1	-1	1
input	'2'	'*'	'('	'3'	'+'	'4'	')'	$

A Matrix Containing the Parsing Results of the Input String 2*(3+4) contains a '-1' which indicates a failed evaluation. For instance, if backtracking occurs at input position four (where the number '3' is present) and procedure pAdditive is called, the parser first checks if a previous computation is stored in the storage matrix. In this case the number 3 is stored and thereby the parser immediately knows that it can advance three steps on the input string and end up at the seventh character of the input string. If the stored value is '-1' the parser knows that a previous call resulted in a failed parse and can thus avoid continuing with the procedure call and instead return a failure response to the calling function. This illustrates how redundant computations and thereby also potential exponential parsing times are avoided with the help of memoization. Calculating the whole matrix in Table1 would be unnecessary since many of the cells are not needed. The idea behind packrat parsing is not to evaluate all of the cells in the parsing matrix, only the results that are needed [10]. This effectively reduces the amount of memory space required during parsing.

F. Scannerless

Conventional parsing methods are usually divided into two phases: the lexical analysis phase and the parsing phase. The tokenization phase is called lexer, lexical analyzer, tokenizer or scanner. The lexical analysis splits the input string into tokens which hopefully corresponds to the permitted terminals of the grammar. This lexical analysis is important for conventional parsers due to their inability to refer to nonterminals for lookahead decisions [6]. Thus, the parser treats the tokens acquired from the lexical analysis as if they were terminals.

Packrat parsers can on the other hand be scannerless, which means that it requires no lexical analysis. When a scannerless packrat parser evaluates different alternatives, it can rely on already evaluated results. This effectively makes a packrat parser able to use both terminals and nonterminals during lookahead [10, 6]. Large parts of the code base of programs may consist of white spaces, comments and other irrelevant information that is not needed for the semantic analysis. A lexical analyzer can effectively disregard such information by simply opting not to create any tokens for them, thus no specific productions for white spaces and/or comments need to be included in the grammar specification of the parser. For a packrat parser that does not use a lexical analyzer, however, this is not the case. A packrat parser that uses no lexical analyzer, the white spaces and comments need to be incorporated into the productions of the grammar.

As previously mentioned, the conventional parsers treat the created tokens given by the lexical analyzer as if they were terminals, and between each token the lexical analyzer disregards any white spaces or comments. To achieve this effect for a packrat parser, a production to manage white space or comments can be created and used after each terminal symbol of the grammar. For instance, the grammar for recognizing arithmetic expression altered in the following way to be able to correctly handle white spaces inside an arithmetic expression:

Additive<- Multitive '+' Spaces Additive / Multitive

Multitive<-Primary '*' Spaces Multitive / Primary

Primary <- '(' Spaces Additive ')' Spaces /Decimal

Decimal <- [0-9] Spaces

Spaces <- ('' / ' \t' / ' \n' / ' \r')*

This grammar is now able to parse an arithmetic expression such as: 2 * (3+ 4).

III. LITERATURE SURVEY

PEGs are a recently introduced technique for describing grammars by Ford in [5] with implementation of the packrat parser. Theory is based upon strong foundations. Ford [18] showed how PRGs can be reduced to TDPLs long back in the 1970s. It was shown by Roman[24] that primitive recursive-descent parser with limited backtracking alongwith integrated lexing can be used for parsing Java 1.5 where requirement is of moderate performance. PEG is not good as a language specification tool as shown in [25]. The characteristic of a specification is that what it specifies is clearly to be seen. But this is, unfortunately, not valid for PEG. Further it gives reasonable performance when C grammar is slightly modified and also in [16] he studied that classical properties like FIRST and FOLLOW where he demonstrated those can be redefined for PEG and can be obtained even for a large grammar. FIRST and FOLLOW are used to define conditions for choice and iteration that are similar to the classical LL(1) conditions, although they have a different structure and semantics. This is different from classical properties like FIRST and FOLLOW where letters are terminal expressions, which may mean sets of letters, or strings. Checking these conditions gives an idea of useful information like the absence of reprocessing or language hiding which is helpful in locating places that need further examination. The properties FIRST and FOLLOW are kind of upper bounds, and conditions using them are sufficient, but not necessary which may results in false warnings In [17] a virtual parsing machine approach is proposed for implementing PEG which is can be applied to pattern matching. Each PEG is converted directly into its equivalent corresponding program Virtual parsing machine then using scripting language excutes the translated program. Creation and composition of new programs are done on fly.

In [7] Robert grimm parsing technique made practical for object-oriented languages. This parser generator employs simpler grammar specifications. Error reporting is also made easy by this parser generator and shown to be better performing parsers through aggressive optimizations.

In [19] cut operator was introduced to parsing expression grammars (PEGs) and when applied to PEG on which packrat parsing is based. Disadvantage is largely addressed with this approach. Concept of cut operator was borrowed from Prolog [6]. It introduces degree of controlling backtracking. An efficient packrat parser can be developed avoiding unnecessary space for memorization by inserting cut operators into a PEG grammar at appropriate places. To show effectiveness and usefulness of cut operators, a packrat parser generator called Yapp was implemented and used. It accepts Parsing Expression Grammar marked with cut operator. The experimental evaluations showed that the packrat parsers generated using grammars with cut operators inserted can parse Java programs and subset of XML files in mostly constant space, unlike conventional packrat parsers. In [12] automatic insertion of cut operators was proposed that achieves the same effect. In these methods, a statistical analysis is made of a PEG grammar by parser generator in order to find the places where the parser generator can insert cut operators without changing the meaning of the grammar and cut operators are inserted at these identified points. Definite clause grammar rules and memoing can be a possible combination for implementation of packrat parser as shown in [20] .Further it points out that packrat parsing may degrade its performance over plain recursive descent with backtracking, but memoing the recognizers of just one or two nonterminals can sometimes give reasonable performance.

Warth [21] tweaked memoization approach used by packrat parser because of which left-recursion even indirectly or mutually was supported. But some experiments were conducted out to show that this is not the case for typical uses of left recursion. In [8] Coq formalization of the theory of PEGs is proposed and with this as a foundation a formally verified parser interpreter for PEGs, TRX is developed. This gives rise to writing a PEG, together with its semantic actions, in Coq and then a parser can be extracted from it a parser with total correctness guarantees. This ensures that the parser will terminate on all kind of inputs and produces output as a parsing results correct with respect to the semantics of PEGs.

In [27] concept of elastic sliding window is used and it is based upon the observation of worst longest backtrack length. Particularly author noted that if a window in the form of small memorization table slides and covers the longest backtrack then redundant calls are avoided since the storage is sufficient enough to store all the results. Practically, it is difficult to get the longest backtrack before parsing as it is runtime entity. Here window is approximated from empirical investigation and if needed may be expanded during parsing.

[28] introduces derivative parsing with memorized approach algorithm for recognition of PEG. Main problem in this algorithm since derivative parsing attempts all possible parses concurrently is to identify which constructs exactly in the current parse tree can match against or consume the current character. This problem is solved by using concept of a backtracking generation (or generation) as a means to take into account for backtracking choices in the process of parsing. Execution of the algorithm is found to be in worst case quadratic time and cubic space. However, it is stressed in this paper that due to the limited amount of backtracking and recursion in grammars when put in practical use and input, practical performance may be nearer to linear time and constant space and requires experimental validation for the same which is in progress. Table II summarizes the comparative study of major packrat parser generators.

TABLE I.   Comparison of Various Packrat Parser Generators

Name of Parser	Language used for implementation	Working Principle	Memory Utilization	Execution Time
YAPP	Object oriented Language Java	Optimized Packrat Parser with CUT operator	Memory requirement has been cut down as cut operator reduces redundant calls	Moderate amount of parsing time required
RATS	Object oriented Language Java	Packrat Parser with some aggressive optimization	Less memory space as some aggressive optimizations used	Moderate amount of parsing time required
Mouse	Object oriented Language Java	Straightforward Recursive descent Parser implemented using PEG with no memorization support	Least amount of storage used	Amount of parsing time is highest among all the parsers as repeated backtracking is not avoided
PAPPY	Functional Programming Language Huskell	Basic Pakrat Parser with memoization	Use of significant storage space	Moderate amount of parsing time required
Nez	Object oriented Language Java	Packrat Parser implemented with elastic sliding window concept	Significant and least amount of storage is used among all packrat parser which use memoization	Moderate amount of parsing time required

IV.   Open Problems in Packrat Parsing

A. Memoization

One of the drawbacks with using packrat parsing is the additional memory consumption when compared with conventional parsing techniques. A tabular approach where the whole m*n matrix is evaluated would require $\Theta(mn)$ space, where m is the amount of nonterminals and n is the size of the input string. However, for a packrat parser, only the required cells in the matrix are evaluated, and these cells are directly related to the input string and not the nonterminals of the grammar [22]. In other words, adding more productions to the grammar may not necessarily increase the storage consumption while increasing the size of the input string will always increase the memory consumption. This makes the required size of the memoization matrix for a packrat parser be proportional only to the size of the input string, thus O(n). Even if the space consumption is upper-bounded by the input string and can therefore be written as O(n) there is a "hidden constant multiple" of n [22].This is because there can be more than n elements in the produced memoization matrix. Conventional LL(k) and LR(k) parsing algorithms only require storage space proportional to the maximum recursion depth that occurs for the given input. This causes these conventional algorithms to have the same worst case memory requirement as a packrat parser. However, a packrat parser is also lower bounded by n and this worst case behavior for LL(k) and LR(k) parsers rarely occurs [10, 22]. In fact, the maximum recursion depth is usually significantly smaller than the size of the input string [22].

B. Maintaining States

A parser for the programming languages C and C++ requires that the parser is able to maintain a global state. The reason is the nature of typedef's for the two languages. The parser needs to be able to distinguish whether the input is a typedef symbol, an object, a function or an enum constant, and change the global state accordingly if the meaning of a specific token changes. For instance, the following C code requires this feature: [7]

        T(*b)[4]
By only looking at this snippet, the parser has no way of

knowing whether T refers to a function call or a typedef name, it is context-sensitive. If it is a function call, the snippet corresponds to accessing the fifth element of the resulting call to function T with the pointer b as input parameter. If T instead is a typedef, the snippet corresponds to b pointing to an array consisting of four elements of type T.

C or C++, however, can still be parsed with a packrat parser that changes its state whenever a variable changes its type [8]. This is because of the requirement that the type of a variable needs to be declared before its usage and therefore no parsing information prior to a definition of a variable is lost. This way, a separate symbol table can be constructed during the parse which keeps track of the type for different tokens. However, for the general case of context-sensitive grammars, packrat parsers may experience exponential parsing time and memory consumption. This is because during parsing a packrat parser assumes that an already evaluated cell of the result matrix is the correct result, and that this value will not have to change. But if a state change occurs the result matrix may have to be re-evaluated to ensure a correct result during backtracking. This can potentially break the guaranteed linear time characteristic due to cells being evaluated multiple times [22].

C. Left recursion:-

Left recursion is an issue in PEG and solution is proposed for the same in [11] by Wrath et al. But this approach fails for some PEGs as shown by Tratt[37] .The solution works for a safe subset of left-recursive PEGs with this approach. By extending this algorithm where allowing left-recursive rules with definite right-recursion to work as expected. In order to parse right-recursive PEGs safely, a number of subtle issues need to be addressed, and the set of right-recursive PEGs safely parseable is less than might originally have been hoped for. Next step obviously is to extend the solutions presented in this paper to tackle with indirect left and indirect right recursion. But this may be quite challenging and may impose further restrictions on valid PEGs. Therefore, this gives rise to a open problem: are PEGs really safe for left-recursion?

D. Error Reporting:-

One important property of parser is to provide good syntax error support. For example, if user enters invalid expression and to recover from it, it is necessary for parser needs to know if it is parsing an array index or, say, an assignment. It is preferable that the parser should resynchronize by skipping ahead to a token. In the later case, it should skip to a; token since top-down parsers maintains a rule invocation stack and is able to report things like invalid expression in array index. Ambiguous context poses a problem before packrat parser since they are always speculating. In practice, recovery from syntax errors cannot be possible because they cannot detect errors until they have seen the entire input.

E. Specification Tool:-

PEG is looked at as a advanced tool for describing syntax and considered to be better than CFGs and regular expressions. The reason behind this is cited as grammar is unambiguous. But though it is an unambiguous specification of a parser, the language specified by it is whatever that parser happens to accept. But the language we want is easily seen? "Specification" means its meaning must be clear to a human reader. "Prefix capture" in PEG is not immediately visible which the main pitfall is. In addition to left recursion, detection of prefix capture is inevitable for any usable parser generator for PEG. To make sure the grammar defines the language required are there any other conditions that must be detected? This gives rise to think in terms of Parsing Expressions. This raises an argument here that BNF make it to understand easier because it better reflects the working of human mind, or because we are using it since long time?

V.   Conclusion and Future Work

In this paper, compressive review is taken about the packrat parsing introduced by Ford in 2002. It presents the state of the art about the development and research about packrat parsing based upon parsing expression Grammar. Specifically this type of parsing is presented by using memoization technique but subsequently it is this memoization which is shown to be hindrance from applying this parsing technique though it guarantee linear time of execution by avoiding redundant calls. Therefore authors focused on this problem so that wide use of this technique is feasible. In addition to this other issues such as left recursion, error reporting also seems to be associated with this type of parsing approach and discussed here about the initiatives made by researchers to address this issue. Future work may be to apply these techniques to wide variety of grammars so that authenticities of these techniques are to be endorsed.

References

[1]   Alfred V. Aho, Ravi Sethi, and Je_rey D. Ullman. Compilers: Principles, Techniques, and Tools. Addison-Wesley Longman Publishing Co., Inc., Boston, MA, USA, 1986.

[2]   Alfred V. Aho and Je_rey D. Ullman. The Theory of Parsing, Translation, and Compiling.Upper Saddle River, NJ, USA, 1972. Prentice-Hall, Inc.

[3]   A. Birman and J. D. Ullman. Parsing Algorithms with Backtrack. Journal of Information and Control, 23(1):1{34, 1973.

[4]   Alexander Birman. The TMG Recognition Schema. PhD thesis, Princeton University,Department of Electrical Engineering, Princeton, NJ, USA, 1970.

[5]   B. Ford. Packrat Parsing: Simple, Powerful, Lazy, Linear Time - Functional Pearl. In Proceedings of the ACM SIGPLAN International Conference on Functional Programming,ICFP, pages 36{47, New York, NY, USA, 2002. ACM.

[6]   Bryan Ford. Packrat Parsing: A Practical Linear-time Algorithm with Backtracking. Master'sthesis, Massachusetts Institute of Technology, Department of Electrical Engeneering and Computer Science, Cambridge, MA, USA, 2002.57

[7]   Bryan Ford. Parsing Expression Grammars: A Recognition-based Syntactic Foundation.In Proceedings of the 31st ACM SIGPLAN-SIGACT Symposium on Principles of Program-ming Languages, POPL '04, pages 111{122, New York, NY, USA, 2004. ACM.

[8]   Robert Grimm. Better Extensibility Through Modular Syntax. In Proceedings of the 2006 ACM SIGPLAN Conference on Programming Language Design and Implementation, PLDI '06, pages 38{51, New York, NY, USA, 2006. ACM.

[9]   Stephen C Johnson. Yacc: Yet Another Compiler-Compiler. Bell Laboratories Murray Hill, NJ, 1975.

[10]   M. E. Lesk and E. Schmidt. UNIX Vol. II. chapter Lex; a Lexical Analyzer Generator,pages 375{387. W. B. Saunders Company, Philadelphia, PA, USA, 1990.

[11]   D. Michie. Memo Functions and Machine Learning. Journal of Nature, 218:19{22, 1968.

[12]   Kota Mizushima, Atusi Maeda, and Yoshinori Yamaguchi. Packrat Parsers Can Handle Practical Grammars in Mostly Constant Space. In Proceedings of the 9th ACM SIGPLAN-SIGSOFT Workshop on Program Analysis for Software Tools and Engineering, PASTE '10, pages 29{36, New York, NY, USA, 2010. ACM.

[13]   Terence J. Parr and Russell W. Quong. Adding Semantic and Syntactic Predicates To LL(k): Pred-LL(k). In Proceedings of the 5th International Conference on Compiler Con-struction, CC '94, pages 263{277, London, UK, UK, 1994. Springer-Verlag.

[14]   R. R. Redziejowski. Parsing Expression Grammar as a Primitive Recursive-Descent Parser with Backtracking. Journal of Fundamenta Informaticae, 79(3-4):513{524, 2007.

[15]   R. Redziejowski. Some aspects of parsing expression grammar. In Fundamenta Informaticae 85, 1-4, pages 441–454, 2008.

[16]   R. Redziejowski. Applying classical concepts to parsing expression grammar. In Fundamenta Informaticae 93, 1-3, pages 325–336, 2009.

[17]   S. Medeiros and R. Lerusalimschy : A Parsing Machine for PEGs. In Proc. PEPM, ACM (January 2009) 105-110.

[18]   R. Grimm. Better extensibility through modular syntax. In Proceedings of the ACM SIGPLAN 2006 Conference on Programming Language Design and Implementation, pages 19–28, 2006.

[19]   K. Mizushima, A. Maeda, and Y. Yamaguchi. Improvement technique of memory efficiency of packrat parsing. In IPSJ Transaction on Programming Vol.49 No. SIG 1(PRO 35) (in Japanese), pages 117–126, 2008.

[20]   R. Becket and Z. Somogyi. Dcgs + memoing = packrat parsing but is it worth it? In Practical Aspects of Declarative Languages, January 2008.

[21]   Warth, A., Douglass, J., Millstein, T.: Packrat parsers can support left recursion. In: Proc. PEPM, ACM (January 2008) 103-110.

[22]   Warth, A., Piumarta, I.: OMeta: an object-oriented language for pattern matching. In: Proc. Dynamic Languages Symposium, ACM (2007) 11-19.

[23]   R. Redziejowski. Mouse: from parsing expressions to a practical parser. In Concurrency Specification and Programming Workshop,September 2009.

[24]   R. Redziejowski. Parsing Expression Grammar for Java 1.5.

[25]   http://www.romanredz.se/papers/PEG.Java.1.5.txt.

[26]   Adam Koprowski and Henri Binsztok. TRX: A formally veri_ed parser interpreter. In Proceedings of the 19th European Symposium on Programming (ESOP '10), volume 6012 of Lecture Notes in Computer Science, pages 345-365, 2010.

[27]   Kuramitsu, K.: Packrat Parsing with Elastic Sliding Window, Journal of Infomration Processing, Vol. 23, No. 4, pp. 505–512 (online), DOI: http://doi.org/10.2197/ipsjjip.23.505 (2015).

[28]   AaronMoss: Derivatives   of   Parsing   Expression Grammars. CoRR abs/1405.4841 (2014)

34

Application of Vague Analytical Hierarchy Process to Prioritize the Challenges Facing Public Transportation in Dar Es Salaam City-Tanzania

Erick P. Massami
Unit for Applied Mathematics
Dar es Salaam Institute of Technology
Dar es Salaam, Tanzania

Benitha M. Myamba
Department of Logistics and Transport Studies
National Institute of Transport
Dar es Salaam, Tanzania

Abstract—Transportation is a key to the economy and social welfare; it makes mobility more accessible and enhances the social and economic interactions. On the other hand, the increase of urban population, pollution and other negative impacts has directly affected the existing transportation system in Dar es Salaam City - Tanzania. As the transportation challenges cannot be overcome simultaneously due to the scarcity of financial resources, a decision support tool is needed to prioritize these challenges. In this study, a composite model of Vague Set Theory (VST) and Analytical Hierarchy Process (AHP) is applied to appraise the challenges. The Vague Analytical Hierarchy Process (VAHP) uses opinions of experts collected from a survey questionnaire. The computational results reveal the ranking in descending order of the urban transportation challenges as poor traffic management, inadequacy of proper public transit service and inadequacy of road transport infrastructure. The results also depict that the VAHP model is a useful decision support tool for transport planners, transport policy makers and other industry stakeholders.

Keywords—*Analytical Hierarchy Process; Vague Set; Urban Transportation; Transportation Challenge; Decision making*

I. INTRODUCTION

The social-economic activities in any nation involve the movement of people and freight from one place to another. Transportation, as a major logistical element, plays a crucial role in this respect. For instance, the non-availability of products and/or services at the right time and right place can lead to negative consequences such as lost sales and customer dissatisfaction. Therefore efficient and effective transportation system is crucial for ensuring social-economic development [1].

Nonetheless, Dar es Salaam, the seaborne gateway in international trade for Tanzania and most of the East and Central African countries has been facing tremendous challenges in urban public transportation resulting from growth in travel demand and vehicular population. These challenges contribute to the malfunctioning of the city's public transport system. Due to resource constraints, it is impossible to tackle the causes of these challenges simultaneously. In addition, various actors may prioritize these challenges differently. Thus, it is essential to apply multi-criteria decision making technique i.e. Vague Analytic Hierarchy Process (VAHP) to optimally prioritize the transportation challenges

in the city – Dar es Salaam. In particular, the Analytic Hierarchy Process (AHP) engineered by Saaty [2] is the most popular instrument in decision making for prioritizing alternatives. The AHP decision making approach combines deductive approach and systems approach of solving problems into one integrated logical framework and this makes it that much more effective in priority setting [3]. As it is hard for a decision maker to assess a factor/sub-factor based on a single number on a proposed scale of Judgement Number of Superiority, the application of the AHP alone could lead to a biased decision. Researchers and/or practitioners have suggested some approaches to overcome this challenge. In this study, we hybridize the AHP with Vague Soft Sets. The assessor's score on a particular factor/sub-factor based on the Vague Set Theory (VST) is given as an interval of crisp values matching with a particular linguistic term. Thus, the assessment of factors/sub-factors becomes much easier and unbiased.

This paper is structured as follows: Section II presents related studies; an overview of vague sets is presented in Section III; modeling procedure based on Vague Analytical Hierarchy Process is developed in Section IV; Section V gives application of the Vague Analytical Hierarchy Process to rank the challenges facing urban transportation in Dar es Salaam city - Tanzania. Lastly, conclusions are given in Section VI.

II. RELATED STUDIES

The challenges facing public transportation in cities have been attributed by continuous growth in urban population, private vehicle ownership, ineffective and inefficient traffic management system and the ineffectiveness of public transport services which are the causes of traffic congestion with direct consequences on social and economic activities [4]. More specifically, the immediate effects of ineffective transportation systems are the rising cost of logistic activities and business services [4]. Arasan [5] describes effective urban transportation factors as adequate road networks, traffic management systems and reliable public transport services.

Harriet *et al.* [1] argue that the existing road transport infrastructure capacity in most cities in the developing economies has reached critical level and is unable to meet the huge demand from the increasing number of vehicles. Miller [6] stipulates that underinvestment in transport infrastructure has negative effects on logistic systems and the entire social and economic activities. Indeed, the rapid growth of China and other Asian countries is stimulated by more sophisticated infrastructure to support transportation and logistics [7].

Effective public transport service is essential for ensuring effective public transportation in urban areas. Xue *et al.* [8] present a study on urban road transportation strategy focusing on the mitigation of GHG emissions and public health damage, taking Xiamen city as a case study. Geng *et al.* [9] analyse the cost effectiveness and environmental benefits of various vehicles taking Shenyang –China as a case study. He *et al.* [10] estimate the energy consumption and CO_2 emissions from China's urban passenger transportation sector up to year 2030. Fan *et al.* [11] formulates a model that minimizes hazmat risk and transportation cost subject to road closure constraints. Fatima and Kumar [12] examine the impact of a new public bus transit system in the city of Bardoli, Gujarat, India. Siedler [13] investigates under what conditions the Bus Rapid Transit (BRT) system can be regarded as the best solution to meet the challenges facing the Oslo metropolitan area.

Studies on effective traffic management are proposed by some researchers and practitioners. Malecki *et al.* [14] investigate the utilization of mobile devices to support traffic management system. Saleh *et al.* [15] propose a mechanism for vehicle routing based on the availability of updated traffic information. Schreffler *et al.* [16] suggest that effective traffic management can improve utilization of road networks at much lower cost than constructing new and expanding existing ones.

The challenges facing the road transportation sector are investigated by some researchers and practitioners. Msigwa [17] points out that the challenges of public transportation in fast-growing cities of Tanzania (e.g. Dar es Salaam) are vehicular growth, inadequacy of parking space, high frequency of accidents, transport infrastructure, and environmental and noise pollution.

The objective of this study is to prioritize the challenges confronting road based public transportation in the Dar es Salaam city-Tanzania. The proposed procedure is based on the hybrid model composed of the most popular decision making tool for ranking and/or selecting the alternatives (i.e. Analytical Hierarchy Process) and Soft Set Theory. We should note that the decision making based on the AHP alone can be biased due to the difficulty of assessing influential factors on the proposed scale of natural numbers. This biasness can be reduced or eliminated by the hybridization of the AHP with Vague Set Theory (VST). When using the VST, the assessor's score on a particular factor/sub-factor is given as an interval of values corresponding to a specific linguistic term.

III.   OVERVIEW OF VAGUE SETS

Let $S = \{a_1, a_2, \ldots, a_m\}$ be the Universe. A vague set over S is characterized by truth-membership function t_v and a false membership function f_v, $t_v: S \rightarrow [0,1], f_v: S \rightarrow [0,1]$, where $t_v(a_i)$ is a lower bound (LB) for the membership degree of a_i derived from the evidence in favour of a_i, $f_v(a_i)$ is a lower bound (LB) on the negation of a_i

derived from the evidence against a_i, and $t_v(a_i) + f_v(a_i) \leq$ 1.The membership degree of a_i in the vague set belongs to the interval $[t_v(a_i), 1 - f_v(a_i)] \in [0,1]$. The vague value $[t_v(a_i), 1 - f_v(a_i)]$ indicates that the exact membership degree $\mu_v(a_i) \in [t_v(a_i), 1 - f_v(a_i)]$, $t_v(a_i) + f_v(a_i) \leq 1$.

IV.   MODELLING PROCEDURE BASED ON VAGUE ANALYTICAL HIERARCHY PROCESS

We develop the Vague AHP model which consists of the following sequential steps:

Step 1: Establish Vague Judgement Number of Importance (i.e. Vague Assessment Scale). In this study, we adopt a scale suggested by Massami [18]. This scale has 0 as the lower bound and 1 as the upper bound. The scale has five (5) intervals each with the width of 0.2 units. The relation between linguistic operator of importance and Vague Judgement Number of Importance is listed in Table I.

Step 2: Establish Vague JudgementTable of Importance (VJTI) of the criteria/sub-criteria for an objective under consideration. This is as defined in Table II.

TABLE I.   THE RELATION BETWEEN LINGUISTIC TERM AND VAGUE JUDGEMENT NUMBER

Vague Judgement Number	[0.0, 0.2]	[0.2, 0.4]	[0.4, 0.6]	[0.6, 0.8]	[0.8, 1.0]
Importance	Very Low	Low	Moderate	High	Very High

TABLE II.   VAGUE JUDGEMENT TABLE OF IMPORTANCE FOR THE CRITERIA OR SUB-CRITERIA

Factor (F_m)	P_1	P_2	...	P_N	$\frac{1}{32}\sum_{n=1}^{N}(a_{mn} + a_{mn}')$
F_1	$[a_{11}, a_{11}']$	$[a_{12}, a_{12}']$	...	$[a_{1N}, a_{1N}']$	$\frac{1}{32}\sum_{n=1}^{N}(a_{1n} + a_{1n}')$
F_2	$[a_{21}, a_{21}']$	$[a_{22}, a_{22}']$	...	$[a_{2N}, a_{2N}']$	$\frac{1}{32}\sum_{n=1}^{N}(a_{2n} + a_{2n}')$
$\vdots$	$\vdots$	$\vdots$	...	$\vdots$	$\vdots$
F_M	$[a_{M1}, a_{M1}']$	$[a_{M2}, a_{M2}']$	...	$[a_{MN}, a_{MN}']$	$\frac{1}{32}\sum_{n=1}^{N}(a_{Mn} + a_{Mn}')$

Note: P_n: Assessor n; $\frac{1}{32}\sum_{n=1}^{N}(a_{mn} + a_{mn}')$: Arithmetic mean of crisp assessment values for factor $F_m, m \in \{1, 2, \ldots M\}$

Step 3: Construct a Crisp Judgment Matrix of Importance (CJMI), C, whose elements are found by using the following mathematical relation.

$$c_{mn} = \frac{\frac{1}{32}\sum_{n=1}^{N}(a_{mn} + a_{mn}')}{\frac{1}{32}\sum_{n=1}^{N}(a_{kn} + a_{kn}')}, \quad \forall m, k \in \{1, 2, \ldots M\} \quad (1)$$

Where $[a_{mn}, a_{mn}']$ is a soft assessment value of factor F_m by assessor n.

Application of Vague Analytical Hierarchy Process to Prioritize the Challenges Facing Public Transportation...

217

Thus, matrix C is given by

$$= \begin{bmatrix} c_{11} & c_{12} & \cdots & c_{1N} \\ c_{21} & c_{22} & \cdots & c_{2N} \\ \vdots & \vdots & \vdots & \vdots \\ c_{M1} & c_{M2} & \cdots & c_{MN} \end{bmatrix}_{M \times N} \quad (2)$$

The entry c_{mn} denotes the number that estimates the relative importance of factor F_m when it is compared with factor F_n for an objective under consideration (i.e. a level with respect to the upper level). The entry c_{mn} must satisfy the following:

a) $c_{mn} > 0$

b) $c_{mn} = \frac{1}{c_{nm}}$ (i.e. the matrix is a reciprocal one).

c) If $c_{mn} = c_{mk} \cdot c_{kn}$, $\forall m, n, k$ then the weights are consistent (i.e. transitive).

d) If $m = n$, $c_{mm} = c_{nn} = 1$. Thus, c_m and c_n are of equal importance with respect to the objective in question.

Step 4: Find a weight vector i.e. priority vector W of order P (i.e. matrix size) satisfying the condition $AW = \lambda W$, the matrix W is called an *eigenvector* and λ is an *eigenvalue*. If the Judgement Matrix is completely consistent, its maximum eigenvalue is equal to the dimension of the matrix i.e. $\lambda_{max} = P$. For matrices composed of elements made of human judgements, the condition $c_{mn} = c_{mk} \cdot c_{kn}$ hardly hold as human judgments are inconsistent to a greater or lesser degree. Consequently, $AW = \lambda_{max} W$ and $\lambda_{max} \geq P$. $(\lambda_{max} - P)$ indicates the inconsistency of the judgements. If $\lambda_{max} - P = 0$ then the judgments are completely consistent.

We define the priority vector W as

$$W = [W_{F_m}], \quad m \in \{1, 2, \ldots M\}$$

Where,

$$W_{F_m} = \cfrac{\cfrac{\sqrt[P]{(\prod_{n=1}^{N} c_{mn})}}{\sum_{m=1}^{M} \sqrt[P]{(\prod_{n=1}^{N} c_{mn})}}}{\sum_{\forall m} \left(\cfrac{\sqrt[P]{(\prod_{n=1}^{N} c_{mn})}}{\sum_{m=1}^{M} \sqrt[P]{(\prod_{n=1}^{N} c_{mn})}} \right)}, m \in \{1, 2, \ldots M\} \quad (3)$$

and $\sum_{m=1}^{M} W_{F_m} = 1$

Step 5: Find the weighted sum matrix (C_W)

$$W = \left[\sum_{m=1}^{M} W_{F_m} c_{mn} \right], \quad n \in \{1, 2, \ldots N\} \quad (4)$$

Step 6: Find the maximum eigenvalue (λ_{max})

The maximum characteristic root of the equation $AW = \lambda W$ is given by

$$\lambda_{max} = \frac{1}{P} \sum_{n=1}^{N} \left(\frac{\sum_{m=1}^{M} W_{F_m} c_{mn}}{W_{F_n}} \right), n \in \{1, 2, \ldots N = M\} \quad (5)$$

Step 7: Calculate a Consistency Index (CI)

The Consistency Index (CI) is given by

$$CI = \frac{\lambda_{max} - P}{P - 1} \quad (6)$$

Step 8: Compute a Consistency Ratio (CR)

A consistency ratio (CR) helps to check the consistency of the judgements and is calculated by dividing the Consistency Index (CI) by the Mean Random Consistency Index (R_P). We use Table III for the mean random consistency index [19].

Thus,

$$CR = \frac{CI}{R_P} \quad (7)$$

If CR = 0 then we have a completely consistency case.

If $CR < 0.1$ then we have a satisfying consistency case (i.e. the judgement matrix is considered to satisfy the unanimity).

If $CR > 0.1$ then we have a non-satisfying consistency case (i.e. the judgements are too inconsistent to be reliable). Thus, a re-examination of the pairwise judgements is recommended until a CR less than or equal to 0.1 is achieved.

TABLE III.   MEAN RANDOM CONSISTENCY INDEX FOR MATRIX DIMENSION P

P	1	2	3	4	5	6	7
R_P	0.00	0.00	0.52	0.89	1.12	1.26	1.36
P	8	9	10	11	12	13	14
R_P	1.41	1.46	1.49	1.52	1.54	1.56	1.58

Step 9: Compute Overall Priority of the 2nd Level Factor (e.g. sub- transportation challenge)

The local priorities of elements of different levels are aggregated to obtain final priorities of the sub-factors as follows:

$$FP_{F_{mn}} = W_{F_m} \cdot W_{F_{mn}} \quad (8)$$

$FP_{F_{mn}}$: The Final Priority of the 2nd Level Factor (F_{mn});
$W_{F_{mn}}$: Local Priority of F_{mn} with respect to F_m;
W_{F_m}: Local Priority of F_m with respect to the goal.

V.   RANKING OF CHALLENGES FOR URBAN TRANSPORTATION IN DAR ES SALAAM

Through reviewing the literature and consulting local experts in the transport industry we identify three main challenges and sub-challenges that have a direct bearing impact on urban transportation in Dar es Salaam City. These prime challenges and sub-challenges are shown in Table IV. The selection of the challenges is also supported by Anin *et al* [20] who argue that an effective transportation system needs to consist of the following optimally combined elements:

transport infrastructure, public transit system and traffic management system.

TABLE IV.   Transportation Challenges in Dar Es Salaam City

Public Transportation Challenge (F_m)	Sub-Public Transportation Challenge (F_{mn})
Inadequacy of road transport infrastructure (F_1)	Inadequacy of road networks with lay-bys (F_{11})
	Inadequacy of parking lot and terminals (F_{12})
	Inadequacy of traffic lights and road sign equipment (F_{13})
Inadequacy of proper public transit service (F_2)	Prevalence of vehicle emissions and noise pollution (F_{21})
	Poor ethical status of drivers and conductors (F_{22})
	Occurrence of traffic accidents (F_{23})
	Inadequacy of road transport service (F_{24})
Inefficient traffic management system (F_3)	Poor management of traffic lights and other signals (F_{31})
	Poor management of drivers and pedestrians' indiscipline on roads (F_{32})
	Poor management of vehicle breakdowns and road accidents (F_{33})

A. Priority Vector Determination

The study uses data from sixteen (16) experts who were supplied with survey questionnaires. This team consists of traffic police officers, practitioners and academia in the road transport subsector. The experts' data is used to compose the Vague Judgement Table of Importance (VJTI) from which the Crisp Judgement Matrix (CJM) is deduced.

1) Assessment of Dar es Salaam City Transportation System

The interviewed experts assessed the transportation system i.e. first level transportation challenges to give the vague judgmentTable V.

We apply equation (1) to get the elements of the crisp judgement matrix obtained by pair-wise comparison of the transportation challenges leading to ineffective urban transportation system as represented in Table VI.

TABLE V.   Vague Judgement Values from the Assessment of First Level Transportation Challenges

Assessor	F_1	F_2	F_3
P_1	[0.8, 1.0]	[0.8, 1.0]	[0.6, 0.8]
P_2	[0.8, 1.0]	[0.6, 0.8]	[0.6, 0.8]
P_3	[0.2, 0.4]	[0.4, 0.6]	[0.2, 0.4]
P_4	[0.4, 0.6]	[0.2, 0.4]	[0.2, 0.4]
P_5	[0.8, 1.0]	[0.6, 0.8]	[0.4, 0.6]
P_6	[0.0, 0.2]	[0.2, 0.4]	[0.0, 0.2]
P_7	[0.4, 0.6]	[0.4, 0.6]	[0.4, 0.6]

	F_1	F_2	F_3
P_8	[0.4, 0.6]	[0.6, 0.8]	[0.6, 0.8]
P_9	[0.4, 0.6]	[0.4, 0.6]	[0.4, 0.6]
P_{10}	[0.4, 0.6]	[0.2, 0.4]	[0.6, 0.8]
P_{11}	[0.4, 0.6]	[0.4, 0.6]	[0.4, 0.6]
P_{12}	[0.4, 0.6]	[0.2, 0.4]	[0.4, 0.6]
P_{13}	[0.4, 0.6]	[0.4, 0.6]	[0.4, 0.6]
P_{14}	[0.2, 0.4]	[0.4, 0.6]	[0.6, 0.8]
P_{15}	[0.4, 0.6]	[0.4, 0.6]	[0.4, 0.6]
P_{16}	[0.2, 0.4]	[0.2, 0.4]	[0.0, 0.2]
$\frac{1}{32}\sum_{m=1}^{16}(a_{mn}+a_{mn}')$	$\frac{41}{80}$	$\frac{1}{2}$	$\frac{39}{80}$

TABLE VI.   Crisp Judgement Matrix of Importance Due to Ineffective Urban Transportation System

Factor (F_m)	F_1	F_2	F_3	Priority Vector ($W F_m$)	Rank
F_1	1	$\frac{40}{41}$	$\frac{39}{41}$	0.3251	3
F_2	$\frac{41}{40}$	1	$\frac{39}{40}$	0.3332	2
F_3	$\frac{41}{39}$	$\frac{40}{39}$	1	0.3417	1

$$c_{11} = \frac{\frac{1}{32}\sum_{m=1}^{16}(a_{m1}+a_{m1}')}{\frac{1}{32}\sum_{m=1}^{16}(a_{m1}+a_{m1}')} = 1; c_{12} = \frac{\frac{1}{32}\sum_{m=1}^{16}(a_{m2}+a_{m2}')}{\frac{1}{32}\sum_{m=1}^{16}(a_{m1}+a_{m1}')} = \frac{40}{41} \quad ;$$

$$c_{13} = \frac{\frac{1}{32}\sum_{m=1}^{16}(a_{m3}+a_{m3}')}{\frac{1}{32}\sum_{m=1}^{16}(a_{m1}+a_{m1}')} = \frac{39}{41}$$

$$c_{21} = \frac{\frac{1}{32}\sum_{m=1}^{16}(a_{m1}+a_{m1}')}{\frac{1}{32}\sum_{m=1}^{16}(a_{m2}+a_{m2}')} = \frac{41}{40}; \ c_{22} = \frac{\frac{1}{32}\sum_{m=1}^{16}(a_{m2}+a_{m2}')}{\frac{1}{32}\sum_{m=1}^{16}(a_{m2}+a_{m2}')} = 1 \quad ;$$

$$c_{23} = \frac{\frac{1}{32}\sum_{m=1}^{16}(a_{m3}+a_{m3}')}{\frac{1}{32}\sum_{m=1}^{16}(a_{m2}+a_{m2}')} = \frac{39}{40}$$

$$c_{31} = \frac{\frac{1}{32}\sum_{m=1}^{16}(a_{m1}+a_{m1}')}{\frac{1}{32}\sum_{m=1}^{16}(a_{m3}+a_{m3}')} = \frac{41}{39}; \ c_{32} = \frac{\frac{1}{32}\sum_{m=1}^{16}(a_{m2}+a_{m2}')}{\frac{1}{32}\sum_{m=1}^{16}(a_{m3}+a_{m3}')} = \frac{40}{39} \quad ;$$

$$c_{33} = \frac{\frac{1}{32}\sum_{m=1}^{16}(a_{m3}+a_{m3}')}{\frac{1}{32}\sum_{m=1}^{16}(a_{m3}+a_{m3}')} = 1$$

We apply equation (3) to get the following elements of the weight vector.

$W_{F_1} = 0.3251$, $W_{F_2} = 0.3332$, $W_{F_3} = 0.3417$

Obviously, the matrix as represented in Table VII is completely consistent i.e.

$$c_{mn} = c_{mk}.c_{kn}, \quad \forall m,n,k \in \{1,2,3\}. \lambda_{max}$$

$$= \frac{1}{3}\sum_{n=1}^{3}\left(\frac{\sum_{m=1}^{3}W_{F_m}c_{nm}}{W_{F_n}}\right)$$

$$\lambda_{max} = \frac{1}{3}\left[\frac{\sum_{m=1}^{3}(W_{F_m}c_{1m})}{W_{F_1}} + \frac{\sum_{m=1}^{3}(W_{F_m}c_{2m})}{W_{F_2}} + \frac{\sum_{m=1}^{3}(W_{F_m}c_{3m})}{W_{F_3}}\right] = 3.0000$$

P = 3 i.e. the matrix dimension

$$CI = \frac{\lambda_{max} - P}{P - 1} = \frac{3.0000 - 3}{3 - 1} = 0$$

$$P = 3, \; R_P = 0.52$$

$CR = \frac{CI}{R_3} = \frac{0}{0.52} = 0$ which means the crisp judgement matrix of importance is completely consistent.

The priority vector in Table VI reveals that poor traffic management is ranked the first urban transportation challenge of the three first level challenges. This result is largely contributed by poor management of drivers and pedestrians' indiscipline on roads (see the weight vector in Table XII). The second urban transportation challenge at the first level is inadequacy of proper public transit service which is aggravated by poor ethical status of drivers and conductors and inadequacy of mass transit service during peak hours (see Table X). The last first level challenge is inadequacy of road transport infrastructure which is largely contributed by the inadequacy of parking lot and terminals (see Table VIII). Nonetheless, the three challenges are approximately of equal significance i.e. 34.17%, 33.32% and 32.51%. Thus, the overcoming process of the three challenges should be carried simultaneously.

2) Assessment of Transportation Challenges Leading to Inadequacy of Road Transport Infrastructure

The experts assessed the factors contributing to inadequacy of road transport infrastructure to give the soft judgement Table VII.

TABLE VII.　Vague Judgement Table Made from the Assessment of Inadequacy of Road Transport Infrastructure

Assessor	F_{11}	F_{12}	F_{13}
P_1	[0.8, 1.0]	[0.8, 1.0]	[0.6, 0.8]
P_2	[0.8, 1.0]	[0.8, 1.0]	[0.6, 0.8]
P_3	[0.0, 0.2]	[0.0, 0.2]	[0.2, 0.4]
P_4	[0.2, 0.4]	[0.2, 0.4]	[0.4, 0.6]
P_5	[0.8, 1.0]	[0.4, 0.6]	[0.2, 0.4]
P_6	[0.2, 0.4]	[0.0, 0.2]	[0.2, 0.4]
P_7	[0.2, 0.4]	[0.0, 0.2]	[0.4, 0.6]
P_8	[0.4, 0.6]	[0.2, 0.4]	[0.2, 0.4]
P_9	[0.4, 0.6]	[0.0, 0.2]	[0.8, 1.0]
P_{10}	[0.4, 0.6]	[0.0, 0.2]	[0.4, 0.6]
P_{11}	[0.4, 0.6]	[0.0, 0.2]	[0.4, 0.6]
P_{12}	[0.4, 0.6]	[0.4, 0.6]	[0.2, 0.4]
P_{13}	[0.4, 0.6]	[0.6, 0.8]	[0.6, 0.8]
P_{14}	[0.2, 0.4]	[0.2, 0.4]	[0.2, 0.4]
P_{15}	[0.4, 0.6]	[0.6, 0.8]	[0.6, 0.8]
P_{16}	[0.2, 0.4]	[0.2, 0.4]	[0.2, 0.4]
$\frac{1}{32}\sum_{m=1}^{16}(a_{mn}+a_{mn}')$	$\frac{39}{80}$	$\frac{3}{8}$	$\frac{73}{160}$

We use equation (1) to get the elements of the crisp judgement matrix represented in Table VIII.

$$c_{11} = \frac{\frac{1}{32}\sum_{m=1}^{16}(a_{m1}+a_{m1}')}{\frac{1}{32}\sum_{m=1}^{16}(a_{m1}+a_{m1}')} = 1; \; c_{12} = \frac{\frac{1}{32}\sum_{m=1}^{16}(a_{m2}+a_{m2}')}{\frac{1}{32}\sum_{m=1}^{16}(a_{m1}+a_{m1}')} = \frac{10}{13} \; ;$$

$$c_{13} = \frac{\frac{1}{32}\sum_{m=1}^{16}(a_{m3}+a_{m3}')}{\frac{1}{32}\sum_{m=1}^{16}(a_{m1}+a_{m1}')} = \frac{73}{78}$$

$$c_{21} = \frac{\frac{1}{32}\sum_{m=1}^{16}(a_{m1}+a_{m1}')}{\frac{1}{32}\sum_{m=1}^{16}(a_{m2}+a_{m2}')} = \frac{13}{10}; \; c_{22} = \frac{\frac{1}{32}\sum_{m=1}^{16}(a_{m2}+a_{m2}')}{\frac{1}{32}\sum_{m=1}^{16}(a_{m2}+a_{m2}')} = 1 \; ;$$

$$c_{23} = \frac{\frac{1}{32}\sum_{m=1}^{16}(a_{m3}+a_{m3}')}{\frac{1}{32}\sum_{m=1}^{16}(a_{m2}+a_{m2}')} = \frac{73}{60}$$

$$c_{31} = \frac{\frac{1}{32}\sum_{m=1}^{16}(a_{m1}+a_{m1}')}{\frac{1}{32}\sum_{m=1}^{16}(a_{m3}+a_{m3}')} = \frac{78}{73}; \; c_{32} = \frac{\frac{1}{32}\sum_{m=1}^{16}(a_{m2}+a_{m2}')}{\frac{1}{32}\sum_{m=1}^{16}(a_{m3}+a_{m3}')} = \frac{60}{73} \; ;$$

$$c_{33} = \frac{\frac{1}{32}\sum_{m=1}^{16}(a_{m3}+a_{m3}')}{\frac{1}{32}\sum_{m=1}^{16}(a_{m3}+a_{m3}')} = 1$$

We apply equation (3) to get the following elements of the weight vector whose set is

$$\{W_{F_{11}} = 0.2969, \quad W_{F_{12}} = 0.3859, \; W_{F_{13}} = 0.3172\}$$

Since $c_{mn} = c_{mk}.c_{kn}, \; \forall m,n,k \in \{1,2,3\}$, the matrix as represented in Table VIII is completely consistent. Thus, $\lambda_{max} = 3$, CI = 0, $R_3 = 0.52$, CR = 0.

From Table VIII, the first challenge associated with inadequacy of road transport infrastructure is shortage of supply of parking lot and terminals to meet the current demand for the facilities (38.59%). Both the Tanzania Roads Agency (TANROADS) and the Municipalities should increase their budget to finance these facilities. The second challenge is the shortage of traffic lights and road sign equipment (31.72%). This calls for the TANROADS and Municipalities to invest more in traffic lights and road sign equipment to be placed at relevant locations. The last challenge is the shortage of road networks with lay-bys (29.69%). Thus, the TANROADS and Municipalities should increase the supply of road networks to meet the current and projected demand.

TABLE VIII.　Crisp Judgement Matrix Due to Inadequacy of Road Transport Infrastructure

Factor (F_{mn})	F_{11}	F_{12}	F_{13}	Priority Vector	Rank
F_{11}	1	$\frac{10}{13}$	$\frac{73}{78}$	0.2969	3
F_{12}	$\frac{13}{10}$	1	$\frac{73}{60}$	0.3859	1
F_{13}	$\frac{78}{73}$	$\frac{60}{73}$	1	0.3172	2

3) Assessment of Transportation Challenges Leading to Public Transit Service

We use the experts' assessments on the transportation challenges associated with the inadequacy of public transit service to give the soft judgement in Table IX.

We apply equation (1) to get the elements of the crisp judgement matrix represented in Table X.

$$c_{11} = \frac{\frac{1}{32}\sum_{m=1}^{16}(a_{m1} + a_{m1}')}{\frac{1}{32}\sum_{m=1}^{16}(a_{m1} + a_{m1}')} = 1; \ c_{12} = \frac{\frac{1}{32}\sum_{m=1}^{16}(a_{m2} + a_{m2}')}{\frac{1}{32}\sum_{m=1}^{16}(a_{m1} + a_{m1}')} = \frac{17}{23} \ ;$$

$$c_{13} = \frac{\frac{1}{32}\sum_{m=1}^{16}(a_{m3} + a_{m3}')}{\frac{1}{32}\sum_{m=1}^{16}(a_{m1} + a_{m1}')} = \frac{41}{46}$$

$$c_{21} = \frac{\frac{1}{32}\sum_{m=1}^{16}(a_{m1} + a_{m1}')}{\frac{1}{32}\sum_{m=1}^{16}(a_{m2} + a_{m2}')} = \frac{23}{17}; \ c_{22} = \frac{\frac{1}{32}\sum_{m=1}^{16}(a_{m2} + a_{m2}')}{\frac{1}{32}\sum_{m=1}^{16}(a_{m2} + a_{m2}')} = 1 \ ;$$

$$c_{23} = \frac{\frac{1}{32}\sum_{m=1}^{16}(a_{m3} + a_{m3}')}{\frac{1}{32}\sum_{m=1}^{16}(a_{m2} + a_{m2}')} = \frac{41}{34}$$

$$c_{31} = \frac{\frac{1}{32}\sum_{m=1}^{16}(a_{m1} + a_{m1}')}{\frac{1}{32}\sum_{m=1}^{16}(a_{m3} + a_{m3}')} = \frac{46}{41}; \ c_{32} = \frac{\frac{1}{32}\sum_{m=1}^{16}(a_{m2} + a_{m2}')}{\frac{1}{32}\sum_{m=1}^{16}(a_{m3} + a_{m3}')} = \frac{34}{41} \ ;$$

$$c_{33} = \frac{\frac{1}{32}\sum_{m=1}^{16}(a_{m3} + a_{m3}')}{\frac{1}{32}\sum_{m=1}^{16}(a_{m3} + a_{m3}')} = 1$$

TABLE IX.   Vague Judgement Values Due to the Inadequacy of Public Transit Service

Assessor	F_{21}	F_{22}	F_{23}	F_{24}
P_1	[0.6, 0.8]	[0.8, 1.0]	[0.6, 0.8]	[0.8, 1.0]
P_2	[0.8, 1.0]	[0.8, 1.0]	[0.6, 0.8]	[0.6, 0.8]
P_3	[0.6, 0.8]	[0.2, 0.4]	[0.4, 0.6]	[0.4, 0.6]
P_4	[0.0, 0.2]	[0.2, 0.4]	[0.4, 0.6]	[0.4, 0.6]
P_5	[0.6, 0.8]	[0.4, 0.6]	[0.2, 0.4]	[0.4, 0.6]
P_6	[0.4, 0.6]	[0.0, 0.2]	[0.6, 0.8]	[0.0, 0.2]
P_7	[0.8, 1.0]	[0.2, 0.4]	[0.4, 0.6]	[0.4, 0.6]
P_8	[0.4, 0.6]	[0.6, 0.8]	[0.4, 0.6]	[0.6, 0.8]
P_9	[0.6, 0.8]	[0.2, 0.4]	[0.6, 0.8]	[0.4, 0.6]
P_{10}	[0.0, 0.2]	[0.2, 0.4]	[0.2, 0.4]	[0.2, 0.4]
P_{11}	[0.4, 0.6]	[0.4, 0.6]	[0.2, 0.4]	[0.2, 0.4]
P_{12}	[0.4, 0.6]	[0.0, 0.2]	[0.4, 0.6]	[0.2, 0.4]
P_{13}	[0.4, 0.6]	[0.4, 0.6]	[0.4, 0.6]	[0.2, 0.4]
P_{14}	[0.8, 1.0]	[0.2, 0.4]	[0.4, 0.6]	[0.2, 0.4]
P_{15}	[0.4, 0.6]	[0.4, 0.6]	[0.4, 0.6]	[0.2, 0.4]
P_{16}	[0.4, 0.6]	[0.2, 0.4]	[0.4, 0.6]	[0.2, 0.4]
$\frac{1}{32}\sum_{m=1}^{16}(a_{mn} + a_{mn}')$	$\frac{23}{40}$	$\frac{17}{40}$	$\frac{41}{80}$	$\frac{7}{16}$

$$c_{41} = \frac{\frac{1}{32}\sum_{m=1}^{16}(a_{m1} + a_{m1}')}{\frac{1}{32}\sum_{m=1}^{16}(a_{m4} + a_{m4}')} = \frac{46}{35}; \ c_{42} = \frac{\frac{1}{32}\sum_{m=1}^{16}(a_{m2} + a_{m2}')}{\frac{1}{32}\sum_{m=1}^{16}(a_{m4} + a_{m4}')} = \frac{34}{35} \ ;$$

$$c_{43} = \frac{\frac{1}{32}\sum_{m=1}^{16}(a_{m3} + a_{m3}')}{\frac{1}{32}\sum_{m=1}^{16}(a_{m4} + a_{m4}')} = \frac{41}{34}$$

$$c_{14} = \frac{\frac{1}{32}\sum_{m=1}^{16}(a_{m4} + a_{m4}')}{\frac{1}{32}\sum_{m=1}^{16}(a_{m1} + a_{m1}')} = \frac{35}{46}; \ c_{24} = \frac{\frac{1}{32}\sum_{m=1}^{16}(a_{m4} + a_{m4}')}{\frac{1}{32}\sum_{m=1}^{16}(a_{m2} + a_{m2}')} = \frac{35}{34} \ ;$$

$$c_{34} = \frac{\frac{1}{32}\sum_{m=1}^{16}(a_{m4} + a_{m4}')}{\frac{1}{32}\sum_{m=1}^{16}(a_{m3} + a_{m3}')} = \frac{35}{41}$$

$$c_{44} = \frac{\frac{1}{32}\sum_{m=1}^{16}(a_{m4} + a_{m4}')}{\frac{1}{32}\sum_{m=1}^{16}(a_{m4} + a_{m4}')} = 1$$

We apply equation (3) to get the following elements of the weight vector whose set is

$$\{W_{F_{21}} = 0.2088, W_{F_{22}} = 0.2825, W_{F_{23}} = 0.2343, W_{F_{24}} = 0.2744\}$$

Table X reveals the following. The first influential factor is poor ethical status of drivers and conductors (28.25%). This necessitates routine training in interpersonal skills and customer service to this group of stakeholders. The training could be offered by the Tanzania traffic policy department, the National Institute of Transport (NIT) or any training firm with expertise in the transport industry. The second factor is inadequacy of road transport service during peak hours (27.44%). As there is no barrier for the new entrants in this particular market i.e. for most routes of the city, the door is open for potential investors i.e. transport operators to provide public transit services. The third factor is the occurrence of traffic accidents (23.43%). As such, all three aspects contributing to road traffic accidents i.e. human element, vehicle element and road environment should be improved by the relevant parties. The last factor is the prevalence of vehicle emissions and noise pollution (20.88%). Consequently, all stakeholders including the Surface and Marine Transport Regulatory Authority (SUMATRA – Tanzania), vehicle owners and operators should take deliberate efforts to overcome the challenge.

TABLE X.   Crisp Judgement Matrix Due to the Inadequacy of Public Transit Service

Factor (F_{mn})	F_{21}	F_{22}	F_{23}	F_{24}	Priority Vector	Rank
F_{21}	1	$\frac{17}{23}$	$\frac{41}{46}$	$\frac{35}{46}$	0.2088	4
F_{22}	$\frac{23}{17}$	1	$\frac{41}{34}$	$\frac{35}{34}$	0.2825	1
F_{23}	$\frac{46}{41}$	$\frac{34}{41}$	1	$\frac{35}{41}$	0.2343	3
F_{24}	$\frac{46}{35}$	$\frac{34}{35}$	$\frac{41}{35}$	1	0.2744	2

Since $c_{mn} = c_{mk} \cdot c_{kn}, \ \forall m, n, k \in \{1, 2, 3, 4\}$, the matrix above is completely consistent. Thus, $\lambda_{max} = 4$, CI = 0, $R_4 = 0.89$, CR = 0.

4) Assessment of Transportation Challenges Related to InefficientTraffic Management System

The experts assessed the factors contributing to inefficient traffic management system to give the vague judgement as represented in Table XI.

We apply equation (1) to get the elements of the crisp judgement matrix represented in Table XII.

$$c_{11} = \frac{\frac{1}{32}\sum_{m=1}^{16}(a_{m1} + a_{m1}')}{\frac{1}{32}\sum_{m=1}^{16}(a_{m1} + a_{m1}')} = 1; \ c_{12} = \frac{\frac{1}{32}\sum_{m=1}^{16}(a_{m2} + a_{m2}')}{\frac{1}{32}\sum_{m=1}^{16}(a_{m1} + a_{m1}')} = \frac{31}{36} \ ;$$

$$c_{13} = \frac{\frac{1}{32}\sum_{m=1}^{16}(a_{m3} + a_{m3}')}{\frac{1}{32}\sum_{m=1}^{16}(a_{m1} + a_{m1}')} = \frac{17}{18}$$

$$c_{21} = \frac{\frac{1}{32}\sum_{m=1}^{16}(a_{m1}+a_{m1}{}')}{\frac{1}{32}\sum_{m=1}^{16}(a_{m2}+a_{m2}{}')} = \frac{36}{31}; \quad c_{22} = \frac{\frac{1}{32}\sum_{m=1}^{16}(a_{m2}+a_{m2}{}')}{\frac{1}{32}\sum_{m=1}^{16}(a_{m2}+a_{m2}{}')} = 1 \quad ;$$

$$c_{23} = \frac{\frac{1}{32}\sum_{m=1}^{16}(a_{m3}+a_{m3}{}')}{\frac{1}{32}\sum_{m=1}^{16}(a_{m2}+a_{m2}{}')} = \frac{34}{31}$$

TABLE XI.   VAGUE JUDGEMENT TABLE DUE TO INEFFICIENT TRAFFIC MANAGEMENT SYSTEM

Assessor	F_{31}	F_{32}	F_{33}
P_1	[0.6, 0.8]	[0.6, 0.8]	[0.4, 0.6]
P_2	[0.6, 0.8]	[0.8, 1.0]	[0.6, 0.8]
P_3	[0.2, 0.4]	[0.0, 0.2]	[0.4, 0.6]
P_4	[0.2, 0.4]	[0.2, 0.4]	[0.2, 0.4]
P_5	[0.6, 0.8]	[0.4, 0.6]	[0.0, 0.2]
P_6	[0.2, 0.4]	[0.0, 0.2]	[0.0, 0.2]
P_7	[0.0, 0.2]	[0.2, 0.4]	[0.2, 0.4]
P_8	[0.4, 0.6]	[0.2, 0.4]	[0.4, 0.6]
P_9	[0.4, 0.6]	[0.0, 0.2]	[0.4, 0.6]
P_{10}	[0.2, 0.4]	[0.2, 0.4]	[0.4, 0.6]
P_{11}	[0.4, 0.6]	[0.2, 0.4]	[0.4, 0.6]
P_{12}	[0.2, 0.4]	[0.4, 0.6]	[0.6, 0.8]
P_{13}	[0.6, 0.8]	[0.2, 0.4]	[0.4, 0.6]
P_{14}	[0.2, 0.4]	[0.8, 1.0]	[0.2, 0.4]
P_{15}	[0.6, 0.8]	[0.2, 0.4]	[0.4, 0.6]
P_{16}	[0.2, 0.4]	[0.2, 0.4]	[0.2, 0.4]
$\frac{1}{32}\sum_{m=1}^{16}(a_{mn}+a_{mn}{}')$	$\frac{9}{20}$	$\frac{31}{80}$	$\frac{17}{40}$

TABLE XII.   CRISP JUDGEMENT MATRIX DUE TO THE INEFFICIENCY OF TRAFFIC MANAGEMENT SYSTEM

Factor (F_{mn})	F_{31}	F_{32}	F_{33}	Priority Vector	Rank
F_{31}	1	$\frac{31}{36}$	$\frac{17}{18}$	0.3106	3
F_{32}	$\frac{36}{31}$	1	$\frac{34}{31}$	0.3606	1
F_{33}	$\frac{18}{17}$	$\frac{31}{34}$	1	0.3288	2

Since $c_{mn} = c_{mk} \cdot c_{kn}, \forall m, n, k \in \{1, 2, 3\}$, the matrix above is completely consistent. Thus, $\lambda_{max} = 3$, CI = 0, $R_3 = 0.52$, CR = 0.

$$c_{31} = \frac{\frac{1}{32}\sum_{m=1}^{16}(a_{m1}+a_{m1}{}')}{\frac{1}{32}\sum_{m=1}^{16}(a_{m3}+a_{m3}{}')} = \frac{18}{17}; \quad c_{32} = \frac{\frac{1}{32}\sum_{m=1}^{16}(a_{m2}+a_{m2}{}')}{\frac{1}{32}\sum_{m=1}^{16}(a_{m3}+a_{m3}{}')} = \frac{31}{34} \quad ;$$

$$c_{33} = \frac{\frac{1}{32}\sum_{m=1}^{16}(a_{m3}+a_{m3}{}')}{\frac{1}{32}\sum_{m=1}^{16}(a_{m3}+a_{m3}{}')} = 1$$

We apply equation (3) to get the following elements of the weight vector whose set is

$$\{W_{F_{31}} = 0.3106, W_{F_{32}} = 0.3606, W_{F_{33}} = 0.3288\}$$

According to experts' views, the first influential factor on inefficient traffic management system in Dar es Salaam city is poor management of drivers and pedestrians' indiscipline (36.06%). This challenge reveals that the Tanzania traffic police department is alleged to provide training to the public on road signs and safety awareness and enforce properly road traffic regulations.

The second factor is poor management of vehicle breakdowns and road accidents (32.88%). Thus, all human, vehicle and road environment aspects need to be improved to curb this problem. The last challenge is poor management of traffic lights and other signals (31.06%). This challenge exists when traffic lights and road signs are not maintained properly. The Tanzania Roads Agency (TANROADS) should carry out routine check and keep abreast of technology (technologies) which can enhance the optimisation of traffic flows.

B. Ranking of the Challenges for Urban Public Transpotationt in Dar esSalaam City

We apply equation (9) to determine the overall priority of the transportation challenges as represented in Table XIII.

TABLE XIII.   MATRIX OF PRIORITIZATION OF TRANSPORTATION CHALLENGES IN DAR ES SALAAM CITY

Factor (F_m)	Local weight (W_{F_m})	Sub-factor (F_{mn})	Local weight ($W_{F_{mn}}$)	Overall Priority $W_{F_m} \cdot W_{F_{mn}}$	Rank
F_1	0.3251	F_{11}	0.2969	$W_{F_1} \cdot W_{F_{11}}$ = 0.0965	6
		F_{12}	0.3859	$W_{F_1} \cdot W_{F_{12}}$ = 0.1255	1
		F_{13}	0.3172	$W_{F_1} \cdot W_{F_{13}}$ = 0.1031	5
F_2	0.3332	F_{21}	0.2088	$W_{F_2} \cdot W_{F_{21}}$ = 0.0696	10
		F_{22}	0.2825	$W_{F_2} \cdot W_{F_{22}}$ = 0.0941	7
		F_{23}	0.2343	$W_{F_2} \cdot W_{F_{23}}$ = 0.0781	9
		F_{24}	0.2744	$W_{F_2} \cdot W_{F_{24}}$ = 0.0914	8
F_3	0.3417	F_{31}	0.3106	$W_{F_3} \cdot W_{F_{31}}$ = 0.1061	4
		F_{32}	0.3606	$W_{F_3} \cdot W_{F_{32}}$ = 0.1232	2
		F_{33}	0.3288	$W_{F_3} \cdot W_{F_{33}}$ = 0.1124	3

Table XIII reveals the overall prioritization of the urban public transportation sub-challenges as follows: Inadequacy of parking lot and terminals; poor management of drivers and pedestrians' indiscipline; poor management of vehicle breakdowns and road accidents; poor management of traffic lights and signals; inadequacy of traffic lights and road sign equipment; inadequacy of road networks with lay-bys; poor ethical status of drivers and conductors; inadequacy of road transport service; occurrence of traffic accidents; and prevalence of vehicle emissions and noise pollution.

As there is limited financial resources attached to the management issues and investment of new facilities to overcome the proposed challenges, the government can use the ranking of the challenges for prioritization purposes. More specifically, the proposed VAHP model can be used as an investment appraisal tool for selecting the best alternative/project in other industries.

VI. CONCLUSIONS

Rapid urbanization in Dar es Salaam city – Tanzania has led to the increased demand for public transport services which in turn necessitates improved transport infrastructure, traffic management and public transit services. Limited financial resources make these transportation challenges to be prioritized and allocate funds accordingly. In this paper, we formulate a multi-criteria decision making problem and appraise the transportation challenges using the Vague Analytical Hierarchy Process (VAHP) Model. The results of ranking of the challenges in descending order are poor traffic management, inadequacy of proper public transit service and inadequacy of road transport infrastructure. The findings also reveal that the hybridization of the AHP with the Vague Sets, improve the consistency of the Crisp Judgement Matrices (CJM). Moreover, the computational results validate the VAHP model which can be applied in other research fields as a decision support tool. Our future research direction is to model a hybrid decision support tool composed of Vague Sets, Soft Sets and Rough Sets to assess rural public transportation challenges in Tanzania.

REFERENCES

[1]   T. Harriet, K. Poku, & E.K. Anin, "Logistics Inefficiencies of Urban Transportation System in Ghana," .*International Journal of Humanities and Social Science*, 3(5): 308-314, 2003.

[2]   T.L. Saaty, "*The analytic hierarchy process: planning, priority setting and resource allocation*," McGraw-Hill: New York, 1980.

[3]   S. Yedla, & R.M. Shrestha, "*Application of Analytic Hierarchy Process to Prioritize Urban Transport Options- Comparative Analysis of Group Aggregation Method,*"Indira Gandhi Institute of Development Research, Mumbai, 2007.

[4]   World Bank, "*Urban Transportation,*"Online available at www.web.worldbank.org (Accessed August 09, 2015), 2011.

[5]   T.V. Arasan, "Urban Transportation systems planning," Unpublished.

[6]   S.Miller, "*The challenges of logistics performance*," Available at http://EzineArticles.com/?expert=sammiller (Accessed August, 2012), 2012.

[7]   A.M. Rodrigues, D.J. Bowersox, & R.J. Calantone, "Estimation of global and natural logistics expenditure: 2002 data update"*Journal of Business Logistics*, 26(2): 1 – 15, 2005.

[8]   X. Xue, Y. Ren, S. Cui, J. Lin, W.Huang, & J. Zhou, "Integrated analysis of GHGs and public health damage mitigation for developing urban road transportation strategies,"*Transportation Research Part D: Transport and Environment*, 35: 84-103, 2015.

[9]   Y. Geng, Z. Ma, B. Xue, W. Ren, Z. Liu, & T. Fujita, "Co-benefit evaluation for urban public transportation-sector-a case of Shenyang, China"*Journal of Cleaner Production*, 58: 82-91, 2013.

[10] D. He, H. Liu, K. He, F. Meng, Y. Jiang, M. Wang, J. Zhou, P. Calthorpe, J. Guo, Z. Yao, & Q. Wang, "Energy use of, and CO2 emissions from China's urban passenger transportation sector-carbon mitigation scenarios upon the transportation mode choices," *Transportation Research Part A: Policy and Practice*, 53: 53-67, 2013.

[11] T. Fan, W. Chiang, & R. Russel, "Modeling urban hazmat transportation with road closure consideration,"*Transportation Research Part D: Transport and Environment*, 35: 104-115, 2015.

[12] E. Fatima, & R. Kumar, "Introduction of public bus transit in Indian cities,"*International Journal of Sustainable Built Environment*, 3(1): 27-34, 2014.

[13] C.E. Siedler, "Can Bus Rapid Transit Be a Sustainable Means of Public Transport in Fast Growing Cities? Empirical Evidence in the case of Oslo," *Transportation Research Procedia*, 1(1): 109-120, 2014.

[14] K. Malecki, S. Iwan, & K. Kijewska, "Influence of Intelligent Transportation Systems on Reduction of the Environmental Negative Impact of Urban Freight Transport Based on Szczecin Example,"*Procedia-Social and Behavioral Sciences*, 151: 215-229, 2014.

[15] Y. Saleh, A. Tofigh, & A. Zahra, "Transportation Routing in Urban Environments Using Updated Traffic Information Provided Through Vehicular Communications,"*Journal of Transportation Systems Engineering and Information Technology*, 14(5): 23-36, 2014.

[16] E. Schreffler, D. Gopalakrishna, D. Vary, D. Friedenfeld, B. Kuhn, C. Dusza, R. Klein & A. Rosas, "Integrating demand management into the transportation planning process: A desk refere3nce,"*Jounal of Institute of Transportation Engineers*, 82(1): 38-41, 2012.

[17] R.E. Msigwa, "Challenges Facing Urban Transportation in Tanzania. *Mathematical Theory and Modelling*," 3(5): 18-26, 2013.

[18] E.P. Massami, "Risk Assessment of Port Competitiveness Based on Vague Soft Sets,"*Transport Policy*, In Press.

[19] H. Shang, (ed.), "Actuarial Science: Theory and Methodology,"Beijing: Higher Education Press, 2006.

[20] E.K. Anin, J. Annan, & F.A. Otchere, "Evaluating the Role of Mass Transit and its Effect on Fuel Efficiency in the Kumasi Metropolis, Ghana,"*International Journal of Business and Social Research*, 3(3): 107-116, 2013.

35

Micro-Blog Emotion Classification Method Research Based on Cross-Media Features

Qiang Chen, Jiangfan Feng
College of computer science and technology
Chongqing University of Posts and Telecommunications
Chongqing, China

Abstract—Although the sentiment analysis of tweet has caused more and more attention in recent years, most existing methods mainly analyze the text information. Because of the fuzziness of emotion expression, users are more likely to use mixed ways, such as words and image, to express their feelings. This paper proposes a classification method of tweet emotion based on fusion feature, which combines the textual feature and the image feature effectively. Due to the sparse data and the high degree of the redundancy of the classification feature, we adopt the canonical correlation analysis to reduce dimensions of data expressed by the text emotional feature and image feature. The dimension reduction of data can maximally retains the relevance of characteristics of the text and the emotional image on the high-level semantic and utilize the support vector machine (SVM) to train and test the feature fusion data set. The results of data experiment on Sina tweet show that the algorithm can obtain better classification effect than the single feature selection methods.

Keywords—tweet sentiment classification; CCA; Text emotional; Image emotional

I. INTRODUCTION

Recently, people witness a rapid development of social networks, such as twitter, facebook, sina tweet and tencent tweet. For example, Twitter, according to reports, the registered users of twitter had outnumbered 500000000 until July 1, 2012. Tweet attracts more than 500000000 users and have about 100000000 messages everyday. Because of the increasing number of tweet users, tweet gains attention and wide space of development. Mining the emotional value of tweet has been extensively studied and applied in many fields, such as business advertisement, social network analysis, public opinion monitoring, cause analysis of accident. At present, the widespread practical technology of sentiment analysis is divided into two categories: (1) the type of adopting emotional dictionary [1]with the help of dictionary counts the amount of positive and negative emotional words in the text and then analyze the emotional polarity of the text according to the difference of positive and negative emotional words; (2)other method utilized machine learning [2]by labeling the training corpus and test corpus and use support vector machine (SVM), "maximum entropy", and KNN classifier to classify emotions. Wang et al. [3] construct a analysis system of Twitter sentiment, which can analyze the emotional tendency of the comments about the presidential election in real time; Agarwal et al. [4] characterized the polarity and part-of-speech of the words to investigate

emotion classification towards the text of tweet based on the kernel tree model and have obtained certain outcomes; Jiang [5] et al. adopt the approaches of relevant and irrelevant to the topic classify emotional polarity, and it can be divided into positive affection and negative affection. Zhiming Liu [6] et al. study three kinds of machine learning algorithms, three feature selection methods and three calculation methods of feature weight for micro blog emotion classification research, but this method fail to consider the impact of emoticon on the emotional polarity of the whole micro blog. Lixing Xie et al. [7] propose muti-strategy sentiment analysis of micro blog based on hierarchical structure which has certain improvement in classification results compared with rules of emoticons, but this method ignores the characteristics of the polarity in the micro blog text.

A new trend of micro blog message is the increase of the visual content, just as users sometimes sent status words with pictures. This is very common, especially mobile phone users, it is more convenient for them to express the mood by photographs, rather than lengthy words. Fig. 1., for example, contains two posts. The one on the right is positive, on the left is negative.

Fig. 1. Microblog messages with images. Left: It is so lucky, beautiful fireworks, Liuyang fireworks awesome .right: People reflect the air hot eyes throat uncomfortable

Obviously, the message of emotion can be expressed more clearly by images rather than words. It shows that the image is meaningful for micro blog emotion classification. To understand the transfer of visual emotion, Borth et al. [8] put forward visual emotional ontology contains emotional detector library and their methods are chiefly concentrated in the image analysis, but the accuracy of image emotional analysis relies on the accuracy of image semantic labels and machine learning. Weining Wang et al. choose line direction histogram to describe the "dynamic" and "static" types of emotional images and completed emotion classification based on the line [9]by studying the relationship of the image line and emotion; When Dai researched the component of the HSV color and the texture parameters in the gray level co-occurrence matrix , he discovered the effects of texture on five kinds of emotion [10];H W. Yoo proposed feature extraction methods combining the feature of color and texture as the core technology, thus set up a general framework of image retrieval based on emotion [11]. T.Hayashi et al., firstly, segmented an image into L*L. Then, take the average color of each image block as the color features of the image. Finally complete the mapping of image bottom-layer feature and the emotional keyword by neural network [12]; Weiwei Lu adopt CSIFT generating emotional visual words, and combine with based on global HSV color histogram ,forming graphical semantic expression types of muti-feature for the image semantics [13]; Xia Mao et al. consider the link between the fluctuations of graphics and emotional reaction and the 1 / f wave theory, then obtain the relationship between image features and the emotion information using power spectrum characteristics of the image [14]; Yali Fu investigate the unique characteristics of the wood's shape and extract the image texture feature of the wood, such as directivity, roughness, strength and contrast, completing the extraction of color features under the L * a * b color space and implementing the classification of images of wood between the "gorgeous" and the "natural" emotion [15].

The existing classification of microblog-oriented emotion primarily consider the emotion of the text. Due to the increasing number of with microblog users who sometimes express their feelings by images, so we consider the emotional characteristics of images and text comprehensively. The textual features mainly include the characteristics of emoticons, emotional dictionary and cyber language; The emotional features of images include the feature of color, texture and shape. We classify emotions of microblog with SVM. In the paper, the main contributions are: (1) consider the characteristics of textural and graphical emotion more comprehensively and classify emotions of Chinese microblog accurately; (2) select feature with Canonical correlation analysis and after dimension reduction characteristics it can maximumly keep semantic emotional correlation between the original text and image characteristics matrix. The proposed algorithm reduce the redundancy and improve the operation efficiency and accuracy.

The rest of this paper is organized as follows: In Section 2, 3 we extract the feature of the textual and image emotion. In Section 4, we reduce the dimension of the original characteristics with CCA. In Section 5,The experimental results and analysis of the new approach has been given. Finally, we summarize the main results of the paper.

II.   TEXT EMOTIONAL CHARACTERISTICS IN TWEET

We summarize the related researches and extract several emotional characteristics of micro blog text with its unique characteristics.

A.   The characteristic of emotional dictionary

HowNet (called HowNet in Chinese), established by Zhendong Dong and Qiang Dong, is one of commonsense knowledge bases of the describing object represented by the concept of English and Chinese   [16].In Hownet, each concept and what it describes is the content of a record and

each word is explained correspond to a number of concepts, the concept is a kind of word semantic description, and, the concept is called meanings, each concept explaned by several meanings original. HowNet the analysis set of emotional words in Chinese contains 3730 positive evaluation words, 3116 negative evaluation words, 836 positive emotional words and 1254 negative emotional words, view words, degree level etc.six parts. National Taiwan University Sentiment Dictionary (NTUSD), an emotional dictionary, which is organized and published by Taiwan University has traditional Chinese and simplified Chinese with 2810 positive words and 8276 negative words [17]. The paper select the simplified Chinese version as the emotional dictionary of feature extraction.

B.   The features of emoticon

Sina microblog platform provides some default emoticons, "emoticons" in crawl down in the text is in the form of being parentheses. For example " " is the expression of the corresponding text "[happy]."A message may contain multiple emoticons.

TABLE I.   ERROR RATE AND PERCENTAGE IN THE GIVEN AREAS

	number	Content
Sina weibo expression	Positive expression34	For example " " corresponds to [happy],accord to" [(.*?)]" regular expression
	Negative expressions 32	For example " ",[hum]) , (,[cry]),

C.   Network language features

With the rapid development of Internet, Internet in the process of communication also generates enormous novel online language network language. We collected 16 positive emotional network words, 24 negative emotional network language. Those words are shown in Table 2.

TABLE II.   THE PART OF NETWORK EMOTION WORDS

Positive network words	Negative network words
counterattack,Very good very powerful, GeiLi	miracle, Ceezy, too delicate to bear a blow, a tear-inducingmisery

III.   IMAGE EMOTIONAL FEATURES OF MICRO BLOG

Low-lever features such as color, texture and shape can express rich emotional information, different color, texture and shape can arouse people's different associations and emotional reaction. However, not every a low-level features are our concerns and needs, the image low-level feature selection has the vital effect on the [18] high-level affective semantic expression of the image.

A.   Color feature

Color is the visual feature of object surface, which is the basic element of the content of the image, and is one of the main perceptual features of human recognition. It can be said that in all the visual features of the image, The color is the most emotional features. Generally, The obvious color was able to attract people's attention and make people have a certain subjective feelings.

Color is represented by color space and HSV color space conform to human visual and psychological feelings, and the color feature don't be affected by illumination and observation angles, also HSV color space quantization results can also be in line with the color feature smaller dimension of visual feature. So the color feature of the image is represented by the HSV space model is appropriate when the semantic image emotion is classified. In this paper, we use the 64 bit histogram method based on the HSV color space to represent the color feature of the image. According to the visual discrimination ability, the tone H, saturation S and brightness V were divided into 16, 4 and 1 respectively. Specific quantitative formula is shown below:

$$H = 15 \begin{cases} 0 & if \ h \in (345,15] \\ 1 & if \ h \in (15,25] \\ 2 & if \ h \in (25,45] \\ 3 & if \ h \in (45,55] \\ 4 & if \ h \in (55,80] \\ 5 & if \ h \in (80,108] \\ 6 & if \ h \in (108,140] \\ 7 & if \ h \in (140,165] \\ 8 & if \ h \in (165,190] \\ 9 & if \ h \in (190,220] \\ 10 & if \ h \in (220,255] \\ 11 & if \ h \in (255,275] \\ 12 & if \ h \in (275,290] \\ 13 & if \ h \in (290,316] \\ 14 & if \ h \in (316,330] \\ 15 & if \ h \in (330,345] \end{cases} S = \begin{cases} 0 & if \ s \in (0,0.15] \\ 1 & if \ s \in (0.15,0.4] \\ 2 & if \ s \in (0.4,0.75] \\ 3 & if \ h \in (0.75,1] \end{cases} V = \begin{cases} 0 & if \ v \in (0,0.15] \\ 1 & if \ v \in (0.15,0.4] \\ 2 & if \ v \in (0.4,0.75] \\ 3 & if \ v \in (0.75,1] \end{cases}$$

(1)

Can be seen, in the three component, the human visual system sensitivity of V, S, H is increased in turn, so according to the H, S, V quantitative series, for three characteristic component , calculation of weights combination can get one dimensional feature vector L can be obtained, it can expressed by the following equation:

$$L = 16H + 4S + V \qquad (2)$$

B. Texture feature

Texture reflects the homogeneous phenomenon of visual features which existing in image, it usually performs irregular in Local but regular in whole, as the clouds, distant lakes. The coarseness, concave-convex and other characteristics of texture can evoke psychological reflection and emotional perception. Material determines the organizational structure of the object surface, so that objects of different materials would create a different psychological feeling.

Tamura texture features is proposed based on the basis of human visual characteristics of texture perception Psychology Research [19] , it divided into six components correspond to six properties of Psychology perspective texture feature, which are coarseness ,contrast, directionality, linelikeness , regularity and roughness. Since the first three components have an intuitive visual sense ,and can directly engender

psychological changes and emotional reactions. Therefore, this paper is to extract the coarseness, the contrast and the directionality of Tamura texture to represent the texture feature of images .The article [20]describes the calculation method of the three texture features.

C. Analyze of Image features in different corpus

These images contain a wealth of features and other semantic information [24], and if color feature, texture feature can distinguish micro-blogging, for the above assumptions, the paper was verified by experiment and found that the image features, texture features in different micro Bo has the ability to distinguish between apparent emotion class, micro-blogging emotion classification has a good effect.

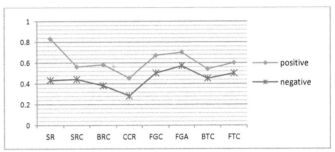

Fig. 2. Image interpretations. We demonstrate how each visual feature distributes over each category of images by the proposed model. The visual features include saturation (SR), saturation contrast (SRC), bright contrast (BRC), cool color ratio (CCR), figure-ground color difference (FGC), figure-ground area difference (FGA), background texture complexity (BTC), and foreground texture complexity (FTC)

Fig.1demonstrates how each visual feature distributes over different emotions the proposed model. For example, in the Happiness category, images tend to have high saturation and bright high contrast, which both bring out a sense of peace and joy. On the contrary, images in Sadness category tend to have lower saturation and saturation contrast, which both convey a sense of dullness and obscurity. Sad images also have low texture complexity, which gives a feeling of pithiness and coherence. The distribution during features value of two types of micro-Bo corpus is significantly different on the color and texture , these two features have a clear distinction. Then use the two features to classify with good results.

IV.   MICRO-BLOG FEATURE REDUCTION AND FUSION

Each feature of micro-blog in different degree reflects the partial information of the researched question, but features redundancy will increase the amount of calculation and increase the complexity of the research problem. Therefore , I hope through quantitative analysis, using less feature subset to express more information, feature selection method is based on the purpose. In this paper, in order to fully exploit the advantages of each feature selection method, a new feature fusion algorithm with CCA, through a combination of two types selection methods to obtain effective integration features. The classification process is as follows:

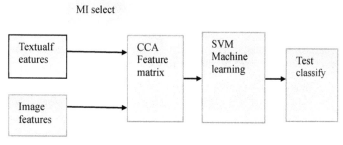

MI select

Fig. 3. classification process

Feature selection methods can be divided into two categories: supervised and unsupervised feature selection methods. Supervised feature selection commonly include: Document Frequency, Information Gain, Chi-Square Statistic, Mutual Information and other methods [21]. IG, CHI and MI is important to measure the degree of correlation of the feature item, but IG is for the category as a whole to consider the importance of a feature item. The DF methods use thresholds to select characteristics which are representative and strong distinguish ability, that use class discrimination lever to measure the importance of the features. These four methods can be used to get have a major impact on the classification of features from different levels, but its drawback is that the calculation of the metric associated with the Corpus categories marked.

The article first with DF method to select the class distinction between good features, then CCA method [22]to reduce redundancy between features and information as soon as possible to preserve the original features information , after feature dimensions ,text and image feature emotional semantic correlation is maintained .CCA always is used in cross-media retrieval [23].

Different types of multimedia data can be co-expressed similar feelings semantics, such as the "smog" image and text(The fog is too terrible 😫) data. In the statistical sense, "terrible smog" there is a correlation between the corresponding image data and text data, this section uses canonical correlation analysis, $X_{(n\times p)}$ showing concentrated extract image data from micro-blog visual emotion feature matrix, $Y_{(n\times q)}$ showing data from text concentrated extract of emotional text feature matrix.So the definition of the correlation of two variables X and Y between the fields as follows: Field variable with n samples, p-variable denoted $X_{(n\times p)}$, additional samples n, q-variable denoted $Y_{(n\times q)}$, in order to maximize to extract the main features of the correlation between X and Y as a criterion, extract from a combination of variable X in L, extracted from a combination of variable Y in M, as follows:

$$X_{(n\times p)} \xrightarrow{W_{X(p\times m)}} L_{(n\times m)};$$

$$Y_{(n\times q)} \xrightarrow{W_{Y(q\times m)}} M_{(n\times m)} (m<p, m<q) \tag{3}$$

Where W_X and W_Y are the feature vector space, also know as the canonical variables. According to equation (1) , the relevant variables with more field variables X and Y is a combination of less variables between L and M interrelated, through the distribution of values to determine the form of space-related distribution of X and Y. Instead, the value W_X, W_Y determined corresponding variables importance. So the question boils down to how to get the canonical variables, the correlation coefficient is defined under p = r(L,M), constraint in equation (3), so that the correlation coefficient is optimized.

$$\rho = r(L,M) = \frac{W_X^T C_{XY} W_Y}{\sqrt{W_X^T C_{XX} W_X W_Y^T C_{YY} W_Y}} \tag{4}$$

$$v(L) = L^T L = W_X^T X^T X W_X = 1;$$
$$v(M) = M^T M = W_Y^T Y^T Y W_Y = 1; \tag{5}$$

In formula (2), C_{XY} represent covariance matrix constructed by $X_{(n\times p)}$ and $Y_{(n\times q)}$. Combined with formula (2) and (3) using the Lagrange multiplier method can be obtained $C_{XY} C_{YY}^{-1} C_{YX} W_X = \lambda^2 C_{XX} W_X$, it will transform the optimization problem to characteristic root problem $Ax = \lambda Bx$. And further according to the formula (1) to give the smallest variables combination of $L_{(n\times m)}$ and $M_{(n\times m)}$, to maximize reveal correlation between $X_{(n\times p)}$ and $Y_{(n\times q)}$.

V. EXPERIMENT

This article is aim to do the positive and negative classification research about related text of most discussed topic on Sina micro-blog. And the data about film and television, people's life and products have been collected. Each field chooses 2000 micro-blog comments as linguistic data. And labels will be added artificially. The results are listed in Table I below:

TABLE III.   THE STATISTICAL RESULTS OF CORPUS

Topic	sample	positive	negative	neutral	sum
Film	The Secret of Grave Robber	600	464	936	2000
Society	smog	236	1250	514	2000
Product	iPhone	1124	320	556	2000
Total		1960	2034	2006	6000

A. Validation method

The text makes accuracy, recall rate, value of F and macro-averaging as the evaluation parameters. Suppose m_{righti} to be the correct amount of micro-blog text classfied to ci. m_{wrongi} is the amount of Micro blog belonging to other kinds of Micro blog wrongly classified to ci. m_{all} is the accurate amount of Micro blog this belonging sort ci.

accuracy of sort ci:

$$Precision_i = \frac{m_{righti}}{m_{righti} + m_{wrongi}} \times 100\% \quad (6)$$

recall rate of sort ci:

$$recall_i = \frac{m_{righti}}{m_{alli}} \times 100\% \quad (7)$$

Value of F of sort ci:

$$Fi = \frac{2 \times precision_i \times recall_i}{precison_i + recall_i} \times 100\% \quad (8)$$

B. The result and analysis of experiment

For each dataset of microblog, 70% of dataset is randomly selected as training set respectively. The other 30% is used as test set. Performance assessment adopts the percentage of the rightly classficated microblog in data sets, i.e,classification accuracy. 20 experiments will do for each of the two algorithms in order to write down the classification accuracy and the average accuracy of each experiment. Matlab2011a toolkit must be used to realize simulation in the system of Windows7.

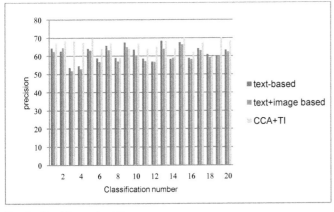

Fig. 4. Precision contrast figure

Above, the horizontal axis represents classification number, a total of 20 times, vertical axis represents classification accuracy. Three methods of classification method respectively represent the text, the text - image method, CCA + TI classification method. Analysis of the results can be seen that the average accuracy between the text method and text- image classification algorithm is similar, although the introduction of image emotional characteristics, but the feature attribute redundancy and feature dimension increasing, make accuracy

rate does not improve. By using CCA method to reduce the emotional characteristics dimension, getting maximum correlation characteristic matrix, and then classified. By comparing the accuracy can be improved by 4%. Illustrate after application of the method, statistical correlation can be maintained after dimension reduction between the text emotional characteristics and image emotional characteristics. Emotional characteristics further reduce redundancy, with improved accuracy.

VI. CONCLUSION

To solve the sparse problem of Microblog -Text emotional characteristics ，we propose a novel approach for Microblog sentiment analysis based on CCA cross-media model (CBM). Previous researches always focus on the text emotion ，neglecting the effect of images emotion with growth of image in the message. Considering more and more people express their feelings through images in Microblog, thus we take images into account in our model. There are three advantages of our method. First, the sentiment of the messages is analyzed by combining the images and texts. Second, this model gives a unified representation of texts and images for cross-media sentiment analysis with CCA method. And the Finally, we use Logistic Regression to relax conditional independence assumption. Experiment results illustrate the effectiveness of our model, with classification accuracy 4% higher than the text-based method.

ACKNOWLEDGMENT

The work is funded by the Natural Science Foundation Project of Chongqing cstc2014 jcyjA00027.The author authors are also grateful to cstc.

REFERENCES

[1] LunWei Ku， TungHo Wu， LiYing Lee， et al. Construction of an evaluation corpus for opinion extraction ［C］ ‖ NTCIR － 5 Japan. 2005: 513-520

[2] DasguptaS， NgV. Mine the easy classify the hard: S semi-supervised approach to automatic sentiment: classification ［ C］ ‖ ACL ' 09: 701 － 709

[3] Wang Hao， Can Dogan， Abe Kazemzadeh. A system for real-time Twitter sentiment analysis of 2012 U. S. presidential election cycle ［ C］ ‖Proceedings of the ACL 2012 SystemDemonstrations， 2012: 115 － 120

[4] Apoorv Agarwal， Xie Boyi， Ilia Vovsha. Sentiment analysis of Twitter data ［ C ］ ‖Proceedings of the Workshop on Languages inSocial Media， 2011:30-38

[5] Jiang Long ， Yu Mo ， Zhou Ming. Targetdependent Twitter sentiment classification ［C］ ‖Proceedings of the 49th Annual Meeting of the Association for Computational Linguistics:Human Language Technologies， 2011:151-160

[6] LIU Zhiming, LIU Lu. Empirical study of sentiment classification for Chinese microblog based on machine learning. Computer Engineering and Applications, 2012, 48（1）: 1-4.

[7] Xing Lixing， Zhou Ming， Sun Maosong. Hierarchical Structure Based Hybrid Approach to Sentiment Analysis of Chinese Micro Blog and Its feature Extraction ［J］ . Journal of Chinese information processing.， 2012, 26(1): 73 － 83

[8] D. Borth, R. Ji. Large-scale visual sentiment ontology and detectors using adjective noun pairs. Proc. of the 21st ACM international conference on Multimedia, 2013, 223-232.

[9] WANG Weining, YU Yinglin, ZHANG Jianchao. Image Emotional Semantic Classification based on Line Direction Histogram [J].

Computer Engineering, 2005, 31(11): 7-9.

[10] Yoo H W, Jung S H, Jang D S, et al. Extraction of major object features using VQ clustering for content-based image retrieval[J]. Pattern Recognition, 2002, 35(5): 1115-1126.

[11] Hayashi T, Hagiwara M. An image retrieval system to estimate impression words from images using a neural network[C]// Computational Cybernetics and Simulation, 1997 IEEE International Conference on. IEEE, 1997, 1: 150-155.

[12] Lv Weiwei. Research on Image Classification Algorithm based on emotion [D]. Beijing Jiaotong University, 2012.

[13] 17 MAO Xia, DING Yu-kuan, Muta Itsuya. Analysis of Affective Characteristics and Evaluation on Harmonious Feeling of Image [J]. ACTA ELECTRONICASINICA, 2009, (z1): 1923-1927.

[14] Fu Yali , Guo Na, Zhang Jiawei . Image kansei feature classification based on color and texture features [J].Journal of Zhengzhou university of light industry (natural science), 2009, 23(6): 118-121.

[15] Lu Quan, Ding Heng. Review of research on image retrieval based on emotion [J]. Information theory and Practice, 2013, 36(2): 119-124.

[16] Dong Zhendong, Dong Qiang. [DB/0L]. HowNet is introduced[2013-7-20]. http://www. kcenagc. com.

[17] Chen Xiaodong .A Thesis Submitted in Full Fulfillment of the Requirements for the Degree of the Master of Engineering:[D].HuBei province:Huazhong University of Science and Technology ,2012.

[18] Liu Zengrong ,Yu Xueli ,Li Zhi . Idengtification of Image Emotional Semantic based on Feature Fusion [J]. Journal of Taiyuan University of Technology, 2012, 43(5): 553-557.

[19] Tamura H, Mori S, Yamawaki T. Textural features corresponding to visual perception[J]. Systems, Man and Cybernetics, IEEE Transactions on, 1978, 8(6): 460-473.

[20] YU Jin. Content based visual information retrieval[M]. Science Press, 2003.

[21] Yang YM ,Pedersen JO . A Comparative Study on Feature Selection in Text Categorization[C]/ / Proceedings of the ICML,1997:412-420

[22] H.Hotelling. Relations between Two Sets of Variates .Biometrika , PP. 321 — 377 , 1936.

[23] Wu F, Zhang H, Zhuang Y. Learning Semantic Correlations for Cross-Media Retrieval [A]. Proceeding of 2006 IEEE International Conference on Image Processing [C], 1465-1468, Atlanta, 2006.

[24] Yang, Y., Jia, J., Zhang, S., et al.: How Do Your Friends on Social Media Disclose Your Emotions. In: Proc. AAAI, 14, pp. 1–7 (2014)

36

The True Nature of Numbers is that they are a Group Associated with the Painlevé Property

Mathematical life structures description hypothesis and notation

Yoshimi Shimokawa
Kiiro Book Store LLC.
Tokyo, Japan

Abstract—The true nature of numbers is that they are a group associated with the moving Painlevé property. In the past, humans considered numbers to be individual entities. The two-point selective ability of living beings can be considered to have established today's mathematical logic. We can consider mathematical logic to have been formed by the minimum condition of a consistent group (There is no discrepancies group) resulting from a light spectrum being transmitted to or reflected on a three-dimensional closed manifold. In other words, examining the characteristics of the light spectrum enables an understanding of the characteristics of human perception, and an understanding of the characteristics of the numbers perceived by human perception. Based on the understanding of these characteristics, humans think about perceiving mathematical logic. What was unfortunate in the past about the logical constructions that started with Gödel, is that they sought for the concept of numbers amid mathematical logic. Cellular automatons have advanced this approach by physicalizing it, and Conway revealed discrepancies by creating actual machines [12].The decimal system, in itself, is simply a notation tool and merely a notation. Owing to the structure of base conversion, it is convenient to use decimals in two-dimensional notations. However, decimals cannot be used in three-dimensional notations; instead, circular numbers are generated. This can be considered the result of using "0," although the concept of writing out a three-dimensional notation consistently should be created separately. With no concept of null ($\aleph$) in the " Set theory and the continuum hypothesis"[5], that the perception of the human body is simply maximizing the margin of classification boundaries in a SVM problem [3]. How to consider maximizing the margin of classification boundaries in perceiving the problem could be thought of as the theme for the theory of numbers. Current, by "The International System of Units (SI)" has been defined, A unit got association that the unified. By using the unit, it will be elucidated also algorithms of the molecular structure in the organism. We need a third algorithm. It is the algorithm of the molecular structure organism, that is"the number of recognition" and "the number of physical"Is an algorithm to unify. In other words, temporary has been described structure in this paper, a common algorithm that is "the number of physical" and"the number of recognition". Once again, it was discussed the number of nature, for that algorithm. In the future, to make a key operation using this algorithm. I wish to apply to display notation the development of new devices.

Keywords—cognitive science; pattern recognition; scale invariance; Painlevé Property

I. INTRODUCTION

Preconditions and Assumptions

If we were to assume that the two-point selective ability has established the present day mathematical logic (the foundation for classification boundaries), it is necessary to understand its characteristics. First, I considered Conway's "puffer train" as a two-point classification boundary figure structure. It has a main body portion that moves independently at half the "speed of light" without interference from fragments, and two "spaceships" that attain two-point discrimination. For considering a nontrivial self-renewal process, a binary method with two-point discrimination provides the required confidence level. When introducing the physical settings on a computer, this is the resulting appearance because the notations on the display are limited to two dimensions.

Next, It is considered why organisms form clod-like continuous shapes from chaotic locations. It is considered examples (of such growth) in nature as well as of organisms that grow in the above mentioned way in nature. Then focused on portions of organisms that remain motionless as objects instead of as growth, on the opposite axis of discrimination. Through the induction of epitope light, plants ultimately produce fruits that can be counted—one, two, three, and so on. Fruits are considered complete after separation from its main body. In other words, the perception of "separation" in the boundary problem is thought of for organisms as being conducted by epitope induction, some other condition (algorithms) for displays. Then examined the boundary problem for this object formation and numbers, and then created 3D figures illustrating the method by which those shapes can be transformed from "Concept 1," which is explained below. By using a three-dimensional multi-connected closed manifold, "the difficulty of classifications" is interpreted along with the state of changes.

Question the continuum hypothesis initial setting

The claim of this research questions the initial settings of the continuum hypothesis. My claim is that numbers are "a simple concept arising from the human awareness of two-point discrimination, and its symmetrical transformation patterns" and that the concepts of the natural numbers 1, 2, 3, 4, 5, 6, 7, 8, and 9 are an expression of how this two-point discrimination is moved. To avoid confusion, the concepts of natural numbers will be referred to below as "Concept 1," "Concept 2," "Concept 3," and so on. Cantor and Gödel focused on cardinality as well as ordinal numbers, but my approach goes a step further, taking the view that cardinality is perceived by the human body, which is created by antigenic epitope induction.

Scope of Analysis and Method

The analysis covers three areas.

1) Organism model analysis
2) Mechanical model analysis
3) Conceptual model analysis
In other words

1) classification boundary epitope induction
2) classification boundary algorithm
3) classification boundary cognition
In other words

1) Analysis of the organism exponentiation conditions save deformation
2) Analysis of the ends of the puffer train and the two spaceships described in The Recursive Universe
3) Analysis of tori (three-dimensional multi-connected closed manifolds) that represent the transformation of Concept 1

To analyze the binary numerical machine minimum model for Conway's puffer train described in The Recursive Universe (Item 2)[12], Be inferred the property of life (in other words, the independence that is characteristic of life), from a different perspective by making a comparison to the conditions of a closed manifold. To analyze the organism model (Item 1), Be inferred numerical formulas from epitope induction, examining "copying" numbers and "control or stop" numbers that can be linked to the binary system. In other words, cell division was interpreted as light induction using copying, and the transformations of Concept 1 (Item 3) were analyzed from the state of perception in which understanding changes when position changes. In other words, the manifold of Concept 3 was displayed.

The minimum figure of perception for considering the logic of numbers is the binary machine minimum model described in The Recursive Universe (Item 2) as the logical theoretical framework. It is considered co-dimensional problems that generate discrepancies in mathematical logic to be inseparable from the structure of perception. It analyzed the structure of the location of visual perception using an organism model, and viewed it along with its constituent equations. Then surmised other examples of this kind of equation being used for other organisms. Then, cognitive recognizes the "concept 1", also, how to recognize a mistake as "concept 2" and "concept 3", I shown in the figure. It was constructed a simple figure with the whether 3D can be deformed in any way from the "Concept 1". Using this 3D multi-linked closed manifold, changes were observed regarding "The difficulty of classification" at the same time.

Comparative analysis targets three, respectively

1) physical status quo analysis
2) physical state compression model analysis
3) cognitive status analysis That is the meaning.

II. ORGANISM MODEL ANALYSIS

A. Number of Visual Perception Iris Structures

First, I used mathematical logic to examine the two-point discrimination structure of two eyeballs. It is considered discrimination to be the margin maximization of a classification boundary in an SVM, and searched for its discrepancies. Vision (i.e., light-gathering) done by organic perception is structured with the structure of the iris (the higher-order equations for "3," "5," and "6"). However, when viewed through a vector analysis of a three-dimensional space, this structure resembles a Seifert surface structure with topology classification E6. It is a 52-dimensional real Lie group composed of four automorphic mappings over four rings. It is a space given by a closed curve C, meaning that it can be created without S and L touching. This is the base of perceptual cardinality. Seifert surfaces are composed of areas with four boundaries and linking numbers. From there, strokes are added to two locations and by folding over to the inner side, three rings overlap on the inside[7]. This is a knot structure called a (p, q)-torus knot, and in two dimensions, it is also a 3 + 1 threshold discrimination structure. Spaces that resemble the horizontal figure eight in two dimensions are two-threshold discriminations, but they can be made consistent (no contact between discrimination spaces S and L) when they have a butterfly stroke structure in three dimensions. In other words, they can be considered a 1-threshold discrimination in three dimensions. This space is a simply connected 3-manifold floating in a temporary 3-sheeted covering space at the center of a simply connected 3 dimensional closed manifold. By using these four homeomorphisms, adjustments are perceived, and far-point perceptions can be surmised.

Fig. 1.   Seifert space, in four of areas, have been constructed. Even when it is overlapped with the complexity, even when just break up into three regions and one of the areas, Linking number of them does not change

From the opposite perspective, even for the same two-point discrimination, a two-point discrimination of an included area is structured from the overlap of three portions. In other words, vision is defined in terms of a simply connected 3-manifold and two-object discrimination, but these can be considered as an E3 multi connected three-dimensional closed manifold. Doing so secures a spot in only one region, enabling a stable and consistent discrimination in the interior.

Organisms perceive the world using the "simply connected three-dimensional closed manifold in a temporary 3-sheeted covering space" as the source of reflection. In other words, it is possible that conditions omitted from this intricate structure are not perceived. To put it differently, the perception used by organisms is one for which this structure is consistent.

From the discussion above, the human visual perception can be considered to be able to discriminate 9 regions (3 points, 3 locations) using the continuum of concentrated light.

B. Number of Epitope Inductions Composing Plants and Animals

Strictly speaking, a two-point discrimination can be considered two special locations in a three-point discrimination of a convex function. Although there is an origin serving as a harness that moves the two locations, in the case of the structure of the spectrum and iris, it indicates the light-gathering act from the outside.

Pursuing this discrepancy reveals the cardinality of numbers and the discrepant portion of the decimal system. It is considered the origin of perception by organisms (which begins with the two-point discrimination) to be Concept 2 and Concept 3, and the final stage of perception by organisms to be Concept 5. The concept currently called "3" can be broken down into "2 + 1," with the "1" portion of "2 + 1" being an adhering item. In other words, It is considered generating Concept 4 to have a common harness. Furthermore, Concept 3 has self-homeomorphism, and Concept 6 is the result of moving unchanged to a higher order and becoming three-dimensional. It is considered the (n + 1) pattern that moves to a higher level and has an external origin acting as a harness to be Concept 7. If considered in terms of the algebraic method, it is what becomes the characteristic function.

Among the Painlevé equations, the third-order equations are the same as the equations representing the structure of the iris, which is the source of visual information. These Painlevé property have four singularities: a moving pole, infinity point, point 0, and point 1. Among these four singularities, the moving pole is the source of the relativity theory and the infinity point is the source of the theory of cosmological inflation. The shape and characteristics of the universe are explained using the characteristics of light. For the dispersion point/separation point directly before point 0/point 1, on the other hand, Dr. Barbara McClintock used the characteristics of light to explain the shapes and characteristics of terrestrial plants [1]. In terms of separation/dispersion, the location affected by the real array is the antigenic determinant (epitope). In other words, the iris perceives both the far point and the dispersion/separation point.

When explained in terms of a garlic that is a pentagon and okra, antigenic determinants that react to light correspond structurally to the origin of the Hasse diagram, and can be considered radicals that manipulate genetic information through the action of light. In terms of signal logic, they correspond to a harness. The types with two axes passing through them may be describable by second-order equations, and types with three axes by third-order equations.

Now It will discuss the shapes of plants. A normal garlic bulb (Photo 1-1) is formed by a Concept 5 epitope, while a garlic bulb with a shifted focal point (Photo 1-2) is formed by a "5 + 9" epitope. An okra pod is formed in an inverted manner by an epitope of Concept 5, but the internal structure of the pod is formed by a seed using 14 epitopes in the inverted cavity. The cross-section of a normal garlic bulb (Photo 1-3) has a mathematical logic in which a complex-plane curve circles while spinning toward the center, with the starting and ending points aligning. In a garlic bulb with a shifted focal point, the epitope formation of Concept 5 becomes shifted such that the end point of the first "lap" does not overlap, causing the H_2O ions (a constituent of the formation) to reverse its polarity and make two "laps" with "5 × 2" − 1. In other words, Concept 1 results in this case because Concept 5 of a normal garlic bulb (which is the "one before" in a quinary calculation) is interpreted as Concept 1 in the epitope. The second "lap" of the shape formation can be considered a covering space in the numerical calculation.

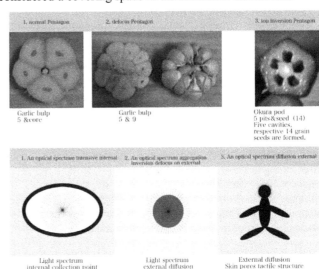

photo1 : 1. normal Pentagon 2. defocus Pentagon 3. ion inversion Pentagon

Fig. 2. Of visual and tactile, perception condensing reversal

Each of the pores along the human skin has individual epitopes, and is sealed by pentagon-shaped molecules. From there, two "tails" extend from each pore, leading to the foliation structures under the skin. For the eyeballs previously mentioned, visual acuity is determined by two-point discrimination with two eyeballs, but the discrimination with human skin may differ according to the day/night lighting and temperature differences. In other words, temperature differences may be used for the detection of the maximization of the margin of classification boundaries in an SVM problem with cardinality[3]. The light structure from the spherical surface used by vision can be considered a Gaussian mapping on the skin in the case of touch, and used in touch perception. Skin cells are replaced in 28-day cycles (peaking after 14 days). Since the human body is also an aggregate formed using the epitopes of Concept 5, it can be inferred that the skin surface (sealed with the epitopes of Concept 5) uses the same identification number as okra (Concept 14) for replacements.

C. Reaction-diffusion Path Estimation and Number of Equations

The panda's coat of fur is a special example of predictable transmission. The panda has a diet of bamboo grass with strengthened epitope paths, and has a coat of fur identified by a distinctive two-color pattern. Juvenile pandas that do not eat bamboo grass do not have the distinctive two-color identification pattern. Among humans, the birthmark known as the Mongolian spot that is prevalent among those of Mongolian descent may be due to an accumulation of B12 cobalamin (which contains a cobalt molecule at its center) at the final portion during the final stage of ecological formation from epitope transmission. The birthmark disappears when the half-life of cobalt (3 to 5 years) has elapsed. The mathematical model of the transmission path of these epitopes simulates a signal network of a group of cells.Pattern of these plants and animals are thought to possible written in mock function, which is a Exponentiation conditions save deformation.

Some examples of epitope inductions with reversed ions are as follows. Among plants, there is the example of lotus petals, which are formed as 16 "2^{2^n}" petals with the third-order equation "n^{n^n}." Epitope induction No. 17 mays occur in the hollow stalk created from negative ions. When the shape of the lotus root is "n^{n-1}" "3^{3-1}", it is created by the second-order equation for "9," which may be because the polarity of the ions in the underwater portion of the lotus root is reversed. Another example is the second molar tooth, which has the same structure as the lotus. The visible portion is composed of four mountain shapes, and the ion-inverted root portion has three prongs. The first-order equation ($n + 1$) that represents Concept 17, can be considered one of the convergence epitopes in the human body. Object programs that represent computer units (binary) can all be the result of the epitopes having a heteroclitic-loop reaction-diffusion path.

III. COMPUTER DISPLAY ANALYSIS: NUMBERS OF ENDS OF THE PUFFER TRAIN AND TWO SPACESHIPS

The ends of the puffer train and the two spaceships described in The Recursive Universe are paired with each other, and are related in three dimensions like points of contact in a Seifert surface. A non-cyclical region with a pulsar and the leading edge of the train are at the top and bottom of both edges, respectively. This arrangement can be considered to be merely the result of planarization of the left/right orientation of molecular structures existing in higher-dimensional worlds, which itself is a polytope of compressed notation.

Ultimately, it is the moving objects that are "fixed," and the puffer train has a bottom and front. In other words, the puffer train has directionality, and the existence of this directionality is considered the true nature of movement. Having directionality implies that symmetry is spontaneously broken. This spontaneous breaking of symmetry is the "movement" that gives a region its independence from the background, or what could be considered "life-like."

The relationship between the main body portion that moves independently at half the speed of light without interference from fragments and the two spaceships that attain two-point discrimination can be expressed by a tau-function relationship represented by three objects aligned in a straight line. When considered as points in a 5-dimensional projected space, they become consistent. The packaged structure is seen in molecules such as collagen. When considered only in terms of mathematical logic, it is the result of a triangular pyramid calculation formula consistently describing self-homeomorphism. For the six tau functions[9], the three dependent variables of the symmetrical forms correspond to the three f variables.

In other words, the fixation of objects is a temporary fastening supported by directionality in at least two directions. It is balance that appears to be stopped, and this is the true nature of "stoppage." To put it differently, the true nature of a three-dimensional closed manifold is supported by equations of at least the third order, and it is a balanced, closed object bearing the potential for movement. The appearance varies according to the dimensions in existence, and it is the portion thought to have a covering space in quantum physics. It is considered interpret this fixed balance as Concept 1.

Both ends of Conway's puffer train and the two spaceships described in The Recursive Universe are a pseudo-open space with a barrier and are closed by two dimensions. However, by making their length massive, they become a simulation of infinity. What this signifies is a pseudo-open model enclosed by straight lines, but this could be a length calculated as a curve. This could also be a pseudo-model for space that humans once perceived to be opening or continually expanding.

New solutions can also be obtained for polyhedral objects by using curves on the surfaces of the Goldberg solid body. The higher-order equations "3," "5," and "6" are used for these solid bodies. When these facts are linked objectively, the logical shapes that form nature can be considered to be dependent on curves. The recognition that straight lines are special cases of curves may further advance the potential of science. "3" can be considered the minimum figure of self-homeomorphism, "5" the minimum figure of the condition of stopping with bridging [8][2], and "6" the minimum figure of dimension-raising using two self-homeomorphisms. Conway created a two-dimensional model of "life" that moves autonomously and has self-homeomorphism. In other words, it can be said that the figure was created which becomes the fixed balance of Concept 1 that is independent from outer space.

However, the Seifert structure of the eyeball represents a 52-dimensional real Lie group E6 (composed of four geometric automorphic mappings over four rings) where it is built infinitely externalized internally [4] [6]. In other words, it can logically be considered a structure able to perceive a far-away point arbitrarily close to a straight line.

IV. ANALYSIS OF TORI (THREE-DIMENSIONAL MULTI CONNECTED CLOSED MANIFOLDS) THAT REPRESENT THE TRANSFORMATION OF CONCEPT 1

A. *Perception Analysis of Concept 1 to Concept 9*

Concept 1

signifies a simply connected three-dimensional closed manifold and a multi connected three-dimensional closed manifold.

Concept 2

signifies the action of maximizing the margin of classification boundaries of two-point discrimination.

Concept 3

signifies the minimum number of automorphic constituents; a polytope towards two dimensions.

Concept 4

signifies center 0 at the time of nonlocal stable opening/closing.

Concept 5

signifies a simply connected higher-dimensional open manifold; a polytope towards three dimensions. For third-order Painlevé equations, "1" and "5" are processed as the same simple group, where "R5/2" and "R1/2" contained in a sphere of radius R are the same covering space of a cyclic group.

Concept 6

signifies $2n + 0$; a diploid of a perfect number with the minimum self-homeomorphism in three dimensions (Concept 3).

Concept 7

signifies $2n + 1$.

Concept 8

signifies $n^3 + 0$; "4" in three dimensions, along with its covering space and origin 0.

Concept 9

signifies $n^{n-1} + 0$; "n^n" in three dimensions, along with its covering space and external origin 0.

The transformation of Concept 1 is represented by tori (three-dimensional multi connected closed manifolds).

The compact theory (Kaluza-Klein Theory) of the co-dimensional portion that encloses the independent Concept 1 described contains a discrepancy [11]. The reason for this discrepancy is a question of how the locations interpreted were changed and the interpretation of locations is related to the problem of perception. Accordingly, It is considered in terms of the number of material structures that support perception as well as the sense of sight and touch, and the number of epitope inductions using characteristics of light that are indispensable for perceiving organisms. When re-examining what numbers are in terms of these locations

covering spaces, It is considered the problem along with its initial settings—living things that perceive numbers. Human perception, in particular, is composed of what resembles a covering space of higher-order equations. The homeomorphism of the mathematical structure of the iris may be reflected in the target and create visual perception.

From the observations above, the true nature of numbers can be considered a creation of the rationality that describes "life." In macro terms, everything can be understood from the shining or reflection of the light spectrum—from the molecular structure of minerals to the trajectories of celestial objects.

Humans have moved from the age of paper and writing instruments used to make compressed notations in two dimensions, to the age of recording transmitted manuscripts enabling uncompressed notation. The age of notation using light has begun. Writing on the two dimensions of paper is a notation method that requires the compression of co-dimensions, and the decimal system is designed mainly to handle this application. Protists are completed in five decimal world,However, achievement that won the longitudinal and movable creatures, Have adopted the decimal system, which was to have a symmetry in quinary. However, notations that do not compress co-dimensions are needed when drawing non-orientable organisms such as sea urchins, oriented manmade structures, the shifting of orientations that occurs in outer space, or the structure of viruses. While computational models already exist, there are no comprehensive concepts or operation keys. Therefore, new connotations for these new notations are required. As the mathematical logic and three-dimensional computations are both ready, keys used to write extra dimensions are required for use as "procedure words."When re-examining the nature of numbers in terms of these types of locations (involving folding co-dimension) covering spaces, I considered the initial settings—living things that perceive numbers. The only reason for doing so was that the locations in which number discrepancies appear are special intermediate-dimensional planes (i.e., co-dimensions), where the locations in which the settings of words, perception, and tools are vague or poorly set. My discussion has been advanced by using "procedure words" instead of "sequences/quantities" as the words of mathematics, defining perception as "two-point discrimination" and using the decimal system as the current tool of notation.

I have derived the problem of the divided perception of a set known in a group from the structure of human perception, which is based on two-point discrimination, by approaching the problem using a model involving simple movements in mathematical logic.

V. DISCUSSION

A. *Control Numbers*

Control numbers are locations having extra dimensions, in which the characteristics of light are noticeable, or locations, where shifts can be created with their reflection angles. "5" is a condition that consistently (There is no discrepancies) closes a boundary as a co-dimensional polytope in a regular polyhedron in three dimensions. Since, in general, it is not possible to solve fifth-order or higher algebraic equations by the Exponentiation root, fixed form transformations using Exponentiation symmetry are not possible. In other words, this means that the path for epitope induction is not definite. Even in the evolved organism of the human body, the fingers, toes, and body as a whole constitute objects that have stopped by dividing into five branches. In other words, the creation of "undividability" can be considered a condition for controlling or stopping convergence. Therefore, Concept 5 is the number that functions as a controller. If observing based on the characteristics of an individual, primitive organism such as sea urchins are independent individuals that have their entire structure formed by a simple equation for "5." Sea urchins have been shaped to withstand the conditions of the highly acidic primitive sea, (in other words, conditions where the state of ions are different that of today) and can be considered to have a shape that is a reaction to the numbers at the rear. The acidic sea can be considered the neighborhood(affect around, and distributed the separation point) condition for creating organisms with acute-angle shapes. In terms of numerical formulas, these organisms may be patterns of manifolds with the origin of epitope inductions (which mammals have inside their bodies) that moved to the outside and have been induced by the 17 types of metals (halogen metals) present in the composition of the sea.

B. Number of Inductions

Contrary to the control numbers, morphogenesis up to immediately prior to the five-dimensional stoppage number depends on the "substitution group." As can be seen from the example of the lotus discussed above, even in a case where the appearance expresses such numbers as "9" for the hollow stalk, with "16" petals and "1" lotus Exponentiation for the flower, it may possess conformity in the group overall simply by virtue of the fact that the root to be taken differs due to ion inversion and swinging back by the substitution group operation. This can be rephrased as it being engaged in monodromy preserving deformation. In other words, the number of inductions is equipped with a Painlevé Property.

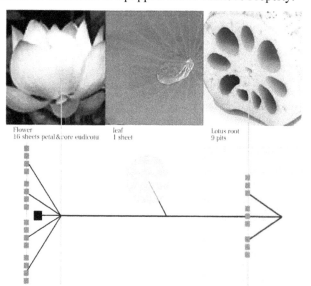

Flower
16 sheets petal&core eudicotu

leaf
1 sheet

Lotus root
9 pits

Fig. 3.   Ion, plus or minus reversal and transformation It was on the basis of the Euler pentagonal theorem

Moreover, if one considers a case in which animals and plants are established as solids to be "Concept 1," this includes an agglomeration (DiscretelySubset)of the discrete parts of number R.

Epitope induction generally consists of two-part division and three-part composition, and is thought to move in accordance with the knot theory. Induction lines that can be calculated using Gröbner bases are thought to exist on the knots or crossings. The number of twists is thought to be related to speed.

C. Perception of Numbers

Initially, the idea for this research arose from wondering if an attempt could be made to prove non-independence using the continuum hypothesis. As my hypothesis, It is considered what the result would be if the perceived numbers "1," "2," and "3" were not independent—in other words, did not have the characteristic of being a sequence. The answer is chaos. However, when It is considered how "1," "2," and "3" could be created as concepts when considering chaos as a single set, I also considered the case of perceiving Concept 1 as Concept 2 in a three-dimensional space, and Concept 2 as Concept 3. As pursued these facts, It noticed that when the concept human perceive as Concept 1 takes on a different appearance, it becomes Concept 2 and then Concept 3. Fig.4 shows the transformation and regeneration of a doughnut-shaped torus of a three-dimensional open manifold normally perceived as "1." Concept 5 viewed from above in three dimensions can appear as "3" or "2" when the representation is compressed into two dimension and viewed from the side. Ultimately, it can be transformed into a state enabling the calculation of its homeomorphism to a simply connected three-dimensional closed manifold. While the numbers discussed here are mere concepts, in practice, they can also be considered characteristics of the light spectrum composing living things.

It is necessary to establish boundary classifications and domain theory that use two-point discrimination cognition, the basis for classification boundaries, and that are in line with reality. It is proper to think of boundary classification as pattern recognition of an n-dimension polytype. The way of approaching the question in the continuum hypothesis was simply regrettable, and it is interesting as training in the method for thinking. Adopting Dr. J H. Conway's expressions of haploid and diploid for doing structural pattern recognition for the cardinality of the number are thought be in line with reality and appropriate[3][4]. This is because structural pattern recognition uses a Hasse diagram and preserves the consistency as a group with an orientation. To phrase it differently, it serves as a method for coming and going through an intermediate dimension consistently(There is no discrepancies) .It is considered as characteristic of the optical spectrum.

VI. CONCLUSION

A. The number of coming and going Topology

Organisms may use these characteristics to construct organic structures. For example, the external appearance of an individual tangerine can be viewed as a simply connected three-dimensional closed manifold, but the internal structure can be considered a transformation of a doughnut-shaped torus of a simply connected three-dimensional closed manifold. The same applies to bulbs of garlic.

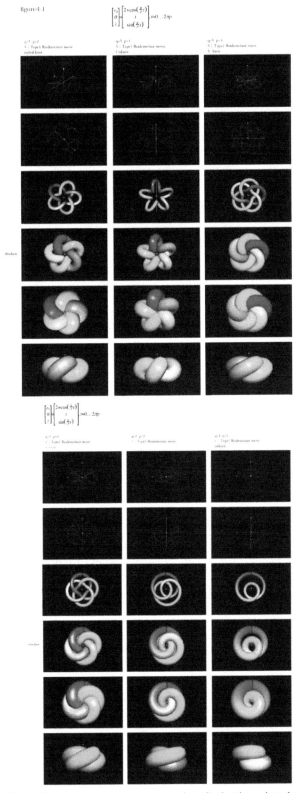

Fig. 4.   The transformation and regeneration of a doughnut-shaped torus of a three-dimensional open manifolds normally perceived as "1"

The "separation" boundary problem may be perceived using substances that function as the smallest grinders during the cell division of an organism. These substances may be related to the 17 types of metals (halogen metals) subjected to epitope induction, have dielectric polarization properties and they may be able to transform into shapes such as Kepler manifolds. It is considered that they form cells while in motion. In other words, they could be considered to have the dielectric polarization characteristics of the 17 types of metals, which is the result of the reactions to epitope inductions.The initial setting of the continuum hypothesis has been examined only by the concept, but some ambiguity remains therein. It is necessary to examine the definition of the number before proving the consistency of the number, and in particular to examine why it has reached the point where it is recognized in that manner.

That decimal is, in a compressed description of the calculation in a two-dimensional, slightly deviated from the phenomenon of a three-dimensional space of reality.

Described above

1) *biological model*
2) *machine model*
3) *conceptual model*
Respectively

1) *4 or more dimensions model*
2) *two-dimensional model*
3) *3-dimensional model*
That is the meaning.

These extra dimensions (intermediate dimension), how to traffic to no contradiction, is a Exponentiation symmetry can be calculated the coating space.

Numbers can be considered to be products of light perception by organisms, and their true nature is that they move subtly depending on the dimensions of their notation. In general, they are a group with the Painlevé property.

In other words, the types of equations described here exist to describe independent organisms, making folds and lowering dimensions for clean convergence when induction has completed. To put it differently, the description of life starts from the symmetry of cell division.When it is assumed that two-point discrimination cognition has established current mathematical logic, it was thought that some condition or other with epitope induction is carrying out the recognition of the boundary problems thereof, but it is precisely this "some condition or other" that may be a Painlevé property that has Exponentiation symmetry.

REFERENCES

[1]   Barbara McClintock "The Significance of Responses of the Genome to Challenge" , Science 1984 vol226 November Copyright©1984 by the Nobel Foundation

[2]   Bruce Alberts, Julian Lewis, Martin Raff, "Molecular Biology of the Cell" , Newton Press Co.,Ltd. 2010 ISBN-10: 4315518670

[3]   Christopher Bishop "Pattern Recognition and Machine Learning" , Maruzen Co.,Ltd. 2009.

[4]   J.H.Conway D.A.Smith "On uaternions and ctonions" , A K Peters,Lte 2003 ISBN 1-56881-134-9

[5] J.P.Cohen " Continuum hypothesis" , TokyoTosho Co.,Ltd. 1972 ISBN 4-489-00339-0

[6] Katsusada Morita " On uatrenions and ctonions and dirac equation" , Nippon Hyoron Sha Co.,Ltd 2011 ISBN 978-4-535-78676-9

[7] Kenji Fukaya " Electromagnetic fields and the vector analysis" , Iwanami Shoten Publishers 2006 ISBN 4-00-006883-0

[8] Linus Pauling "A Molecular Theory of General Anesthesia" , Science 7 July 1961 vol 134 November 3471

[9] Masatoshi Noumi "Painleve equation" , Asakura Publishing Co.,Ltd. 2000 ISBN 978-4-254-11554-3

[10] Tosaka, Nobuyoshi " Solution and application of differential equation" , University of Tokyo Press 2010 ISBN 978-4-13-062913-3

[11] Yukio Matsumoto "Basis of the manifold" , University of Tokyo Press 1988 ISBN 4-13-062103-3

[12] William Poundstone" The Recursive Universe" , Nippon Hyoron Sha Co.,Ltd , 1990

Permissions

All chapters in this book were first published in IJARAI, by The Science and Information Organization; hereby published with permission under the Creative Commons Attribution License or equivalent. Every chapter published in this book has been scrutinized by our experts. Their significance has been extensively debated. The topics covered herein carry significant findings which will fuel the growth of the discipline. They may even be implemented as practical applications or may be referred to as a beginning point for another development.

The contributors of this book come from diverse backgrounds, making this book a truly international effort. This book will bring forth new frontiers with its revolutionizing research information and detailed analysis of the nascent developments around the world.

We would like to thank all the contributing authors for lending their expertise to make the book truly unique. They have played a crucial role in the development of this book. Without their invaluable contributions this book wouldn't have been possible. They have made vital efforts to compile up to date information on the varied aspects of this subject to make this book a valuable addition to the collection of many professionals and students.

This book was conceptualized with the vision of imparting up-to-date information and advanced data in this field. To ensure the same, a matchless editorial board was set up. Every individual on the board went through rigorous rounds of assessment to prove their worth. After which they invested a large part of their time researching and compiling the most relevant data for our readers.

The editorial board has been involved in producing this book since its inception. They have spent rigorous hours researching and exploring the diverse topics which have resulted in the successful publishing of this book. They have passed on their knowledge of decades through this book. To expedite this challenging task, the publisher supported the team at every step. A small team of assistant editors was also appointed to further simplify the editing procedure and attain best results for the readers.

Apart from the editorial board, the designing team has also invested a significant amount of their time in understanding the subject and creating the most relevant covers. They scrutinized every image to scout for the most suitable representation of the subject and create an appropriate cover for the book.

The publishing team has been an ardent support to the editorial, designing and production team. Their endless efforts to recruit the best for this project, has resulted in the accomplishment of this book. They are a veteran in the field of academics and their pool of knowledge is as vast as their experience in printing. Their expertise and guidance has proved useful at every step. Their uncompromising quality standards have made this book an exceptional effort. Their encouragement from time to time has been an inspiration for everyone.

The publisher and the editorial board hope that this book will prove to be a valuable piece of knowledge for researchers, students, practitioners and scholars across the globe.

List of Contributors

Marimpis Avraam
Computer Science Department Aristotle University of Thessaloniki, AUTH Thessaloniki, Greece

Majida Ali Abed
College of Computers Sciences & Mathematics, University of Tikrit, Tikrit, Iraq

Hamid Ali Abed Alasad
Computers Sciences Department, Education for Pure Science College, University of Basra, Basra, Iraq

Eugene S. Kitamura
Department of Computer Science, National Defense Academy Yokosuka, Japan

Akira Namatame
Department of Computer Science, National Defense Academy Yokosuka, Japan

Hadji Salah and Ellouze Noureddine
TIC department LR SITI ENIT BP 37 Belvédère 1002 Tunis, Tunisia

Rosa Andrie Asmara
Graduate School of Science and Engineering Saga University Saga City, Japan
Informatics Management Department State Polytechnics of Malang Malang, Indonesia

Toshiya Katano
Institute of Lowland and Marine Research Saga University Saga City Japan

Eugene S. Kitamura and Akira Namatame
Department of Computer Science, National Defense Academy Yokosuka, Japan

Sabah Al-Fedaghi
Computer Engineering Department Kuwait University Kuwait

A Joukhadar, I Hasan, A Alsabbagh and M Alkouzbary
Dept. of Mechatronics Engineering University of Aleppo, Aleppo-Syria

ShengJun Cheng
School of Computer Science and Technology Harbin Institute of Technology Harbin 150001, China

Jiafeng Liu and XiangLong Tang
Harbin Institute of Technology Harbin150001, China

Kohei Arai, Indra Nugraha Abdullah and Hiroshi Okumura
Graduate School of Science and Engineering Saga University Saga City, Japan

Masanoori Sakashita
Information Science, Saga University Saga, Japan

Osamu Shigetomi and Yuko Miura
Saga Prefectural Agricultural Research Institute Saga Prefectural Government, Japan

Harjot Kaur
Dept of Comp. Sci. and Engg. GNDU Regional Campus, Gurdaspur Punjab, INDIA

Karanjeet Singh Kahlon and Rajinder Singh Virk
Dept of Comp. Sci. and Engg. Guru Nanak Dev University, Amritsar Punjab, INDIA

Steven Ray Sentinuwo
Department of Electrical Engineering Sam Ratulangi University Manado, Indonesia

Anik Nur Handayani
Electrical and Information Technology, State University of Malang Malang, Indonesia

Dalia Kass Hanna and Abdulkader Joukhadar
Mechatronics Department University of Aleppo Aleppo-Syria

Khaled Nasser ElSayed
Computer Science Department, Umm AlQura University

Masaya Nakashima
Department of Information Science Saga University Saga City, Japan

Masniah
College of Informatics and Computer Management STMIK Banjarbaru Banjarbaru, Indonesia

Sri Redjeki, M. Guntara and Pius Anggoro
Informatics Engineering Department STMIK AKAKOM Yogyakarta, Indonesia

Obuandike Georgina N.
Department of Mathematical Sciences and IT Federal University Dutsinma Katsina state, Nigeria

Audu Isah
Department of Mathematics and Statistics Federal University of Technology Minna, Niger State

John Alhasan
Department of Computer Science Federal University of Technology, Niger State, Nigeria

Irina Topalova
Faculty of German Engineering Education and Industrial Management Technical University of Sofia, Bulgaria Sofia, Bulgaria

Fahim Akhter
Department of Management Information Systems College of Business Administration King Saud University, Saudi Arabia

Nikos Tatarakis and Ergina Kavallieratou
Dept. of Information and Communication System Engineering, University of the Aegean, Samos, Greece

Nagy Ramadan Darwish
Department of Computer and Information Sciences, Institute of Statistical Studies and Research, Cairo University, Cairo, Egypt

Ahmed A. Mohamed
Department of Information System, Higher Technological Institute, 10th of Ramadan City, Egypt

Bassem S. M. Zohdy
Department of Business Technology, Canadian International College, Cairo, Egypt

Dewa Bagus Sanjaya
Lecturer of Civics Education Ganesha University of Education Singaraja, Bali, Indonesia

Dewa Gede Hendra Divayana
Lecturer of Information Technology Education Ganesha University of Education Singaraja, Bali, Indonesia

Mahamadou Issoufou Tiado
Department of Mathematics and Computer Science, University of Abdou Moumouni, UAM Niamey, Niger

Abdou Idrissa
University Institute of Technology University of Tahoua Tahoua, Niger

Karimou Djibo
Department of Mathematics and Computer Science, University of Abdou Moumouni, UAM Niamey, Niger

Amit Gupta
Professor, Department of ECE Chandigarh University, Gharuan, India

Surbhi Bakshi
Associate Professor, Department of ECE Chandigarh University, Gharuan, India

Shaina
Research Scholar, Department of ECE Chandigarh University, Gharuan, India

Mandeep Chaudhary
School of Engineering & Digital arts University of Kent Canterbury,UK

Husein Hadi Abbas Jassim, Kawther B.R. Al-dbag and Hind R.M Shaaban
Faculty of Computer Science and Mathematics University of Kufa Najaf, Iraq

Zahir M. Hussain
Faculty of Computer Science and Mathematics University of Kufa Najaf, Iraq
Adj. Prof., School of Engineering, ECU, Australia

Chinedu Pascal Ezenkwu, Simeon Ozuomba and Constance kalu
Electrical/Electronics & Computer Engineering Department, University of Uyo, Uyo, Akwa Ibom State, Nigeria

Miguel Leon and Ning Xiong
School of Innovation, Design and Eginering Malardalen University Vasteras, Sweden

Takuji Maekawa, Toshihisa Maeda, Hiroshi Sekiguchi and Noriyuki Masago
LSI Production Headquarters Rohm Co., Ltd. Kyoto City, Japan

Manish M. Goswami
Research Scholar, Dept. of Computer Science and Engineering, G.H.Raisoni College of Engineering, Nagpur, India

Dr. M.M. Raghuwanshi
Professor, Department of Computer Technology, YCCE, Nagpur, India

Dr. Latesh Malik
Professor, Dept. of CSE, G.H.Raisoni College of Engg., Nagpur, India

P. Massami
Unit for Applied Mathematics Dar es Salaam Institute of Technology Dar es Salaam, Tanzania

Benitha M. Myamba
Department of Logistics and Transport Studies National
Institute of Transport Dar es Salaam, Tanzania

Qiang Chen and Jiangfan Feng
College of computer science and technology Chongqing
University of Posts and Telecommunications
Chongqing, China

Yoshimi Shimokawa
Kiiro Book Store LLC. Tokyo, Japan

Index

Printed in the USA
CPSIA information can be obtained
at www.ICGtesting.com
JSHW051430221024
72173JS00006B/1429